Jung's Life and Work

A list of Jung's works appears at the back of the volume.

Jung's Life and Work

INTERVIEWS FOR *MEMORIES, DREAMS, REFLECTIONS* WITH ANIELA JAFFÉ.

C. G. JUNG AND ANIELA JAFFÉ

EDITED BY SONU SHAMDASANI

WITH THOMAS FISCHER AS CONSULTING EDITOR

Translated by Heather McCartney and John Peck

🄟 PHILEMON SERIES

Published with the support of the Philemon Foundation
This book is part of the Philemon Series of the Philemon Foundation

PRINCETON UNIVERSITY PRESS
PRINCETON AND OXFORD

Published by Princeton University Press
41 William Street, Princeton, New Jersey 08540
99 Banbury Road, Oxford OX2 6JX

press.princeton.edu

GPSR Authorized Representative: Easy Access System Europe - Mustamäe tee 50,
10621 Tallinn, Estonia, gpsr.requests@easproject.com

ISBN 978-0-691-19322-9
ISBN (e-book) 978-0-691-26634-3
Library of Congress Control Number: 2025943708

British Library Cataloging-in-Publication Data is available

Editorial: Fred Appel and Tara Dugan
Production Editorial: Karen Carter
Jacket/Cover Design: Ben Higgins
Production: Erin Suydam
Publicity: William Pagdatoon
Copyeditor: Francis Eaves

Jacket/Cover Credit: INTERFOTO / Alamy Stock Photo

This book has been composed in Sabon LT Std

Printed in the United States of America

10 9 8 7 6 5 4 3 2 1

Contents

Jung in his library, 1959. Photo by Henri Cartier-Bresson. © Fondation Cartier-Bresson, Magnum Photos.

Acknowledgments

THE PHILEMON FOUNDATION gratefully acknowledges all its donors, and in particular former president Judith Harris, whose support made this edition possible. I thank her and Tony Woolfson for their unwavering commitment to Jung's unpublished works and my editing of them. I am indebted to the Foundation's board—Caterina Vezzoli, Janet Tatum, Ann Blake, Claire Francica, Audrey Punnett, and Joseph Meneghini—for their stewardship of the enterprise, along with former board members.

At an early stage of discussions, Ulrich Hoerni examined the issue of the possible publication of the interviews for *Memories, Dreams, Reflections* on behalf of the Society of Heirs of C. G. Jung. This enabled the editorial project to be seriously considered. Robert Hinshaw, representing the estate of Aniela Jaffé, and Thomas Fischer, together with the board of The Foundation of the Works of C. G. Jung, were instrumental in securing and enabling the publication of this volume.

Peter Fritz of the Paul and Peter Fritz Literary Agency managed contractual arrangements and facilitated the release of material which later appeared, heavily revised, in *Memories, Dreams, Reflections*, from Random House, with support from Rolf auf der Maur of Vischer AG on copyright matters. I thank the Paul and Peter Fritz Agency and The Foundation of the Works of C. G. Jung for permission to cite from Jung's unpublished letters.

Thomas Fischer has been involved at every stage of the project: coordinating efforts on behalf of the Foundation for the Works of C. G. Jung, negotiating with rights holders, advising on editorial decisions, verifying transcriptions, reviewing translations, and assisting in the resolution of footnote queries. Medea Hoch undertook the painstaking transcription of the notes of the Interviews; she and Bettina Kaufmann meticulously checked and verified the text. Carl Christian Jung reviewed the edited manuscript, consulted relevant material from the Jung papers at ETH Zurich, and provided sections from Aniela Jaffé's manuscript *Erlebtes und Gedachtes*, also held there. At the Jung Family Archive in Küsnacht,

Susanne Eggenberger-Jung provided detailed information on Jung's day-to-day activities during the period in question, along with copious answers to specific queries. Andreas Jung contributed insights into Jung's family relationships and ancestry, while Ulrich Hoerni offered valuable information on aspects of Basel local history. I am deeply grateful to both of them for their recollections of their grandfather over many years.

Robert Hinshaw reviewed the edited manuscript, and I thank him for his longstanding engagement with and thoughtful discussions around this project.

It has been a pleasure to work with Heather McCartney and John Peck on the translation. With the latter, this marks the completion of a collaboration spanning the translations of Jung's *Red Book* and *Black Books*, which has been an education in linguistic "piano tuning."

At Princeton University Press, Fred Appel has overseen the project, and it has been a pleasure to continue a longstanding collaboration. Karen Carter managed production with impeccable care; Francis Eaves provided meticulous copy-editing, bringing a fine linguistic ear to the text and a sharp eye to the notes; Ross MacFarlane provided timely assistance with the proofs; and Virginia Ling created a resourceful index.

At the C. G. Jung Papers Collection of the ETH Zurich Library, Yvonne Voegeli and Claudia Briellmann provided key materials. At the Beinecke Rare Book and Manuscript Library, Yale University, Mary Ellen Budney and Dolores Colon supplied materials from the Kurt and Helen Wolff papers.

Dangwei Zhou kindly shared information from his forthcoming intellectual biography of Richard Wilhelm, and Gaia Domenici provided information on Jung's school years from the Basel State Archives.

I am grateful to the University of Illinois Library Special Collections for copies of Jung's correspondence with H. G. Wells and the Minnesota Historical Society for copies from Jerome Hill's papers.

Magnum Photos granted permission to reproduce Henri Cartier-Bresson's photograph of Jung and of Jung with Aniela Jaffé (with thanks to Michael Shulman). The Eranos Foundation permitted the use of Margaret Fellerer's photograph of Kurt Wolff at Eranos (with thanks to Ricardo Bernardini).

My work on this project began with a conversation in 1988 with the late Michael Fordham, who recalled that the early drafts of the first chapters of *Memories, Dreams, Reflections* were "far madder" and significantly different from the published version. I am indebted to him for encouraging my historical research. In 1990 I discovered an editorial typescript of the book at the Countway Library of Medicine at Harvard Medical School, which contained substantial material omitted from the final publication. Richard Wolfe, then curator of Rare Books and Manuscripts, kindly permitted me to make a copy.

This discovery led to a correspondence with the late Aniela Jaffé, who informed me that the interview notes forming the basis of *Memories, Dreams, Reflections* had been given by Helen Wolff to the Library of Congress following Kurt Wolff's death; however, these were not on access. These notes had been transferred to Princeton University Press and subsequently donated by them to the Library of Congress in 1983 with a ten-year restriction. Thanks to the Press—particularly Eric Rohmann, Debbie Tegarden, and the late William McGuire—I was granted access to them in 1991.

In 1992, Michael Eigen gave me the opportunity to present my findings in public at the National Psychological Association for Psychoanalysis. The following year, my research intersected with that of Alan Elms, resulting in a collegial exchange. Ximena de Angulo shared vivid memories of Jung, Helen and Kurt Wolff, Richard Hull, Aniela Jaffé, and her mother, Cary Baynes. She also gave access to her mother's papers and was a constant source of encouragement throughout my historical research.

Studying the editorial correspondence surrounding the creation of *Memories, Dreams, Reflections* occasioned uncanny moments of *déjà vécu*. This edition would not have been possible without the steadfast support of Maggie Baron. I am grateful to Philip Bechtel for his assistance at a critical juncture.

Kurt Wolff at Eranos in August 1951. Photo by Margarethe Fellerer. © Margarethe Fellerer.

Abbreviations

1925	C. G. Jung, *Introduction to Jungian Psychology: Notes of the Seminar on Analytical Psychology Given in 1925*. Edited by William McGuire; revised, updated, and with a new introduction by Sonu Shamdasani. Philemon Series. Princeton, NJ: Princeton University Press, 2012.
BA	Bollingen Archives, Manuscript Division, Library of Congress, Washington, DC.
BB	C. G. Jung, *The Black Books: Notebooks of Transformation, 1913–1932*, 7 vols. Edited by Sonu Shamdasani; translated by Martin Liebscher, John Peck, and Sonu Shamdasani. New York: W. W. Norton, 2020.
BL	Beinecke Rare Book and Manuscript Library, Yale University, New Haven, CT.
BP	Cary Baynes Papers, Wellcome Collection Archives, London.
CLM	Countway Library of Medicine, Harvard Medical School, Boston, MA.
CE	*Critical Edition of the Works of C. G. Jung*, 26 vols. General editor Sonu Shamdasani; edited by Gaia Domenici, Martin Liebscher, and Christopher Wagner; translated by Caitlin Stephens with Astrid Freuler. Princeton, NJ: Princeton University Press, forthcoming.
CW	*The Collected Works of C. G. Jung*, 21 vols. Executive editor William McGuire; edited by Sir Herbert Read, Michael Fordham, and Gerhard Adler; translated by R. F. C. Hull. Bollingen Series. New York and Princeton, NJ: Princeton University Press, 1953–83.
EG	Aniela Jaffé, "Erlebtes und Gedachtes bei C. G. Jung." ETH Zurich University Archives.

ETG   *Erinnerungen, Träume, Gedanken von C. G. Jung*, Aufgezeichnet und herausgegeben von Aniela Jaffé, Zurich: Walter Verlag, 1962/1983.

ETH   ETH Zurich University Archives, ETH Library, Swiss Federal Institute of Technology, Zurich.

FJL   *The Freud/Jung Letters: The Correspondence Between Sigmund Freud and C. G. Jung*. Edited by William McGuire; translated by Ralph Manheim and R.F.C. Hull. Bollingen Series. Princeton, NJ: Princeton University Press, 1974.

JFA   Jung Family Archives.

JP   C. G. Jung Papers Collection, ETH Zurich University Archives, ETH Library, Swiss Federal Institute of Technology, Zurich.

Letters   *C. G. Jung Letters*, 2 vols. Selected and edited by Gerhard Adler in collaboration with Aniela Jaffé; translated by R.F.C. Hull. Bollingen Series. Princeton, NJ: Princeton University Press, 1973 and 1975.

LC   Library of Congress, Washington, DC.

LH   Lucy Heyer Grote Papers, University of Basel Archives.

LN   C. G. Jung, *The Red Book. Liber Novus: A Reader's Edition*. Edited by Sonu Shamdasani; translated by Mark Kyburz, John Peck, and Sonu Shamdasani. Philemon Series. New York: W. W. Norton, 2012.

MDR   C. G. Jung, *Memories, Dreams, Reflections*. Recorded and edited by Aniela Jaffé. New York: Vintage, 1963/1989.

Reflections   Aniela Jaffé, *Reflections on the Life and Dreams of C. G. Jung*. From conversations with C. G. Jung, with "Historical Commentary" by Elena Fischli; translated by Caitlin Stephens. Einsiedeln: Daimon Verlag, 2023.

SE   *The Standard Edition of the Complete Psychological Works of Sigmund Freud*, 24 vols. Edited by James Strachey in collaboration with Anna Freud, assisted by Alix Strachey and Alan Tyson; translated by James Strachey. London: The Hogarth Press and The Institute of Psycho-Analysis, 1953–74.

VA   C. G. Jung, "Von den anfänglichen Ereignissen meines Lebens," Jung Family Archives.

Introduction

"A book with living fire in it": On the Interviews for *Memories, Dreams, Reflections*

SONU SHAMDASANI

IN THE FALL OF 1962, Pantheon announced the publication of *Memories, Dreams, Reflections* as Jung's "interior autobiography": "One of the world's greatest explorers of the depths of man's thoughts and actions has, in this volume, attempted to fathom his own unconscious being."[1] *Memories* swiftly became a bestseller. Writing in *The Listener*, Gerhard Adler noted "Nowhere else has the man Jung revealed himself so openly or testified to his crises of decision and the existence of his inner law."[2] For Kathleen Raine, "Jung's life, even so fragmentarily revealed, invites comparison not with profane autobiography, but with the lives of Plotinus and Swedenborg, the lives of the saints and sages, interwoven with miracle."[3] In an article entitled "Dreams from the Plutonian Realms," a reviewer in the *New York Herald Tribune* wrote, "Here is the man himself, a strange man, with the treasures he brought back from the strangest of odysseys."[4] In *The Sunday Telegraph*, J. B. Priestley suggested that anyone unacquainted with Jung's work should start here before venturing into his collected works. The chapters on his childhood were "matched only by a few of the greatest novelists and poets."[5] In *The Sunday Times*, Cyril Connolly likened it to "Yeats' Byzantium" in prose.[6]

---

[1] Pantheon, Fall Catalogue, 1962, p. 14.

[2] Gerhard Adler, "The Memoirs of C. G. Jung," *The Listener*, July 18, 1963, p. 85.

[3] Kathleen Raine, "A Sent Man," *The Listener*, August 22, 1963, p. 284.

[4] *New York Herald Tribune*, May 12, 1963.

[5] J. B. Priestley, "Bold Self-Scrutiny of a Dreaming Giant," *The Sunday Telegraph*, July 7, 1963.

[6] Cyril Connolly, "Jung: Poetry and Wisdom," *The Sunday Times*, July 7, 1963. For critical reviews, see Philip Rieff, "C. G. Jung's Confession: Psychology as a Language of

Even a Freudian critic, Edward Glover, concluded that "this book of memoirs will continue to be read with fascination by future generations when some of his more formal works are respectfully interred in psychological libraries."[7]

Since then, it has been regarded as the single most authoritative source of information concerning Jung's life and work. Its reception did much to set the template for how he and his works have been viewed since, both pro and contra. With sales nearing a million in English alone, it has sold far more than any other work by Jung. In short, it is the work by which he has come to be known by the public at large, and if someone has read only one work by him, the chances are that it is *Memories, Dreams, Reflections.* Consequently, its impact has gone far beyond Jungian circles. As James Olney remarked, in this memoir, "Jung finally offers what he had been so reticent about in his theoretical writings: a comprehensive statement of his profound experience in and his achieved understanding of the human condition."[8] As such it provided the critical hinge between felt experience and Jung's theories, in the making of a psychology. It has been a notable exemplar of a modern form of psychological biography and autobiography, narrating a life from dreams, visions, and inner experience.[9]

The work was the brainchild of the legendary publisher Kurt Wolff. It was compiled and edited by Aniela Jaffé on the basis of interviews she conducted with Jung, largely between 1957 and 1958, supplemented by Jung's own memoir concerning the early years of his life, and some other biographical materials, with Kurt Wolff's active involvement. However, behind the scenes of the published work, there lay an unsuspectedly complex tale of composition, editing, publication, and alleged censorship, as the parties involved came into conflict concerning how to shape and present what came to be regarded as Jung's final testament.

In 1993, Jaffé's original interviews with Jung were placed on open access in the Library of Congress in Washington, DC. These revealed that

---

Faith," *Encounter,* 22 May 1964, pp. 45–50; Erich Fromm "C. G. Jung: Prophet of the Unconscious," *Scientific American*, September 1, 1963, pp. 283–90 and Hans Eysenck, "Patriarch of the Psyche," *The Spectator*, July 19, 1963, p. 86.

[7] Edward Glover, "Illuminations from Within," *The New York Times*, May 19, 1963, p. 26.

[8] James Olney, *Metaphors of Self: The Meaning of Autobiography* (Princeton, NJ: Princeton University Press, 1984), p. 90.

[9] See Olney, *Metaphors of Self.*

much significant material had been completely omitted in the published version, and that much material had been heavily edited.[10]

Moreover, while the published version of *Memories, Dreams, Reflections* was cast in the form of a chronological life narrative, the Protocols of the original interviews show Jung ranging across an array of subjects in an associative manner in a single interview, and indeed, actively discovering meaningful connections that he himself had hitherto not suspected, aided by Jaffé's sensitive questioning and Kurt Wolff's prompting. Thus the interviews present not only recollections of times past, but a critical chapter in Jung's evolving self-understanding and the elaboration of his work, and critically, a window into his own personal cosmology, as elaborated in his *Red Book* and *Black Books*, and only hinted at in his published writings.

This introduction narrates the events leading up to the commencement of the project. Editorial discussions which took place as it unfolded have been placed in the footnotes to the Interviews in a chronological sequence, and a short epilogue narrates what followed.

The Myth of Jung's Life

In the prologue to *Memories, Dreams, Reflections*, Jung stated that he had now undertaken to tell the "myth" of his life.[11] His way to discerning this myth had its inception in his self-investigations more than forty years prior. It was from the autumn of 1913 onward, first in the *Black Books*, then in the *Red Book: Liber Novus*, that Jung started to reevaluate and reappraise his life. In 1950, he recalled that after completing *Transformations and Symbols of the Libido* in 1912, he was driven to ask himself,

[W]hat is the myth you are living? I found no answer to this question, and had to admit that I was not living with a myth, or even in a myth [. . .]. I did not know that I was living a myth, and even if I

---

[10] One contemporaneous reviewer seems to have suspected some of this: "If rumour can be credited, certain relevant passages about his sexual and marital relations have been omitted at the request of the surviving family. This omission—or deletion—is unfortunate in the case of a man whose personal experiment in open erotic relationships influenced the marriage of more than one patient who came to him for advice. One would like to know his final judgement in maturity upon his efforts to maintain a continuing bipolar relationship between two psychologically contrasting types, a Griselda and an Iseult." (Lewis Mumford, "The Revolt of the Demons," *The New Yorker*, May 23, 1964).

[11] *ETG*, p. 10, *MDR*, p. 3.

had known it, I would not know what sort of myth was ordering my life without my knowledge. So [. . .] I took it upon myself to get to know "my" myth.[12]

The Black Books commence with Jung addressing his soul, after being absent from her for more than a decade. On November 12, 1913, he asked her, "Shall I tell you everything I have seen, experienced, and drunk in?"[13] He then recounted to his soul the pivotal dreams in his adolescence that persuaded him to opt for a career in medical science, and how this led him to move into the contemporary world and away from the soul. Following this, he narrated his more recent dreams of the white dove with the twelve dead and the Austrian customs official with the twelfth-century knight that heralded a return to his soul. In Liber Novus he contrasted the spirit of the times and the spirit of the depths: the former characterized by use and value, and the latter which ruled the depths of everything contemporary and led to the things of the soul.[14] As he saw it, having followed the spirit of the times for the previous decade, the time had come to heed the spirit of the depths. From the outset of his self-investigation, memories from his childhood surfaced, which he went over a number of times. His reconnection with his playing and building activities brought back to the surface his dream of the underground phallus.[15] Thus a reappraisal of his childhood and youth was a key component of the first phase of Jung's self-investigation.

As this process evolved over the following decade, it saw the emergence of a complex imaginal cosmology—in other terms, the myth of his life. While not biographies in any conventional sense, The Black Books and Liber Novus contain Jung's spiritual testament, his mythography. Liber Novus could be considered a new form of Bildungsroman: in the language of Jung's psychology, it presented the story of his process of individuation, and how he managed to find his orientation and recover a sense of meaning in his life.

Alongside his work in The Black Books and Liber Novus, Jung sought to translate insights from these works into a conceptual language aimed at a medical and scientific audience. In his published writings, metaphysical and theological questions tended to be bracketed out, as belonging

---

[12] Symbols of Transformations (1952), CE 22; CW 5, pp. xxiv–xxv.
[13] C. G. Jung, Black Book 2, p. 149.
[14] LN, pp. 119–23.
[15] See below, pp. 39–40.

outside the purview of an emergent science of psychology. This did not mean that Jung considered them insignificant, or that such considerations were absent from his life. This wider penumbra came strongly to the fore once more in the Interviews.

In the early 1920s, Jung had Cary de Angulo re-transcribe the text of *Liber Novus* from the calligraphic version. His discussions with her at this point indicate that he was attempting to find the right form in which to publish the work. On October 2, 1922, de Angulo noted his comments:

> Meyrink you [Jung] said could throw his [material] into novel form and it was all right, but you could only command the scientific and philosophical method and that stuff you couldn't cast into that mould. I said you could use the Zarathustra form and you said that was true, but you were sick of that. [. . .] Then you said you had thought of making an autobiography out of it.[16]

In 1924, these deliberations gave rise to a striking literary experiment, in the form of a novella.[17] This work consists in a letter exchange between "Jung" and a man eleven years his elder, by the name of A. E. The latter had consulted "Jung" between 1913 and August 2, 1914. Now, years later, he sent "Jung" a manuscript which he had since written describing his experiences, requesting that "Jung" publish it. From the content of the letters, it is clear that A. E. is none other than Jung himself, and the manuscript in question was evidently *Liber Novus*, for which this letter exchange would serve as an introduction to a pseudonymous publication. In his letters, A. E. recounted to "Jung" his apocalyptic train visions from the autumn of 1913, his early philosophical readings, and critical events in his childhood which he had not told him at the time of their first encounter, which he now saw to be connected with the material in his manuscript. He viewed these not as causal instigators, but as marking his first encounter with "the foreign guest." Taken together, these formed critical constitutents of his own "myth." These experiences would later feature in the Interviews: Jung's underground phallus dream, his encounter with the figure of a Jesuit, and the wooden manikin he had carved.[18] A. E. saw these experiences as containing *in nuce* the conflict

---

[16] *LN*, p. 65.

[17] C. G. Jung, *The "Foreign Guest": An Autobiographical Novella by C. G. Jung*, ed. Sonu Shamdasani, trans. Caitlin Stephens, Philemon Series (forthcoming).

[18] See below, pp. 39, 41, and 45.

between animal impulses and morality, an issue which was prominent when he first went to consult "Jung." This novella shows how Jung attempted to use events from his childhood and youth as a preface to a pseudonymous publication of *Liber Novus*, and how he saw these as being connected as chapters in the emergence of the myth of his life. As we shall see, this theme would come to feature prominently in the Interviews, as well as in Jung's memoir, "From the Earliest Experiences of my Life."

Aside from his intimate circle and close associates, Jung did not share details regarding his life or inner transformation with a wider public. The first presentation to a wider circle took place in 1925, in his seminars at the Psychological Club in Zurich. Jung began by noting,

> No one seriously interested in analytical psychology can fail to have been struck with the astonishing width of the field embraced by it, and so I have thought it would be useful to all of us if, in the course of these lectures, we could obtain a view of that field. At the beginning, I would like to give you a brief sketch of the development of my own conceptions from the time I first became interested in problems of the unconscious.[19]

Here, his intellectual biography would serve as an introduction to the whole field of analytical psychology. He presented his intellectual development from his medical school days: his studies in philosophy, and explorations in psychical research. He followed this with his collaboration with Freud, and a detailed presentation of his self-experimentation, focusing on the initial period, between October and December 1913.

As opposed to the lyrical and evocative language of the second layer of *Liber Novus*, Jung here employed his psychological concepts; or, to be more precise, he attempted to show how he derived his psychological concepts from his reflections upon these encounters. As he tellingly noted, "I drew all of my empirical material from my patients, but the solution of the problem I drew from the inside, from my observations of the unconscious processes."[20] The remainder of the seminar was taken up by group discussion of Rider Haggard's *She* and Marie Hay's *The Evil Vineyard*.

Though the "A. E." manuscript was not published, it established the template whereby Jung presented and commented on some of his mandala

---

[19] *1925*, p. 3.
[20] *1925*, p. 35.

paintings and dreams in his scholarly works, as belonging to anonymous patients.[21] One example of this type occurs in his unpublished book on alchemy and individuation in 1937, which evidences Jung's continued meditation on the transpersonal aspects of his childhood experiences.[22] This study was intended as the introduction to what was to be his major work on these subjects. Strikingly, he began this manuscript not with Wolfgang Pauli's dreams—as he eventually did in *Psychology and Alchemy* in 1944—but with an anonymized account of his major childhood dream of the underground phallus. He then elaborated an extended amplification of this dream, drawing out from it the following motifs: the "cohabitatio permanens" (the permanent pregnancy and divine incest), the eternal self-renewal of the God, the androgynous primordial being, and the conjunction of opposites. His discussion of these then formed the subject of the remainder of his manuscript.

Jung's study of this dream was connected with his research project on the subject of childhood dreams in the 1930s, which resulted in a seminar at the ETH Zurich. Among the questions asked were these: What is the earliest childhood dream you remember? Did you have this dream again in later life? Does the dream have a new meaning in terms of subsequent life developments? Have you had precognitive dreams, dreams of a cosmic character, dreams in relation to the death of others?[23]

TOWARDS A BIOGRAPHY[24]

Before considering initiatives towards a Jung biography in the 1950s, it is important to consider the status of the biographical in Jung's psychology. In his autobiography, Goethe had described his works as "fragments of one great confession."[25] In *Beyond Good and Evil* (1886) Nietzsche noted, "It has gradually become clear to me what every great philosophy

---

[21] See "Commentary on *The Secret of the Golden Flower*" (1929), CE 11; CW 13, mandalas A3, A6, and A10; "The Psychological Aspects of the Kore" (1941), CE 16; CW 9.1, "Case Z," §§ 358–82; "Concerning Mandala Symbolism" (1950), CE 16; CW 9.1, figures 6, 28, 29, and 36.

[22] JP.

[23] C. G. Jung, "Traumprobleme" (Martin Liebscher ed, Philemon Series, forthcomiing); C. G. Jung, *Children's Dreams: Notes of the Seminar Given in 1936–1940*, ed. Lorenz Jung and Maria Meyer-Gross, trans. Ernst Falzeder with Tony Woolfson, Philemon Series (Princeton, NJ: Princeton University Press, 2008).

[24] The following sections draw in part on Sonu Shamdasani, *Jung Stripped Bare by His Biographers, Even* (London: Karnac, 2005), ch. 1.

[25] Johann Wolfgang von Goethe, *The Collected Works, Volume 4: From My Life: Poetry and Truth, Parts 1–3* (Princeton, NJ: Princeton University Press, 1994), p. 214.

has hitherto been: a confession on the part of its author and a kind of involuntary and unconscious memoir."[26] In psychology, the subjective conditioning of knowledge had been debated in terms of the "personal equation." As William James observed in 1890, most psychologists made their own personal peculiarities into universal rules.[27] This issue lay at the heart of Jung's *Psychological Types*. He argued that in psychology, conceptions "will always be a product of the subjective psychological constellation of the investigator."[28] Correspondingly, it would not be possible to understand the genesis of the work of a psychologist without taking these subjective determinants into consideration. In 1929, Jung formulated it as follows: "philosophical criticism has helped me to see that every psychology—my own included—has the character of a subjective confession."[29]

At the same time, reformulating what constituted the "subjective" lay at the center of Jung's work. In his view, the more deeply one went into one's subjectivity, the more one encountered a wider terrain of collective determinants: in the language of *Liber Novus*, the powers of the depths, or, in the language of Jung's psychology, the dominants or archetypes. To give due recognition to such factors would require something other than a conventional biography.

In the history of modern psychology, psychiatry and psychotherapy, a number of prominent figures wrote memoirs or autobiographies: Auguste Forel, Stanley Hall, Emil Kraepelin, and Wilhelm Wundt, for example. In psychoanalysis, Freud, Ernest Jones, and Wilhelm Stekel published autobiographical works. Commencing in the 1930s, the American psychologist Carl Murchison edited a series of volumes for which important psychologists such as Édouard Claparède, Pierre Janet, William McDougall, Jean Piaget, William Stern, J. B. Watson, and many others were persuaded to write autobiographical contributions.[30] Consequently, there

---

[26] Friedrich Nietzsche, *Beyond Good and Evil: Prelude to a Philosophy of the Future*, trans. Marion Faber (Oxford: Oxford University Press, 1998), p. 14.

[27] William James, *The Principles of Psychology*, vol. 2 (New York: Henry Holt, 1890), p. 64.

[28] *Psychological Types* (1921), CE 9; CW 6, § 9.

[29] "The Freud–Jung Opposition" (1929), CE 11; CW 4, § 774.

[30] *A History of Psychology in Autobiography*, vol. 1 (1930), ed. Carl Murchison [for Claparède, Janet, McDougall, Stern, i.a.]; vol. 3 (1936), ed. Murchison [for Watson, i.a.]; vol. 4 (1952), ed. Edwin G. Boring, Heinz Werner, Herbert S. Langfeld, and Robert M. Yerkes [for Piaget, i.a.] (Worcester, MA: Clark University Press, 1930–). Murchison did not approach Jung for this project, but he had asked Jung to contribute to his volume *Psychologies of 1930*. Jung had declined, recommending his assistant H. G. Baynes instead (Murchison to Jung, November 2, 1928, JP). Baynes did not contribute to the volume.

was significant interest in Jung's biography, both in the public at large and within Jung's circle.

Since the time that she prepared her edition of Jung's 1925 seminar, Cary Baynes had been contemplating a biography of Jung.[31] Over the next few decades she was taken up with her translation of the *I Ching*, but when she met Jung after the war in 1946, she discussed the possibility with him but when. Jung's view was that "there might be something in it."[32] Over the next few years, Jung's attention began increasingly to turn to his own past: on January 2, 1949 he wrote to Alwina von Keller, "I also find myself at this time in a retrospective phase and am occupied again fundamentally with myself for the first time for 25 years, in that I collected and put together my old dreams."[33]

In 1951, Cary Baynes outlined a plan for a biographical study to Emma Jung involving a three-way collaboration:

> Now with respect to the plan for getting C. G. to set down the curve of development of his ideas. Of course it is contained in his works, but it seems to me that one should take advantage of the degree of his consciousness to make it explicit instead of having to be dug out by the industrious and missed altogether by the majority, even of those who are able to profit most by knowing it. I think his pioneer work is such a treasure to the human race that there ought to be a clear indication in his own words as to how it came about that he was able to push consciousness to the highest point yet achieved by any individual with the chain unbroken, you might say, back to antiquity [. . .]. C. G. took on the cruxification, I think it can be called that, of struggling through the integration process [. . .]. I am just concerned to have for the first time a record of the individuation process from the person who carried it further than anyone else. Now it seems to me that the Red Book would serve as the core of the record, and that therefore it would not be too much of a labor on C. G.'s part with you and me to do the spade work. I was thrilled to know, by the way that you thought well of this idea of mine. But I must say, when I ask myself if I really think I could fill the right function in this enterprise, my knees begin to tremble and all of the difficulties loom large on the horizon.

---

[31] Jung to Jaffé, January 20, 1954, JP.
[32] Cary Baynes to Emma Jung, May 15, 1951, JFA.
[33] JP. Jung wrote these down in the continuation of *Black Book 7*.

I know perfectly the goal I am after, but I have not yet thought out any sort of a working plan that I could submit to you and C. G.[34]

As Cary Baynes had transcribed Jung's *Red Book* (and had urged Jung to publish it), she was ideally placed to undertake such a project. This was not intended as a conventional biography, but rather sought to present Jung's own account of his individuation process.

Meanwhile, there was interest in Jung on the part of documentary makers. In 1950, the filmmaker Jerome Hill proposed a documentary on him. Together with Erica Anderson, he did some filming of Jung in Küsnacht and Bollingen in 1951. Cary Baynes and Kurt Wolff saw the footage, and were impressed by how Jung came across. However, Jung was critical of it, and the project was eventually abandoned.[35] In a conversation on October 16, 1953 with Hill and his cousin, the anthropologist Maud Oakes (who collaborated on the project), Jung commented, "I am trying to see how you can visualize or exteriorize any of my ideas."[36]

In 1952, Lucy Heyer, the ex-wife of Gustav Heyer, proposed a biography of Jung, which was to be published by Daniel Brody of Rhein Verlag, the publisher of the Eranos yearbooks. She had had analysis with Jung and Toni Wolff in the 1930s, and her brother Fritz Grote had been a school contemporary of Jung's in Basel. She intended to base her work on extended interviews with Jung, which would set it apart from all other works on him.[37] Initially, she had proposed to collaborate with Cary Baynes on the biography. On September 5, 1952, her daughter Ximena de Angulo wrote to Cary Baynes about this project after a conversation with Jung, indicating that Jung was of a view that he wouldn't proceed with Lucy Heyer's project unless she undertook it in collaboration with Cary Baynes:

---

[34] Cary Baynes to Emma Jung, May 15, 1951, JFA.

[35] Cary Baynes to Emma Jung, July 12, 1951, JFA.

[36] "Interview with C. G. Jung on October 16, 1953, in Küsnacht, near Zurich," p. 5, Jerome Hill Papers, Minnesota Historical Society. For Maud Oakes's work on Jung's Bollingen Stone, see her *The Stone Speaks: The Memoir of a Personal Transformation* (Wilmette, IL: Chiron Publications, 1987). Scripts and letters related to the film are in the Jerome Hill Papers. In 1991, some footage edited by Jonas Mekas was released as *Carl G. Jung by Jerome Hill, or Lapis Philosophorum* (available on YouTube: https://bit.ly/LapisPhilosphorum [accessed April 23, 2025]). In 1957 Hill's film on the French theologian and humanitarian Albert Schweitzer (1875–1965) won an Oscar for the best documentary.

[37] On July 25, 1951, Lucy Heyer sent Jung a synopsis in five chapters (JP). On Lucy Heyer, see Yael N. B. Gsell, *Lucy Heyer-Grote (1891–1991): Ihr Leben im Wandel der Zeit* (Hamburg: Tredition, 2021).

He [Jung] very definitely wants you to undertake it. [. . .] C. G. said he didn't see why you should have such doubts and fears as to your competence, that you had done the 1925 Notes admirably, and he visualized this as a sort of amplification of that technique. He said that in itself the idea of a biography gave him a certain discomfort, that he certainly would never write an autobiography (as he also said in Bollingen two years ago, when I questioned him on your behalf) but that he realized that circumstances were making it necessary. I had the impression that he would very much like that it be done in a way that he could control, so no nonsense would issue, not by some nincompoop after his death. I asked him if the interview method you had thought of would not be very tiring for him, and he said, oh no, that wouldn't be so bad, that he could do it quite well.[38]

In Jung's view, Cary Baynes was critical to this project, and he saw it as "an amplification" of the 1925 seminar. The factor which was overcoming his aversion to a biographical enterprise was the increasing realization that someone was bound to undertake one anyway.

On reading Lucy Heyer's outline, Cary Baynes saw much value in her project. However, it was clearly much more extraverted than her project based on Jung's interior journey as charted in *Liber Novus*. While Heyer intended to give much emphasis to Jung's forebears, Baynes considered Jung's work as marking a caesura in history, which provided a new illumination on all that had gone on before.[39] In addition to the differences in conception, it was not clear to her how they would collaborate on a practical level. Ximena de Angulo tried to persuade her mother to do so, indicating that in her view, Lucy Heyer was too much in awe of Jung, her feelings were hurt too easily, and she was insufficiently conversant with his ideas.[40] She added that he had indicated that he thought that Heyer did not know him well. As we shall see, in contrast to his collaboration with Jaffé, it appears that at no point did Jung make available to Heyer his *Black Books* or *Liber Novus*, either to use or to consult. On September 26, Ximena de Angulo wrote again to her mother:

I think there is a real danger of an outsider horning in, Jung seemed to imply that when he said to me that he saw the time had come to

---

[38] Ximena de Angulo to Cary Baynes, September 5, 1952, BP.
[39] Ximena de Angulo, personal communication to the editor.
[40] Ximena de Angulo to Cary Baynes, September 5, 1952, BP.

have a project of this sort undertaken. Reporters are constantly now trying to interview him, and it won't be long before some enterprising person saw the chance of a book being got out on him.[41]

Lucy Heyer had requested funding from the Bollingen Foundation, and Paul Mellon subsequently agreed to support the project out of his own funds.[42] On October 7, 1952 Jung wrote to Cary Baynes on the matter:

> I have insisted from the beginning that you should come in. You represent an entirely different point of view which is presumably rather important. At all events, I would like you to join in and collaborate with Mrs. Heyer, and you had better hurry up before I am getting altogether too senile![43]

Meanwhile, Lucy Heyer prepared an outline of her biography, which proposed a study of Jung's life coupled with a comprehensive contextual location of his work in Western intellectual history and its contemporary reception.[44] Cary Baynes withdrew from the project.[45]

Jung gave Lucy Heyer a volume of Ernest Jones's Freud biography so that she might get a sense of what had been written about him, remarking to Cary Baynes, "I am curious to see how Lucie Heyer is going to proceed: I still don't see exactly how she is planning to catch the bird."[46] As the project proceeded, Jung had increasing reservations concerning Lucy Heyer and her appropriateness for the task. In addition, his qualms concerning the possibility of a biography had not receded. On April 4, 1954 he wrote to Baynes:

> Concerning our dear Lucy Heyer I get more and more the feeling that you have left me holding the baby. She would like to see me at least once a week, so that I could produce a biography for her. I

---

[41] Ximena de Angulo to Cary Baynes, September 26, 1952, BP.

[42] Paul Mellon to Lucy Heyer, April 14, 1953, BA.

[43] BP (original in English).

[44] Reproduced in Shamdasani, *Jung Stripped Bare*, pp. 15–17.

[45] Olga Froebe-Kapteyn to Jack Barrett, January 6, 1953, BA. For Lucy Heyer's ms., see LH (Basel University Library). On her ms., see Florent Serina's (somewhat uncharitably titled) "Lucy Heyer-Grote, Hapless Hagiographer of C. G. Jung, with a Hitherto Unpublished Memory of Jung's Infancy," *Jung Journal: Culture & Psyche* 15, no. 1 (2021): 83–102.

[46] March 28, 1954, BA (original in English).

have tried to produce some flies for her to catch, but I don't know whether she got anywhere with that game. I must say I never would have thought of helping somebody as far away as Lucy Heyer to write my biography. You just muscled her in, and I, thinking she might alleviate your task, said yes, and you just faded out. I'm quite unable to continue this funny kind of playing at a biography. You could just as well ask me to help that foolish American Radio-Company to produce myself in the form of a film.[47] I don't go to church on Sundays with a prayer-book under my arm, nor do I wear a white coat, nor do I build hospitals, nor do I sit at the organ. So I'm not fodder for the average sentimental needs of the general public. And that will be so with my biography. There is just nothing very interesting in it.[48]

The interviews do not appear to have proceeded to Jung's liking. On September 9, 1954 he wrote to Cary Baynes that "in all the interviews I have had with [Heyer] so far, I found nothing from which I could conclude that she would be capable of producing something that would look like an intelligent biography. I must say, I am for a biography, an utterly uninteresting case, so I don't wonder that she doesn't get anywhere."[49] In response to her request for further funding from the Bollingen Foundation, Jack Barrett wrote to ask Jung if he thought this advisable.[50] Jung's reply indicates a less than enthusiastic response to the work she had done:

Up to the present, I haven't seen a line of what she has written about my biography. A while ago, I told her it would be nice to see once something of all the interviews I had given her. But up to now I have seen nothing. I am not sure at all whether she has worked out something or not. I always wondered what she was going to do about her interviews, but I couldn't say that I have got any idea of it. You will understand that under these circumstances I have grown progressively less keen to entertain the dear old lady and I have

---

[47] Notwithstanding this comment, Jung subsequently consented to several filmed interviews: an interview with Stephen Black in July 1955, a portion of which was broadcast on BBC TV's *Panorama*; in August 1957, a lengthy interview with Richard Evans; and in October 1959, an interview with John Freeman for his BBC *Face to Face* program.
[48] BP (original in English).
[49] BP (original in English).
[50] November 16, 1954, *BA*.

regretted the loss of time rather precious to me. Thus, if I may express my view of the situation, I shouldn't weep many tears if somebody would lead the sad lady kindly away. I must say with my limited imagination I cannot conceive how she could possibly construct a biography of myself, but not being a literary man I would hardly know how to go about in writing a biography.[51]

On this basis, Mellon decided to provide a "modest sum" to see Heyer to the end of 1955, to enable her to get into shape the material she had collected. A few months later, however, Jung had decided to terminate the project. Heyer had sent Jung a manuscript, and he replied on February 2, 1955,

My decision in no way indicates a negative judgement on your intelligence or your ability, but springs entirely alone from my understanding, that in my case the abyss between my damned obligations and duty is really terrible. This would make me completely discouraged, if I entrusted myself with such a task.[52]

In an undated letter to Daniel Brody which appears to be an explanation for the termination of the project, Jung wrote,

I have gained the impression from what I have read that my life does not at all contain the matter from which one could make a biography worth reading. I feared this from the beginning and for that reason also never could imagine, how one would be capable of externalising a plausible image of a life [Lebensbild] from a long chain of banalities and inconspicuous things.[53]

Heyer wrote to her ex-husband Gustav Heyer that after her initial shock, she was grateful that Jung had terminated the project, given her struggle with the writing.[54] From her papers, it appears that she had completed chapters on Jung's childhood and youth, an account of his complex psychology, and notes on his ancestry. The materials she sent

---

[51] November 24, 1954, BA (original in English).
[52] JP.
[53] JP.
[54] Gsell, *Lucy Heyer-Grote*, p. 167.

Jung were evidently drawn from these. From the contents, it is clear that Jung had spoken to her about a number of the dreams and episodes from his childhood that he would later narrate to Jaffé.[55] In retrospect, these sessions could be regarded as a rehearsal or dry run for *Memories, Dreams, Reflections*. Now, instead of the anonymized presentations that Jung had tried in his "A. E." manuscript and in his published works, the material would be clearly acknowledged as his own. Reading Heyer's chapters on Jung's childhood and youth, one may surmise that Jung found disturbing the manner in which she combined narration of episodes he had told her with her own interpretations.

During this period, Jung continued to receive a number of inquiries regarding an autobiography or biography of him. Jung's replies indicate a strong resistance to both possibilities. In 1953, Henri Flournoy, the son of Jung's mentor, the Swiss psychologist, Théodore Flournoy, relayed to Jung the question of a Dr. Junod as to whether he had written an autobiography, or intended to do one.[56] Jung replied, "I have always mistrusted an autobiography because one can never tell the truth. In so far as one is truthful, or believes one is truthful, it is an illusion, or of bad taste."[57]

Jung was no less sanguine concerning the possibility of a biography of his life. In a reply to John Thorburn in 1952, who had suggested that Jung should commission one, he wrote,

[I]f I where you I shouldn't bother about my biography. I don't want to write one, because quite apart from the lack of motive I wouldn't know how to set about it. Much less can I see how anybody else could disentangle this monstrous Gordian knot of fatality, denseness, and aspirations and what-not! Anybody who would try such an adventure ought to analyze me far beyond my own head if he wants to make a real job of it.[58]

---

[55] LH.

[56] Henri Flournoy to Jung, February 8, 1953, JP. In a similar vein, on January 13, 1948 Jung wrote to Antonios Savides, "An autobiography is the one thing I am never going to write. Such things are never quite true and they cannot be made true. I've seen enough autobiographies in my lifetime and the essential things were lacking in every one of them." *Letters*, vol. 1, p. 489.

[57] Jung to Henri Flournoy, February 12, 1953. *Letters*, vol. 2, p. 106 (original in French, translation modified). In a dedicatory note to a collection of his offprints for Jürg Fierz, Jung simply wrote, "I myself have a distaste for autobiography." December 21, 1945 (*Letters*, vol. 1, p. 404).

[58] Jung to John Thorburn, February 6, 1952, *Letters* 1, pp. 38–39 (original in English).

In 1954, Jung gave an interview to Cleonie Carroll Wadsworth, in which he commented on his suitability as the subject for a biography:

> Someone wants to write my biography but it is foolish. I am a simple Bourgeois. I seldom travel—I sit here and write or walk down my garden—my life has not been dramatic. Now old Schweitzer is dramatic—playing the organ, working in a long white coat among the palm trees or going with the bible under his arm to preach—or healing people. No one knows what I am doing and it is not paintable and you cannot take a picture of it.[59]

Meanwhile, after the collapse of Lucy Heyer's project, the search for a suitable biographer continued. On May 5, 1956, Cary Baynes explained to Jung that she had never been interested in writing about the extraverted side of Jung's life, and had never considered that Lucy Heyer could have written about the introverted side, adding, "I don't think anyone but you can as a matter of fact."[60] She proposed another candidate in the form of Eugen Böhler, given his cultural background and understanding of Jung's work. Böhler was a professor of economics at the ETH Zurich, and he had applied Jung's work in the economic sphere.[61] Regarding the introverted side, she thought that Böhler could possibly get enough information from Jung to cover this.[62]

IMPROVISING JUNG'S MEMORIES

Kurt Wolff was one of the legends of European publishing. Among the authors he published were Kafka, Meyrink, Pasternak, Grass, Frisch, Musil, Trakl, Broch, Valery, Walser, Buber, Rolland, Tagore, Benjamin, and Jaspers. He was described in *The New York Times* as "a tall courtly man who exudes old world charm" and "one of the most distinguished book publishers of the 20th Century."[63] He worked closely with his wife, Helen, who was actively involved in the Jung project. Kurt Wolff Verlag was

---

[59] Interview with Cleonie Carroll Wadsworth, March 1, 1954, CLM (original in English). The would-be biographer referred to is evidently Lucy Heyer.

[60] Cary Baynes to Jung, May 5, 1956, JP.

[61] See Gerhard Wehr, ed., *C. G. Jung und Eugen Böhler: Eine Begegnung in Briefen* (Zurich: Hochschulverlag, 1996).

[62] Cary Baynes to Jung, May 5, 1956, BP.

[63] *The New York Times*, September 3, 1961, p. 8, and October 23, 1963, p. 41.

known as the "Expressionist" publishing house.[64] He was in effect one of the architects of European modernist literature. After emigrating to the USA, Helen and Kurt Wolff founded Pantheon Books in 1942, which did much to introduce modern European literature in the English-speaking world. Pantheon Books was the publisher of the Bollingen Series, of which Jung's *Collected Works* was subseries XX. The Bollingen Series was vital for the financial survival of Pantheon Books.[65]

Wolff's ethos is captured in the following statement:

> Either you publish books you think people ought to read, or books you think people want to read. Publishers in the second category, publishers, that is to say, who slavishly cater to the public's tastes, do not count in our scheme of things[; . . .] for publishing activity of this kind you need neither enthusiasm nor taste.[66]

Kurt Wolff had been an enthusiast for Jung's work for a long time. He considered Jung to be a "great thinker and a visionary."[67] They first met in the 1920s. He recalled hearing Jung at Count Keyserling's School of Wisdom in Darmstadt and meeting him in Munich in the early twenties.[68] The first present that Kurt Wolff gave his future wife Helen Mosel had been a copy of Jung and Wilhelm's *The Secret of the Golden Flower*.[69] Although a decade younger than Jung, Wolff shared with him a deep background in European humanist culture. This cultural affinity formed the basis of their relationship. Their collaboration would in turn help make Jung's work accessible to an Anglo-American audience far removed from this.

---

[64] On Kurt Wolff, see Barbara Weidle, ed., *Kurt Wolff: Ein Literat und Gentleman* (Bonn: Weidle Verlag, 2007); Alexander Wolff, *Endpapers: A Family Story of Books, War, Escape, and Home* (New York: Grove Atlantic, 2020). On Helen Wolff, who played a far more prominent role than has been realized, see Marion Detjen, "'At my death, burn or throw away unread!' Zum Hintergrund des Hintergrunds," in Helen Wolff, *Hintergrund für Liebe* (Bonn: Weidle Verlag, 2020), pp. 119–215.

[65] Helen Wolff, cited in A. Wolff, *Endpapers*, p. 191.

[66] Kurt Wolff, "On Publishing in General and the Question, How Do an Author and Publisher Come Together?," in Michael Ermarth, ed., *Kurt Wolff: A Portrait in Essays and Letters* (Chicago: University of Chicago Press, 1991), p. 9.

[67] Kurt Wolff to Aniela Jaffé, October 8, 1958, BL. (Unless otherwise noted, Kurt Wolff's letters are in German).

[68] On the School of Wisdom, Kurt Wolff recalled "with gratitude some truly valuable lectures by men such as Max Scheler, Richard Wilhelm, and C. G. Jung" ("Rabindranath Tagore," in Ermrath, *Kurt Wolff*, p. 122); Kurt Wolff to Jaffé, November 1, 1957, BL. For Jung's recollections of Keyserling, see below, pp. 123–28.

[69] Helen Wolff to Jung, November 12, 1958, BL.

For years, Kurt Wolff had unsuccessfully tried to get Jung to write an autobiography. In the early fifties, they met at the Eranos conferences in Ascona.[70] In 1956, the theme was "Man and the Creative." At that meeting, Wolff took another tack, and suggested that his friend Jolande Jacobi, herself a Viennese émigré, undertake a biography of Jung in the form of interviews. The model for this was Eckermann's *Conversations with Goethe*. Jacobi declined, and proposed Aniela Jaffé for the task, because, as Jung's secretary, it would be easier for her to ask questions concerning his life in free hours.[71]

This arrangement was to work out well. After the collapse of Lucy Heyer's project the preceding year, Kurt Wolff's renewed approach was well timed. Jung had in effect already come round to the inevitability of a biography being written, and considered that it would be better if he had a hand in shaping it. To Richard Hull, the translator of Jung's *Collected Works*, Wolff described how

> for several years he had tried to persuade Jung to write [an autobiography], how Jung had always refused, and how finally he (Kurt) hit on the happy idea of an "Eckerfrau" to whom Jung could dictate at random, the Eckerfrau being Aniela Jaffé.[72]

Aniela Jaffé was born in Berlin in 1903.[73] She initially studied medicine, though her interests shifted to psychology. She went to the Uni-

---

[70] On July 17, 1953, Wolff sent Jung a clipping of a case concerning synchronicity from *The New York Times Magazine* and wrote, "happily thinking back to the pleasant hours spent with you at Round Table at Olga's in '51 and '52." (JP). This was a reference to the Eranos conferences. Elsewhere, he recalled that "I was never able to convince C. G. Jung that *Das grüne Gesicht* [*The Green Face*] was a bad novel—Jung thought very highly of it." Wolff, "On Publishing in General," p. 13.

[71] Jaffé, draft foreword to *MDR*, Rascher Verlag archives, Zentralbibliothek, Zurich, p. 1.

[72] Richard Hull, "A Record of Events Preceding the Publication of Jung's Autobiography, as Seen by R.F.C. Hull," July 27, 1960, BA. In an undated note of "subjects mentioned in correspondence with Jaffé," Kurt Wolff referred to the project as the "Jung–Eckermann book" (BL). The Eckermann/Goethe analogy was not lost on Jung: see below, n. 127.) On July 21, 1958 Wolff wrote to Kyrill Shabert, "You have asked me why I am so excited, you even said obsessed, by this manuscript. You know that I have tried for years, unsuccessfully, to persuade Jung to write his autobiography, that I had just about given up hope, when, all of a sudden in late fall 1956, he changed his mind." (BL).

[73] Information on Aniela Jaffé is drawn from her interview with Gene Nameche (CLM, Jung Biographical Archive), from her essay "From Jung's Last Years" in her *From the Life and Work of C. G. Jung*, trans. R.F.C. Hull and Murray Stein (Einsiedeln: Daimon Verlag, 1989), and from Elena Fischli's "Historical Commentary" to Jaffé's *Reflections on the Life*

versity of Hamburg to study with the prominent child psychologist William Stern (1871–1938). In 1929 she married Jean Dreyfus (1904–1985). Dreyfus was Swiss, and it was through her marriage that she acquired a Swiss passport. She wrote her doctoral dissertation on "The Social Behaviour of Children in Kindergarten," under Stern. However, due to the advent of the Nazi regime and the expulsion of Jewish academics, including Stern, she was unable to have a doctoral viva and so to graduate. On refusing to give a Nazi salute, she was expelled from the university. On Stern's recommendation, she emigrated to Switzerland and went to Zurich, working at the Balgrist Clinic and the Burghölzli asylum. She also worked as a freelance secretary for Professors Gideon and von Tscharner. In 1937 she separated from her husband. During this period, she attended one of Jung's seminars on children's dreams at the ETH. She then began an analysis with Jung's student Liliane Frey-Rohn (1901–1991), who in turn sent her to work with Jung. Her analysis with him commenced in 1937. In 1939 she presented a case study in Jung's "Children's Dreams" seminars.[74] In 1947, she became the secretary of the newly founded Jung Institute in Zurich (a part-time position). During this period, she would undertake tasks for Jung, such as writing letters, doing research in libraries and commenting on manuscripts. In 1950 Jung included her essay on E.T.A. Hoffman in a collection of his writings.[75]

In 1955 Jaffé became Jung's secretary. Her schedule with him began with dealing with correspondence from ten to twelve o'clock. She later recalled, "I must confess that the approach of the old magician never lost its excitement in all those years. With my inner ear I still hear it to this day."[76] In an interview with Gene Nameche, she recalled that after Jung's wife's death,

> I answered many letters for him, he did not feel at all like doing that work. I read my tentative answers to him—sometimes he corrected a word or a sentence, sometimes it was all right. After a certain time

and Dreams of C. G. Jung (Einsiedeln: Daimon Verlag, 2023; hereafter: Reflections). See also Remembering Jung #11: A Conversation about C.G. Jung and His Work with Aniela Jaffé (DVD), C. G. Jung Institute of Los Angeles.

[74] See Jung, , Children's Dreams, pp. 279–90.

[75] Aniela Jaffé, "Bilder und Symbole aus E.T.A. Hoffmans Märchen 'Der goldne Topf'" (Images and symbols from E.T.A. Hoffman's fairy-tale, "The Golden Pot"), in C. G. Jung, Gestaltungen des Unbewussten (Formations of the unconscious) Psychologische Abhandlungen 7 (Zurich: Rascher Verlag, 1950).

[76] Jaffé, "From Jung's Last Years," p. 139.

he began to be interested again in what he got from the world and I stopped writing in his name.[77]

This working arrangement shows the level of trust that Jung showed in Jaffé, allowing her to write in his name, and mediate his relation to the world. At the same time, she continued her own researches, publishing her book on death dreams and ghosts in 1959.[78]

Aware of what had happened with Lucy Heyer's project, and possibly having read Heyer's manuscripts, Jaffé wrote a portrait of Jung in *Du* in 1955 in which she noted,

> The greatness of this life does not lie outside. Personal details: studies, career, professional positions, honors, travels and encounters are only pointers, outward markers, between and behind which the fullness of human experience plays out, and the great arc of the soul's development spans.
>
> The discrepancy between the relative inconspicuousness of this researcher's life and the inner density and fullness could overwhelm every biographer; for it befits only the man himself who bears such a life, who has given it form and also been shaped by it to report, reveal or draw a veil over his experiences. To allow the contemporary world and the night world to have a share in his innermost.
>
> Yet for the observer who seeks to understand this life its polarities will also be significant: they correspond to the differentiation between the personal world of consciousness and the impersonal one of the not-I, of the limited world of consciousness and the vast world of the psyche or the unconscious.[79]

This clearly articulates her sense that what was significant in Jung's life was his spiritual development, and the challenge this posed to biographers. What was required was a biography that gave due prominence to the unconscious nightworld. As she saw it, it was ultimately only Jung himself who could write this.

The discussions with Kurt Wolff evidently continued to reverberate in Jung's mind. Immediately after the Eranos conference in 1956, Jung

---

[77] Aniela Jaffé, interview with Gene Nameche, p. 11, CLM, Jung Biographical Archive.
[78] Aniela Jaffé, *Death Dreams and Ghosts* (Einsiedeln: Daimon Verlag 1999 [1959]).
[79] Aniela Jaffé, "Carl Gustav Jung," *Du: Schweizerische Monatsschrift*, April 1955, p. 22.

was visited by his friend the psychiatrist E. A. Bennet. Bennet noted Jung saying on August 30,

> At breakfast C. G. spoke of the difficulties implicit in the idea of anyone writing his biography; he said it would require a full understanding of his thought, and no one understood it completely. Freud's life, he said, could be easily described because his thought was simply laid out. But with him it was more complex, for unless the development of his thought were central to his biography it would be no more than a series of incidents, like writing the biography of Kant without knowing his work.[80]

As illustration, Jung described how his 1913 dream of slaying Siegfried was a turning point in his life.[81] On his return to England, Bennet followed up the possibility of undertaking a biography himself. On September 5 he wrote to Jung, recalling their discussion of Dr. Howard Philp's suggestion that Philp write a biography of him. Ruth Bailey had then suggested to Bennet that Bennet should write one, as Philp had now recently suggested as well. He added that it would be helpful if he could collaborate with a member of Jung's family, such as his daughter Marianne Niehus. On October 10 Jung replied to Bennet,

> As you know, I am a somewhat complicated phenomenon, which hardly can be covered by one biographer only [. . .]. Therefore I should like to make you a similar proposition, namely that you proceed along your line as a medical man like Philp has done on his part as a theologian. Being a doctor you would inquire into the anamnesis of your patient and you would ask the questions and I would answer as a patient would answer. Thus you would move along the lines of your habitual thinking and would be enabled to produce a picture of my personality understandable at least to more or less medical people. Philp certainly would produce a picture of my religious aspect, equally satisfactory. Since it is undeniable that one of several aspects is medical, another theological, a biography written by specialists in their field has the best chance of being accurate, although not comprehensive in as much as the specifical

---

[80] E. A. Bennet, *Meetings with Jung: Conversations Recorded During the Years 1946–1961* (Zurich: Daimon Verlag, 1982), August 30, 1956 (p. 61).
[81] *LN*, pp. 160–61.

psychological synthesis would demand somebody equally at home in primitive psychology, mythology, history, parapsychology and science—and even in the field of artistic experience.[82]

For Jung, the solution to the perspectival limitations stemming from the personal equation of the biographer lay in having multiple biographies undertaken, from different disciplinary standpoints.

Unaware of these parallel developments, Kurt Wolff wrote to Jaffé on October 24,

> From Dr. Jolande Jacobi I learned that she told you about a Jung book which I had discussed with her in August in Ascona. I now learn from Dr. Jacobi that Professor Jung, as yourself, responded favourably to the idea, and I am very happy about it. When you have thought the matter over and discussed the whole project in more detail with Dr. Jung, please let me have an outline and a tentative list of contents. I suppose Dr. Jacobi has told you that I feel it would be most desirable to present the material in a very direct way, Eckermann-like, or rather, giving Jung's memories of people, places, and events in his own words in the first person singular "as told to Aniela Jaffe."[83]

A work presented in the first person would clearly be regarded as more authoritative than a biography written in the third person. Kurt Wolff was asking Jaffé to continue "writing in Jung's name."

Jaffé proceeded to discuss the project with Jung. On November 9 she replied to Wolff, indicating that Jung was not in principle disinclined, but suggested taking the whole thing as an experiment. The main issue was the question of time, as Jung was easily tired. Jung suggested that he would prefer that these conversations take place at Bollingen. Evidently

---

[82] Jung to Bennet, October 10, 1956, JP (original in English); Philp had also been considering a biographical work on Jung. After modifications, the outcome of Bennet's project was his *C. G. Jung* (Wilmette, IL: Chiron Publications, 2006 [1961]); the outcome of Philp's was his *Jung and the Problem of Evil* (London: Rockliff, 1958). Jung's replies to Philp's questions were also reproduced in *CW* 18 under the title "Jung and Religious Belief" (*CE* 25). In a later diary entry Bennet recorded a conversation with Mrs. Niehus, to whom he had shown his introduction: "She said my approach was quite different from Mrs. Jaffé's and pressed me to continue. She said mine was more masculine, and the fact that another biography was in preparation should not prevent me from going on with it." Bennet, *Meetings with Jung*, March 24, 1959 (p. 111).

[83] Wolff to Jaffé, October 24 1956, BL (original in English).

encouraged by her response, Wolff told Jaffé that it would take a few months for the project to take shape.[84] He subsequently informed Herbert Read that in the last analysis it was Jaffé who persuaded Jung to undertake the task.[85] For Jaffé, the project was supremely important. She informed Alwina von Keller that she regarded her role as the "catalyzer" in it as the most fundamental in her life.[86]

Meanwhile, Gerald Sykes (1904–1984), an author and literary critic who had written a favorable review of Jung's *Psychology and Alchemy* in *The New York Times* and had met him in Ascona in 1955, wrote to Jung that on December 4, 1956 William McGuire had informed him that Kurt Wolff "has had an idea that I should go to Zurich, spend as much time as possible with you, and write a sort of Eckermann about you."[87] Jaffé was quick to reply on Jung's behalf on December 11:

> Dr. Jung said that at the present moment two biographies are in the making and a third one will start in springtime. So, he said, that for the moment he has enough to do providing the different biographers with his memories and thoughts. He is convinced that you would understand this difficulty and that he cannot make up his mind to begin a fourth one. That would be too much for him.[88]

A few days earlier, on December 7, Bennet had written to Jung developing plans for his biography: "You kindly replied last month and made the valuable suggestion that I might address a few questions to you."[89] He then appended four questions, mainly about Jung's childhood. A few days later, Jung replied that it would take him too long to give written answers, so invited him to stay for ten to fourteen days over the winter holidays. He reflected,

---

[84] Wolff to Jaffé, November 13, 1956, BL.

[85] October 27, 1959, BA.

[86] Jaffé to Alwina von Keller, August 25, 1959, JP (filed with Jung's correspondence to von Keller). Unless otherwise stated, Jaffé's letters are in German.

[87] Gerald Sykes to Jung, December 7, 1956, JP. It is not clear whether Sykes was directly in touch with Kurt Wolff at all, or whether this just came through William McGuire, based on what he may have heard. To Gene Nameche, Sykes recalled that Kurt Wolff "wanted me to go to Zurich and do a book based on conversations with [Jung]": interview with Gene Nameche, p. 6, CLM, Jung Biographical Archive. On Sykes, see below, p. 295.

[88] JP. The "two biographies" underway evidently refers to Bennet's and Philp's projects, and the third is Jaffé and Kurt Wolff's.

[89] Bennet to Jung, December 7, 1956, JP.

The whole thing is a ticklish task and it seems to be rather difficult because the average reader would hardly be capable of understanding what it is all about. I have been exposed to so many misunderstandings that I am rather scared to tell the truth about my biography, as I see it. I should therefore prefer, you should first try to find your way through the jungle of memories.[90]

Bennet stayed with Jung in early January, and his notes of his discussions with Jung record a number of reminiscences.

At that time, Jung already had exclusive contracts with Routledge and Kegan Paul, the Bollingen Foundation, and Rascher Verlag. For another publisher to manage publish Jung's "autobiography" would be quite a coup, though clearly a challenge that Kurt Wolff was up for. In an article entitled "On Luring Away Authors, or How Authors and Publishers Part Company," Wolff wrote,

Every country in the world has strict laws about white-slave traffic. Authors, on the other hand, are an unprotected species and must look after themselves. They can be bought and sold, like girls for the white-slave trade—except that in the case of authors it is not illegal.[91]

As Wolff saw it, the work was not intended for Jungians, but for general readers. As he later remarked to Cary Baynes, he hoped that it would be a book which would "lead the outsider inside the work."[92] Due to the involvement of another publisher, the book did not go down the same editorial channels as the rest of Jung's work.

On January 7, 1957 Kurt Wolff inquired as to how Jaffé was getting on with the project, and asked whether she had started taking notes. From the outset, he was an active editor, suggesting the approach she should take, as well as some of the questions she should ask, as if he saw her as his proxy. This would later lead to considerable tensions. He gave indications of some of the topics he would like to see covered:

It has come to mind that I have given you very few hints about the many subjects which in my opinion should be included. It would be wonderful, for instance, if you could get Jung to talk a little bit

---

[90] Jung to Bennet, December 10, 1956, JP (original in English).
[91] Ermarth, *Kurt Wolff*, p. 21.
[92] Wolff to Cary Baynes, September 18, 1959, BP.

about his feelings towards animals, about the characteristics of various nationalities (the British, the Germans, etc.), how he feels about the primitive people he has come to know, some pages about his reactions to children, to the sexes, and then of course to single personalities such as Charcot, Freud, etc., etc.[93]

As a model, he directed her to Paul Claudel's recently published *Improvised Memories* (1954).[94] This work was based on a lengthy series of radio interviews with Claudel, in which Jean Amrouche questioned him on his life.

Jaffé was concerned by the relation of her project to Bennet's undertaking. On January 11 she wrote to Kurt Wolff that "Professor Jung takes the view that Bennet's and my work would not overlap, not only because we are two very different personalities and characters but ultimately because my perspective will be a different one from Bennet's."[95] She thanked Kurt Wolff for his suggestions, but had a different perspective:

One can hardly ask him such "normal" questions as his view on different nationalities. But his relationship with animals will play a role—like when a pair of snakes took up residence on the shore near his tower for whom he regularly put out a saucer of milk, as well as a dog in whose eyes he saw his deceased father, or a bird who sat on his spade when he was digging up potatoes and in whom he greeted the "ghost" of a beloved friend who had passed on. This is his "manner." The proximity of the dead in general, I'd like to say: the proximity of the beyond, as well as a quite extraordinary connection with nature. My guiding principle would be: Jung and nature—inner and outer. Inner nature includes dreams and everything that belongs to that. Outer nature is the earth.[96]

From the outset, and following the perspective she had presented in her *Du* article, Jaffé had a clear conception of the type of work she was intending, which was at significant variance to what Kurt Wolff had in mind: this was to be no conventional biography, but, to use the language of Jung's 1958 memoir, it was to be a study of Jung's "personality

---

[93] Wolff to Jaffé, January 7, 1957, BL (original in English).
[94] Paul Claudel, *Mémoires improvisés* (Paris: Gallimard, 1954).
[95] Jaffé to Wolff, January 11, 1957, BL.
[96] Jaffé to Wolff, January 11, 1957, BL. On the episodes mentioned, see below, pp. 246–47.

no. 2." As he had had already confided striking episodes to her, the first task would be to get him to relay these again.

She added that Jung had given her permission to use his 1925 seminar, in which he discussed some of these episodes. Furthermore, there was a "very thick book" with fantasies from which Jung had developed his theories, and she asked whether this would be of interest to Wolff. As for questions regarding Freud and Charcot, these could be left to Bennet (as she didn't find this aspect interesting).[97] She continued,

> Quite a while ago he once told me how, as a young boy, he had made himself manikins, sort of homunculi, and of how he had experienced a type of identification with a stone, heralding the alchemist to come, and things like this [. . .]. Concerning the unfolding of the story, Jung prefers me to keep to "inner material," so to dreams and fantasies.[98]

As to procedure, Jaffé wrote that she had been tempted to put questions to Jung when she went over the post with him, but had refrained from doing so, as she saw how easily he tired. Jung had indicated that he would prefer to deal with her questions while in Bollingen.[99]

On January 16 Wolff replied, indicating that he didn't think that Bennet's project would clash. He gave a strong indication to what he was looking for: "Let us by all means avoid for ourselves the word and idea of a 'biography.' After all, the whole idea of the book is that it should not be a biography, but as nearly as possible an autobiography."[100] He was glad that she had started looking at Claudel's book, and added, "This, by the way, would be the ideal title for our book, indicating exactly what I have in mind."[101] In contrast to the Claudel book, he recommended that

---

[97] When Bennet's book appeared, before her own, Jaffé found to her great consternation that Jung had also told Bennet a number of the dreams and key episodes that he had confided to her. Kurt Wolff wrote to Cary Baynes, "Aniela has fits about the book and I well understand why: Jung told Bennet not all but quite a lot of the stuff he dictated Aniela for the autobiography—many of his dreams for instance, among them the Basler Münster dream—and now his book comes out before the autobiography will be published in Spring. Aniela feels cheated by the Master." Kurt Wolff to Cary Baynes, July 20, 1961, BP.

[98] Jaffé to Wolff, January 11, 1957, BL.

[99] Jaffé to Wolff, January 11, 1957, BL.

[100] Wolff to Jaffé, January 16, 1957, BL.

[101] The first contracts for the work, dated October 25, 1957 describe it as a work "tentatively titled 'Carl Gustav Jung's Improvised Memories'" (BL).

the Jung book, I think could be improved by reducing the part of the interviewer in favor of more talk by the interviewee. Your idea to give substantial space to Jung's relation to nature seems to be excellent, and I think it would be excellent to use material from early seminars. Maybe, you could transcribe the seminar texts into something more direct. What I am aiming at for the whole book is as much direct speech by Jung as possible.

I strongly feel, of course that the book should not be confined to the one subject nature, but should have reminiscences from Jung's childhood, his adolescent years, etc., etc.,—as much as you can get out of him.

When I mentioned names like Charcot and Freud and Jung's experiences with them, I did not, of course, have in mind Jung's position with regard to Freud as a scholar (a subject that has been treated at sufficient length in other publications), but informal observations of Freud as husband, father, friend—in other words, as a personality—and this goes for the other famous people too.

To give another example: When I had the pleasure of spending with my wife an hour with Jung in Küsnacht in late January of 1954, we talked about Bachofen and Burckhardt, and in an extremely lively way Jung told how he remembers these two great figures as students from his student days in Basel; how Bachofen, the wealthy patrician, arrived at the University in his coach, impeccably dressed, and how Burckhardt, carrying a large heavy portfolio with the photographs to be shown students, entered the university in his shabby old jacket, etc., etc. And he went out telling how in those years the memory of the time Nietzsche spent at Basel University was still alive with many people.

And finally it would be wonderful if you could bring Jung to tell you in a relaxed hour a little about his family background, his growing up in the family, how he felt about his parents and brothers and sisters, how and when he outgrew the family ties.

And all this should go into the manuscript in *direkte Rede*, Jung speaking in the first person. I could imagine that a half-hour here and there, in Küsnacht or Bollingen, just the time Jung takes out of serious work for a cup of tea or walk in the garden, would give you an opportunity to assemble such material gradually. Perhaps in the beginning you will even forget about how to group and organize the material and will just take down whatever you can, keeping in mind that you should try to get material of as much variety as possible.[102]

On January 20 Jaffé replied, thanking Wolff for his very important suggestions. She related to him that the previous Friday, completely unexpectedly, Jung had said that he wanted to tell her his earliest childhood memories, which she immediately took down stenographically. These memories were precious and moving. She added,

> If one only knew what lay in seeds which later blossomed, these small experiences become terribly important. They then contain an almost mysterious profundity. Jung did not tell me these broader associations; he assumes that I understand them; something he explicitly emphasized.[103]

She wasn't sure that she grasped all these connections, so wondered if it would be possible for her "to appear in this autobiography as a 'speaker', so to speak, explaining the colourful events on stage in everyday garb and in a low voice."[104] She added that Jung had told her that he wanted to speak to her often, not systematically, but of whatever occurred to him. She thanked Wolff for his suggestions, which were very helpful, and was glad that he wasn't expecting something systematic—ordering the material was a secondary question, which could be left till later. Clearly, Jung felt comfortable narrating such intimate memories to Jaffé, to whom he did not need to spell out all the connections to his later life and work.

Wolff was happy to receive this news, which seemed to present an ideal solution:

> What could be nicer than Jung's spontaneous willingness to speak to you of his early childhood memories—here we have "improvised memories." At other times he will perhaps tell you about his years at the Gymnasium, or his student years, whatever; and in the meantime perhaps other topics as well. You are completely right to leave your notes in their original form for now—other than that, "editing" should be avoided as far as possible; arranging and collating material etc., are a matter for later on.[105]

[102] Wolff to Jaffé, January 16, 1957, BL (original in English).
[103] Jaffé to Wolff, January 20, 1957, BL.
[104] Jaffé to Wolff, January 11, 1957, BL.
[105] Wolff to Jaffé, January 26, 1957, BL.

Like Lucy Heyer, Jaffé undertook a series of regular interviews with Jung, which she noted in shorthand. She then typed out her notes, and sent copies regularly to Kurt Wolff.[106] To Helen Wolff, Jaffé described her approach:

> Actually I have only spoken and asked questions very little. Jung spoke from the heart. Sometimes we were both silent for a long time, until something new emerged within him.—In any case it was important to Jung that he himself came out "purer," even at the cost of completeness or form.[107]

In retrospect, she noted that she had "sometimes asked questions and made remarks and on rare occasions there were others present who did the same."[108] As she had not mastered shorthand, "whenever possible [. . .] I did write up and edit my notes later the same day, adding any additional recollections of what Jung had said, and rendered everything into a readable style while endeavouring to maintain Jung's direct and free style of expression."[109] To William McGuire, she later recalled that Jung "spoke and followed a sort of Freudian line of assocations. When I came home, I took a cup of tea, went immediately to the typewriter: copied my notes and filled them out with what was still in my ears."[110]

Following the first session on January 18 (with a brief addendum the following day), Jung continued his narration of his childhood experiences on January 25. The project was then interrupted, as Jaffé became seriously ill and was hospitalized.[111] It recommenced at the end of March. On March 21 Kurt Wolff wrote to her, glad to hear that she had recovered after a month in hospital. He responded positively to her suggestion "to include in our book such material as you have put down in the past about remarks Jung made, stories he told, etc." He added, "In putting questions to Dr. Jung, I am sure you will have in mind the desirability of rounding out the various phases of his life with experiences, with meetings with personalities who became important to him, etc."[112]

In her introduction to *Memories, Dreams, Reflections*, Jaffé wrote,

---

[106] Jaffé to the editor, January 1991.
[107] Jaffé to Helen Wolff, October 14, 1958, BL.
[108] *Reflections*, p. 8.
[109] *Reflections*, p. 9.
[110] Jaffé to William McGuire, November 26, 1981, Jung Collection, LC.
[111] On February 2 and 20, Jung wrote to her with concern and advice regarding illness and recovery (JP).
[112] Wolff to Jaffé, March 21, 1957, BL.

It had been proposed that the book be written not as a "biography" but in the form of an "autobiography," with Jung himself as the narrator. This plan determined the form of the book, and my first task consisted solely in asking questions and noting down Jung's replies.[113]

From March 30 onward Jaffé continued her "biography hours" with Jung on a regular basis.[114] Writing to Kurt Wolff in 1958, she characterized these hours as follows: "Conversation with him [. . .] was like a storm wind, no, like a hurricane that swept over me. I knew that it was not Jung who was speaking here, but his creative daimon, and that there was nothing else to do but submit to it."[115] On receiving the installments of her notes, Wolff marked them up extensively (though it does not appear that his edits were conveyed back to her). From April, she started arranging the material thematically and chronologically into chapters. The first drafts of these took seven months to prepare.[116] Meanwhile Wolff, together with Wolfgang Sauerlander, had independently started to compile material from her notes into chapters.[117]

At the beginning of January 1958 Wolff showed the manuscript of the Interviews to Cary Baynes, who described her impressions to Jung:

I went into the Wolffs' without an Ahnung that I was going to read a book with living fire in it. I was conscious as I read, that I was in a sort of passionate participation with your crucifixion, it was mine too, and everything was involved in the way you handled it. Then the outside world melted away and I was THERE, that is, in a state of being wholly new to me; I knew for the first time, but what I knew I absolutely cannot report. This I cannot understand. Do you think I got into the region beyond Maya? I did not think that anything like this would be permitted to me. It marks a climax in my life [. . .]. Irrespective of its effects on me, this is a profoundly moving book, and it is so right the way it is written, that the contents are

---

[113] *MDR*, p. 7.

[114] Jaffé to Wolff, January 10, 1958, BL.

[115] Jaffé to Wolff, October 19, 1958, BL.

[116] Jaffé to Wolff, November 13, 1959, BL.

[117] Wolff and Sauerlander's compiled chapters can be found in folders B–G of the protocols of the Interviews (Jung Collection, LC). Sauerlander (1911–1976) was a fellow German émigré, who became a production manager at Pantheon. He later worked for the Bollingen Foundation, edited and translated the collected works of Bertolt Brecht and co-edited the German edition of the Freud–Jung letters.

out of prying, monkey hands. Also it is the right introduction to the Red Book, and so I can die in peace on that score![118]

Another reader of the Interviews who felt similarly moved in a profoundly participatory manner was Helen Wolff. On March 13, 1958 she drafted a letter to Jung conveying her impressions of what she had read:

The special thing about your form of communication is that it will immediately bring about an active reaction in the reader. One involuntarily gets into a dialogue with what has been read. Be it childhood memories, dreams, the final visions—the effect is an expansion of consciousness, an activation of one's own content, an abandonment of the normal limits of the known and the circumspect.

To meet a person who so radically surrenders to his daimon is something extraordinary—how extraordinary is one who lives so long and faithfully with one's self perhaps not fully consciously. The fact that you have found a form of communicating these experiences in a completely natural, non-hermetic, unmysterious way, allowing the reader to participate in the self-expression of one's own self, with absolute impartiality—that makes your book into something unique, almost eerie in its effect. So one wants to continue the conversation with the book to infinity, because here is someone who has exceeded the normal mortal limits, has an idea of the greater consciousness in which we are included, and which opens up to us this consciousness, as far as a man is able to open it up.

Just as it is so extraordinarily personal, the manuscript has such a great fascination and becomes universally effective.[119]

Jaffé conveyed to Helen Wolff Jung's response on hearing her reaction:

That's how I feel about life, as a tremendous stream. It is painful to be outside this stream, and to be in the stream is a painful delight. But to be outside is no delight. One is then so to speak, very glad to be in it, but it is only a reward for one's own cowardice, and one pays for it with spiritual constipation. How one can live so half-cocked is a complete mystery to me.[120]

---

[118] Cary Baynes to Jung, January 8, 1958, BP.
[119] Helen Wolff to Jung, March 13, 1958, BL.
[120] Jaffé to Helen Wolff, March 18, 1958, BL.

With greater detachment, but no less excitement, Kurt Wolff conveyed his impressions to his colleague at Pantheon, Kyrill Schabert:

> After reading the first installment I realized that Jung was (and he still is) writing this book with a directness and immediacy I hadn't dared to hope for. The aliveness and freshness of the great old man [. . .] are really incredible. When in February I expressed to him my admiration for the way he is writing this book, he said, "It's one of the pleasant advantages of old age not to care any more what other people may think or say, but just to speak without inhibition in all sincerity how one feels." It's this human grandeur, the sovereign truthfulness of the memories that impresses and excites me so much.[121]

We are now in a position to follow Jung's reminiscences and reflections, in the sequence in which they originally unfolded, and without the subsequent deletions and revisions, by many hands. Jung was a great raconteur, and spoke colorfully and with much humor of the people and situations that he encountered in his life, ranging from Einstein, William James, Count Keyserling, Leo Frobenius, Thomas Mann, Theodore Roosevelt and H. G. Wells to anonymous patients. As a psychologist, he took a lively interest in quirks of behavior, happenstance, and twists of fate. A lot of this, however, which was precisely what Kurt Wolff was seeking, was omitted. More personal material, such as Jung's discussions of his relation with Toni Wolff, as well as speculations on the possibilities of her reincarnation, in comparison to that of his wife, was also omitted, along with religious and metaphysical speculations that Jaffé felt the world was not ready for. The stark language with which Jung recalled his childhood and youth was toned down. These changes significantly tilted the resultant book towards inner biography, without some of the significant relationships within which this was embedded.

The Interviews shed incomparable light on the composition of *Memories, Dreams, Reflections*, and enables one to see the extent of the collective editorial work that shaped the latter. What was to be taken as Jung's final testament was by no means a solitary enterprise, stemming from his pen alone. However, this, together with the omitted materials, is not the sole value of the Interviews. Beyond the omissions, the largest gulf between the Interviews and *Memories* lies in the manner in which the

---

[121] Kurt Wolff to Kyrill Schabert, July 21, 1958, BL. Original in English.

material was recast in the latter into a chronological narrative, obscuring the work of memory, with its multiple threads: the continual back-and-forth between the past, the present, and the intemporal in Jung's recollections, in search of what connected them and what might lie behind such connections, that is all-pervasive in the Interviews.

As powerful as the impact of *Memories* on the reading public for more than half a century has been, the responses of Cary Baynes and Helen Wolff to the Interviews raises the possibility that its effects on its reader may be of a significantly greater order. For a contemporary reader, the Interviews are as close as one can get to being in Jung's study and hearing him speak spontaneously about his life, reminiscing about times past in a manner that is in turn questing, profound, witty, and melancholic. Now, with the extensive publication of Jung's works and correspondence since the appearance of *Memories, Dreams, Reflections*, and particularly *Liber Novus* and *The Black Books*, we are better able to grasp the interconnections between Jung's life and work that emerge here, and in so doing, discern his myth in the round.

Editorial Note

Aniela Jaffé did not preserve her shorthand notes or original typescript. In 1983, in the context of the copyright disputes around her second book drawn from the protocols of the Interviews, she noted, "The Protocols do not correspond verbatim to what Jung told me during the interviews in a free talk. In working out my notes I did an immediate editing, in order to formulate a readable and coherent text."[122] She added that as Kurt Wolff's intention was that the work should be "as near as possible an autobiography," "the questions and remarks I made during the interviews were omitted from the Protocols right from the beginning."[123] Wolff marked up, copy-edited, and made comments on his copy of the Protocols. He did not send these to Jaffé, but they may have been discussed when they met. From September 1958 onward Jaffé's "biography hours" with Jung continued, but she stopped sending notes of these to Wolff, following the deterioration of their relationship. Instead, she just sent him draft chapters when they were completed.

In 1977, Helen Wolff gave this copy of the Interviews to Jack Barrett, in his capacity as president of the Bollingen Foundation. He passed it to Herb Bailey at Princeton University Press, which had taken on responsibility for the Bollingen Series. Extracts were translated by Ximena Roelli de Angulo, to enable Paul Mellon to read them: she wrote to William McGuire that "it's like hearing C. G. talk again, his characteristic rhythms are there, I feel Aniela must have taken down quite faithfully what he said, I mean largely in his own words."[124] At Paul Mellon's suggestion, the copy was donated to the Library of Congress in 1983, with a ten-year restriction.

---

[122] "Concerning the Protocols," Jung Collection, LC. This statement was made in the context of the disputed copyright claims around "Erlebtes und Gedachtes" (see below, p. 36).

[123] "Concerning the Protocols," Jung Collection, LC.

[124] Ximena de Angulo to William McGuire, October 1, 1979, Jung Collection, LC.

The present edition is based on this copy of the Interviews, which runs from January 18, 1957 to September 19, 1958. The pages were stamped with numbers by William McGuire, in the order in which they were originally received (which was somewhat haphazard). Here, the Interviews have been placed in a chronological sequence. McGuire's numeration has been retained, inserted in the text in square brackets, for ease of cross-reference. The copy of the material in the Library of Congress is in seven folders, starting with the bulk of the Interviews (folder A), followed by draft chapters at various stages of editing. Three later entries, those for June 13, 1958, August 1958, and September 19, 1958 are in folder B.[125]

On October 23, 1958, Jaffé informed Kurt Wolff that she had a new plan to group the material thematically, and add to it some fictive dates, so that it would be "a type of spoken diary."[126] One section of material dealing with Jung's psychiatric and psychotherapeutic work—not found in the first dated sequence—was arranged in this manner, and given sequential dates from February 1 to March 1, 1957 (folder G). Jaffé was actually seriously ill during this time and did not meet with Jung. As it is not clear when the discussions which gave rise to this material originally occurred, it has been placed here in an appendix (Appendix 1), without the fictive dates. Material from some of the Interviews (e.g., March 7, 1958; June 13, 1958) which was interspersed with this has not been given twice.

A close transcription noting all subsequent changes has been prepared. The aim of this edition has been to present an easily readable reconstruction of the original conversations, insofar as this is possible. Consequently, Kurt Wolff's subsequent copy-editing has not been reproduced. Jaffé's handwritten corrections have been followed, given her procedure as noted above. Spelling mistakes (particularly as regards names) have been silently corrected. Narrating events at several decades remove, Jung's recollection of details and dates was subject to the passage of time, so should be taken with caution. Where possible, correct dates have been given in the footnotes.

---

[125] Folder A also included material which is not part of the Interviews: excerpts from discussions on September 21 and October 10, 1956, and notes of discussions Jung held with pastors on January 26, 1957 and with the Curatorium of the Jung Institute on June 22, 1957. The excerpt from September 21, 1956 has since been published in *Reflections* (pp. 177–78). The material from November 10, 1956 has been included as an appendix (Appendix 2) here, due to cross-references to it. The other discussions will be published in *CE*.

[126] Jaffé to Wolff, October 23, 1958, BL.

In 1980 Jaffé prepared a second manuscript, "Erlebtes und Gedachtes bei C. G. Jung," which she described as "loose ends" which she didn't include in *Memories, Dreams, Reflections*, and signed a contract with Bonz Verlag for this.[127] A copyright dispute ensued with the Society of Heirs of C. G. Jung, and the work did not appear. In 1991, shortly before her death, she prepared a further edited version of this manuscript. The copyright issues were resolved, and it was published in 2021 under the title translated as *Reflections on the Life and Work of C. G. Jung* (hereafter: *Reflections*). It contained thematically grouped edited and elaborated excerpts of the Interviews. Some excerpts from the January 1957 to September 1958 period which are missing in the manuscript of the Interviews in the Library of Congress have been inserted in this edition, drawn from Jaffé's earlier (less edited) manuscript, "Erlebtes und Gedachtes." Excerpts from discussions between November 1958 and May 1961, which may be found in *Reflections*, have not been included here.

After completion of the Interviews, the material went through many rounds of editing and generated a voluminous correspondence. The aim of this edition has been to present the original Interviews as a critical source of information regarding Jung's life, work, and their interrelation. Evolving editorial discussions pertaining to the work (rather than contractual issues) have been recorded chronologically in the footnotes. It has not been the aim to present the material as the pre-stage of *Memories, Dreams, Reflections*, nor to chart the full editorial history and controversies surrounding the work. As fascinating as these subjects are, this would require a volume in itself. Cross-references to the published English and German versions of *Memories* have been given, indicating where material was reproduced in a direct or edited manner. Already in 1961, Kurt Wolff noted that "the comparison of the original ms. with the protocols will greatly interest Jung researchers."[128]

---

[127] Jaffé to McGuire, March 22, 1981, McGuire Papers, *LC*. A copy of this manuscript is in the *ETH*.

[128] Kurt Wolff to Bernhard Peyer, September 12, 1961, BL.

The Interviews

Jung in his library with Aniela Jaffé, 1959. Photo by Henri Cartier-Bresson. © Fondation Cartier-Bresson, Magnum Photos.

Interviews, January 1957–September 1958

[4]

JANUARY 18, 1957

Yesterday I thought about the earliest memories of my life. I was about two years old so the memory is rather vague. I was in a pram in the shade of a tree. It was a beautiful, warm summer's day with blue sky and the sun was shining. I awake to the amazing beauty, see the sun sparkling through the leaves of the trees.—That is my earliest memory and it was all absolutely wonderful. Colorful and splendid.[129]

Later, between my third and fourth years, probably closer to the fourth or even fifth—in any case four—is when memories of places begin, so it is easier to place them in time.

The first memory, as I lay in my pram under the tree in the sun, is more of a vague impression. The first definitive memory is of a dream and my experience with a Catholic priest.[130] I have the feeling that the experience is connected with another dream that I locate in about my fourth year.

[131]The presbytery stood on its own next to Laufen Castle and there was a big meadow (this is reality, not a dream). In the dream I was standing on this meadow and suddenly I saw a dark, square hole, bricked up at the sides. I had never seen it before. Immediately I ran towards it and peered down into it. Then I saw a stone staircase, about a meter wide, leading about twenty steps down. Down below was a vaulted room. There was a door there. Covered with a green curtain. I observed a large black curtain, made as if from embroidered fabric; like brocade, it looked

---

[129] See *ETG*, p. 13, *MDR*, p. 6
[130] See below, p. 41.
[131] See *ETG*, p. 18, *MDR*, p. 10. Jung was born on July 26, 1875 at Kesswil, by Lake Constance. Six months later, his family moved to Laufen near the Rhine Falls.

quite lavish. I was very curious about what might be behind it and I pushed the curtain to one side. And then I saw a square room in dim light. There was not much light there, but it was just light enough to make out the details. Where the source of light was, I do not know. The room was vaulted, the floor was slabbed with stone, and a red carpet ran from the entrance to the back narrow corner at the end of the room. There, there stood a small pedestal, so at the end of the room. This room was perhaps five to six meters wide and about [4/5] double the length, or perhaps ten meters long. At the end of this room, opposite the entrance at the narrow wall, two or three steps led up to a podium and upon this stood a golden throne, a wonderful, rich golden throne. I am not sure, but perhaps there lay a red cushion on the top. It was a wonderful seat, like in a fairy-tale, a proper royal throne. Upon this stood something which I took to be a tree trunk; the diameter was about fifty to sixty centimeters. A massive form, reaching almost to the ceiling. It was four to five meters high and at the top it had an eye. Not an eye that could see, but it appeared to me like an indistinct head. The whole thing was of course an erect phallus.—As I saw this, I heard the voice of my mother although I knew she was not close by. She called: *Yes, now look at that, the man-eater!* Then I got the fright of my life and awoke in fear.[132]

This emotion showed up again in another experience with the Catholic priest, as the fear that I felt at the sight of him was not new to me, since it was as if I had thought this could have been the man-eater. [Drawing in illustration of Jung's experience.][133] [5/6]

---

[132] In 1937 Jung presented this dream in an anonymous form in his unpublished book on alchemy and individuation. In this manuscript, he then developed an extended discussion of the motifs which he drew out from the dream: the "cohabitatio permanens": the permanent pregnancy and divine incest, the eternal self-renewal of the God, the androgynous primordial being, and the conjunction of opposites. These amplifications then formed the subject of the remainder of his manuscript (forthcoming, edited by Martin Liebscher, Philemon Series).

E. A. Bennet noted, "At the time of the dream he felt he must not speak of it; he never did mention it till he was sixty-five years of age, when he related it to his wife, and the silence was next broken when he told it to me." (However, Jung had also narrated the dream to Lucy Heyer). Bennet added, "Years later he got glimpses of what the dream meant. Thus in adolescence when his own physical development came he realized that the mysterious object on the cushion, like and unlike a tree trunk, might be a phallus [. . . . It] was only in later years that he recognized it as the phallic archetype, the principle of creativity which is expressed in many forms, such as the resurrection of life, the minaret, the pillar—like grave monuments in Turkey, Assam and elsewhere." E. A. Bennet, *C. G. Jung* (Wilmette, IL: Chiron Publications, 2006 [1961]), pp. 10–11.

[133] No illustration follows.

[134]The experience was such that I was (in reality) playing on the door-step at the front of the house. On the opposite side I saw a figure wearing a cassock. I thought it was a woman but realized that it was a man. I thought, now that's a Jesuit! I became terribly afraid and ran into the house, ran to the attic where I holed up and hid myself away. I was frightened for my life. I peered out of the attic window and then saw that there was no one left around. Only when I was entirely sure of this did I dare to come out again. I had had a hellish shock.

I recalled how my father had spoken with colleagues about the danger of the Jesuits.[135] I did not know what this was. But I knew the word *Jesus* from my child's prayers. I thought: They are devils, that is why they are in disguise. Then I had an anxious panic just as in the dream of the phallus.—The Jesuits, Catholics *per se*, are the "completely other."

Some two to four years later I made an excursion with my parents to Arlesheim (I was then about six or seven years old). There was a Catholic church there.[136] The first I had ever seen. I was desperate to look inside.[137] But as I went through the doors, I stumbled and fell down and wounded my chin. It bled and I screamed terribly.

[138]Another big memory comes from this time, at the same age of six or so, when my father traveled with me to Thurgau to visit friends.[139] They had a castle on Lake Constance. They couldn't get me away from the water. Waves from the steamer came all the way inshore, the sun sparkled on the water. The vastness of it! This was an unimaginable pleasure, a wonder beyond compare. At that time the idea took root that I had to live by a lake and that one simply could not live apart from water.

Then we moved to Klein-Hüningen.[140] There we lived out of town, across from Hüningen Castle.[141] This was on the Rhine. There was water there alright.

[142]I never told anyone about the dream of the phallus during my youth. The Jesuit was also a part of this mysterious realm. But from then on,

---

[134] See *ETG*, p. 17, *MDR*, p. 10

[135] After the defeat of the Catholic cantons in the Sonderbund war, Switzerland banned Jesuits from clerical activity in 1848, and they were expelled. This ban was only lifted in 1972.

[136] Presumably the cathedral of Arlesheim, which was consecrated in 1681.

[137] See *ETG*, p. 23, *MDR*, p. 16.

[138] See *ETG*, p. 14, *MDR*, p. 7, where it is stated that he went with his mother.

[139] Thurgau: a canton in eastern Switzerland.

[140] Jung's family moved to Klein-Hüningen near Basel in 1879.

[141] Hüningen Fortress was built at the end of the seventeenth century, and was razed to the ground in 1815 after the defeat of Napoleon.

[142] See *ETG*, p. 28, *MDR*, p. 22.

doubts always arose in me when I was subjected to religious teaching, and they said that such and such is beautiful or good. For then I always thought, "But [6/7] something else remains deeply secret and people do not know this." This other had to do with the Catholic church. It was an "opposite," it was the other extreme.[143] For a long time, I associated my childhood experience with the Catholic church. I could not step into a church without secret fear of the Jesuits and of keeling over, of blood and keeling over and Jesuits. That was the tone shrouding all this. But it has always fascinated me. If they said that certain people were Catholic, I could not help feeling a secret fear, and it persisted.

Then I remember that when I was still very small, I had some unpleasant eczema on my body, for a long time.[144] Often, I was unable to sleep, and I used to scream. When I was about three years old, I remember that my father took me in his arms and carried me up and down in my room. He sang me his old student songs. I actually recall one of them that I liked a lot, and which always calmed me. It was the so-called song of the father of the land: "Keep still, all now turn their heads to this sound."[145] This is sort of how it began.—I always remember my father's voice singing over me.

Something else occurs to me about the eczema: I had a lot of injuries. Once I almost fell through the railings of the railway bridge into the Rhine. The nanny was just about able to grab me by the coattails. I always had long scars on my head. This was true right into my puberty.

This was connected to my parents' marriage.[146] It didn't work, my mother was once away for a while, perhaps a couple of months, and I remember that a girl fostered me.[147] I still recall how she took me in her arm, and I laid my head on her shoulder. She had black hair and an olive complexion. It struck me that she was different from my mother. This impression later became a component of my anima. This type.

Funnily enough, at that time my mother-in-law to be occasionally came over and took me out for walks.[148]

---

[143] See *ETG*, p. 23, *MDR*, p. 16.

[144] See *ETG*, p. 14, *MDR*, p. 8.

[145] "Alles schweige, jeder neige / Ernsten Tönen nun sein Ohr" (Everyone be silent, each now incline / His ear to serious sounds) begins an eighteenth-century German student song composed by August Niemann. It became the song of the *Landesvater*, a students' ceremony during which their caps are pierced by a sword.

[146] See *ETG*, p. 15, *MDR*, p. 8.

[147] In "On the Early Events of my Life" Jung dates this to 1878, adding, "An aunt (Gusteli), a spinster, about 20 years older than my mother, was looking after me then." (*BB* 7, p. 235). This would have been Augusta Weiss-Preiswerk (1825–1904), Jung's mother's sister.

[148] Bertha Rauschenbach (1856–1932).

When I was aged four we arrived in Basel (1879). There, the small village of Worth was situated on the other bank of the Rhine.[149] I remember how a pretty, very young and friendly girl with blue eyes and blond hair took me for walks there. It was autumn and the sun shone through [7/8] the golden leaves, and yellow leaves lay on the ground. This was the first impression of my mother-in-law to be. She lived in a village which belonged to my father's parish.

My mother was away for some months.[150] This is why I always had a feeling of mistrust whenever the word "love" was mentioned. When I heard it, I always became suspicious. For me, the feel of the feminine means natural unreliability; one can never depend on it. "Father" means, for me, reliability and impotence. This is the handicap I started with. Later this impression was revised: I believed I had friends, but I was disappointed by them and I was suspicious of women and was not disappointed.

At New Year 1875/76 we moved to Laufen. In the winter of 1878/79 to Basel.[151] I don't recall the move.

But there's another memory: a fine summer evening. My mother had taken me out in front of the house and shown me the Alps.[152] You could see the mountains quite clearly on that fine evening. "Look at that now, the mountains are all red." This was the first time I was conscious of seeing the Alps.—Then I heard that the next day a school trip was taking place and desperately wanted to join in and was terribly sad that I was told I was still too little.

[153]Then another memory: I recall that the maid came rushing into the house, the fishermen had landed a corpse and they were asking if they could secure it in the washhouse. (I was four years old at this time). The washhouse is still there. This fascinated me extraordinarily and I was determined to see the corpse. My aunt strictly forbade it.[154] But then I broke free and managed to get into the washhouse. But inside, the doors were locked so I went around the outside of the house; there the drainage pipe from the washhouse was situated. I saw water and blood flowing out of it. This fascinated me.

---

[149] See *ETG*, p. 15, *MDR*, p. 9.

[150] See *ETG*, p. 15, *MDR*, p. 8.

[151] Jung's family moved to Laufen in 1879.

[152] See *ETG*, p. 13, *MDR*, p. 7, where it is stated that it was an aunt who showed this view to him.

[153] See *ETG*, p. 14, *MDR*, p. 7.

[154] "My aunt": Augusta Weiss-Preiswerk (see n. 147 above).

[155]And another memory: I was sitting on a high-chair in the dining room in the rectory with a cup of warm milk and bread nuggets in front of me. This had a characteristic aroma and it was the first time that I was conscious of the aroma. It was a moment in which I became conscious of the sense of smell. This is one of the earliest memories. [8/9]

At that time a great flood occurred.[156] The entire meadow in front of the house was under water. On the upper Rhine a bridge collapsed, and fourteen people drowned and were washed away by the Rhine. I remember having seen the corpse of a middle-aged man, in a black frock coat. He lay there half covered in sand, his arm over his eyes. This keenly fascinated me.—It also fascinated me to watch a pig being slaughtered. To the horror of my mother, I observed this process with intense interest. She almost died of horror. She found this a terrible thing. And the dead man, it simply interested me.

Next come the school memories. Something surprising happened there: I was the best pupil by far,[157] and was terribly bored in school. In arithmetic I was bad because I had an over-active imagination. In the first or second class of primary school, aged about six or eight, I preferred to play with the girls. I always had a crowd of girls after me. The boys were much too klutzy and dull. The girls were livelier, not so klutzy. I much preferred to play with them. We played on the street.

Then when I was ten, I went to the *Gymnasium* in Basel.[158] Aged eleven, I had the dream of the cactus (see later).[159] This made a profound impact upon me. Then strange things began to happen. At about that time a type of strange experiences began, not actually depressive states.[160] I was self-absorbed and had the feeling of there being a mystery which one should be able to explain, and I didn't know what it was, but attempted to give expression to it. I always thought it would be possible to find something, perhaps in nature, which would shed light upon it. Or

---

[155] See *ETG*, p. 13, *MDR*, p. 6.

[156] See *ETG*, p. 22, *MDR*, p. 15. On December 28, 1882, the River Wiese flooded and the Tumring bridge collapsed, killing fourteen men who were crossing it.

[157] From Jung's school reports, it appears he always had very good grades, and was usually either first, second, or third in the class.

[158] In 1886 Jung started at the Unteres Gymnasium (lower secondary school) in Basel on Munsterplatz, which had been founded in the eleventh century. From 1891 to 1895, he attended the Oberes Gymnasium (upper secondary school), and remained there till 1895, passing his *Maturität* examination on March 30. Both Jacob Burckhardt and Friedrich Nietzsche had taught there.

[159] See below, n. 242.

[160] See *ETG*, p. 28, *MDR*, p. 22.

where the mystery might be. At that time my interest grew in plants, animals, and stones. I was always in search of something mysterious. In my conscious life I was raised as a Christian and was Christian in my religion but always with the qualification that "It is not so certain!" and "What about what is under the ground? That is also the mystery."

You might say I was afraid of sexuality. But such worries would be superfluous in my case, since I grew up with farm boys and had seen everything [9/10] there was to see. For me, that was unproblematic nature.

The experience with the stone is connected to this. This was between my ninth and tenth year.[161] I used to often sit upon a stone on the slope in our garden. And there I engaged in quite remarkable ponderings. I thought: Now I'm sitting here in this meadow, and I say "I" and the stone could also say "I." It could say, I lie upon this slope, and something is sitting upon me, and then it was as if I were inside the stone, or as if the stone was identical with me, so as if I were this stone. That was completely unclear. This feeling of a remarkable and fascinating darkness.

Later my mother often used to relate that she had thought I was melancholic. But this was only a preoccupation. I was able to squat upon this stone for the longest time, it held something fascinating for me.

When I later read Greek mythology, I found that Zeus used to sit upon a stone when he had troubles in love. He sat upon his stone in Euboea or Crete.[162] For me, it was not love troubles but the question of who I actually am. Out of this developed then something Other.

[163]Back then, I used a pencil case such as primary school children have. Inside there was also a ruler. I carved the top part of this into a sort of head so that a small man emerged out of the ruler. I put it into the pencil case. I also made for him a little coat and a small bed out of pieces of fabric in the box. Then I put a couple of oblong stones inside that I had found on the banks of the Rhine. I decorated these with some paint. And this was the great mystery for me. I concealed this box: "No one is allowed to see this!" In our house we had an ancient attic. I climbed up on to the beams and deposited the little box in the darkest possible place

---

[161] See *ETG*, p. 26, *MDR*, p. 20.

[162] In his copy of *The Magic Art and the Evolution of Kings 1*, the first volume of J. G. Frazer's *The Golden Bough*, Jung drew a line in the margin by the following passage: "Zeus is said to have often cured himself of his love for Hera by sitting down on a certain rock in the island of Leucadia. In these cases it may have been thought that the wayward and flighty impulses of love and madness were counteracted by the steadying influence of heavy stone." (3rd edn [1911], p. 161).

[163] See *ETG*, p. 27, *MDR*, p. 21.

so that no one could see it. From time to time I visited it and looked at it. Then I wrote upon small rolls of paper, I don't know what I wrote, but they were also a part of it. This whole story then completely sank away and was forgotten. I don't know what became of it. Perhaps the box is still there today. For me, it was the great mystery.[164] When I was reading in preparation [10/11] for *Transformations and Symbols of the Libido* in 1911, this whole story came back to me, when, in my reading, I came upon the soul stones of the primitives. Churingas.[165] (A cache close to Arlesheim was discovered with decorated soul stones.) I used to always creep into the attic when I was certain that no one could see me, climb up onto the beams and look at the box with the little man and the stones. I don't know what I was thinking of by doing this. It's remarkable how everything was already prefigured in childhood!

January 19, 1957

[166]This phallus and what I've told you about the carved little man at the end of the ruler, this is the same as the figure in the garden in Küsnacht that I made much later. The unconscious supplied me then with the name for the first time. I called the figure Atmavictu = "the breath of life."[167] This is what later gave me the starting point for my concept of dementia praecox,

---

[164] See *ETG*, p. 29, *MDR*, p. 22.

[165] It was through reading Lucien Lévy-Bruhl's *The Mental Functions* at this time that Jung came across the discussion of the churinga by Baldwin Spencer and F. J. Gillen in their work *The Central Tribes of Northern Australia*. On this, see Sonu Shamdasani, *Jung and the Making of Modern Psychology: The Dream of a Science* (Cambridge: Cambridge University Press, 2003), pp. 295–97. In October 1910 Fritz Sartorius-Preiswerk had found a neolithic burial site near Arlesheim, which contained painted stones. The British archaeologist Arthur B. Cook and Swiss ethnographer Fritz Sarasin likened these to the Australian churingas. See Jürg Sedlmeier, *Die letzten Wildbeuter der Eiszeit: Neue Forschungen zum Spätaläolithikum im Kanton Basel-Landschaft* (Basel: Schwabe, 2015), p. 164.

[166] See *ETG*, p. 29, *MDR*, p. 23.

[167] "the breath of life": in English in the original. Atmaviktu (as it is spelt there) first appears in *BB* 6, in 1917. Here is a paraphrase of the fantasy of April 25, 1917 (pp. 288–92):

> The serpent says that Atmaviktu was her companion for thousands of years. He was first an old man, then he died and became a bear. Then he died and became an otter. Then he died and became a newt. Then he died again and came into the serpent. The serpent is Atmaviktu. He made a mistake before then and became a man, while he was still an earth serpent. Jung's soul says that Atmaviktu is a *kobold*, a serpent conjuror, and is himself a serpent. The serpent says that she is the kernel of the self. From the serpent, Atmaviktu transformed into Philemon.

> For the wooden carvings and subsequent stone carving of Atmavictu, see the Foundation of the Works of C. G. Jung's *The Art of C. G. Jung* (New York: W. W. Norton, 2018), cat. nos

or even for the archetypes. Think of the mentally ill patient and his vision of the sun phallus.[168] This is the origin of the spirit. In the Greek text, it is called the origin of the spirit on duty. It is something which produces a spirit. The Atmavictu in the garden is represented with a hoe: this signifies agriculture. This whole is however ultimately a Kabir, cloaked in a "little coat," shrouded in the "kista" and supplied with life force (the stone). These are all things that only became clear much later. When I was a child it was just like what I observed later among the native Africans: first they do it, and they do not know it. Only much later is it thought about.[169] [13]

JANUARY 25, 1957

[170]Goethe's mystery was that he was an alchemist. He understood his life as an *opus magnum*, or *divinum*. So he is correct in saying that *Faust* was

---

67, 68, 69, and 70 (pp. 148–50). Jung was referring to the time when he was in England in 1919. Atmavictu plays a crucial role in a series of paintings in *LN* in 1919 and 1920.

[168] Jung is referring to Emil Schwyzer, a patient at the Burghölzli, whom he, and principally his assistant Johann Honegger, studied. In 1912 Jung claimed that the motif in Schwyzer's vision was the same as was present in the Mithras Liturgy, which Schwyzer could not have been familiar with (*Transformations and Symbols of the Libido*, CE 6; CWB, § 179). The Mithras Liturgy begins (in Albrecht Dieterich's translation), "First origin of my origin, first ground of my ground, first spirit of the spirit in me, firstborn of the spirit." Later on, reference is made to "the origin of the wind in action." *Eine Mithrasliturgie*, annotated by Albrecht Dieterich (Leipzig, B. G. Teubner, 1903), pp. 3 and 7. The Schwyzer case formed one of the paradigms for Jung's conception of the collective unconscious. See Ronald V. Huggins, "C. G. Jung, J. J. Honegger, and the Case of Emil Schwyzer (the 'Solar Phallus' Man)," *Phanês* 4 (2021): 82–151.

[169] On January 20, 1957 Jaffé wrote to Kurt Wolff thanking him for his very important suggestions. She wrote,

> Last Friday quite unexpectedly Jung said to me that he wanted to narrate his childhood memories. That was the moment! I have produced a rich harvest of stenographic notes! [. . .] The following should be said about them: these memories, as Jung has related them, stretch back as far as the pram and are moving, interesting and, in part, delightful, as childhood experiences can be. Any reader of such an 'autobiography' would notice this and feast on them. But this is not all. When one knows just how many seeds are contained there that later blossom, these small experiences become terribly significant. Then they contain an almost incredible profundity. Jung did not mention these further associations; he assumes that I understand them; and so I wondered if it would not be possible for me to appear in this 'autobiography' as a 'speaker' who explains in everyday clothes and a quiet voice the vivid events taking place on the stage. You will be able to understand this better from the notes.
>
> Jung said he now wants to narrate his life to me more often, but, for heaven's sake, not systematically, but only what occurs to him each time. This is what I have been waiting for, for only in this way can one acquire the living *prima materia*. [BL]

[170] See *ETG*, p. 209, *MDR*, p 206.

his "principal work" and hence, that his life is defined by Faust. You can see that, for him, in a spectacular way this is his living substance, vitally alive and active.[171] With Thomas Mann, I always had the feeling that he has such a differentiated sense of culture, intellect, and feeling that he can see everything correctly without his life somehow being gripped by it.[172] This turned me off. I recoiled from him. He terrified me, like one of those South American vampires who fly around at night sucking blood from toes while people sleep.[173] I had the feeling that he would suck me dry. Immediately I broke off the connection and withdrew. He invited me to associate with him but I was not able to.

[174]I once had the same feeling with H. G. Wells. I met him once and this encounter is depicted in his novel *The World of William Clissold*. He described the episode there. I met with him one evening after my lectures in London. We got into conversation about psychiatry and mental illnesses. I sketched out a typical case of paranoia for him, delusions of grandeur and so on. During the exchange Wells fell completely silent. He sat in a corner, motionless.

And then a completely incomprehensible phenomenon occurred: although he was a rather small, chubby, extraverted, and talkative man, in that moment he fell completely silent, in that chair in the corner, and seemed to be getting smaller and smaller. In the end he shrank like a ball, a small, fat gnome with little legs and arms, only about this tall [Jung gestured about 60 centimeters in height]. While I was speaking, I kept having this illusion of the "little man," and when I had finished, there he was sitting once again in his familiar form, as before. "What was going on there?"[175] [13/14][176]

---

[171] Jung discussed the alchemical elements of *Faust* in his lecture "*Faust* and Alchemy," in Irene Gerber-Münch, *Goethes Faust: Eine tiefenpsychologische Studie über den Mythos des modernen Menschen; Mit dem Vortrag von C. G. Jung, Faust und die Alchemie* (Küsnacht: Verlag Stiftung für Jung'sche Psychologie, 1997).

[172] There is one extant letter from Thomas Mann to Jung, dated April 1, 1929, in which Mann thanks Jung for sending him a recent publication, of which he expressed his appreciation (JP). Mann lived in Küsnacht from 1933 to 1938 at Schiedhaldenstrasse 33 (about half an hour's walk from Jung's house), and they had a mutual friend in the Hungarian classicist Karl Kérenyi. On Jung and Thomas Mann, see Paul Bishop, "'Literarische Beziehungen haben nie bestanden'? Thomas Mann and C. G. Jung," *Oxford German Studies*, 24, no. 1 (1994): pp. 124–72.

[173] Vampire bats in South America feed on blood, including that of humans.

[174] See E. A. Bennet, *Meetings with Jung: Conversations Recorded During the Years 1946–1961* (Zurich: Daimon Verlag, 1982) January 28, 1955 (pp. 50–51).

[175] "Da" was here typed over "mir" ("there" replacing "with me").

[176] See H. G. Wells, *The World of William Clissold* (Poughkeepsie, NY: House of Stratus, 2002 [1926]), pp. 57–61. According to Wells, he met Jung in 1924 on the evening after the last of the latter's lectures on analytical psychology and education at the International

The next thing Wells wrote was *Christina Alberta's Father*,[177] where the figure of a mentally ill person makes an appearance. Then followed

---

Congress of Education in London, which was on May 13. Curiously, the narrator in Wells's novel recounts an occurrence that happened to him at times during his youth and early manhood: "The visible world, remaining just as bright and clear as it has ever been, would suddenly appear to be *minute*. People become midgets, the houses and furniture, dolls'-houses and furniture, the trees mere moss-fronds. I myself did not seem to shrink to scale, it was only the universe around me that shrank. This effect would last for a few seconds or for a few minutes, and then it would pass away." (pp. 7–8).

On July 25, 1924 Jung replied to a letter from Wells, agreeing to meet him again in Zurich. Later, on receiving a copy of Wells's book, Jung wrote to him once more: "It was indeed a great surprise to me that you remembered so well what we were talking about. Thank you very much." (September 11, 1926; both letters are preserved in the H. G. Wells Papers, University of Illinois.)

[177] On reading this book Jung praised it highly to Wells: "It is such an essential description of all the essentials of a case of such a borderland kind, that one almost imagines that you had seen such a good fellow of the Preemby [type?] from very close quarters. It is grand. You got him, the Hero malgré lui of our days. You know in the early beginning of the Christian Aera it was the rite of the Deificatio in the pagan mysteries, now it is a disease, sometimes it remains even a mere stomach trouble [. . .]. God has become a nervous disease in our days—the only way to demonstrate to the homo sapiens of our days that there is a superior will in each of us, that contradicts our rationalism. Freud was the last attempt at rationalizing even the unconscious mind." (Jung to Wells, September 11, 1926; H. G. Wells Papers, University of Illinois). Albert Edward Preemby is the protagonist in Wells's novel *Christina Alberta's Father*. A mild-mannered, retired laundryman and widower, Preemby undergoes a dramatic transformation following his wife's death. He becomes convinced that he is the reincarnation of Sargon, the ancient king of Sumeria, destined to restore order to a post–World War I world. In 1928 Jung again referred to the novel: "[a] most excellent account—taken from life, so to speak—of such an inner transformation" (*The Relations Between the I and the Unconscious* [1928], *CE* 10; *CW* 7, § 270. See also §§ 284 and 332). Elsewhere, Jung referred also to Wells's novels *The War of the Worlds* and *The Time Machine*.

On October 29, 1928 Jung informed Wells that he would be receiving an invitation from the *Neue Zurcher Zeitung* to contribute to a series of articles about his psychology: "I have been discovered in my country. It is really the first time people pay any attention to my existence [. . .]. It would certainly help my position in Switzerland, when such a great and famous man like yourself says a few words in my favour [. . .]. I am in a terribly hampered situation. You would really help me, if you would say, that my work has meant something to you." (H. G. Wells Papers, University of Illinois). On November 3, 1928 Wells replied that he had written to the *Neue Zürcher Zeitung* indicating that "it was not for writers like him to sit in judgement upon scientific men of your calibre." He added, "I find your work [. . . (illegible)] valuable to me, I refer to it constantly in conversations with my friends." (JP).

On November 18, 1928, the *Neue Zürcher Zeitung* published Wells's response to their invitation, in which he wrote, "It would be [. . .] demanding if I were to judge him as a man of science and a philosopher—that must be left to his peers. But as a writer and as one who is vividly concerned with all questions of the human soul and the development of human society, I find in the thoughts and writings and in the experimental results of Dr. Jung an incomparable inspiration, a bright light on my darkness and treasure trove of material for reflection." (p. 9). This was followed by an extract from *The World of William Clissold*. This formed part of several tributes to Jung's work in this issue of the newspaper.

Finally, on November 25, 1937, Jung thanked Wells for sending him his work "Anatomy of Frustration," commenting on the importance of this subject (JP).

The World of William Clissold. That evening with Wells is depicted in it as a hodge-podge of conversational fragments from our visit: everything mixed up and not a word of what I had said about psychoses, which had been the main point of the evening.

After the evening with Wells, I was half dead with exhaustion. That is why since then I avoid people who are not defined by a "principal task." That is also why I steered clear of Thomas Mann.

[178]The principal task in my own case began in my eleventh year. My life is suffused with and encompassed by one purpose: namely, to penetrate into the mystery of the personality. Everything can be understood from this central point, and when people assert that it's all about nothing but "volte-faces,"[179] that is simply crazy. They do not see that everything pertains to the same theme: so *Transformations and Symbols of the Libido* is simply paradigmatic of the transformation in this one person.[180] At that time I outgrew my friendship with Freud, which marks the beginning of my independent path as a scientist. Everything in this nexus is interwoven.[181] And then comes the question: What does one do with the unconscious? One response is the book on *The Relations between the I and the Unconscious*.[182] [183]Then comes the *Types* book, being an exploration of the points of view that limit the scope of judgment. It is the personality type that limits judgment from the outset. So with that the question arises: Where is unity if everything is only a relative point of view?[184]This is where the concept of Tao comes in, and the meeting with Richard Wilhelm and all my mandala drawings which relate to this.[185] For example, the image of the city with the fortress wall (in the *Golden*

---

[178] See *ETG*, p. 210, *MDR*, p. 206.

[179] Jaffé noted here, "Jung is referring to a dissertation in the USA in which it was claimed that his work oscillated from one pole to another. (Swartley)." This appears to refer to the Canadian psychologist William Swartley (1927–1979), who was active in the human potential movement, and founded primal integration. He studied for a while at the Jung Institute. On March 17, 1953, he sent Jung an account of some dreams, recalling that they had met at a party for students at the Jung Institute in 1948 (JP).

[180] *Transformations and Symbols of the Libido* (1912), CE 6; CW B. This was the study of the fantasies of Miss Frank Miller. See Sonu Shamdasani, "A Woman Called Frank," *Spring: Journal of Archeytpe and Culture* 50 (1990): 26–56.

[181] See *ETG*, p. 210, *MDR*, p. 206.

[182] The second work in CE 10; CW 7.

[183] See *ETG*, p. 211, *MDR*, p. 207.

[184] See *ETG*, pp. 200–201 and 211, *MDR*, pp. 197 and 208, and below, pp. 105–6.

[185] For Jung's mandala drawings and paintings, see *The Red Book*. pp. 80–97; *Art of C. G. Jung*; and Sonu Shamdasani, "Expressions symboliques: Jung, Dada, le Mandala et l'art de la folie," in Edith Alleart Bertin, ed., *Jung et élan créatur* (Noville-sur-Mehaigne/Maransart: Espreluète/L'Arbre Soleil, 2018), pp. 269–324.

Flower).[186] When I did that, I had to ask myself: Why is this so Chinese? I was impressed by [14/15] the Chinese manner although, extrinsically, there was nothing Chinese in it. Yet so it seemed to me.

And then, right at that moment came the letter from Wilhelm containing the manuscript of the *Golden Flower* and the invitation to annotate it. And so I immediately dove right into the manuscript.

When I had arrived at this central point (Tao), then began my confrontations with the world; I began to give many lectures and to write smaller texts. I gave brief lectures in many places back then.[187] While doing this I came across alchemy, and that occurred through a dream. Unfortunately, I can no longer tell you just when that was: it came sometime in 1926/27. I know that it came three to four years before I was acquainted with the first alchemical text and not long after the First World War.[188] Sometime in the mid-Twenties—before or after Africa, probably after, and so, in 1926. This is the dream I had then.

[189]I was in the South Tirol; the war was on, and I am at the Italian front and traveling back from the front with a man of small stature, a farmer on his wagon with his horse. (Association: at the beginning of the First World War, I traveled with a farmer upon such a horse and cart in Holland.)[190] Around us grenades were exploding, and I think, "We've got to get out of here," and it is very dangerous. We arrive at a tunnel which we must drive through, crossing a bridge. The vault of the tunnel has been partly damaged by shells. I see that the bricks might fall down, and the situation is frightening. Then we get through the tunnel and now there's the sun and the area is like Upper Verona. I see Verona lying beneath me and it is in full beautiful sunshine.

We emerge into the green, blossoming Lombardy plain, we see the rice fields, olive trees and so on. It's as if a burden were lifted and I travel through the fine, spring landscape and then I see how, along the street,

---

186 *CE* 11; *CW* 13, A10, and *The Red Book*, image 163.

187 A number of these lectures were collected in the edited volumes *Contributions to Analytical Psychology* (1928) and *Seelenprobleme der Gegenwart* (Problems of the soul in the present time) (1931). For details of some of Jung's lecturing activity around 1927 and 1928, see *BB* 7, 243 n. 273 and 245 n. 276.

188 Jung is referring to his reading of the *Artis auriferae volumina duo*. On Jung's acquisition of his collection of alchemical books, see Thomas Fischer, "The Alchemical Rare Book Collection of C. G. Jung," *International Journal of Jungian Studies* 3, no. 2 (2011): pp. 169–81.

189 See *ETG*, p. 206–7, *MDR*, p. 202. Jung also narrated this dream to Bennet: Bennet, *Meetings with Jung*, January 5, 1957 (p. 75).

190 At the outbreak of the war, Jung was in Scotland, in Aberdeen, and returned to Switzerland via Holland, picking up Maria Moltzer on the way (JFA).

there is a large building of vast proportions, like the castle of a Duke di Ferrara or Este.[191] There stands a very characterful palace with many annexes and outbuildings, rather like the Louvre or the Tuileries. The road winds past the castle [15/16] into a large courtyard. The small coachman and I walk through a gate into this courtyard, and we look back through another gate out into the landscape. I thought we now had it in mind to view the castle: to the right is the front of the castle, leading up to the courtyard, on the left are the servants' quarters and the stables, the hen-house, the barns where the cattle are housed, and so on. These annexes extend out far to the left.

While we are still in mid-courtyard, something completely unexpected occurs: both gates slam shut with a bang. The farmer next to me jumps down from the carriage seat and says, "Now we're trapped in the seventeenth century!" I think, yes, this is true! Yet what can be done? Now we'll be trapped for years! But then the thought comes to me: Afterwards I will get out again.

Following this dream, I read volumes about world history in order to find something, anything, that might account for the dream. In vain. Yet the seventeenth century is the high point of alchemy.

In 1930/31 *Artis auriferae*, volume two, containing the *Rosarium philsophorum,* landed in my hands.[192] In 1931 I began to read the *Rosarium*. When I was reading from it one night, it suddenly occurred to me, "That's your dream! This is it!" Until then the dream had preoccupied me without my having been able to crack the nut. Now I knew: now I am condemned to study the whole of alchemy!

And by studying alchemy, all the experiential material that I had accumulated in my practice fell into place. I now had the historical pattern,[193] and I was able to see what things meant. Until then, I had thought that everything seemed to be Chinese; indeed, there were similar ideas in play, but there was no pattern, no total picture.

---

[191] Ferrara, in northern Italy, was a commune ruled by the house of Este. Jung may have been referring to the Castello Estense in Ferrara. He had some blank postcards from Ferrara, which he may have visited on his trips to Italy in 1914 or 1932.

[192] See *ETG*, p. 208, *MDR*, p. 205, The *Rosarium philosophorum* is a series of woodcuts, a version of which was included in the *Artis auriferae* (1593), a compendium of alchemical texts. In 1946 Jung used this as the basis for his study *The Psychology of the Transference*. On Jung's reading of the text, see Christopher Wagner, "A Case of Projection: The 'Sol and Luna' *Bildgedicht* and the 'Alchemy' of Carl Jung," M.Phil dissertation, University of Cambridge, 2011. Jung's personal collection of alchemical works can be viewed at https://www.e-rara.ch/alch/nav/classification/1133851 (accessed April 24, 2025).

[193] "pattern": in English in the original, here and below.

I needed a long time to find the threads of meaning in the alchemical treatises: I noticed in the *Rosarium* that typical modes of expression were present, which are repeated, over and over again. Of course, at first, I could not understand them. So, for example, "solve et coagula"[194] and so on. I knew that this was repeated multiple times. [16/17]. Then I thought, "God, what does this mean?" Then I said to myself: Now I must create a lexicon with cross-references[195] in order to understand the meaning behind it all. So I wrote up thousands of key words, this was a purely philological procedure. It was a phenomenal job of work.[196]

You see, this too is the "man eater,"[197] whose imposition of such a task consumes one with fire. In this case, it is not others whom he consumes by fire, but his very own foundations. When Thomas Mann says that Goethe consumed men [See *Lotte in Weimar*, conclusion],[198] that too is the man eater. The same motif is also to be found in the Christian communion. Nietzsche says, "One spark from the fire of truth is sufficient to consume a scholar's life or to ignite it in flames." (Or some such thing he said.)[199] With Thomas Mann, the feeling is a sinister thing: his understanding of it is exquisite, but he stays at one remove; he lives vicariously.

I must reflect on my relationship with the environment when I was a boy, and what a difference this possession of a mystery made.

About the dream of the castle from the seventeenth century: the war and the shells falling from the sky, these are shots coming from the other

---

[194] "Dissolve and coagulate."

[195] "cross references": in English in the original.

[196] Jung's philological deciphering of alchemy took place in a series of eight copy books, together with an index volume (these were compiled with the collaboration of Marie-Louise von Franz). The first volume, dated 1935, is titled, in English, "Treasure Hunting." Call slips in these volumes indicated that Jung conducted extensive research back in the Basel University Library in the winter of 1935. Among other locations he worked at were the Zurich Zentralbibliothek and the British Library. The second, third, and fourth volumes were assembled by Marie-Louise von Franz. See Alfred Ribi, "Zum schöpferischen Prozess bei C. G. Jung: Aus den Excerptbänden zur Alchemie," *Analytische Psychologie* 13 (1982): 201–21. For photographs of these, see Sonu Shamdasani, *Jung: A Biography in Books* (New York: W. W. Norton, 2011), pp. 172–88.

[197] See Jung's childhood dream of the underground phallus, above p. 40–41.

[198] See Thomas Mann, *Lotte in Weimar*, trans. H. T. Lowe-Porter (London: Secker & Warburg, 1947), ch. 9.

[199] The reference is to Nietzsche's statement in "Schopenhauer as an Educator," in his *Untimely Meditations* (Cambridge: Cambridge University Press, 1997 [1876]): "For a spark from the fire of justice fallen into a scholar's soul suffices to enkindle and purify his life and strivings, so that he no longer knows any rest and is for ever expelled from the lukewarm or frosty mood in which scholars usually accomplish their daily work." Translation by R. J. Hollingdale, p. 173.

side, from the enemy. They are the effects worked on me coming from the shadow side. Which means that the war that had been happening outside is now going on within.
[27]

I have often been asked how I came to write the book *Answer to Job*.[200] It is a matter of a very complex situation which had bothered me for a long time, and in which finally all sorts of determinants came together. And then the time was right.

I have observed on principle that evidently there are those who are incapable of understanding that one can write something "for its own sake," can think about things without putting them to the test.

The more or less obvious reason was that I had previously written *Psychology and Alchemy*, in which I had represented Christ as a symbolic figure.[201] And there I had expounded the doctrine of salvation, taking the opportunity to critique the idea of *privatio boni*. Consequently, the engagement with medieval natural philosophy, which is extraordinarily interesting for psychology, prompted me to assess for myself what the actual God image in these philosophers was all about, or, to be more precise, the symbolic modifications of the God image, which actually point in the direction of a *complexio oppositorum*. And this awoke in me the memory of Job. In a way, Job expects that God will come to his aid against God.

On the other hand, many questions from the public and from patients had required me to express myself more clearly and definitively regarding the religious questions of modern man. But I hesitated to do so for many years because I was very aware of what a storm I would unleash. One cannot help it if one is gripped by the urgency and difficulty of this problem. I therefore considered myself compelled to represent this whole problem in the form of an experience, sustained by subjective emotions. I also did this with a specific aim, because in this way I wished to forestall the impression that I was out to proclaim an eternal truth. I wanted it to be simply the voice and inquiry of an individual who hopes for and expects the thoughtfulness of the public.
[38]

---

[200] See Jung's "Prefatory Note" to *Answer to Job* (1952), CE 23; CW 11, pp. 357–58.

[201] See Jung, *Psychology and Alchemy* (1944), CE 17; CW 12, part 3, ch. 5, "The Lapis–Christ Parallel."

[202]I must describe to you my relationship to the environment when I was a boy. This possession of a mystery—what a difference that made! I see it as the essential feature of those early years: the mystery. This is something of the utmost significance for me: the cache of these wooden figures and stones where I tried to give form to the mystery. This later disappeared completely from my mind. Only in 1910/11 did I recall it again when I was writing *Transformations*. It was when I read about the soul stones. "My God, this is what you used to do!"[203]—that was also when I had the experiences of feeling both two and one: at that time, I was already at the *Gymnasium*.

[204]When I was eleven or twelve, I was a guest at some friends of my parents at Lake Lucerne, and I had been emphatically warned not to get up to any escapades with the boat. Paying no heed, I immediately went out onto the lake standing up back at the stern and rowing from there—exactly what I had been told not to do. Of course, I got a mighty talking to from our host. That seemed quite reasonable. But afterwards in my room I had a terrible attack of rage: how could this uneducated fellow have presumed to say such a thing to me! This was so disproportionate that I became suspicious myself: You are reacting as if you are the devil! And at the same time, you know that the other person is completely correct. Then it became clear to me that a second person was hidden inside me, and was already adult. This duality was hugely underlined by a second experience from that time, namely of the image of God who shits upon Basel cathedral.

[205]I was eleven or twelve years old. On a splendid spring day after leaving school, I came into the cathedral square. I felt at peace and was looking forward to the fine day and I saw the beauty of the cathedral, the sun glittering on its roof. The whole day was set to be happy and contented. And just then I had the feeling that I had to think something [38/39]. Something quite specific, but what I did not know. And there was something else in me that would not permit this specific thought. A terrible time began for me because I always wanted to think something I did not know and something else would not allow it. Night after night, I had to bear this conflict and struggled against this pressure or

---

[202] See *ETG*, p. 2, *MDR*, p. 22.
[203] See above, p. 45.
[204] See *ETG*, p. 39, *MDR*, p. 33.
[205] See *ETG*, p. 42, *MDR*, p. 36.

compulsion to think this unknown thought. All of a sudden, one night I had a vision, in which God shits upon the cathedral and the turd is so enormous that the roof collapses under its weight. Now I knew that this was the thought, and I was full of fear and horror that God would punish me for this blasphemous thought.

But then something altogether unexpected happened: I suddenly felt completely free and cut loose, knowing that God was not angry with me but had assimilated me into his grace. Now I knew what an experience of grace was. I was liberated to an unbelievable extent. But then came the reflections: I wondered, just who thought that? I myself certainly had had no such thought. And who could have given me this thought? Neither my mother nor my father; and then I went back through my relatives and everyone I knew, not a single one who in my view could have come up with such an outrageous thought and given it to me. Indeed, none of them was compelled to come up with anything like it. And so finally down unto the last generation, I came to Adam and Eve, and I reflected on the temptation narrative; and there I found it: they too had to think something that they had no desire to think at all. Therefore, I concluded that it was God himself who inspired them, like me, so that I was compelled to think it was either that or the devil. They made me think it. This experience and these ponderings have influenced my whole life. [39/40]

Such was the tangible proof, if I had ever spoken of it, that stones fall from the sky, for now I had one in my pocket. And this experience is connected with the earlier mystery, the dream of the phallus in the underground temple.[206] But this did not as yet initiate any demonstrable effect at that time. I cannot recall—until the moment when I became conscious, when I was an adult. From then on came moments when I found myself in a remarkable mood: that we were living not in 1889, but in 1789.[207]

[208]Once when we lived in Klein-Hüningen a carriage came by from the Black Forest, an ancient green rig hung with leather tackle, and cambered wheels just like on carriages from the eighteenth century. Then it was as if I went crazy: "This is it! This is from my time!" That's how it was. And then came a peculiar *sentiment écoeurant*,[209] as if someone had stolen something from me, or as if I had been cheated of my own beloved prehistory. The carriage was a relic from that: *This is what it was!* I can't

---

[206] See above, p. 39–40.

[207] See *ETG*, p. 41, *MDR*, p. 35. 1789 was the date of the beginning of the French Revolution. *MDR* has "1786" and "1886," following *VA*.

[208] See *ETG*, p. 40, *MDR*, p. 34.

[209] *sentiment écoeurant*, in French in the original: "sickening feeling."

describe what it was: a longing, a feeling of homesickness, or: *Yes, that was it!*

And the other experience also pointing to the eighteenth century: this was an ancient piece of terracotta consisting of two figures. It portrayed old Dr. Stückelberger, a well-known figure in the life of Basel from the eighteenth and the beginning of the nineteenth centuries. The other figure was a patient of his and she was sticking her tongue out with her eyes closed.[210] There was a legend about the two of them and it went like this: Old Stückelberger was once crossing the bridge over the Rhine, and, good God, there was this old patient coming towards him and jabbering something at him. Old Stückelberger says, Yes, yes, something must be wrong with you. Put out your tongue and close your eyes! This she did, and in that very moment he ran away from her, but she remained standing there with her tongue outstretched, much to the amusement of everyone. This old character Stückelberger was wearing buckled shoes and I was convinced: I had worn those very shoes. [40/41] This drove me crazy. Yes, but they were my shoes! It's true! I can still sense those shoes on my feet and I couldn't account for how I came to have this crazy feeling. What was it about this eighteenth century? I could not grasp it.

So when I had this dream of the cathedral, finally there was something I could get my hands on. This was a great mystery. That was when I also remembered the phallus in the underground temple.[211] And this had a remarkable effect: I was a completely normal boy. I played all the tricks that a boy usually gets up to. I was known to be a bit of a tearaway and so on. This was completely normal and is very uninteresting. I was always something of a ringleader in my class, and if something happened, I got the blame. Even if I was not guilty, they thought so, because they used to attribute all sorts of hoodlum behavior to me. But my inner feeling was always this: there is a mystery here. A mystery that in fact is very shameful to me. I have stumbled into something wicked, something naughty, something sinister and at the same time a sort of accolade. And this had the effect that sometimes I felt the overwhelming urge to speak of it—not of these dreams however, but rather to hint that there were remarkable things about which one knew nothing. I was never tempted actually to

---

[210] Dr. Jakob Stückelberger (1758–1838), was a professor of practical medicine at the University of Basel. There were widely reproduced terracotta figurines of him with a widow, Mrs. Ochs ("ox," or "oaf"), depicting the anecdote that Jung narrates here.

[211] See above, p. 39–40.

speak about them. I knew you could not do that. I first spoke about the phallus dream when I was sixty-five years old, and the other one I perhaps shared with my wife, but also not until I was well into my later years, because there was still a heavy taboo connected with it, originating in childhood.[212] I would never have been able to talk about it with friends. It was shrouded in much too heavy a taboo.

All the same I felt a remarkable pressure to talk about it, yet to what end was not clear, whether to probe, or to discover whether other people had had such experiences. I never succeeded in even finding a trace [41/42] of it in others. So I got the feeling of being either an outcast or a chosen one, either cursed or blessed. I soon came to take it as something like a special grace from God, or that I was somehow cursed by something so hot that one could not even touch it. In time, these thoughts disappeared from the surface again.

[213]My mother said to me that I was often depressed at that time. In fact, I was not depressed; I was preoccupied with the mystery. At the time it was a remarkably blessed reassurance to sit on top of this rock.[214] This liberated me somehow of doubts. The conflict ceased when I thought that I was this stone. It had no uncertainty, had no pressure to unburden itself and has remained imperishable for centuries. I am only a passing phenomenon which dissolves into all possible emotions, like a flame which soon flares up and then dies out.

And then there were these rather unclear feelings again. And the so-called "depression," these were simply times when these feelings came up. There came profound doubts about everything my father said. You must also not forget:[215] in my mother's family there were six ministers, and on my father's side it was not only my father who was a minister but also two of my uncles.[216] I heard many religious conversations and theological discussions, sermons and so on. In this I always had the feeling, "Yes, yes this is all very fine. But what about the mystery? And the mystery is also the mystery of grace. You know nothing about any of this, and you

---

[212] See n. 132 above.

[213] See *ETG*, p. 48, *MDR*, p. 42.

[214] See above, p. 132.

[215] See *ETG*, pp. 47–48, *MDR*, pp. 41–42.

[216] These appear to have all been from the Preiswerk side of the family: Samuel Gottlob Preiswerk (1825–1912), four of whose sons also became pastors; and Eduard Preiswerk–Friedrich (1846–1932), who also had a son-in-law who was a pastor. Sophia Preiswerk was married to the pastor Edmund Fröhlich (1832–1898). Taken together, on his maternal side, Jung had two great-grandfathers, one grandfather, one great uncle, and four male cousins who were pastors. Two female cousins were also married to pastors (JFA).

don't know that God even wants you to do wrong, that I must think of damnable things in order to experience his grace." Everything that the others said was completely relative. I thought, for God's sake, someone must know something about it! Somewhere the truth must be found. I researched in my father's Bible. I read many articles in the philosophical lexicon. (This was Krug's lexicon from the beginning of the 'forties.[217] Back then Schopenhauer was the most recent addition, and it is now more than one hundred years old). In this lexicon, however, the articles I read were completely in the style of the times. I read the articles about "God," "Trinity," "spirit," [42/44] and "consciousness." I devoured them but grew none the wiser for it. Every time, I always concluded: They too don't know anything about this either! This led me later to study philosophy. I read Schopenhauer and Kant, beginning in my thirteenth and fourteenth years.[218] At that time, I also read a book on Christian dogma by Biedermann.[219] (His daughter married one of my uncles!) My great-grandfather's brother married Schleiermacher's daughter.[220] He was Johan Sigismund von Jung. Schleiermacher converted my grandfather from Catholicism to Protestantism.

[221] During this period of philosophical study, I was confirmed. This is when the famous story happened with my father: he taught me the catechism. This bored me terribly, it was utterly unspeakable. Once I was leafing through the small catechism trying to find something interesting and my glance fell upon the paragraph about the Trinity. At this I grew excited, for this had awakened my interest. When it was finally the time for this section and the long-awaited hour arrived, my father simply said, "We'll skip this section now. I myself don't know what one is supposed to think about it." With that my hope was buried. I did admire my father's

---

[217] In Jung's library there is a copy of the four-volume second (1832–38) edition of the German philosopher Wilhelm Krug's (1770–1842) *Allgemeines Handwörterbuch der philosophischen Wissenschaften* (Leipzig: F. H. Broadhaus, 1827–34).

[218] See *ETG*, p. 62, *MDR*, p. 56.

[219] Alois Biedermann (1819–1885) was a Swiss theologian and professor of theology at the University of Zurich. He wrote *Christliche Dogmatik* (Berlin: Reimer, 1885).

[220] See *ETG*, p. 399. Friedrich Schleiermacher (1780–1849) was a major German Protestant theologian. On May 4, 1953 Jung wrote to Henry Corbin, "Your intuition is astounding: Schleiermacher really is one of my spiritual ancestors. He even baptized my grandfather—born a Catholic—who by then was a doctor [. . .]. The vast, esoteric, and individual spirit of Schleiermacher was a part of the intellectual atmosphere of my father's family. I never studied him, but unconsciously he was for me a spiritus rector." *Letters*, vol. 2, p. 115. On Jung and Schleiermacher, see Matei Iagher, "Jung and the Psychology of Religion: A Preliminary Sketch," *Phanês* 1 (2018): 58–82.

[221] See *ETG*, p. 68, *MDR*, p. 52.

honesty, but that did not help me with the fact that thenceforth all religious talk bored me to death.

Still I hoped that the mystery of the communion would turn on a light for me, but once again this was nothing but pure realism and made no impression upon me. It was a rather chilly morning and this cold sip of wine! And this bread, when I very well knew the baker who had baked it! From the bottom of my heart, I pitied my father for having to celebrate this as if it meant something. I came out of there as if an extremely unpleasant task had been carried out.—The most interesting thing was that I been given a fine black Sunday suit, a type of frock coat with a split tail at the back! You could stick the handkerchief back there, that was the cat's pajamas! All my internal preparation for this, that was all in vain! I [43/44] never went to communion again. I simply *could* not. My father never forced me to go. He himself suffered terribly from religious doubts. I always hoped that I would be able to spell out to him what grace was so that he could also experience it, but that never happened. He thought I was simply an unbeliever who had been ruined by school.

At that time I pushed further into philosophy and gradually developed a downright resistance to theology. I began to study Kant and Schopenhauer.

I then went to the *Gymnasium*. There was not a single one of my teachers who inspired me, and I was indescribably bored.[222] One teacher was a university professor, a very clever chap. He taught Latin.[223] He often sent me to the university library instead of keeping me in the Latin class. Because I already knew Latin from my sixth year. My father taught me. So I had to fetch books for him during the exercises which I then pored over with delight, taking the longest possible route back to school. But boredom was not the worst thing by far.

[224]Once, among the many essay topics, which were not exactly stimulating, there was an interesting one. I took it very seriously and constructed my sentences with great care. I handed it to the teacher in the joyful expectation that perhaps I had written the best essay, or at least one of the best.[225] Whenever he returned essays, he would always discuss the best essay and the others in order of their grade. Mine was not the first, nor

---

[222] See *ETG*, p. 49, *MDR*, p. 43.

[223] Jung's Latin teachers at the *Gymnasium* were Carl Grob, Theophil Burckhardt-Biedermann, and Jakob Oeri.

[224] See *ETG*, p. 69–70, *MDR*, p. 64–65.

[225] Jung's grades in the *Gymnasium* from 1891 and 1895 were almost uniformly excellent (Basel Staatsarchiv).

even the second or third. Every other student took their turn ahead of me, and as the weakest effort had finally been discussed, the teacher puffed himself up threateningly and said, "Jung's essay is the best by far, but he reeled it off the cuff carelessly and without effort. For this reason, he does not deserve a grade."—I interrupted him: "That is not true, I never worked so hard on an essay [44/45] as on this one." "That is a lie!" he cried, "Look at X there" (namely, the boy who had produced the worst essay). "X made an effort. He will go far in life, but you will not succeed because one cannot succeed with mere cleverness and cheating." I was silent, and from then on I never worked at my German lesson.

At that time, I began to leaf through the principal teachings of Bacon of Verulam in Latin,[226] as well as other books which I no longer recall.

Then there was a Greek teacher who unfortunately identified himself with Plato.[227] He was also an old hypochondriac with a cross-cut beard. He sort of represented "mass, number, and weight." Right proportion is the sine qua non!—such was the slogan he physically embodied, but his teaching of Plato was first-rate.

We had one Latin teacher, he was a complete fool although I did learn a whole load of living Latin from him.[228] But he had a stomach neurosis and was a neurotic of the first order. He yelled and blustered at us, but he gave excellent lessons. We read Caesar and Cicero with him. Due to his excellent lessons, he made an impression on me.

Then we had a teacher for religious studies.[229] He was a specialist in the history of the Reformation. I can't tell you the torture I had to bear with him! Such terrible boredom! He wheeled out the entire jargon of the theologian. The "path of salvation," God's expectation of salvation, and so on. This all seemed to me like madness. For me, God was a terrible mystery, and what the teacher said only bored me horrifically, and none of it was true. [45/46]

[230]I had great trouble deciding what I wanted to become. Mostly I was drawn to things Egyptian and Babylonian. I imagined becoming an archaeologist. But I had no money to study elsewhere and there were no

---

[226] Presumably, Francis Bacon (1st Baron Verulam)'s *Novum Organum: sive indicia vera de interpretatione naturae* (*The New Organon, or True Directions Concerning the Interpretation of Nature*) (1620). This was a canonical work in the formulation of the notion of scientific method.

[227] Jung was taught Greek by Emanuel Probst and Theodor Plüss.

[228] See n. 223 above.

[229] Rudolf Staehelin (1875–1943). He was the author of, among other works, *Huldreich Zwingli: Sein Leben und Wirken nach den Quellen dargestellt*, 2 vols (Basel: Schwabe, 1895).

[230] See *ETG*, pp. 89–90, *MDR*, p. 84.

teachers for that in Basel. So that plan was useless. At first, I registered as a student of Philosophy II, meaning to study the natural sciences. And this is what happened: when I considered career choices, I wanted to become something to do with the discovery and the understanding of antiquity, undertaking excavations or deciphering Egyptian texts and so on. Then I realized that, well, no, I can't become this; because then I can only ever be a teacher. And I would rather have been anything than a teacher. I had to do something connected to nature. Then came two dreams that determined my path.[231]

In the first dream I am walking into a wood along the bank of the Rhine. It does not really exist in the way I saw it in the dream. In the deepest part of the woods, I came across a small hill, and there I began to dig. And there I found bones from prehistoric animals. This aroused an incredibly passionate interest and then a cry arose in me, "Ah, it's not antiquity but nature that I want to study!"

And then came a second dream. Again, there was a wood, permeated by streams. In the darkest place was a round pond. And in the pond, there was the most amazing creature I have ever seen: a circular thing, shimmering in many colors, consisting of many small cells or organs formed like tentacles. The whole creature was about a meter in diameter. And this set off a wave of interest, and now I knew I had to decide for the sciences. So, I enrolled as a student of Phil. II. But then, even before the term began, I had another idea: it had to be zoology. But then you'll have to be a schoolteacher, so then, botany—though that too leads to teaching—I cannot hope for anything else as I have no money. And then after further consideration I figured that a doctor too must study science and, indeed, must acquire a much more comprehensive education, including anatomy, physiology, physics, and so on, each being an integral part. That seemed much better to me—I would study medicine. And that's what I enrolled to do.[232]

---

[231] On November 15, 1913 Jung noted these dreams in *Black Book* 2, in a different order: "I think further back to my nineteenth year of age, when a dream decided upon my career choice: First I saw, in a dense undergrowth of a solitary region, a quiet dark water, a pond, and in its middle swam the most fantastic of animals, roughly comparable to a many-colored jellyfish. This animal aroused in me the highest intellectual curiosity, so that I awoke with a pounding heart. And soon thereafter I had a second dream: I was in a dark forest, where I found a small hill like a charcoal kiln. I poked it with my foot and discovered in it to my greatest surprise the bones of prehistoric animals, which also sparked off the greatest curiosity in me. These dreams motivated me to the study of the natural sciences and that led me to medicine." (pp. 153–54).

[232] On April 18, 1895 Jung entered the medical school of Basel University.

[233]I have forgotten to mention something: I was between twelve and thirteen years old. The fact that I was far in advance of my class plays a part in this. We had eight lessons of Latin per week. I was already well advanced because my father had already taught me Latin from when I was five. So, I was horribly bored in school. I knew no one with whom I could have talked. My father was very nice, and I liked him very much. But he was either preoccupied or grumbling. He was eager to discuss philosophy with me, but in religious matters he maintained that one must believe and not think. The boys I knew—of course they were nothing much. So I was completely alone. I had my sister, but she was ten years younger than me.[234] I was closest to my mother. But soon I found that she was not enough for me in conversation. Mostly she admired me, and that was not good for me. So, I was mostly alone. But I preferred it that way. I played on my own, went wandering alone, dreamed or went walking in the woods alone. School was an abomination to me. Once, after school when classes had ended, I was waiting for someone. Then one of the other boys came along, kicked me, and I stupidly fell and hit my head on the curb of the pavement. I had a head injury; a cerebral concussion. I was a bit dazed for half an hour. Soon I felt better. But from that date onward I used to have fainting fits, mostly in the mornings around eleven or twelve o'clock. This was due to the fact that I left the house at 7 a.m. after only drinking only a cup of milk and sometimes not even that. So I was simply hungry. My father consulted various doctors. Of course, nothing helped. [47/48] I myself knew exactly that they would find nothing. The moment I fell, in the blink of an eye I knew with utter clarity: Now I have an excuse, I don't have to go to school any more. In the end, when the doctors found nothing, they supposed that it must be some kind of traumatic epilepsy. Then I was taken out of school, for me a dream come true.[235] I was able to be free, daydream for hours, draw, go out on the water, be in the woods. At that time, mainly I drew battles or furious warriors or ancient castles under attack or on fire. All combative scenes, or pages full of grimacing faces which still appear to me sometimes before dropping off to sleep, constantly moving and changing. By contrast Leonardo is a joker![236] Some of these

---

[233] See *ETG*, pp. 36–37, *MDR*, pp. 30–31.

[234] Gertrud Jung (1884–1935). See below, p. 94–95.

[235] This would have been in late 1887/early 1888, as Jung spent a month at the beginning of 1888 in Winterthur (probably with his uncle).

[236] In his *Treatise on Painting*, Leonardo da Vinci wrote, "I will not omit to introduce among these precepts a new kind of speculative invention, which though apparently trifling, and almost laughable, is nevertheless of great utility in assisting the genius to find

grimaces have predicted the deaths of other people, for example. It is not without its problems!

Now that I no longer had to go to school, I was able to immerse myself in the world of the mysterious. There were the trees, a lake, the marsh, the stones and animals. All of this was wonderful. More and more I hid away from the world—with a quiet feeling of bad conscience. Once one of father's friends came to see him and I overheard them: "And how is your son?"—"Oh," said my father, "this is a difficult case. They think it's epilepsy." I knew precisely that it was not, but it suited me damn well at the time! "We have lost our means, what will become of the chap?" I heard my father saying, full of worry. And this struck me like a thunderbolt. I got straight onto my Latin grammar and began to grind away and after ten minutes I had the most splendid fainting fit. I simply slipped from the chair and after a few minutes I came around. And carried on. "For goodness' sake, you do not have fainting fits!" I said to myself. And I went on working. After thirty minutes the second fainting fit came along! "And now you're really going to get down to work!" And then no more fits occurred and after a couple of days I went back to school and then I had no further episodes of fainting. After that the whole enchantment had vanished. That was when I learned what a neurosis is! [48/49]

I have always known that nothing is. I am not sure whether I had told anyone. At that time, I also read a lot, especially about religious questions. I read what I could find about God and the Trinity.

But again, I encountered the same thing: this neurosis was once again my mystery, being at the same time a shameful mystery and later a defeat for me as well. Yet from then on this led to a keenly marked precision and great diligence, both of which I still have today. Sometimes then I even worked from three o'clock until six in the morning before going to school. I rose regularly at 5 a.m., sometimes at 4 and one time even at 3 a.m., in order to work. From then on I undertook my tasks with the utmost seriousness, because I had a mortal fear that I could fall into temptation and vanish from the world. This was a mortal fear in me. Then began my conscientiousness, not for the sake of worthy repute but conscientiousness for my own sake! I knew how I had been in the wrong towards myself, just as I was the one who had disgraced myself, the donkey.

---

variety for composition. By looking attentively at old and smeared walls, or stones and veined marble of various colours, you may fancy that you see in them several compositions, landscapes, battles, figures in quick motion, strange countenances, and dresses, with an infinity of other objects. By these confused lines the inventive genius is excited to new exertions." Translation by John Rigaud (London: J. Taylor, 1802), p. 84.

No one else was to blame. I myself was the condemned deserter. But what had led me on this detour was my passion for being alone, the enchantment of being solitary; this was still inarticulate in me. Nature seemed to me full of wonders into which I wanted to plunge. Every stone, every plant, they were all alive and indescribable! At that time I sank deeply into nature, sort of crawled into its being and was detached from the whole world of humanity. There was not a single soul with whom I could have spoken. I had friends, but they were all just lads and I always had the feeling that I was an adult man. At fourteen my nickname in the *Gymnasium* was "Father Abraham"!

[237]My entire youth can be understood through the lens of the mystery. Through it I entered into an almost unbearable loneliness. It was my great achievement of that period that I resisted the temptation of speaking to someone about it. At that time my relationship to the world prefigured what it is today: I am also alone today because I know things and must presage certain things that others do not know and mostly do not wish to know.

That a marvelous creature lay undisturbed in this clear, deep water, half immersed, this was indescribably wonderful. I had this dream [49/50] before my high-school diploma, aged around nineteen. Back then, my favorite subjects were zoology and botany.[238]

[239](Maternal) grandfather Preiswerk. He discovered that he was constantly surrounded by spirits. For this reason, my mother had to sit behind him when he wrote his sermons to prevent the spirits from accosting him from behind. He was born in 1800 and had a distinctly poetical tendency. He had a girlfriend. It was not intimate, but all the same a relationship. My maternal grandfather wrote a famous poem, "We had built a stately house . . ." It is in the *Teutschen Liederbuch*.[240] [241]
[61]

---

[237] See *ETG*, p. 47, *MDR*, p. 41.
[238] See above, p. 62.
[239] See *ETG*, pp. 405–6.
[240] "Wir hatten gebauet ein stattliches Haus" is the first line of a famous student song written in fact by August Daniel von Binzer in 1819. In 1912 Jung cited a hymn by Samuel Preiswerk from the *Gesangbuch für die Evangelisch-reformierte Kirche* (no. 170) in *Transformations and Symbols of the Libido* (CE 6; CW B, § 534). Preiswerk's hymns are available at https://hymnary.org/person/Preiswerk_Samuel (accessed April 24, 2025).
[241] A two-month gap ensues: on March 2, Jaffé informed Kurt Wolff that she had been in hospital for a month after an influenza infection (BL).

MARCH 30, 1957[242]

I went to the *Gymnasium* when I was ten years old. I have told you about the traumatic neurosis.[243] That was in my eleventh year. I was never angry towards that schoolmate for knocking me to the floor. He was sort of "appointed" to do so. I never held it against him. He was an innocent lad. From my side there was a devilish arrangement in the mix. I hated school. I wanted much rather to be alone and play and build my fortresses out of earth and stones. So, I fantasized and lost myself in daydreaming. Then it happened that I was confronted by reality for the first time. Namely, when I heard my father saying to a friend, "We have forfeited our assets and now the boy is in this situation! What on earth can he do if he can't learn anything properly?"

That was the collision with reality. "Aha, so one has to work!" went through my head. I was eleven years old. From then on, I became a studious child.

[244]At that time it so happened, on the long way to school from Klein-Hüningen to Basel, that a moment came when I sort of emerged out of mist and knew, now *I* am. Behind me was a sort of vaporous wall in which I was not yet. But then in that moment *I* happened to *myself*. Prior to that I had been present, but everything as it were only happened to me. Now I knew: Now I exist, now I am present. Now I must have volition, and this happened at that time.

---

[242] On March 3, Jaffé wrote to Kurt Wolff that she had now read the Claudel volume and was startled by the active role of the interlocutor. By contrast, she saw her role as follows: "in reality I only listen; and the little questions I throw in now and then—'Didn't your dream about the cactus come then?' or: 'What did your mother say about the experience?'—are completely uninteresting for the reader. Jung is by nature a great story-teller, who continuously translates the stream of inner images into words. I'm careful not to interrupt that even when he digresses—which happens often—because those detours are full of surprises." She then asked Wolff whether he would agree to her including remarks that Jung made in other contexts within this work (BL).

On March 18 Jung wrote to Jaffé that he had just got back from Bollingen and informed her that he had "finished painting the ceiling in Bollingen and done more work on my inscription." (*Letters*, vol. 2, p. 351).

On March 21 Kurt Wolff replied to Jaffé, "Your idea to include in our book such material as you have put down in the past about remarks Jung made, stories he told, etc., seems to me excellent. I would certainly suggest you doing so [...]. In putting questions to Dr. Jung, I am sure you will have in mind the desirability of rounding out the various phases of his life with experiences, meetings with personalities who became important to him, etc., etc." (BL).

[243] See above, pp. 63–64.

[244] See *ETG*, pp. 38–39, *MDR*, p. 32.

[245]This is linked to the experience with Basel cathedral: how I came out of the *Gymnasium* yard at twelve noon. into the cathedral square; the sky was a gorgeous blue and the sun was shining gloriously, the roof of the cathedral sparkled in the light, the sun reflected from the roof tiles. I thought to myself: The world is beautiful and the church is beautiful and, above it and higher than all, God sits on his golden throne.—Then came an opening and there was something there which I was unable to think. Now, you know the reflections that consumed me then and that I came to the idea that God had created Adam and Eve in such a way that they had to think what they did not want to think. He compels them to think something so that he knows that they are obedient. And he can also demand something that man must do for religious reasons even if it is evil. [61/62]

It was obedience that had brought me grace. From then on, I knew what grace was.

After I had thought what I was compelled to think, this experience brought me the concept of the greatness of divine grace. I was at God's mercy. The only thing that matters is that one fulfills his will. Otherwise, one is abandoned to nonsense. From that moment on, my ultimate responsibility began. Why did he shit on the cathedral? For me this was a hideous thought. Then came the notion that God might be something hideous and then came the feeling: everything is beautiful and good, one must obey the father, one must go to school, *but* above all stands the command of God. For me this was a very fearful and dark matter. This overshadowed my life. And I became very preoccupied.

Secretly in these days I searched in my father's bible for a definition of God. But what I experienced there was a formidable mystery. And I also experienced this as my own inferiority. I am simply a devil or a swine, I thought. Something degenerate, and then with a certain gratification I read in the gospels about the pharisees and the collectors, that it was precisely the degenerate who were the chosen ones. (God have mercy on me, a sinner!) It impressed me, for example, that the unfaithful steward is praised,[246] and that Peter, the waverer, is called the rock.

[247]The greater my feelings of inferiority were, all the greater did the grace of God appear to me. I was never sure of myself. When my mother once said, "You were always a good boy," I could hardly believe it. Me?

---

[245] See *ETG*, pp. 42–43, *MDR*, pp. 36–37.
[246] Luke 16:1–13.
[247] See *ETG*, p. 47, *MDR*, p. 41.

That was news to me. I always thought that I was someone damaged or inferior. Which was also connected with the fact that I grew up with peasant boys and heard of everything. There was no sordid villainy I didn't know about. I grew up with animals and peasants. It was all very close to the earth. The lads from distinguished families always seemed much finer to me. In any case, then, I soon saw that all is not what it seems to be, [62/63] but only the cloak over a tail. At first this impressed me powerfully. I also noticed quite early that my parents' marriage was not a good one.

Alongside my schoolwork I tried to orient myself in philosophical questions. At that time, I read Bodmer's history of dogma.[248] At eighteen I began to read philosophical articles in Krug's lexicon,[249] and in school I also read Schopenhauer.[250] Later, during my university years, I read Kant and Nietzsche.[251]

[252]Regarding the first dream that I have already told you and which influenced my career plans: in the dream I was in an unknown forest, very primeval and quite wild. Back then we had such wild woods on the river islands of the Rhine. It had not yet been rechanneled but flowed through many tributaries. There were marvelous woods there where I roamed, daydreaming around, exploring the plants and so on. I looked for animals, immersing myself in everything that was connected to natural science.—Once I won a first prize at school: Wossidlo's book *Lehrbuch der Zoologie*.[253]—So in the dream I was in such a forest and I came

---

[248] No such work has been located. From Jung's earlier recollection, it seems that the work he had in mind was Biedermann's *Christliche Dogmatik*.

[249] See above, p. 59.

[250] Jung's copy of Schopenhauer's *The World as Will and Representation*, bearing his nameplate, is dated 1897. On May 4, 1897, Jung took out a copy of Schopenhauer's *Parega und Parapilomena* from the Basel library. (Basel library checking records).

[251] The Basel University Library checking records show that the first volume of Kant that Jung took out was his *Lectures on Psychology*, on January 30, 1897 and that on March 23 he took out volumes 7 and 8 of Kant's works. This would have included his *Anthropology from a Pragmatic Point of View* and his post-1781 essays. He took out the fourth volume of Nietzsche's *Werke* (*Daybreak*) on May 15, 1897, and two months later, on July 1, he returned to take out the second and third volumes (*Human, All Too Human*), together with *Beyond Good and Evil*. On Jung's reading of Nietzsche, see Paul Bishop, *The Dionysian Self: C. G. Jung's Reception of Nietzsche* (Berlin: Walter de Gruyter, 1995); Martin Liebscher, *Aneignung oder Überwindung: Jung und Nietzsche im Vergleich* (Basel: Schwabe, 2011); Gaia Domenici, *Jung's Nietzsche: Zarathustra, The Red Book, and "Visionary" Works* (London: Palgrave Macmillan, 2019).

[252] See above, p. 62; *ETG*, p. 89, *MDR*, p. 85.

[253] Paul Wassidlo, *Lehrbuch der Zoologie für höhere Lehranstalten sowie zum Selbstunterricht* (Berlin: Wiedmannsche Buchhandlung, 1886).

upon a small hill, a round hill like a grave tumulus and there I began to dig, and I came across the bones of prehistoric animals. This penetrated me with uncanny force.

Before that I had been given as a gift a picture atlas about prehistoric animals, which I had adored. It had interested me keenly. Also, at this time I rapaciously read Darwin.

[254]The second dream came a few weeks later. This one became crucial, as it occurred during my high-school graduation exams. After the second dream I wanted to study natural sciences at university. In this dream there was another primeval forest, dark and mysterious, it was a natural pond. In fact, there really was such a pond from which a stream came. And I saw in the middle of the water, as if suspended, a gelatinous, transparent, partly colored mass consisting of many cells, and radially formed, and this creature was a marvel. I awoke completely entranced with the thought: I must study natural sciences! At the start of the semester, I switched to medicine. I wanted to do research, not teach. My idea was that studying medicine would bring me far greater opportunities and that as a doctor I would be able to develop further in some direction. From the harmony of both philosophical and scientific studies, things soon came to a head. Above all because in 1897 I got to know a medium with whom I undertook many séances during 1898–1899.[255] Then I gained an insight into the extraordinary workings of the psyche, and this was pivotal for what I would do later.

Nine days after my state examinations, I arrived in Zurich as an assistant doctor at the Bli.[256] What is also significant: at seventeen or eighteen I had fallen in love with an older cousin, a cousin on my mother's side.[257] Of course she noticed nothing of my feelings; for I would rather have done anything than let on about it!

---

[254] See above, p. 62; *ETG*, pp. 89–90, *MDR*, pp. 85–86.

[255] See *ETG*, p. 113, *MDR*, p. 106. Jung is referring to his séances with his cousin Helene Preiswerk. On this, see Stefanie Zumstein-Preiswerk, *C. G. Jungs Medium: Die Geschichte der Helly Preiswerk* (Munich: Kindler, 1975) and Sonu Shamdasani, "'S. W.' and C. G. Jung: Mediumship, Psychiatry and Serial Exemplarity," *History of Psychiatry* 26, no. 3 (2015): 288–302. In 1925 he dated the inception of the séances to 1896 (*1925*, p. 3).

[256] Throughout the text, Jung generally referred to the Burghölzli as the "Bli." Jung's exam took place on November 26, 1900, and he started at the Burghölzli early the following month on December 11.

[257] Louise Preiswerk (1874–1957) (nicknamed "Luggi"), the sister of Helene Preiswerk. See Zumstein-Preiswerk, *C. G. Jungs Medium*. Jung gave Louise a copy of Du Prel's works, *Das Rätsel des Menschen* and *Der Spiritismus*, with the dedication, "For his dear cousin Luggi, a little book worthy of consideration by a beautiful soul." (p. 142).

I'd like to tell you something else about prescience. Mostly it is simply prescience, but not a premonition. So, I had a dream long after the death of my sister:[258] it was in Basel at a garden party. My sister was there, and I was amazed; for I knew that she had died. I also saw Dr. Schmid,[259] who was also dead by then. But others who were present were still living. Then I saw that a woman I knew well from Basel was strolling with my sister, yet she was still alive, although since she was in my sister's company she had evidently already been grazed by death. I thought, "She is earmarked," though in the dream she was completely and clearly conscious to me. Rather as if I knew this evening that today you visited me and I spoke with you, but then I make a small adjustment in consciousness like this: I awake but no longer know who you are. [63/65].—That's how it was for me with respect to that lady: I might have torn my hair out but still couldn't for the life of me remember who she was. In my mind I went through several acquaintances in case something might ring true. Nothing!—A few weeks later I received the news that Miss Häussler had met with an accident.[260] Immediately I knew that it was her I had seen in the dream but had not remembered. She was from Basel, and I knew her quite well. She was in treatment with my wife. (She had been in a manic-depressive state and was able to get clear of it. What still remained was a phobia of Paris. After her cure she thought that for once she would dare to go to Paris. She traveled there and was killed in a car accident!)

When we enter this world, it is terribly raw and brutal and repugnant and of divine beauty. This is nature: cold as stone and splendid as the finest love. And I say to myself: This continues after death. This is still nature and things can happen which would make you aghast. For example, take a man who starts off as a young lad with very tender stirrings of the heart, but what has become of him after thirty or forty years? And Gottfried Keller said the same of young girls, how innocent they looked and

---

[258] See *ETG*, p. 306, *MDR*, p. 303. Jung noted this dream and the related episode in the continuation of *Black Book* 7, writing however that he dreamed it three to four months before the death of his sister (in 1938) (*BB* 7, pp. 170–72). On July 14, 1957 Jung related to Bennet another dream he had after the death of his sister: Bennet, *Meetings with Jung*, p. 98.

[259] Hans Schmid (1881–1932), psychiatrist and friend of Jung. Between 1915 and 1916 Jung and Schmid had a correspondence on theoretical matters, which played a critical role in Jung's thinking concerning psychological types. See John Beebe and Ernst Falzeder, eds, *The Question of Psychological Types: The Correspondence of C. G. Jung and Hans Schmid-Guisan, 1915–1916*, trans. Ernst Falzeder, Philemon Series (Princeton, NJ: Princeton University Press, 2013).

[260] This appears to be Elisabeth Heusler, who was a patient of Emma Jung's. On December 3, 1931 Jung wrote to her thanking her for an invitation to a lecture (JP).

what then becomes of them later! One could say: They become this nature, they grow into it and become these devils that they precisely are also in eternal nature. And then the dead come into a different nature. They are born into it through death and assume the color and pitch of that nature. For "there" is also some sort of nature, it too is somehow of God.

It is possible that the process of emanation, of God from the Godhead, is continued onward.[261] Otherwise our existence has not the least trace of meaning, and the whole of creation would be utterly meaningless. It is also the case that it pushes right at the boundary, one must have a springtime belief if one believes in meaning. It is a question of temperament as to what one believes will prevail: absurdity, meaninglessness, or meaning.[262] Although, if meaninglessness were to absolutely prevail, the fulfillment of meaning would disappear to an increasing extent with higher development. But that is also not the case. Probably, as with all metaphysical questions, it is both [65/66]: God is meaning and absurdity, or he has meaning and absurdity.[263] I have the anxious hope that meaning must prevail or win the battle, for it is in fact a battle. May it win out!
[11]

APRIL 24, 1957[264]

[265]In my first big childhood dream I was initiated into the mysteries of the earth, that is, there was a burial in the ground, and it took a very long time until I resurfaced again. This was in order to bring the greatest possible amount of light into the darkness. For this reason, it is completely irrelevant whether people understand something of what I have said, whether a dozen people understand my ideas, or two or three dozen. The main thing is that these things have been said. Perhaps then, I have said enough.
[67]

---

[261] The differentiation between the Godhead and God and the emanation of God from the Godhead play an important role in the thought of Meister Eckhart.

[262] Jung took up the relation between *Sinn*, *Unsinn*, and *Übersinn* in the prologue to *LN* (pp. 120–21).

[263] See *ETG*, p. 360, *MDR*, p. 359, where this sentence is reproduced with "Leben" (life) replacing "Gott" (God).

[264] On April 19, Jung wrote to Aniela Jaffé asking her to bring some pipes to Bollingen, and indicated that the "Rosencreuzian ABC-Booklet with the breakthrough visions" could possibly be found in the Zurich Zentralbibliothek or in the Basel University Library (JP).

[265] See above, p. 39, and *ETG*, p. 21, *MDR*, p. 11.

May 4, 1957

[266]My student years were a pleasant time for me. A time of friendships. Yes, it was a pleasant time. I had good friends, and everything was animated intellectually. Back then I gave all sorts of talks in the Zofingia Society in Basel.[267] This was a color-wearing association. I cannot remember about what. I remember one of them: on Ritschl's theology.[268] This seemed completely ridiculous to me. I read the fat tome he wrote; I can't recall the title.[269] And his theology!—Just imagine this: he compares the event, the life of Christ, along with his epiphany, to a great freight train being shunted. At the back, the locomotive shunts the carriages, then the jerk goes through the entire train, and at the front a wagon is set in motion! This is how the impetus of Christ is supposed to have gone through the centuries!

Then I gave a talk about Schliemann and his excavations in Troy. I delivered a large presentation on this. But this was still in my schooldays in the *Gymnasium*.

The beginning of my student years—that was when I read Schopenhauer and Kant. *The Critique of Pure Reason*. And Eduard von Hartman and Carus.[270]

---

[266] See *ETG*, p. 102, *MDR*, p. 97.

[267] The Zofingia Society is a Swiss student debating society, with sections in university towns. Jung became a member of the Basel branch of the society on May 18, 1895, and its chairman in 1898. For his lectures there, see CE 1; CW A.

[268] See Jung's "Thoughts on the Interpretation of Christianity, with Reference to the Theory of Albrecht Ritschl" (1899), CE 1; CW A.

[269] Albrecht Ritschl (1822–1889) was the most prominent German Protestant theologian at that time. He attempted to synthesize Kant and Luther. He was opposed to mysticism and pietism, and saw Christianity as a moral outlook rather than a direct relation to God. He stressed the ethical development of man in community. His major work was *Die christliche Lehre von der Rechtfertigung und Versöhnung* (1870–74), translated as *The Christian Doctrine of Justification and Reconciliation*, ed. H. R. Macintosh and A. B. Macaulay (Edinburgh: T. & T. Clark, 1900).

[270] While discussing a dissertation written by an American student, Ira Progoff, with Ximena de Angulo, Jung protested against the common Freudocentric misreading of his work, stating that his own conceptions were "much more like Carus than Freud" and that Kant, Schopenhauer, Carus, and von Hartmann had provided him with the "tools of thought." Ximena de Angulo, "Comments on a Doctoral Thesis," in William McGuire and R. F. C. Hull, eds, C. G. *Jung Speaking: Interviews and Encounters*, Bollingen Series 97 (Princeton, NJ/London: , Princeton University Press, 1977/Picador, 1980), p. 207. Jung checked out Eduard von Hartmann's *Die Philosophie des Unbewußten* (*The Philosophy of the Unconscious*) from the Basel University Library on January 15, 1898, his *Das Ding an Sich und seine Beschaffenheit* (The thing-in-itself and its nature) on September 13 that year, and his *Die Selbstzersetzung des Christenthums und die Religion der Zukunft* (The self–decay of Christianity and the religion of the future) on October 18. On

And then in 1898, due to my interests in occult phenomena, I got to know the somnambulist.[271] This event had been heralded about three weeks previously by an extraordinary experience: namely, that a table, our dining table from my grandmother's trousseau, suddenly split in two with a loud bang. The crack extended over half the depth of the walnut table. This is how it happened: I was working for some sort of exams and was in an adjoining room. In the room itself my mother was sitting at the window. When it happened, she was terribly shocked. She always had all sorts of ideas about spirits and the devil knows what. For example, she said, "Bacteria, what do you want with those? They are spirits!" (And how does Portmann describe viruses today? Just recall the lecture about hydrophobia in Ascona!)[272]

[273]And the story with the knife, [67/68] that was oil to the fire. A knife in the drawer suddenly broke into four pieces with a violent bang. I still have the knife in my possession even today. I stood helpless before these phenomena. I then went to a good knifesmith and asked him, "Can you tell me how this happened? The knife was in the drawer. What happened there?"—The smith explained that one would need to clamp it and then sort of chip it off in order to break it in this way. Or if one dropped rocks on it from a great height.—But the knife was in the breadbasket in the sideboard, and it split with a similar bang to a pistol shot. Altogether there

---

Schopenhauer and Hartmann, see Angus Nichols and Martin Liebscher, eds, *Thinking the Unconscious: Nineteenth Century German Thought* (Cambridge: Cambridge University Press, 2010).

[271] See *ETG*, p. 111, *MDR*, p. 105. On November 27, 1934 Jung narrated this episode together with the episode which follows regarding the exploded knife to J. B. Rhine, and commented, "According to my idea these two facts are connected with an acquaintance I had made just in those days. I met a young woman with marked mediumistic faculties, and I had made up my mind to experiment with her. She lived at that time at a distance of about 4 km. She hadn't come anywhere near to my house then, but soon after the series of séances with her began. She told me that she had vividly thought of these séances just in those days when the explosions occurred. She could produce quite noticeable raps in pieces of furniture and in the walls. Some of those raps also happened during her absence at a distance of about 4 km." *Letters*, vol. 1, pp. 181–82.

[272] In 1958 Jung wrote, "'Absolute knowledge' occurs not only in telepathy and precognition, but also in biology, for instance in the attunement of the virus of hydrophobia to the anatomy of dog and man as described by Portmann" (*A Modern Myth: Of Things Seen in the Skies* [1958], CE 26; CW 10, § 636). Adolf Portmann's lecture was entitled "Die Bedeutung der Bilder in der lebendigen Energiewandlung" (The meaning of images in living energy transformation), published in *Eranos-Jarbuch 1952* (vol. 21): *Mensch und Energie*, ed. Olga Frobe-Kapteyn (Zurich: Rhein Verlag, 1953), pp. 325–57; see pp. 353–54.

[273] See *ETG*, p. 112, *MDR*, p. 105.

were three drawers. The knife was in the right one, at the front. It broke into four pieces with smooth cutting surfaces.

Shortly after this I made the acquaintance of this medium. This interested me extraordinarily. I had read a lot about the phenomena in romantic literature. *The Seeress of Prevorst* and that sort of thing.[274] Also the old spiritualist literature about the Fox sisters, Zöllner, on Mrs. Espérance, Alan Kardec, Aksakow and all the books on this which are still in my library today.[275]

The medium was a cousin of mine.[276] My mother had many brothers and sisters who lived very scattered, and we did not know them all.[277] I then became acquainted with the young medium's branch of the family. She was fifteen-and-a-half years old. She had already held séances at home with her sisters. I had heard about these and was interested myself.

[278]The séances with me took the following course: I had to darken the room, so we were in twilight. She then sank into a trance. Then she spoke

---

[274] Justinus Kerner, *Die Seherin von Prevorst. Eröffnungenüber das innere Leben und über das Hineinragen einer Geisterwelt in die unsere*, 2 vols (Stuttgart, J. G. Cotta'sche Buchhandlung, 1829); *The Seeress of Prevorst, Being Revelations Concerning the Inner-Life of Man, and the Inter-Diffusion of a World of Spiritsin the One We Inhabit*, trans. Catherine Crowe (London: J. C. Moore, 1845). Jung took Kerner's book out of the Basel University Library only on August 17, 1897; in 1933–34 he devoted five lectures to a detailed reading of it. See Ernst Falzeder, ed., *History of Modern Psychology: Lectures at ETH Zurich, Vol. 1: 1933–1934*, trans. Falzeder, Mark Kyburz, and John Peck, Philemon Series (Princeton, NJ: Princeton University Press, 2018), pp. 38–70.

[275] The birth of modern spiritualism is attributed to the Hydesville rappings in 1848, when Maggie Fox (1833–1893) and her sister Kate (1837–1892) claimed to be in communication with a peddler who had been murdered in their house five years previously. Together with their sister Leah (1814–1892), they gave public demonstrations of mediumship throughout the United States. "Mme d'Espérance" was the pseudonym of a controversial English physical medium, Elizabeth Hope (1855–1919). Among other works on spiritualism, Jung's library holds the following: Alexander Aksákow, *Animismus und Spiritismus* (Leipzig: Oswald Mutze, 1894); Allan Kardec, *Das Buch der Medien: Ein Wegweiser für Medien und Anrufer über Art und Einfluss der Geister*, trans. Franz Pavlicek (Leipzig: Oswald Mutze, 1891); and Friedrich Zöllner, *Die transcendentale Physik und die sogenannte Philosophie* (Leipzig: L. Stackmann, 1897). Jung's advocacy of spiritualism at this time is apparent in his 1897 Zofingia lecture, "Some Thoughts on Psychology" (*CE* 1; *CW* A).

[276] See *ETG*, pp. 113–14, *MDR*, pp. 106–7.

[277] Jung's mother's siblings were Samuel Gottlob (1825–1912), Auguste Dorothea (1828–1904), Lucas Albrecht (1829–1908), Maria Sophia (1831–1914), Rudolf Johannes (1832–1895), Wilhelm Adolf (1835–1856), Carl Heinrich (1836–1856), Gustav Adolf (1837–1913), Salome Elisabeth (1839–1899), Johannes (1842–1909), Eduard (1843–1844), and Eduard (1846–1932): information from Zumstein-Preiswerk, *C. G. Jungs Medium*, where some further details are also given (p. 132).

[278] For Jung's descriptions of the séances, see "The Psychology and Psychopathology of So-Called Occult Phenomena" (1902), *CE* 2; *CW* 1, §§ 45–71; Zumstein-Preiswerk, *C. G. Jungs Medium*, pp. 53–54; and Jung's manuscript notes, *CE* 1.

in a different voice and also produced knocking sounds. She lay on the sofa. Next to this was a small table. This was in front of me: a round table on a column with three legs. The noises came from the column of the table. One could precisely determine where the knocking was coming from. She also claimed to see all sorts of spirits. I myself never saw anything. I only wrote down what she said. In my dissertation I only mentioned the main points. [68/69]. Then she began to cheat, whereupon I gave up the matter. That was after we had held perhaps one or two years of séances together. Later I wrote my line about it: it operated like a sort of personality development. Later she became an extraordinarily efficient and gifted seamstress, although she died young. She had a studio in Paris with twenty-two employees.[279] Later she made a skirt for my wife which was the finest she had ever had. It was isabelline in color. She [Jung's wife] appeared to me in a dream wearing this dress after her death.[280]

This understanding of the development of the personality took shape around 1900. The whole thing made an infinitely strong impression and threw up many problems for me. It also very much prompted me to study Kant.

I remember it was in that period—it was 1900—early summer, something remarkable once happened: on Saturday afternoon I went on a long solitary walk. I walked for a good three hours. Then, as I wandered through the woods and fields all alone, I noticed that my thoughts revolved anxiously around my mother and my sister. I imagined them at home. We lived in the country at that time. We had no, or barely any, neighbors.

Then gradually the fantasy came to me that my mother had been burgled and that my mother and sister might have been murdered and perhaps also the young maid. I thought: Crazy ideas, ridiculous mood! And I was annoyed that my walk was so disturbed. Then my fear increased, whereupon I finally turned around and went home. I went faster and faster and, in the end, I was galloping home as fast as I could. I stopped before the front door and thought: When you enter, you'll find a bloodbath. And there was nothing!—What had happened there?

I had imagined that in the autumn of 1900, you'll sit for the state exam, and then I'll seek a position as assistant in a mental hospital.

---

[279] In 1902, Louise Preiswerk reported, "Helly is now the first tailor in the best and most highly regarded couturier. Her studio is located in near the Madeleine, in the finest quarter. Rich ladies are fighting for the chance to get a dress designed by her." Zumstein-Preiswerk, C. G. *Jungs Medium*, p. 100.

[280] See below, p. 187.

[69/70] I had already written to Eugen Bleuler that I would like to work as an assistant doctor with him.[281] At the time he was the most well-known psychiatrist. Nothing was happening in Basel. He replied to me that he would get back to me. Then he wrote some time later that I could start with him as an assistant doctor as early as December 1900.—So, on that walk my thoughts were preoccupied with the idea that I wanted to go away from home. I wanted to get right away from Basel. One was so stuck in tradition there. It was also a very conservative element in me as well, it suited me, but at the same time I also feared it.[282]

One day, when I was fifteen, I was waylaid by a storm; I can tell you it was a real hurricane; I felt myself caught up in a tremendous wind, in a whirlwind, roaring about with the strength of a hurricane and carrying everything away. I wrote a poem about it then and gave it to my mother.[283]

---

[281] Eugen Bleuler (1857–1939), director of the Burghölzli from 1898 to 1927. On July 15, 1900 Bleuler wrote to Jung,

> A long time ago I received a reference from Prof. Müller regarding your effectiveness at the public hospital there. In the expectation of soon receiving a notification or similar from yourself, I temporarily shelved it. Now the architect Mr. Jung reminded me again of the matter and I am taking the liberty of inquiring of you whether you are minded to apply for an assistant doctor post at the Burghölzli. If everything takes its natural course, such a post will probably be available before the spring of 1901, certainly before the autumn of 1901. In October 1901 a job change will take place in any case." [JP]

In October 1900 Jung wrote in his diary,

> Prof. Bleuler offered me a post as assistant doctor, directly after the exams. I have accepted.—If I now pass my exam and take up this post, then my outer self has achieved a milestone.
>
> And my inner self? A bit more peace, the years have brought a bit more traction. But I'm wavering like a will of the wisp in the infinite. I am still expecting the unknown, something great and unspeakable, more with that anxious oppressive haste, which set off nightly visions in me, in faith, I believe, of men, of salvation of the world, the original mystery will have revealed itself and, new spheres will have opened up with the force of thunder. [JFA]

[282] At the end of April 1900, Jung noted in his diary, "For many people the moment comes when they have been at home for the longest time where they no longer feel with the family, they can no longer join in with traditional cares and interests. This moment is approaching for me. I feel that something new is inserting itself into my empirical personality." (JFA).

[283] Lucy Heyer narrated the following regarding Jung's birth and this poem: "This friendly and mildly temperate landscape was struck by a severe catastrophic storm, a rare natural event at this ferocity, just as the child was being taken for baptism in the church. The home-bound young mother was anxious to see the young one safely brought through the ferocity and the eclipse. In the family, this event fell into oblivion until fifteen years later the boy wrote a poem that described a storm catastrophe. He dedicated it to his mother,

She said to me, "It's a wonder to me all the things that you come up against!" This was a spiritual storm, it was terrible, it was a world storm

---

and only at that moment she remembered again how threateningly the storm God had accompanied the baptism of her firstborn on that day of baptism in late summer 1875. When Jung related this poem and his mother's reaction, he noticed that he had often had such inspirations as this poem, contents foreign to consciousness that corresponded to an objective event, which imposed themselves on him and sought expression. That storm poem, which was for a long time in the possession of the mother, was unfortunately later lost" (LH, "Biographie von Carl Gustav Jung," "Kindheit," p. 1). As indicated by Florent Serina, the poem described here appears to correspond to the following poem in Jung's papers:

"Thoughts in a Spring Night"
"And believing themselves to be wise, they
have become fools."
"The old has gone; see, all
has become new."
Wildly raging storms roar through
the spring night, that darkness,
shaking the withered trees, waking them
into new life. Look!
The old oak keels over, rotten,
long since reduced to propping up
a shell of hoarfrost—for the young year's storms
broke its elder strength.
Roaring resounds through the forest
with the tree's fall. The storm
sweeps overhead, waking the young,
stirring them into life and on
into growth—
heaving, surging, rising
on the flood of sap to break
the dormant pip's dark
sheath. On to life, on into the
light!
Christians! Hear the admonition!
Are you deaf, blind, sleeping?
Don't you feel the new era's
mighty downpour? Waken to it! Live!—
spur the spirits onward, doff
yesteryear's curled, powdered wig.
Don't you ever feel in your heart?
Eternally new, eternally old,
never the same yet always the same.
Oh, you may never recognize it
because it is smaller and yet greater
than mankind's dead wisdom;
because it is nearer and yet further
than you can reach with your knowledge.
Listen! Marvel: it is life,
and life is God!

that simply wiped out an entire old world that had been carrying me. I was simply carried off by this storm. It was also simply *my* storm. An indescribable event. From then on, I was filled with the thought: Now something is coming!

And indeed, then came the medium, but that was almost ten years later. Back then everything was still firmly established for me. There was the Habsburg monarchy, there was Bismarck, a German Reich, the French Republic. They still spoke of Napoleon, of the Apatucci.[284] I was shown shrapnel from the bomb that had dropped on the cathedral square in 1811.[285] One had the feeling of a continuity and security: things have always been like this and will always be like this, and everything is wiped away by this world storm. At that time, for example, a man such as Ostwald could say: There can be no more wars, the nations are far too connected through economic relationships.[286]

Now, the vision of murder that I had on my walk: that was the farewell to my mother. My mother was awkward and needy.[287] She lived with my sister;[288] but my sister was six years younger than me.[289] [70/71] My father died in 1896 and then I stepped into my father's shoes. For example, I had to give my mother the housekeeping money on a weekly basis because she could not manage the household or money. So, it was very hard for her if I were to go away. But I knew that I must.

The epigraphs are from Paul's Epistle to the Romans (1:22) and Second Epistle to the Corinthians (5:17). On this poem, see Paul Bishop, "C. G. Jung and 'Naturmystik': the Early Poem 'Gedanken in Einer Frühlingsnacht'," *German Life and Letters* 56, no. 4 (2003): 327–43; and Florent Serina, "Lucy Heyer-Grote, Hapless Hagiographer of C. G. Jung, with a Hitherto Unpublished Memory of Jung's Infancy," *Jung Journal: Culture & Psyche* 15, no. 1 (2021): 83–102. The manuscript of the poem is dated 1893 (JP).

[284] The French general Jean Charles Abbatucci (1770–1796), who was originally from Hüningen. Jung would have been familiar with his bust in the eponymous Abbatucci Square there.

[285] The year was actually 1815: see Niklaus Stark, *Basel im Visier der Festung Hüningen* (Basel: Druckerei Dietrich, 2021), pp. 44–45.

[286] In 1916 Jung criticized Wilhelm Ostwald's statement, in the latter's *Die Philosophie der Werte* (Leipzig: Alfred Kröner, 1913), pp. 312–13, regarding the need to stop preparations for wars which would never take place: see "The Psychology of the Unconscious Processes," in C. G. Jung, *Collected Papers on Analytical Psychology*, ed. Constance E. Long, 2nd edn (London: Baillière, Tindall and Cox, 1917 [1916]), p. 398.

[287] See *ETG*, p. 119, *MDR*, p. 112.

[288] At this time, Jung was living near his mother and sister in Binningen near Basel (in an old house that belonged to a wealthier uncle who allowed them to stay there after the death of Jung's father). Jung's mother and sister later lived in Seestrasse 177, a short walk from Jung's own house.

[289] Kurt Wolff noted here, "Something needs to be said about Basel before this."

Basel was far too parochial for me. Back then, for the Baselers, their town was everything: on the far side of the Birs was where "misery" began![290] Later, when I came to Basel on a visit they always used to ask: When are you coming back? They did not understand at all that I had gone away, for only in Basel are things as they should be! And foreign parts, that's a misery.—For my mother it was very difficult that I left, but she took it very courageously. In Basel you are defined once and for all: there, I was the son of Jung, the parson. I belonged in a certain set,[291] a sort of "pious set," and there, you could only sense resistance towards it. I did not wish, nor was I able, to allow myself to be pinned down.

[292]In 1896 my father died after a long illness. He had been ill for a year with cancer of the pancreas. This is a chapter in its own right. Even in the confirmation classes with him, I was alone. I was so terribly bored by it. I was enormously excited about the chapter on the Trinity and then came the disappointment that you know about.[293] Everything my father taught me in these classes felt like dry felt in the mouth. I always thought: I'm chewing papier mâché or I have felt in my mouth. Then I thought: Finally, something's coming that has some meaning. And then my father said: Now, the chapter on the Trinity. I don't understand anything about it myself, we'll skip this. From then on it was all over! I then noticed that my father himself had the greatest difficulties. He was also a pastor for the insane asylum,[294] and there he had been infected by the skepticism of the doctors who reduced everything psychic to chemical secretions and who had a wretched philosophical education. He believed that the mind was nothing but a secretion of the brain.[295] [71/72]

---

[290] "In Basel, you are defined once and for always" was added above here in type and then typed over.

[291] "set": in English in the original.

[292] See *ETG*, p. 100, *MDR*, pp. 96–97.

[293] See above, p. 58.

[294] In 1886 the Friedmatt Basel asylum was founded, and Paul Jung became the pastor there until his death.

[295] In 1805 Pierre Jean Georges Cabanis had written that "[t]he brain after a fashion digests impressions; [. . .] it organically performs the secretion of thought." (*Rapports du physique de du moral de l'homme* [Paris: Caille et Ravier, 1815], p. 129). In 1845 Wilhelm Griesinger commenced his textbook by asking rhetorically, "What organ must necessarily and invariably be diseased where there is madness? [. . .] Physiological and pathological facts show us that this organ can only be the brain; we therefore primarily, and in every case of mental disease, recognise a morbid action of that organ." (*Mental Pathology and Therapeutics*, trans. Lockhart Robertson and James Rutherford [London: New Sydenham Society, 1867], p. 1). The reductionist and materialist outlook dominated mid- to late nineteenth-century German psychiatry.

I knew that this was a swindle. I had already read Kant's philosophy, at least in Krug.[296] I understood something of epistemology and knew that the whole of materialism is rubbish. But my father had let himself be influenced by it. He did not want to think. I always wanted to discuss things with him and get him to think. There were some very bitter arguments. In the end, I noticed that to a large extent he had lost his faith. I was very sorry for him. Once I heard him pray for faith. That made a terrible impression upon me. In this respect I had no difficulties whatsoever. I knew about the fallacy[297] of materialism, I knew that these are the ultimate things about which one can say nothing, just as little as one can say anything about God.

Since that moment when I experienced God shitting on the church, I knew that I was in the hands of something greater.[298] I knew: I am destined, it's above my head. I am singled out, and that gives the feeling as if a personal being were appointing me.—From that moment on, I felt myself responsible, for I knew I had to respond with my entire being to what was leading me. I often thought: Poor father, you torment yourself with your faith! One is destined; one must do things that one does not wish to. That is proof enough. This has nothing to do with matter, any more than with faith. Aged eleven, I had to sit up at night and ponder how it was that I had to think such things. In this lies the key to everything.

My father wore himself into the ground with his doubts.—I must say that in a certain sense I was glad for him that he could die. And in a certain sense too for myself. It was a burden, for he was terribly at odds with himself and consequently had terrible moods. He always said to me, "Oh, you always want to think! One must believe."[299]—I used to think to myself: I don't need to believe. I have experienced it!—So it always amused me to provoke theologians because they had so deeply disappointed me.—And if it came to that, none of them stood firm. For me, [72/73] God shitting on the church was a bloody event.[300] This turned my life around. For on my own I never would have arrived at this obscenity.[301] But my father didn't have an inkling of such an experience. So, in the end

---

[296] W. T. Krug, *Allgemeines Handwörterbuch der philosophischen Wissenschaften* (Leipzig: F. A. Brockhaus, 1832). See *ETG*, p. 66, *MDR*, p. 61.

[297] "fallacy": in English in the original.

[298] See above, pp. 55–56.

[299] Cf. *ETG*, p. 49, *MDR*, p. 43.

[300] See above, p. 63.

[301] "So it was also a liberation" was obscured by overtyping over here.

it was a liberation when he died. He had sort of given up on me. I never again went to communion and not even to church if I could avoid it.

My father was a terribly decent man and did not dare to reproach me, because he knew where he himself stood. He would have preferred to have left his ministry. He suffered terribly from his doubts and the intractability of his situation rendered me speechless. I could no longer speak with him about my interests. It all wounded him. Then to top it all, natural science: that seemed to him to be the source of all evil. For it proves that everything is nothing but matter! He was a feeling type, but had no wish to think. And his feeling did not impress me at all. When he spoke of "eternal bliss" and "salvation" and so on it was grief and pain to me, because I knew his doubts.

Also, my parents' marriage was not harmonious. My mother was sometimes hysterical.[302] She lived in a fantasy world and had every possible medical condition. I always had the feeling that these illnesses were not real. After my father's death she was better.

Once, the following happened to my mother: I was already in my first clinical semester. I come back home. My sister comes towards me, very troubled. She says my mother has a high fever. I felt her pulse. It was quick and I took her temperature. It was 39.5 degrees [Celsius]. But then I had the feeling that something was not right. So, I ask her, "Where have you been this afternoon?"—She said she had been in town to see her aunt, as she was very unwell.—But now it came out that, at the aunt's, a distant relative, she had seen the corpse of this woman's sister who had died of heart disease. She had seen the dead woman there, comes home and was now ready to die. I say to her, "Now you are imagining that you must die. [73/74]. You have just let the corpse make a very great impression on you!"—In half an hour the fever had gone!

My mother knew about the relationship between myself and my father. Once she said to me: Your father died in time for you. This affected me terribly, this "for you." But I felt: Now this is the storm. And it tore loose an element of times past. But in its place a bit of manliness and freedom entered me.

I moved into my father's room after his death.[303] And then something very remarkable happened: about six weeks after his death he came back

---

[302] In *VA*, Jung wrote, "At that time, my mother was in hospital in Basel for some months. Presumably with hysteria due to disappointment with her husband whose heroic period had expired with his final exams." (Continuation of *BB* 7, p. 235.)

[303] See *ETG*, p. 101, *MDR*, p. 96.

in a dream. Suddenly there he was, and he said he was coming back from his holidays. He had fully recovered and was now coming home. I thought there would now be a thunderstorm because I had moved into his room. But not at all!—But I had fundamental feelings of inferiority. I had imagined that he was dead and all the time here he was, looking hale and hearty!—After a few days he came again: he said he had come home again. I reproached myself that I thought he had died, and he told me he was feeling fine.

At the time, I had a lot of doubt about what one should think about life after death.[304] No one could take the feeling away from me that I was appointed to do what God wishes and not what I wish. But as to whether we have immortality, that was something else.

It was clear to me that great things would happen in my life, that I had a destiny to fulfill. But I was uncertain about immortality.

These were the first dreams since my childhood that made a colossal impact upon me. I kept asking myself: What does it mean that my father shows up in this way? He was completely "real." These dreams were a profound experience for me.

He did not come back in a dream again until 1922. (In February 1923 my mother died.) But then he returned "as if from a long journey." I had not dreamed of him since 1896, but then came a dream a half year before my mother died. [74/75]

[305]In the dream, my father came to me, the doctor. I was already in Küsnacht then. I was extremely pleased that he came to me, and I wanted to tell him everything, about my family, the children, my wife, my house, about my *Types* book that had just been published. I wanted to tell him all this. But I noticed that he was very preoccupied and rather embarrassed. Then he asked about marital psychology and I gave him a talk about it.[306]—Six months later, my mother died, after an illness lasting only two days, aged seventy-five. One cannot take this dream as proof, but it is a clue.

---

[304] On this issue, see Sonu Shamdasani, "'The boundless expanse': Jung's Reflections on Life and Death," *Quadrant* 38, no. 1 (2008): 9–32.

[305] See below, p. 267. In *BB* 7 Jung noted (January 8/9, 1923), "I dreamed that my father had returned from a long journey. I thought, now for once he can come into my house and see my family, whom he never knew. But he wanted to consult me concerning his marriage and I had to explain to him the psychological relationship in marriage." (p. 232). Jung's mother actually died on January 9, 1923.

[306] See "Marriage as a Psychological Relationship" (1925), *CE* 10; *CW* 10. On July 14, 1957 Jung narrated this dream to Bennet: Bennet, *Meetings with Jung*, p. 98.

After my father's death came my student days. It was a mental liberation for me no longer to have to bear, hopelessly and impassively, my father's suffering. On December 10, 1900 I finished my student days. I was able to start as an assistant doctor immediately. With that, my whole youth was over. My friends scattered and everything was gone. I was alone.

[307]For the first half year I did not leave the hospital. I knew I had to adapt, and now I knew I must learn something. My entire medical knowledge acquired during my studies was useless. So, I simply worked all the time. The others thought I was melancholic, because they did not understand that I was always in the library or in my room reading. I read the old volumes of the *Zeitschrift für Psychiatrie*,[308] I studied the history of psychology, and I thought about my dissertation.[309]

At the Bli, a topic had been suggested to me around schizophrenia, then called "dementia praecox."[310] I made my proposal to Professor Bleuler and remarkably he accepted it immediately. Then I began the associations experiment.[311] At this time I was also very impressed by research into the anatomy of the brain. I assisted in the laboratory when brain dissections were being carried out. It was a Dr. von Muralt who led this.[312] These studies impressed me greatly. But I always wanted to know

---

[307] See *ETG*, p. 120. *MDR*, p. 52.

[308] *Die Allgemeine Zeitschrift für Psychiatrie und psychisch-gerichtliche Medicin*, which was founded in 1844.

[309] "On the Psychology and Pathology of so-called Occult Phenomena" (1902), *CE* 2; *CW* 1.

[310] On the work on dementia praecox at the Burghölzli at this time, see Brigitta Bernet, *Schizophrenia: Entstehung und Entwicklung eines psychiatriches Krankheitsbild um 1900* (Zurich: Chronos Verlag, 2013). Bleuler shared Jung's interests in psychic research: in the 1920s and 1930s, they conducted séances with the mediums Rudi Schneider and Oscar Schlag. Aniela Jaffé, *From the Life and Work of C. G. Jung*, trans. R.F.C. Hull and Murray Stein (Einsiedeln: Daimon Verlag, 1989), p. 10.

[311] See C. G. Jung, ed., *Studies in Word-Association: Experiments in the Diagnosis of Psychopathological Conditions Carried Out at the Psychiatric Clinic of the University of Zurich, Under the Direction of C. G. Jung*, trans. M. D. Eder (New York: Moffat, Yard, 1916).

[312] Jung refers here to Alexander Ludwig von Muralt (1869–1917). In 1901, von Muralt published his dissertation on moral insanity. Jung, in the conclusion to his own dissertation, thanked "my friend Dr. Ludwig von Muralt for his kindness in handing over to me the first case mentioned in this book (case of Miss E.)" (*CW* 2, § 150). In 1903 von Muralt gave a course on hypnotism and psychotherapy. When he was on sick leave from the Burghölzli (1903–04), Jung, who had left the Burghölzli in October 1902, stepped in and deputized for him, from October 1903, and in April 1905 formally assumed the position of *Sekundararzt*, roughly equivalent today to clinical director. In 1905 von Muralt became the director of the Davos Sanitorium. He was married to Florence Hull Watson (1867–1964), a doctor from Philadelphia. He died of tuberculosis.

what, in the final analysis, he saw in it. Yet I received no reply to this question.

Dr. Alexander von Muralt, he was a great comfort to me in my isolation then. I was not very close to Bleuler.[313] [75/76] He was a cross between peasant and schoolteacher. And being from Basel, I was terribly spoiled. There, I belonged to a sort of aristocracy, also of the spirit. There was a highly cultured tradition discernible in conversation and in people's background, sensed as cultivated. That all went missing in Bleuler. But all the same, I valued Zurich, for the air was free. There was no ancient haze there, the brown haze of the centuries; that was not present. But it seemed to me like a conglomerate of a peasant population. Von Muralt on the other hand, he was an aristocrat, and this was my caliber.

I seemed on the whole very unlikeable to people then. Some admired me, others hated me. I was a Basel native; I had the Basel *médisance*,[314] I liked making macabre jokes. But my vexation and my thoughts were lost on them. They had never heard of theological disputes. In Basel, I was accustomed to such contentious debates. You were able to take a classical education for granted in any conversation. We could debate about the different styles in Cicero, even among medical students. That was simply a part of how it was.

Jacob Burckhardt once had to move house, and naturally this set off in one a whole barnyard of emotions. He also had a baby grand piano, and one of the giant fellows who had turned for the move simply lifted it up onto his shoulder and carried it away. Whereupon Burckhardt cried, "Good heavens, it's Atlas!"—That is Basel. You had to have been there![315]

As medical students we argued about Schopenhauer, Kant, and different theological perspectives. It was an educated and mentally interesting

---

[313] Bennet notes the following comments of Jung in his diary: "Bleuler: he had a latent psychosis and was afraid to go into matters, but he was a good psychiatrist, a good organizer" (September 16, 1959); "Bleuler—B. discussed all the material in his book on Psychiatry with his colleagues and very largely with Jung who gave Bleuler his ideas freely; he never thought of doing anything else. But Bleuler never mentioned this help in his book. He gave Bleuler many examples and his interpretations of them and these Bleuler used." (September 18, 1959) (Bennet Papers, ETH).

[314] *médisance* (French): "gossip," "backbiting."

[315] Jacob Burckhardt (1818–1897): Swiss historian, one of the founding figures of art and cultural history. He is best known for his 1860 work *Die Kultur der Renaissance in Italien* (published in English in 1878 as *The Civilization of the Renaissance in Italy*) He held a professorship in Basel until his retirement in 1893. Jung in part took over Burckhardt's understanding of the cultural historical role of primordial images: see *Transformations and Symbols of the Libido* (1912), CE 6; CW B, § 56n.

environment. This was not present in Zurich. I became a close friend of von Muralt. The friendship endured until he married. A proper American, a proper animus-hound. She managed to destroy the friendship because she was envious.—Then I became a senior physician. Von Muralt got tuberculosis and had to go to Davos. There he became a lung specialist.

I was very interested in histology and even taught a course in it.[316] I loved that; it was marvelous for me. I taught my colleagues [76/77] about it and then I began to do brain dissections and to dye them. But I worried about it and asked von Muralt, "What is the point of this actually? What can one see in the brains of schizophrenics (Dem. Prac.)?" Answer: "You can't see anything at all in them."—"Why do we do it then?" "We just do it," was the reply. That was it, and then I only entered the laboratory full of doubts. One day, von Muralt came no more. I asked him why. "Now I am engaged in photography," he said.—"But that has nothing to do with brain dissection?"—"No, that is just a sport!"—So, this is how it is, I thought, and I threw myself into the associations experiment.

After the doctoral examination, from September 1 through 9, 1900 I made my first trip.[317] I went to Munich. With a legacy from a distant relative, an uncle by marriage, who had dealt in fine art with all sorts of people and had made a good profit from it.[318] Out of this money, I paid the examination fees and with the rest, I traveled to Munich and considered myself terribly well-traveled.—On November 30, 1900 I went to the theater for the first time, to see *Carmen*.[319] Before that, I had not had the money to do so; I was too poor. Later in Zurich I couldn't take part very much in society because I only had a couple of pairs of trousers and a couple of shirts. After my father's death, my mother had 2,200 francs per year. And four people had to live off that! For my university studies I received scholarships.

Before the Munich trip, I had been abroad only once: I went to Belfort on foot;[320] and once I made a fourteen-day trip with 60 francs. I traveled

---

[316] Some histological diagrams by Jung have survived (JFA).

[317] The exam was on November 26, according to an entry in Jung's diary. "September" is an error: the trip was actually in December. The diary entry further notes, "Munich, Augsburg, Ulm, Stuttgart, Karlsruhe," indicating the places Jung visited (JFA).

[318] Stephanie Zumstein-Preiswerk notes that it was the antiquities collection of his maternal aunt Auguste Preiswerk that Jung had helped to sell (*C. G. Jungs Medium*, p. 99); also, that it was actually his maternal uncle Eduard Preiswerk who gave him a loan for his studies. See *ETG*, p. 102, *MDR*, p. 97.

[319] Georges Bizet's opera, which had premiered in 1875.

[320] Belfort: in France, about 65 km from Basel.

as far as Lake Como and then we hiked for fourteen days. This was with a friend,[321] an exceptionally taciturn person. For 50 centimes, we could spend the night in a hay-barn.—This friend later became a chemist; he was an exceptionally taciturn person.

I recall the time when I was once given a box of cigarettes. I felt like a prince. They lasted a whole year. I allowed myself only one on Sundays.— When I was in Paris for the first time, I lived on one franc a day. I was already a doctor then. I stayed in the Hôtel des Balcons in the rue Casimir Delvigne, a student hostel.[322]

There I learned to speak like a Parisian.—I would not like to have missed this time of poverty. A cigar, or getting something really good to eat now and again—these are simply things that one learns to appreciate.

I have been placed in my life's task by fate. From the very beginning I had a sense of destiny. Even as early as the collision with the priest. That too had incredible significance; it made the Catholic church significant for me. The dream of the cathedral was the collision with Christianity and the great world storm is like a new edition of God shitting on the church.[323]

[324]The symbolism in my childhood dreams disturbed me terribly: the phallus, and that God shat on the church. I wondered: Who is actually speaking that way? Who has such effrontery to portray a phallus so nakedly? Who is speaking such that God shits on his church? So outrageous and disgusting. The violence of the image, the filth bursting down! I always asked myself if it was not the devil who had arranged this. I never doubted that it had been God or the devil who was speaking in this way and who makes me think it or not think it. I certainly felt that it was not me. I was only eleven years old! But these are the decisive events of my life. It then dawned on me: It is up to me; a problem has been posed to me to which I must give an answer. And who is posing the problem? To this day no one has answered that question for me. And I knew that no one could at all. I knew that I must answer this myself from my innermost being: I was alone before God, utterly alone. None of my friends would have been able to answer. I never spoke about it with anyone.

---

[321] Jung had fifteen blank postcards from Lake Como, and also visited there in 1909 and 1914 (JFA).

[322] The hotel, in the Latin quarter, still exists, under the name of Grand Hôtel des Balcons, rue Casimir Delavigne 3, near the Jardin du Luxembourg. Jung painted the view from it: see *Art of C. G. Jung*, cat. no. 24 (p. 82). Jung was in Paris from November 5, 1902 to January 19, 1903.

[323] See above, p. 55.

[324] See *ETG*, p. 53, *MDR*, p. 47.

All this gave me the feeling: I am not one among others, I am only alone with God. God alone is asking me these terrible things. I was occupied with this throughout my entire childhood and youth. One has to do the other things too: studying, working. But in the background, you are alone with God. This gave me the strength to set out on my path. [78/79]

I have no need to doubt or to seek. I was always already at my bench: now you do this, now this or that must be done. This feeling simply ran through everything. The one who had given an answer when I was alone, that was the one who had always been; the one even before my birth. He belonged, for example, in the eighteenth century. Always, when I was "there," when I was no longer alone, I was somewhere back in the centuries. That was the one who is forever. I sort of went back into the centuries. People noticed this. Even in school they called me Father Abraham.[325] The conversations with that "other" were my most profound experiences: on the one hand, the bloodiest of battles, on the other hand, the supreme delight. That is why I am in fact never alone, because I never relied on others. Naturally some reliance, but not in the final analysis. I can endorse what Hans Hopfer, a pupil of Holbein says: death is the ultimate of things.[326] I yield to no one.

There was a feeling of an unparalleled certain destiny, an inner certainty, although I could never prove it. But to me it was proven.

When I decided to become a psychiatrist, all my friends said it was crazy. I too really thought it was probably a blunder. But I simply knew: This is how it has to be. Or: This is what I am and now it's do or die. Although I knew nothing of psychiatry, I even had terrible resistances against it. [79/80]

MAY 16, 1957

Today I want to tell you another dream that I had about my father.

[327]It was more or less the last dream in a series of others, and it began with me making a visit to my father in the dream. He lived in the

---

[325] See ETG, p. 71, MDR, p. 64.

[326] In 1958, in A Modern Myth, Jung wrote, "One would therefore wish many people the compensating attitude of the anima in our dream, and would recommend them to choose a motto like that of Hans Hopfer, a native of Basel and pupil of Holbein: 'Death is the last line of things. I yield to none.'" (CE 25; CW 10, § 696).

[327] See ETG, pp. 221–22, MDR, pp. 217–18. Jung noted this dream in the continuation of BB 7, dating it "March 1948" (pp. 151–53).

country; I don't know where. It was a house in the style of the eighteenth century, very spacious, and it had some large outbuildings, and there were crypts within them, and my father was the custodian there. They said that this house had originally been an inn, a sort of inn at a spa where many princes and nobles and famous people of all kinds used to stay, and they said some of these had died and were buried in these crypts. And now my father was the custodian there.—I had an association with "the illustrious ancestors," and moreover, unlike before, my father was now a great independent scholar, as I discovered. Then I was in his study, and curiously Dr. Brunner from the Brunner sanatorium in Küsnacht was also with me:[328] he was about my age, along with his son who now has the sanatorium. And as I say my father was also there.

I don't know if it was in response to a question from me, or whether he wanted to explain something of his own accord; in any case, he fetched down from a rafter a large bible for this purpose; it was like the Merian Bible which I own in my library and which is such a thick tome, and this bible was bound in a shiny fish skin.[329] He opened it to a passage in the Old Testament, I assume it was in the Pentateuch, and now began to give an exegesis of this passage, and so quickly and in such a scholarly way that I was not able to follow. I gathered only that he conveyed heaps of learning, including linguistic knowledge whose meaning I could only infer intuitively, but which I could not understand. He spoke in a rush, so quickly, and I observed that Dr. Brunner next to me caught not a bit of it. He understood absolutely nothing, and his son began to laugh. They were remarkably dull people [80/81]; I knew that Brunner was thinking my father was obviously in some kind of senile fit of enthusiasm. But I knew that this was no pathological excitement, and that it was very important to him, fascinated as he was by what he was presenting, and that was why he was speaking with such haste. (Brunner represented this dumb medical

---

[328] Dr. Theodor Brunner (1877–1956) was a psychiatrist who since 1908 had run a private sanatorium in Küsnacht, established in 1840 by his grandfather. It was located close to Jung's house on Seestrasse. Theodor Brunner had friendly relations with Jung. An advertisement from 1911 indicates that the sanatorium served nervous and mental patients, convalescents, and those in need of withdrawal from alcohol and morphine. It promised individualized medical treatment in a magnificent location with lakeside garden promenades: *Monatsschrift für Psychiatrie und Neurologie* 30, no. 1 (1911).

[329] There is a copy of the Merian Bible in Jung's library. It was printed in 1630, with illustrations by Matthäus Merian the Elder (1593–1650) to Luther's translation. In the continuation of *BB 7*, Jung added the following note to this motif: "The various references to fishes is probably related to the fact that in the winter and spring of 1948 I was writing a work on the symbol of the fish." The reference is to his researches which culminated in *Aion* (1951), *CE* 21; *CW* 9.2.

standpoint that naturally clings to one. That is my shadow in its second or third edition).

Then the scene changed, and we were in front of the house across from a kind of large barn where it seems firewood was stored. There was a terrible commotion, as when large pieces of wood fall down or get thrown around. It was like poltergeists. And I had the impression of at least two workers being involved. But my father implied to me that it was not workers, but that the rear house was haunted. And then we entered that house and there I saw that the place had very thick walls. In one wall we went up a staircase to the first floor; then we stepped out of the wall into the first floor of the house, and that was like the Diwan-i-khas (council chamber) of Sultan Akbar in Fatehpur Sikri.[330] It was the precise image of this: namely, a round gallery from which four bridges led into a central basin. It was a proper mandala, and in the middle was another round seat, where the sultan sat and spoke to his advisers who sat along the walls behind the bridges. The basin rested on a massive column reaching down into the ground floor. This is true in reality. And then I suddenly saw— this is now the dream, no longer the depiction—that leading from the middle a steep staircase went up the wall and at the top was a small door and my father said: Now I will bring you into the ultimate presence, and then he kneeled down and touched the ground with his forehead and I did the same and also kneeled, and was very moved. But for some reason I could not get my forehead fully down to the ground. Perhaps a millimeter remained between my forehead and the ground. But I had made the gesture with him. I suddenly also knew that above the door at the top lived Uriah, King David's general, isolated in a chamber, whom King David had betrayed by seducing his wife.[331] That shameful deed!

[332]Then comes the dream with the fish laboratory, but it is associated with dreams I had before I discovered alchemy. Then dreams came where the same motif kept presenting itself, that next to my house there was yet another, yet another wing which I did not know. I was always amazed in the dream and then woke up because of it.

---

[330] Fatehpur Sikri, near Agra, was built in the latter half of the sixteenth century, and was the capital of the Mughal empire for about ten years. The Diwan-i-Khas, built in red sandstone, was the "Hall of Private audience" of the Emperor Akbar. Jung visited there on December 23, 1938. Sulagna Sengupta, *Jung in India* (New Orleans: Spring Journal Publications, 2013) p. 113.

[331] See 2 Samuel 11.

[332] See *ETG*, p. 206, *MDR*, p. 213.

But once a dream came in which I really ended up in the other wing. There was a great library within it, originating in the seventeenth century. Great, fat volumes lined the walls, bound in pigskin. Many works also originated in the sixteenth century. Among these volumes there were different ones which were decorated with copperplate engravings, engravings of a completely strange nature such as I have never seen before.

Later after the dream of the bible bound in fish skin, I dreamed that my house had a large adjoining wing which I had never entered. I thought I must have a look at it some time. The addition was in front of the veranda. Then I went over to it. There was a large double door and I went through it. I was suddenly in this room. This is what it was like, there was another corridor and there was a laboratory and there, in front of the window, was a table covered with glassware and all the paraphernalia of the laboratory. This was my father's workplace. But he was not there. On the walls, upon the beams, were hundreds of glasses with every imaginable sort of fish; I was extremely astonished: now my father is engaged in ichthyology!

As I stood there, suddenly Hans Kuhn was there.[333] I had noticed a curtain there. This billowed open from time to time as if a strong wind was blowing. I said to Hans that he should check whether a window was open. He went over there and after a while he came back with a deadly serious face. I saw [82/83] immediately: Something has happened to him! Hans said only, "Yes, there is something, it is haunted!" And I saw that he was profoundly shocked. The expression of terror and a deep seriousness was in his face. Then I went in myself.

There was another door leading into my mother's room and it was now quite remarkable: there were all sorts of chests hanging, perhaps five in every row, and a garden door led into the open air, into the garden. Each of these chests was hanging above the ground, so that a gap of two feet remained. The chests were like small garden houses: in each there were two beds, but there were no people there and it was incredibly weird. I knew that this was the place where my mother, who then had already died, is visited, or where she had opened sleeping accommodation for

---

[333] Hans Kuhn's family lived about half a mile from the tower at Bollingen. He worked as Jung's Bollingen "factotum," helping with the building of the tower, gardening, chopping wood, cooking, and sailing. Helene Hoerni recalled him as a "true helper" of her father, always ready to do anything. He would eat with the family, and often stayed over ("A Memoir of Bollingen," unpublished, pp. 17–19). Around 1932, Jung got him a position with one of his American patients in Zurich, Alice Crawley, for whom he worked as a servant and chauffeur. Crawley let him continue to work for Jung at the tower. See *Letters*, vol. 1, pp. 42–44 (January 1, 1926) for a letter of Jung's to Kuhn. For further details, see Barbara Hannah, *Jung: His Life and Work: A Biographical Memoir* (New York: G. P. Putnam's Sons, 1976), p. 233.

visiting spirits. For spirits who come in pairs, sort of spirit couples, who spend the night or rather the day there. It reminded me of the small towers with the small stone lanterns on the top like they have in southern France for wandering spirits. You need them especially during the twelve nights.[334] Now I went through the middle door of the corridor: there is a door, where does it lead to? I thought. Then I came into a massive hall, like the lobby of an American hotel. There were armchairs and little tables around and a brass band[335] was playing. They were playing loud music which I had been aware of the whole time without knowing where it came from. I thought that the billowing of the curtain was connected to it. In the hall there was no one, but the large band belted out their tunes—dances and marches.—For me, music means emotional life. This music means an extremely ostentatious conviviality or worldliness. Behind this loud facade, no one would have intuited the other which was also there.

This lobby is like the caricature of my bonhomie, and behind it is the fish laboratory and the reception hall for the spirits. My father's room, the fish laboratory, was an uncanny place; an uncanny silence prevailed there, a great mysterious silence, and one had the feeling: Here lives the night. But the lobby,[336] this is the world of the day, and here it was also entirely light.

In my mother's room there was only a subdued light; in father's laboratory there was a bright sort of scientific light. The hall was like that of the Blackstone Hotel in Chicago,[337] [83/84] with a glaring luxury like a sumptuous[338] lobby or like the Plaza Hotel in New York[339]—with columns and concomitant splendor. Where your knees weaken when you go through the door. In every regard the most extreme worldliness in great style.

Then comes the last dream, it was like this: I had met a Catholic priest, a small stocky man who reminded me at first of G. Fr.[340] Though it was not

---

[334] That is, from Christmas day to the eve of Epiphany.

[335] "brass band": in English in the original.

[336] "lobby": in English in the original.

[337] Known as the 'hotel of the presidents', the Blackstone Hotel would have just opened when Jung was in Chicago in 1910 (see n. 1037 below).

[338] "sumptuous": in French in the original, *somptueuse*.

[339] In March 1910 Jung went to Chicago to treat his patient Medill McCormick (1877–1925) (see below, n. 1037). In 1936, Jung gave a lecture on "The Concept of the Collective Unconscious" to a large audience at the Plaza Hotel in New York. See Jung, "Is Analytical Psychology a Religion?" in McGuire and Hull, C. G. *Jung Speaking*, pp. 94–98.

[340] Presumably, Gebhard Frei (1905–1967), a Swiss psychologist and Catholic priest. He was the president of the Society for Catholic Priests, and lectured at the Jung Institute in Zurich. He had a lengthy correspondence with Jung (*JP*).

G. Fr. but he reminded me of someone, of an American. It could have been old Professor White, the psychiatrist.[341] I was still a young man when I got to know him, he was a famous personality, exceptionally intelligent. So, a sort of *mixtum compositum* of both of them. A small stout man, and he said to me that he wanted to introduce me to a great personality, but he did not say who it was, and then he went with me into a Baroque church, like a Jesuit church, and there, rather apologetically, he said he had to perform his prayers. He made the sign of the cross and prayed. I stood in the background while he did this, staying close to the door.

When he was ready, he went with me out of the church through an inner courtyard to a large building from the same epoch, and there was a very fine staircase with wrought-iron banisters going inwards, sweeping upwards in an arc and ending at a double door. It was also in the style of the end of the seventeenth or start of the eighteenth century.

We crossed this bridge, and he rang an old Gothic bell at the double door and the door opened and there stood my father, at least a head taller than I, and he had on a clerical collar and clerical habit, a black cassock and a high black cravat, like a Catholic priest, but at the same time he had the air of a *grand seigneur* with very high responsibility. He looked exceptionally superior and very clear. I saw the background on both sides next to him: a massive hall, two storeys high, filled with books, as large as the reading room of the British Museum. A gallery led around the walls at half height.

(Uriah[342] = prefiguration of Christ, the God-man, who is abandoned by God himself. This is the ultimate present.)

The enlivening things always came from my father (in the dream).[343] [84/85]

---

[341] William Alanson White (1870–1937) was for several decades the superintendent of St. Elisabeth's Hospital in Washington. He corresponded with Jung and invited him to St. Elisabeth's in 1913. On his work, see Suzanne Hollman, "White's Restraint and Progressive American Psychiatry at St. Elizabeth's Hospital," unpublished PhD Thesis, University College London, 2020.

[342] See above, p. 89.

[343] On May 28, 1957 Kurt Wolff wrote to Aniela Jaffé on receiving further sections of the protocols of the Interviews, "I am delighted with them. There is a naturalness of tone which gives one the feeling of hearing Jung himself speaking. You are so right to keep the first-person narrative and I strongly feel that one should do as little editing of the material as possible. Nothing seems to me more important than to keep the convincing sincerity, artlessness and immediacy of these communications." On May 30 Jung wrote to Esther

JUNE 7, 1957[344]

Today I want to tell you about my mother—"It sounds so wondrous!"[345] My mother was a very good mother to me. She had a great animal warmth; she was a very good cook and was immensely homely. She was very fat and she, oh she could gossip so with everyday people, could turn her ear to people, that was so harmless, a harmless babbling, and then she had all the conventional, traditional opinions that one can have and then again, on the other hand, she had an unconscious personality that was somehow powerful. Then she would suddenly say things that were outrageous, so that even as a boy of eleven or twelve I was conscious of this, or even earlier.

The first time I became aware of it was probably in my ninth year. She had—I can't remember what it was about—some kind of anxieties or fantasies, so she spoke to me about it.

Whenever she spoke to me in this way, she always took me for far older than my age, like an adult. She evidently said to me everything that she could not say to my father.—At that time, she had prompted me to go to a friend and to her older brother in order to speak to them about it.—Thank God both were not at home. It was some sort of difficult issue—I can't remember what it was about. It troubled me very much, I believe it concerned my father or financial matters. She could exaggerate and dramatize wildly.

You know what women can be like! She had a certain hysterical disposition and therefore she could dramatize, and this made a disproportionate impression on me. I used to run into town to my old uncle and old friends when it happened. I can say it was a *providentia specialis* that both were not at home. I did not tell my mother that I had been out looking for them. When I came home, she started up again on the same theme; but this time in a completely harmless way so that everything dissolved into blue mist. This really shocked me. [85/86] And from then on, I divided everything my mother said by two and thenceforth was no longer taken in by her. This was like a stone that fell into the gears. I only half trusted my mother then, and I took a critical position in relation to her.

Harding that he was occupied with the proofs of *Present and Future* and was now working on his book on flying saucers. *Letters*, vol. 2, p. 362.

[344] The same day, Kurt Wolff sent Jung via Jaffé a copy of Alan Watts's *The Way of Zen*, which he had just published (New York: Pantheon, 1957).

[345] Kurt Wolff noted "*Faust II.*" (Faust to Mephistopheles, "The mothers! Mothers! It sounds so wondrous!" [Act 1, sc. 3, 1. 6220]) See *ETG*, p. 54, *MDR*, p. 48.

But then came those moments when her second personality emerged; it was then so much to the point[346] and so true that I shook before it. On the one hand I had a good, proper mother–son relationship. Until about my ninth year.

I was the only child. Then my sister was born, and she was *toto coelo* different from me.[347] She was as if born to be a spinster. She was sickly, tender, in part really so, in part *malade imaginaire*,[348] she was pitied by her mother from the start as a poor little mite, which always irritated me. I said to her, "If you raise her like this then nothing will become of her!" She did not marry but later she acquired a fantastic attitude. I can only say, she was a born lady[349] with an unbelievable attitude. That is how she also died. She went to have an operation that was thought to be simple and harmless. She died from it. But then it came out that beforehand she had put all her affairs in order with the utmost precision. She had always and in all circumstances had a fabulous attitude. She never complained, never moaned or anything. She was a stranger to me, but I had great respect for her.

I had a passionate nature, full of illusions. Although my sister also always had illusions. She always fell in love with the wrong one. One saw quite clearly: She doesn't really mean it. But it was impossible to discover what she really did mean. But even as a child, something peculiar was expressed in her: in her books she did not write her name, [86/87] but she used a noble name as a form of *nom de plume*. Naturally marriage did not fit into this attitude at all. Unless it were to a man who realized what this ideal represented for her. But there was no chance of that. Also, she did not embark on this with any seriousness. I always had to think of a noble convent for young ladies when I thought of her.

I myself was far more emotional. In my turmoil I often wondered: What on earth is wrong with you? In my "storm and stress" period I kicked out in every direction and was full of emotions. My sister on the other hand was always relaxed, although fundamentally she was very sensitive. She preserved a fabulous form, which totally impressed me.

Remarkably, my grandfather Carl Gustav Jung also had a single sister who was also quite a lot younger than he was, and who lived in a

---

[346] "to the point": in English in the original.

[347] See *ETG*, p. 119, *MDR*, p. 112.

[348] As in the original: a reference to Molière's play, *La malade imaginaire* (*The Imaginary Invalid*) (1673).

[349] "lady": in English in the original.

noblewomen's convent.[350] And Goethe also had a single sister, Cornelia,[351] who had the remarkable symptom of urticaria on the neck,[352] so that she could never wear a low-cut dress and go out. And just think, just like my sister![353] This is a highly suspicious case and often gave me pause for thought.

The curious thing about my mother was the two personalities, one of which emerged only in very rare moments, the other a homely, rather gossipy old woman who was loved by the whole area. She got on well with everyone.

My mother had no music, had nothing of art; only literature. For example, when I was about sixteen years old, she directed me towards *Faust II*.[354] She had an exceptional literary gift, taste and depth. But that didn't have any proper outlet for expression. It remained hidden behind a really dear, fat old woman who was very hospitable and was an excellent cook, and who rambled on in a gossipy way and had a great sense of humor—but then again a dark, great figure emerged which possessed an inviolable authority—and no bones about it.[355] I knew precisely: If I tried to speak to her about this, she wouldn't know anything about it at all.

I understood it better later when such things also happened to me.[356] For example, the story of the man whose entire life story I recounted without knowing him! You know this don't you? No? So: I had been married for about two years and a friend of my wife was getting married and we

---

[350] Johanna Karolina Jung (1796–1871) was single, lived with her parents, and cared for her mother after the death of her father. Towards the end of her life, she lived in a sanatorium and nursing home in Achern.

[351] Cornelia Friederica Christiana Schlosser (*née* Goethe) (1750–1777).

[352] A skin condition that produces a red, itchy rash.

[353] In *ETG*, Jaffé added the following note: "On the death of his sister Jung wrote the following lines: 'My sister Gertrud lived with her mother in Basel until 1904. Then she moved over to Zurich where they lived together in Zollikon until 1909 and after that, until her death, in Küsnacht. After her mother's death in 1923, she lived alone. Her outer life was quiet, withdrawn and played out in a narrow circle of friends and relatives. She was polite, friendly, good-natured and denied her environment any curious glimpses of her inner world. In this way she also died, without complaint, not mentioning her own fate, in perfect composure. She departed a life that had fulfilled itself, untouched by judgment and self-disclosure.'" (p. 119). From June 1902 to January 1903 Gertrud spent time learning French at the home of the village pastor in Château d'Oex. In 1904 she moved with her mother from Basel to Zurich. From 1906 to 1908 she worked as a nurse at the Burghölzli, and enrolled in a nursing college in 1910. She helped her brother with secretarial work until 1925, when he hired a full-time secretary, as well as assisting with the household and the children. She also taught handicrafts the Arbeistelle für Gebrechtliche (Workshop for the frail).

[354] See *ETG*, p. 65, *MDR*, p. 60.

[355] "and no bones about it": in English in the original.

[356] See *ETG*, p. 56, *MDR*, p. 51.

were invited to the wedding. It was a friend whom I did not know at all. My wife had met her in a *pension* in Paris. [87/88] She had been in Paris for a year as a young girl and had got to know this friend when she was there. I knew absolutely no one from the girl's family. The wedding did not take place in Zurich. So, we sat down to eat and there were tables each of eight people. Opposite me sat a middle-aged gentleman, with a fine full beard who was introduced to me as a lawyer. I declared myself to be a psychiatrist and got into conversation about forensic psychology. At that time, I was just getting underway with the associations experiment. He was a very intelligent man and we had a lively conversation. Then we reached the point where we could no longer agree. I can't remember what it was. I thought: Now how can I make it clear to him?

I thought about it and then began: Let's take the case that someone does this or that . . . and so on and so forth. I only know that I concocted an entire story—as an example—with many decorative details. As I was speaking, I myself was amazed at some of my own touches: how did I come to be relating this in so much detail? Then I noticed how he had acquired a completely altered expression and had withdrawn quite remarkably.

A remarkable silence spread over the table. Awkwardly, I stopped speaking. After a while a gentleman sitting to my left said: I believe it has stopped raining!—Oh my God, I thought, what just happened there? Thank God we were already at the dessert stage. I then stood up, went into the lobby of the hotel, crept into a corner—behind a couple of potted plants—lit myself a cigar and thought: Now consider with precision what you said!—Then to my astonishment not even the merest memory of it remained!—In that moment, the gentleman came—the one who had spoken of the weather. "Oh there you are! How on earth did you come to commit such an indiscretion?"—"Indiscretion?" "Yes, this story you told!" "But I concocted this story!"—And what emerged? It was the exact history of my conversation partner. He thought, however, that no one knew about it. But in reality, of course everyone knew about it. I said, "But I don't know this gentleman at all! I just made up this story!"— "But you told it with all the details!"—And in that moment, I couldn't even recall the theme! It was as if deleted from my mind.

By the way, Zschokke relates something similar in his *Selbstschau*.[357] He went once to eat at an inn, where a youngish man sits at this table.

---

[357] Heinrich Zschokke (1771–1848), a prominent German (later Swiss) writer. The two-part *Eine Selbstschau* (Aarau: Heinrich Remigius Sauerländer, 1842) was his

Suddenly Zschokke sees this other man quite clearly stealing a sum of 256.50. And he cried out, "But how did you come to steal the money?" Immediately the man stood up. He had just come from the robbery.

Such things often happened to me. That I would suddenly know something that was absolutely true but which I could not possibly know. It seemed to me as if it were my own idea. More than once, for example, it happened with patients. There were cases, even before the patient had arrived, I knew that I would take the view: I will speak first—in general I tend to let the patient speak first—I must say to him that I think this and this. Then I tell him this and then it happens very frequently that he says: But you are telling me the dream I dreamed!—Or think of the little Jewish woman of whom I dreamed; that helped me to resolve the entire case in eight days.[358]

It was much the same with my mother: she did not even know what she was saying but with it was a voice of absolute authority and it was always precisely what was needed for the inner situation.—She said to me one time—I had already been married for seven years; it must have been about 1910. I was an absolutely faithful husband and even before marriage I had had no adventures so to speak. I was always anxiously correct with women. One evening my mother came casually into my study. Before that she had been inside at most on two other occasions. She came in and sat down on the patients' chair, looked at me and said, "I only wanted to say something to you." [89/90] "Yes, what is it then?"— "You know too few women. You should know more women!" Then she stood up and left. I sank fourteen fathoms deep into the earth. This hit home! This was something quite fantastic! I was in fact at that time just engaged with the anima problem.[359]

And that is how my mother was in things both great and small.

As when I was involved in my associations experiment, about which she had absolutely no clue. I lived then in the Zollikerstrasse.[360] I had

---

autobiography. Jung also referred to the anecdote that follows in 1958, in "A Psychological View of Conscience," CE 25; CW 10, § 850. In 1903, in his dissertation, Jung referred to Zschokke's book (citing pp. 247–48) as containing examples of intuitive knowledge ("On the Psychology and Pathology of So-Called Occult Phenomena," CE 2; CW 1, § 147). See also Zschokke, *Das Schicksal und der Mensch* (*Eine Selbstschau*, part 1), pp. 269–70.

[358] Jaffé noted here in the text, "(Note: This dream and the story of the little Jewish woman is noted in other papers. Can be added here.)" See below, Appendix 2, pp. 403–4.

[359] On September 29, 1910, Toni Wolff commenced her analysis with Jung.

[360] After returning from Paris, Jung got married, in February 1903. After their honeymoon, he and Emma Jung stayed in an apartment at Zollikerstrasse 198, from April 26,

wallpapered the whole room with graphs. One day she visited me, looked around in my room and then she said, "What's that then?"— "These are experimental studies that I'm working on at the moment." I had a certain pride that I was doing such a thing.—But back then I had no clue about what significance these complexes would have. I was just finding out what the disturbances in the experiment signified and that they were associated with complexes. My mother looked around the room, then she said—also in her second voice—suddenly standing there like a judge, "Oh, you really think that is something?" This was like the Delphic oracle. I might just as well have thought that I did not value it highly enough as that I might overestimate it. Basically, however, she was expressing my own unacknowledged doubt. It struck me so powerfully that I could not lift a pen for three weeks. It confronted my doubt, to the absolute core, as to whether what I was doing meant something.

It is always difficult for me to accept that my judgment is wrong. But she voiced my unacknowledged fear. She spoke as with a voice which sounded different from her usual voice, but very serious, and as if she had wanted to draw my attention to the thought that my work was indeed something and at the same time she was expressing the doubt as to whether there was anything really in it. Almost in the same breath she said, "I don't understand anything of all this"—This was like the Delphic oracle: "Like this or in fact not like this." When you cross the Rubicon, you will destroy a kingdom![361] Therefore, yes! In fact, she simply underlined the significance of the moment. [90/91]

She did the same with her other utterance about women. I was then in the middle of an anima problem. And that she spoke of *many* women! If the anima is one single woman, the man actually will never get away from

1903 to September 1904, when they moved into an apartment in the Burghölzli. In May, Jung did some work at the Burghölzi, deputizing for doctors on military service. Later, he took up a post at the Burghölzli again, when von Muralt left after contracting tuberculosis.

[361] Cf. Heraclitus, "The Lord whose Oracle is in Delphi neither indicates clearly nor conceals, but gives a sign." (fragment 33 [D 93]): Charles Kahn, ed., *The Art and Thought of Heraclitus: An Edition of the Fragments with Translation and Commentary* (Cambridge: Cambridge University Press, 1979), p. 43. In 49 BCE, after Julius Caesar's conquest of Gaul, the Roman senate ordered him to disband his army and return to Rome. Disobeying, Caesar decided to cross the Rubicon river, which marked the border between Rome and its northern provinces, with his army, leading to civil war, and eventually, to the rise of the Roman Empire. The episode Jung was recalling was actually the following: Croesus the king of Lysia (b. 565 BCE) asked the Delphic Oracle whether to begin a campaign against the Persian Empire. The oracle replied that if he attacked the Persians, he would destroy a great empire. Croesus went to war, which led to his own downfall.

her. It *must* be many. As with a woman when she hooks an adored pastor, she never emerges from this if she can't worship other Gods. She must also learn to take other paths of thought. For this reason, she cannot develop her animus either if she does not have a relationship to another man apart from her husband. For the woman, the man whom she loves is the container of the spirit, and a woman I am interested in would hardly make an impression on me if I did not see in her, for example, the quality of a Goddess. No, I would not be in the slightest bit interested in her otherwise.

It was precisely the type of woman whom as a younger man, as a student, I carefully avoided that was the one who later took on the anima quality for me. For I was not permitted to marry an anima, that would have been a terrible catastrophe. I would have simply murdered such a woman, or she me. When I was still a young student, I met a girl who interested me terribly. I met her at the house of some friends. Then I had an inner warning. After that I kept as far away as possible from her. She had the anima quality. Later she committed suicide.—When I was a doctor at the Bli and was involved with schizophrenics, whom I did not understand, I often thought: If I could just sleep one time with a schizophrenic or at least with a hysteric, to "understand" them. But they were precisely the ones whom I anxiously avoided.

The traces of hysteria in my mother were so repulsive to me.[362] What the truth really was one had to ascertain through endless divisions and subtractions. This is how a fateful, significant purpose appears initially in projection. And then instead of seizing this purpose, one can perceive it as actual only in the other person. One needs others in order for it to become actual.

[363]For this reason, due to my contention partly with the ancient world, partly with Christianity, I was never able to go to Rome. I could go to Pompeii (after *Transformation and Symbols*) [91/92] and there I saw the paintings and frescoes, including those from the Villa dei Misteri. These things stirred me in a directly erotic way, they caused a sort of inner excitement when I first went to Pompeii in 1912.[364] I would have so liked to travel to Rome, but I was not able to. Rome would have been an

---

[362] See above, p. 81.

[363] See *ETG*, pp. 291–92, *MDR*, p. 287.

[364] Jung visited Pompeii in early March, 1913, on the way by ship to America. He brought back twenty-one blank postcards. The "Villa of Mysteries," on the outskirts of Pompeii, contains a series of striking frescoes, taken to depict the initiation of a young woman into the mysteries of Dionysus. See Linda Fierz-David, *Women's Dionysian*

excitement within me of an entirely different order. And when I decided to go to Rome eight years ago (1949), when I went to collect the tickets, I fainted. What is Hecuba to you?[365] What is she to me? Rome is an anima to avoid. I am always amazed by the people who are able to go to Rome as, for example, to Paris, or London, or who are able to live in Rome. If one did not know, then one would be able, then you would not know what was happening to you. Then you would think that it was destiny and not know that it was Rome. What I am saying now also refers in part to the fact that Rome made me very ill.

I was familiar with the north of Italy and have been as far as Florence without any damage, and in the south, in 1912, I traveled from Genoa by ship to Naples and from there to America.[366] I stood at the rail as we sailed along the coast at the same latitude as Rome. I thought to myself: Beyond there is Rome, there lies Rome. That was like an incendiary point. Rome is the ancient world, still extant; this means that living spirits are around which are infinitely more significant than, for example, the spirits around in Pompeii. In Rome, these are important and dangerous spirits. There, there is such an incredible profanity that one is out of one's depth.

I got an inkling of ancient profanity in Naples when I watched the people there: purely animalistic faces, in the sense of the Kali of Samothrace.[367] Remarkable demonic cripples and such things. I was constantly anxious of being contaminated by something. Grotesque monstrosities and I don't know what. There, I had a foretaste of ancient ferality. My tour guide in Naples: I went out to eat with him in the evening and still had a couple of hours before I had to be back on the ship. In a polite voice he quietly said that he could show me something very interesting: a brothel. "No, thank you." Then he looked at me sidelong and said, once again in a very polite voice: "There are also very pretty [92/93] boys."— "No, absolutely not!"—Then he sank into a long contemplation. Again, he looked at me doubtfully. Then he said very amiably that he knew a place where there were wonderful goats![368]

Initiation: The Villa of Mysteries in Pompeii, trans. Gladys Phelan (Dallas, TX: Spring Publications, 1988).

[365] Hecuba was the wife of King Priam of Troy; an allusion to Shakespeare's *Hamlet* 2.2, when a roving player recites a speech by Aeneas describing the king's death and Hecuba's grief. Shamed by the performance, which moves the stage audience, Hamlet resolves to avenge his father's murder.

[366] This trip was in March 1913.

[367] Presumably, a reference to the statue of winged Niké, the Greek Goddess of victory, currently in the Louvre museum in Paris.

[368] In Jung's fantasy of January 5, 1914 the anchorite Ammonius recounted how "I felt an insatiable greed to see the world, I drank wine, wallowed in pleasure and wholly turned

I felt this spirit of the ancient world, this hideous profanity and the hidden animal spirit, in Pompeii. It didn't faze me. Think of Rome: the animal fighting and gladiatorial combat of the ancient cults. Back then the savagery was unimaginable. And this spirit still lives today.

There was such an enormous difference between the two personalities in my mother. As a child, I often had anxiety dreams about her. By day she was a loving mother. By night she seemed uncanny—simply uncanny. She was like a seeress who is also some kind of animal. Like a priestess in a bear pit. Archaic, and also profane. Profane like the truth and nature. This was the "natural mind."[369] But this gift is associated for me with the fact that I can see a person as they are, as they are in their deepest mind. I can let myself be deceived by people in their thousands and back again, yet all the same I know exactly what the other person really is. Like a dog who lets itself be tricked but then can always still sniff it out. This is an absolute *participation mystique* with the other. And it has everything to do with the "eye of the background." I am in constant touch with this background. All I know is that the entirely primitive aboriginals who have these totem ancestors[370] are also creators of the world. The archaic nature in me has something to do with such a background.

JUNE 14, 1957

(Question regarding Richard Wilhelm)[371]

[372]At that time, I painted the mandala published in *The Golden Flower* and which has such green and yellow tones; and it seemed somehow Chinese to me. "That is actually something rather Chinese," I thought, and when I had completed it, as if by return came the manuscript from Wilhelm about the *Golden Flower*. He had never before ever proposed anything like this to me.[373]

Of course, I knew his works: the translation of the *I Ching* of Zhuang Zhou and so on.[374]—I first met him at the conference in Darmstadt, with

---

into an animal. When I climbed ashore in Naples, the Red One stood there, and I knew that I had fallen into the hands of evil." (*BB* 3, p. 118).

[369] "natural mind": in English in the original. See *ETG*, p. 56, *MDR*, p. 50.

[370] "totem ancestors": in English in the original.

[371] Jaffé replaced this with "My Relationship with Richard Wilhelm:" On June 9 she informed Kurt Wolff that the theme of the next discussion would be Jung's relations with Wilhelm, Flournoy, and Keyserling (BL).

[372] See *ETG*, pp. 200–201 and 380–84, *MDR*, pp. 197 and 373–77.

[373] Jung, "Commentary on *The Secret of the Golden Flower*" (1929), CE 11; CW 13, A10; *LN*, image 163.

[374] Jung had an extensive collection of Wilhelm's works in his library.

Keyserling, and then we invited him here to give a talk at the Psychological Club.[375] That is how I got to know him. The first time I had seen him was in Vienna with Dr. Jacobi.[376] No, it was not with her, but with Keyserling and then afterwards with Mrs. Jacobi. That came later. In the Kulturbund, they had a conference in Prague where we were also received by Benesch, and the prince primate of Bohemia was also there in a fine white robe.[377] So I got to know him at the Darmstadt conference, but I can't remember when it was. I reckon it was around 1924 or something like that.—Back then he wrote an article in the *Neue Zurcher Zeitung* for my sixtieth birthday.[378] You can look up the details.

At that time I was very interested in the East; I had already encountered the *I Ching* in English in the *Sacred Books of the East* and I engaged with the *I Ching* for the first time at the beginning of 1920 and began to experiment with it myself; in fact this was in 1924.[379] I did not yet know Wilhelm then (it was probably 1926 when I met him). I was always thinking about the *I Ching* but never got as far as properly studying it until the summer of 1924; I know this as I had some reed stems cut for me by Hans Kuhn (a young servant, driver, gardener, assistant, a native of Bollingen). For I wished to do the classical *I Ching* with the yarrow stalks. So, I sat on the ground under the one-hundred-year-old pear tree with the *I Ching* next to me and practiced the technique. In those holidays I occupied myself with this very intensively. It was terribly problematic for me to get the thing to work and then Wilhelm's *I Ching* was published which I got hold of immediately. In it, I saw that he had also understood the thing [94/95] the same way as I had figured it out for

---

[375] It was on December 15, 1921 that Wilhelm gave his first lecture to the Psychological Club, on the invitation of Adolf Keller. On Keyserling, see below, pp. 123–28. Jung's first presentation at Keyserling's School of Wisdom in Darmstadt was actually in 1927.

[376] Jolande Jacobi (1890–1973), analytical psychologist, was vice-president of the Kulturbund in Vienna, where Jung spoke in 1928. She obtained a PhD in psychology at the University of Vienna in 1938 and emigrated that same year to Zurich. She was a key instigator of, and was prominently involved in, the C. G. Jung Institute in Zurich (established 1948), and was the author of a number of publications developing analytical psychology.

[377] Jung spoke in October 1928 in Prague at a conference of the Association for Intellectual Collaboration. He presented "The Soul Problem of Modern Man" (*CE* 11; *CW* 10). "Benesch" is presumably be Edvard Beneš (1884–1948), the Czechoslovak foreign minister at the time (later president).

[378] Richard Wilhelm, "Meine Begegnung mit C. G. Jung in China" (My encounter with C. G. Jung in China), *Neue Zürcher Zeitung*, January 21, 1929, pp. 1–2. On April 19, 1960 Jaffé informed Wolff that Jung wanted this article included as an appendix to their book (BL).

[379] There are notes of some hexagrams in Jung's appointment book for 1920, indicating that he was already experimenting with it around that time (JFA).

myself, but he knew Chinese so he could fill in the gaps which remained for me.

In Prague, nothing important happened, and then I saw him in Zurich where he spoke at the Club.[380] Then I had the chance of speaking with him comprehensively about the *I Ching*. He told me a lot about China, and he mainly struck me as a European with an explicitly Christian attitude and appearance, which was familiar to me, as both of the Blumhardts were known to me. The elder Blumhardt was his father-in-law.[381] (He came from Bad Boll.) I had also read the book by the elder Blumhardt, *Der Kampf von Möttlingen*, in which he describes an exorcism.[382] It is a very impressive book. And then I knew the younger Blumhardt indirectly through many Baselers who had been in Bad Boll.[383] They made a kind of pilgrimage there in order to get rid of their sins. The younger Blumhardt had a good and fatherly manner of relating to people. Wilhelm married his daughter.[384]

[385]So, I was oriented towards Wilhelm because I knew his whole background well. I met him and he was completely Chinese. He was deeply impressed by Chinese culture and said to me once, "My one satisfaction is that I have never baptized a Chinese."[386] He was a missionary in China. He had immediately been deeply impressed by this ancient culture and devoted himself to it intensively. He became completely assimilated into it. He had taken on completely the Eastern point of view. He interested me for this reason, because I knew—actually, via an indiscretion—that he had been affected by a woman in China and this had become a big problem for him.

---

[380] Wilhelm first lectured at the Psychological Club on December 15, 1921, at the invitation of Adolf Keller. His last lecture at the Club was on January 19, 1929. His translation of the *I Ching* appeared in 1924.

[381] Johann Christoph Blumhardt (1805–1880), a prominent German Lutheran theologian. It was actually his son, Christoph Blumhardt (1842–1919) who was also a German Lutheran theologian, who was Wilhelm's father-in-law.

[382] *Blumhardts Kampf: zuverlässiger Abdruck seines eigenen Berichts über die Krankheits- und Heilungsgeschichte der Gottliebin Dittus in Möttlingen* (Stuttgart: Verlag goldene Worte, 1971 [1850]). There is a copy of this book in Jung's library.

[383] See n. 381 above.

[384] Salome Wilhelm (1879–1958).

[385] See *ETG*, p. 380, *MDR*, p. 375.

[386] However, on July 28, 1910 Wilhelm wrote to his wife that he had just baptized his first Chinese boy, Erich Heinrich Li, who was the son of Li Deshuen and Margarete Krueger (Wilhelm Papers, Bayern Akademie der Wissenschaften, Munich). On Wilhelm's life and work, see Dangwei Zhou, "Richard Wilhelm (1873–1930): An Alternative Way to Bridge the East and the West," unpublished PhD thesis, University College London, 2022.

As a Christian he got into a conflict with China. For there, this conflict does not exist; in China, there is a first wife and a second wife.[387] But, ascetically, he decided upon the "one wife." That was his mental restriction. But everything else about him was Chinese. But where it got under his skin, he couldn't go any further. And when he returned to Europe, Christianity completely absorbed him. There he drew a line. [95/96]

He was very interested in my psychology and arrived as a matter of course at this problem, namely, that of the anima. But this could not come into the open or he would have got into trouble with his wife.—I better understood certain commentaries in the *I Ching* after I knew about this story. I had the same problem and I know I was rather disappointed by him. Initially he made an impression on me because of his Chinese culture, and I thank him very much in this respect. But when I discovered *this*, then doubt arose within me and I noticed that when I offered psychological points of view, he was exceptionally interested as long as it was about something objective, about meditation; then everything was okay. But when I attempted to approach the actual problem, then I noticed some hesitation in him because then it was close to the bone. Later I confirmed this.

This is what happened: I visited him in Frankfurt.[388] I attended a lecture he gave. By this point he was out of his Chinese period and had lapsed into the style of a missionary. I went to him and said, "My dear Wilhelm, don't take this the wrong way, but I have the impression that you have reverted back to the West again." And he admitted it to me: Yes, the Western atmosphere had taken him over again.—I said to him that it was a pity. He should introduce the East to the West and the West should not obliterate everything again.

Later I invited him to visit me: he was already getting attacks of tropical sprue then. I thought it looked rather suspicious. But he did not wish

---

[387] Wilhelm had a long relationship with Marie Luise (Lisel) Bahr. Her family were from Germany, and her father was a merchant in Qingdao. She married a German, who was captured by the Japanese when they invaded and taken as a prisoner to Japan. Bahr studied Latin and Greek with Wilhelm during the war. Wilhelm's wife learned of the affair in 1919 and they considered a divorce. Bahr continued to accompany Wilhelm on his travels. When he was appointed as scientific advisor to the German embassy in Peking in 1922, Bahr became his private secretary and assisted in his translation of the *I Ching* during their last two years there. They returned to Germany in 1924, and Bahr became a staff member at the China Institute at University of Frankfurt.

[388] Jung was in Frankfurt from October 24 to 26, 1928. His first trip there was in 1906, when he stopped there on the way back from attending the Congress for Experimental Psychology in Würzburg with Emma Jung.

to make a fuss about it. I heard later that he had to go to the hospital in Frankfurt and that he was suffering from tropical sprue. Then I heard that he was not doing so well, and that he had chronic diarrhea. I traveled to Frankfurt to visit him, found him in hospital where he had leukemia.[389] Then I knew he was lost. He said to me then, "You know what, it's all twisted. If I get over this illness, I'm coming to Zurich to see you."

That was my last conversation with him. "Everything's got to change, it's all twisted." He was defeated by his problem. Everything found its climax in the question of whether he accepted his anima problem or not. That's the decisive question; there nothing can be done. That is where we get down to truly bloody reality. [96/97]

He really could have said "yes" to China: but he was too Christian and too much of a missionary to engage with his problem. He remained hanging, and that's the criterion. He was obliged to return to Europe after being in China for twenty years and he returned as a fully Chinese man. He should have been able to get beyond our Christian prejudices. And he should have remained true to his nature. In the East this matter is simply understood differently: there, you can have the spouse and perhaps a mistress. It makes a tremendous difference whether this question is responded to with a "yes" or a "no." One cannot go a step further if this question is answered with a "no." It is equally the case if one sorts it out in the Western way: with a type of recklessness, and doesn't see the problem inherent within it. The Christian had also let himself be scared off in this respect.

My mother's other nature, that was the voice of nature which uttered the deep truths, shocking truths. I measured everything against that nature; this was for me the uppermost moral law; that was decisive for me. These are things which one cannot say out loud here.

[390]Before Wilhelm died, I had an apparition: one evening as I was going to bed, after some time it was as if it was getting lighter in my room. And suddenly I saw a Chinese man in a blue cotton garment; he had his hands in the sleeves and I saw every detail, every thread of the fabric, and he bowed down deeply before me as if he wanted to tell me something. This made me resolve to return to Frankfurt to see Wilhelm. That was in late autumn of the year before he died. I saw every detail as

---

[389] On April 6, 1929 Jung wrote to Wilhelm to arrange to meet him on April 11 in Frankfurt, en route to a conference in Nauheim (Wilhelm Papers, Bayern Akademie der Wissenschaften, Munich). The comment here suggests that he also paid him another visit later that year.

[390] See *ETG*, p. 384, *MDR*, p. 377.

a matter of fact. When I returned to Wilhelm, he told me he kept dreaming of Asian places, barren places through which he was walking; it was
clearly China—the China he had left! The desolation: that is what he had
left, that was the desert within him that he had not fulfilled in his life in
order to remain well. He lacked the humility to accept his sin and to
carry it out. Only in this way would he have paid the price that would
have let him say that he was a sinful man, one who had paid the cost. If
the unfaithful steward had not cheated his master, [97/98] he would not
have won his praise.[391] One cannot be redeemed from sin that one has
not committed. Fate had destined this problem for him.

I know the moment I was faced with the problem of T. W. After the
analysis, I had discharged her in the appropriate way, despite my feeling
how much affection I had for her. Then after a year I had a dream in
which I was with her in the Alps. We were in a rocky valley. Suddenly I
heard the elves singing within the mountains and T. W. was about to disappear into the mountain. Then I thought: This cannot be, this must not
be. That is when I wrote to her again.[392]

I had a whole series of dreams at that time: I had a really terrible
dream: there was a woman who was a stone from the center of her body
down, but on top she was still alive. Yet I knew that I had given this
woman an injection in her spinal cord so that she had turned to stone.
This was absolutely horrific to me, and then came the experience of how
I swam out into the lake and noticed how I got a cramp. I made the vow:
If the cramp eases and I am able to swim back, I will give in.

In the dream of the rockface I thought of the elf king.[393] I heard the
quiet voices of the elves and I noticed how she was sinking away into the

---

[391] See Luke 16:1–13.

[392] In a diary entry of December 29, 1924 Toni Wolff noted that twelve years before, on
Jung's return from America, she went to him and "spoke of relationship." Toni Wolff,
Diary B (Toni Wolff Papers, p. 98). On November 5, 1913, in *BB* 2, following his account
of the dream around December 1912 of the dove that transformed itself into a small girl
and then back into the dove, Jung noted, "My decision was made. I had to give all my faith
and trust to this woman." (p. 156). In March 1913 he went to America again for five weeks.
Decades later, Toni Wolff noted in her diary, "The feeling is somehow similar to 1913, when
C[arl] went to America and we separated—and yet we couldn't do it afterward." (*Diary* K,
September 25, 1937, p. 151). This suggests a separation may have taken place at this time.
In a diary entry of March 4, 1944 Toni Wolff referred to "31 years of relationship and
34 years of acquaintance" (*Diary* M, p. 84). This confirms that her relationship with Jung
began at some time in 1913.

[393] "Erlkönig" (1782) is a poem by Goethe. A father riding a horse is carrying his son at
night. The boy sees the elf-king, who tempts the boy to go with him. The boy calls out to his

mountain, and I snatched her away out of it.[394] Then I knew: Now it is unavoidable. I was then also in danger for my life.

As I was working on the unconscious, that was even before when I was engaged with Gilgamesh and had to help the giant.[395] Even more than when I shot the hero, and I could not understand the dream.[396] This was the attitude which had hindered me. It appeared to me like a weakness of will on my part, but the dream presented it in reverse: the hero must be murdered. It seemed to me that I was like a hero who is victorious. The dream says: You must simply kill this hero. This exaggeration of the will was at the time being demonstrated by the Germans. *Siegfried*

---

father, who offers naturalistic explanations of the apparition. The boy is then killed by the elf-king.

[394] *EG* adds here, "The anima requires her sacrifice, I may no longer evade it. It is a matter of life and death. / What a power drive it would have released if I had evaded the anima! I would never have risen above it. But in this way a relationship of crucial significance developed. During the difficult period of my inner exploration she was a companion of profound psychological and human insight. She offered me support and fulfilled the role of the anima in the finest sense. For me she was fertile earth." (pp. 54–55).

[395] See *BB* 3, January 8, 1914, pp. 119–20, where Jung gave the figure his earlier name, Izdubar, which had been based on a mistranslation. In 1906 Peter Jensen had noted, "It has now been established that Gilgamesh is the chief protagonist of the epic, and not Gishtubar or Izdubar as assumed previously": Jensen, *Das Gilgamesch-Epos in der Weltliteratur* (Strasbourg: Trübner, 1906), vol. 1, p. 2.

[396] *BB* 2, December 18, 1913:

I was with an unknown youth, a brown savage, in a mighty mountainscape before daybreak. The eastern sky was already light. Then Siegfried's horn resounded over the mountains with a jubilant sound, and we knew that our mortal enemy was now coming. We were armed and lurked beside a narrow rocky path to murder the hero. Then he came high across the mountain on a chariot made of the bones of the dead, in a white garment with black mystical figures, and drove with unbelievable boldness over the steep rocks and arrived at the narrow path where we lay in wait. As he came around the turn, we fired at the same time and wounded him fatally. My companion left me in order to attend to the hero one last time, that, is to finish him off. Thereupon I turned to flee. A terrible rain swept down. I bounded nimbly up an incredibly steep path and later helped my wife, who followed me at a slower pace, to ascend. Some people mocked us, but I didn't care, since this showed that they didn't know that I had murdered the hero.

But after this dream I went through a mental torment unto death. And I felt that I must kill myself, if I could not solve the riddle. I knew that I must shoot myself, if I could not understand the dream.

Gradually it dawned on me that *the highest truth is one and the same with the absurd.* [pp. 174–75]

See also Bennet, *Meetings with Jung*, August 30, 1956 (pp. 61–62).

Line.[397] "Where there's a will, there's a way." I thought then: I must just shoot myself if I do not understand the dream.[398]

[399]Théodore Flournoy–I knew him previously before I met Richard Wilhelm.[400] I already knew him when I was still a doctor at the Bli. Then I read the book *Des Indes à la planète Mars*,[401] and I wrote to Flournoy. I wanted to translate this book into German. I received no reply for six months, then came a letter in which he apologized profusely for taking too long to reply: unfortunately, a translator had already been appointed. I visited him several times in Geneva.

Then when I got to know Freud and I saw what his limitations were, I visited Flournoy and persuaded him to attend one of the congresses.[402] I had the feeling there of still being far too young to be independent. I still needed support. I needed someone I could talk to, about problems which concerned us both scientifically. About somnambulism, for example. I assumed the concept of the "imagination créatrice" and I took over from Flournoy the case of Miss Miller which I published in *Transformations and Symbols of the Libido*.[403] His ideas were completely in line with mine and they greatly enriched me. I had no one who shared my interest in this regard. So, from time to time I went to Geneva and talked things over with him.[404] Unfortunately he died soon after that. He was already an

---

[397] The Siegfried Line, or *Westwall*, was a German defensive line, nearly 400 miles long, built from 1936 along Nazi Germany's western border, from the Netherlands to Switzerland.

[398] Jaffé inserted the dream here from the 1925 seminar (pp. 61–62).

[399] See *ETG*, p. 378.

[400] Théodore Flournoy (1854–1920) was a Swiss psychologist, and professor of psychology at the University of Geneva.

[401] Flournoy, *Des Indes à la planète Mars: Étude sur un cas de somnambulisme avec glossolalie* (Paris: F. Alcan/Geneva: Ch. Eggimann, 1900); translated into English as *From India to the Planet Mars: A Case of Multiple Personality with Imaginary Languages*, ed. Sonu Shamdasani, trans. D. Vermilye (Princeton, NJ: Princeton University Press, 1994).

[402] The congress took place September 5–9, 1913 in Munich. Jung presented "The Question of Psychological Types" (*CE* 7; *CW* 6).

[403] Frank Miller (1879–1927), an American costume lecturer who had briefly studied with Flournoy in 1900 and corresponded with him. See Shamdasani, "Woman Called Frank"; Sam Ryals, "Miss Frank Miller: Jung's Sherpa from Alabama," *Quadrant* 58 (2018): pp. 25–40. Jung's analysis of Miller was based on her article "Quelques faits d'imagination créatrice subconsciente," *Archives de psychologie* 5 (1905): 36–51, with an introduction by Flournoy. The article was written to exemplify his psychological reading of mediumship.

[404] There was close informal collaboration between the Association of Analytical Psychology, which was founded in 1914, and Flournoy. In 1915, two sessions were held discussing Flournoy's work *Une mystique moderne*, and other joint discussions appear to have taken place. Jung published his paper on psychological types in Flournoy's journal,

old man when I made his acquaintance. At the time I needed a counter-balance to Freud. Because his manner simply did not suit me. That devaluing manner, sniffing out the inferior and sexuality, I did not like that at all. I could have turned to Janet,[405] but I could not have learned much from him. From Flournoy I learned how to immerse myself devotedly in a case, and that is why I also carried a case of his to completion. Out of it emerged a modeling of one aspect of the collective unconscious processes. I had already been interested in finding these associations in the mentally ill. But Flournoy also helped me to see these things more clearly. He saw them much more as a whole. With Freud, much was contorted in the service of a prejudice. Flournoy saw with objectivity what was happening, and he approached the case carefully and comprehensively within a wide horizon. [101/102] He was cultivated and distinguished; it all did me a great deal of good. With Freud one always noticed his background. Of course, he was very bright, but nothing more. *Il n'avait pas d'étape,*[406] namely, the *étape* of cultured parents. Flournoy—he was through and through a fine, cultured gentleman, mentally conciliatory, with the proper proportions; that was highly beneficial. In fact, I met him before Freud, and it was when I was with him[407] the last time, that was in Munich at a congress where the split with Freud took place.[408]

I wanted to hear his views about Freud. He said very accurate things about him. He was, after all, a professor of philosophy,[409] with a very clear mind, and he put his finger on the right points: Freud's Enlightenment worldview being very one-sided and so on. And that was my overriding impression with Flournoy: he had an excellent mind, a truly objective

---

Archives de psychologie, in 1913, and also "The Structure of the Unconscious," in 1916. Flournoy was also actively engaged in trying to arrange a French translation of Jung's *Transformations and Symbols of the Libido* (Flournoy to Alphonse Maeder, June 29 and November 12, 1916 (Maeder Papers).

[405] Pierre Janet (1857–1947), French psychologist. On Jung's relations with Janet, see John Haule, "From Somnambulism to Archetypes: The French Roots of Jung's Split from Freud," *Psychoanalytic Review* 71, no. 4 (1984): 95–107; Sonu Shamdasani, "From Geneva to Zurich: Jung and French Switzerland," *Journal of Analytical Psychology* 43, no. 1 (1998): 115–26. See also C. G. Jung, *Comptes rendus critiques de la psychologie francophone*, ed. and trans. (into French) Florent Serina (Lausanne: Éditions BHMS, 2020).

[406] "He didn't have the level."

[407] That is, with Freud.

[408] The International Psychoanalytic Association Congress in Munich was held on September 7–8, 1913.

[409] Flournoy had both a medical and a philosophical background. In philosophy, he specialized in Kant. In 1891, he was appointed professor of psychophysiology at the University of Geneva. At his insistence, this was discipline was placed in the Faculty of Sciences, rather than the Faculty of Philosophy.

approach that was striking to me next to Freud's. Freud had a dynamic and penetrating manner. He wanted something from his cases. Flournoy did not want that. He looked on from a distance and he saw things clearly. Freud got himself mixed up in the psychology of the unconscious.

Through Freud's influence I acquired knowledge but was not enlightened. But Flournoy schooled me in one's distance from the object and kept it alive in me. The more descriptive way of doing things, without presupposition or participation—he had a lively, warm interest in the case. He was a philosopher and a psychologist, was also a friend of William James, and was strongly influenced by James's pragmatism.

I made the acquaintance of William James in 1909, at Clark University. I visited him there twice.[410] In 1912 I returned to the USA and took a long walk with him.[411] Even at that point he said already he could feel his heart. Soon after that he died. He was a fine man, a tall slim apparition, a gentleman,[412] a very fine, organized man. Freud did not suit him. He had the opportunity to make his acquaintance. I must say Freud did not tolerate the comparison. James had a very objective and genteel attitude and we got on together splendidly as regards valuing the religious factor in the psyche. He had a similar effect upon me as Flournoy. Both

---

[410] On September 26, 1909 William James wrote to Flournoy regarding Jung's visit to the Clark conference: "I went there for one day in order to see what Freud was like, and met also Yung [sic] of Zurich, who professed great esteem for you, and made a very pleasant impression. I hope that Freud and his pupils will push their ideas to their utmost limits, so that we may learn what they are. They can't fail to throw light on human nature; but I confess that he made on me personally the impression of a man obsessed with fixed ideas. I can make nothing in my own case with his dream theories, and obviously 'symbolism' is a most dangerous method. A newspaper report of the congress said that Freud had condemned the American religious therapy (which has such extensive results) as very 'dangerous' because so 'unscientific.' Bah!" Robert Le Clair, ed., *The Letters of William James and Théodore Flournoy* (Madison, WI: University of Wisconsin Press, 1966), p. 292. Possibly on this occasion, Jung presented James with a copy of his dissertation. On the Clark conference, see John Burnham, ed., *After Freud Left: A Century of Psychoanalysis in America* (Chicago: Chicago University Press, 2012).

[411] James died in August 1910. However, Jung did visit America in March 1910, to visit his former patient Medill McCormick in Chicago, so (see below, n. 1113). In his foreword to his 1912 Fordham lectures Jung wrote, "I have taken as my guiding principle William James's pragmatic rule: 'You must bring out of each word its practical cash-value, set it at work within the stream of your experience. It appears less as a solution, then, than as a program for more work, and more particularly as an indication of the ways in which existing realities may be changed. *Theories thus become instruments, not answers to enigmas, in which we can rest.* We don't lie back upon them, we move forward, and on occasion, make nature over again by their aid.'" CE 7; CW 4, p. 86.

[412] "gentleman": in English in the original.

strengthened within me the universalistic point of view, but both Flournoy and James were rather contemplative men and far too sensitive to get directly in touch with the object. [102/103] Both were too sensitive to let themselves be touched directly by the object whereas Freud let himself be affected by the object; but due to the narrowness of his intellectual horizon he also let himself be overcome by the object.

Freud's psychology is a feminine psychology in which, biologically, sexuality is an enormous issue. For a woman, sexuality has a social flavor, it is a socially important issue and can even be a business. Whereas for a man it does not play such an important role. For the man it is a physiological function absolutely without social significance, with the consequence that it becomes a highly mystical issue which nonetheless is mostly denied. You must never forget Gérard de Nerval's "une femme ordinaire de mon siècle!"[413] "What, this is supposed to be important?" The other aspect of such an attitude is the anima and her mystery.

Flournoy was very similar to James in relation to his practical knowledge of human beings or in relation to problems thrown up by the feminine. James held himself back much further. He was rather dry, and sexuality was locked in a dark chamber. With Flournoy, there was a warm understanding, but also a great conventional anxiety which I shared with him. I found Flournoy humanly warmer and more relational with me than James.

James had a similar breadth of horizon to Flournoy's—perhaps a greater breadth. But when it came to participation in life, then James became quite thin. In personal conversation he was uncommonly amiable, human, everything was fine, but blood was missing. He was also quite physically thin, and long. Yet he was a commanding man, a very fine man! Also, in relation to psychology Flournoy was much more naturalistic than James. James was only a philosopher. He once did parapsychological experiments with the medium Mrs. Piper,[414] and recognized the importance of this

---

[413] The citation is from Nerval's *Aurélia*, where the possessive is "notre" (our); "I have read the inventions of poets too seriously and have made a Laura or a Beatrice out of an ordinary woman of our century." Craig Stephenson, ed., *On Psychological and Visionary Art: Notes from C. G. Jung's Lecture on Gérard de Nerval's "Aurélia,"* trans. Gottwalt Pankow (Princeton, NJ: Princeton University Press, 2015), p. 121. The woman in question was Jenny Colon (1808–1842), an actress and singer.

[414] Leonora Piper (1857–1950), one of the foremost trance mediums. See the volume of James's writings edited by Gregory Shushan, *Mind Dust and White Crows: The Psychical Research of William James* (Guildford: White Crow Books, 2024). James's last study of Piper appeared in 1909: "Report on Mrs Piper's Hodgson-Control," *Proceedings of the Society for Psychical Research* 23 (1909): 2–121.

access to the unconscious. His friend Hyslop was professor of mathematics in New York, who became general secretary of the American Society for Psychical Research.[415]

James and Hyslop made an agreement: whoever of them died first should, wherever possible, give the other a sign. James died first. At first nothing happened. A few months after the death of James (back then they had regular correspondence between the various parapsychological, or spiritualistic, circles in different countries)[416] [103/104] a message came from the circle in Dublin that a spirit had come forward in one of the various séances who had claimed to be William James. It said they should write to Hyslop and remind him of the "red pajamas."[417]

They wrote this to Hyslop. He racked his brains on what all this might mean. He assumed it was expressing something that only Hyslop and James could know. For if it were something that only the two of them would know, then it could be regarded as a proof of identity. That is how Hyslop understood it. But he did not understand what James—or his "spirit"–meant by this. And he racked his brains about it. He told me this personally. He went over everything that might be considered in this regard. Until he went back to memories from their student years in Paris, where he lived with James and where James had had some red pajamas, and Hyslop had always laughed at him about them. For Hyslop this was a very big deal. He considered this to be a proof of identity.

He told me then about another case: he was working with four or five mediums and was doing séances with them. Once a female "spirit" appeared. She said she was called such-and-such, and had lived in another

---

[415] James Hervey Hyslop (1854–1920), a psychologist and professor of ethics and logic at Columbia University. On July 10, 1946 Jung wrote to Fritz Künkel, "I once discussed the proof of identity for a long time with a friend of William James's Professor Hyslop in New York. He admitted that, all things considered, all these metapsychic phenomena could be explained better by the hypothesis of spirits than by the qualities and peculiarities of the unconscious. And here, on the basis of my own experience, I am bound to concede he is right. In each individual case I must of necessity be skeptical, but in the long run I have to admit that the spirit hypothesis yields better results in practice than any other." *Letters*, vol. 1, p. 431.

[416] These were known as the cross correspondences, and have been the subject of longstanding study in parapsychology. See Trevor Hamilton, *Arthur Balfour's Ghosts: An Edwardian Elite and the Riddle of Cross-Correspondence Automatic Writings* (Exeter: Imprint Academic, 2017).

[417] The source for this anecdote is Hyslop's "Poltergeist Phenomena and Dissociation," *Journal of the American Society for Psychical Research* 7, no. 1 (1913): 1–56, at pp. 36–37. Jung mentioned the same anecdote in his November 22, 1933 lecture on the interpretation of visions, correctly describing the pajamas there as pink: see C. G. Jung, *Visions: Notes on the Seminar Given in 1930–34*, ed. Claire Douglas and Mary Foote, Bollingen Series 99 (Princeton, NJ: Princeton University Press, 1997), vol. 2, pp. 1187–88.

town, a small place, and she had died at a certain time and asked them to send greetings from her to her daughter. She gave the address, and they found the daughter in reality and this "spirit" (they had asked for identifying features) also said, "Before my death I wore a gray shawl[418] for many years which my daughter made." So, they found the daughter and asked her whether she knew something that would be characteristic of her mother. Yes, she could: she always walked round wearing a gray neck scarf! (The medium naturally did not know this family).—Another "spirit" announced that he had died in the year 1600 and that his grave could be found in a small cemetery. There was a gravestone. No one knew about this. After a long search, the gravestone was indeed found.—Here, though, there was still the possibility of a cryptomnesia.[419] [105/106] But in the example of the woman, it is unthinkable.

I am convinced that one is still present after death and, indeed, very personally. But only for a certain time, and then comes a change. Then the mystery begins.—Think of the last dream I had of my wife.[420] How she appeared to me in her beautiful garment, quite youthful. But it was not her, though it said it had been arranged for me, as a sort of portrayal of her. And yet it was her whole being.

JUNE 20, 1957

Dream:

[421]I was on the second floor of a house, that is, the house had two floors, and I noticed that I was in a kind of living room furnished in a somewhat comfortable way, with fine pieces partly in the Baroque style, partly the Renaissance. Some were also Rococo, thus late Baroque. It was around the period from 1650 to 1750, with a few earlier echoes hinting at the sixteenth century. There were also beautiful old paintings on the walls. It seemed to be my house and I was amazed about this. Suddenly it occurred to me that I was on the second floor and did not know how the lower storey was furnished. I went down quite a few stairs and arrived at the first floor. There,

---

418 "shawl": in English in the original.

419 Flournoy's concept, of what was presented as a memory but was actually a forgotten impression that had been through a process of subconscious elaboration.

420 See p. 75 above.

421 See *ETG*, pp. 163–64, *MDR*, pp. 158–59, and *1925*, pp. 23–24. On January 16, 1952 and September 26, 1959, Jung discussed this dream with Bennet: Bennet, *Meetings with Jung*, pp. 35–36 and 117–18. Bennet noted, "When he reflected about it later the house had some association in his mind with his uncle's very old house in Basle which was built in the old moat of the town and had two cellars; the lower one was dark and like a cave." (p. 118).

everything was arranged in a medieval style: flagstones out of red brick. Everything was very old, this entire section of the house. It dated from at least the fifteenth or sixteenth century. I walked around, and it was so dark—indeed very ancient. I thought: Now I must explore the entire house, and then I found an old heavy door. I opened it and discovered a staircase leading to the cellar. It was a very old staircase. I climbed down and found myself now in a beautiful, vaulted room that looked very ancient. I wondered when it had been built. I explored the walls and discovered that they contained Roman brickwork. So that was a wall from the Roman period. Between the stones were layers of brick, arranged in certain patterns, and when I saw that I knew: This is Roman. My interest had now reached its peak. I examined the floor more precisely for a second time. This was of flagstones, and in one of them I discovered a ring. I pulled on it, the flagstone lifted, and I saw a narrow staircase of stone steps, leading once again into the depths. Down I went. Within the rock there came a low cavern, and there thick dust lay upon the ground and within it lay bones and broken pots, very primitive, and perhaps two human skulls. They looked archaic and were half decomposed. I was hugely interested in this.

I told this dream to Freud on our joint American trip.[422] [106/107] He didn't have a clue what to make of it. I had some sort of an idea of what the dream could mean, namely a type of illustration of the psyche. But I did not say this to him for I did not trust my own judgment at that time. I noticed that he kept coming back to those skulls. I was supposed to discover a wish within it. What did I think about the skulls? And who did they originate from? I thought it must be from someone whose death it would be worth wishing for. So I said: My wife and my sister-in-law. I said that because I thought it was in line with his theory. I felt exactly that this was not correct, but I went along with his intention. I wanted to learn from him after all, he had to know better than I! I thought: What does he really want? For God's sake, whose death am I supposed to desire? My mother was still alive at that time. Nothing in me pointed to the idea that I wished her death, nor of my wife or my sister-in-law in fact. But you can just go along with it! Then it would be as if Freud were exonerated! This episode showed me that he was completely powerless in the face of such dreams.—I thought: Now the devil take me if I cannot get at what this dream actually means![423]

---

[422] See below, pp. 289–91. In 1925, Jung said that this dream occurred on the way back from America (p. 23).

[423] Bennet noted that Jung narrated the following to him regarding this dream: "In reply to Freud's statement that the dream represented a death wish, he suggested his wife, to which Freud replied, 'Yes . . . it could be that. And the most likely meaning is that you

Then I said to myself: I wake up in an old house as if I had awoken in an earlier generation. The bygone was still animated, as with certain old houses in Basel where people live for centuries among ancient furniture. The ground floor of the house in the dream gave the impression of being uninhabited; it was like a museum. In the cellar there were no pots—nothing—empty. But the second floor, where I was, that was "lived in"[424] and possibly there was another storey above me. The first floor, that is the one which pointed to history. What impressed me at that time were the historical indications in Freud, such as the Oedipus complex, the Pompeii fantasies in the Villa dei Misteri, Jensen's *Gradiva*.[425]

These were the first indications where I noticed that when confronted with them Freud is completely helpless. I also saw that he had a completely different understanding of the dream than I had. I take the dream as it is, *tel quel*; it struck me as peculiar that the dream as Freud imagined it [107/108] had a tendency to deceive. For me, dreams were nature. The eyes too don't wish to deceive us, but one deceives oneself because the eyes are short-sighted. One hears amiss because the ears are not good, but the ears don't wish to deceive us. The unconscious seemed to me from the very beginning to be something natural, a purely natural function completely independent of consciousness. I always thought of it that way, for a long time before I met Freud. For example, in my dissertation and in the deliria of the mentally ill.[426] Such was the first dream.

The second dream, this one came later, around 1911.[427] I remember well that it was a very hot summer that year. The motif of the hot sun marked the dream: thus, I was in an Italian town (where you have the southern sun!) and it was exactly midday, between twelve and one o'clock.

---

want to get rid of your wife and bury her under two cellars.' Jung was unsatisfied with this interpretation in personal terms." Bennet noted that "Jung felt that Freud's handling of the dream showed a tendency to make the facts fit his theory." Bennet added that as Jung reflected on the dream, he saw the house as representing the exterior of his personality, and the inside of the house, the interior of his personality, containing historical layers. Thus the house possibly represented the stages of culture. To Bennet, he said, "It was then, at that moment, I got the idea of the collective unconscious." Bennet, *C. G. Jung*, p. 88.

[424] "'lived in'": in English in the original.

[425] Wilhelm Jensen, *Gradiva* (Frankfurt: S. Fischer Verlag, 1902). This formed the basis of Freud's 1907 study, "Delusion and Dream in Jensen's *Gradiva*." On reading it, Jung praised it highly to Freud, writing, "Your *Gradiva* is magnificent." (May 24, 1907: *FJL*, p. 26).

[426] Jung's understanding of dreams in his early work draws on a wide range of non-Freudian conceptions. See Shamdasani, *Jung and the Making of Modern Psychology*, section 2, "Night and Day," pp. 131–32.

[427] See *ETG*, p. 167, *MDR*, p. 164; *BB* 2, p. 160; and *1925*, pp. 40–41. It seems from *BB* 2 that the dream occurred in 1912 (p. 155).

I knew it was twelve, for people were coming out of the shops. This Italian town was built on the hills.

This reminded me of a certain place in Basel, the Kohlenberg.[428] The valley running through Basel is the Birs Valley. On the right bank is the Münsterberg, on the left, the Nadelberg, and on this embankment there is an old castle: Wildegg.[429] But this is well into the town and now the main guard house is there; next to it is the ancient church of St. Leonhard. On the brow of the hill where the castle is situated, a street descends, consisting of nothing but steps. It leads down into the Birs Valley. The actual route makes a detour. All the alleyways leading down are stepped alleyways.—So I went down these steps to Barfüsserplatz.

But it was an Italian town, or one can also say, it had an absolutely southern character, and the sun was at its zenith. It was hot and radiant. An intensive radiance, a high midday summer sun. It was very hot just then; it was 1911 and then people came towards me out of the shops of the town where the people are heading home at this time for lunch. Such a rush hour. And among these people there was a knight in full armor. But the armor was like this: he [108/109] had a great helmet covering his face and this helmet only had eye slits. And he had on chain mail armor and above this he was wearing a white over-garment, so that one saw only the arms and hands. One could not see his face because he was wearing a helmet. At the front and the back of the garment was a large red cross. I thought: How remarkable! I was impressed by the fact that no one in the throng on the street noticed him, no one passing him turned towards him or looked back after him. It was exactly as if we were completely invisible. I was utterly astonished: Where did he come from? You can imagine what an impression it would make if a crusader should suddenly come into the middle of a crowd! He came directly towards me, up the steps. And then I noticed that no one seemed to perceive him. Then the question arose in me: What is this then? And then it was as if someone said to me (but there was no one there to say it): Yes, that is a regular appearance here! Always between twelve and one o'clock he passes by here, and no one pays any attention. And then I awoke. The dream made a colossal impression upon me, you can imagine. I did not know what to make of it.

---

[428] A steep elevation in the old town in Basel.

[429] Schloss Wildegg is a baroque castle in Kanton Aargau, around thirty miles from Basel, not in Basel itself.

[430]And then a little while after that—some weeks or months later—I had the dream that I was somewhere in Austria, or in the Tirol, in a rather mountainous area near the border, and then came a uniformed figure, an older man, an Austrian customs official with the old imperial-royal cap,[431] and he had such a remarkably morose face and was rather stooped, a man of about sixty years, so an older man but still fit for duty. He walked past me without paying me any attention. And then there were some people, and someone made a remark: he walks around here; he is already long dead, a proper ghost! It was not nighttime, however, but daytime, heading towards evening, and I was instructed by someone that he was not real but the ghost of a deceased customs official here.—At this, Freud immediately came to mind. He had little similarity externally with Freud; he was a rather morose old man and completely uneducated, who simply walked past me. Then the "censor" came to mind. There were also "censors" in the Austrian bureaucracy. [110/111] Which led Freud later to formulate the "superego."[432] I never liked this because nature was absent from it. The concept of the superego seemed to me like a state authority, something created by man. Even the border, that is not natural, but something artificial, and nature itself does not follow the shape of it, it has forests and fields on both sides. So now a customs official is the expression of public order, and that is why the censor occurred to me (the excise? Old expression associated with customs). This is what came to mind about customs. This was the very embarrasing inspection of the sacks, bags, and suitcases at the border. And then analysis occurred to me. (I later received the proof of this from a female patient who had dreamed of me as a customs official who pulled things which she did not know she had out of her suitcase).

The border alludes to the border between consciousness and the un-conscious. One must however also keep in mind the situation at that time in Austria. Austrian bureaucracy, that was quite something. Only, considering the great esteem which I then had for Freud, it struck me powerfully that I would dream of him in such a way. What sort of remarkable propensity is this in me?

---

[430] See *ETG*, pp. 167–68, *MDR*, p. 165. In *BB* 2 and in *1925* Jung narrated this sequence as part of the same dream, rather than two dreams, with the customs officer appearing in the southern town before the knight. The version in *ETG* follows *BB* 2 and *1925* in this regard.

[431] "imperial-royal": "kaiserlich-königlich," or "k.-k.," referring to the Austro-Hungarian "dual monarchy" (1867–1918).

[432] "The I and the It" (1923), *SE* 19.

At that time, under Freud's influence, I had largely abandoned my own judgment, otherwise I would not have been able to go along with him. I told myself: For now, you are abandoning your judgment. Freud is much more intelligent and experienced than you. For now, simply listen to what he says. And now, to my sorrow, there in the dream I had noticed the similarity between Freud and the customs official. But why should the dream represent Freud in this way? This was, of course, a compensation for my over-valuation. The dream said: Now for once you ought to regard him in this way. And then I dreamed of him as an old Austrian official of the old Austrian regime.

In the old Austria, the concept of "society" was a "shibboleth." One could say, a saint's image, a treasured concept or apparition. Such is society: one imagines fine houses, fine clothes [110/111] and carriages, villas and castles.—I went to such a palace belonging to the Countess of Schönborn. This was in Vienna.[433] And there, for example, it was worth making fun of everything that proclaimed, or believed in, "society." Here in Switzerland, it is not worth it, because that does not exist for us. But in Austria everything that has authority—church, state, aristocracy—all of that was "belittled"[434] and it was worth making jokes about it. Such was the style at that time in such countries. There is always a class that is simply against everything.

Jewish society tended to be "against everything" because the Jews were treated very scandalously at that time; a crass anti-Semitism dominated, and the aristocrats reinforced it. Many Jews were socialists. This found expression when the prime minister was murdered by a Jew named Adler.[435] Socialism took over the leadership. It played a role in society at the time as communism does today. The opposites then arose from the social structure of the state and society: Jews and socialists on the one hand, and the nobility on the other, which for its part then spilled over into National Socialism. (Prince Starhemberg).[436]

Freud was on the side of the Jewish intelligentsia which was overflowing with jokes about the church, the nobility, the state, and everything, in fact. We don't know this here at all. It was there that I encountered this

---

[433] Franziska Gräfin von Schönborn-Buchheim (1866–1937). This was probably during Jung's visit to Vienna in 1928.

[434] "'belittled'": in English in the original.

[435] Karl von Stürgkh (1859–1916), Austrian prime minister, was assassinated by the social democrat politician Friedrich Adler (1879–1960). Adler was sentenced to death, but later pardoned and given an amnesty.

[436] Presumably Prince Ernst von Starhemberg (1899–1956), Austrian vice-chancellor with fascist sympathies.

impression for the first time. Now I had the impression of this customs official in the dream: an old, careworn official. And the impression that I had of Freud: a careworn, old man who had to bring everything down and who had not gotten what he wanted. He believed this disappointment was connected with the fact that he was a Jew.—I do not have what I would like to have either, I too am not recognized, simply because people are too stupid to accept something new.—Freud got his title of professor (his professorship) due to the fact that he treated the mistress of a minister. She then arranged it with her boyfriend.[437] That is how it was back then in the old Austria.[438]

It is remarkable that both the knight and the customs official were seen only by me, for they were completely antithetical figures. The knight, he was unbelievably full of life. The customs official was shadowy, and, overall, the whole of the first dream was unbelievably numinous, while the other was the opposite. The customs guard, such is one who was as yet not able to die, a fading apparition. The knight, that is an extremely lively apparition which however has never been understood.—Of course, I thought about this a great deal, about this sort of "elevated" figure. Later, this motif reappeared when I dreamed that I was in the "Alyscamps," these being the Elysian fields near Arles.[439]

There is an avenue of sarcophaguses there, reaching back into the Merovingian period.[440] There is a church there,[441] situated in an ancient Roman temple, and it was in those centuries that the great men were

---

[437] Freud was first proposed for the position of "professor extraordinarius" (honorary professor) by the internist Hermann Nothnagel and and psychiatrist Richard von Krafft-Ebing in 1897, and this was supported by the Medical Faculty of the University of Vienna. It was turned down by the Ministry of Education. On March 11, 1902, Freud informed his close friend Wilhelm Fliess that he asked his former patient Elise Gomperz to intervene. She visited the minister, Wilhelm von Hartel, who indicated that the proposal would need to be renewed. Freud then got Nothnagel and Krafft-Ebing to do this. As nothing seemed to be forthcoming, according to Freud another of his patients, Baroness Marie von Ferstel, intervened. She met the minister and "secured his promise through a mutual friend that he would give a professorship to her doctor, who had cured her." She offered in addition the gift of a modern painting to the gallery he wished to establish. The Modern Gallery did receive her gift of a painting by Emil Orlik in 1902: see *The Complete Letters of Sigmund Freud to Wilhelm Fliess, 1877–1904*, ed. and trans. Jeffrey Moussaieff Masson (Cambridge, MA: Harvard University Press, 1985), pp. 456–57; also Henri F. Ellenberger, *The Discovery of the Unconscious: The History and Evolution of Dynamic Psychiatry* (New York: Basic Books, 1970), pp. 452–54.

[438] The last sentence was added handwritten by Jaffé.

[439] Alyscamps is a Roman acropolis near Arles in Provence, southern France. In Greek mythology, the Elysian fields were where the heroes on whom the Gods bestowed immortality dwelt.

[440] The Merovingian dynasty ruled the Franks from the fifth to the eighth century.

[441] The medieval church of St. Honoratus.

buried in Arles.—Now I dreamed—but this was only in 1913 or so—that I came from the town. It was just as in Arles, a similar avenue, also with these sarcophaguses. There were pedestals with flagstones upon them, and on these lay the dead, not of stone, but mummified in a remarkable way. They lay there just as one also sees in burial chapels: the knights lay there in their armor, on their backs with folded hands. This is how the dead lay in my dream, with folded hands, in their clothes on the flagstones, and I saw only a long row and I looked at the first one, he was from the thirties of the nineteenth century. As I was studying his clothes with interest, suddenly he moved his hands. He unfolded his hands and became alive, and he only did this because I was looking at him. I had a very unpleasant feeling and I went on further and came to another figure, from the eighteenth century. And it was exactly the same: as I looked at him, he moved his hands and became alive. So, I went along the entire row, until I arrived as it were in the twelfth century, namely at a crusader in chain mail armor, lying there with folded hands. I think: He is really dead. He gave me the impression of being made of wood, it was as if he were carved. I looked at him for a long time and thought: Now he is really dead. [112/113] And then I saw that in fact the finger on his left hand began to move. And this was the knight.[442]

[443]This is the time when alchemy began and the quest for the Holy Grail.—When I was sixteen years old, I read the Grail legends and they made an incredible impression on me. It was permanent, and that early childhood impression, it was immediately associated with the apparition of the knight in the dream. From there, I also arrived at what occupied the hiatus between the age of chivalry and antiquity. Naturally I meditated on the dream for a long time and I researched how it happens that there is a hiatus there.—The time of the Holy Grail has always greatly fascinated me; there must be a great mystery in it, I said to myself. At the time when I dreamed that, I was writing *Transformations*. I had not yet included the Grail legend in it because my wife was already working on it.[444] So what was it all about, "the treasure hard to obtain"? It was likely that here lay the answer to the question that Christianity leaves

---

[442] See below, p. 276.

[443] See *ETG*, pp. 169–70, *MDR*, p. 165.

[444] See *ETG*, p. 218, *MDR*, p. 215, and Emma Jung and Marie-Louise von Franz, *The Grail Legend*, trans. Andrea Dykes (Princeton, NJ: Princeton University Press, 1998). On Emma Jung, see Emma Jung, *Dedicated to the Soul: The Writings and Drawings of Emma Jung*, ed. Ann Conrad Lammers, Thomas Fischer, and Medea Hoch (Princeton, NJ: Princeton University Press, 2025).

unanswered. Quite simply because Christianity is not focused upon that question. Then I attempted to transport myself into the time before the Grail knights and simply fell into an answerless darkness. And then, as I sort of descended to the third century, I had the feeling: Now it's starting to get lighter. I had the feeling: There a part of me lives and it came out in my work on the unconscious—such are, of course, the Gnostics to whom the figure of Philemon also belongs.[445] How he appeared to me, that it was with me, as if I had come into the form that was right for me. The other figures, they were like a continuity from father to son, whereas the relationship with the Gnostics, that was like spiritual kinship. The other was not a spiritual kinship but rather one of blood, of the body.

I meditated about the knight dream for a long time; I had the persistent feeling that it was about a great adventure that required a heap of courage and chivalrous virtue. More I did not know. It had to be something like a military quest that demanded much knightly virtue as well as spiritual service. Like the knights of the Holy Grail and the Minne singers.[446]

And for me, all this was associated again with the dream of the *tabula smaragdina* that came in 1912.[447]

[448]On the dream of the *tabula smaragdina*: The Holy Ghost is a bird, a messenger, coming out of the blue sky like Noah's dove or something.[449] In the dream it was a thoroughly religious experience; it was a white bird.

---

[445] See below, p. 130.

[446] *Minnesang*: a tradition of romantic poetry and songs that flourished in Germany between the twelfth and fourteenth centuries.

[447] In 1913, in *BB 2*, Jung noted this dream as follows: "I dreamed at that time (it was shortly after Christmas 1912), that I was sitting with my children in a marvelous and richly furnished castle apartment—an open columned hall—we were sitting at a round table, whose top was a marvelous dark green stone. Suddenly a gull or a dove flew in and sprang lightly onto the table. I admonished the children to be quiet, so that they would not scare away the beautiful white bird. Suddenly this bird turned into a child of eight years, a small blond girl, and ran around playing with my children in the marvelous columned colonnades. Then the child suddenly turned into the gull or dove. She said the following to me: 'Only in the first hour of the night can I become human, while the male dove is busy with the twelve dead.' With these words the bird flew away and I awoke." (pp. 17–18). In *1925* Jung noted that "there flashed across my mind the story of the *Tabula smaragdina*, or emerald table, which is part of the legend of the Thrice Great Hermes. He is supposed to have left a table on which was engraved all the wisdom of the ages, formulated in the Greek words: 'Ether above, Ether below, Heaven above, Heaven below, all this above, all this below, take it and be happy.'" (p. 43). Aniela Jaffé added here a lightly copy-edited excerpt from the 1925 seminar, which recounted the dream, Jung's visions on the way to Schaffhausen, and the commencement of Jung's active imaginations (see *1925*, pp. 42–45). Jung also narrated this dream to Bennet. Bennet, *Meetings with Jung*, January 5, 1957 (p. 75).

[448] See *ETG*, pp. 175–76, *MDR*, p. 172.

[449] Cf. Genesis 8:11.

And it transformed itself into the young girl, the same age as my daughter who was seven years old at that time.[450]—The image in the dream refers to the archetype of the "wise old man" which, for his part, was the father of the anima. On the individuation path of a man, after the archetype of the wise old man comes the spiritual mother, for the wise old man is the "ancient son of the mother."[451] She is the one, Sophia, who is abandoned by God, while God then married Israel instead.—The twelve dead, these are the twelve apostles, time. These are also spirits who have gone on ahead and who must be taught, who must be educated. For example, in Goethe this took the form of teaching the *puer aeternus*. (Cf. *Faust II*, closing scene).[452] In the afterlife, he teaches the dead. Twelve is a sacred number. In the dream, while the "old man" is occupied with these dead, while he is teaching them in the evenings from eight until twelve o'clock, then he is free of the anima. One cannot directly approach the "lord of the dovecote." [116/117] There is an illustration in Rome in an early Christian church where Christ appears as an epiphany, surrounded by a crown of doves.[453] This is a parallel to the dream. The wise old man is the "lord of the doves," the epitome of wisdom. The mother of the "ancient son" is the *mater coelestis*, Isis.[454] [118]

June 27, 1957 (Addendum)

[455]When I was engrossed with psychology and alchemy—no, to be more precise, it was when I was giving the seminar on Ignatius of Loyola[456]— once, in the night, I had a vision of Christ. One night I awoke and there, at the foot of the bed, I saw a crucifix. Not quite life-sized. It was very clear and couched in a bright light. In this light, Christ was hanging on the cross and then I saw that it was as if his entire body were made of gold, as if of green gold. It looked wonderful. I was scared to death by it. Just then I was particularly engrossed by the Anima Christi. There is a very beautiful

---

[450] Agatha Niehus-Jung (1904–1998).
[451] An alchemical expression.
[452] In 1949 Jung presented a talk to the Psychological Club on "Faust and Alchemy," included in Gerber-Münch, *Goethes Faust*.
[453] Possibly the twelfth-century mosaic in the Basilica of San Clemente in Rome.
[454] On the celestial mother, see *BB 5*, p. 270.
[455] See *ETG*, p. 214, *MDR*, p. 210.
[456] See Martin Liebscher, ed., *Jung on the Ignatius of Loyola's "Spiritual Exercises": Lectures at the ETH Zurich, Volume 7: 1939–1940*, trans. Caitlin Stephens, Philemon Series (Princeton, NJ: Princeton University Press, 2023).

meditation by Ignatius on it.[457] And then this happened to me in the night! Naturally, it was a matter of the "aurum non vulgi."[458] And when I understood that, I was comforted. That is simply the living quality seen by the alchemists not only in people but also present in inorganic gold. Such is the Anthropos poured out into the whole world, the *Filius macrocosmi*.[459] This spirit is poured out into inorganic matter; he is also in metal and stone. For me this means that the Christian imagination penetrates into matter. That is also what the alchemists wanted to express.

[18]

JUNE 28, 1957

I got to know Count Keyserling at his conferences in Darmstadt.[460] I was invited at Keyserling's request by the Grand Duke of Hessen-Darmstadt,[461]

---

[457] "Anima Christi" is the title of a prayer that Saint Ignatius placed at the beginning of the *Spiritual Exercises*. Jung commented on this in his ETH lecture of November 22, 1940: Liebscher, *Jung on the Ignatius*, pp. 243–55.

[458] "aurum non vulgi": "uncommon gold." The Roman expression "aurum nostrum non est aurum vulgi" (our gold is not the common gold) was used to distinguish genuine value from imitation. It was much used by the alchemists; for example, in the *Rosarium philosophorum* (*Artis auriferae volumina duo*, p. 220).

[459] In "The Visions of Zosimos" (1938), Jung wrote, "In the sixteenth century Khunrath formulated for the first time the 'theological' position of the lapis: it was the *filius macrocosmi* as opposed to the 'son of man,' who was the *filius microcosmi*" (CE 15; CW 13 § 127). On Khunrath, see Peter Forshaw, *The Mage's Images*, vol. 4: *Occult Theosophy in Heinrich Khunrath's Early Modern Oratory and Laboratory* (Leiden: Brill, forthcoming).

[460] Count Hermann Keyserling (1880–1946). In 1920 he founded the School of Wisdom in Darmstadt, where it organized annual conferences, the presentations being published in *Der Leuchter*. In 1923 Keyserling invited Jung to lecture there. Jung declined, as he had to attend an international conference in the autumn, and as he had to go to England in the summer, he couldn't go the Darmstadt to meet Keyserling before the following winter (March 31, 1923, JP). On November 19, 1925 Keyserling wrote to Emma Jung to ask her to use her influence on her husband to have him accept an invitation to their next congress to speak on "the geology of the soul" and to forward the invitation to Jung in Africa (JP). Jung spoke at the 1927 symposium, and again at the tenth anniversary of the School of Wisdom in 1930. On this occasion, he was accompanied by Emma Jung, their daughter Marianne, Toni Wolff, and Cary Baynes. In 1931 Keyserling spoke in Zurich at the Psychological Club (Toni Wolff to Keyserling, December 6, 1930, JP). On the School of Wisdom, see Suzanne Marchand, "Eastern Wisdom in an Era of Western Despair: Orientalism in 1920s Central Europe," in Peter Gordon and John McCormick, eds, *Weimar Thought: A Contested Legacy* (Princeton, NJ: Princeton University Press, 2013), pp. 341–60. In *Reflections*, Jaffé noted that on numerous occasions Kurt Wolff had wanted Jung to speak about Keyserling, particularly given that it was at the School of Wisdom that he himself first met Jung (p. 53).

[461] Ernst Ludwig, Großherzog von Hessen und bei Rhein (1868–1937). In November and December 1926 Keyserling and Schmitz discussed the best way of inviting Jung to stay

and even stayed with my wife in the grand duke's castle.[462] I also got to know Frobenius there.[463] Keyserling was already known to me through his book *The Travel Diary of a Philosopher*,[464] but I had never met him in person before. But I had heard of him earlier from Oskar H. Schmitz.[465]

There's a good story about this: Keyserling asked Schmitz to explain my types—my *Types* book—to him. I was suspicious that Keyserling could not read at all because he was too much in love with his own thoughts. So, Schmitz took it in hand and explained the types to him. He also told him that he himself was an introvert, and that Keyserling was

---

with the grand duke. On December 4, Schmitz wrote to Jung that the hotels and restaurants in Darmstadt were bad and that as the School of Wisdom didn't have great funds, they put up speakers in private houses. The grand duke had asked if Jung would stay with him. Schmitz added, "The grand duke is a very simple person and the grand duchess even more so; both are hospitable, and in the English sense which famously means leaving the guests in peace and not having to devote oneself to them, etc. The socializing is limited to lunch and black coffee where different speakers are invited in turn, among them, this time, Wilhelm, Scheler, Much, etc., and this should interest you. In the evenings one meets in a relaxed way at one's leisure with the conference participants at Hotel Traube." Goedela Keyserling, ed., *Sinnsuche oder Psychoanalyse: Briefwechsel mit Graf Hermann Keyserling aus den Tagen der Schule der Weisheit* (Darmstadt: Gesellschaft der hessischen Literaturfreunde, 1970), p. 70. On January 7, 1927 Jung replied, "I gladly accept the invitation to the grand duke's, although I do not know how come I am receiving this honor. My wife will probably come, too. Must I write to the grand duke personally? How and where? Is he called 'Royal Highness?'" C. G. Jung, "Letters to Oskar Schmitz, 1921–1931," *Psychological Perspectives* 6, no. 1 (1975): 79–95 at p. 85. On January 13 Keyserling wrote to Jung indicating that the grand duke and his wife had invited him to stay at the New Palace from April 24 to 30 (JP). Subsequently, after the grand duke's death, his widow wrote to Jung inviting him to contribute to a book she and her son were compiling in which friends and collaborators would recall their encounters with her husband (Eleanore von Hessen to Jung, October 29, 1937, JP). Jung sent a memoir, recalling the deep impression that his stay there and the grand duke had made on him: in particular, "[t]o experience the past and history as the living present: the majesty of royal blood is an emanation of a destiny enhanced a hundred times, the mana of an apostolic succession of great faces." This gave Jung an "insight into one of the great mystery of human history" (JP).

[462] Schloss Wolfsgarten, the former hunting lodge of the ruling family of Hesse-Darmstadt, built in 1724.

[463] Leo Frobenius (1873–1938), German ethnologist and archaeologist, who specialized in Africa. His conception of the "night sea journey" in *Das Zeitalter des Sonnengottes* (Berlin: G. Reimer, 1904) played an important role in Jung's *Transformations and Symbols of the Libido*. See below, p. 126. Frobenius and Jung both spoke at the 1927 meeting. Jung presented "Die Erdbedingtheit der Psyche" (CE 11; CW 8 and 10) and Frobenius presented "Erdenschicksal und Kulturwerden."

[464] Hermann von Keyserling's book *Das Reisetagebuch eines Philosophen* (Munich: Verlag Von Duncker & Humblot, 1919), in English *The Travel Diary of a Philosopher*, trans. J. H. Reece, 2 vols (New York: Harcourt, Brace, 1925), was a bestseller.

[465] Oskar A. H. Schmitz, (1873–1931), German writer, whose interests included psychoanalysis and yoga. For Jung's letters to him, see E. Jung, "Letters to Oskar Schmitz." In 1932 Jung wrote a preface to his posthumous "On the Fairytale of the Otter" (CE 12; CW 18).

an extravert. But Keyserling protested; no, he was introverted.—If ever there were someone who was not introverted, it was he, Keyserling! Then the pair of them had such an argument that Keyserling challenged him to a duel! They sought out their seconds, who then saw how crazy the whole thing was and attempted to get them to make up. Finally, Keyserling withdrew the challenge. They did not speak to each other for half a year. But afterward they could not leave it alone, although gradually there was a rapprochement, until finally everything returned to equilibrium. So ridiculous! At least that is the story I was told.[466]

Keyserling had a lady friend,[467] a very beautiful woman, but an absolute horse. A classical beauty. Though one cannot ever say "beautiful." She was a mare, no, better: a stallion. Strikingly beautiful and an important personality. She came to see me once.

When I was with Keyserling I was completely flooded. His words cascaded over me like a torrent. I could never get a word in. [18/19] I saw him several times, and he always talked without stopping. I remembered that famous meeting between Professor Windelband and Carlyle in Heidelberg.[468] Afterwards they asked the professor: So, Herr Professor, how was your visit? He replied by saying that he had spoken for two hours on the matter of holy silence!—That was Keyserling! Part of his talk was always brilliant. But one was snowed under.[469] When he held forth, from sheer exhaustion I could no longer give ear to that constant torrent. Why did he have to spout, I wondered. Does he want to prove something to himself? As if there was an urgent need for him to make other people realize that he was present and that he absolutely wanted to show something. But I wouldn't say that I found a thread to follow anywhere. I'd be unable to

---

[466] For Keyserling's correspondence with Schmitz, see G. Keyserling, *Sinnsuche oder Psychoanalyse*.

[467] This appears to be the Argentinian writer and publisher Victoria Ocampo (1890–1979). On her meeting with Jung, see "Victoria Ocampo Pays Jung a Visit," in McGuire and Hull, *C. G. Jung Speaking*, pp. 82–84. She is designated as 'X' in Jung's letters to Keyserling of April 23, August 13, and December 24, 1931 (*Letters*, vol. 1, pp. 82–86). On Ocampo and Keyserling, see Amy K. Kaminsky, *Argentina: Stories for a Nation* (Minneapolis: University of Minnesota Press, 2008), ch. 5 (pp. 70–97); Craig Stephenson, *The Correspondence of Victoria Ocampo, Count Keyserling and C. G. Jung: Writing to the Woman Who Was Everything* (London: Routledge, 2022).

[468] Wilhelm Windelband (1848–1915) was a neo-Kantian Philosopher, who held a chair in Heidelberg. In his *History of Philosophy*, trans. James H. Tufts (New York: Macmillan, 1901 [Ger. orig. 1891]) he praised Carlyle's work. On Jung's relation to his work, see Shamdasani, *Jung and the Making of Modern Psychology*, pp. 35 and 95. In *Past and Present* (London: Chapman and Hall, 1943) Carlyle wrote of the significance of silence.

[469] "snowed under": in English in the original.

summarize a single exchange or recall what he had spoken about. Because it was simply too much. It was completely amusing or brilliant, but always torrential, so it was futile to converse with him.

The grand duke who had invited me, he was a very friendly gentleman. During the intervals he often sat working at his embroidery frame.

But then there was someone else in Darmstadt: an occultist. He reminded me of a figure at court from the eighteenth century. A nobleman, with a large black hat. He reminded me of Count Cagliostro, Count St. Germain.[470] He interested me because he was so formal and correct. In the innocuousness of this princely court, he was a sort of dark figure. As a *tenebrio*—not a "grey eminence." Something like a Rosicrucian or alchemist.

And then Frobenius was there too. He was exceptionally interesting. He had unbelievable vitality and intelligence and great ethnological knowledge, but ideas simply raged through him. He was very intense and lively and very amusing. An original. For example, he possessed some trousers made of tanned lion skin. [19/20] He left the tail on them and occasionally he would wag it. That is what I was told. He himself told me that he had built a grass hut near Munich, just as the negroes build them, and he lived in it. With him I had a couple of very good exchanges. But you know how these people often are: one noticed his lack of manners. And his ideas ran away with him. Much like Keyserling, he spoke only of himself. With very little understanding of the ideas of others. In that he showed his lack of culture; that was quite clear with Frobenius. Whereas in the case of the "dark prince," he had culture.

At one meal, a brother of the Kaiser was present. He was called Heinrich.[471] He told how he had fled Berlin in the Spartacist uprising (1918).[472] He and his entourage came out of the city to a gravel pit and one of the Reds jumped on the running board of his car. Heinrich himself shot him. I was struck forcibly by the backdrop of barbarism evident there.

---

[470] In *Reflections*, this figure is identified as Kuno Ferdinand von Hardenberg (see below, n. 582). In 1923 he published a book with Keyserling and Karl Happich, *Das Okkulte* (Darmstadt: Otto Reichl Verlag, 1923). Count Alessandro di Cagliostro was the alias of Guiseppi Balsamo (1743–1795), an occultist and magician. The Comte de St. Germain (d. 1784), whose true name and origin remain unknown, was an eighteenth-century (probably) German alchemist, musician, and adventurer.

[471] Prince Albert Wilhelm Heinrich of Prussia (1862–1929), brother of Kaiser Wilhelm II.

[472] In January 1919 a hundred thousand workers went on strike in Berlin, led by Karl Liebknecht and Rosa Luxemburg, in an attempt to replicate the Russian revolution. This was known as the Spartacist uprising.

It impressed me that Keyserling could at times suddenly express himself with great humility. But that was only at certain moments when one could sense a certain admirable modesty in him. But that was all drowned out in a torrent of words. Yet I never had the impression of a tasteless vanity, rather of an involuntary sense of entitlement. He simply could not do anything else. He had to prevail in the face of the tribulations of the time. He was an aristocrat, and that fact wants to assert itself and must assert itself *à tout prix*.[473] That's what was actually behind it. That was his nature. So I said of him that he was not a person but a phenomenon.[474] That pleased him inordinately. Less so when he wrote *The Travel Diary of a Philosopher* and his crazy idea of founding a spiritual monastery for intellectuals. I said to him then: Am I now to imagine Count Keyserling as a lay brother [20/21] doing the kitchen chores? For the essence of a cloister is submission and humility! He didn't like hearing that.

Keyserling was an important man; even more: he was an impressive phenomenon who simply could do nothing other than assert himself. There was an aristocrat in him that was destined to come to the fore. Although to play what role one did not actually know. Such is the tail-end of aristocracy,[475] the last squeal of entitlement, which is legitimized by dint of aristocracy and which also one might accept for that reason. But the content would not have declared it. He had no message which one could hear in any discernible way. One wondered what he did in fact bring. It was only the reaction of an aristocrat at the end of his rope.[476] That was the Baltic in him, the complete baron who is simply a grand-seigneur.[477] Indeed his grandfather was the noble marshal in the Baltic, an absolute gentleman.[478] And this grand-seigneur in Keyserling, that was something in its own right, though he was a *roi sans royaume*.[479] He claimed that originally he had been a very shy man. Yet the needs of the time compelled him to bruit things about. He even became over-loud, as if he had to break through a wall. All in all, that flowed out of him like a feudal personality beating a retreat. This role he portrayed with all the merits and demerits of the aristocracy.

---

[473] *à tout prix*, in French in the original: "at any cost."

[474] See Jung's response to Keyserling's book *Das Spectrum Europas*: "The Meaning of the Swiss Line in the European Spectrum" (1928), CE 11; CW 10, §§ 903–4, and his review "The Rise of a New World" (1930), CE 11; CW 10.

[475] "tail-end of aristocracy": in English in the original.

[476] "at the end of his rope": in English in the original.

[477] "grand-seigneur," in French in the original.

[478] Count Alexander von Keyserling (1815–1891).

[479] *roi sans royaume*, in French in the original: "king without a kingdom."

His wife was the granddaughter of Bismarck.[480] So in Darmstadt I had a glimpse of the German aristocracy, predominantly the north German version. There were certain people among them, specifically an older sister of Countess Keyserling.[481] She lived in Potsdam. She was a personality, a real lady.[482] You know: deportment, aristocracy, very imposing. Whereas with Keyserling himself there was an undercurrent of brutality. The horses' stable was just next door. This countess reminded me of the English aristocracy. There were the same grand gestures. She was a lady. For example, when the Russians invaded, she wrapped them around her little finger. She knew how to get along with scoundrels. With Keyserling himself, the whip was palpable in the background. [21/22] There was a violent manner to him, whereas this Bismarck lady, she was quality. I got on very well with these people. I understood them, until the brashness began which they all shared. A certain cynicism which, in fact, in many cases was simply a sign of heightened sensitivity.

The Origin of the Method of Active Imagination
[483]This dates right back to the beginning. Here is how it began: in the autumn, in October 1913, I had these visions while on the train that were repeated a few weeks later, once again on the railway when I was traveling to Schaffhausen.[484] I believe it was connected to that fact that I was crossing the Rhine towards Germany. The route to Schaffhausen takes you over the Rhine and that is the spiritual border with Germany. Schaffhausen is for me a sort of German enclave in Switzerland, being rather identified with Germany. It is already on the other side of the Rhine. And there I became aware that something must be wrong, and that was after my definitive split from Freud.

[485]Then I decided: From now on I don't want to impose any more theoretical presuppositions on my patients. I just want to wait and see what they bring, and I simply focused upon what chance brought. I said to myself: What I want is simply to observe what happens without theoretical presuppositions. Then came the dreams and also fantasies that they brought. I would ask them: What comes to your mind in this connection? And they responded to it and gave me their associations. I had to help

---

[480] Countess Maria Goedela von Bismarck (1896–1981).
[481] Princess Hannah Leopoldine Alice von Bismarck (1893–1971).
[482] "lady": in English in the original.
[483] See *ETG*, pp. 178–79, *MDR*, pp. 175–76.
[484] See below, p. 151.
[485] See *ETG*, pp. 174–75, *MDR*, p. 170.

them understand these things logically, not according to theoretical pre-suppositions. This process led me into an incredible multiplicity of aspects. I saw very soon that it was right to take dreams *tel quel*;[486] for that is what is intended, these are the facts we must proceed from. Everything else is fantasy. At that time, I simply wanted to see how the patients engaged with it. So more and more the need emerged [22/23] for a sort of—how should I put it—the initial need for a criterion, or an orientation. Then the visions on the train came, and I myself needed such an orientation all the more.[487] I thought, "I have misgivings that the images in these visions portend revolution." And I could not imagine that at all. Therefore, I decided that it must have something to do with me. So I must be in danger of a psychosis, I concluded.

[488]Further dreams followed, in the spring of 1914 (April, May, June), the three dreams of a polar frost arriving in mid-summer, and the land being turned to ice. So, for example, the whole region of Lorraine was frozen. This is the place where the first skirmishes of World War I took place. Everywhere I looked the landscape was completely devoid of people. And this vision repeated itself three times, each time in mid-summer. I was then on my way to Aberdeen where I was to give a lecture on schizophrenia at a congress.[489] I arrived there on July 28, 1914 and I was full of apprehension that something would happen. For these visions, these are fate. It also seemed to me like fate that I had to speak on the theme of schizophrenia.

Then, foreseen by no one, the war broke out on August 1. At that juncture I thought that now I had to reflect upon myself; I must know what is actually going on.[490] I remembered that until 1900 I had kept a journal, and so I thought this would be a possibility for me to attempt to observe myself.[491] It would be an attempt to meditate on myself, and so I began to describe my inner states. These portrayed themselves within me in metaphors: for example, I am in a desert, and the sun was unbearably hot (sun = consciousness). Thereafter came the long visions that you

---

[486] *tel quel*, in French in the original,: "just as they are."

[487] See *ETG*, p. 179, *MDR*, p. 176.

[488] See *LN*, pp. 224–25.

[489] Jung spoke on "The Importance of the Unconscious in Psychopathology" at a meeting of the British Medical Association, July 24–31, 1914.

[490] In *LN*, Jung wrote, "And then the war broke out. This opened my eyes about what I had experienced before, and it also gave me the courage to say all of that which I have written in the earlier part of this book" (p. 476).

[491] Jung resumed writing in this journal in the autumn of 1913, after an interval of eleven years. See *BB* 2.

know.—Then the voice said, "This is art."[492] It was the voice of a patient who had a crazy animus and who unfailingly provoked the anima in me. I knew this already, that it was not the person, but the anima within me that said this. She was a very lively figure in me.

Soon after that the figure of Elijah appeared and out of him Philemon developed.[493] Philemon, who brought an Egyptian-Gnostic-Hellenist [23/24] mood with him, a clearly Gnostic hue, because he was actually a pagan. He was simply a superior way of knowing and he taught me psychological objectivity, the actuality of the soul. He enacted this dissociation: namely that between me and my mental object. Previously it had been what I formulate, then it became a thing, and he personified that thing. He formulated this thing that I was not and voiced everything that I had not thought. For one thing, I perceived that he was speaking it. I took him to be speaking sort of in sermons.

When I was writing the *Septem Sermones* I was forced to speak that way myself.[494] Until then it was spoken only by him. At the beginning, when I realized Philemon, it was as if he objectively confronted me. It was like that first experience with the voice of the anima. Something is in me to say something I do *not* intend to say, that is perhaps even said against me. I also came to see this with Philemon: but it can also be said for me. Those apparitions also taught me to see that there are things that I do not make but which make themselves.

The *Septem Sermones*, that was later, when Philemon lost his absolute autonomy.

[495]The figure of Philemon first appeared to me in a dream when I was at the beginning of encountering the unconscious. I saw him: there was a blue sky, but it was moving as if it were a sea and also covered in clouds. But these clouds were like ice floes and it was as if these floes were being dispersed and the water was breaking through. Thus the blue sky became visible there. Suddenly from the right a winged creature appeared. It sailed

---

[492] See below, p. 240–41; and Bennet, *Meetings with Jung*, January 8, 1957 (p. 76).

[493] See *ETG*, p. 186, *MDR*, p. 182.

[494] In the first version of *Sermones* in *The Black Books*, the *Sermones* are spoken by the "I" to the dead (*BB 5*, pp. 282–83). In the version in *LN*, they are spoken by Philemon (pp. 508–9).

[495] See *ETG*, p. 186–87, *MDR*, p. 182. The first form of Philemon actually appeared in a fantasy of January 27, 1914 (*BB 4*, pp. 227–28). In his appointment book for January 3, 1919 Jung drew a sketch of Philemon flying, which evidently formed the basis of a painting: see *Art of C. G. Jung*, cat. no. 64 (p. 143). For a black and white photo of the painting, see Gerhard Wehr, *An Illustrated Biography of Jung*, trans. Michael Kohn (Boston. MA: Shambala, 1989), p. 72.

through the sky. I tried to make it out: it was an old man with bulls' horns and a set of keys in his hand and with the wings of the kingfisher on his back. This was Philemon! I then painted this picture and when I had finished it, I found a dead kingfisher on the shore. That was the only time in my life that I found a kingfisher. I had it stuffed and installed it in my library.[496]

My perspective was lost through the ice floes. That is the image of a dissociation, and the synthesis appeared to me in Philemon. And that was further underlined by a synchronistic phenomenon. It was as if I were struck by thunder when I found the bird.

[497]Later the figure of Philemon was relativized by the arrival of Ka. (The king's Ka is his earthly form, his stone soul). The Ka soul, that is the stone soul. It came from below, out of the earth, it came as if from a deep well. And this is how I depicted it: the lower part of the figure is from stone or metal. It is like a herm made of metal.[498] Right at the top, Philemon hovers in the light. You can see his wings. The daimon has something daimonic,[499] Mephistophelian about him. He is holding a surreal bejeweled figure in his hand, and in the other, a pen with which he is working on it. He says, "I am the one who entombed the Gods in gold and precious stones." He is a counterbalance to Philemon, for he has a lame foot and cannot walk on the earth. Philemon is the spiritual aspect, he is "the meaning."—The lower is the strength of nature, he is the one who makes everything actual, and who also robs it of meaning; who replaces meaning with beauty, through the "eternal reflection." "Amidst colored reflection we have life."[500] But the meaning, that is the lord of the garden, that gets lost.[501] In time, both figures became real and were then integrated. The urge to creation arose and then I had to express the meaning myself.

[502]This is how the *Septem Sermones* came into being with their peculiar language. The dead came to me. I did not want to write this; I had no

---

[496] This has not been found.

[497] See *ETG*, p. 188, *MDR*, p. 184. The figure of Ka first enters in a fantasy of October 18, 1917 (*BB* 7, p. 163). Jung carved a sculpture of Ka: see *Art of C. G. Jung*, cat. no. 49 (p. 119). See the fantasy of February 14, 1918 (*BB* 7, pp. 174–75).

[498] A herm (or herma; from classical Greek *hermes*) is a sculpted head or bust surmounting a squared columnar base, often with genitalia carved at the appropriate height, placed in suitable public locations in ancient Greece to serve an apotropaic function.

[499] In the typescript, "The daimon has" replaced "Philemon also has."

[500] *Faust II*, Act 1, sc. 1, l. 4727: While gazing at a rainbow, Faust says, "Amidst colored reflection we have life."

[501] At the end of *Scrutinies*, Philemon addresses Christ: "Welcome to the garden, my master, my beloved, my brother!" (*LN*, p. 554).

[502] See *ETG*, pp. 193–94, *MDR*, pp. 190–91; *BB* 5, pp. 282–83 and *BB* 6, pp. 207–8.

notion of what they wanted from me. But there was a great disturbance and then things began to be haunted: my oldest daughter saw a white figure walking through the room.[503] The other one told me that she had her blanket torn away from her three times in the night. And my son had a terrifying night terror dream. In the morning he painted it, while he otherwise never painted pictures. He called it the "picture of the fisherman": a river flows through the middle of the picture [25/26] and a fisherman with an angling rod stands on the bank. He has caught a fish. The fisherman has a chimney on his head out of which comes fire and smoke. From the other side of the bank comes the devil: he is cursing that there are no fish for him. But an angel is painted above the fisherman who says: You may not do anything to him; he is only catching the evil fish! My son normally never paints!—He painted this picture between Friday and Sunday. On Sunday towards five o'clock—the two girls were in the kitchen—the doorbell started ringing like crazy! They checked to see who was there but there was absolutely no one there. They looked all over the place! The air was thick, I tell you. I said only: Now something must happen. The whole house was rammed full of spirits. They were right under the doors and you had the feeling that the house was full of them. Naturally the question was present in me: For God's sake, what is going on? Then they cried in chorus, "We are returning from Jerusalem where we did not find what we were looking for."[504]—That is how *Septem Sermones*

---

[503] In 1923 Jung recounted this episode to Cary Baynes:

One night your boy began to rave in his sleep and throw himself about saying he couldn't wake up. Finally your wife had to call you to get him quiet & this you could only do by cold cloths on him—Finally he settled down and went on sleeping. Next morning he woke up remembering nothing, but seemed utterly exhausted, so you told him not to go to school, he didn't ask why but seemed to take it for granted. But quite unexpectedly he asked for paper and colored pencils and set to work to make the following picture—a man was angling for fishes with hook and line in the middle of the picture. On the left was the Devil saying something to the man, and your son wrote down what he said. It was that he had come for the fisherman because he was catching his fishes, but on the right was an angel who said, 'No you can't take this man, he is taking only bad fishes and none of the good ones.' Then after your son had made that picture he was quite content. The same night, two of your daughters thought that they had seen spooks in their rooms. The next day you wrote out the 'Sermons to the Dead,' and you knew after that nothing more would disturb your family, and nothing did. Of course I knew you were the fisherman in your son's picture, and you told me so, but the boy didn't know it. [cited in *LN*, p. 40]

[504] See *BB 5*, January 30, 1916 (p. 283). In a fantasy of January 17, 1914 the dead Anabaptists led by Ezekiel had first appeared, and they were heading to Jerusalem to pray at the holy places (see *BB 4*, p. 207).

begins: it began to flow out of me and in three evenings the entire thing was written.[505]

That was 1916 and in fact I wrote it also on the occasion of the founding of the Psychological Club. I thought to myself that it would be a gift to Mrs. McCormick on the Club's inauguration.[506] And there was one thing that was interesting: hardly had I put down my pen than the entire company of ghosts imploded. The room became peaceful and the atmosphere pure. By the next evening something had built up again and then the same thing happened again.

This was all between 1914 and 1917.

Philemon—he was an incredibly mysterious figure. At times he was almost real. He was a figure of fantasy.[507] [12]

AUGUST 2, 1957

Question about bad conscience.

[508]As a child I always had a bad conscience, without justification. Such that I even wrote alibi notes. I have never understood why I suffered from such a bad conscience. Probably it was because I had detected the atmosphere of my parents. I was oppressed in my conscience without my being able to account for it. When I really did get up to something, I felt immediately relieved. For then I knew where that belonged.—So, a bad conscience can transgress.

Such transgressiveness also applies to depressions, to anxiety and so on, and also to the feeling of a bad conscience. The evil conscience is a type of anxiety, a special case of anxiety. It can often happen that one is overcome by anxiety that has no content. Think of phobias or the more or less unjustified anxiety that a fire could break out. Such a person might well say: I know very well that this is my phobia, but he feels anxious all the same.

[509]Among primitives a palaver is organized because the whole tribe feels damaged, magically damaged, when a robbery took place. Or when

---

[505] The composition of the *Sermones* actually lasted till February 8, 1916 (see *BB* 4, p. 227).

[506] The Club was founded through a gift of 360,000 Swiss francs from Edith Rockefeller McCormick. The first meeting was held on February 26, 1916.

[507] On July 9 Jung wrote to Aniela Jaffé from Bollingen regarding ethics. *Letters*, vol. 2, pp. 379–80.

[508] See *ETG*, p. 37, *MDR*, p. 31.

[509] See below, pp. 217–20.

an abortion is concealed, then all are affected. Not the fact that it happened, but that it was concealed, therein lies the guilt. Pig sacrifices are then offered to the Great Mother because it was concealed, and the Goddess must be appeased.—Then we come to the concept of collective guilt. This is an instinctive reaction that when something has gone wrong, then it has gone wrong not just for one person, it has gone wrong for all. [127]

AUGUST 3, 1957

[510]I want to tell you today about my adventure in the Baptistry of the Arians in Ravenna that took place in 1932.

I had been to Ravenna with acquaintances eight years before and I knew the baptistry very well.[511] When I now saw it again eight years later, this time with Miss Wolff, it seemed to me to be completely changed, completely different than I had remembered it. Even on my first visit to Ravenna, the mausoleum of Galla Placidia had made a very particular impression on me, it fascinated me to a high degree, without my being able to account for my fascination to myself. The second time it was exactly the same; and again, I got into this peculiar mood when I was at the mausoleum of Galla Placidia. Immediately after the mausoleum we went to the baptistry of the Arians and what struck me first and foremost was a remarkable blue light that wondrously filled the space. I could not account for where the light came from; at that moment the wonder of it did not enter my mind.

Now I saw to my great astonishment that where, in my memory, there had been windows—but in that moment I was no longer thinking of the windows—now there were four large, incredibly beautiful mosaics there. One depicted the baptism in the Jordan, the second the Children of Israel crossing the Red Sea, the third was unclear and faded from my memory soon after I had seen it. It might perhaps have been the cleansing of the leper by Naaman in the Jordan and it was similar to the depiction of this miracle in the old Merian Bible. I have the Merian Bible in my

---

[510] See *ETG*, p. 288–89, *MDR*, p. 284. Jung narrated this episode to Bennet: Bennet, *Meetings with Jung*, January 9, 1957 (pp. 80–81).

[511] Jung's previous visit to Ravenna, with Hans Schmid, was actually eighteen years earlier, in April 1914. On April 5 that year, Jung wrote a postcard to Emma Jung indicating that they planned to go to Ravenna the following day. From Jung's appointment book, it seems likely that the trip in 1932 took place between September 11 and 30, while Emma Jung was in London with their youngest daughter Helene Hoerni-Jung.

library. The fourth mosaic in the west of the chapel, that was the most impressive: we had started viewing the frescoes from the left-hand side, this was the east wall. Then finally we reached the west wall, and there was the finest mosaic: of Christ extending his hand to Peter as he sank under the waves. There we stopped for at least twenty minutes, and we discussed the remarkable notion that baptism originally represented a mortal danger. It was originally a proper "immersion" which evoked the danger of drowning. [127/128] I have the clearest memory of this mosaic, in the finest detail: the blue of the sea and even the individual tiles of the mosaic which I examined. I sought to decipher the banners emerging from the mouths.

After we had left the baptistry, I dashed to Alinari,[512] in order to buy myself photographs of the mosaics. Of course, I found nothing there. I decided against seeking further as time was pressing. We still wanted to go to San Vitale.[513] So I spared myself this purchase for later. On the next day we departed, and I never managed to get back to Alinari. But when I was back in Zurich, I did commission Dr. Meier to obtain some photographs, as he was traveling soon afterwards to Ravenna.[514] Immediately after my return home, I mentioned in a seminar this extremely remarkable notion of baptism and the frescoes.[515] Of course Dr. Meier was also unable to obtain the photographs and when he himself went into the Baptistry of the Arians it became clear to him that such mosaics did not even exist! But the memory of them is permanent and as if carved in stone.

At that time the details of the story of Galla Placidia were still quite unknown to me. I then concerned myself with it in more detail and found out that during an extremely tempestuous crossing from Byzantium to Ravenna she had sworn that, if she were spared, she would build a

---

[512] Alinari: a well-known photographic company.

[513] The sixth-century Basilica of San Vitale, on the outskirts of Ravenna.

[514] C. A. Meier (1905–1995), analytical psychologist, first president of the Jung Institute in Zurich, who succeeded Jung in his professorship at the ETH Zurich.

[515] In his seminar of October 12, 1932 on Kundalini Yoga, Jung gave the following description: "But if you study the beautiful mosaic pictures in the Baptistry of the Orthodox in Ravenna (which dates from the fourth or the beginning of the fifth century, where the baptism was still a mystery cult), you see four scenes depicted on the wall: two describe the baptism of Christ in the Jordan, and the fourth is St. Peter drowning in a lake during a storm and the Savior is rescuing him." C. G. Jung, *The Psychology of Kundalini Yoga*, ed. Sonu Shamdasani, Bollingen Series 99 (Princeton, NJ: Princeton University Press, 1996), p. 16. On May 5, 1954 Jung wrote to Richard Hull apropos his seminar notes: "There is one particular story which must be excluded, because it is entirely impossible, and that is the story of the baptismal symbolism in the Battistero degli Ortodossi in Ravenna." Jung Collection, LC.

chapel and portray the dangers of the sea. She fulfilled the oath with the construction of the church of San Giovanni in Ravenna, which she had decorated with suitable mosaics. In the Middle Ages, San Giovanni was destroyed by fire, but in the Ambrosian Library in Milan there is still a sketch of a mosaic depicting the dangerous crossing. But at the time I knew nothing of that.[516]

When Dr. Meier returned and reported that there were no such mosaics in the baptistry, Miss Wolff could not believe it! We had both seen them quite clearly! [128/129]

That is one of the most extraordinary things that has ever happened to me. It was unutterably beautiful. Inexplicable. Perhaps it is associated with the great danger to the anima experienced on the crossing through the sea of the unconscious. In this, the man runs incredible spiritual dangers. This is always represented in the mysteries as a mortal risk.

I still remembered exactly the powerful impression that the mausoleum made on me the first time—eight years before the experience. That was already an indescribable fascination. I went there with Dr. Schmid. We cycled down there from Switzerland which we enjoyed incredibly.[517] Even then I had a fantastic impression, but I have no idea what went into that fascination. It seemed to me somehow incredibly significant, I had no idea why and knew nothing about Galla Placidia.

Yet even the first time I thought: What is it about Galla Placidia? Therefore, Ravenna remains for me an amazing experience because it is beset with something that I cannot substantiate.—When I was there with Schmid, the anima was already a known factor.

Such experiences make an incredibly deep impression. I can still see myself entering the Alinari shop and I know for certain that afterwards we went to San Vitale.[518] [129/130]

---

[516] The Biblioteca Ambrosiana, a historic library in Milan founded in 1609.

[517] In his memoriam for Schmid, Jung wrote: "I remember a highly enjoyable bicycle tour which took us to Ravenna, where we road along the sand through the waves of the sea. This tour was continual discussion which lasted from coffee in the morning, all through the dust of the Lombardy roads, to the round-bellied Chianti in the evening, and continued even in our dreams." (CE 12; CW 18, § 1715).

[518] On December 7, 1957 Kurt Wolff wrote to Erwin Panofsky inquiring regarding the possibility that what Jung saw may have been mosaics at another location (BL). On May 3, 1958 Jung gave the physicist Max Knoll the following account of what he saw (as relayed by Knoll to Cary Baynes, July 19, 1959, BL)

Arose in connection with an idea about the conception of baptism as initiatory trauma (like water hole in the cave into which the intitiate was pushed). / He was first with a friend in the tomb, whose interior seemed particularly impressive to him

Once I was in a very melancholic mood. I went on a long walk starting at Scuol,[519]and got as far as the Cheu de la Stria ("stria" means witch).[520] I sat on a bench and lit a cigarette. All of a sudden, I sensed something above my head and when I turned around, I saw that a goat was sniffing at the smoke! I put the cigarette into its mouth and behold! She held it between her lips which of course looked very funny. Then I gave her another, but she ate that one. And as I continued sitting there, all of a sudden I felt something on my cheek: the goat was rubbing her head tenderly against mine! Then of course my melancholy completely disappeared!— The remarkable thing is that the "strias" are thought of as being goats.

I was later in the Val del Strega (this is the same area); there I saw a man who twenty years before had met a *strega* and since that time had never spoken another word. When one loses one's way and meets a goat one can easily decide to follow it believing it would be going back to the goat shed. But far from it! Goats can lead you terribly astray. That is

---

this time (as if filled with blue light). Then they went to the window level (1) Baptism of the Jordan (2) Red Sea (3) Lazarus (4) Sinking Peter (Galilee) clear and distinct. [. . .] Jung learns that Galla Placida had a votive image of the same content placed at this place because of the rescue from distress at sea on the voyage from Constantinople, but that it was destroyed in the 12th century. A sketch of it is still in the Ambrosiana.

Ron Huggins has convincingly shown that what most likely happened was that Jung mistook the figure emerging from the water in the baptismal scene on the ceiling of baptistry for Peter, rather than a personification of the River Jordan, and linked this with the Latin inscriptions in the four arches: "Jesus, walking on the sea, takes the sinking Peter by the hand, and at the command of the Lord, the wind ceased" (paraphrase of Matthew 14:29–32); "Blessed are they whose iniquities are forgiven, and whose sins are covered. Blessed is the man to whom the Lord hath not imputed sin" (Psalm 32 [31]:1–2a); "When Jesus had laid aside his garments, and put water in a basin and he washed the feet of his disciples" (paraphrase of John 13:4–5); "He hath set me in a place of pasture. He hath brought me up, on the water of refreshment" (Psalms 23 [22]: 2, Douay-Rheims). Ronald V. Huggins, "What Really Happened in Ravenna? C. G. Jung and Toni Wolff's Mosaic Vision," *Phanês* 3 (2020): pp. 76–115. Huggins argues, "Jung and Toni Wolff go to see the Baptistery of the Orthodox. Jung begins translating and explaining what is written above the arches. When he comes to the one about Peter sinking, he starts to make connections to other links between baptism and death in the larger iconographical program of the baptistery. He points out the mosaic in the centre of the ceiling that seemed to him to represent a combined scene of the baptism of Jesus by John and the saving of Peter from sinking down in the water. He calls her attention as well to the three stuccos of Daniel, Jonah, and the triumphant Christ. Afterwards he recalls all these details as being presented in four mosaics. But the ultimate organising basis for his memory was provided by the four arches with their Latin inscriptions." (p. 108).

[519] Scuol: a region in the Engadine.

[520] "Cheu de la Stria" (Romansch): "the Witch's Head," a rock outcrop in the Engadine. Italian *strega* (see the next paragraph) also means "witch."

apparently what happened to that man: he was out hunting and returned home completely at his wits end and confused. He had even thrown away his gun, his clothes were torn, and he had been away several days. He never spoke again![521]
[131]

AUGUST 16, 1957

[522]The life of a person is an extremely questionable experiment. Only numerically is it an incredible phenomenon. It is so fleeting, so unsatisfactory, that it is simply a miracle that something might come of it. That became very clear to me even as a young medical student, and I thought it would be a veritable miracle if I myself were not destroyed prematurely. So to me, life has always seemed like a plant that lives from a rhizome. The actual life of the plant is not visible at all. It is hidden in the rhizome. The visible plant lasts only one summer. Then it decays. It is an ephemeral emergence.

What remains from what I have created? Perhaps one day it will gather dust in the libraries, and no one will know about it. And what had survived from what my father, the pastor, knew? He was an Arabist and knew seven oriental languages.[523] Nothing of that remains for me.

No one can take everything from what I have created. Everyone takes a small part. And despite this, I continue to work and *must* go on working? Man is a phenomenon. He enacts it as a singular occurrence which comes and then decays. Like the blossom on the rhizome. Just consider the flowering of imperial Rome: in complete safety one could travel to Constantinople from Rome. With stagecoaches, and in only five days. Back then you could travel more safely than today. Back then they also built ships bigger than the ones built in Europe a hundred years ago. Massive grain ships. Then all of that disappeared and it was hundreds of years before such things appeared again. The post also functioned superbly back then, throughout the Roman empire. Then it stopped. And

[521] On August 5–8 Jung had filmed interviews with Richard Evans (McGuire and Hull, C. G. *Jung Speaking*, pp. 276–352).

[522] See *ETG*, p. 11, *MDR*, p. 4.

[523] See pp. 79–82 above. Johann Paul Achilles Jung's dissertation at the University of Göttingen was entitled "Ueber des Karäers Jephet arabaische Erklärung des Hohenliedes." Among the languages he knew were Arabic and Hebrew. On Jung's father's philological work, see Joel Ryce-Menuhin, "Jung's Father, Paul Achilles Jung and the 'Song of Songs': An Introduction," in Ryce-Menuhin, ed., *Jung and the Monotheisms: Judaism, Christianity and Islam* (London: Routledge, 1994), pp. 233–40.

not until the princes of Thurn and Taxis was something painstakingly rebuilt.[524] One has—when one thinks of all this becoming and fading away—the impression of absolute futility, but on the other hand, one always has the feeling: Down below, there is something that remains. What one sees is the blossom and that withers, the rhizome remains. That is why what I have described as the "becoming conscious of being" seems to me so vital. That pushes into "the rhizome." Fundamentally, I have developed Schopenhauerian ideas further. He said that man holds a mirror up to God,[525] and shows that the world is full of suffering. But that fails to express life and therefore I say further that an existence without suffering is also imaginable. But that can be the case only if a consciousness is present that knows it is not suffering. To have a consciousness only of suffering: that does not express life.—In the East one strives to overcome the thousand things. But that is insufficient. One might assume that such awareness would also be an eternally enduring fullness; then the unconscious would be the void.[526] But in this void, the fullness would also be already present. Consciousness is the representation of the world. [132/133]

AUGUST 1957[527]

In an infinite world painful limitation no longer exists, and contained within it is also the possibility of a complete evolution. Life in the fourth dimension no longer has limited expansion, but instead is unlimited expansion. As a consequence, here and now I am dreaming of a far greater capacity. However, I can engender this unboundedness around me only by not considering that what I am is my own "property." It is a suchness, but not *my* gift, *my* beauty, etc. And when one knows that, then one's desires change accordingly. When one understands that and really feels it, one is already connected to the unbounded in this life. Then one feels limited only when one has limited intentions. Not being world enough for oneself—that is the basis for envy and jealousy. Also, in a relationship

---

[524] The princely house of Thurn and Taxis: in the sixteenth century the Taxis family became the imperial couriers of the Holy Roman Empire, the service that subsequently became the Imperial Reichspost. When that was dissolved at the beginning of the nineteenth century, the company maintained a monopoly as the Thurn-und-Taxis Post.

[525] In this clause, Jaffé changed "Mensch" (man) to "Intellekt" (intellect), and "Gott" (God) to "Wille" (will), by hand.

[526] Cf. Jung's description of the pleroma in the first sermon to the dead (*LN*, p. 509).

[527] At some time in August, Jung thanked Kurt Wolff for sending him Alan Watts's book on Zen, adding that "the psychology of Zen, as you know, has long interested me" (JP).

it is crucial whether, within it, boundlessness is given expression or not. Because eternity is the essential thing. As far as the questions of humanity are concerned, it makes no difference whether someone is a man or a woman. The decisive question in life is: Are we related to the infinite or not? That is the real criterion. Then we can put personal sensitivities to one side. We still have them, these sensitivities, but they no longer define us.

What defines a relationship is boundlessness. The other things are personal characteristics that play a part when one assumes rights of possession. When one fails to know that this boundlessness is the essential thing, then one misplaces what defines one in futilities, in things that are absolutely not definitive.

The more false the possession is, the less satisfactory, and the more one insists that one is young or beautiful, or can do something or has something, because what is essential is not present. Then one makes up stories as if that were the essential thing. What makes you happy, what is really alive and lasting, is the infinite. Then one can no longer insist that one amounts to something because of this or that. One counts for something because of the essential; and if one does not have that, then nothing works at all.

I can have boundlessness only if I am quite finite. The self is the greatest confinement of man. It is the experience of "I am *only* that."[528] In the consciousness of the self is found the narrowest of confinements, but this is tied to the infinity of the unconscious. If I experience eternity within me, then I am limited and eternal, the one and the other. That is the fusing together into the one.

By being singular in my personal combination, meaning incredibly limited, I then have the possibility of consciousness of the infinite. But only then.—For this reason, it is so important in an epoch like ours where one must be conscious, to be conscious of one's uniqueness. In an aeon that aims exclusively at the enlargement of consciousness, it is imperative that one have objective and actual insights rather than insisting on non-essential "possessions." [134/135]

I once had a patient whom I pulled out of a habitual depression. It was mainly psychogenic. Soon after, he married a woman who had chosen him mainly for his money. Of course, she immediately worked against me out of jealousy. I had agreed with him if something happened to him that he should turn to me straight away. But he did not do that. When I saw the wife for the first time, I knew immediately: Something evil is going on

---

[528] Cf. "tvat tvam asi" (that which you are), *Chandogya Upanishad* 6.8.7.

there. As often happens with women who do not really love their husband and they destroy his friendships. They want him to completely belong to them because they themselves in fact do not belong to him. This is the core of every jealousy.—Then the man got a depression, a year after the wedding. But he said nothing to me about it.

[529]At that time, I gave a lecture in Bern. I arrived at the hotel around midnight—people had stayed behind after the lecture—then I went to bed and could not go to sleep for a long time. Around 1 a.m, no, nearer 2 a.m., I finally fell asleep. But not much time had passed, I must have been asleep for only a relatively short time.—Then at 2 a.m. I awoke, believing that someone had come into my room. The door flew open, and someone was in the room. I immediately put on the light, there was nothing. I thought perhaps someone had come to the door by mistake, so I opened the door to the corridor, everything was dead silent. Strange, somebody really did come into the room!

Then it occurred to me that I had been awoken by something crashing into my forehead and then colliding at the rear wall of my skull.—The next day I received a telegram that that patient had committed suicide at precisely that time. Later I learned that the bullet had got stuck in the rear wall of his skull. I had awoken in high anxiety. I thought: By God, someone has come into the room! I could not imagine what might have happened. What devil has appeared? The emotion of the patient or his anxiety communicated itself to me. The whole evening, I had been strangely restless and nervous. The clock is five hours ahead. So, in New York it happened in the early evening.[530]

---

[529] See *ETG*, p. 143, *MDR*, p. 137.

[530] The patient in question was George French Porter (1881–1927). He was an American businessman, collector, and philanthropist from Chicago and a patient of Jung and of William Alanson White. It was on Porter's invitation that Jung traveled to America in 1924–25, and Porter financed the trip. In September 1926 he suffered a neck injury from a car accident, and in February 1927 he was planning to visit Jung in Zurich. On February 24 he shot and killed himself. The news was carried on the front page of that day's *Chicago Tribune*, which reproduced his suicide note to his wife, in which he wrote, "This fate was on me—the inevitable conclusion to a twisted life." The *Tribune* described him as a "sufferer from melancholia." Barbara Hannah noted, "When he died [. . .] Jung was much distressed and said that if he had only known about George Porter's difficulties he would have gone to America at once to do all he could to help him." Hannah, *Jung: His Life and Work*, p. 158. His estate was worth $5 million, and he bequeathed Jung $20,000. Franz Jung informed William McGuire that it proved to be "mining stock of slight value": McGuire, "Jung in America, 1924–1925," *Spring: An Annual of Archetypal Psychology and Jungian Thought*, 1978: 37–53. See *Chicago Tribune*, February 24 and May 6, 1927; and *New York Herald Tribune*, March 4, 1927. For a further account of this episode with further details and reflections, see below, p. 249.

This is an example of the communicability of anxiety. Another example, [135/136] not from my own experience, is the following: a six-year-old girl wakes in the night with anxiety and runs to her mother. Her mother was in that moment about to commit suicide and was saved by her daughter. [136/137]

[531]When I was a student, already in the clinical semester, I once came home very tired and sat down on the sofa and was almost falling asleep; and then very quietly and distantly I heard a beautiful alto voice singing an aria in the style of Handel. Due to my great tiredness, I began to drop into slumber but without *actually* sleeping. In this state akin to sleep I heard this voice quite close by, much closer than before. As if it had come into the next room. A beautiful voice. I listened for a long time, and I also perceived something like a distant musical accompaniment. "Curious," I thought, "but there is no one there! And anyway: no one can sing like that, no one has such a wondrous voice." Then I got closer to waking up and the voice faded further away again. But it still sounded ravishingly beautiful. I could not understand at all what it was.[532]

I recalled this voice as I sat that winter evening in Bollingen, and I heard the kettle singing as the water simmered.[533]

I had a similar experience yesterday evening. In my internal ear I perceived a song of Brahms. As if a great female singer was ministering to me in the most gentle way: "I'll sing you the Brahms song and then you'll fall asleep for sure."—Just like that! It was wonderful, simply wonderful. And then I slept like a baby.

AUGUST 25, 1957

Question about his kinship with Goethe.

[534]My great-grandmother and her sister were involved, I don't know exactly how, in the theater in Mannheim. Goethe was there, and it is said that this Sophie Ziegler,[535] who was my great-grandfather Jung's wife, had a child with him (Goethe). Schiller was in Mannheim at that time.

---

[531] The fragment that follows is from *EG*, p. 62.

[532] In 1907 Jung referred to a "young colleague" who, on finishing his dissertation, "was impelled to whistle for half the day Handel's 'See, the Conquering Hero Comes.'" *CE* 4; *CW* 3, § 115.

[533] See below, p. 262.

[534] See *ETG*, p. 399.

[535] In a letter of December 30, 1959 to his cousin Ewald Jung, Jung commented on Sophie Ziegler's mental illness. *Letters*, vol. 2, pp. 527–29.

The two Ziegler sisters moved in these artistic circles. So, it is alleged that this child was my grandfather. He himself mentions nothing of this in his biography. But it was simply generally known. It was common knowledge. My great grandparents' marriage was unhappy. This we know. And she suffered from depressions. It was taken for granted that her son was by Goethe. Later she was on friendly terms with Lotte Kestner,[536] who later settled near my grandfather. This Lotte Kestner was like an aunt to my uncles, the children of Prof. Jung. For example, she often visited with them as, by the way, did Liszt,[537] in order to see my grandfather. It was something that was taken for granted. He himself never spoke about it. But one could say it is not impossible. My grandfather told how he saw Goethe in Weimar, but only from behind! My grandfather moved from Mannheim to Heidelberg and studied there. His father was a resident of Mannheim. But my grandfather did not get on well with his father, he was completely different from him. He converted to Protestantism under the influence of Schleiermacher.[538] He was a private scholar at the military academy and read physics and chemistry. He was close friends with the Reimer household.[539] Mrs Reimer was like a mother to him. He met the Schlegels and the Tiecks.[540] But that is striking too: he came to Berlin and was immediately received in all of these literary circles. He himself had a certain poetic gift. One of the poems was published in the *Teutschen Liederbuch*.[541] He was a member of a student fraternity, a friend of the murderer of Kotzebue (Sand),[542] and for that he spent thirteen months incarcerated in the Berlin city prison. Then he was banned from Prussia and went to Paris [137/138] where, in precarious circumstances, he met Alexander

---

[536] Charlotte Buff-Kestner (1753–1828). In 1772, Goethe fell in love with her, but she was already engaged. This formed the background of his novella *The Sorrows of Young Werther* (1774).

[537] The famous Hungarian composer and pianist Franz Liszt (1811–1886).

[538] See above, p. 59.

[539] Ximena de Angulo noted that the context suggests that this must have been Friedrich Wilhelm Riemer (1774–1845), a literary historian who worked in Goethe's household, and edited his works ("A. J.'s Protocol," p. 27, filed with the protocols of the Interviews, Jung Collection, Manuscript Division, LC).

[540] Friedrich Schlegel (1772–1829), German poet, critic, and philosopher; Ludwig Tieck (1773–1853), German poet, novelist, and critic. Both were leading figures in the Romantic movement.

[541] Carl Gustav Jung (the elder)'s "Blaue Nebel steigen von der Erde auf (Abendlied 1813)" appeared in the popular student songbook the *Allgemeines Deutsches Kommersbuch* (1858).

[542] Karl Ludwig Sand (1795–1820), German student and member of the *Burschenschaften* student fraternity, who was executed for the murder in 1819 of the conservative dramatist August von Kotzebue (1761–1819).

von Humboldt.[543] Then he became an assistant doctor with one the of the best-known surgeons. Then Humboldt wrote a reference for him to Prof. . . . in Basel.[544]

The remarkable thing: my grandfather had only one sister.[545] She lived in a convent for noble ladies. She came to Basel only once or twice to visit her brother and she never married. Goethe also had a sister. Of whom he related that she could never go into society because she had urticaria, and my sister suffered from the same malady. I too have only one sister.—Very little is known about my grandfather's sister, but from her character she appears to have been quite similar to my sister: she had a rather stiff demeanor. I already told you that my sister had a fanciful demeanor. I always had the feeling that the three of them had something in common: Cornelia Goethe, my grandfather's sister, and my sister.[546] [547] [138/139]

SEPTEMBER 23, 1957

Dream of Toni Wolff.[548]
She returned. It was as if a sort of misunderstanding had happened that she had died and she had come back to go on living a further part of her life as if she had died through a misunderstanding and now she was back again.

I can understand this only as the anima.

(Question whether this could refer to a possible reincarnation.)
With my wife I have the feeling of a much greater detachment or distance. With Toni, it struck me that she is still close by.

(Question whether it is not literally conceivable that something that was not settled in life must now be made up for in another life.)

---

[543] Alexander von Humboldt (1769–1859), German naturalist and explorer.

[544] Humboldt's recommendation was to Bürgermeister (mayor) Johann Heinrich Wieland, and the letter is reproduced in Huldrych M. Koelbing, "Die Berufung Karl Gustav Jungs (1794–1864) nach Basel und ihre Vorgeschichte," *Gesnerus* 34 (1977): 318–30. Koelbing also reproduced a letter he received from C. G. Jung in 1954 about his grandfather.

[545] See above, pp. 262–63.

[546] See above, pp. 94–95.

[547] Over September 1–7, 1957 Jung participated in the International Congress of Psychiatry, held in Zurich. His paper "Schizophrenia" was read out by his grandson, Dieter Baumann (1928–2020), psychiatrist and analytical psychologist.

[548] This dream has not been found, but Jung had similar dreams of Toni Wolff on April 4, 1953, January 5, 1954, and November 26, 1956 (*BB* 7 [continuation], pp. 194, 202, and 226).

My wife achieved something that Toni did not achieve.—The reincarnation would be an incredibly profound revival of actuality. Even though something profound animates actuality, that is still no criterion for it actually being the case. However, one cannot prove it that it is not so. That would be as if one did not know the healing properties of plants and then one was to eat certain plants during an illness and find that they had a very good effect. Then one would not doubt the healing powers. For example, the effect of digitalis was known long before one knew anything of digitalis. One found out through experience what effect it had. One discovered the healing effect of a plant from practical experience.—The criterion of a metaphysical truth such as reincarnation could be located in the fact that this idea brings with it some healing potential or a reanimation of actuality. Just as there are plants, like coca for example, that have a refreshing effect, this too has it; and this has been known for ages, for thousands of years, the Indians knew it well and used it. A frozen Inca boy was found high in the mountains where he had been offered as a sacrifice. He is seven hundred years old. And he had coca leaves in his hand. So coca was already used back then, [139/140] and it was known for simply having this effect. So there could also be ideas that have this effect and therefore, one simply has them; whether they can be proved is another question. It is not a sure thing whether a strange healing effect does not dwell within this thought. Whether perhaps metaphysical processes are taking place that are absolutely imperceptible to us, that cannot be ruled out.

I just might be conscious of the impression that Toni was still closer to the earth, that she was able to manifest herself to me better, whereas my wife is on another level into which I cannot reach. Toni is where one might be able to reach her. I have deduced from this that she was much closer and so then she is naturally closer to the sphere of three-dimensional existence and would therefore have the chance to slip back into existence. With her I have the strong impression, or in fact the knowledge, that she has not achieved that state where a continuation of three-dimensional existence of life would have no more meaning. If that means anything, it means that you reach certain levels of insight, that you then no longer have to return. Higher insight inhibits the wish to be reincarnated. This is nirvana, that one escapes the three-dimensional world. But when karma remains unresolved, then one falls back into desires, one puts oneself back into the world in order to live it, perhaps even from the insight that something must still be completed.

(Question about the origins of Bollingen)[549]

[550]At first there was only the one (large) tower. Then the building was added that now stands in the middle, between the two towers. The first tower originates from 1923, then in 1927 the central building was added, but only the small outer room, the lower work room, and the guest room. In 1931, there followed the lower small fireplace and the small tower, and again four years later, in 1935, the outer annex was added, containing the small house within it. Over twelve years the various parts of the building were developed. And then twenty years passed, and I completed it: so that's the fourth one. It's as if the house grew together with me, and everything is highly symbolic.

[551]In 1903, with the associations experiment, my actual work had begun, I mean my actual creative work.[552] I consider this to be my first scientific work. The dissertation,[553] that did not yet express my own ideas. But with the discovery of complexes in the unconscious, it began for real.

Then the next thing was in 1917 with the French edition of the *Relations*,[554] but I found that everything was still completely hanging in the air. Then I decided that I had to come down to earth and that I must also respond to Freud and Adler. So, then the *Types* book emerged, and through that I came down to earth. (In 1912 the book on *Transformations* was published which initiated the split from Freud).[555] What was crucial in my coming down to earth was the *Types* book. It was finished eight years after the split from Freud.

[556]Integral to this "coming down to earth" was my representing in stone my innermost thoughts, my very being as it were, and that had to be, so I thought at the time,—in the form of a round hut. And that was the beginning of Bollingen. At first, I didn't want a tower, but only to make the building a single-storey structure. The idea was a round

[549] Jung first acquired his land at Bollingen on the upper shore of Lake Zurich in 1922. In a postcard to Otto Duthaler written on October 27, 1920 he described his plan for it to be a "just a room for refuge": see Wehr, *Illustrated Biography*, p. 68.

[550] See *ETG*, p. 227, *MDR*, pp. 223–24.

[551] See *ETG*, pp. 210–11, *MDR*, pp. 206–7.

[552] Jung and Franz Riklin, "Experimental Researches on the Associations of the Healthy" (1904), *CE* 3; *CW* 2.

[553] "On the Psychology and Pathology of So-Called Occult Phenomena" (1902), *CE* 2; *CW* 1.

[554] Published as "La structure de l'inconscient," *Archives de psychologie* 16 (1916): 152–79.

[555] *Transformations and Symbols of the Libido* (1912), *CE* 6; *CW* B.

[556] See *ETG*, pp. 227–28, *MDR*, pp. 223–24.

building with a stove in the middle. I wanted to build just a fairly primitive dwelling. Then only when I had begun to build did it occur to me that it must have two storeys. It must not simply huddle near the ground. Then I began to paint the walls. In the [141/142] kitchen there is a painted sculpture depicting the individuation process. I started that in 1923. Bollingen was a great thing for me, because word and paper were not real enough for me. I had a confession to declare in stone. This seemed to be a totally crazy idea, but I just did it, and while I was living within it, during the first four years, I had the feeling it was not enough, more must be added. The tower was like a place of maturation, a maternal womb, a maternal figure, in which I was able to be again as I am; I could be the person I most authentically was. The tower was as if I had been reborn in stone. Like a realization of what has been previously thought, or a realiztion of what is inherent within me. A representation of individuation. A monument "aere perennius."[557] And this also had a therapeutic effect.—That was true even in the first years when only the large tower was there. Then came the feeling: That is not everything, more must still be added.

So then came the cellar, the small work room, the guest room. The original idea of the hut was that it should be a round room with the stove in the center and beds on the walls. But that was not sufficient. A proper house had to be added. And after a further four years I had the feeling: Everything has still not been said, something more must yet be added. In its current form, it is still too primitive. The spiritual distinctiveness is not yet in it. It was too simple and chthonic. So, the extension with the chapel was added. And that was enough until I got the open space. I had the feeling that we needed still a piece of land, a piece of earth. I must have a bigger space under the heavens. And this piece was again a thing "on its own," like a separate undertaking. As I was making it, it became clear to me; it expressed itself in this way: My wife associates the tower with the kitchen. Here, spiritual and physical are intermingled: bedroom and kitchen at the same time. And within it were the spiritual symbols as images on the walls. But this was too mixed for me. The one must be distinguished from the other. Thus the second tower emerged, representing Toni Wolff, and the space in the open air. The chapel is something exclusively spiritual.[558] Inside, I projected myself onto the walls. Partly as a process

---

[557] From Horace, *Odes* 3.30: "Exegi monumentum aere perennius" (I have erected a monument more lasting than bronze).

[558] Referred to in *ETG* simply as a "secluded room" (p. 228, *MDR*, p. 224).

of growth from below, and partly as an influx from above. But the fourth was still missing. That was the small house between the towers. So, originally it was a trinity and a discrete quaternity. Then I saw that the rear building that was so hidden away in the ground, that was *me*! Not until my wife had died was I able to build up the rear section. Before that I could not. It seemed to me to be presumptuous self-emphasis.

Originally, I wanted to erect this hut on the island opposite. Due to a political affair in the locality I could not acquire the land there. This area is the landscape of St. Meinrad.[559] This is ecclesiastical land that used to belong to the monastery of St. Gallen.[560] And the distinctive charm of the lake captivated me from the very beginning. So, it had to be on the lake, come what may.

Bollingen expresses my relationship to the contemporary environment, as if an ancient seed has sprouted. It all comes from the fact that it is like my relationship to nature; and that is exquisitely historical.

SEPTEMBER 30, 1957[561]

When I compare myself as I am today with what I was at the beginning! Such an incredible difference: I have, so to speak, never recovered from my early life.[562] All my work, everything that I have achieved intellectually comes from these original sources of imaginations and dreams that I have related to you. Nearly fifty years have passed since then.

The imaginations started in 1912.[563] It's not quite fifty years ago. Everything that I have done in my later life is contained within them, partly in the form of tremendous emotion, partly formulated quite incompletely. It's as good as I was able to formulate it at the time, with my limitations in language. I was simply hopeless under it all. I made a great effort to follow the psychic presuppositions out of which these images appeared.[564] It's as if massive individual blocks were crashing down upon me that barely hung together. One thunderstorm released the next. And I was able to express this only in extremely clumsy language. It's a miracle that it

---

[559] Saint Meinrad of Einsiedeln (799–861), an ascetic hermit. The thirteenth-century St. Meinrad chapel in Bollingen is not far from Jung's tower.

[560] Initially an eighth-century Carolingian abbey, with one of the finest surviving medieval libraries.

[561] Kurt Wolff was in Zurich during this time and had meetings with Jaffé and Jung.

[562] See *ETG*, p. 196, *MDR*, p. 192.

[563] See *BB* 2.

[564] See *ETG*, p. 180, *MDR*, p. 177.

didn't break me into pieces. Others would have been shattered by it. For example, Schreber, he's one who was broken by it.[565]

These were matters that didn't concern me alone. I already had the feeling back then that there was a message to the world, coming to me with superior force, and I knew it was not yet the right language in which I was writing it down. I would still need to translate it. My scientific work then developed out of it. The first form, that was a type of elevated common sense.[566] I was not hearing it only for myself, but also for everyone else.

The phallus of the first dream must not be interpreted only in a Freudian way.[567] In a certain sense, however, it should indeed be interpreted in a Freudian way, because the phallus is a primal experience. But it is not the penis. It's a question of the terrible, mythological presence, like the sacred phallus that is worshipped underground in India.[568]

So things came to me in this form, in these imaginations; I wrote them down as they were presented to me. It presented itself to me in such a way that I don't know what sort of relationship I have with it, since it simply besieged me and I wrote it down.[569] The language that is the style of archetypes; that's how they speak. In part, it's a style that's embarrassing to me, and which gets on my nerves, as if someone is dragging their nails on a board, or like a knife on a plate. And that's how it was because I didn't know what it was all about. And so I had absolutely no choice.

Sometimes it was as if I was hearing with my ears. Sometimes I felt it in my mouth, as if my tongue was formulating words, and then I would

---

[565] Daniel Paul Schreber (1842–1911), a German judge who was eventually institutionalized. In 1903, he published an account of his experiences in *Denkwürdigkeiten eines Nervenkranken* (Leipzig: Oswald Mutze), translated as Schreber, *Memoirs of My Nervous Illness*, ed. and trans. Ida Macalpine and Richard A. Hunter (London: W. Dawson, 1955), which Jung cited in 1907 several times in his *Psychology of Dementia Praecox* (CE 4; CW 3). Schreber's work was the centerpiece of Freud's "Psycho-Analytic Notes on an Autobiographical Account of Paranoia (Dementia Paranoides)" (1911), *SE* 11. ETG and MDR replace the mention of Schreber with "Nietzsche and also Hölderlin and many others" (pp. 180 and 177 respectively). Michael Fordham recalled encountering Jung reading Schreber around these years. When asked why he was reading him, Jung stated that some of his prophecies turned out to be valid (Fordham to the editor, personal communication, 1988). Jung's copy of Schreber's book has many annotations. On Schreber, see especially Zvi Lothane, *In Defense of Schreber* (Hillsdale, NJ: The Analytic Press, 1992).

[566] "common sense": in English in the original.

[567] See above, pp. 39–40.

[568] A reference to the Shiva linga.

[569] See *ETG*, p. 181, *MDR*, p. 177.

hear myself whispering a word. Under the threshold of consciousness everything was alive, and there, everything was already expressed.

[570]At that time, I was so full of emotions that I used yoga exercises I had learned in order to switch off my emotions. I had to do these exercises in order to master the terrible inner excitation. But, of course, since I wanted to be aware of what was happening, I did the yoga exercises only to a certain degree in order to calm myself down and only until I was able to work with the unconscious again. I only restrained the emotions so that I was calm once again. When I had recovered, when I had the feeling of being myself again, then I had to relax control again and give the word to the kleshas,[571] whereas it is the aim of the Indians to completely eliminate the kleshas through yoga. If I had just stayed with the emotion, it would have torn me to shreds or I would have been able to split off from it and then I would have landed in a neurosis and would have been torn apart by it anyway. Therefore, it is my view that one is healed if one is able to find the images that lie behind the emotions—behind the emotions that are causing the neurosis.

These images, they all came to me from within, without external events being present which could have explained them. My dreams and visions, they didn't come from outside, but rather they were in the air. They were also precognitions; for example, the premonitions of the war in 1914.[572] We lived in a peaceful world and there were no personal entanglements either. They first came through the work on *Transformations and Symbols of the Libido*. A great deal was stirred up by that.

[573]In 1912, when I drew a line under the manuscript, I wondered, "What have you written, what on earth is this? [145/146] That is the

---

[570] See *ETG*, p. 180. *MDR*, p. 177. It is not clear what yoga exercises Jung engaged in. However, Fowler McCormick, recalling an analytical interview with Jung in 1937, spoke of Jung's recommendation of a procedure not without similarities to the *savasana asana* of Hatha Yoga: "Dr. Jung said that under periods of great stress the one thing which was useful was to lie flat down on a couch or a bed and just lie quietly there and breathe quietly with the sense that [. . .] the wind of disturbance blew over one." Fowler McCormick interview, p. 17, CLM, Jung Biographical Archive.

[571] Georg Feuerstein defined these as follows: "The kleśhas provide the dynamic framework of the phenomenal consciousness. They urge the organism to burst into activity, to feel, to think, to want. As the basic emotional and motivational factors they lie at the root of all misery": Feuerstein, *The Philosophy of Classical Yoga* (Manchester: Manchester University Press, 1980), pp. 65–66.

[572] See above, p. 128.

[573] See *ETG*, p. 174, *MDR*, p. 171. In his 1925 seminar, Jung recalled,

When I finished the *Psychology of the Unconscious*, I had a peculiarly lucid moment in which I surveyed my path as far as I had come. I thought: 'Now you have the myth in which man has always lived. And in which myth does man live today?—In the Christian myth, one might say. Do you live in that?—If I must be honest, no; I could not claim that I live in the Christian myth. For me, it's not what I live.—Then do we no longer have a myth?—Yes, apparently, we no longer have a myth.—Yes, but what is your myth, from which you live?"

Then it became unpleasant, and then I stopped thinking.—A year later, in October 1913, the two visions came while on the journey to Schaffhausen;[574] in 1913 in winter, around Christmas, I had the dream of the white bird; and then in spring—April until June 1914—three times I had the same dream of the onset of the polar frost; and that was a precognition of the war.[575] I know that even before the dream of the white bird arrived I was completely suspended. And I couldn't make anything at all of the dream. I did not know what it meant. [149]

OCTOBER 1, 1957 (BOLLINGEN, WITH KURT WOLFF)[576]

(Discussion of the difference in style in the books by Jung compared with the biographical notes, dreams, fantasies, etc.)

[577]Jung: The one is the *prima materia*, the other is a more or less successful effort at integrating this hot matter into a world. These first imaginations and dreams are like fiery, fluid basalt out of which, later, stone is formed from which one can make something. The fire, that is the passion which resides in this fire; this lava stream has compelled it, and everything has arranged itself quite naturally.

---

key to mythology and you have the power to unlock all doors.' But then something within me said: 'Why unlock all these doors?' And then I found myself asking what I had done after all. I had written a book about the hero, I had explained the myths of past peoples, but what about my own myth? I had to admit I had none; I knew theirs but none of my own, nor did anyone else have one today. Moreover, we were without an understanding of the unconscious. Around these reflections, as around a central core, grew all the ideas that came to partial expression in the book on types. [*1925*, p. 26]

See also his preface to the revised 1952 edition, *Symbols of Transformation* (CE 5; CW 5, p. xxiv).

[574] See above, p. 129.

[575] See above, p. 129. The dream of the white bird occurred around Christmas 1912.

[576] In the early autumn of 1957, Kurt Wolff visited Switzerland prior to going to the Frankfurt Book Fair. On August 13, he wrote to Jaffé that while he would be meeting with Swiss publishers, his main intention was to meet up with her (BL).

[577] See *ETG*, p. 203, *MDR*, p. 199.

(Question as to whether the material for his works comes more from within or from outside.)

I am the most accursed dilettante that has ever lived. I wanted to achieve something in my science and then I encountered this lava stream, and this then arranged everything. I say dilettantism because I live from borrowing; I constantly borrow knowledge from others.[578] What I have done on alchemy and in psychiatry is, in part, original work. Aside from this, I rely on taking cultural material from outside, and I call this dilettantism because I have not created it myself. It was all amassed, and I was somehow able to elucidate it. This is how I also experienced alchemy: I amassed it.

Alchemy, this did not come from within. I read books for about fifteen years in order to find a sort of set of clothes for this primal revelation that I wasn't able to master myself.[579] It cost me forty-five years to capture in some measure the things that I wrote down in the vessel of my work at that time. There were dangerous experiences; for those visions—that is also the material that destroys people. My earliest experience in this regard was Nietzsche. I saw this with him, how a man is destroyed by the plenitude. There is a fullness of power and of imaginative possibility contained in those images.

(Question as to whether *Septem Sermones* would perhaps be in the appendix)[580]

If those records (also from the *Red Book*)[581] are to be taken into consideration, then it should probably be included in the chain of events. It is also one of the events. [149/150]

(On Graf Kuno Hardenberg from Darmstadt)[582]

It was Graf Hardenberg[583] who issued the deportation order from Prussia to my grandfather. He was banned from Prussia because he was a

---

[578] Jaffé added here, by hand, "(Reference to his scientific precision)."

[579] See n. 196 above.

[580] On November 6, 1957 Jung wrote to Jack Barrett of the Bollingen Foundation, "Mrs Jaffé is also authorised to use [. . .] the *Septem Sermones*, as I have already stated in my letter of October 3rd." The *Sermones* were included in the US and German editions of *ETG/MDR*, though not in the first UK edition.

[581] "*Red Book*": in English in the original.

[582] Kuno, Graf von Hardenberg (1871–1938), a painter, art historian, writer, and museum director, who was a friend of Großherzog Ernst Ludwig (see n. 461 above).

[583] Karl August Fürst von Hardenberg (1750–1822), prime minister of Prussia.

friend of Sand who had murdered Kotzebue.[584] He was imprisoned for thirteen months. He was professor of physics and chemistry at the Prussian military academy. So Hardenberg was always the *bête noir* in the history of my grandfather. For this reason, I could not bring his name to mind. My grandfather did gymnastics with Jahn,[585] and was also at the Wartburg festival.[586]

After the deportation he went to Paris. One day he was lying on a bench in the Bois de Boulogne. A man stopped before him and addressed him: "So who are you?" He had recognized that he was a German and spoke to him directly in German. My grandfather told him his sad fate. And who was it who had spoken to him? None other than Alexander von Humboldt.[587] He recommended him to the surgical department of the Hôtel Dieu in Paris. He worked there for several years as a surgeon. And later he went to Basel.

[588]My father was born in Basel. My grandfather married a French aristocrat (de Lascelles)[589] and brought her to Basel. That was his first wife and not my father's mother. This first wife had one single child, a daughter, my aunt, and she married the son of the publisher, Reimer, in Berlin. My grandfather was old Mrs. Reimer's sort of "son."[590] She mothered him and he was in a circle there with Schlegel and Tieck, and he heard Schleiermacher preach. He was Catholic and was converted by Schleiermacher.[591] I did not know Schleiermacher. I read his works only much later. It is astonishing how much of Schleiermacher permeated my grandfather.[592]

Curiously, my grandfather did not get along well with his father, he was completely different from him.[593]This great-grandfather came from Mainz and then went to Mannheim, later to Heidelberg and studied there.

---

[584] See above, p. 143.

[585] Friedrich Ludwig Jahn (1778–1852), a Prussian gymnastics teacher and nationalist, regarded as the *Turnvater*, "father of gymnastics."

[586] A meeting in 1817 of five hundred Protestant students at Wartburg Castle, near Eisenach, protesting against the reactionary politics of the German Confederation, and calling for the formation of a nation state.

[587] See above, p. 143.

[588] See *ETG*, p. 400.

[589] Virginie de Lassaulx (1804–1840).

[590] See above, p. 143.

[591] See above, p. 59.

[592] See above, p. 143.

[593] See *ETG*, p. 237, 399, *MDR*, p. 232.

In the Napoleonic campaign, he headed a military hospital. He had a brother, Sigismund von Jung; he was the Bavarian chancellor.[594]

My family first came to Switzerland in 1822 with my grandfather. After the French first wife of my grandfather had died, he married again, but this wife died very quickly from tuberculosis. She was a Rayenthaler;[595] he then married the daughter of the mayor of Basel.[596] Reimer had another son who married my aunt. The young Reimer later took over the Zeller insane asylum.[597] Old Zeller, he was a Swabian;[598] he was [150/151] the first significant psychiatrist in Germany.

My grandfather's third wife was the daughter of the mayor of Basel.[599] Her maiden name was Sophie Frey. Her father, the mayor, is buried in the cloister of Basel cathedral. And through this marriage the Jungs became Basel patricians. My father is the son of the third wife; he married the daughter of the antistes of Basel.[600] This was the Protestant bishop of Basel.

[601]And now we have reached the time of Burckhardt and Bachofen.[602] I saw both of them as a schoolboy. I often came across both. Burckhardt also taught at the *Gymnasium*; I came across him daily. He shuffled so and looked rather awkward; he was not exactly dressed very elegantly. He wore a large cravat and high collar. Bachofen, on the other hand, trav-

---

[594] Sigismund von Jung (1745–1824), probably the Johann Sigmund Jung also known as "Columella," his code name in the Bavarian Enlightenment secularist secret society the Illuminati.

[595] Elisabeth Catherina Rayenthaler (1810–1833).

[596] Sophie Frey (1812–1855), the daughter of Johann Rudolf Frey (1781–1855).

[597] The Winnenthal insane asylum at Winnenden in Baden-Württemberg, southwest Germany.

[598] Ernst Albert Zeller (1804–1877) directed the Winnenthal asylum from 1834 until his death.

[599] See *ETG*, p. 404.

[600] Emilie Preiswerk Jung (1848–1923).

[601] See *ETG*, pp. 102, 118, *MDR*, p. 101. In *Reflections*, Jaffé indicated Jung's comments about Bachofen and Burckhardt were replies to a question from Kurt Wolff (p. 31). Kurt Wolff had recently published *Letters of Jacob Burckhardt*, ed. and trans. Alexander Dru (New York: Pantheon, 1955).

[602] Johann Jakob Bachofen (1815–1887), jurist and historian, best known for his *Das Mutterrecht: Eine Untersuchung über die Gynaikokratie der alten Welt nach ihrer religiösen und rechtlichen Natur* (Stuttgart: Krais & Hoffmann, 1861), abridged and translated by David Partenheimer as *An English Translation of Bachofen's "Mutterrecht" ("Mother Right") 1861: A Study of the Religious and Juridical Aspects of Gynecocracy in the Ancient World*, 5 vols (Lewiston, NY: Edward Mellen Press, 2003–7) The copy in Jung's library is from 1897, and bears Toni Wolff's bookplate. In 1952 Jung said that Bachofen "influenced my understanding of the nature of symbols" (De Angulo, "Comments on a Doctoral Thesis," p. 208).

eled in a wonderfully elegant coach. He was rich; he had nine million! That was some money back then! He was the owner of the famous White House and I saw him there very frequently.[603] There was also a so-called Blue House next to it. He always wore overtight trousers; he was humorous. Do you know, such thin trousers and stripes and a sort of frock coat; he was very elegant and had a proper pot belly and he looked like a child; he had a round child's face, a proper child's face.

Once Burckhardt had to move to a new house. He came through the front door and watched a furniture remover undertaking the removal. Burckhardt owned a baby grand piano. And the man simply lifted it up onto his back. Burckhardt was completely astounded: Good Lord, it's Atlas!—This was Burckhardt.

Because Burckhardt made such scornful remarks about Bachofen, I began to be very interested in Bachofen. Burckhardt's sister was the grandmother of one of my friends, and I knew all the stories about the grandfather.[604] My friend, he looked like Jacob Burckhardt. He had exactly the same round face and also had the same lisp when he spoke! This was Oeri. The Oeris are a noble house from Zurich that later went to Basel.[605]

I knew all the jokes going around about Jacob Burckhardt from Oeri: he was very important and at the same time he had such childish, [151/152] neurotic traits. Burckhardt had no relationships with women. He was simply a very sensitive introvert. He never married; due to his sensitivity he was too far away from that, far too shy to create a relationship with a woman, and this is why he remained infantile. All the malicious remarks that Burckhardt made about Bachofen and Nietzsche irritated me and made these two men the object of my interest.

I studied Nietzsche before I began psychiatry. I never saw him; he had already retired before my family came to Basel.—Nietzsche was anything

---

[603] A property on the Rheinsprung in Basel.

[604] See *ETG*, p. 102.

[605] Albert Oeri (1875–1950) was a Swiss historian, journalist, and politician. He was the son of Jung's Latin teacher Johann Jakob Oeri, who had been a friend of Jung's father. For many years Oeri was the editor of the *Allgemeine Schweizer Zeitung*. In the 1930s he was an active opponent of National Socialism, and co-founded the National Resistance Campaign. He was a member of Liberal Democratic party, and from 1931 to 1949 and had a seat on the Swiss National Council. Jung wrote to his widow that with his death, "my last living friend has also departed." Jung to Hanna Oeri, December 23, 1950 (*Letters*, vol. 1, p. 569). Jung wrote an obituary for him (JP), which was incorporated in *ETG* (pp. 102–3; this was not reproduced in *MDR*). In 1935 Oeri contributed a piece, "Some Youthful Memories," to the *Festschrift* volume for Jung's sixtieth birthday, *Die kulturelle Bedeuntung der komplexen Psychologie* (see McGuire and Hull, *C. G. Jung Speaking*, pp. 3–10).

but well-off. He was privately supported. I had another friend, a Vischer,[606] whose parents supported Nietzsche. There were people in Basel who realized that he needed support.

(Astounding that Burckhardt had such different tastes than we do today. Question about the transformation of taste through the centuries).
It is astounding what Burckhardt did not see in Italy, and how he saw.[607] He even found no way of relating to Ravenna! But these are simply the transformations of taste. Goethe did not see Giotto![608] That is a psychological prejudice that accompanies secular transformations. A genius is also subject to the fashion of the day because he is a mouthpiece of his time. It is astounding how limited Burckhardt was in his judgment: this inability to recognize Ravenna! And yet, all in all, there was a cosmopolitan and international atmosphere in Basel at that time. I saw the difference when I came to Zurich. It felt as if I had relocated to a village. The relationship of Zurich to the world is not one of spirit, but of trade.

In Basel too there were tradesmen, the *Bändeliherren*.[609] They made the necessary money for the others who were intellectually connected to the world. One section of the Baselers were proper hucksters and money makers, but then this money flowed profitably to the university.—One must also not forget that Basel is a border town, so this extraordinary syncretic spirit developed between France, Germany, and Switzerland.

But the language in Basel was not French, as it was, for example, in Bern, but it was strictly Basel-German. It is in the Sundgau, and it lies nearer to the Alsace than to Zurich. After the Middle–High German period it took another turn away from the developments in the language. We could directly read a Walter von der Vogelweide from Swiss German.[610] As early as the pre-Reformation period, the German language developed more in the direction of the Sundgau than in the rest of

---

[606] See *ETG*, p. 102. Andreas Vischer (1877–1930). After his medical training, he eventually became the director of the missionary hospital in Urfa, Turkey. Vischer was also part of the Basel Zofingia society, and later visited Jung when he was in Paris.

[607] The reference is to Burckhardt's major work of 1860, *The Civilization of the Renaissance in Italy* (see n. 156 above). As the title makes clear, Burckhardt's focus here was on the Renaissance. Jaffé noted in *Reflections* that Jung's remarks were in reply to a statement of Kurt Wolff that Burckhardt's "measure of aesthetic value differed greatly from modern assessements" (p. 33).

[608] While visiting Padua, Goethe did not visit the Scrovegni Chapel, containing Giotto's frescoes.

[609] *Bändeliherren*: literally, "ribbon men," who organized networks of rural home silk weavers around Basel, whose work they financed and sold.

[610] Walther von der Vogelweide (ca. 1170–ca. 1230), famous German lyrical poet.

Switzerland.—Because Basel was also rather isolated due to its cultural development, the phenomenon developed that locality was used as a shield. It's very characteristic of Switzerland in general that locality is used as a shield and a defense. This is a sign of mistrust that the Swiss have by nature. It's typical for Basel that they said of someone whose house was located a small distance from Basel that they were from "beyond the Birs."[611] Whoever does not in live in Basel, lives in "misery." When I went to Zurich, they asked me, "So, when are you coming back? Can you really live in Zurich then?" That's Basel!—Even today I still have a painful weakness for Basel but it's no longer what it once was. I myself still belong in that time where there was a Bachofen and a Burckhardt.

(The topic turned to Wolfskehl, George and so on.[612] I forget the question).
One of their group came to me once and wanted to study my psychology; he was a doctor.[613] But he could not understand the particular psychological point of view. (It was in the Nazi period.) I always thought: Goodness, is he mentally normal? He visited me here and we walked round the lake and one morning, we were strolling up and down along the shore. Suddenly I saw that a bird was flying around us. But it was in fact no bird, but a bat. I thought: What the devil! What on earth is this, a bat in the middle of the day. I thought, now this is a small miracle—a bat in the belfry![614] The next day as we walked around the lake again, the bat returned. "Now it's coming for me and the other one!" The other fellow

---

[611] The Birs is a river that forms the border between Basel and Birsfelden.

[612] Stefan George (1868–1932), German symbolist poet; Karl Wolfskehl (1869–1948), German Jewish writer and friend of George. In 1892 George started publishing a literary periodical, *Blätter für die Kunst*, and gathered around him a group of acolytes known as the George-Kreis (George circle). This included figures such as Friedrich Gundolf, Ernst Kantorwicz, Ludwig Klages, Wacław Rolicz-Lieder, Alfred Schuler, and Albert Verwey. Kurt Wolff knew Georg, and Pantheon published a translation of his poems in 1943. See Lothar Helbing and Claus Victor Bock, eds, *Stefan George: Dokumente seiner Wirkung* (Amsterdam: Castrum Peregrini Press, 1974).

[613] The context suggests that this was Gustav Richard Heyer (1890–1967). Heyer participated in the Stefan George circle in his youth. He worked in Munich and was a member of the Nazi Party from 1937 to 1944. Jung wrote positive reviews of his books *Der Organismus der Seele* (1932) and *Praktische Seelenkunde* (1935) in 1933 and 1936 (*CE* 12 and 13; CW 18, §§ 1774–79). He met Jung in 1928 and had an analysis with him in 1930. Around 1936/37 Jung broke off relations with him. From 1937, he was the training director of the German Institute for Psychological Research. Among his analysands was Rudolf Hess. See Geoffrey Cocks, *Psychotherapy in the Third Reich: The Göring Institute* (New Brunswick, NJ: Transaction Press, 1997).

[614] "a bat in the belfry": in English in the original.

also saw it. It was a bit much for him.—The next day he departed for Munich. He wrote to me then of how he had wanted to go back to work the next day, but he did not feel well, and he had a rather peculiar headache. Then he went walking outside of the town and—there was the bat again! [153/154] He is the only one of my pupils who got completely caught up in Nazism.—The world of George, of homosexuality, these are an integral part of Nazism.[615] They are an expression of its origins. It's a shame George was a poet!

(Freud belongs completely to the nineteenth century. It was essentially about overcoming the nineteenth century.)[616]
But in this nineteenth century quite particular values prevail that one perhaps could recognize only later. The transition from the nineteenth to the twentieth century was an utter catastrophe. It hit me very hard and was very *contrecoeur*.[617] In the twentieth century an entire world perished. I lived through that and paid for it with a great loneliness.

(The orthodox Freudians are people of the nineteenth century)
With Freud himself, I was not surprised. He fitted wonderfully into the Viennese milieu of the nineteenth century. He simply could not see beyond it. He went crazy through his discovery in the next century. But he did not recognize this.

(Question whether the later Freud himself was "Freudian" in the strict sense?)
Later he began to work on concepts which in actual fact were no longer Freudian. That began before London; there was a transformation in him. He saw himself compelled to go along my lines, but he was not able to admit this to himself.

(With Einstein it was similar, in that he no longer understood the ideas of later physicists. But he was completely indifferent to that. "Feel free to carry on!")

---

[615] Stefan George was homosexual. His work was taken up by the Nationalsozialist-ische Deutsche Arbeiterpartei, but he himself was critical of Hitler and Nazism. (Homo-sexuals were persecuted under National Socialism and sent to concentration camps.)

[616] In 1932, in "Sigmund Freud in his Historical Setting," Jung wrote, "Freud [. . .] is an answer to the nineteenth century. That is indeed his chief significance." CE 12; CW 17, § 52.

[617] *contrecoeur*, in French in the original: "with reluctance," "against my will" (lit. "against the heart").

I also knew Einstein.[618] He explained his theory of relativity to me and I had him at my house several times for that purpose. He is a man who, on the one hand, is incredibly naïve, endearingly naïve.

The tragic thing with Freud was that he believed he could keep everything under his hat with his paw on top, but that simply did not work. That is impossible and this is why all his better pupils walked away. Adler, Rank—he was his "own child," and I was the "crown prince."[619] [154/154]

(Question about his grandfather's second wife)
She was a Reyentaler.[620] She was a waitress from the student pub in Basel. He married her out of revenge. In fact, he had tried to win the daughter of the mayor, but the family rejected him. At that time, he was nothing, only a young professor, and given what they were like in Basel, he was nothing! And then he went right into the student pub and married the waitress. But she then died of tuberculosis along with her children.

---

[618] On February 25, 1953, Jung wrote to Carl Seelig,

I got to know Albert Einstein through one of his pupils, a Dr. Hopf if I remember correctly. Professor Einstein was my guest on several occasions at dinner, when, as you have heard, Adolf Keller was present on one of them and on others Professor Eugen Bleuler, a psychiatrist and my former chief. These were very early days when Einstein was developing his first theory of relativity. He tried to instill into us the elements of it, more or less successfully. As non-mathematicians we psychiatrists had difficulty in following his argument. Even so, I understood enough to form a powerful impression of him. It was above all the simplicity and directness of his genius as a thinker that impressed me mightily and exerted a lasting influence on my own intellectual work. It was Einstein who first started me off thinking about a possible relativity of time as well as space, and their psychic conditionality. More than thirty years later this stimulus led to my relation with the physicist Professor W. Pauli and to my thesis of psychic synchronicity. With Einstein's departure from Zurich my relationship with him ceased, and I hardly think he has any recollection of me. One can scarcely imagine a greater contrast than that between the mathematical and the psychological mentality. The one is extremely quantitative and the other just as extremely qualitative. [*Letters*, vol. 2, pp. 108–9]

Einstein's second and third periods in Zurich were 1909–11 (as extraordinary professor at the University of Zurich) and 1912–14 (as professor of theoretical physics at the ETH Zurich). On January 18, 1911 Jung wrote to Freud, "Last Sunday I invited Bleuler over to my place [. . . and] we spent the whole evening talking with a physicist about something far removed from our usual concerns—the electrical theory of light." (*FJL*, p. 384).

[619] Alfred Adler (1870–1937) and Otto Rank (1884–1939) were both prominent members of Freud's circle. In 1912 Adler left to form his own school of Individual Psychology; Rank broke with Freud in 1926.

[620] See above, p. 153.

The other friend, not Oeri, he was called Vischer.[621] He was a doctor of medicine and practiced in Urfa in Mesopotamia. He was at a hospital there—I forget the name of it. He was a sort of missionary doctor and went to Asia Minor during the persecution of the Armenians by the Turks. [147]

OCTOBER 3, 1957

(Jung on his work)

Spiritually I have anticipated a few hundred years, meaning that I have been transposed a few hundred years into the future. That is why I am considered "wise"; and when they say this of me, I seem ridiculous to myself. I fell into an immense hole; that is the fact. My only merit is that I did not drown in it, but I saved my life from it. "Glad to have escaped death," that could be the motto of this autobiography (inscribed in Greek).[622]

My knowledge developed out of the visions and dreams; it was the anxious means by which I wormed my way out of the hole; it was the only option; otherwise, the whole material would have hung upon me like sticky burs, like marsh plants, if I had not removed every little piece from me with the greatest care. Otherwise, it would have been like drowning in a pot of honey. That is what people do not do; they let it rise, perhaps observe it, but they do not take the trouble to understand it and to draw the moral consequences. But when they do not do that, then they fall ruinously into the material.

[623]It is a tremendous responsibility having such images imposed upon you. It gets hold of a person with superior force. But if they believe it can be achieved through science, then that is a stupendous error. For whoever does not regard their perception as an ethical responsibility degenerates into magic. The perception then turns the person into its mouthpiece. That can have good effects, but it also has destructive effects if the ethical responsibility is not recognized. And it not only destroys others, but also the person themselves. The consequences of such imaginations reach into the very depth of life. Otherwise people are devoured by them, and it operates unconsciously—as magic—through them. Why did Goethe write

---

[621] See above, p. 156.

[622] In *ETG* Jaffé noted that Jung recommended this as the motto for the chapter "Confrontation with the Unconscious" (p. 180 n. 4).

[623] See *ETG*, p. 196, *MDR*, p. 193.

Faust? He tried to save himself, but because he ultimately did not know that, he was not saved, but died from it.

You will also see what is driven by fear in my imaginations, to be precise, in the attempts to show how one escapes from this terrible entanglement. In the chapter on the fight with the devil, there you see that quite clearly.[624] Or, for example, the chapter [147/148] with Gilgamesh-Izdubar.[625] It is really crazy; why must I break my head about how to help the dead giant? But I knew: If I do not do my utmost, then I have lost the battle. Then I might claim for a long time that it was merely a fantasy.[626] I would still know, though, that I had failed.

I gave it my all to find the solution, quite unperturbed by how ridiculous it was. I had to find a formula that held the entire meaning of this fantasy, and I would be liberated from it despite this. I paid for this ridiculous solution I found with the insight that I somehow had captured a God. These imaginations are literally a hellish mixture of the most sublime and the most ridiculous. This cost me a tremendous amount, that I was trapped by ridiculous unrealities as in a mouse trap, and that I was able to free the victim only with the greatest courage and effort of will. No one could understand this. I myself did not understand it for the longest time. It is exactly as if someone were drowning in a bathtub and is fooled that it is the ocean.

[627]The *Red Book* is the attempt at an elaboration in the sense of a revelation. It was my hypothesis that if I am equal and faithful to the summons, doing the best that I was able to do, I would then be able to liberate myself. But then I saw for the first time that this by no means achieves the liberation. It became clear to me that I still had to come back completely again to the human side. I understood that I had to return to solid ground, and that is science. I had to draw concrete conclusions from these insights. I gave my life for this. The elaboration in the *Red Book* was necessary, but with it came also the insight into ethical responsibility. I paid with my life and I paid with my science.[628] Only that freed me, the one as well as the other.
[156]

---

[624] "The Red One," *Liber Secundus*, ch. 1, *LN*, pp. 212–13.
[625] "First Day," *Liber Secundus*, ch. 8, *LN*, pp. 277–78.
[626] To be able to carry the wounded Izdubar to find healing for him, Jung's "I" convinced him that he was a fantasy: "Second Day," *Liber Secundus*, ch. 9, *LN*, pp. 293–94.
[627] See *ETG*, pp. 191–92, *MDR*, pp. 188–89.
[628] The last clause was typed over the following: "and that is my devotion to science."

OCTOBER 4, 1957[629]

[630]There was an epoch in my life—it must have been roughly after completing *Transformations and Symbols of the Libido*—in which I played a great deal, as if I were still a child.[631] It was after I had finally separated from Freud, so around 1912, when I felt completely disoriented and I decided at the time, "Now I will make no more interpretations to my patients," and then I noticed that they brought me their dreams spontaneously, and their visions. I asked nothing except, "What do you mean?" "Where does that come from?" "What do you think about it?" And then the interpretation emerged quite spontaneously. I abstained from every point of view. I regarded the material only on its own terms and brought no theoretical presuppositions to it. At the same time, I felt completely disoriented.

[632]This feeling of disorientation was so strong that I thought I must have a psychic disturbance. Twice I thought through my whole life in every detail. I always thought perhaps something lay in my past that I could not see, and which could be considered the cause of the disturbance. But this retrospection too was completely fruitless. Then I thought, "I know nothing at all, so I will now simply do what occurs to me."

Then it occurred to me that I had a period in my youth, perhaps aged ten, when I passionately liked to play with bricks. Building was a favorite pastime for me. I was always building houses out of small stones, or castles or forts, and I made very complicated things with gates that I arched over two bottles. With great attention to detail, I accomplished this with small stones which for the most part I had gathered myself; so, digging and delving and all sorts of funny things. This amused me enormously and it came back to me when I was in that period of disorientation.

---

[629] On this day, Aniela Jaffé wrote to Kurt Wolff, "Prof. Jung today got started once again on the biography. He is now very interested himself but asked me to inquire of you whether you would not take the view that perhaps 15 percent commission could be paid. This request seems justified as he is making available material that is important to him and one can probably count on a high print run." Wolff replied on the following day, "I find that one should not discuss economic matters with Dr. Jung, but should accept his wishes." (BL) In *Reflections*, Jaffé noted that Wolff had read a part of her notes on a visit to Zurich at the end of September for the first time, and requested that Jung speak about his impressions of art, literature, and music. Wolff was particularly interested in the paintings in Jung's house in Seestrasse (p. 23).

[630] See *ETG*, p. 177, *MDR*, p. 173.

[631] See *ETG*, p. 174, *MDR*, p. 170.

[632] See *ETG*, p. 177, *MDR*, p. 173.

I thought, good, now I'll just do that! I gathered together some stones from a stony patch in the garden, some from the lake shore, some from the water, and I began to build little houses and a castle and then I thought there also needed to be a church so I made a square building for a church, with a hexagonal drum upon it and an arch, and then I thought [156/157] a church also needs an altar. But I resisted. I shied away from putting an altar inside it. But one day I was walking along the lake and I was thinking about how to complete the building of the church; I was gathering stones from the shoreline and then, all at once, I saw a red pebble: it was a square pyramid about two centimeters high. This square pyramid, it was a fragment that had been smoothed into this shape by the water, by rolling in the water. A product of pure chance! When I found this stone it became clear to me immediately that it should serve as the altar. I placed it in the middle of the transept crossing, and as I did, it occurred to me, this is the underground phallus from my childhood dream, and I thought: Now it is satisfactory.[633] Then I began to meditate and I wondered: What are you actually doing there? You are building a proper town; you are performing this as a ritual; and then I had the feeling: This is mythology! And then I went to the *Black Book*.

Building, that was the beginning. I always did my building after lunch. As soon as I had finished eating, I played in this way until it was time for my patients to come back. Until 2 p.m., or sometimes even until three, and in the evening if I finished early, then I also worked on building. In that way I clarified my thoughts at that time, and I noticed that a fantasy was in me. Then I wrote it down in the *Black Book*.

This type of thing kept on happening to me: if ever I got stuck, I painted a picture and carved stones, and in every case this was a *rite d'entrée*[634] for subsequent thoughts.

Everything I have produced this year (1957) and last year, so, *Present and Future* and *A Modern Myth*,[635] came out of the work in stone that I did after my wife's death.[636] Including the small model of Bollingen I made—that was also such a *rite d'entrée*.[637] Through this work I reconnected with creativity again.

---

[633] See above, p. 39; and *Art of C. G. Jung*, cat. no. 9 (p. 61).
[634] *rite d'entrée*, in French in the original: "entry/initiation procedure."
[635] CE 26; CW 10.
[636] See *Art of C. G. Jung*, cat. no. 78 (p. 169).
[637] This appears not to have survived. Ulrich Hoerni saw it once, and recalls (personal communication to the editor), "In 1955 C. G. Jung modelled in clay the tower and the

The consummation of my wife, her ending, and what became clear to me in this, took me out of myself enormously. It took a great deal to re-settle myself again.[638] The first thing I felt at the time was: I have yet to become what I myself am. I had the feeling that—if I express it in the language of the house in Bollingen—I can no longer disappear between the two towers, but I must now begin to put the emphasis on myself. So the middle building, that represents me myself, was now enhanced with an upper storey.

There is an important dream I'd like to tell you that also occurred at that time. But I am not entirely sure when exactly it took place. But you can find that out, for it was close to the time when I was painting the mandala that's depicted in the *Golden Flower*.[639] After I had painted it, I received the manuscript that Wilhelm sent me. This mandala actually represents a castle; it always made a strongly Chinese impression on me. The dream is from this period when I was painting it. And this dream is depicted in the image in the *Golden Flower*; this image is a fantasy form arising from the dream.

At that time, I was enormously preoccupied with ideas about where unconscious production ceases, what its purpose is, and I was thinking of it as a development that runs in a singular fashion from the past into the future. I did not think of it as a line of development circumambulating around a center. And then I had this dream:[640] I found myself in a city; it was dirty, filled with smog, it was raining, and it was dark, it was night-time. It was Liverpool. I was walking through this city with a vague num-ber of Swiss people, perhaps half a dozen of them. I had the feeling we had come from the sea, from the port, and the actual city was in fact above, high up on the cliffs. We went up towards it. Now it was like Basel: the market was below, and then the Totengässchen alleyways lead to an upper plateau, where St. Leonhard's and St. Peter's churches are.—So we went along a dark, dimly lit street. It was terribly sinister. We went through this darkness to the upper town. We arrived at the plateau and there, a wide

---

adjoining land, presumably to the scale of 1:100. Occasionally he could be observed sitting on the veranda of his house in Küsnacht, working on it. The vegetation around the tower he represented with model trees from a toy shop. The entire model measured 40×40 cm and was painted in attractive colors. Unfortunately the paint on the inside peeled off a few months later."

[638] See *ETG*, p. 228, *MDR*, p. 225.

[639] *LN*, image 159. See *ETG*, p. 200, *MDR*, p. 197.

[640] Jung recorded this dream on January 2, 1927. *BB* 7, pp. 239–40.

prospect opened up before us. It felt like a larger square surrounded by regular districts. In the center there was a small lake and in the middle of the lake was an island upon which stood a single tree. We walked along the lake and talked together about the disgusting weather of this filthy city, and this darkness. We could not imagine how on earth one could ever live in this city.

I had already noticed before that in the center of the island stood a magnolia tree, covered all over in blossoms and couched in a radiant light with an absolutely paradisical beauty.

Meanwhile the conversation continued. They said a Swiss man lived in this city, at one of the intersections. In the image I marked this point with a magnolia-red dot. He lived there on that corner. And they could not understand how a Swiss man would be living in such a smog-filled city. How on earth could he ever tolerate it. I thought: I know why he lives there: he sees the beauty of this magnolia tree. It had an absolutely celestial beauty that was so perfect one cannot describe it. It was a sun-kissed island of celestial beauty. And an old magnolia tree, densely covered with blossoms. And that in the middle of winter!—Even in the dream I understood that this was the mystery of life. Liverpool is the pool of life. And as I had this thought, that was when then I woke up.

So, this dream, that is my inner situation. I can still see these grey-yellow raincoats, gleaming in the dampness of the rain and everything being terribly joyless. That is how I feel. But I have the inner vision of this celestial beauty, and it is because of this that one can live at all. And then I saw: This is the definitive thing, this is the goal. One cannot get away from the center. The center is the goal, and everything was organized towards this center. From this, I recognized that the self is an archetype of orientation and of meaning. The one Swiss man, that is the I. He lives in one of these filthy streets at one of the intersections. He is a small replication of the center. I know the I is not the center, not the self, but from there, I have a view of the divine wonder. However, I do not live from that, rather I live excentrically so to speak. The small light seemed to me like a reflection of the great light; so, even excentrically, there was something there that reminded me of the primal vision.

After this dream I gave up drawing or painting mandalas. I then understood that there is no linear line of development [159/160] but initially, it is as if development leads upwards from below, up the mountain. That is a unitary linear development. But only when one is at the top, then one sees the great expanse and within it the lake, the island, and the tree of light. I saw something similar later in India: in the temples they have a water pool, and from the reception hall of the temple the God is led processionally to the the pool. He rests in the reception hall.

This dream describes the pinnacle of the entire unconscious development. It completely satisfied me because it completely expressed my situation. I was totally isolated at that time. I knew I was involved with something great that no one understood. This clarification by way of the dream made it possible to observe objectively what was suffusing me. The manuscript that Wilhelm sent me at that time was also the first thing I could connect myself to. I felt the affinity.

The small sidelight was, for me, the I; it was like a memory of the magnificent tree in the center.—The others did not see the tree; I alone saw it. It was as if the sun were shining there, but at the same time, it was as if the blossoms were self-luminous. It was as if this tree were standing in the sunlight. There, it was the full brightness of the day, and it was unbelievably beautiful. Where we were standing, it was dark, cold, and rainy night.

Without such a vision my life would have lost all meaning. But here, the meaning was expressed.

When I split from Freud, I knew then that now I was falling into the unknown. I knew nothing beyond Freud, and I risked the step into the darkness. But then, when such a dream comes, that's an act of grace.

(Question about the strongest impressions from literature)
There are two things that belong to my earliest memories. The earlier one, that's the Grail legend. That was my favorite book. I used to start reading it over again as soon as I had finished it, back to back. That was something absolutely wonderful to me. Since then I knew about the Grail figures. [160/161] I was incredibly fascinated by them. But I never mentioned it in my works because, very early on, my wife began to write about the Grail legends.[641]

The second great literary impression, when I was fifteen or sixteen years old, was *Faust*.[642] My mother said to me, "Now you must read *Faust*." It made the greatest impression on me. Yes, it was *the* book and everything else paled into insignificance beside it. Then there were individual poems by Goethe, but nothing comes close to this impression.

---

[641] See above, p. 120, and *ETG*, p. 169, *MDR*, p. 165.
[642] See *ETG*, p. 65, *MDR*, p. 60.

Then, somewhat later, so when I was a student, I got to know Hölderlin, and that was the poem *Patmos*,[643] and for me, that was the pinnacle. There is something in it of the island with the magnolia tree.[644] "But in the light / Up high blossoms the silver snow; / And witness of eternal life / On unreachable walls / Ancient, the ivy grows. . . ."[645]

And then Mörike's *Orplid*, a splendid poem.[646] I was completely astonished that the other pieces by Mörike were so mediocre. This one poem towers high above all the others.—With Hölderlin, much is mannered, or it has exaggerated emotionality, but *Patmos*, that's the real thing, and *Orplid*. Hugo Wolf set it wonderfully to music in a song.[647]

And then curiously in parallel with my reading of Schopenhauer—he was the first philosopher I read—Vischer's book *Auch Einer* also somehow made sense to me.[648] And then Schopenhauer began, and Kant, and

---

[643] Friedrich Hölderlin (1770–1843) wrote the first version of *Patmos* in 1802. In 1912, Jung would submit the poem to a psychological analysis, finding echoes in it of the Christian mysteries, Mithraism, and Gilgamesh: *Transformations and Symbols of the Libido* (1912), CE 6; CW B, §§ 651–52. Asked in 1954 to write about Hölderlin, Jung replied, "It is now up to the younger generation to open up a few locked doors, perhaps with the help of the keys I have wrought. I see no one at present who could tackle Hölderlin. Such a work is reserved for a distant future." Jung to Mrs. Oswald, *Letters*, vol. 2, p. 193. On Jung and literature, see Shamdasani, *Jung: Biography in Books*.

[644] See above, p. 165.

[645] Friedrich Hölderlin, *Patmos*, v. 3, ll. 8–12.

[646] Eduard Mörike (1804–1875): Jung refers to his *Gesang Weylas* (1831):

You are Orplid, my land!
Gleaming from afar;
your sunny shore steams with mist from the sea,
which moistens the cheeks of Gods.
Ancient waters rise
rejuvenated around your hips, child!
To your divinity
kings bow, who attend you.

[647] Hugo Wolf (1860–1903), an Austrian composer of *Lieder*. A rendition of his *Gesang Weylas* (1888) performed by Dietrich Fischer-Dieskau and Sviatoslav Richter is available at https://www.youtube.com/watch?v=j78AWwfk7eQ (accessed April 25, 2025).

[648] Friedrich Theodor Vischer (1807–1887), *Auch Einer: Eine Reisebekanntschaft* (Stuttgart: Deutsche Verlags-Anstalt, 1884). Jung referred to this in 1898 in his diary (p. 2). In 1914 Jung noted in *BB 3*, "I hardly dare say that Izdubar's fate is grotesque and tragic, for that is what our most sacred life is. Fr. Th. Vischer's A[uch] E[iner] is the first attempt to elevate this truth to a system. He rightly deserves a place among the immortals." (p. 130). In 1921 he wrote, "Vischer's novel, *Auch Einer*, gives a deep insight into this side of the introverted state of the soul, and also into the underlying symbolism of the collective unconscious." *Psychological Types*, CE 9; CW 6, § 627. In 1932 he commented on Vischer in his *Psychology of Kundalini Yoga*, p. 54.

then I was at it in earnest. In later German literature, there's too much psychology in it for me. Much interested me, but it didn't move me in the depths.

I also read Shakespeare's plays and the sonnets, but I experienced them always as typically literary. Even the poetry, yes, it's quite good, but it didn't touch me.—Then I'd rather have Schiller with his ethical pathos; I could relate to him. Of course, I saw the beauty of individual poems but that was only like individual flowers that one finds on the path, and I could not say this or that had made a particular impression on me. But from Mörike, the *Orplid* poem stands out and that is unforgettable. And [161/162] Holderlin's *Patmos* and Goethe's *Faust*.

Goethe's dramas—his style, his grand style, that's too ponderous[649] for me. I read the *Conversations* with Eckermann with great interest but at the same time that's also comic.[650]

Wilhelm Meister,[651] well, now that's very good, but it made no real impression on me.

[652]And then Nietzsche moved me. Above all *Zarathustra*—that moved me powerfully; he became a heavy problem for me. What happened to Nietzsche there? It's Nietzsche's encounter with the old wise man, which however still hovered in the air, in a non-real beyond. The other writings by Nietzsche, they affected me intellectually,[653] but the *Zarathustra* affected me in a human way.—*Faust* always seemed to me like a personal legacy. This story is not finished. A residue remains to which one must make a response.

Faust and *Zarathustra*, they are on the same level, so to speak, they became starting points for me for what is my own.

And then Schopenhauer, that vision of the world, the pessimistic world view, I shared it sometimes, but sometimes I didn't.

With Kant, it was the careful, precise work of differentiation of what belonged to me, of what lay within my reach and of what lies beyond it,

---

[649] "ponderous": in English in the original.

[650] Johann Peter Eckermann (1792–1854), *Gespräche mit Goethe in den letzten Jahren seines Lebens*, 3 vols (Leipzig: F. A. Brockhaus, 1836–48); a recent translation is *Conversations with Goethe*, trans. Allan Blunden (London: Penguin, 2022)).

[651] Goethe, *Wilhelm Meisters Lehrjahre* (1795–96); *Wilhelm Meisters Wanderjahre, oder Die Entsagenden* (1821); translated together in two volumes by Thomas Carlyle as *Wilhelm Meister's Apprenticeship and Travels* (London: Chapman & Hall, 1984).

[652] See *ETG*, p. 109, *MDR*, p. 102.

[653] Lucius Apuleius, *The Golden Ass*. Jung was particularly interested in its account of the initiation and deification of the initiate in the ancient mysteries. He referred to it in 1912 in *Transformations and Symbols of the Libido* (CE 6; CW B, p. 496 n. 30) and in *1925* (p. 106).

and where we cannot reach to without harm. What I encountered later were, for the most part, things of only psychological interest.

Yes, the world of the *Odyssey*—that was splendid, in part also the *Aeneid*, the *Eclogues*, especially the fourth,[654] and some poems by Horace.—Then, later, Apuleius was a great experience for me. From him I always got a whiff of the ancient problem of psychic transformation; for that reason, he made a very strong impression on me. But only relatively late did I get to know him. Then I was already familiar with the unconscious. The Greek dramas had little attraction for me, even Plato didn't actually interest me very much; he did not speak to me. Of the Greek philosophers, my favorite was Heraclitus. He had incredible intuition. [162/163]

And as far as visual art is concerned, I'd like to tell you my earliest memory about that:[655] in my parental home, in the eighteenth-century vicarage in Klein-Hüningen, we had a dark living room, containing all the good furniture and old paintings. An Italian painting depicting David and Goliath. It was an exact copy from the studio of Guido Reni.[656] The original is in the Louvre. I don't know how it came to be in our family. And yet another fine old painting hung there, that's now with my son.

I often secretly crept into this dark, secluded room in order to look at this beauty. That was the only beauty I knew. I could look at those paintings for hours.

And once—when I was still a boy of six—an aunt, my mother's sister, showed me the stuffed animals in the museum in Basel.[657] We spent a long time there because I wanted to look at everything in great detail. At 4 p.m. the bell rang to announce that the museum was about to close. So, we had to go, but I did not want to leave the showcases. Yet my aunt insisted that it was time to leave. By now, the main exit was closed, and we had to take a different route to the stairs. My aunt opened the doors leading to the antiquities gallery. We had to pass through them in order to reach the stairs. And suddenly I saw these amazing sculptures! Quite overcome, my eyes wide open, never had I seen something so beautiful. I was full of amazement and could not get enough of the sight. But my aunt

---

[654] Virgil's fourth *Eclogue*, the so-called "messianic eclogue," was that which Augustine saw as a prefiguration of the birth of Christ: see *The Eclogues*, trans. Guy Lee (London: Penguin, 1984), p. 55.

[655] See *ETG*, p. 22, *MDR*, p. 15.

[656] Italian Baroque painter (1575–1642). This painting is currently in Jung's house in Küsnacht.

[657] See *ETG*, p. 22–23, *MDR*, p. 15–16.

tugged at my hand.—I kept dragging my feet behind her and wanted to see yet more of this beauty. Then my aunt cried, "You odious boy, close your eyes, you odious boy, close your eyes!" Only in that moment did I notice that the figures were wearing fig leaves, they were naked! I had not seen that before. This was my first encounter with fine art! My aunt was full of indignation as if she were being led through a pornographic establishment. [163/164]

Later when I was at the *Gymnasium*, I often visited our art collection in Basel. As a schoolboy I was keen on Holbein and Böcklin and I adored the old Dutch masters.[658] I started my own copperplate engraving collection. In Basel, they were very keen on art thanks to the influence of J. Burckhardt. I own prints by Boucher,[659] and by the oldest aquatint artists. I browsed around a lot in the *bouquinistes* in Paris,[660] and in 1902 I picked up a whole range of pieces there; I also found a Dürer engraving there. I own two prints by Dürer, a woodcut and a copper engraving.[661]

I'm very well acquainted with eighteenth-century copper engravings. When I was in Paris I went to the Louvre pretty much every day and I can't tell you how often I viewed the *Gioconda* there.[662] I chatted there with many copyists and I had a copy of a Frans Hals done for myself.[663] Later in Florence, I had a copy done of the painting *Viellesse et jeunesse* by [Domenico Ghirlandaio][664] as well as the *Adoration in the Forest* by Fra Filippo Lippi.[665] For a year I almost exclusively immersed myself in

---

[658] Hans Holbein (1497–1543), German painter renowned for his portraits; Arnold Böcklin (1827–1901), Swiss symbolist painter.

[659] François Boucher, French Rococo painter and etcher. Before his marriage, Jung gave his fiancée a print of a Boucher by Gilles Demarteau, which hung in their home.

[660] *bouquinistes*: Parisian second-hand and antiquarian booksellers who ply their trade in stalls along the banks of the River Seine.

[661] In 1906 Jung and his wife visited the Dürer house in Nürnberg (JFA).

[662] Leonardo da Vinci's painting also known as *The Mona Lisa*. See above, p. 63.

[663] The painting was a family portrait of Paulus van Berestyn van der Eeem, which is now attributed to a contemporary of Hals, Pieter Claesz Soutman. Jung had it copied in 1902 by Léontine Lemée.

[664] Domenico di Tommaso Bigordi, known as Ghirlandaio (1448–1494), Florentine Renaissance painter. The painting, *Age and Youth*, from around 1490, depicts an old man and his grandson, and is in the Louvre. The copy made for Jung by Giulia Cheli Capella (1875–1919) is in his house. Jung collected twenty-five postcards from Florence, bearing witness to his interest in its artworks.

[665] Filippo Lippi (1406–1469), early Renaissance Florentine painter (and Carmelite priest), among whose pupils was Sandro Botticelli. The painting known as the *Adoration in the Forest* dates from ca. 1460. It was originally an altar image which hung in the private chapel of the Palazzo Medici Riccardi in Florence, and is currently in the Berlin state museum.

art. Before I came to the Bli. Then I had no more time. I also collected tinted German woodcuts.

I became familiar with Egyptian art in the Louvre. I was at the Bli from 1900 until the autumn of 1902, directly after my state examinations. Then I went to Paris for half a year and after that to England for two months. In Paris I mostly attended lectures given by Janet, went to the insane asylums and to some hospitals.[666] But I left medicine to one side whenever possible. I went tirelessly to the museums and absorbed the works of art into myself.

In Paris, there were two things that occupied me; one was fine art and the other was *la misère qui a froid, la misère noire.*[667] I read statistical works about the social conditions in Paris in order to form a picture for myself. Paris made a terrible impression on me. On the one hand this beauty and on the other this terrible poverty. Basically, I was in a terrible state at that time. I had never seen anything like that before. All the misery of humanity . . . I was preoccupied at that time with dark thoughts about the blackness of the abyss and feelings of a *grande compassion*[668] were present in me. I often thought about Buddha there. I knew about him from Schopenhauer.[669]

---

[666] Janet's lectures at the Collège de France at that time were on the experimental and comparative study of emotion in the sane and the ill. See *Compte-rendu des cours au Collège de France de Monsieur Pierre Janet, chaire de psychologie expérimentale et comparée* (Paris: A. Chahine, 1926). On December 14, 1902, Jung wrote to Andreas Vischer that he was attending two hours of Janet's class each week. He slept late, often went around in the omnibus for an hour, was painting in watercolors, and had an English class at the Berlitz school. He was listening to music, but understanding it no better than before (JP). Cf. Bennet, *Meetings with Jung*, January 12, 1957 (p. 86).

[667] *la misère [. . .] noire*, in French in the original: "the misery [or poverty] that feels the cold, black misery." In *Rome*, the second of his novel cycle *Lourdes-Rome-Paris* (1893–1898), Émile Zola (1840–1902) wrote, "Oh! the cold misery, it is the excess of social injustice, the most terrible school where the poor learn to know their suffering, become indignant about it and swear to put an end to it, even if it means bringing down the old world!" On May 1, 1900 Jung noted in his diary, "What a splendid expression of Zola's: 'indifferent nature' (*Lourdes*)," and that "right at this decisive moment fate cast Zola's *Lourdes* into my hands: what a coincidence! The impression is quite incredible."

[668] *grande compassion*: in French in the original.

[669] Arthur Schopenhauer was the first Western philosopher to become seriously interested in Buddhism. In *Die Welt als Wille und Vorstellung* (1818) he wrote, discussing religions, "If I were to take the results of my philosophy as the standard of truth, I would be obliged to concede to Buddhism the pre-eminence over the rest. In any case it must be a satisfaction to me to see my teaching in such close agreement with a religion which the majority of men upon the earth hold as their own." Schopenhauer, *The World as Will and Representation*, trans. R. B. Haldane and J. Kemp, (London: Kegan Paul, Trench, Trübner & Co., 1886), vol. 2, p. 361.

It was puzzling to me that people were able to find Paris entertaining. I [164/165] was far too affected by the tragedy of it. I went to the morgue in the Halles and to the poor quarters. Paris was either wonderfully beautiful, tasteful, magnificent, or an abyss of poverty. That was very hard for me to bear. I used to do some painting myself at that time: landscapes of northern France, small watercolors.[670] And once a large cloud painting,[671] and then smaller sketches, just a few. One I painted all night until 4 a.m., a landscape from memory; this foreign landscape that made a very curious impression on me; the color and the atmosphere.[672] I went for many long walks in Paris and the surroundings, alone: Fontainebleau, Versailles, Trianon and so on. The reminders of Napoleon. I was completely imbued by French.[673] I also read many French novels at this time. Afterwards, for a long time, I used to read the *Matin* and from 1904, the *Daily Telegraph* because of the Russo–Japanese war. And also for the English language. I acquired a large vocabulary in this way.

In Paris I spoke like a Frenchman. I threw myself right in with the people, I always ate in small, relatively poor bistros, talked with ordinary people, on the street, in the shops and the bistros. I even mastered the slang quite well.—If I had later had more opportunity to speak, I would have retained impeccable French. Back then the French were leaders in psychiatry. I was very familiar with the French professional literature.

When I arrived in London, after I left Paris, my English was still very imperfect.[674] It was difficult for me to make the transition. In 1904 during

---

[670] See *Art of C. G. Jung*, cat nos. 23, 24, 25, 26 (pp. 81–84).

[671] See *Art of C. G. Jung*, cat. no. 27, (p. 85). This was painted at Christmas, and was dedicated to Emma Jung.

[672] Probably *Art of C. G. Jung*, cat. no. 28 (p. 86). This bore the inscription "2. XII. 1902. A reminiscence from better times. It may not be perfectly executed, but *ut desint vires, tamen est laudanda voluntas* [though the power may be lacking, the intention is good]."

[673] "imbued by French": in English in the original. In Paris, Jung also looked up his cousin Helene Preiswerk. On January 2, 1903 he wrote to her inviting her to the theater, and on n January 11 he wrote suggesting a meeting on the following Sunday at the Théâtre Sarah Bernhardt: "Théroigne de Méricourt will probably be performing, and she is very fine. But *Résurrection* at the Odéon is even better and *Le Joue* at Mme. Réjane's is more amusing." Zumstein-Preiswerk, *C. G. Jungs Medium*, illustrations following p. 135.

[674] Jung was in London for ten days in January 1903. According to Franz Jung, he had a private language tutorial from 5–6 p.m. each day (cited in William McGuire, "Firm Affinities: Jung's Relations with Britain and the United States," *Journal of Analytical Psychology* 40, no. 3 [1995]: 301–26). While there, he explored the city of London and visited museums (including the British Museum, the National Gallery, the Victoria and Albert Museum, the Wallace Collection, and the National History Museum). After his honeymoon Jung and his wife visited London again for eight days.

the associations experiment, I had had American pupils who infected me with their Americanisms.[675] Thank God I lost them.

Oxford was the highpoint of my stay in England. That was right up my street. I will never forget my enthusiasm when I saw the colleges for the first time. And the conversations there! After dinner, a silver crescent was passed around containing snuff tobacco! And then followed black coffee with cigars and liqueurs and then we conducted intellectual conversations in the style of the eighteenth century. Only men were present because we wanted to speak exclusively in an intellectual way. [165/166]

I've yet to tell you how I met my wife: I was about twenty-one and once I went to Schaffhausen. I was going to visit Mrs. Rauschenbach there, an old acquaintance of my father. He had been a minister in Laufen from 1874 to 1879 and his parish consisted of three villages. In one of the villages, in Uhwiesen, was a very influential man who owned the guesthouse Zum Hirschen, a stately old country guesthouse.[676] Rauschenbach was a retired colonel; he had led the ordnance provision of the army in the border occupation of 1870–71; he was an important personality.[677] Theirs was an old family who had owned this guesthouse for more than a hundred years. He had a very beautiful daughter, and she was my mother-in-law. She took me for a walk when I was a young boy. I told you about that.[678]

Seventeen years later I had a friend in Schaffhausen and my mother said to me, "If you are going there to see your friend, do go and see old Rauschenbach."[679]—This I did, and I saw this girl standing at the top of the stairs, about fourteen years old, with pigtails, and then I knew: That's my wife. This deeply shocked me. I knew: Now I have seen my wife. I told my friend, who said, "Well, you've always been crazy."—Six or seven

---

[675] A number of American psychiatrists went to study with Jung at this time, some on Adolf Meyer's recommendation. In 1907, Jung co-authored articles with Frederick Peterson (1859–1938) and Charles Ricksher (1879–1943) on the associations experiment. On January 21, 1907 Peterson wrote to Meyer, "Jung is in every way charming, and I think he has genius." Another who visited was the American psychiatrist and psychoanalyst Trigant Burrow (1875–1950). In an undated letter to Meyer, Burrow wrote, "Jung is certainly the man for me and I am having a most valuable course with him. He is enthusiastic and stimulating as a teacher and personally I have found him very congenial quite apart from the work." (Adolf Meyer Papers, Alan Mason Chesney Medical Archives, Johns Hopkins University).

[676] This was built around 1850 on the Landstrasse, Uhwiesen, and still exists today.

[677] This is actually Emma Jung's maternal grandfather, Johann Schenk-Müller (1832–1902).

[678] See above, p. 43.

[679] See ETG, p. 406.

years later I married her! At the mere sight of her I thought: That's my wife, and it was absolutely certain.[680] Even today I can remember precisely standing in the street telling my friend. With absolute certainty, the same certainty with which I predicted to Freud that the bookcase would crack, which then also actually happened.[681]

OCTOBER 12, 1957[682]

Yesterday I dreamed something that has often repeated itself. I have this same dream over and over again. It's a long story where I was in doubt about something or there was something undecided; it occurred to me that it might also have something to do with cooking. Yes, it has something to do with what I'd like to describe as Bollingen no. 2.[683] It's this idea that I had two Bollingens; the other one is not on the lake but on a plateau, in a relatively flat region. Perhaps near a river, but not on the water. It's linked to the idea of meadows, and it's always a house which I knew didn't fully satisfy me; I had not built it and therefore gave it up.

And that's something to which I always connect a certain doubt and also certain questions. Beyond doubt is simply that I often forget that it exists and always have a sort of guilty conscience. Just as one, for example, can also have a guilty conscience towards objects. I look in sorrow at my sailboat which I no longer use and at times even forget about. It's the same with this house.

How can one not use a house for many years? And immediately comes the thought: Now I must take care of my house once again. And do I even

---

[680] In August 1899 Jung wrote in his diary,

E.R. I am in love; I love with that searching yearning that Swedenborg so wonderfully describes: the anticipation of the other self, the unity preparing for heavenly, eternal times. Does she think of me? Does she know it? Could I have deluded myself? Is she not the destined one? I cannot believe that my feeling has deluded me. It must be her [. . .] E.R. In the dark shades of the trees, in the bright rooms of sunny nature I see only her, the sweet one in her familiar stature, in her bright dress with the red ribbons, she, who is so intimately akin to my soul. Does she know it? Does she feel my love regardless of the extent of space that separates? [JFA]

The reference is to Swedenborg's conception of conjugal love. Jung had taken out Swedenborg's book on this topic from Basel University Library on October 18, 1898 (Basel University Library checking records).

[681] Kurt Wolff added here, "makes good transition to Freud chapter."

[682] On October 10, 1957 Aniela Jaffé wrote to Jung conveying her impression that "The *Black Book*, in its 'imperfection,' is so incomparably more gripping than the *Red Book*." (JP).

[683] No record of this dream has been located.

have such a house? Of course, this house exists, but I haven't seen it for many years. What sort of state will it be in then? These are all thoughts and questions that repeat themselves with this dream.

In this last dream one small detail had changed: an old farmer's wife, she has the key to the house, and she lives somewhere in the neighborhood. It is an old house that loosely belongs to a village. It has no garden and no specific land belongs to it. It simply stands there in the fields. It's also questionable whether it stands by a road, or whether it's on a hill. It's a rather characterless house, with four walls and an absolutely undistinguished door and inside it's simply divided into rooms. Downstairs, there's a larger room with a fireplace. In the earlier dreams there was always this idea: that there's something in this room, something that I've painted and forgotten about or something like that. [167/168]

It was always sparse, because I had skimped or had to skimp. And then, what was new now in this dream when it came yesterday was that the house consisted of two wings that stood perpendicular to each other. The lower windows are small, and upstairs it has larger windows. The shutters are closed. It looks a bit like an abandoned farm in northern Italy or southern France. Towards the south of France there are farms like this where the houses are very small downstairs and the upper row of windows is larger.

Only one detail is important now: the keys are in the hands of an old woman, a farmer. It's a country where nothing much happens, where an isolated, abandoned house attracts barely any attention. It would be interesting only near a city where possibilities exist for its use.

I never know exactly what I have left behind in the house. How is it furnished? Only absolutely necessary things are inside. Everything is a bit poor and mismatched. It does not correspond to my taste; there is little originality in it: a normal, utilitarian door, everything done in the cheapest way. It's as if I had built it in a time when the necessary materials had not been available. So, a first draft of something.

In the earlier dreams, I thought the kitchen was downstairs. Now the large room was on the first floor. In the dream I was in this house and wanted to take a look at it. As I did this I was thinking: One can't simply leave it standing empty. It was like when I had made my children aware that something was still around which they knew nothing of.

So, I went up to the first floor in the dream but with no memory of a staircase. Upstairs was quite a large room that was also commodiously furnished. Fine carpets lay on the floor, Persian carpets. The room was furnished with a certain comfort, as a sort of living room. In fact, amazingly comfortable. For what purpose? It was a first attempt to isolate myself in the country where nothing can disturb me, where I can be alone because I always suffer from not being able to be alone. Now, in the dream it was as if I had rediscovered it and regret that I do not come more often, that it is always closed up. I experienced it as a faithlessness that I had forgotten the house, but I do not get to understand what this house might actually mean. [168/169]

A house represents a life situation. One is within it as in a situation. It has something to do with Bollingen, like a shadow of Bollingen. Bollingen was originally planned as a round hut; for I wished to know how one feels in a centrally planned building.[684] That was a quite outrageous idea. I also had the plan to place the stove in the center. In contrast with that, this house is rather conventional. This dream preoccupied me in the night. Once it had disappeared, I was able to recall it through one detail. This dream is repeatedly mixed with active imagination which begins in the dream itself: how the house could perhaps be renovated, that it is not a new house but an old house whose remarkable character already belongs in history. I can't connect any experiences with this house, sometimes it appears like a fantasy. In the dream it was as if it stood on the far side of the lake, a counterpart to Bollingen, a type of antecedent of it. And the doubt is always present: Is that really the case? And then: How can one forget it? And then one wakes up and is still full of doubt. This time it was as if I had consciously engaged with solving the question of this house in order to do something with it. It reminds me of how urgent it felt finally to complete Bollingen. But if only I knew what it might be all about.[685]

Of course, that's it, it clicks! The *Red Book* too was never completed.[686] And even in and of itself, it is incomplete: it's simply that I have now seen that the things I say in it must still be brought into a form in which they can be introduced to the world. I knew from the very beginning that one would never be able to do that in the form as it was expressed in the fantasies. That sounds like prophecy and that I'm extremely averse to that. It's the raw material that just flows out. But the

---

[684] See *ETG*, pp. 227–28, *MDR*, pp. 223–24.

[685] Jaffé added here, "(My interpretation suggestion: this is surely about the fantasies from the Red and Black Books!)."

[686] In the spring of 1959, Jung took up the calligraphic folio of *The Red Book* again to try to complete the last incomplete painting (image 169). He also took up the transcription of the text into this volume (pp. 171–89), before breaking off again mid-sentence. He then wrote an afterword in his regular script (*LN*, p. 555).

whole person is simply not in that. For that reason, one must not overestimate the unconscious. For example, Nietzsche felt himself to be a whole person in his *Zarathustra*; he did not see beyond it. [169/170]

But I have always taken a critical stance towards it. I am, after all, not a poet-philosopher like Nietzsche who believes in his involuntary creation. I have always said: It is being spoken in this way, but it is not I who speaks. I only hear it, and I experience it as deplorably impoverished. I was simply pulled down into this stream, and I felt as if I were in it. But at the same time, I always preserved my capacity to critique it. I sort of did it while grinding my teeth because I was not in full agreement with it. That is why, aside from *Septem Sermones*, I have also released nothing of it in the world. They were something self-contained. And so the "house" remained unfinished—until today!

Question about the interpretation of the dream (after the murder of Siegfried).[687]
I saw a magnificent garden in which figures were walking around dressed in white silk. Each was surrounded by a unique, gossamer-like, colorful luminous aura; one red, another blue and green. These lights permeated me spiritually and sensorily. . . .[688]

It's a sort of intermediate realm (in the original version of the dream this expression arises for sure). The idea was that when one is confronted with the shadow—as happened through the experience of the Siegfried dream—then the idea comes; I'm stumbling into a twilight zone: I am that and yet I am something else. And this duplexity portrays itself: as "I" plus my aura. Something that I am and something other that is different from me. It is an intimation of the unconscious that curiously extends far beyond me. Like the halo of the saints.—That has a remarkable effect on one's attitude towards a person. When one is in the company of several people and one knows them and is aware of their shadow, then one sees these people as they are, but they are also something completely other. They are surrounded by an extraordinary sphere. They live in a supernal color-imbued sphere that circumscribes their "other" state. This came to me as a vision of the afterlife where people are what they are in their wholeness and not as they seem to be here. The halo of the saint also

---

[687] See *BB* 2, pp. 174–75, and above, p. 107.
[688] *BB* 2, p. 175.

characterizes his transcendent light-form, his soulful being. I had the feeling of the[689] [170/171]

This dream is a compensation to the darkness of the shadow. The meaning extends to another form of being in which people live in their wholeness.

During the years 1914–18, I lived fully within myself; I was as if in a dream the whole time. I practiced my profession properly, but in the main I wrote these things and painted. I already knew T. W. then.[690] Previously I had a Dutch patient, a crazy minx, who had a massive transference to me.[691] She constellated the anima in me. In the beginning when writing these things, I heard a voice whispering to me, "That is art," and that was her voice. This woman had psychiatrist X on her conscience,[692] for example. She also made out to him that he was a misunderstood artist and he believed it and had a breakdown because of it. She was exceptionally engaged and in a certain sense intelligent, very skillful and aesthetically gifted. She believed that the unconscious was simply art. I always told her that I would not concede that: it is not art; it is nature. Dr. X, however, let himself be conned into this thing and was ruined by it. That's how dangerous it is. He did not live from his own self-recognition, however, but from the recognition of others. And that's dangerous. I knew her from 1912 until 1918.

T. W. had quite incredible fantasies at the beginning of her analysis, a complete outbreak of the craziest fantasies, also of a cosmic nature. But at the time I was so involved with my material that I could barely go into hers. But her fantasies, they proceeded exactly along my lines.[693]

---

[689] This page breaks off mid-sentence.

[690] Toni Wolff was brought by her mother to Jung for analysis on September 20, 1910 at the age of twenty-three. She had fallen into a depression following her father's death.

[691] Maria Moltzer (1874–1944). On Moltzer, see Sonu Shamdasani, *Cult Fictions: C. G. Jung and the Founding of Analytical Psychology* (London, Routledge, 1998). In 1905, Moltzer started working at the Bircher-Benner Clinic in Küsnacht. Jung's first reference to her is in a letter to Freud of September 8, 1910: see *FJL*, p. 352. On the breakdown of Jung's relationship with Moltzer, see Sonu Shamdasani, "Introduction" to *BB* 1, pp. 62–63. After 1918 they had no further contact. Jung also narrated this episode to Bennet: Bennet, *Meetings with Jung*, January 8, 1957 (p. 76).

[692] Franz Beda Riklin (1878–1938). Riklin was Jung's collaborator on the associations experiment at the Burghölzli, and married Jung's cousin, Sophie Fiechter. Riklin increasingly forsook analysis for painting, and became a student of Augusto Giacometti. His artistic career was not commercially successful, and he later returned to psychiatric work.

[693] On Jung's relationship and collaboration with Toni Wolff, see Sonu Shamdasani, "Introduction" to *BB* 1, pp. 27–33 and 60–61.

I was in a terrible darkness at that time. Everything was so difficult and so incomprehensible. I found my way through this labyrinth only because I thought I must obey a higher will and endure although I understood nothing. And then I wrote up this madness and had crazy resistances to it. I felt as if I were something that had been thrown out on the street. And when I later read of the alchemical stone "in via ejectus," [171/172][694] then I used to think, Well, yes, I know something about that. I felt utterly worthless and ridiculous. I was as if stripped of all human dignity and pursued by a deplorable nonsense that I could not understand. That first began to clear away with the end of the war.

In 1916 I painted my first mandala, after writing the *Septem Sermones*.[695] Of course I did not understand the mandala. I could say that the air cleared itself when I showed the door to the Dutch woman who wanted me to think that what I was doing was art, and again when I began to understand the mandala drawings, and that was in 1918/1919. Then I was in the Château d'Oex, *commandeur du rayon anglais des internés de guerre*.[696] There I drew a mandala every morning in my military notepad.[697] I was still in a state of indescribable chaos at that time. The relationship with T. W. had begun and through it I had landed in chaos, so that I no longer knew which way was up. So, I had a sort of military notebook, a sort of exercise book, and in it I sketched a small mandala every day and in that way it was as if I had a feeling for that day, as if a photograph of the day had been taken. I observed every day how it changed.

Then I received a letter from this Dutch woman which got so incredibly on my nerves. The next morning a part of the mandala had broken out and that is how I came to realize what the mandala actually is: Formation–Transformation, eternal mind's eternal recreation.[698] And that is the self. Such is the cryptogram delivered to me daily about the state of my self. There I saw how the self was at work.

---

[694] Jung cited this in *Psychology and Alchemy* (1944), CE 17; CW 12, § 103.

[695] On January 16, 1916, Jung painted a sketch which he later elaborated as the painting *Systema mundi totius* (*BB 5*, p. 273). The *Sermones* took place between January 30 (*BB 5*, p. 282) and February 8 (*BB 6*, p. 226).

[696] Jung was on military service at Château d'Oex from June 11 to October 2, 1917, as "commander of the British section of war internees."

[697] A sequence of twenty-seven mandalas has survived (see *Art of C. G. Jung*). Jung later recopied and elaborated these in the calligraphic volume of *LN*. The sequence was not always daily.

[698] The reference is to Goethe's *Faust II*, Act 1, sc. 5, ll. 6287–88. Mephistopheles is addressing Faust, giving him directions to the realm of the Mothers.

This whole series of mandalas from Château d'Oex is reproduced in my *Red Book*. That was at a time when I still did not understand anything of it. But it seemed to me to be incredibly significant. And I tended it like a precious pearl. I had the feeling that I was now getting at something central. But naturally I had to ask myself: What did these cryptograms mean?

Once at that time I had a vision of a red clay tablet that was recessed into the wall of my bedroom, and upon this were curious hieroglyphs which I did my best to copy the next day while feeling there was something within it, that is, a message, but I didn't know what.[699]—But then when I was painting the mandalas, it was then that the living idea of the self came to me for the first time. [172/173] It corresponds to the microcosmic nature of the soul, and it seemed to me like the monad that I am and which is my world. The mandala represents this self. I don't know how many mandalas I have drawn. There were very many, certainly around twenty or more, and then I always wondered: Where does this process lead, what is its goal? I felt with great precision: I could not choose a goal of my own volition, I saw simply that I must completely give up. I failed at it: I wanted to get further with the scientific working-through of the myths. That was my goal. But not a word of it! I had to go through this process of the unconscious; I had to allow myself first to be carried away by this stream without knowing where it was leading me. At first, when I began to paint the mandalas, I saw that all paths that I trod and all steps that I took led back again to one point: namely, to the center. The mandala became an expression for all paths. A unitary development manifests its summit at the beginning.

This process of the inner images stretched out over years. Even fifteen years ago or so I did a drawing, or perhaps it was twenty years ago. But I did not elaborate on this drawing. At the time it was becoming ever clearer: the mandala is the absolute center. It became clear to me in the years between 1917 and about 1920 that the goal is the self. There is no linear development; there is only a circumambulation. And this gave me inner strength. Otherwise, the whole experience would have driven me crazy, or the people around me would have gone crazy.

T. W. was caught up in a similar stream of images. I had apparently infected her, or I was the instigator[700] who stirred up her fantasies. Hers

---

[699] Jung incorporated this motif in images 89 and 90 in *LN*. On October 7, 1917, Jung's soul asked the black magician Ha to translate these hieroglyphs (*BB* 7, pp. 152–57).

[700] "instigator": in French in the original, "instigateur."

and my own were involved in a *participation mystique*. It was a common stream, and a common task. As I gradually became conscious of mine, I gradually became the center; and to the extent to which I came to these insights, she also found her center. But then she got stuck somewhere, and that was because I had become too much the center that functioned for her. Therefore I was never allowed to be different from what she wanted or needed me to be.[701] She was pulled into this terrible process in which I found myself, and I was just as helpless in it as she. I simply did my utmost to hold onto my orientation, or rather, to find it.

I did the mandala drawings between 1917 and 1918. I went to Château d'Oex on two occasions.[702] And these drawings showed me the self in its salvific function, and that was my redemption.—I was unable to speak to anyone about my inner experiences. Often, I had to sort of grip hold of the table so that I would not fall apart. I had terrible moments back then, and repeatedly I had the feeling that it would destroy me. Only with Toni Wolff was I able to talk about it, but she was in the same soup and was without orientation.

Even my wife was not able to help. It was absolutely terrible. But meanwhile my wife had come awake at that time and began to study physics, mathematics, Latin and Greek. The animus became lively in her at that time. And in all this tumult, I had to be a normal father and husband, and I had to be a doctor and everything. That I managed to bear it at all was a matter of brute strength. Anyone else would have fallen apart from it. But there was a daimonic strength in me.

At that time I was also completely isolated from the association I had founded and whose president I was.[703] I had also withdrawn from the university because I had the feeling, "I can't go on. I have such an exposed situation and I can't possibly speak about what is taking place within me."[704] For eight years I had lectured at the University of Zurich. At that time, I quite consciously sacrificed my academic career. For I found that it was something so terrible that was happening to me here,

---

[701] Toni Wolff's surviving diaries from 1924 confirm Jung's recollections here.

[702] In addition to his time at the Château in 1917, Jung was there from November 2 to December 14, 1918.

[703] The Association for Analytical Psychology was founded in the summer of 1914. It was made up of around ten analysts (Jung to Poul Bjerre, April 2, 1917, JP). It met roughly fortnightly, until 1918, when the meetings merged into those of the Psychological Club.

[704] On April 20, 1914, Jung resigned as a lecturer from the medical faculty of the University of Zurich (the same day he resigned as president of the International Psychoanalytic Association: *FJL*, p. 551). He had begun lecturing there in 1904.

and that this would fill up my life. But I couldn't take this to any university. So you see, I was ready for every venture.

When I was in England in 1924 and I saw the British Empire Exhibition in Wembley where all the nations were represented, as I arrived at the exhibit for West Africa and entered into a negro village, there was a certainty within me: I must go to Africa, no matter the cost.[705] The atmosphere of the primitive appealed to me. I had to see that *in situ* and I had to experience how it once was. For I always had the feeling, that in this stream of images I had fallen into something that was already there.

[706]Philemon, he was a Gnostic. He was terribly real to me. I walked up and down in the garden with him. Philemon was my spiritual guru.—At the time I lived in a completely strange world. I knew only that if I did not stand firm then there would be a catastrophe and then another terrible madness happened; and it was clear to me: cost what it may,[707] I had to get to the bottom of it. I must find the meaning of what I was now experiencing.

This stream of the unconscious began with the dreams that I had in 1912–14, so in the second half of life, and that spread out over about twenty years. I can say that I first reached my bedrock when I came across alchemy. The Gnostics, they were still too far way. At first I came across the Gnostics, even before alchemy. Philemon was a Gnostic. And then, around 1920, came the dream that I was trapped in the seventeenth century, and later alchemy began to interest me, and only then did I understand the dream.[708]

[709]I had already read Silberer. But he had mainly used certain late material and he applied Freudian interpretations. These late alchemical texts

---

[705] See *ETG*, p. 257, *MDR*, p. 253 (date corrected to 1925). The British Empire Exhibition was held at the newly built Empire Stadium (later renamed Wembley Stadium), from April 1924 to October 1925: contemporary Pathé newsreels of it are available on YouTube, for example at https://www.youtube.com/watch?v=b6gY0shGXN0, and the footage at https://www.youtube.com/watch?v=0Qz65qzRPM which includes views of the African village (accessed April 25, 2025). Jung gave lectures in London in May 1924 at the New Education Fellowship, and was in England again in the summer of 1925, where he gave a summer school at Swanage, in Dorset.

[706] See *ETG*, p. 187, *MDR*, p. 182.

[707] "cost what it may": in French in the original, "côute que côute."

[708] See *ETG*, pp. 206–7, *MDR*, p. 203.

[709] See *ETG*, pp. 207–8, *MDR*, pp. 204–5. Herbert Silberer (1882–1923) was a Viennese psychoanalyst. Jung had a series of offprints from Silberer's work in his library, with dedications, as well as a copy of his book *Probleme der Mystik und ihrer Symbolik* (Vienna: Hugo Heller, 1914) with a dedication. In this book, Silberer commented on an anonymous Rosicrucian text of 1795, *Secret Figures of the Rosicrucians from the Sixteenth and*

are very confused and baroque, and are almost incomprehensible if one does not already know the interpretation. Yet it is also clearly recognizable that they contain mythological motifs. Therefore it was only when I became familiar with the text of the *Golden Flower*,[710] and saw how my unconscious had anticipated this, that alchemy opened up to me and I thought: Oh my God, this amounts to something after all.

The text of the *Golden Flower* is pure Chinese alchemy. Silberer brought only Freudian or "anagogic" interpretations, and I didn't like that; it seemed so banal. I couldn't make much of it. It was only through the *Golden Flower* that one saw something: there I am . . . , there I saw; I should really get to know these old texts.

I commissioned a Munich-based book dealer to keep me informed when he got hold of alchemical volumes. The first one to come into my hands was the *Artis auriferae*, volume 2.[711] But at first these volumes remained untouched for a year. I looked at the pictures and thought: Goodness, what sort of madness is this, it's impossible to understand. But no, you must really look at this more closely. Then one winter, [175/176] I began. Then I found it terribly exciting: it looked to me like blatant rubbish, yet from time to time came intimations that this was a mystery concerned with something that I understood and recognized. That this was my language! And then I saw: It's really fantastic, this thing, I *must* understand it!

It was 1931 when this started. When I began to understand, for the first time I had the feeling that now the bridge is built between past and present.[712] Now I could somehow go over into the past. Previously, I had had no roots. The traditions between Gnosis and the present were torn down. People such as Baader,[713] they said damned little to me. That was

---

Seventeenth Centuries, and referred mainly to seventeenth- and eighteenth-century alchemical materials. He subjected these to an analytic and anagogic mode of interpretation, drawing on Jung's *Transformations and Symbols of the Libido*. On Jung and Silberer, see Christine Maillard, "Herbert Silberer (1882–1923) et Carl Gustav Jung: Genèse et enjeux d'une théorie de l'alchimie," *Recherches germaniques* 9 (2014): 79–96; and Julia Gyimesi, "The Unorthodox Silberer," *Imágó Budapest* 6, no. 4 (2017): 33–58.

[710] See above. p. 52.

[711] *Artis auriferae quam chemiam vocant* (Of the art of producing gold which they call chemical) (Basel, 1593). Jung's copy is viewable at https://www.e-rara.ch/cgj/content/titleinfo/1344381 (accessed April 25, 2025). This was a compendium of classic alchemical texts. See Thomas Fischer, "The Alchemical Rare Book Collection of C. G. Jung," *International Journal of Jungian Studies* 3, no. 2 (2011): 169–80.

[712] See *ETG*, p. 204, *MDR*, p. 204.

[713] Franz von Baader (1765–1841), German mystical theologian. The works of Meister Eckhart and Jakob Boehme were particularly important for him.

only a pale imitation of the original, sweetened in mysticism. Or Görres, he was the same.⁷¹⁴ This mysticism was unsympathetic to me because the dark substance was missing; and it was precisely that which I found in alchemy. Not in vain was it called the "black art." In the Coptic, it was called *chem*: the black earth of Egypt.⁷¹⁵ And that is connected to the black Isis, the black mother Isis; she is in fact the first alchemist. In the Hathor temple at Edfu, they found inscriptions of an alchemical nature, from as early as the Roman imperial period, and Isis was the alchemist *par excellence*.⁷¹⁶

The darkness played a decisive role in my life from childhood on. Just think of the experience of God shitting on the church.⁷¹⁷ And once when I was still a young student, and I was very insecure back then, I always had the wish, if I could only once have an immediate experience of the eternal, or a vision of God. Then I had the feeling, and that was in a dream, where I thought: Now it's coming, now I will finally experience it! There was a door, and I understood that when one opened this door, then this experience will come, then one will see. Then I opened this door and what was behind it? A great heap of manure, and upon it lay a huge mother sow.

Can you imagine what a terrible impression that made upon me? Not quite as bad as the experience with the Basel cathedral, but still nearly as bad.⁷¹⁸ The sow, that's an aspect of Demeter and that is Isis. But I did not yet know that back then. It made a terrible impression.

The years I have told you of when I pursued the inner images, that was the most important time of my life.⁷¹⁹ Everything else can be traced back to then. It began then and the later details hardly matter any more. My whole life consisted of working on what broke out of the unconscious at

---

⁷¹⁴ Joseph Görres (1776–1848), German theologian. Among his works were *Die christliche Mystik*, 5 vols (Regensberg: G. J. Manz, 1836–42), which Jung cited in 1905 "On Spiritualistic Phenomena," CE 3; CW 18, § 700.

⁷¹⁵ In Coptic, the name for Egypt was "Kmt," which meant "black earth." This was the root of the Greek word for chemistry, *chemeia*.

⁷¹⁶ The Edfu temple to Horus, on the banks of the Nile, dates from the Ptolemaic dynasty (constructed 237–57 BCE). A project directed by Dieter Kurth is underway at Academy of Sciences of Göttingen to prepare a complete transcription of all the temple's inscriptions. In "The Visions of Zosimos" (1938) Jung commented on an alchemical text "From Isis to Horus," in which an angel brought Isis a vessel of shining water. He noted, "A text from Edfu says: 'I bring you the vessels with the God's limbs [i.e., the Nile], that you may drink of them; I refresh your heart that you may be satisfied.'" CE 15; CW 13, §§ 97–98.

⁷¹⁷ See above, pp. 55–56.

⁷¹⁸ Ibid.

⁷¹⁹ See ETG, p. 203, MDR, p. 199.

that time and flooded over me like a mysterious stream and threatened to destroy me. That was substance and material for more than one life. Everything that came later was only the external classification, the scientific reworking and the integration into life. But the numinous beginning that contained everything, that was then.

My daughter Gret told me yesterday that her son Dieter, when he was a young boy, went once to see his great-grandmother in Schaffhausen.[720] She was still alive then, He got up to some mischief and she swore at him. Then he looked at her in rage and said to her reproachfully, "You can't curse the dear Lord!" That is child psychology!

When I was eleven, around that time, I was once going along the street and suddenly I stood still because suddenly I knew something very important: it was as if I had stepped out of mist.[721] I knew: I have always been in this mist and now I know that I exist. I was eleven years old then. After that, came the experience of the traumatic neurosis and that terrible story of God shitting on the church. And the rock I meditated on, and that I felt identical with.

Once as I sat in the garden I heard my daughter Marianne,[722] aged about five years old, talking with her doll as she pushed her in a small baby carriage in front of her. She could not see me. She said to her doll, "Do you know what, we are royalty, Jungs!"

And when I [177/178] was three years old, once a younger brother of my mother came to visit. Back then I had a small wooden horse that was nailed to a board with wheels, as a toy. My uncle said to me, "Little boy, gee up horsey, play now!?" I told this to my mother—she told me the whole story later. "Why is the man speaking so stupidly?" I was, I don't know which: God or royalty; for how can the man speak so stupidly to me as if I am only a small child. That is how children are, they still have something of the knowledge of the original and whole person; they are still close to the pleroma where the eternal images are alive. That is child psychology, but you won't find that in any textbook! [178/179][723]

---

[720] Gret Baumann-Jung (1906–1995) was a noted astrologer; her son Dieter Baumann (1928–2020) became a psychiatrist and analytical psychologist.

[721] See *ETG*, pp. 38–39, *MDR*, pp. 32–33.

[722] Marianne Niehus-Jung (1910–1965).

[723] The following day, Jaffé wrote to Kurt Wolff about this discussion,

"In the meantime the unconscious has helpfully played its part: an oft-repeated dream of Jung's which he was never able to understand came again. And in interpretation it

OCTOBER 16, 1957

The trip to India (1938/39) signified a caesura in my life. I acquired a completely new conception of evil.[724]

When I was in India I was chiefly concerned with the question of evil.[725] While there I came to see that there is no other way than taking on full responsibility for accepting evil, otherwise one cannot accept the good either, and we remain outside the divine antinomy, and we have not realized our wholeness. When we avoid the danger of evil, then we also avoid the good. There is nothing to be done about it. India, and what I experienced there, signified for me the conclusion of the Christian problem. I noticed there that the whole of Indian spirituality has just as much evil as good, or to put it another way: to the same degree that evil is lacking, so is the good lacking. There, the moral problem does not play any role as it does with us. We always want to strive for the good or degenerate into evil;[726] but the Indians feel absolutely outside of good and evil. They seek to achieve this state through yoga. That is the state of *nirdvandva* in which they liberate themselves from the opposites. But as a result, neither good nor evil has sufficient distinction, and that brings about a certain stasis. One doesn't fully believe in evil, one doesn't fully believe in good. The good is not very sharply defined; it is what is more or less *my* good; what appears to be good to me. The goal is not moral perfection but rather the liberation from things. *Neti neti.*[727]

But that is where my objection arises. For me, there is no liberation *à tout prix.*[728] I cannot be liberated from anything that I have not encountered or experienced; but rather I can be liberated only after a full

---

became very clear that it was necessary to open up his 'personal material.' It is hard to imagine anything better happening!

Tomorrow or the day after I will send the protocols to New York. Again, there are some very personal parts about Toni W in there which to me seem important and valuable as she was the companion of his early years with all her tremendous disturbances. These are for your eyes only and I hope it will not be troublesome that I am burdening you with the entire undistilled prima materia." [BL]

[724] Jung arrived in Bombay on December 16, 1937 and was in India and Ceylon (Sri Lanka) until the beginning of February 1938. He wrote up his impressions of India in two articles in 1939: "The Dreamlike World of India," and "What India Can Teach Us" (*CE* 16; *CW* 10). On Jung's India trip, see Sengupta, *Jung in India.*

[725] See *ETG*, p. 279, *MDR*, p. 275.

[726] "or we take the" was obscured by overtyping here.

[727] *Neti neti*: a Sanskrit expression meaning "not this, not that," which features prominently in Jnana yoga and the Advaita Vedanta school of textual exegesis in Hinduism.

[728] *à tout prix*, in French in the original: "at any cost."

surrender to it and a full participation in it. If I abstain from this participation, then that neglects one side. Or, on the other hand, if the participation is too difficult for me, I feel myself compelled to declare, "Non possumus."[729] Of course, there are reasons why I cannot completely abandon myself to it. However, one must then be aware that one has failed in something essential. One must then be aware: I have failed in such and such, and so neither was I able to liberate myself from it. [179/180]

Real liberation is possible only when I have done what I honestly[730] could. And where I had to shirk away from it, then I know that unfortunately I have left *this* task unfinished.

Once I read a French author whose name I sadly forget. He said that one cannot gain mastery of one's passions, but one can only live them, and in that way, overcome them. That is correct. A man who has never gone through the hell of his passions has never overcome them. Then they are only next door in another house, and if he doesn't pay attention, then without his seeing it, a flame might ignite and spread to his own house. If one gives up too much, leaves too much behind, or quasi-forgets it, the possibility always exists that what is given up or left behind will return again. That's why people who have given up a great deal must, before their death, catch up on what they have neglected in their life.

I always think about the dream I had of my wife after her death, where she appeared to me as an image that contained something of her.[731] And as I saw her in this lovely dress that she wore as a young woman, that the medium had made for her—the one with whom I experimented before my doctoral thesis, who later had an excellent couture salon in Paris[732]—I had a quite extraordinary impression in the dream: my wife was not friendly, and not unfriendly, not serious, and not cheerful; she was like an image, and it was as if it had been provided for me and this is how I was supposed to keep her in my memory. The way she looked at me cannot be described in any other way than "objective." She looked at me as someone looks at another person objectively. Not "yes," not "no," but simply objectively. Like when I receive a letter from someone I do not know, then

---

[729] "Non possumus" (Lat.): "We cannot," deriving from the refusal of the Martyrs of Abitinae to submit to persecution under Roman emperor Diocletian (304 CE) and used in Roman Catholicism to express doctrinal intransigence.

[730] "honestly": in English in the original.

[731] See *ETG*, p. 300, *MDR*, p. 296.

[732] See above, p. 75.

I regard that letter quite objectively. There is not the slightest emotional reaction to it, for it is simply objective. [180/181]

I believe that this objectivity is part of a completed individuation. If I cannot see others objectively, then I cannot see myself objectively; and if I can't see myself objectively, how can I then see others objectively? "Objectively" means detached from all value judgments, so, from what we call an emotional attachment. A tremendous amount is due to these emotional bonds in us; but they also contain many of one's own projections and it is important to take them back in order to achieve this objectivity.

Emotional relationships are actually relationships of desire. When desire ceases, only then can wholeness be reached. As long as I still desire, I can't be objective; then something else is in the mix, a wish, a need. And that prevents an objective perception. This objective perception, this seems to be the central mystery. Only then is a true *coniunctio* possible.[733]

For example, how can I recognize my anima if I do not see women objectively? And how could I understand women if I do not know about my anima? And this perception is incredibly important for the integration of wholeness. But these are truths that are damned difficult for us to grasp because they seem to prevent emotion. Yet that is why emotion is also eminently important, because it entangles us in relationships, and ultimately every relationship faces a projection that it is important to reclaim. It can hardly be understood how someone can come to this way as it is so infinitely difficult. But every step on this way is a step towards liberation.

In every emotional relationship a compulsion is present, and that is also an impairment of the relationship. Every emotional relationship presents the other with a compulsion; it is burdened with compulsion, for one expects something from the other. And that expectation means that projections are still present that are yet to be taken back. [181/182]

It seems that emotional relationships are more important for the woman than the man. But with the man it's his accomplishments and what he achieves in life that are important for him and in which he is unfree and bound. Neither is better than the other. [182/183]

---

[733] The *coniunctio* (Lat.: "union" or "sacred marriage") is a term which features in alchemy, signifying the union of opposites, such as sulfur and mercury, or the king and the queen, leading to the creation of the philosopher's stone. For Jung, this represented the uniting of psychic opposites in the individuation process. See *Mysterium Coniunctionis* (1955–56), CE 24; CW 14.

OCTOBER 18, 1957

I've been once again mulling over the question of publication of what I am telling you about my life. One cannot write a biography without telling the truth. We already have enough misleading biographies. Naturally one can also say: *Mysteria revelata vilescunt*.[734] And they are very unusual things that I've experienced. But in fact, nothing is given away if I tell them. I belong to the world, I do not belong to myself. One is somewhat exposed; and then it's questionable whether one somehow feels a bit resentful about it. But there's already been so much rubbish said about me, so a little more or less, that doesn't bother me.

It was 1938/39 when I was in India. It heralded a very important new chapter in my life. And then, the next caesura, an incredibly drastic one in my life, that was my illness in 1944. India, that's a chapter inasmuch as I had not yet been under the direct influence of a foreign culture. Before then I had never been able to engage in conversation with leading representatives of another worldview.

I had already been to Africa. But there, I had no contact with great minds or any sort of significant personalities. In Africa, I passed through as a tourist, so to say. That was in 1921.[735] I was not able to converse with anyone who could be said to represent the spirit of North Africa. The only Arab I spoke to was my tour guide. And I traveled through Egypt as a foreigner in the same way. Later in the course of my trip I did speak with negroes in their own language; consequently, I got a direct impression of their psychology.[736] But that was too far down the scale. It was a relatively primitive state of mind that did not directly concern me.[737] But

---

[734] *Mysteria revelata vilescunt*: "Mysteries which are revealed are profaned." Jung used this expression in a letter he wrote three days earlier to John Trinick, who had sent him the manuscript of his book on alchemy, *The Fire-Tried Stone* (Marazion: Wordens of Cornwall, 1967), adding, "In trying to reveal that which no mortal being is able to conceive, we distort and say the wrong things. Instead of creating light, we conceal in darkness, instead of lifting up, we expose the treasure to ridicule and contempt. Instead of opening a way, we barricade it by an inextricable snarl of paradoxes." *Letters*, vol. 2, p. 395.

[735] In 1920, Jung accompanied his friend Hermann Sigg on a trip to Tunisia. From Jung's appointment book and letters to Emma Jung, it appears that he left Zurich on March 6, arriving in Marseille the following day, sailed from Marseille to Algiers on March 10, then proceeded by train to Sousse, where he stayed from March 15 to 18; he was in Sfax on March 22, Touzeur on March 23, Nefta Oasiso on March 24–25, then back to Sfax on March 25, on to Sousse on March 26, and back to Tunis on March 29.

[736] Jung appears to be referring here to his 1925 trip to Africa. See below, pp. 217–20.

[737] See *ETG*, p. 278, *MDR*, p. 275.

in India there's a highly differentiated culture with a very particular spirit. And there I had the opportunity to speak with representatives of this spirit, to compare with the European spirit, and to really engage with that foreign spirit. That was incredibly important for me. I spoke with the guru of the maharaja of Mysore, Prof. Iyer.[738] [183/184] Then with [Dasgupta],[739] the author of the book about the philosophy of yoga, and then with a series of others whose names are not well known. It was incredibly impressive for me to see the way in which the problems that concern us, for example, the problem of good and evil, to see how they are integrated into Indian spiritual life, whereas for us it's simply not integrated. This same matter has also always interested me extraordinarily when I discussed it with educated Chinese. I saw how it's possible for so-called "evil" to be integrated at all, without one "losing face," as it were. I learned this mainly through the cult of Kali Dhurga, also later through Kundalini yoga.[740] I saw the cult of the Kali Dhurga in Kalighat in Calcutta.[741] Anyone can go inside there. I was extremely impressed by the

---

[738] V. Subrahamanya Iyer (1869–1949), Indian philosopher. He represented India at the International Congress of Philosophy in Paris in 1937, where he met Jung, who invited him to Küsnacht. They corresponded on the relations between Indian and European thought: see Iyer to Jung, August 25, 1937 (JP), and Jung to Iyer, September 16, 1937. *Letters*, vol. 1, pp. 235–36. They met again while Jung was in Mysore. On July 27, 1938, Iyer wrote to Jung that "often have the university men thought of going to you since and sitting at your feet to learn the secret of diving into the unfathomable depths of the human mind" (JP). An obituary by A. R. Wadia (*Philosophy* 26, no. 96 [1951]: p. 96) stated that Iyer's "originality lay in trying to prove *Advaita* on the basis of Western science. [. . .] He] had no faith in mysticism or religion": See his *The Philosophy of Truth, or, Tatvagnana: A Collection of Speeches and Writings* (Salem, MA: Mrs. Rukmani Kuppanna, 1955). Cf. Bennet, *Meetings with Jung*, January 9, 1957 (p. 78).

[739] Jaffé left a space here for the name. The context suggests that Jung was referring to Surendranath Dasgupta, whom Jung met in Calcutta and invited to Zurich to lecture at the Psychological Club the following year. His main work was *Yoga as Philosophy and Religion* (London: Kegan Paul, 1924).

[740] See Jung, *Psychology of Kundalini Yoga*.

[741] The Kalighat Kali temple. The present structure dates from around two hundred years ago. Jung's companion on the trip, Fowler McCormick, recalled, "As we would go through temples of Kali, which were numerous at almost every Hindu city, we saw the evidences of animal sacrifice: the places were filthy dirty—dried blood on the floor and lots of remains of red betelnut all around, so that the colour red was associated with destructiveness. Concurrently in Calcutta Jung began to have a series of dreams in which the colour red was stressed. It wasn't long before dysentery overcame Dr. Jung and I had to take him to the English hospital at Calcutta [. . .]. A more lasting effect of this impression of the destructiveness of Kali was the emotional foundation it gave him for the conviction that evil was not a negative thing but a positive thing [. . .]. The influence of that experience in India, to my mind, was very great on Jung in his later years." Fowler McCormick interview, pp. 25–26, Jung Biographical Archive, CLM.

darkness in the monkey temple at Benares.[742] That's a Shiva temple full of monkeys, and it's incredibly uncanny. My impressions in India were not actually due to individual people, or individual places, but rather to the whole atmosphere. You can't put your finger on it.

It was incredibly interesting to me to speak with people for whom the moral problem was not uppermost, as it is with us in the West. It's terribly difficult to talk about it and to make clear what I mean. For it also cannot be said that these conversations then made the integration of evil acceptable to me, but rather, I simply saw only that good and evil are, as it were, relative. And consequently they are then somehow of nature, and so correspondingly within nature. And for the same reason, they must not only stay unconscious but also could be lived consciously with meaning. In that case, they are no longer what they were before when they were still unconscious. Made conscious, good is no longer good, and evil is no longer evil, and the devil no longer has a tail, and the opposite can also be included in the divine and be expressed, for example, in a feminine form. In the Middle Ages, when they said, [184/185] "vir a deo creatur, mulier a simia Dei,"[743] it meant that the woman is "the opposite," just as the devil is the opposite to God. But yet, one cannot say: She *is* a devil. She simply represents the other who is also possible.

This is very difficult. It's true: one could say it's really daft that I, at my age, with my experience, do not yet know about good and evil. But people simply do not understand that one might have logical concepts of it without actually having it. They simply confuse the words with what it actually is. Otherwise, so much naïvety would not be possible, such as for example, that I claim to make woman and the devil the "fourth," as a completion of the Trinity, and that I believe woman is the devil. What ignorance! People have no real conceptions of good and evil. They think morality is whether one follows the moral law or not. But that is absolutely not a moral question. Such a question begins at all only when the moral law no longer provides any information. But it's simply terribly difficult to describe this phenomenon of good and evil more precisely. And one encounters astonishing incomprehension when one ventures into this domain.

---

[742] Possibly the Sankat Mohan Mandir, dedicated to Hanuman, known as the "monkey temple." Hanuman is depicted as a man with a monkey's face.

[743] "Man is created by God, woman by the ape of God" (i.e., the devil). Jung cited this in "An Attempt at a Psychological Interpretation of the Dogma of the Trinity" (1942), CE 16; CW 11, § 262.

The other great caesura in my life was my illness in 1944 when I had the visions.[744] In actual fact it is not much. It was a big deal only as I was experiencing it, but when it comes to consciousness, then it appears insubstantial.

Back then when the visions came I was not lucid, but for me they were terribly impressive things that were being played out. That must have been when they gave me oxygen and camphor, and when they thought that I was going to die. I was at the utmost frontier and I don't know if it was a dream or an ecstasy, I was simply high up in the room and saw the globe far below me couched in an indescribably beautiful light, through which the contours of the globe were shimmering like silver. I saw the sea, deep blue, and I saw the continents. Under my feet lay Ceylon, and I saw before me [185/186] the subcontinent of India. And the earth, it was as if my field of vision could not encompass it, but I saw clearly that it was a sphere shimmering through a wonderful blue light. I could just see the Red Sea and the red-yellow Arabian desert, as if the silver of the earth had taken on a red or russet hue. In some places it was speckled dark green and looked like oxidized silver, quite colorful. On the left side I saw a great expanse, that was the Arabian mainland, then came the Red Sea and far behind on the left side, at the top, I could just make out a tip of the Mediterranean Sea.

Later I once asked the physicist Markus Fierz how high one would have to be above the earth to have this vast perspective.[745] He calculated it as 2,400 kilometers! That's how high I stood in the air above Ceylon to see all that. My vista turned chiefly towards Europe. The rest appeared to me only indistinctly. But I also saw the snow-capped mountains of the Himalayas. But there it was rather misty or cloudy. I did not look to the right.

It is somewhat naïve to speak of "right" or "left," for I was simply in space. And I knew that I was in the process of leaving the earth. While I was beholding all that, in reality I was in a coma. But I can tell you that was the most magnificent and most magical thing I have ever seen.

My nurse told me she thought I was dying then. In a state of shock, she said to me later, "It was as if you were surrounded by a bright light like one sees with the dying."

---

[744] See *ETG*, p. 293, *MDR*, pp. 289–90. On February 11, 1944, Jung fell and broke his fibula. He was taken to Hirslanden hospital, where he had a heart thrombosis. He was there till the beginning of July (JFA).

[745] Markus Fierz (1912–2006), Swiss physicist, and the son of Jung's student the analytical psychologist Linda Fierz David. He was an assistant to Wolfgang Pauli and in the 1950s was a professor at the University of Basel, before succeeding Pauli at ETH Zurich.

After a while, I turned away from Ceylon. I had been standing with my back to the Pacific Ocean. Then I turned towards the south. That is actually irrelevant, but it seemed to me as if I was making a turn or a rotation. There, I saw at a short distance in space an incredibly dark block of rock, like a massive meteorite. About the size of my house, or even larger, and in it, there was a door hollowed out. One sees such rocks on the coast of the Gulf of Bengal. There, they have carved temples into such rocks, hewn out of ancient blue-black granite. That is what my rock was like. It had an entrance, and this led into a small anteroom, where on the right there was a stone bench, and upon it a thoroughly black Indian was sitting in the lotus position, wearing a white robe. [186/187] I knew that he was expecting me. He was in a perfectly peaceful state and anticipated me in this way, in total silence. I saw that a door led into this anteroom and this door was framed high up with small alcoves in which there was coconut oil in small apertures, and small wicks were immersed in that oil which were all lit and flickering with small flames. I saw this for real in the temple of the holy tooth in Ceylon,[746] in the ancient temple city of Kandy. (It's in the mountains and I went there from Colombo; a small train takes you up there). So, that was the door leading into the rock, completely framed by several rows of these small oil lamps. It was like a crown of small flames. At the front, two steps were hewn out, leading into the anteroom, and I knew the Indian was expecting me. I knew that, although he said nothing.

While I was approaching this step something very significant occurred: I had the feeling that everything was falling off me, or rather as if everything was being stripped away from me; everything that I believe, or that I desire or thought, was taken from me. This entire phantasmagoria fell away from me, or was taken away from me, and that was an extremely painful process. And I had it all, everything that I had lived and had done, everything that had happened around me, I *had* it all or it was now with me. I consisted of it so to speak; I consisted of my history, and I absolutely had the feeling that this is now me: I am this bundle of facts. That was a feeling of the most extreme poverty but at the same time of great contentment. I had nothing of which I could say: This I can demand or desire; but I was objective, I was what had been.

When I wanted to go up to this step that led into the rock temple—but they were, of course, only made out of air, as it were—then from the right,

---

[746] The Dalada Maligawa in Kandy, said to house a tooth of the Buddha. Jung visited Kandy at the end of January 1930, with Fowler McCormick.

from below, coming up from Europe, there came an image, upwards. And it was Haemmerli,[747] my doctor, and he was surrounded, or his image was surrounded, by a golden laurel wreath, or a chain was wrapped around him. I knew him: Ah, there's my doctor who's been treating me; but now he's showing up like a prince, like a basileus of Kos.[748] Even Haemmerli in reality was only an avatar of this Basileus who actually once existed. He now came to me in his primal form and, seemingly, I too was in my primal form—but I did not perceive that—but I think it was the case. So, like an image, he came floating up out of the depths towards me, and then an exchange of thoughts took place us between us. He had a message to convey to me. He was delegated from the earth: there were protests against my leaving, I was not allowed to leave and must return.—I was terribly disappointed; for in that moment the whole vision stopped. I was deeply disappointed: now it was all in vain! This defoliation that had been an extremely painful process for me, that was now all past.

From then on, it took a good three weeks until I could really make up my mind to live again. During the day, I could not eat because I had a such a disgust[749] at doing so. I had a beautiful view through the window

---

[747] Dr. Theodor Haemmerli (1883–1944), a noted heart specialist. Among his patients were Paul Klee and Rainer Maria Rilke. He died on June 30, 1944, and Jung then wrote to Alwina von Keller on July 6 that Haemmerli, like Heinrich Zimmer, "died on the eve of his fame. This seems to be a particularly critical moment." *Letters*, vol. 1, p. 345. On October 25, 1955 Jung wrote to Haemmerli's brother Armin, "Your letter from Kos moved me deeply, since your late brother, who attended me when I had my cardiac infarct in 1944, was associated with Kos in a mysterious way. In my delirious states the image of your brother appeared to me, framed by the golden Hippocratic wreath, and announced—at that point I was already 2,500 km away from the earth and was about to enter a rock temple hollowed out of a meteorite—that I had no permission to go any further from the earth but had to return to it. From the moment of this vision I feared for the life of your brother, since I had seen him in his primal form as Prince of Kos, which signified his death. I discovered only afterwards that the great physicians of Kos styled themselves as (kings). On April 4, 1944 I was allowed to sit up on the edge of the bed for the first time, and on that day your brother took to his bed, never to rise again." *Letters*, vol. 2, p. 273. As Gerhard Adler noted, the Greek island Kos was the birthplace of Hippocrates, and was famed for a sanctuary of Asculepius. Barbara Hannah noted that "Jung was still distressed by the idea that [Haemmerli's] death might be connected with his own almost miraculous recovery. He pointed out that Zeus himself was said to have killed Aesculapius by a thunderbolt because he had brought back patients from death. Later in the Aesculapian sanctuaries, doctors might save any lives they could among their patients but were forbidden to bring anyone back from the dead. Should they break this law, they had to pay for it with their own lives. Jung was somewhat consoled, however when he heard that a friend of Dr. H.—another well-known Zurich specialist—had been distressed about him several months *before* Jung's illness began." Hannah, *Jung: His Life and Work*, p. 277.
[748] *basileus*: Greek term for a "king/sovereign."
[749] "disgust": in French in the original, "dégoût."

out onto the Institute for Epileptics and the Albis.[750] But for me, that was like a painted curtain with black holes in it. It was like a page of newsprint with photographs and holes in it, and I had absolutely no relationship with it. I kept thinking: Now I must squeeze myself back into the system of boxes. It seemed to me as if a three-dimensional world had been artificially constructed behind the horizon of the cosmos where everyone was sitting in their little boxes. And now I was supposed to pretend once again that this was something! That felt to me like a terrible prison, and I was angry beyond measure that I should ever find this acceptable again, this world. There, I had been utterly joyful that finally everything had fallen away from me, but now it was again as if I—like all the others—was suspended by threads inside such a box. When I was in space, I had been weightless, and there, nothing had weighed down on me any more.

And then there was still something that I must elaborate further: as I was approaching the temple in the rock, I was certain that I was entering a luminous room—I simply knew this!—and there were gathered all those people to whom I actually belonged. I would finally now understand what causal chain I belonged to: I would know finally what came before me and what would become of my life. My lived life seemed to me like a story, with no beginning and no end, and that was now cut off again as if with scissors. Nothing but questions arose: Why has your life taken this course? Why did he bring these preconditions with him? What did he do with it? What will be the result of it? I knew I would have received an answer to all these if I had stepped inside the rock temple. And there, I would have joined those people who had lived something similar to me. I knew that I would suddenly see why everything was as it was. That was unimaginably enchanting: in the universe this rock was floating, and I myself was floating in the universe.

During the day I was always terribly depressed. I felt miserably weak; I hardly dared move and I kept thinking: Now I must return to this grey old world. I was resistant to Dr. Haemmerli because he had brought me back to life. On the other hand, I was worried about him: "For God's sake, his life is in danger! He appeared to me in his primal form! And if someone has achieved this form, then it is the case that he must soon die. Then he already belongs to that company of people who belong to him!"

Then I had the thought that he had to die—in my place. I wanted to speak to him about it and he did not understand me. I was angry with him and thought, "Why does he keep pretending that he does not know

---

[750] Albis: a mountain range visible from Zurich.

that he is a Basileus of Kos? That he has already taken on his primal form? He wants to make me believe that he doesn't know it." And this upset me terribly. My wife reproached me for being so unfriendly towards him. And I know I positively resented him for not wanting to speak about all of this with me. "For God's sake, he must take care, he can't be so heedless, I'd like to speak with him about it so that he does something to take care of himself." I was convinced that he could be in danger because in space he had met me in his primal form.

In actual fact I was his final patient. On April 4, 1944[751]—I remember the date precisely—I was allowed to sit on the edge of the bed for the first time, and on this same day he took to his bed and never got up again.—I heard then that he had occasional attacks of high fever, and very soon afterwards he had died. He was a good doctor; there was something genial about him. Otherwise, he would not have appeared to me as the Prince of Kos! [189/190]

Then every night, between twelve and one o'clock, I experienced a ludicrously peculiar state of mind. At first, I slept until about midnight. Then I came to myself and was in a completely altered state for about an hour. I was as if unburdened: I was happy and at peace. I felt as if I were floating in space, as if I were hidden in the lap of the universe in an incredible emptiness, but filled with the utmost feeling of happiness. "Now that is eternal blessedness." One cannot experience that; it is far too wonderful. It was an absolute and infinite and complete feeling of happiness that filled me. My surroundings also seemed enchanted.

In the beginning, it seemed to me that my nurse was an old Jewish woman. She always warmed up food for me—in reality—at any hour of the night, and it seemed to me as if she were preparing ritual kosher meals for me. I then ate with gusto. It seemed to me as if she had a blue halo around her head. She was an old Jewess, much older than she was in reality, and she prepared ritual meals for me.

I was in the Pardes Rimonim, the orchard of pomegranates. That is the title of a Kabbalistic tract (M. Cordovero).[752] And the marriage was taking place of the Tiferet with the Malchut. Or, I was the rabbi Simon ben Jochai,[753] whose marriage was celebrated in the afterlife. It was the

---

[751] See n. 747 above.

[752] *Pardes rimonim* (Orchard of pomegranates) is a Kabbalistic work composed in 1548 by Moses ben Jacob Cordovero, the influential leader of a mystical school based in Safed, in the Damascus *eyalet* of the Ottoman Empire.

[753] In an undated letter to Rivkah Schärf, probably written in 1944, Aniela Jaffé thanked her on behalf of Jung: "Please thank Miss Schärf in my name, and tell her that I am

mystical wedding, but this was performed in terms of[754] Kabbalistic ideas.

So that was wonderful; that was indescribable. I always thought: So that's the orchard of pomegranates. That's the wedding of Malchut with Tiferet.[755] I don't know if I played a role in it also, but I myself was it; I was the wedding. And my blessedness was that of a wedding. Then it abated and gradually transformed. The marriage of the lamb in the festively adorned Jerusalem had come. I cannot describe what that was like in detail. It simply was so. These were indescribable states of blessedness. "I am the marriage of the lamb." Angels were present, and light, and I don't know what.

And that too disappeared again, and then came the idea, and that was the final thing: then I went along a far valley, right to the end, where there was a gentle mountain range. And at the end of the valley was an ancient [190/191] theater; it lay beautifully in the green landscape. And there, in this theater, the hierosgamos[756] was taking place. It was a theater with Greek columns, there were Greek dancers, both male and female, there. And on a couch bedecked with flowers, all-father Zeus and Hera were consummating the mystical marriage. That's the ancient idea of the hierosgamos. And all that was magnificent. So night after night I floated in utmost blessedness, "surrounded by images of all creatures."[757]

And then these motifs combined and became fainter and I gradually drew closer to the earth again, and about three weeks after the first vision these states stopped completely. Mostly they lasted only about an hour, and then I went back to sleep. And towards morning, I already felt: Now this grey morning is returning, now the grey world is coming. What madness, what a terrible madness! For these inner states, they were so fantastically beautiful; in contrast, the earth was downright ridiculous.

At that time someone visited me, and I was still so close to that other world when she gave me her hand to hold. And it seemed unbelievably brutal and real to me. This touch was of a terrible materiality and reality

---

especially thankful to her for the Kabbalistic literature that she had got for me before my illness. It was especially helpful for me in the darkest hours of my illness" (quoted by courtesy of Nomi Kluger-Nash).

[754] "in terms of": in English in the original.

[755] See *Mysterium Coniunctionis* (1955–56), CE 24; CW 14, §§ 18–19, § 568 and §§ 591–92.

[756] "hierosgamos" (sacred marriage): the ritual union between divine counterparts, usually a God and Goddess, to be found in a wide range of traditions.

[757] A citation from Goethe's *Faust II*, Act 1, sc. 5, l. 6289.

which I could not yet tolerate. Anything but closeness! Any closeness was completely unbearable to me.

But do you know, one cannot ever imagine this beauty and this intensity of feeling. And then came the contrast, the day; I was terribly tormented and was absolutely at the end of my tether. Everything irritated me. Everything was too material and had a repulsive taste. But at night: everything was alright.

But I still remember exactly: in the beginning, in the pomegranate orchard, there, I asked the nurse to excuse me if I should harm her. For there was such a holiness in space, and that could be harmful for her. She, of course, did not understand that. It was the great holiness of space, and I feared that would be unbearable for others. Therefore I apologized for this, I could do nothing about it. This holiness, it was very dangerous. It was quite unbelievably enchanting and indescribable, this presence of holiness. That was like an atmosphere. I understood that one speaks of the "scent" of the Holy Spirit. That was it. There was a pneuma present in space of unbelievable holiness. And that was the *mysterium coniunctionis*.

In India I learned to say yes to the unification of the opposites. But that is too difficult, one cannot explain that to people, one cannot refer to that; it is a wonderful mystery. With Paracelsus, I encountered similar ideas; he also struck me to the core. And in the *Paracelsica*, I called it the tremendous mystery for the first time.[758]

OCTOBER 21, 1957[759]

I've given much thought to what I told you on Friday, these visions and experiences during my illness in 1944. What so affected me about it was

---

[758] *Paracelsica* (1941), CE 16, comprised Jung's essays "Paracelsus as a Physician," CW 15, and "Paracelsus as a Spiritual Phenomenon," CW 13.

[759] On this day, Aniela Jaffé wrote to Kurt Wolff, "Last Friday I had another wonderful 'biography session.' Jung told me about the death visions that he experienced during his serious illness in 1944. And also about India." On October 24, Wolff wrote to her asking for information about The Red Book and The Black Book, and asked for a copy of Jung's Africa and India diaries, together with sections from the The Red Book and The Black Book that could be included in the work (BL). On October 27 Jung wrote to Jaffé authorizing her to publish her notes from their conversations, and to supplement these with excerpts from autobiographical notes, such as The Red Book, The Black Book, his Africa diary, his "Impressions from a Trip to India," and the 1925 Seminar. He also agreed to the inclusion of the *Septem Sermones ad Mortuos* as an appendix. He granted her the rights on the notes of their interviews, on the condition of equally split royalties (JP). On October 29, Jaffé replied to Wolff with information regarding the items he asked about. She indicated that for this project, an excerpt from The Black Book would come under consideration. She

that it was so objective and not just felt. It was real and so entirely genuine. I would never have thought that one could experience something like that in such a state. Or that such a state would be possible at all. It was a feeling of eternal blessedness. We cannot imagine this at all. After I told you about it, I gave much thought in particular to the idea of this objectivity.

We are scared of the term "eternal." But this was the blessedness of a non-temporal state, where present and past and future are one. It is, in actuality, a wholeness and it is objective. Nothing is oriented in time any more, and, further, nothing can now be measured according to temporal concepts, but it is a state, for example, a feeling state, which one cannot imagine.

How would it then be if I were the same as I was the day before yesterday, and today, and the day after tomorrow? Then something would not yet have begun, something else would be most clearly present, and something else again would have already happened or have ended, and all that would be one. The one thing that remains to be felt is a totality, an iridescent wholeness, in which all experiences are contained: where there is anticipation for what is beginning, surprise for what is happening now, and satisfaction about the outcome already contained within it. That is a complete objectivity.

And this experience is, in turn, linked to the dream about my wife in which she produces the image for me that contains the beginning of our relationship and all our life events spanning fifty-three years, and which also contains the end.[760] In the face of this wholeness, one can't keep up. For this is an indescribable whole that one is pulled down into, full of emotion, or one is quite objective, and one is both at the same time.

Those visions of 1944 were the most incredible thing that I have ever experienced. From the force of those images I concluded that I was very close to death.

I'd suggest you read that small article (in *Reader's Digest*). There, someone is sitting at the bed of a dying man and holds their hand tightly. The dying man says to him that he should let go, he should not hold him back. Ahead, there is actually something very [193/194] important. When he would arrive at that place, then he would have a wonderful

hadn't yet read Jung's Africa journal (BL). On November 2 Jaffé wrote to Jack Barrett that "his permission to use his autobiographical writings is only given for those parts of these writings, which I insert in the so-called 'autobiography.' But there is no permission to publish anything of this material beyond that autobiography" (BA).

760 See above, p. 75.

prospect.[761]—That's it. That's how it was for me. It seemed to me that I was robbed; everything was stripped away from me and then I was suddenly in a quite different position. At first I had the feeling of absolute annihilation, of being robbed, of being plundered, and then suddenly it was all perfectly one and the same. Suddenly it was all quite in the past; it was a sudden *fait accompli*, without any sort of back-reference to what came before. There was no regret about it, that something fell away or was taken away. On the contrary. I had everything that I was and I had only that. *Omnia mea mecum porto.*[762][194/195]

OCTOBER 23, 1957

(Dream of an acquaintance who was close to death:[763] she has been to the "afterlife," there was a school class there in which deceased friends of hers were sitting in the front row; this signified that the woman was now coming to join them. And they were all extremely excited about her arrival.)

This dream seems to me incredibly significant. It portrays the newcomer who is just now coming to join these other dead as if they were bringing "news," that is, the things that consciousness had acquired on earth in the interim. For there in eternity, there is no progress. That is the reason man develops and consciousness develops on the earth; since something new can be acquired. But in eternity nothing new is attained; nothing becomes conscious; for everything is "one" there, and something can become conscious only if it is taken apart so that the one is differentiated from the other. That can take place only in time, not in eternity.

What a person "takes over" with them at death seems to be exceptionally important. And the insight into this destiny of man and of consciousness is an important contribution to the purpose of life; it conveys an aspect of life which has never yet been considered.

The proposition of the dream also concurs with my own experience with the unconscious. When I was working with the unconscious—and

---

[761] The reference is to the condensed version of Norman Vincent Peale's *Stay Alive All Your Life* (Hoboken, NJ: Prentice-Hall, 1957), in *Reader's Digest*, October 1957, under the title "Beyond Death There Is Life": "Dr. Leslie Weatherhead, of London, says that once he sat on the bed of a dying man and held his hand. 'I must have gripped his hands more tightly than I thought,' Dr. Weatherhead said, 'for the patient said a strange thing. "Don't pull me back . . . It looks so wonderful further on!"'" (p. 90).

[762] "All that is mine I carry with me," variously ascribed to Stilpon the Stoic and Bias of Priene.

[763] Cf. *ETG*, p. 307, *MDR*, p. 305.

the unconscious corresponds in a certain regard to the "afterlife"—I saw then that the unconscious figures were each, in turn, uninformed about what was actually happening. Mead had the same experience.[764] He published around sixteen to eighteen volumes on mystical literature, predominantly about Gnosticism. He really achieved a great deal in this research. Then later, in his more advanced years, he devoted himself to spiritualism and did many experiments with mediums. He himself wrote to me about it—I believe they were the last letters before his death. And what he wrote to me was extremely interesting. He had a medium through which an ancient Gnostic had manifested, namely Valentinus.[765] [195/196]

He, Mead, had literally thrown himself at him in order to learn from him. But "Valentinus" had preempted him and besieged him with questions, for he wanted to know what had happened on Earth in these two thousand years. So Mead had to tell him about philosophy, about science, about history and so on. The sciences in particular interested "Valentinus"; unfortunately Mead did not understand much of this; but he told him the mystery of the railway and of airplanes. Valentinus was absolutely delighted, said this was amazing and that he must tell his friend Basilides.[766] With that, his manifestation ended, and he did not appear in the séances for a long time. But once, much later, he returned again with new questions. He reported that he had seen Basilides, that he'd had to seek him out for a long time, and finally he had found him up high on a mountain where he was meditating. He, Valentinus, had gone to great trouble to reach him and told him everything that had happened on Earth in the meantime. But Basilides had been completely skeptical, saying: Valentinus thou dreamest![767] This expresses splendidly the relationship between consciousness and the unconscious; you can also say: between this

---

[764] G.R.S. Mead (1863–1933), English theosophist and specialist on Hermeticism and Gnosticism. On Mead, see Clare Goodrick-Clarke and Nicholas Goodrick-Clarke, eds, *G.R.S. Mead and the Gnostic Quest* (Berkeley, CA: North Atlantic Books, 2005). Jung possessed many of Mead's works.

[765] Valentinus (100–160 CE) was a major Gnostic theologian. On his work and his school, see G.R.S. Mead, *Fragments of a Faith Forgotten*, 2nd edn (London: Theosophical Publishing Society, 1906 [1900]), pp. 284–310.

[766] Basilides, A major Gnostic figure in Alexandria in the first century CE. On Basilides, see Mead, *Fragments*, pp. 253–84. Jung credited his privately published *Septem Sermones ad Mortuos* to Basilides: he explained in a letter to Alphonse Maeder of January 19, 1917, "I could not presume to put my name to it, but chose instead the name of one of those great minds of the early Christian era which Christianity obliterated." *Letters*, vol. 1, p. 34.

[767] Basilides's phrase is in English in the original.

side and the beyond. The same goes for the butterfly dream of Chuang Tzu.[768]

[769]I still recall when I was first working with the unconscious that the figures of Salome and Elijah played a great role. Elijah later transformed himself into Philemon; Salome became my anima.—Very much later, about one or two years later, they showed up again in my fantasies and to my greatest astonishment they behaved as if nothing had happened, whereas in reality the most outrageous things had happened. Yet both of them knew absolutely nothing about it. I had to start from the beginning again in telling them everything. That astonished me no end.[770]

Now what does this mean? It means that both had in the meantime gone into eternity and were therefore unaware; they were simply uniformed or unconscious. In the same way, God is not informed either, but must allow himself to be informed through a consciousness, through a human being. That is in fact the most noble task of consciousness, therein resides its absolute meaning. And that is why life is a *mysterium*.

The lunatic Schreber expressed this idea: [196/197] God was compelled to keep nearer to Earth in order to see what sort of remarkable things were happening there.[771] And Schreber goes on to report that because God drew close to Earth, great miracles happened.[772] "Miracles abound," as he puts it.[773] These thoughts or images destroyed poor old Schreber's consciousness, but ultimately they arise as consequences from the unconsciousness of God. For when it is said of God that he is omniscient, his knowing is only a knowing in eternity, and that means, in essence, not knowing; for there are no contrasts in eternity. It is one single all. Whatever contents there are in eternity must iterate in time in order to be known. For knowing and consciousness always mean this and not that. And this unfolding of the one out of the other can take place only in time.

---

[768] "Once upon a time, I, Chuang Tzu, dreamt that I was a butterfly, flitting around and enjoying myself. I had no idea I was Chuang Tzu. Then suddenly I woke up and was Chuang Tzu again. But I could not tell, had I been Chaung Tzu dreaming I was a butterfly, or a butterfly dreaming I was now Chuang Tzu? However, there must have been some difference between Chuang Tzu and a butterfly! We call this the transformation of things." *The Book of Chuang Tzu*, trans. Martin Palmer with Elizabeth Breuilly, Chang Wai Ming, and Jay Ramsey (London: Penguin, 1996), p. 20.

[769] See *ETG*, p. 309, *MDR*, p. 306, and *BB 2*, pp. 179–80.

[770] See *BB 6*, May 3, 1916, pp. 234–35.

[771] See Schreber, *Memoirs*, p. 231. (On Schreber, see n. 565 above).

[772] Schreber, *Memoirs*, p. 234.

[773] Schreber, *Memoirs*, p. 232.

In the dream I told you, the spirits of the deceased are interested in those who are newly arriving in order to hear from them an account of further, new levels of consciousness, and in order to acquire real insight.[774] As an example, this is why my *Septem Sermones* also started with the dead returning from Jerusalem because they did not find what they were seeking there.[775] And what they did not find in eternity they were now seeking from human beings. I was always amazed by this lack of knowledge.

One can consider this a dying person's dream, and it threw an illuminating light upon these associations. That, in fact, one can "know" only here on Earth and can learn something new only here. And first and foremost: that this life is of incredible importance for the salvation of the world. What one brings over at the end of life is incredibly important.

I also had the experiences of a "gathering" in the visions of 1944. And even during this vision, a dream occurred to me that I had during my confrontation with the unconscious, during the work on *Transformations*.[776] I had had a dream of such a "gathering." That was around 1911. At the time I was on a cycling trip to northern Italy with a friend.[777] On the way home, we traveled via Pavia to Arona on the lower part of Lago Maggiore. I had it in mind to cycle along Lago Maggiore and through the Tessin as far as Faido, in order to take the train back to Zurich from there. But during the night when we were in Arona, I had a dream: I was in a gathering of people who were sort of [197/198] my tribe, or "my" people, people who belong to me. And these were people from all different centuries. There was, for example, a gentleman with a full-bottomed wig who spoke to me in Latin and I was also supposed to reply to him in Latin. I understood him because I had learned Latin, but of course I couldn't go as far as answering him in Latin. I felt hugely ashamed of that and this feeling was so intense that I woke up because of it.

Immediately upon waking, I thought of my work, *Transformations*. There was no further thought of continuing the cycle tour, because I felt compelled to take the train home immediately. I had massive feelings of

---

[774] See above, p. 200.

[775] The *Sermones* commenced with the dead saying, "We have come back from Jerusalem, where we did not find what we sought!" January 30, 1916 (*BB 5*, p. 283). Two years earlier the dead Anabaptists led by Ezekiel had gone to Jerusalem to pray at the holy places (*BB 4*, p. 207).

[776] See *ETG*, p. 309, *MDR*, p. 306

[777] The bicycle tour Jung referred took place in October 1910, with Wolfgang Stockmayer (see *FJL*, p. 359).

inferiority, and that is why I had to get back to work as quickly as possible. Only later did I understand the meaning of the dream: for this man in the full-bottomed wig also wanted to ask me something and I did not yet know the answer; it was too early back then, I had not yet traveled far enough. Then I went home right away, for I could in no way sacrifice three more days for a cycling trip.

Those crazy people who always think it's the ones in the afterlife who know. No, it's precisely the opposite, if someone knows, it's us.

This possibility of finding the meaning of life is true not only for special people, because it applies to all, since that is the very thing for which they exist. It's that way in nature: countless seeds are sown, some grow, and what grows bears fruit, while the rest wither due to unfavorable conditions. Jesus said the same in his parable: countless seeds fell among thorns and countless on good soil.[778]

When I first dared to think of God as being unconscious then straight away all these insights and realizations came, but I had to fight my way through hideous undergrowth. For what was eternally unconscious is incredibly difficult to extricate. [198/199]

OCTOBER 24, 1957

If I say that in the unconscious there is an absolute knowledge—religiously put: that God is omniscient—there is no contradiction in my saying that only man, or consciousness, can have knowledge. As a human being, I am a creature who knows that I know. Man is conscious of his knowledge, whereas this, this all-being, is not conscious of its knowledge; knowledge is simply present, and presumably extends into the smallest details of the cosmos and nature. For in nature things arise that appear to derive from an intelligence.

Think of the symbiosis of two animals or animals and plants. And, for example, how does the hydrocephalus virus behave?[779] It behaves as if anatomy is familiar to it. For example, if one cuts out the lens of a salamander's eyes, this lens repairs itself from the surrounding tissue, although it is not specifically designed to do that. Or a certain type of wasp needs the flesh of a caterpillar for its young, so she must put a caterpillar among the eggs and what does she do? She stings this caterpillar in the spinal cord in one particular spinal ganglion where the motor center resides, and

---

[778] See Matthew 13:1–23.
[779] See n. 73 above.

then the caterpillar is lamed. And how does she know to do this? The bees can even transmit their "knowledge"; they can share it with others. These are intelligent actions, but whether they are aware of what they are doing, that we don't know. Or whether they are aware of their knowledge, that we know just as little. Of ourselves, we know that we know, or that we know to a certain degree. Where it transcends that, then such effects take place as they did with Freud.

Eros also belongs to man's actual knowledge.[780] Eros is an energy in contradistinction to Logos: a relational function. It creates and destroys relationships. Eros is also a very negative force. And although I can recognize things, this insight is naturally only discriminatory. There, everything could be separated from everything. One could compare one separate thing with another, but there could be no action that corresponds to the insights, as for that to occur, it needs Eros. The insights must bond with a feeling, with a value judgment.

Someone with an inferior feeling can hardly be selective from among his insights. For this, sheer comparison is not sufficient. While he may be able to compare, he does not arrive at constructive action [199/200] because he does not feel under obligation. The feeling of obligation towards the insights, that is Eros. I can have an important insight, but this can leave me fully cold as a human being. But because I have Eros, then it makes an impression on me, and in consequence my action is also determined by it. If I have no Eros, then absolutely nothing arises out it. No action arises out of insight alone, for I am not further involved. If I only observe the insight, or the "truth," then that in itself achieves nothing.

If I am involved and draw conclusions from it, or feel myself under obligation, then that takes place in time and temporal processes arise from it. We experience Eros therefore only as a temporal process. If no more time takes place—that is, in the "afterlife" or in the unconscious— then Eros is simply the expression of an identity. Because in the "afterlife" or in the unconscious, everything is one. The Eros we know always wants to make two things into one, he is a force that joins what is separated. And that is unnecessary in the afterlife because there, everything is one and together.

Eros binds facts together. So if a house burns down in the neighborhood, that can leave me quite cold; or else I am affected by it in my feeling, and through Eros, who connects separated things, it might even be

<hr>

[780] See *ETG*, p. 356, *MDR*, p. 353.

that the burning house is connected to my own inner state so that a "sympathy" between it and me exists. So that synchronicity is present.

Thus the relatedness of man and woman, the archetype of Eros, is the image for intrinsic oneness. From this comes the Platonic idea of the primal being as the hermaphrodite.[781] Or the pederasty of the ancient world, that seeks to identify the one with the other and wants to say: This is what you are! And out of these things determined by Eros arises the idea of the Self as a unity out of many. And that is why Eros is no longer necessary in the intrinsic self, or in the "afterlife," because he has then attained his goal. He has already made all into one. [200/201]

Logos creates twoness and separates; Eros creates oneness from the many. And these two phenomena are possible only in three-dimensional space: that is, in time. So, when I am in such a space which I have separated from myself, then the original knowing is not so far away from me since, after all, I came originally from the oneness. The knowledge of this oneness is still in me. Eros comes to the aid of this dark knowledge; for this reason one lifts his unconscious knowledge into the light through love. Because one comes together through Eros and then one recognizes what one already always knew. *Qui amat cognoscit.*[782] Man's knowing is a recognition; as Plato says too: every knowing is a remembering.[783]

Man inquires about everything he is separated from. In the afterlife, he cannot find the answer, because he is in a state of unity there and is only as far as he was able to get.

God's knowing is always something less than what we know on this earth. This is why God turns to man. His behavior is a reflection of my own behavior. Man's feeling leads him to insight. He loves something, is interested in something, fascinated by something, and does not know why. But he can find out the reason if he goes after this feeling and, at its end, arrives at knowing Eros refers not only to the relationship between person and person. It goes much further.

This is how I experienced, for example, the wall paintings in Pompeii,[784] the entirety of ancient art, but mainly the paintings and the relics of the life of antiquity; these were absolutely erotically fascinating for me, almost like a sexual arousal. They were in fact for me like the direct manifestation of the life of antiquity. That was a terrible fascination. That

---

[781] See Plato, *Timaeus* 90–91.
[782] *Qui amat cognoscit* (Lat.): "He who loves, knows."
[783] Plato, *Phaedo* 72e.
[784] Presumably the "Villa of the Mysteries." See above, p. 99.

stopped only when I wrote *Transformations and Symbols of the Libido*, in which I understood something of the spirit of antiquity. And only after that was I able to go to Pompeii. Before that, to go to Pompeii was an unfulfilled dream; I could not go there because I did not yet have any relationship to it. And when I had written *Transformations*, then the relationship was there and I was able to go.—That wasn't enough for Rome because of the transition into Christianity which I didn't understand at the time. And when I understood it later, I was no longer physically capable of doing so. [201/202]

The great oneness is already before us. It is not possible to be caught up in something in which you are not caught up in from the absolute beginning, and you could know nothing of something if there were not already an unconscious knowledge of it present within you. However, it is in the unconscious, and you must bring it into consciousness. And Eros helps us in this meaning-making task. "A good man, through obscurest aspiration, still has still an instinct for the one true way."[785] In this regard, one does not regret any so-called stupidity, for even in that there always resides an inner necessity; and one never regrets what one has really lived. Even when it is apparently regrettable or it causes suffering, through it one has recognized something and wrested it from the darkness that has reigned for all eternity. A world that is known is a different world from the one that is not known, one that arises and fades away and never entered into consciousness. It did indeed have knowledge of itself but without knowing that it knew. That is how it is for primitives. They do not know that they know; they are not self-conscious; they are completely unconscious.

A good example is the Old Testament God who does have knowledge, but does not know this knowledge. Even the fact that God is a God of love is still no knowing of this knowledge.

Consciousness that really knows about this knowledge has cosmic significance. That is why I believe that we bring a knowing of this knowledge over to the other side at the end of our life. And that the Godhead must empty himself of his Godhead over and over again in order to take on human form, in order to create these experiences. One must, that is, be separate in order to know separateness. Only what is different from God can really know. For as long as God is the whole, it cannot know anything, it is all, in and of itself. When I am this world, I cannot know it. This is the meaning of the mystical remoteness of God; but it is a

---

[785] Quoted from the prologue to Goethe's *Faust*, ll. 328–29.

desolate state which is Lucifer. No one sees more clearly the beauty of God than the devil. His fire is the fire of a passionate longing for God which he cannot himself fulfil. [202/203]

It has never entered my head that someone might ever think I have found eternal truth. Theologians reproach me with this because they themselves are used to speaking only of eternal truth. You can't even dream of saying this about me. I am discerning a state of truth,[786] nothing more. If the physicist says the atom is like this or like that, and produces a model of it, he will not believe that this model signifies an "eternal truth." The theologians are not familiar with scientific thinking, with the consequence that misunderstandings occur due to an easy displacement of the concept or the presupposition. No scientist thinks that he has postulated an eternal truth. But these theologians, they're so used to pronouncing upon eternal truths.

When I met Freud for the first time in Vienna, we spoke for thirteen hours without interruption.[787] We made a sort of *tour d'horizon*,[788] and on that occasion I sought to hear his view about parapsychological phenomena, and I asked him about what he thought of precognitions, for example. He naturally rejected this at that time, due to his materialist prejudices. By the way, Bleuler was exactly the same, though later he became a spiritualist; he was ridiculed terribly after he had laughed at me for twenty years.[789] So later he became open to his own experiences.—Then Freud had to acknowledge that this is no mumbo-jumbo when even he later observed such phenomena himself.[790]

When I mentioned the possibility of such phenomena and said to Freud that I had also had certain experiences—quite aside from the literature that was already available at the time—he wheeled out such a platitudinous positivism that it was difficult for me not to respond with a counterblast that would have been too offensive. There was such an absence of philosophical reflection in his remarks that it made my stomach turn—as if "science" were the be-all and end-all. Such drivel! Not the

---

[786] "state of truth": in English in the original.

[787] See *ETG*, p. 153, *MDR*, p. 149. Jung and his wife, together with his then student Ludwig Binswanger, visited Freud in March 1907. The first meeting was on March 3. For Binswanger's recollections of this, see his *Sigmund Freud: Reminiscences of a Friendship* (New York: Grune and Stratton, 1957).

[788] *tour d'horizon*, in French in the original: "overview."

[789] Bleuler maintained an interest in psychical research: see n. 310 above.

[790] See Freud's "Psycho-Analysis and Telepathy" (1921/1941), *SE* 18, pp. 177–93.

true "science," but as if the "science of today" had already declared the ultimate and final word, whereas I was convinced we are absolutely nowhere near any ultimate truth. [203/204]

791While Freud was still speaking, I had the peculiar feeling that my diaphragm was made of iron and was glowing: in a glowing diaphragmatic vault. And in the same moment such a loud creaking took place in the bookcase directly next to us—we were sitting in front of it—that we were both terribly alarmed that the thing was about to fall down on us. This is exactly what happened. I said to Freud, "Now, that's a so-called catalytic exteriorization phenomenon"—"Oh no," he said, "that is total nonsense!" "But no," I replied, "you are mistaken, Herr Professor. And to prove that I'm right I now predict that there will be another creaking any minute!"—Then he looked at me in amazement and sure enough: at that moment there was another indescribably terrible creaking in the bookcase!

I do not know where this certainty came from. But I knew for certain that it would happen again, and that was indeed the case.—Freud looked at me horrified. I don't know what he was thinking or what he was looking at, whether he thought the bookcase had gone mad or whether I was crazy. There was such a creaking that we both believed the bookcase was about to fall upon us. This episode awoke in him a mistrust of me, for something like that is not possible, that sort of thing has no place in his worldview. In consequence, I somehow got completely off on the wrong foot with him. Afterwards I had the definite feeling that I had done him an injury. Afterwards I never spoke to him about this matter again. That took place in our first conversation.

I had observed similar things before: whenever I was in a situation where there was something unconsciously fateful for me contained in it, then a thing like this took place, such as knocking sounds, or such striking so-called catalytic manifestations as creaking furniture. And always precisely at that moment when such a situation was manifesting.—For example, when I made my first visit to the woman who would become my mother-in-law, when there was not even the merest notion of how

791 See *ETG*, pp. 159–60, *MDR*, p. 155. This event actually took place on Jung's second visit to Vienna with Emma Jung, March 25–30, 1909. On April 16 Freud wrote to Jung that he continued investigating this after Jung left, and noted that in one room there was a constant creaking where Egyptian steles rested on the bookshelves. In the second room, where they heard the noise, he had since heard it repeatedly, when there was no direct connection with his thoughts. *FJL*, p. 218.

our later relationship would develop,[792] I had to wait for a moment in the sitting room, and suddenly this creaking began in the furniture! And then I thought: My goodness! It's kicking off again! You know about how I had seen my wife for a moment standing on the stairs [204/205]—she was fourteen years old at the time.—And naturally with this impression in mind, I was waiting in the sitting room and had hardly been there a moment when it began! I knew that there was something fateful for me here. And I also knew it at that time with Freud: Something fateful is going to happen. For there is a knowledge in me that belongs to the future, that I am already aware of at the moment but without knowing it. In my unconscious, in my inner tension, a knowledge is present. That is how it was back then with my mother-in-law, and it was the same with Freud. At the time I did not yet know anything of the psychology of these phenomena. I knew that they took place, but I knew nothing more. (Supplement this with Freud letters!)[793] [794]

---

[792] See above, p. 43.

[793] Here followed excerpts from Freud's letters to Jung of April 16, 1909, May 12, 1911, and June 15, 1911, regarding occultism and parapsychology.

[794] The contract between Pantheon Books and Aniela Jaffé for "a work tentatively entitled 'Carl Georg [sic] Jung's Improvised Memories'" was dated October 25, 1957. On October 29, Jaffé wrote to Kurt Wolff that Jung would be on holiday till November 4. She indicated that given the nature of the work, she wanted to leave the submission date open-ended. Regarding the Red Book, she wrote that he already had "Die Wiederfindung der Seele." Jung had given her six volumes of the Black Books just before going to Bollingen. She was to go through them carefully to see what should be used for the proposed publication. She described the contents of the Red Book and the Black Books. Jung was still writing in the seventh volume, about matters such as the death of his wife, and she doubted that he would give this to her. She concluded, "I find it wonderful that you are accompanying the creation of this book with so much interest and engagement. I must confess that I myself am also already completely drunk with it. It is such an extraordinary life and above all: it is lived in such an extraordinary way, experienced and filled in such an unusual way, that one has never heard anything like it. The great thing is that Jung himself is now enjoying the telling of it." In an undated reply to Wolff's letter of October 30, Jaffé further narrated Jung's comments about The Red Book and The Black Book. She considered the publication of these at this juncture as being closed. On October 31 Wolff asked her to transcribe the sections from these that she was considering for inclusion.
On November 1 he wrote to her, "I thought that in a few cases you might have an opportunity to ask him to supplement what he told you at other times (for instance, the 'formidable secret,' the dream and the story of the little Jewess, the dream of the white bird, and the dreams from the big cold, etc.)." (See above, p. 55, below, pp. 403–4, above p. 121 and above p. 129, respectively.) He indicated that he was happy to see that much of what he would have liked to be covered had been, and gave a list of other subjects he would like to see addressed, such as what Jung felt about his psychiatric practice, and why he eventually gave it up; what he felt about marriage, his experience as a paterfamilias, his relation to children in general, his own, and his grandchildren; and what the importance of puberty was in development. It would be good too if he could expand on his comments on "the

NOVEMBER 8, 1957

Answer to Job developed out of the *Aion* book in which I began to engage with the psychology of Christianity.[795] Job is for me a sort of prefiguration of Christ. Both are connected through the idea of suffering. With Christ, it is the sin of the world that causes the suffering. And who is guilty of this sin? Well, it's God who created it, who committed this deception and who must now himself suffer the destiny of humanity. I understand evil as a metaphysical reality—that is, as contained in God himself. If one does not accept this, if it is not contained within God, then where is it? Then it is in man, and we cannot go along with that. It was not we who made the world. We are ourselves creatures of this world.

We are now at the end of the aeon of the fish, and a new aeon is beginning, in which everything that has been excluded from man thus far must now be added.[796] Until now we saw the good in God and the source of evil in man. But logically one could just as well also say the opposite. In future man himself will be recognized as the source of good and evil. They are qualities of the self. And this transition into humanity can take place because over the course of the aeons God has drawn closer to man. He became a man in his son, and he will incarnate in every individual person, this is what the Bible says. This is what the end of my *Job* book is about. In this sense, God incarnates in every individual—"Ye are

---

advantage and disadvantage of education," which he had mentioned in relation to Thomas Mann (see above, p. 53). Wolff referred to Jaffé's letter of October 13, in which she "mentioned a dream Dr. Jung had had repeatedly was eventually treated by him as a call to confide his most personal material to you (I suppose this is the dream of the unfinished house). I think it would be good to have this dream somewhere inserted." He was also interested in hearing whether music had been of importance to Jung, as well as architecture (especially in Egypt). He wondered if Charcot had made an impression on him, and wanted to hear his ideas regarding nationalities and races. Regarding the structure of the work, he thought it important to minimize the gaps in the narratives. He added that it was important for her to let Jung speak of whatever was on his mind, but that there would be occasions when she could encourage him to speak on certain subjects. In a postscript, he noted that it would be important that Jung's sense of humor be conveyed in the book. On November 2 Jaffé wrote to Wolff, "it is a great joy to me that you experience the visions of 1944 so similarly as I. It was an unforgettable afternoon when Jung described them to me: we sat in the garden and he even carried on speaking after the sun had set. It was an evening when summer was giving way to fall. For me that was the quintessential Jung." (BL).

[795] See *ETG*, p. 219, *MDR*, p. 216.

[796] The reference is to the conception of the Platonic month, or aeon, of Pisces, which is based on the precession of the equinoxes. Each Platonic month consists of one zodiacal sign, and lasts approximately 2,300 years. Jung discusses the symbolism attached to this in *Aion* (1951), CE 21; CW 9.2, ch. 6. See Liz Greene, *Jung's Studies in Astrology: Prophecies, Magic and the Qualities of Time* (London: Routledge, 2018).

Gods!"[797]—we are the source of good and evil. Which animal launched a Sputnik or invented an atomic bomb?[798] These are divine powers that have come into man and they are not good. But we are ourselves creations of God. He made us. We can give up the idea that God is good. The best we can say is that he is both good and evil.

It absolutely does not mean that I am against Christianity if I say such things and if I have written about them. Nor am I against the Church. But I am thinking Christianity onward. It's what has happened to me that has prompted this thinking onward in me.

Before I went to India, I felt that the problem of evil was about to land. [28/29]. That was the reason behind the fateful invitation to India.[799] There are educated people there you can speak with. They are convinced that they themselves are Atman. Such an idea has just as many advantages as disadvantages. For these Indians, concepts of good and evil applied to the Atman are completely irrelevant categories; one cannot say anything about them in relation to the Atman. When the Indian says he is an Atman it does not mean that he is good, but it does mean that he is somehow connected to God.

It is not a matter of the good God incarnating in man, but also just as much his dark side. But the incarnation of the good is an extremely frightening experience because, in any case, it is beyond human, and it even annihilates life. One cannot simply be good. For example, the life of a hermit is a good life but a crushed human life. And moreover, when the good is present, then evil must be added in, for the one is only possible or conceivable thanks to the other. It is the overabundance of the Godhead, and the all-consuming magnificence of the Godhead, that go naturally to both polarities, in both directions, not only the one side. Not only towards good or only towards evil.

When I am at the end of my life, I will not only have to give an account to the good God but also to the dark God. Giving an account to the darkness means whether I have paid my tribute to life; that means: Have I really lived or not? But that counts only if I am also conscious of the darkness that I have lived. It can barely even be expressed that one must also live the darkness if it is required of me. People do not

---

[797] See Psalm 82:6 and John 10:34.

[798] On October 4, 1957 Russia had launched *Sputnik* 1, the first satellite to orbit the earth.

[799] See above, p. 186, and pp. 189–91.

understand this, or they misunderstand it. Saint Paul was quite close to awareness of the darkness within him: "For I do not do the good I want to do, but the evil I do not want to do—this I keep on doing."[800] So he had a messenger of Satan who compelled him to blaspheme. That is an astonishing disclosure from Paul. A Peter or a John, to my mind, they're far less likeable, because they did not have the awareness that Paul possessed. They were unaware of their dark side.

Before I went to Africa for the first time in the spring of 1920, I knew the unconscious only as a subjective phenomenon and I was even less clear about the unconscious of other people.[801] Naturally I saw a certain correspondence between me and other people, but that was all within my subjective bandwidth. But now I wanted to see what an unconscious looks like where life is lived at a deeper level of consciousness. I also wanted to have lived for once in another world where everything is much more primitive, in order to see whether I would then have reactions like those of primitive people. That is why it was important to me while I was there to write up all my dreams. But I had only one single dream that was about a negro.[802]

The face of this negro appeared oddly familiar to me. Wherever had I seen him before? I had to think for a long time before I figured it out. At last it came to me: it's my hairdresser from Chattanooga in Tennessee! So an American negro! So I concluded that I must protect myself. For in the dream the negro had a massive curling iron which was glowing red hot, and I feared he would burn my skull with it. He wanted to impose negro hair upon me; he wanted to make my hair "kinky."[803] I had to pay attention to this warning of the unconscious. I saw that this unconsciousness, this primitiveness, was a danger to which one can fall victim only all too easily. When one is surrounded by Blacks, one gradually takes on their appearance; that's known as "going black."[804]

I remember still an old Englishman whom I met in Africa, a man who had lived there for a long time. He asked me why I'd come to Africa. I explained to him that the negroes and the life of primitive people interested me. Then he gave me this advice: "You better study Europeans under

---

[800] Romans 7:19.

[801] See above, p. 214–17.

[802] See *ETG*, pp. 275–76, *MDR*, pp. 272–73, where this dream is attributed to Jung's later African trip.

[803] "'kinky'": in English in the original.

[804] "'going black'": in English in the original.

African conditions!"[805] And in this he was not wrong. [30/31] It was my intention to study my "mind"[806] under these primitive conditions.

In the spring of 1920 I was in Africa for the first time, but only in Arabic North Africa.[807] I traveled to Algiers and from there along the coast as far as Tunis. From there I went south into the desert, towards Hoggard.[808] In the desert we traveled on mules, gorgeous animals that mostly walk at a fast trot. We arrived at an oasis, and I stayed there a few days and joined in an extremely interesting festival. In the morning I awoke early and I heard the busy sound of many people and the grunting of camels. And as I opened the shutters—I was staying in very modest accommodation; a Frenchman had a small guesthouse there but that was full of desert sand and the wood of the doors was completely warped by aridity and had wide cracks in it—I looked out and the whole place was full of hundreds of camels. The Arabs with their animals had streamed in from all over the area in order to render service to the marabout for two days. The marabout was a prince who exercises a religious function. He is also the administrator of alms to the poor. And over those two days they worked on a piece of the oasis, digging out small channels and planting. It was intended as a benefit for the poor from which the marabout distributed alms to the poor. And so they headed off to work with drumming and great noise and danced as they worked. They were as if intoxicated, and it was not without danger. I stopped nearby with my tour guide and observed everything. It was extraordinarily interesting.

And then when I came back, I had an extremely impressive dream. It was the dream of the Arab prince.[809]

On the final day before I sailed from Tunis to Marseille, I dreamed I was in an Arabic city; and there was a fortress there, and it was depicted in the dream. The city lay upon a flat plain and was surrounded by a city wall. It was—not untypically for that region—surrounded by a moat. If memory serves, the ground plan was square and there were four gates. I stood before a wooden bridge [31/32] leading over the water, towards one of the gates. It was a dark, horseshoe-shaped gate, and I thought: I'd like to see this city with its fortress from the inside. When I was in the center of the bridge a very handsome dark man came out of the gate; he was an elegant and regal figure, a youth in a white burnous. He evidently lived in

---

[805] *Sic*: quoted in English in the original.

[806] "'mind'": in English in the original.

[807] See *ETG*, p. 242, *MDR*, p. 238.

[808] Probably the Hoggar Mountains in the central Sahara (southern Algeria).

[809] See *ETG*, p. 246, *MDR*, p. 242, and *BB* 7, December 25, 1922 (pp. 222–23).

the fortress, and I thought that perhaps he might be the residing prince there. As I stand in the center of the bridge, he attacks me and tries to beat me to the ground or to throw me into the water. We wrestled with each other and finally we both fell into the water. There he tried to push me under. No, I thought, that's going too far! And then I pushed him under the water! Yet I knew that he had not drowned but had come back to life. Afterwards we sat in the fortress. In a large octagonal room. It was completely white, the walls of grey marble, very simple and very beautiful, and along the walls there were sofas. In the middle was a gorgeous carpet. I sat on one of the low sofas, and in front of me on the floor was a parchment with fine black lettering, written in an exceptionally beautiful style. On milk-white parchment. The young Arab prince with whom I had just wrestled sat to my right, and I put my arm around his shoulder. I explained to him that he must now read this, that I had triumphed over him, and therefore he must now read the book. I had the feeling that this was absolutely vital. But he was not keen on doing that and bristled against it.—I did not know what sort of book it was. But I had the feeling that it was sort of *my* book. I now had power over him.

This dream made a crazy impression on me: I had evidently gone to Africa in order to find my shadow, the darkness. I was conscious that I wanted to see the world with other eyes than those of a European. And I also made a whole heap of small observations which were very interesting.[810] But this dream said to me: in the kingdom of the dark man, there is a city and within it is a fortress, so that the round resides in the square. There is a central dome, an octagon. That is the Divan, the reception room of the prince. And now, I am there and dictating to him, and the darkness almost overpowered me. [32/33]

At the end of my trip I had an attack of infectious enteritis. It came because I ate the food of the Arabs. You see, I *ate* the land. I ate black dates and I ate couscous, and everything the Arabs ate and drank, and I probably contracted enteritis from this. I ate it all in order to incorporate the land within me. I did the same in India. When I came home from India, I had amoebic dysentery. I had the feeling: So now, India is inside me; now, it has penetrated me.

There are some very remarkable things. For example, that a man falls in love with a girl while knowing she has gonorrhea. He shudders at facing it but the fascination is greater, and so despite this he must sleep

---

[810] Jaffé added the following note in the margin by hand: "Not yet had the chance to ask about them."

with her.—That's the mystery of the anima. That is how it is with these men: instead of giving himself to the soul of the woman, which is a mystery, he assimilates the poison that is in her body. He lets himself be poisoned by the collective—gonorrhea is a collective illness—and thereby reaps the revenge of the anima. Since one did not consider the "soul," in order to get "soul" one must take a prostitute. Such men abuse the woman or the feminine and, for this, they reap not the collective unconscious but collective illness. It ends with a poisoning. How the collective unconscious poisons and destroys if one does not know about it! But if one knows about it, then it is an enlightenment.

And the young man, the Arab who came towards me, he was a piece of the soul of Muslim North Africa. A sort of quintessence of North Africa; and my shadow took on this form. Naturally he wanted to destroy me as a European. I was not permitted to penetrate into the mystery of the Casbah; after all, I'm a European who is hated in any case. I always had the scent of blood in my nose back then.

I had the same when I was in Berlin in 1934.[811] I was not in Berlin for more than three or four days. And I could not bear it any longer there. I had to get away because I could not bear the scent of blood one minute longer. I knew exactly: A terrible thing is in the offing. As quickly as possible I headed for Copenhagen. "The Gods seek to ruin you, I hasten so as not to die with you!"[812] Mussolini was in Berlin at the same time. That made a terrifying impression on me.[813] [33/34]

I had the same feeling in Tunis back then and in North Africa. It was of course the perception of hate towards the Europeans which was present even then.

I was very struck in North Africa by a homosexuality reminiscent of antiquity.[814] Because the Arabs have not yet been able to found a state, they were still at the stage of male friendships. These are a sort of

---

[811] In Jung's "Agenda" there is a diary entry for March 22, "Meeting of the Zentralblatt." The pages for following days are blank, suggesting that he may have gone to Berlin for this. In May he was in Bad Nauheim for the congress of the International Medical Society for Psychotherapy.

[812] Jaffé noted, "Schiller, 'The Ring of Polycrates.' This poem was written in 1797."

[813] Mussolini's visit to Berlin was actually September 27–30, 1937. In an interview with H. R. Knickerbocker in 1938, "Diagnosing the Dictators," Jung recalled, "I saw the Duce and the Führer together in Berlin the time Mussolini paid his formal visit; I had the good luck to be placed only a few yards away from them, and could study them well." He then went on to relay his impressions of the two: see McGuire and Hull, C. G. Jung Speaking, pp. 126–27. Jung went on to attend the Ninth International Medical Congress for Psychotherapy in Copenhagen, October 2–4.

[814] See ETG, p. 243, MDR, p. 239.

precursor to the founding of the *polis*. Even today there's still a lot of homosexuality there. And do you know, I'll never forget the sight: in these splendid palm gardens they stroll about in their flowing white garments, their arms around each other's shoulders, exceptionally handsome men of noble stature. A splendid sight from an aesthetic point of view. Here, homosexuality had the creative goal of founding a state. One cannot say that the homosexual is not a creative person *per se*. Cultural history has far too many examples of the opposite. The most one can say is that where homosexuality is not genuine but represents an avoidance, a flight from engagement with the opposite sex—perhaps because of a mother complex—then in that case, the genuine creative force of the man cannot find its elaboration.

I did not have any contact at that time with educated Arabs. The most highly educated Arab I spoke to was my tour guide.

In the years 1925/26 I went to Africa for the second time, this time to Kenya, Uganda, the Sudan, and Egypt.[815] I covered three thousand kilometers including several hundred kilometers on foot. The other stretches were covered by ship or by rail.

I was very interested in the dreams of the negroes, but I got to hear only very few of these. "Only the witchdoctor still has dreams," I was told, and when I asked him he said, "Yes, my grandfather, he still had dreams," but that he himself did not! Since the Whites have been in Africa no more dreams arise![816]

Once a man told me a dream. This was an old negro sitting at home who had quite a large herd of cows that were grazing over a broad expanse of land. The negroes have a very close relationship to their cattle, as if they knew the individual animals personally. Now this old negro had a black and white cow. He dreamed she gave birth to a calf at a bend in the river, in the bay. He did not know that this animal was pregnant. He sent a couple of young boys to the appointed place and sure enough, they found the cow who had indeed given birth to a bull calf. This is the sort of dream they have, but otherwise nothing is dreamed.

Africa was for me a colossal affirmation, an incredible affirmation: I saw quite clearly how we Europeans are quite similar to these people.

---

[815] See *ETG*, p. 257, *MDR*, p. 253. Jung traveled with Peter [i.e., H. G.] Baynes (1882–1943) and George Beckwith (1896–1931). They were later joined by Ruth Bailey. On Jung's travels to Africa and New Mexico, see Shamdasani, *Jung and the Making of Modern Psychology*, pp. 316–28. On Jung's trip to Africa, see Blake W. Burleson, *Jung in Africa* (New York: Continuum, 2005).

[816] See *ETG*, p. 269, *MDR*, p. 265.

The primitive is no different from us, he is only much simpler but also much more profound. He is still connected with the whole of nature in a still crepuscular way. He does not have the enlightened, concentrated consciousness that we have.

I experienced there the interpretation of myths and of numinous narratives which are enormously valued by these people. I saw the attachment to mysteries and magical customs, but that is the same for us. You only have to go deep into the country or look behind the scenes: very soon the primitive arises in us too, alive with its magical customs.

What made a deep impression on me was an unbelievably unprejudiced acceptance of feeling impressions. When I had an impression that a place might be unpropitious (cf. the teachers' conference of April 1957!)[817] then that was considered to be real. Then it was extremely likely that my feeling was correct, and it was respected. I got on splendidly with the negroes in regard to feelings.

Once I took part in a great festival with them where the negroes were performing their war dances.[818] That was in Uganda in an absolutely remote area, and they told us later we were crazy to travel through there alone. One night these people made a huge fire and the women and children clustered around it. Then the men came in their full war paraphernalia with their glittering spears, and they began to dance their war dances. The whole group of men danced right up close to the fire and then they swerved back again and they did this over and over again. I danced with them. But the dance became wilder and wilder, and finally the men began to boil over and I knew: Now it's time to stop [35/36] or else it's going to get extremely dangerous. So I took my rhinoceros whip—I was completely unarmed otherwise—and I cracked it hard and swore at them in Swiss German. And then the eighty to a hundred people scattered. It was a marvelous experience: a wonderful moon, everything was as if enchanted. At ten o'clock at night it was still 34 degrees [Celsius]. They danced so malleably at the knees and they swayed about—hell!—as if driven into the fire and swaying back again. But when it got to midnight then it began to go over the top, the whole time the men singing their wild war chants. It sounded wonderful, sublime. The chants were melodious and not unmusical, wailing like the Indians do. The negroes are very musical. And added to that was the rhythm of the drumming, getting constantly faster. That is the rhythm of blood; it was fantastic!

---

[817] Jaffé added the following note in the margin by hand: "detailed protocol available!"
[818] See *ETG*, p. 274f., *MDR*, p.270f.

In these dances and this music, the negroes are completely beside themselves, they get into a state of possession, become berserk; they make crazy jumps in the air in the dance and all sorts of fantastic things. It was a completely wild horde and I noticed that it was extremely dangerous, and the thing looked damned peculiar. It all depended on me not losing my head. My boys[819] were fearful right from the beginning and hid themselves away. Then I cursed in a loud voice and called out, "This business ends here." I could speak and write Swahili. But these people can't speak Swahili, but I called out what they say in Swahili when a thing is finished: Schauri kisha! And then I said: Now all go home, you rascals, and I cracked the whip. They absolutely loved this, and it amused them terribly. They all then ran away laughing, like schoolboys. I was only playing at being angry and of course the people noticed that I was only playing at it, but it was exactly the right thing to do; it worked. They loved me and they consciously did not want to do anything to me, but in a state of intoxication they no longer know what they're doing. And when I noticed that, I chased them all home, the entire herd of wretched swine, and cursed them in Swiss German. And behold: it worked. That was the first time in my life that I knew with absolute inner certainty what to do. [36/37]

I remembered that the Sarasin brothers had such war dances performed for them in Celebes and one of them was seriously injured by a dancer's spear.[820]

We later heard that an "official" from Uganda who took the same route shortly afterwards had been murdered by the negroes in the same spot. He probably did not know how to tackle the people. Perhaps he was in a bad mood and did not find the correct tone.

The next day, two trucks appeared. They had been sent by the district commissioner to pick up the Europeans. We asked them how the D.C. knew that we were there. We just do!—In Africa things that are new are picked up very quickly. Of course, we were so glad about it. It was a very unhealthy area, swampy, and a proper black and white fever area. The water that one found there was terrible. Only afterwards did it become clear that the people were supposed to have picked up someone entirely different. But we were glad that the cars came and we drove off with

---

[819] "boys": in English in the original.

[820] The Swiss naturalists Paul and Fritz Sarasin published an account of their anthropological expeditions in Celebes (Sulawesi, Indonesia): *Reisen in Celebes: Ausgeführt in den Jahren 1893–1896 und 1902–1903*, 2 vols (Wiesbaden: C. W. Kreidel, 1905).

much aplomb. I learned only later that this was an absolutely wild tribe who had as yet not been reached by colonization. But we got on very well with each other: we gave them safety pins and cigarettes as gifts and they were terribly pleased with them.

[208]
NOVEMBER 15, 1957[821]

Yesterday I had a dream I'd like to relate to you: in the dream I'm on a journey, or at a station. The impression is a little vague, I can't quite grasp it. So I'm somehow in a foreign country and there's a large building. Perhaps a station building or something like that, and I'm standing outside. And there's a sort of hangar; it's an airfield. There are no planes there; but a wide field spreads out before me, as far the horizon. A dark expanse. Stretching into infinity. And there is an awareness in me that I'm on a journey.

And then comes the part that I remember very clearly, but no, it's basically also unclear, of course. It's like this: the background was like a train standing on a track. We're standing by the engine—a lot of people—and I'm with father and mother. It was more that I knew they were there than that I saw them exactly. And I was on a journey with my father and my mother, and we were in festive clothes; and I knew we're returning from a wedding that had taken place in a foreign country a long way away. Father was wearing a top hat and I'm also wearing a top hat; that is, I'm holding it in my hand along with my hand luggage. Rather uncomfortable. I think: How ridiculous, why did I not take a hat box with me? I look at the top hat, in fact it looks a bit "crumpled." Mother was somewhat clearer than my father and we were, as I said, on the way home from a wedding. And then it struck me: My sister is absent. Of course: she's the one who got married!—So the country we were returning from must then be the afterlife—whatever that is called!

My sister died in the thirties; last night I thought about this dream in all sorts of ways until it suddenly occurred to me: My sister is missing! And then it suddenly became clear to me that this wedding can apply only to my sister. My sister as my anima.—I never had a close relationship with her. She was a very peculiar person. I told you about

---

[821] This entry is followed by a second lightly revised version of the opening section (pp. 221–24), which is not reproduced here. The main change is the deletion of information regarding Jung's sister and of the subsequent discussion of the sister as anima figure.

her and about her extraordinary way of being.[822] I always had to admire her. She died from an operation which was really only a mild intervention, but she was fully aware that it was now a matter of life and death. [208/209] I only just made it to her deathbed for I'd had no idea about the reality of the situation, and then it all happened quite quickly.

So in the dream I'm now my parents' son. I was an adult, around forty years old, so more in the middle years of my life. When my mother died, I was already in the second half of my forties, and my father died as early as 1896.

The dream was as if I had only been on a journey, or rather on a return journey. But in the course of the dream, it became quite clear that it was a return journey. Even in the first part of the dream, on the airfield, it was quite clear that I was coming back from a great distance, from a cosmic distance. There was a vast expanse and depth of space before me. Darkness! The motif of the return journey continues in the second part of the dream.

The top hat is a notable dream detail which at first I could not make anything of. It makes someone taller, doesn't it; it allows him to appear taller, that is its purpose. One is then more important because one is taller. This is correct "there," in the afterlife. Here, it's an impediment. In the last dream I acquired trousers that were far too big for me. That's very awkward when one returns to earthly circumstances! So we were standing on the platform next to the train engine. I don't know: had we disembarked from the train? We walked from the engine along the length of the train as if we were seeking a carriage to board. The whole thing was somehow as if we wanted to board the train in Vienna or Paris in order to travel home, but as if we were essentially coming from much further away.

When one is on the platform, one is *à niveau*.[823] But there was something extraordinary there: father was walking to my left and he stood, or he was walking, much higher than I, as if his feet were at the height of my head. Mother was walking to my right and her feet were at half the height of father's. I myself had the feeling of being a rather squat figure. [209/210]

The large expanse of the airfield had something alarming about it: it was dark, the early hours of the night, but it was further into the night, and an unimaginably vast expanse, an emptiness—a colossal emptiness. And there was this hall, this hangar, very spacious and lofty. I stood right

---

[822] See above, p. 94–95.
[823] *à niveau*, in French in the original: "on the level."

at the outermost edge of this field and before me was this colossal expanse; and I was occupied with this "departure" or "arrival."

My sister as anima is self-explanatory. Yesterday I was concerned with something I've read. You know: Fate.[824] There are remarkable things in it. There was the story of the boy five or six years old who had a cerebral-spinal influenza, a sort of sleeping sickness, and he was in a coma for fourteen days. Afterwards he was semi-conscious for about four months. And during that time he kept having the same dream: there's a curtain in his room. He goes up to it and opens it and goes through it, and there is a wonderfully tended path leading into a magnificent garden. He arrives at a large house, like a palace; he rings the bell and the door is opened by a beautiful young girl. She plays beautiful hymns on the piano for him.— This dream also came again later from time to time. He was the son of very poor parents who lived in the Colorado desert. The boy was now convinced that the young girl who appeared to him in the dream was actually a living person. So he went out on his travels in order to seek her.— One day he arrived at a town in the Midwest. He went into the church and to his utmost amazement he heard the hymns he had experienced in the dream. When the service ended he stood at the door of the church and a young girl stepped out who was in actual fact the young girl from the dream. He addressed her: "Hello Joan!" And she was indeed called Joan. She was about fifteen years younger than him, so she had not even been born when he had dreamed of her! And just imagine: it turned out that she had also had the same dream many times. I've never read anything so remarkable.

Now the sister in the dream, she is a sort of personification of my unconscious, or the anima. So she's got married. Therefore, she must have somehow entered into a vital connection. I have the feeling that my exhaustion has something to do with it, [210/211] with this colossal distance that I had to return from. I have the feeling of a great achievement: I must return, I must scale things back, I must take off the top hat, bring my legs down to earth again. My father's feet were at the height of my head. But that wasn't even up in the air, it was simply how it was!

The "cross-cousin-marriage"[825] pattern occurred to me in relation to this wedding. The son is marrying mother's brother's daughter. So that's

---

[824] Jaffé noted here, "Magazine. Cf. Dec. 57." The reference is to an account by J. O. Jackson, "Behind the Dark: He Ran into the Huge White House in His Dream World—and into a Baffling Mystery of the Human Mind," in *Fate Magazine* December 1957, pp. 67–78.
[825] "cross-cousin-marriage": in English in the original (as also below). Jaffé noted here, "Cf. 'Psychology of the Transference'" (1946): see CE 19; CW 16, § 433–34.

a cousin. Or mother's uncle's daughter. So in the dream, my sister would also have thus married a male cousin of mine. In reality, I have a male cousin who's still alive and living in Lausanne as a musician.[826] His mother comes from the Holzach line; that's an old Basel patrician lineage very burdened with schizophrenia. But the dream has nothing to do with this cousin.—So I would marry the daughter of my mother's brother. And my sister would marry the brother of my wife. Or, if my sister marries, then I would marry that husband's sister. Then it would be correct. In this, my sister's husband would have something particular about him, for he comes from the "other side." And this woman I'm marrying, she would have to be a non-real woman, a cygnet, or a fairy, or a witch. And this, again, is linked to Morgan le Fey and the Merlin problem.

Merlin, he disappears in the forest—"he goes to Bollingen!" Do you know what I wanted to carve on the back of the stone in Bollingen?— "Le cri de Merlin."[827] Merlin is a tremendously important figure because he represents the real solution. He is the son whom the devil spawned with a pure virgin. He's a magician, but he's not actually evil. His figure represents the attempt of the unconscious at that time to bring forth a figure parallel to Parsifal. Parsifal corresponds to the Christian hero. Although Merlin's not accepted; that is why he's in exile—and hence "le cri de Merlin"! Something in me has always identified with this figure. My wife got stuck on this problem in her work on the Grail. It's an incredibly difficult set of issues. Merlin is more significant than Parsifal, infinitely more significant. He is the actual figure, the great tragic figure from this whole epic. [211/212]

Merlin was, of course, enchanted by his fairy, enchanted into the forest, after she had robbed him of the mystery: which means that, externally, his meaning has never been assimilated. Just think: at that time, in the twelfth century, the time was not yet ripe for its assimilation. The "cri de Merlin" proves that he is present in an unredeemed form. His history is not finished and he is still around. One could perhaps say that the mystery of Merlin has been preserved in alchemy. There is even a tract

---

[826] At this time, Jung's only living cousin was Rudolf Jung (1882–1958), who was an opera singer. On May 11, 1956 Jung wrote him a letter regarding carcinoma, Huxley, symbols, and mescaline. *Letters*, vol. 2, pp. 297–98.

[827] "Le cri de Merlin," in French in the original, here and below: "the cry of Merlin." See *ETG*, p. 232, *MDR*, p. 228. Legend has it that the cry of Merlin could be heard in the forest after his death. On Merlin, see Emma Jung and Marie-Louise von Franz, *The Grail Legend* (London: Coventure, 1986), pp. 347–400, and von Franz's "Le cri de Merlin," ch. 14 in her *C. G. Jung: His Myth in Our Time*, trans. William Kennedy (New York: C. G. Jung Foundation for Analytical Psychology, 1975), pp. 269–87.

Aenigma Merlini, although it should actually be called *Aenigma Merculi-ni*.[828] But it is noteworthy that the Merculinus or Mercurius transformed into a Merlinus.

Parsifal and Merlin, they are actually brothers; or the one and the other form: that is, the visible and invisible figure of one and the same form. The visible figure is the accepted one, while the dark one remains unconscious. For one cannot, of course, assimilate it, although it gradually draws closer to consciousness. These are ultimately the opposites of God which can neither be fully assimilated in either one direction or the other. Merlin is to Parsifal what Mephistopheles is to Faust. One could compare Faust with Parsifal's fool. And Merlin would be Mephistopheles. The great tragic figure in *Faust* is in fact Mephistopheles. He accomplished the deeds. Even Merlin does all sorts of very positive things.

In my case, Philemon corresponds to him, and then came Ka, who's a magician but who makes things real.[829] In our time the opposites have come closer together; hence the realization of man and his shadow, of the problems of the opposites and all that. "I am both!" This is the result of the incarnation. The extension of consciousness on both sides. It cannot go only towards one side. In *Faust*, it is very clearly indicated: Faust, who is only an inept philosopher, becomes the doer of great things with the help of Mephistopheles. He actualizes them as a man. Faust has both sides, and in the murder of Philemon and Baucis,[830] he's already the devil himself. In my life I always considered it my task to right this wrong. The great deeds should not destroy the past. This is why I am with my parents in the dream. I did not accomplish something new in opposition to my parents. I preserve the cultural traditions only as much as I can. Whereas in *Faust*, the idea becomes clear that the old is nefariously murdered by the new.

Notably, Merlin is not the nefarious innovator. He is, rather, much more subtle. It is a highly significant thing, this problem of Merlin. It is very intertwined with the problems of our time.

In the dream there's something else that's remarkable: namely the color black. On such occasions one wears a festive black, like at weddings, funerals, and so on. When old ladies participate in such occasions they wear black attire, as men do in any case: a black smoking jacket

---

[828] Merlinus, "Allegoria de arcano lapidis," in the *Artis auriferae volumina duo*. Jung discusses this text in "The Psychology of the Transference" (1946), CE 19; CW 16, § 472.

[829] See *BB* 7, October 22, 1917 (pp. 162–63).

[830] Kurt Wolff noted, "Cf. Goethe, *Faust II*, Act 5."

with a black tie, or a dark frock coat. Here, he [Jung's father in the dream] has a white tie but it's a black suit. Now this scene by the engine, there was a certain blackness in it, the feeling of black clothes. And on this airfield, the vista was also rather black, not a blue distance, but it had a blackness within it, not dark, but blackish. And it was also the same with the engine. It had black, shiny metal components. This blackness simply expresses the *nigredo*,[831] in and of itself.—And that matches very well with the atmosphere of Merlin who represents the darkness. It was as if some soot had been mixed in with everything, or rather a metallic quality, a coal smoke. But the atmosphere was not smoky, it was simply blackish.

And for me, the cross-cousin-marriage problem is connected with this: I'm giving my sister away to a male cousin who is of course also my cousin. In the fairy-tale,[832] it reads that the sister gets the unknown man and that the man marries the unknown woman. Now in the dream, I definitely did not have a wife, but logically, the unknown woman would have to be a match for me. So the wife on the dark side, and my sister married the magician. That is curious.

In fact, we always link ideas of light with the concept of the "beyond." And I don't believe that at all. For me, the darkness is always missing in that. The light is very beautiful but where then is the other half of God?—If I may fantasize about it I would say: the ideas we get to hear about the beyond are ideas [213/214] which are very strongly determined by people's prejudices, by which I mean the ultimately luminous nature of the beyond.

I have another idea about this: the world is consistent to such a great extent that any beyond that is utterly free of oppositional tension would be highly unlikely. My own idea is that there must be something else to it that resists fitting into our worldview. For example, the fact that there is such an insurmountable separation of the deceased from human beings. Why? That's something against which feeling absolutely rebels. I am utterly convinced that after death something happens, that it continues, but in a way completely unknowable to us. I say to myself: If this world of the beyond were all light and goodness and simplicity (because non-dual), then blissful communiqués would have to take place among nothing but

---

[831] Kurt Wolff noted, "cf. Jung, *Psychology and Alchemy*, p. 219." The *nigredo*, or blackening, is the initial stage of the alchemical process. CE 17; CW 12, §§ 334–35.

[832] Kurt Wolff noted, "cf. Jung, *The Practice of Psychotherapy*, p. 222." Jung referred there in "The Psychology of the Transference" to an Icelandic fairy-tale which corresponds to this anecdote. CE 19; CW 16, § 426.

blissful spirits; and there's no talk of that. Half of the actual reports that we have are sinister. Not only are there blissful experiences, there are also dark spirits who maybe have something good to do.

And think of the black rock that showed up in my death visions in 1944.[833] It always gave me something to think about. It was the hardest granite and it was dark; in fact it was terrifying. When I think of that otherworldliness—my thoughts circle very much around astronomical things—then I think: It's completely impossible that we land on some lovely flowery meadow. The world we pass on into will be magnificent and terrifying, just as the Godhead is. That might simply be a law that always applies.

So what sort of a story is going around in my head? It's the story of a woman who had lost her husband shortly after her wedding. He had fallen in the war. Then she had a dream in which she rediscovered her husband. He led her to a beautiful spot where there was a splendid garden. She said to him that she wanted to stay with him forever. But he responded that it was not permitted, because she had a body and she had a task to fulfill in life. Then she asked him whether he could not do something to her body so that she could stay there. But he explained to her that she was not allowed to stay. Then she awoke. And from then on she never dreamed about him ever again. Just imagine! [214/215]

I'm constantly amazed that I don't dream about my wife. Why? I cannot dream of my wife. And Miss Wolff too is completely lost to me since the dream containing the hint that she has reincarnated. Of my wife I have no trace of a dream; that is, there are no dreams in which I have the feeling that it is more than a memory, but only ones in which it is an "as if." And it has been that way from the moment when my wife presented herself to me in the dream as a "picture."[834] That was "actual," or rather, the communication that this picture was presented for me, that was actual, or to put it otherwise, such was the intention of the presence. But from that moment on, I have had no more dreams in which I had the feeling of a presence, but much more the feeling of an implacable demarcation, of a separation.

And then there's something else that's remarkable: every time that I visualize the problem of the separation and the beyond and attempt to consolidate it within myself, then my thoughts wander off into a suggestively sexual fantasy; as if it were diverted into such a suggestion, whereas

---

[833] See above, pp. 192–200.
[834] See above, p. 187.

it is now going in exactly the opposite direction. Naturally, I see what is going on: the objects of this world, as it were, have been made artificially interesting to me when in fact I'm mostly indifferent. In this case, where one would like to feel some connection, this inner deflection is particularly shocking.[835] There is an element of brazen ghastliness within it.— All that is for me an allusion to this black atmosphere or to an aspect of the timeless intrinsic being which we somehow do not see or are even intended not to see.—In the usual fantasies about the beyond, a heap of wishful thinking comes in. But if the beyond were only a luminous and beautiful concern, then I could not possibly imagine what the reality is that is "here." *This* world is so gruesome that the "other side" can't somehow be completely different. I believe the idea that there is heaven *and* hell, that this idea is much better.

For example, in my vision of 1944: [215/216] this almost black rock, it was so absurd that I thought: That is like a dark blot, such a lump. The earth below looked completely transfigured, but this cold block of granite swimming in space, this was so incredibly absurd! And it was right there that my spiritual relations were to be found. I always have the idea that the Hades of the Greeks was not such a stupid concept. There people return to their own. There the philosophers speak with each other on the shady Asphodel meadows, and for the "righteous" it even looks "righteous" there.

What was so exhilarating in my vision of 1944 was the liberation from the burden of the body and the liberation from all meaninglessness. One enters into such a fullness of meaning that this experience is absolutely indescribable. Everything became incredibly meaningful; and I knew: Now I'm reaching the solution to all the questions of my life. I received the answer to the question: Why was it all like this? What did it mean that I had this life? What came before? What will come afterwards? There was something incredibly positive in it. Hence the ecstasy when I was absolutely liberated from time and body. That was incomparable, and that is how I imagine the "beyond." And despite this, there is also darkness there. Certain sorts of limitation must hold there. I can't imagine that the suffering of the world simply comes to an end. For when the opposites are no more, then there is nothing. There must, I imagine, be a sufficient abundance of a personal being on hand that cannot exist without being set apart from non-being. So one can't get around that.

---

[835] "shocking": in English in the original.

I have the idea that one finds out after a longer time where the limits of this liberated state are to be found. Somewhere there are limits, or somewhere there is also a world-defining necessity. For there must be a creative necessity present that, for example, decides which souls must be reborn or which even wish it for themselves. I could even imagine that certain souls experience the state of three-dimensional existence as more blessed than their immortality. It is questionable how much we take over with us of the completeness or incompleteness of our human existence.

It's a very familiar motif that one still has something to do on the earth and that the "spirits" [216/217] set much store by this being accomplished. One can imagine that someone with a failed life is simply bound to repeat it once again in order to make it right,—so that this thought of God is realized. "Encore une fois"[836]—I have come to think that it is a matter of something voluntary: that one person emphasizes their conviction of reincarnation and the other the opposite, the singularity of one human life. A generalized doubt seems to prevail about this. It's likely that, as in all such cases, both are true. In one case life must not be repeated, in the other case it must be.

[837]In some people one can detect a remarkable sense of shared destiny with their ancestors. I would express this in the idea of an impersonal karma that resides in the family and that is passed on from father to son. I had a very strong feeling that I am affected by the unfulfilled aspects of my parents and grandparents, and going even further back. That I have to answer the questions that had presented themselves even then, but that received no answer at that time. I always had the feeling: If this story about Goethe is true, then it is also extremely likely from within.

For example, I had some research done into my coat of arms.[838] It was painted by my grandfather. It is completely impossible that we had no coat of arms beforehand. The Jungs in Mainz had a type of phoenix as their heraldic animal, connected to "youth."

Now, my grandfather had strong resistances to his father and that was why he altered his heraldic arms, quite defiantly. But now it contains the problem of the cross, and moreover it's a blue cross, pointing to a spiritual carrying of the cross. It faces a blue cluster of grapes. Of course, that's Dionysus, and the cross indicates Christ. That's completely appropriate. The center is a golden star, the symbol of individuation, and because my

---

836 "Encore une fois," in French in the original: "once again."
837 See *ETG*, p. 237, *MDR*, p. 233.
838 See *ETG*, p. 236, *MDR*, p. 232.

grandfather was a freemason, he repeated every symbol three times, but I then simplified it.—His painting this coat of arms shows that [217/218] he was also confronted with this problem of the opposites, yet in the writings he left there is no trace of awareness of that.

In freemasonry, though, this opposition is also to be found, but it is expressed as the opposition of Christ and John. It is also found in the Templars. At the entrance to John's chapel in Bubikon (Kanton Zurich) there is a carving: two angels bearing a platter with the head of John the Baptist.[839] One thinks it is the chapel of Saint John. But it's John the Baptist who's meant here, who did not betray the mysteries. In the Mandaen Book of John,[840] the conversation is between John and Jesus. John reproaches him that he has betrayed the mysteries. But Christ replies that the lame walk and the blind see and the deaf can hear. The conversation ends without resolution; both maintain their standpoint. But John was never fully convinced that Jesus was the Messiah.—From these contexts it becomes clear that in the Scottish Rite's high degrees of freemasonry, Christ is replaced by John the Baptist. John was sacrificed, after all; he was sacrificed by the powers of darkness, and he stands for blood. Salome, the incestuous daughter of Herod, loved him; she loved the holy man, but he did not love her. His head was opposed to returning her love! He privileged the light and did not accept the darkness that was seeking the light—although she did not know it. But if she had only been an unchaste woman, then she would not have loved John! And it was precisely this that he should have noticed! He should not have rejected her. But no one has ever said what Salome's love could have meant.[841]

Essentially the opposition between Christ and John, including the version in the Mandaean Book of John, is also the problem that is hinted at in *Faust* and inadequately resolved, and which reappears in my coat of arms.

[842]What I have told you today are all memories. These are the questions and reflections in which I have lived, and which have preoccupied me. In a certain sense, they are also the basis of my writings. For those

---

[839] The reference is to the chapel of the Ritterhaus Bubikon (Bubikon Commandery), a fortified monastery complex of the Knights Hospitaller (Order of St. John) dating from the twelfth century.

[840] A holy book, written in Mandaic Aramaic, of Mandaeism (also known as Nasoraeanism or Sabianism), a Gnostic, monotheistic religion with Greek, Jewish, and Persian influences practiced by an ethnic group based in the Mesopotamian region, predominantly Iraq. John the Baptist is especially revered.

[841] Cf. *BB* 2, December 21, 1913 (pp. 180–81).

[842] See *ETG*, p. 302, *MDR*, p. 299.

are essentially nothing other than ever-new attempts [218/219] to find an answer to the question of the interplay between "this side" and "the beyond." But I have never uttered anything of these reflections. For I would have had to write them, but that means to animate them, and one can't do that. Now I'm simply saying it. It needs the proximity of death to be able to say these things: *Μυθολογεν*—to mythologize—to tell stories![843] That was it.

The significance of the inner images that accompanied me throughout my life made everything personal seem unimportant. What does this banal reality mean alongside that? But on the other hand, this became my most important concern: the earth. The dominance of otherworldly images so caused me to dig deeply inside myself in order not to be washed away. But they also alienated me from life.—That is why my coat of arms is so important. In the center it has the transcendent function, the star of individuation, which embraces both sides. The blue cross is extended between spiritual opposites. The blue cluster of grapes gives us red wine, and that is the color of blood.

[844]My grandfather who painted the coat of arms was a grand master of the Swiss Lodge of Freemasons, and that meant something back then. He had no relationship to these ideas. Among his posthumous papers I found only one page where he is "philosophizing."[845] He was a very extraverted person. And this is how the page read: "Yes, yes, one needs to have thought about these more serious things at some time, and these are the 'ultimate things' about which one thinks." "Thinking" for him, however, was only a casual thought, and then nothing more happened with it. He was a great organizer, enormously active externally, but there was no depth to it. Very brilliant, humorous, eloquent, and an absolutely striking personality. I myself have swum in his backwash: yes, yes, Professor Jung, he was something! His scientific achievement was not massive, but he was a great organizer. He completely restructured the medical curriculum at the University of Basel. [219/220]

First, he reordered the anatomy curriculum. He was professor of anatomy, then surgery, and an internist. Under him the Merian wing of the university was built. That was the one belonging to the former margravial palace of the Margrave of Baden-Durlach; and then he built the first

---

[843] *Μυθολογεν*: probably μυθολογείν (Greek infinitive form); if so, however, this verbal counterpart to the noun μυθολογία (*mythologia*) is Jung's neologism.

[844] See *ETG*, p. 236, *MDR*, p. 232.

[845] Some manuscripts from C. G. Jung the elder have survived, but this one has not been identified.

lunatic asylum in Basel, and then—as I said—he founded the "Institute for Hope" for mentally disabled children. It was not at all in his mentality to look inwards.

When I painted the ceiling of the loggia this summer in Bollingen,[846] I really had to think hard about why he came to change the emblems on the coat of arms in this particular way. I could really not have found a more expressive set of arms. What if he had chosen, for example, the cubic stone of the freemasons![847] But no, this was simply how it was! I assume that he was a sensation type and such things happen to them. They have quite fantastic intuitions. He was very multifaceted in his sphere of influence. He began with physics and chemistry. Back then these things fitted together in a much smaller patch than today. And in fact, he was very shrewd. Evidently, he studied the whole area of medicine most thoroughly. That was in Heidelberg. And instead of a dog he had a little pig that he took for walks, to the amusement of the whole of Heidelberg.

NOVEMBER 22, 1957

[848]Yesterday I heard about a tribe of Indians in Labrador that has no Gods, no daimons, no rituals, for everyone has a "great man"[849] within themselves. And he sends dreams to each individual; and when one is interested in these dreams and lives according to them, then he sends more and better ones. But if one does not listen to the dreams, then the "great man" becomes enraged and then it becomes dangerous and then he sends ruinous dreams! The religion of this tribe consists in paying attention to the "inner man." And what's most remarkable of all: this "inner man" is portrayed as a four-part mandala! When one considers this, it's like the ancient Indian philosophy based on the *Upanishads* which begin with Prajapati speaking to "his own greatness."[850] You see, this is the "great man"; he said he was alone and wanted now to create something outside of himself; and with that, he split into man and woman.

---

[846] Jaffé added a note: "There, Jung painted his own coat of arms and those of his wife and his sons-in-law."

[847] The pointed cubic stone of freemasonry symbolizes the completion of the work.

[848] "On the dream" was obscured by overtyping here.

[849] "'great man'": in English in the original, here and below.

[850] Possibly "Praśna Upaniṣad": see Patrick Olivelle, trans., *Upaniṣads* (Oxford: Oxford University Press, 1996), pp. 278–87.

This is truth in a nutshell.[851] A completely unimpaired realization of the original state of affairs, just as with that Indian tribe. That is religious experience without projection. That is how it's discovered, and such is the original experience of man. The question as to whether it is experienced in this form, or rather in projection, is likely a question of more or less pronounced introversion or extraversion. Accordingly, things are experienced either more subjectively, or more externally.

Postscript on the coat of arms.[852]
The five-pointed star in the middle as a symbol of individuation is the unrealized self.[853] If it were reflected, then the star would have four or eight aspects or rays. But the five-radial star, that is originally a petroglyph of man: there are four limbs and a head. The head is simply an appendage of the body, simply a protuberance. Man is a five-rayed star as long as he is unconscious. In the coat of arms, that is quite correct, for like this, it always signifies the departure point. Self-becoming begins, as it were, in the five-rayed star. [224/225]

I'd like to give you the inner thread that runs through the succession of my works.[854] To do so I must begin essentially with the years 1914–1917 when I was occupied with the unconscious. That lasted about three years, and then it abated. Only when it had become quieter was I able to think about it objectively and begin to think about it scientifically. Then *The Relations Between the I and the Unconscious* emerged.[855] And I did the preliminary work on the *Types* book. It seemed to me that through my engagement with the unconscious I had become conscious of my self. Therefore, I was able to confront the unconscious objectively: but only after I was no longer inside the magic mountain. The *Types* book also pertains to this, addressing the question: How do I relate to the external world? Another question also plays an important role here: that is, how do I differentiate myself from Freud and how from Adler? When I attempted to answer this ques-

---

[851] "the truth in a nutshell": in English in the original.

[852] See above, p. 228.

[853] Cf. the blue star in the seventh sermon, which is described as "the God, the goal of man" in BB 6, February 8, 1916 (p. 227), and Jung's painting of a star: *Art of C.G. Jung*, cat. no. 62 (p. 138).

[854] See ETG, p. 208, MDR, p. 206.

[855] *The Relations Between the I and the Unconscious* (1928), CE 10; CW 7: chronologically speaking, Jung is referring here to his 1916 essay "The Structure of the Unconscious," in Jung, *Collected Papers on Analytical Psychology*, which was later revised and expanded as *Relations* CE 8, CW 7.

tion, I encountered the type problem. I worked a great deal of literature into this, as you know. Spitteler's work played a very special role in this, particularly *Prometheus and Epimetheus*.[856]

But in *Relations* I determined only to a certain degree that I was referring to the unconscious, though I said nothing about the unconscious as it is and still had no knowledge that it is a process. As yet, nothing of that is in it. I first completed *Relations* and then came the *Types* book containing the[857] exploration of my relatedness to the world, to man, and to things, and which clarifies the different aspects of consciousness.—After that came a series of individual essays and lectures that I wrote after my re-entry into the world, somewhat in contrast to my inner preoccupations and in response to the questions that had been put to me. These are the papers in *Seelenprobleme der Gegenwart* and *Wirklichkeit der Seele*.[858] Then it gradually became clear to me that the relationship to the unconscious unleashes an actual process of development that, for example, has found its deposits in the systems of religion. In particular, I was interested at that time in Gnostic ideas, because they evidently engaged with the unconscious, in contrast to Christianity which is not concerned with the unconscious but possesses a highly differentiated and cultivated mythology. With Christian ideas [225/226] I always had the feeling of being far below this differentiated doctrine. I myself confronted a primal world, and that was also true of the Gnostics, who also grappled with these things, although they were not able to indicate what it was that fascinated them. For these were, in part, terribly sinister things, contaminated with the world of drives.

Then the past began to animate itself to me and I dreamed of the dead who come to life. I told you about these dreams, didn't I?[859] At that time I explored a great deal in the history of religion, and I saw how gradually Christianity grew out of and differentiated itself from a primitive state of mind, and how the Gnostic idea containing every possible thing is related to a primitive form of religion. Then I grew distinctly irritated that I had found no historical transition from Gnosticism—or Neoplatonism—to the

---

[856] Carl Spitteler, *Prometheus and Epimetheus: A Prose Epic*, trans. James Muirhead (London: Jarrolds, 1931 [1880–81]). See *Psychological Types* (1921), CE 9; CW 6, ch. 5, "The Type Problem in Poetry."

[857] "the" was typed over "my."

[858] C. G. Jung, *Seelenprobleme der Gegenwart* (Contemporary problems of the soul) (Zurich: Rascher Verlag, 1931); Jung, *Wirklichkeit der Seele* (Actuality of the soul) (Zurich: Rascher Verlag, 1934).

[859] See above, p. 120.

present. But then in the twenties I had the dream of being trapped in the seventeenth century and of the beginnings of alchemy.[860] In alchemy I found the missing link[861] between the present and Gnosticism, and only with that did it become possible for me to properly engage with my unconscious and to understand the process of the unconscious, the transformation of symbols. And moreover, that made it possible for me to understand the unconscious in its primitive form and to figure out what I had experienced in the years 1914–1917. In those years I didn't read a single scientific book. After *Transformations* I wasn't able to read another book; these experiences had completely lain waste to me. They had shattered the whole of my joy in conscious work. I also withdrew from the university then because I felt myself unable to lecture in that state. It had completely cut me off from the world. Then I saw what that means: *this* world and the real world. At that time I was able to see only the external world in contrast to the inner world. Today I know about the interplay of the two worlds, but back then I did not.

[862]And yet, of course, I needed—particularly at that time—a foothold in "this" world, and for me that was my family. It was hugely important that I also had an ordinary life as a counterweight to this terrible internal world. My family, that was always for me the foundation to which one was able to return, which proved to me that I was also an ordinary person. Because these unconscious contents, they could drive me over the edge. But my family and the fact that I [227/227] knew I had a Swiss medical diploma, I had a wife and five children, I live at Seestrasse 228 in Küsnacht; these were facts, that was my actuality, which kept proving to me: I really do exist, I am not just a blank page blown about by the spirit like a Nietzsche, who had completely lost his identity because he had only the inner world. Nietzsche was completely uprooted and floated above the ground, and that is why he is also unreal and insubstantial, and that unreality was for me the epitome of horror. For "I" meant *this* world and *this* life; and also even when I was so lost and worried, I still always knew that this meant this life. If I then reach the limits of this life or arrive in another world, then all well and good, then we'll grapple with the problem! But right now, nothing is meant but this life. So my family was always a blessed reality and guarantee for me that I am real, for I often seemed to myself to be unreal in the face of these

---

[860] See *ETG*, pp. 204–5, *MDR*, pp. 200–201.
[861] "missing link": in English in the original.
[862] See *ETG*, p. 193, *MDR*, p. 189.

unconscious contents. But the family, they were always like a plumbline for measuring the depths, or a sextant for figuring out where one is.

[863]And now to return to the sequence of my books, it's essential to point out that the books published from 1927 onward already reflect on questions of worldview as well as confronting the religious question. First would come *Psychology and Religion*, and next the *Paracelsica*.[864] The second essay, "Paracelsus as a Spiritual Phenomenon," contains much that is significant from the standpoint of the worldview question. The Paracelsian writings are a highly original thing which clearly contain the question of alchemy, although in a later form. That prompted me to represent the nature of alchemy, and to be precise, its relationship to psychology, or one could also say: alchemy understood as religion. And with that I was upon the ground that correlated with my experience of the years 1913–1917. For the alchemical experiences, they were my experiences.

[865]In *Psychology and Alchemy*, the central problem was of course the *coniunctio*.[866] And that led to the *The Psychology of the Transference*.[867] In general since I wrote *Psychology and Religion*, I saw that the alchemical problem [227/288] has very many aspects because analytical psychology flows together with alchemy in a quite remarkable way. Of course, for me, that was quite an ideal experience, and it fascinated me to a high degree because I had found the historical counterpart to the psychology of the unconscious, which until then had been hanging in the air.

[868]Alchemy is a bridge leading from Gnosticism to Christianity, and through it my psychology acquired a historical foundation. Otherwise it would have remained a mere phantasmagoria. This comparative foundation gives my psychology substance. I wrote my psychology out of the knowledge of my clinical experience and my own experiences, and it was in this connection that I viewed alchemy. It was important for me to place my specific experience upon the ground of reality, and to this the historical foundation also belongs. Otherwise, people would have always understood all this only as a fantasy—which they still do today. I considered my main obligation to be the grounding of my own experience and

---

[863] See *ETG*, p. 213, *MDR*, p. 209.

[864] *Psychology and Religion* (1938), CE 15; CW 11; *Paracelsica* (1942), CE 16; CW 13 and CW 15.

[865] See *ETG*, p. 216, *MDR*, p. 213.

[866] *Psychology and Alchemy* (1944), CE 17; CW 12.

[867] "The Psychology of the Transference" (1946), CE 19; CW 16.

[868] See *ETG*, p. 203, *MDR*, p. 201.

my patients' experience, and I could not do that without a bridge back to Gnosticism. I could not prove this bridge; I was simply missing a piece. The further development of Gnosticism was apparently missing. One had always assumed that had simply ended; and one did not see that Gnosticism, for example, had been continued in Kabbalah and in alchemy. One thought there was nothing there apart from Christianity and perhaps a few philosophers. Or, for example, Eckhart,[869] but he is neither in the Gnostic tradition nor in that of alchemy.

So after *Psychology and Alchemy* the next book was *The Psychology of the Transference*. There I wanted to show to its full extent how my psychology lines up exactly with alchemy, or vice versa, in order to get to the bottom of analytical psychology. Nothing is achieved by the publication of case histories, for then one can always say it was arbitrariness on my part. I sensed it as a task that I was destined to fulfill: to bring my knowledge of the unconscious into the actuality of our spiritual tradition.[870] Above all else, the central question is to be found in that connection, [228/229] and that is the main problem, the practical problem of medical psychotherapy: namely, the transference—in this Freud and I are completely in agreement. So after I had dealt with this problem in *The Psychology of the Transference*, then followed the problem of mapping the symbolism of the unconscious in line with Christianity. That's the *Symbolism of the Spirit* book where I consider the dogma of the Trinity.[871] And also an exploration of certain aspects of Buddhism in "The Psychology of Eastern Meditation."[872]

Another question close to my heart was the libido theory: that is, I wanted to show that libido was an almost quantitative concept—in contrast to the hazy concepts of other psychologies that have no inner connection (for example Wundt's psychology),[873] but represent only accumulations of individual facts. I also wanted for psychology the connection that is emerging across the sciences: namely, the common energetic theory; and that is why I wrote "On the Energetics of the Soul."[874]

---

[869] In *VA*, Jung recalled that in his youth, "only in Meister Eckhart did I feel the breath of life, not that I understood him." *ETG*, p. 74, *MDR*, pp. 68–69.

[870] See *ETG*, p. 216, *MDR*, p. 212.

[871] C. G. Jung, *Symbolik des Geistes* (Zurich: Rascher Verlag, 1948); "Attempt at a Psychological Interpretation of the Dogma of the Trinity" (1942), *CE* 16; *CW* 11.

[872] "The Psychology of Eastern Meditation" (1943), *CE* 16; *CW* 11.

[873] Wilhelm Wundt (1832–1920), philosopher and psychologist, a central figure in the formation and institutionalization of experimental psychology as well as ethnopsychology.

[874] C. G. Jung, "Über die Energetik der Seele," in *Über die Energetik der Seele* (Zurich: Rascher Verlag, 1928); "On the Energetics of the Soul," *CE* 11; *CW* 8, pp. 3–66.

[875]My attempt at a confrontation of analytical psychology with Christian intuitions naturally led to the central figure of Christ, and I considered the problem of "Christ" in *Aion*,[876] or to be more precise, the Christ problem that emerged from the confrontation of this figure with psychology, or of psychology with this figure. It's always both sides. In *Aion* my concern was not chiefly to determine what sort of parallels might arise but rather it was about a psychological concept of the central figure of Christ. No longer purged of all contingencies, but as it presents itself in history; for example, how Christ was astrologically predicted, and how Christ must be understood from the spirit of that time. That is what I wanted to portray, with all the remarkable marginal notes surrounding it.

Christ stands at the beginning of the double sign of Pisces, and the psychological view cannot get around its ambiguousness, or recognizing the ambiguousness of God: for example, the "Lead us not into temptation."[877] That then led directly to my *Answer to Job*;[878] for Christ is the suffering servant of God, and Job was that also.—Besides, as I showed in *Aion*, a remarkable synchronicity emerged: namely, Christ appears with the start of the new aeon, and therefore there is a synchronicity between his appearance and [229/230] the objective event that the vernal equinox brings into the sign of the Fishes. Christ is the lord of the new aeon. Out of this arose the problem of synchronicity which I then dealt with separately.[879]

The figure of Christ is thus so significant because the collective mentality of that time condensed upon the person of Jesus, an unknown Jewish prophet; that is why he became such a powerful figure. At the time there were only a few who thought he was the Messiah. For the Greeks and the Romans of that time, the idea of the Messiah was as long as it was broad; it did not interest them. But the idea of the Anthropos, which has both an ancient and a particular Jewish tradition, that was pivotal. The Anthropos, the son of man! The ancient Anthropos idea has its roots in Egyptian Osiris; that is an Anthropos, and the link originates there. The idea of the Anthropos captured humanity; it corresponds to the *Zeitgeist*, and fundamentally the person of Jesus went back a long way beyond that.

---

[875] See *ETG*, p. 215, *MDR*, p. 211.

[876] *Aion* (1951), CE 21; CW 9.2.

[877] "The Lord's Prayer": Matthew 6:9–13.

[878] "Answer to Job" (1952), CE 23; CW 11.

[879] "Synchronicity: An Acausal Connecting Principle" (1952), CE 23; CW 8.

I am often asked about the man Jesus. Of course, I can only respond
with some reservations because the sources are very scarce. Viewed as a
man, I would assume that he had the mentality of an illegitimate child,
namely a strong autoeroticism for which he is compelled to compensate.
If the father is absent, then the task of filling the father's place falls to the
son. Because he has been mother's little husband from the beginning.
Then there's always the danger that in such cases self-consciousness is
pushed to pathological limits. Such traits are also evident with Jesus: for
example, when he's speaking with the scribes in the temple and even allows his mother to depart—which impresses her no end.—For she has
always been his wife! "Woman, what have I to do with you!"[880]—there
he treated her simply as *genus femininum* and with that begins his
real lack of relationship to women. He developed into what I call the
"*puer aeternus* type," who then goes through the world without com-
mitments because he never lets himself be beguiled by a relationship
with a woman.[881]

All this makes him especially suited to become a union of God with
men. And as a *puer aeternus*, he is, of course, a never-fulfilled promise
to a woman—like a Catholic priest. Towards Mary, Martha's sister, he's
not really referring to the female sex; rather, he's reacting to the adoration from his female follower, but the personal relatedness is missing.
That must also be understood in the spirit of that time, that he was operating in a male society—the women of that time, they of course went
along with this! It was simply sex and nothing more. However, it becomes clear from the New Testament that a spiritual relationship with a
woman is also possible; perhaps one can understand the relationship
with Mary in this way. And Jesus was able to do this thanks to the unat-
tachedness of the *puer aeternus* who is so bound to mother that the
thought would never enter his head of looking at another woman.—And
in order to preserve this purity towards woman he must of course leave
the devil, for the devil might tear him out of his childhood heaven. Jesus
is apparently unconscious of his relationship with his mother, he knows
nothing about this inner dependence, and for this reason he is out of
this world. He has a spiritual connection only with the disciples, and,
interestingly, with those beneath him. He has no relationship to his spiritual superiors of his day who are also present. Of course, that can be

---

[880] John 2:4.
[881] See Marie-Louise von Franz, *The Problem of the Puer Aeternus: A Psychological Study
of the Adult Struggle with the Paradise of Childhood* (Zurich: Spring Publications, 1970).

linked to his extremely intensive spiritual task, or to a lack of education, so that he does not engage at all with the ideas of this world. If he was a pupil of John—which is highly likely—then he was an Essene and so belongs to those who are not concerned with this world, but only with their relationship with God.[882] The Essenes must have been a thoroughly monastic outfit. So, in the beginning is the fatherless son, he himself is the little father and the little husband, and therefore develops in the direction of the spiritual. He remained contained in the mother. Only when a man really gets to grips with a woman [231/232] must he grapple with the mother. Interestingly the Catholic church considers him as one with the mother. "The woman and her seed will crush the head of the serpent,"[883] showing the unity of mother and son which the devil will destroy. This is reminiscent perhaps of the ancient Goddess of the city of Jerusalem, Astarte with her son Tammuz.[884] That is the ancient primal image of the God who dies early which is completely a function of the mother. The *puer aeternus* in fact lives in his consciousness of the mother world, which for him is the world of the spirit. The other, the real world, that is what Jesus calls "this world," which he experiences as evil, and in it he is a stranger. He is not concerned about these real people. He lives according to his own law and this is the world of the mother. For this reason, earthly responsibility is absent for the man Jesus. It is a typical case, only it is very noticeable that the archetype has become real in this pure form. I have no doubt that Jesus lived.

For the woman, the spiritual world is the world of the father; for the man, it is the world of the mother. The invention of the Church is a typically masculine creation, for that is the mother, and it was arranged as an inner world. The Church is typically a mother, and her servants, the priests, are collectively her "sons," or castrati of the Great Mother, exactly as in the Cybele cult.[885] For example, the Pope has his housekeeper—she is called the "Virgo fortis," the formidable Virgo who tyrannizes him, which is naturally the shadow of the mother; the Pope is the primary servant of the Church, of the mother, and so he is the patriarch and at the same time he is

---

[882] The Essenes were prominent as a Jewish sect from the second century BCE to the first century CE. The key source of information regarding them is Flavius Josephus's *The Jewish War* (75 CE).

[883] Genesis 3:15.

[884] Tammuz was the son and consort of Astarte (or Ishtar), a Babylonian Goddess.

[885] Cybele was the Phrygian mother of the Gods, later identified by the Greeks with Rhea. In 1938 Jung wrote that "the effects of a mother-complex on the son may be seen in the ideology of the Cybele and Attis type: self-castration, madness, and early death." "Psychological Aspects of the Mother Archetype," CE 13; CW 9.1, § 162.

the son![886] And in addition this mother has many other children: all of the clergy. The woman naturally sees the father in the personal figure of the Pope, and what he says goes: that is her truth. For men, being contained in the mother is mostly cloaked by being contained in some group or other—for example, the Church. "In the womb of the church," or one also says, "in the womb of the gathering." These groups, they are always a woman. And the gathering is also a woman. [232/234]

[887]Thinking about the Christ problem led me then to the great problem: how does the appearance of the Anthropos, construed psychologically, the "self," the "great man," express itself in experience? I sought to give the answer to this problem in *On the Roots of Consciousness*.[888] There arises the interplay of the unconscious and consciousness. And finally comes the *Mysterium Coniunctionis* in which I take up the original idea that came to me after *Psychology and Alchemy*: that is, to represent the entire extent of alchemy, a type of psychology of alchemy or an alchemical foundation of psychology. In this way psychology is situated in actuality and the whole is underpinned. Now it could stand, and with this, my task was fulfilled. In the moment where I reached the foundation, I encountered the outermost limit at the same time, the transcendent, about which nothing more can be said.

It was one of my main concerns to place my work in the great cultural tradition. That began very early with me. I was still very young, about sixteen years old, when I read *Faust* for the first time.[889] Even then I found that it had an erroneous ending, that it should be reworked. When later I was working on the unconscious, I immersed myself fully in the world of *Faust*. But I knew: I cannot simply look at things, I must *do* something with it. But I formed an attachment to *Faust* and therefore my inner figures bear names from *Faust*. Philemon for example. This quite incidental figure of the old man became a central figure for me, specifically an

---

[886] Presumably a reference to Sister Pascalina Lehnert (1894–1983), who served Pope Pius XII as a housekeeper and secretary from 1917 to his death in 1958. See Charles Theodore Murr, *The Godmother: Madre Pascalina; A Feminine Tour de Force* (New York: Charles Murr, 2017).

[887] See *ETG*, p. 225.

[888] C. G. Jung, *Von den Wurzeln des Bewusstseins: Studien über den Archetypus* (Zurich: Rascher Verlag, 1954). This collection comprised Jung's essays "On the Archetypes of the Collective Unconscious," "On the Archetypes with Special Consideration of the Anima," "The Psychological Aspects of the Mother Archetype," "The Visions of Zosimos," "Transformation Symbolism in the Mass," "The Philosophical Tree," and "Theoretical Reflections on the Essence of the Psychical."

[889] See above, p. 166.

acknowledgment of what Faust had overlooked and had not accomplished. Respect for eternal human rights, the appreciation of the ancient and the continuity of culture and history of ideas. I had the need to bring this entire experience of the unconscious from my early years into a historical framework in order to demonstrate it as a general human experience. For otherwise it would be easy to claim that it was all only my subjective fantasy. It was incredibly important for me to show the world that we have an unconscious full of meaning and not a dirty pot full of perverse things. This always terribly got on my nerves, this devaluation of Freud's. [233/234]

Since there is only one world, and what we call "the beyond," or the unconscious, an invisible world, sort of a background world, standing behind our reality, it is to be assumed that a similar split is also present there as here. It will be good and not good. But naturally one must always keep in mind that fundamentally we do not know whether anthropomorphic projections have any validity. We must only make an attempt to form some sort of conception of the communications from the "great man" who sends us such intimations in dreams. Woe to him who makes no conception of it! He is the loser! We must attempt to form an image in fear and trembling. And one must know exactly where one ceases with intimations, and never assume that one is completely right. But it is absolutely vital that one make some sense of it. One must be able to prove to oneself that one has tried to form a conception. One can always say: The inner man means nothing. But that is an insult to it and if it is obliterated in this way, then it emerges somewhere else. When, for example, evil happens to someone then that comes from the fact that one has insulted the self and it is taking revenge in that way. And conversely, it may even be necessary to do the right thing for ourselves even when it is apparently immoral. The self decides. As a child I always made an effort to be on the side of good. And the more I tried, the more devilries came out that I did not want at all and that horrified me. So you see, this being good according to prescription, that can be quite false. One should stand up for one's convictions and overcome cowardice, otherwise one can deny one's greater being.

One can say that a child is unaccountable, and nature does not ask us what we know. We get typhus whether we know that there are bacteria or not. But when we know it and do nothing, then that is madness, and it takes revenge. [234/235]

The difficult question now is how we can ever know the will of the self. Dreams are not always unambiguous, or easy to interpret. Man is set

down in reality with an extremely incomplete consciousness and inadequate knowledge, and no devil bothers with him. It is only this inner figure who gives him hints here and there. If he fails to understand himself then it is his own funeral.[890] If he has a feeling of helplessness, then he can receive all sorts of help through his own naïve endeavors, if he does not strive against it, since the help might come in a form that seems quite unpleasant to him. Often something appears quite pernicious to us; but if we were uninhibited, then we would say that perhaps the right thing lay within it. But in society it is immoral, which means that it does not conform to morals and customs. If I were to wear a red top hat that would be indecent. The primitives still understand how to listen to the intimations of the "great man." Then there is the story of the Indian chief to whom a "great spirit" appeared when he was forty years old. He said to him: Now you must sit with the women. He took that quite literally and understood instinctively that he would now be transformed into a woman. So from then on, he wore women's clothes and from that moment on he acquired a great spiritual authority. As it were, he was transformed into a woman—but such a thing would not be okay with us.—I have come by my entire knowledge of the unconscious only through my stupidity and my lack of knowledge. And by falling in love with women. I saw that I had to say "yes" to it, and then the next dream brought the white bird and the *Tabula smaragdina*.[891] Then the anima appeared. I would never have become conscious otherwise.[892]
[249]

DECEMBER 6, 1957

[893]I recall a dream where I'm on some sort of walking trip. I'm walking on a back road through a hilly landscape, the sun is shining, and I have a vast panorama all around me. Then I arrive at a small wayside chapel, the door is a little ajar, so I go inside. To my astonishment upon the altar

---

[890] "his own funeral": in English in the original.

[891] See above, p. 121.

[892] Pages 236–48 of the Interviews are a copy of pp. 224–35, so are not reproduced here. Judging by a letter from Jaffé to Jung on November 26 (JP), Jung was in Bollingen at that time.

On December 5 Cary Baynes wrote to Jung conveying Kurt Wolff's excitement on reading the protocols of the Interviews. She added that when she read the first twenty-five pages, her impression was that "Mrs Jaffé has caught your way of expressing yourself down to a dot, and you sound entirely uninhibited as you said you would be in talking to her." (JP).

[893] See *ETG*, p. 326, *MDR*, p. 323.

there is no image of the mother of God nor of Christ, there was nothing but flowers, a wonderful arrangement of flowers. And only then do I see that in front of the altar, facing towards me, a fakir sits in the lotus position, deep in contemplation. And as I take a closer look at him, I realize that he has my face! That was a terrible shock, and I awoke with the thought: Aha, so this is who is meditating me! He has a dream, and that is me; and I felt that when he awakes, then I am no more.—That was a dream after my illness in 1944.

Of course, the dream is only portraying an allegory, but one can pursue the image further: I assume that my self, that can never fully realize itself—inasmuch as it is autonomous—is engaged in meditation, like a yogi, and through meditation is manifesting in an earthly form. It is a sort of materialization as if through a medium. In this earthly form, as this self, it can have experiences of the three-dimensional world. In my case it must have been primarily for reasons of increased awareness that it completely forgoes otherworldly existence, and indeed in an ultimately religious attitude. In the dream the chapel alludes to the religious position. It's like when someone puts on a diving suit in order to go diving in the sea; this figure takes on human form in order to enter three-dimensional existence. Here, it naturally has a different form from what it has "there," and it is here in order to acquire awareness. I have the feeling that this is connected to my extraordinarily passionate thirst for knowledge.—That is the strongest thing about me—to be able to return richly laden. With this strong desire it has created for itself a sort of secondary consciousness.

This dream and its associations could give an insight into the state of mind of a dead man who has reached the conclusion [249/250] that he knows too little, so he has thought himself into the three-dimensional world by means of an incredible thirst for knowledge, until he knows what is happening and is aware of it. The three-dimensional world seems to me like a system of coordinates: here, what is broken down into coordinates and x-axes is all one and synthesized "there." "There" it is a sort of primal image, with many shades, but neither is there a specific awareness, nor does it impart one, but it is much more a cloud of awareness, or something like that. Of course, it depends on the nature of the self, on what it is made for, as to what causes it to immerse itself again in the three-dimensional world. I could imagine that a need exists to experience and to become aware of what it would be like to live as a criminal or perhaps as a saint. Perhaps in someone who was not satisfied with the morality of his existence, whose self might have the burning desire to experience the very dark or the very light. The goal is always the attainment of as much awareness as possible and this also includes a profound insight into the shadow.

In my case it was quite certain that I came into this world for the sake of awareness, for I was born with an inexhaustible drive for awareness. My ultimate goal is an ever- increased awareness. But that is of course an individual prejudice. One must also add that awareness represents an essential issue for a man. It is for him perhaps the ultimate. And, for example, I could well imagine that a dead woman who has experienced the normal female destiny might very much miss that she never had a spiritual relationship to a man and that this might be a strong enough motive for an entire human life. It would be exactly the same for a man who, for example, was stuck in an occupation full of painful spiritual limitations because he had absolutely no means of satisfying this spiritual desire, as when a dead man like this arrived at the thought of risking another chance at life exclusively for the purpose of awareness! [250/251]

If one carries such thoughts around, along with some others that have preoccupied me since my childhood, then naturally one stands alone in the world. That became clear to me very early on. It was most clear in the period from 1914 to 1917, when this irruption of the unconscious and the strong desire to understand assumed its first potent form. I knew this: that's something I could not speak of to anyone; it would be misunderstood immediately, and I cannot properly explain it even to myself. And yet I knew that I must show that certain things in human experience are real, not only in mine; but that they are often repeated—that is why alchemy was so crucial to me. But I knew that I could find the connection to the world only if I made the most intensive effort to teach humanity a completely new *manière de voir*.[894] If I were not to succeed in that then I knew I was condemned to absolute loneliness. The worst thing was that at first, I, myself, did not understand, and even now I am far from understanding everything. Infinitely many questions crowd in on one which far exceed this life. For instance, this relationship to the "beyond." I imagine it in a far more complicated way than people imagine it. A sort of economy exists there that reaches right into the divine. I believe in fact that something happens in the world in order to become conscious. Becoming conscious and the creative are closely linked.

---

[894] *manière de voir*, in French in the original: "way of seeing."

[895]Solitude arises not because one has questions that are not yet resolved but because one knows things that others do not know, and then one is already solitary, then one is an outsider. That began for me with the dream I had as a child,[896] of God and the cathedral in Basel. And this: in my life I missed terribly having no masculine company with whom I could have spoken freely. Men could only misunderstand me. To the majority of them most of the psychic facts I am presenting are nearly completely unknown. Their rational thinking cannot keep up. I present them with experiences and facts completely unknown to them, yet they act as if they knew it all precisely. [251/252] But who already knows these things? They think they grasp alchemy while assuming that it was all about chemistry. The insights that it involved for me and which I was seeking were, when I began to work them out, not to be found anywhere in humanity and that is why I had to pursue my own original experiences. This is why I undertook the experiment of the coming to terms with my own soul (*The Black Book*). Back then I devoted myself to my soul.[897] I loved her, and I hated her. She taught me and I taught her. When we do not understand what is taking place within us we will have no connection with other people and none with the world, with the cosmos. Only by understanding the universal within me have I found relationships with people. Even back then I believed of course that I had them. But basically, others did not concern me. The strong desire to understand the mysteries of the soul did not let me go; it was like a compulsion to think things. But it was not only a compulsion, for it was also my own will, my temperament, and it was actually what I always wanted. That is why as a young doctor I always wished I could have a schizophrenia myself or at least a love affair with a schizophrenic woman in order to know what is going on in these people.

It's not the thirst for knowledge itself, but the thing that I find, the possession of knowledge, that has isolated me; for at first there was no one there who was able to understand it. And strictly speaking, I'm relating things to you now that I was not able to explain previously, to anyone. Inasmuch as you gain something from it you too are set apart from humanity. What you know causes you to be alone. But the opposite likewise is true: for this knowledge accounts for why such people understand the

---

[895] See *ETG*, p. 357, *MDR*, p. 356.

[896] Here "how God shits on the cathedral" was obscured by overtyping.

[897] *BB* 2, November 12, 1913 (pp. 149ff.).

meaning of community and from them community can also emanate. To find community under the banner of banality has little point. Only, it holds together what one has, and the others do not have. This is why for primitives, community is always bound up with mystery. Community is a type of mystery cult.—The freemasons do not form a real community. [252/253] That is the pointless aping of community. For what they know are not mysteries; there is too much that is artificial in it all. They know too little about those things to keep them secret or they do not understand what is meant by them. For example, why, in the lower degrees, Christ plays the greatest role, while in the higher degrees it's John the Baptist.[898]

There are very remarkable forms in which the dead can reveal themselves. Even dead animals! For example, I once had a boxer dog called Pascha and whenever I was digging in the garden he sat next to me and greedily ate the cockchafer grubs that my digging uncovered. Then he died and I was very sad about his death. Then I was digging one time and a small robin redbreast landed and sat close to me and began to eat the cockchafer grubs just as Pascha used to do. Finally, it even sat on the shovel and waited to see the grubs being dug up. I was very moved and thought, "That's my Pascha coming as the soul of a bird and eating the grubs." But then I was annoyed and thought, "You're just hallucinating after all!" Then I called my wife so that she could see for herself. "Just come and take a look at this!" She came but she was only about fifteen meters away when the robin flew away; but she did still see it.[899]—That was about twenty years ago.

And just think: on the day Miss Wolff died, two years ago, I was in Bollingen and Hans Kuhn (the gardener and chauffeur, born in Bollingen, a young man), brought a pile of dry wood down to the house. So there was a whole pile of brambles. Then he came to me and in some embarrassment said that it was curious but there was always a bird around who did not want to leave; he could not understand it. I immediately went to see and there was another robin. He was perched on the branch of a tree and—quite remarkably—allowed me to get very close and would not leave our presence. It sat there for over an hour. When it turned dark it came into

---

[898] On John the Baptist in freemasonry, see Tobias Churton, *The Mysteries of John the Baptist: His Legacy in Gnosticism, Paganism, and Freemasonry* (Rochester, VT: Inner Traditions, 2012).

[899] See Jung's sculpture for a dog's grave, *Art of C. G. Jung*, cat. no. 71 (p. 151).

the yard and [253/254] sat on this dry undergrowth. Hans knew that it was the day Miss T. W. had died, and he wondered to me whether that was not her soul. I had already noticed how he was reacting and had thought the same to myself.[900]

Pascha was altogether an extraordinary animal; once I went down the steps in the garden and he was standing at the bottom looking at me expectantly. Now that was exactly the expression in my father's eyes. And immediately I thought: That's my father looking at me! I was positively thrown into disarray by this impression. I cannot explain it to myself.[901] But that's what the primitives say: that the spirits of the dead can manifest in all sorts of animals, near to the grave and the house. Unfortunately, I can't remember now what happened in reality in that regard. In my memory it seems to me rather like an indistinct situation.

It's not at all possible to know about the "beyond" and the relationship to the dead and about the dead's relationship to us. We do not know what happens to the dead. But what we do have are intimations from the side of the unconscious but which we mostly do not accept because we think this is all just an irresolvable question. But I take the view that if we do not know something, then we can intellectually dismiss it. I don't know the reason the universe came into being. I must "dismiss" this. But when an idea presents itself to me—for example, from dreams or communications—then I want to pay attention. I want to have a specific conception, for only in that way does awareness come into being. One simply accepts at first what is offered; for it is very important that there is not too much that I must intellectually dismiss. On the other hand, I also cannot wait until a completely satisfactory answer appears, but I must dare to take a view. While I cannot prove that things are as I have described them to you, one can also not prove that they are not so. And I am of the view that the unconscious is most likely to be able to say something about it. So I often used to dream in times gone by that I was making the mistake of not recognizing certain [254/255] hints from the unconscious for what they were. It also seems to me something all too

---

[900] Ximena de Angulo noted, "The only strange thing about these two episodes is that C. G. should never previously have noted a red-breast behaving in this way: bird-lovers have observed this behaviour numberless times. It is characteristic of the European robin and is frequently mentioned in bird and garden literature." "A. J.'s Protocol," p. 37.

[901] Cf. the following lines in LN: "Your dog robs you of your father, who passed away long ago, and looks at you as he did." Liber Secundus, "Dies II," ch. 5, p. 260.

god-almighty-like[902] to act so loftily and to say that we know nothing, when the unconscious gives me a chance and shares something with me. The unconscious can share other things with me that I could not know otherwise: for example, synchronistic phenomena. I must be critical only enough to know that the communications are always subjective phenomena that might be correct or not. But because I know nothing else, I want to accept as a hypothesis what the unconscious says to me, and to see how it works. Whether it agrees with me or not. But the hypotheses that I have made for myself about the beyond have never turned out badly for me. Naturally I will not write a book of revelation about it, but I will humbly[903] acknowledge that I have some superstition about it. However, superstition is the earliest form of science. All science began with myth. And what I am telling you about it are myths.

The reason for my hypothesis is that the unconscious can occasionally communicate very important things that one simply does not know.[904] I remember I was once traveling home from Bollingen by train; it was the time of the Second World War. I had a book with me that I wanted to read. I was traveling third class and placed the book next to me. I was not able to read a word, for as soon as we departed I was overcome by the memory of someone who had drowned. It was the memory of a military service accident where someone had drowned after swimming out too far in the lake. I myself had personally warned him about it because I had seen that he lacked due caution. This image came back to me on the journey to Bollingen and I could not shake it off. That freaked me out and I thought: What on earth's the matter? Has an accident happened?— And indeed, there had. I left the train in Erlenbach and went home still preoccupied with this idea.[905] At home my second daughter's children were all standing around. She and her family were living with us at that time for she had returned to Switzerland from Paris because of the war.[906] The children were all looking so stunned and I asked: What on earth's the matter? And then they told me: Klaus, the youngest, had nearly drowned. He had fallen from the boathouse into the water. It's very deep there and he could not swim; the older ones helped him out of the water.

---

[902] "god-almighty-like": in English in the original.

[903] "humbly": in French in the original, "humblement."

[904] See *ETG*, p. 305, *MDR*, p. 302.

[905] Erlenbach: a village about a twenty-minute walk from Küsnacht.

[906] Gret Baumann and her four sons stayed with C. G. and Emma Jung for three years during the war. See Monika Wittman, "In Memoriam: Gret Baumann Jung," *Psychological Perspectives* 31 (1995): 9.

And it was at the precise time that I had boarded the train. The unconscious had given me an intimation. Of course, I can say: That is all nonsense, I have no reason to dwell on that memory. But behold: it had a meaningful association. So it simply was a piece of information. Therefore: why can the unconscious not give me further information about other things?

[907]I have told you the story of how I sensed a dull pain in my head during the night when my patient shot a bullet through his head. At the time I was in Bern, and he was in Chicago. When one takes into consideration the time difference, I felt the pain at the same time as he was committing suicide.[908]And something else occurs to me: my wife had a cousin. She was also interested in me. She was a pretty, congenial person. I noticed her interest but her family did not suit me and I kept my distance, I was very careful. She then married but it was not a happy marriage. And then I only saw her very occasionally at large family gatherings. So there was no relationship between us. Then I heard that she had a very remarkable illness: bleeding in the cerebral membrane, and immediately I thought, that's a serious matter. But soon she was better. One night I dreamed that the bed next to me where my wife was sleeping was a deep pit with walled up sides, rather antique, and it was like a grave. Then I heard a deep sigh as when someone gives up the ghost, and then a figure sat up in my wife's bed in a white robe. The figure resembled my wife. Curious black signs were woven into the robe and the figure hovered up out of the grave. I woke up and woke my wife and quickly looked at the clock. It was three o'clock. I immediately thought, "Someone has just died, that's for sure. This dream is too curious. There's something particular about it." At seven o'clock there was a knock at the door. It was a telegram informing us that my wife's cousin had died at 3 a.m. in Basel.[909]

When one knows such things from the unconscious then one gets a certain reverence for its powers. And when the unconscious has repeatedly given one such information, then one finally thinks, well alright, everyone knows that and I'm a know-nothing. And if I know nothing, and someone comes along who is in the know, am I right in claiming that he is a stupid devil? Perhaps what he says is quite right?

---

[907] See *ETG*, p. 143, *MDR*, p. 137. The patient was George French Porter (1881–1927). See above, p. 141.

[908] See *ETG*, p. 306, *MDR*, p. 303; *BB* 2, November 26, 1913 (p. 158).

[909] Hedwig Sturzenegger, *née* Bendel (1876–1912). See *BB* 2, November 26, 1913 (p. 161).

[910]Prof. Heinrich Zimmer?[911] Well, we drank and smoked together, and I took him out in my sailing boat and we got on together very well. And once he told me how the first thing by me he had ever read irritated him so much that he had thrown the book against the wall—it was *The Secret of the Golden Flower*—then he found he had to read it again and then he saw what I meant by what I am saying. That's quite an anecdote. I'm sure you can use that!

(Question about the scene in the *Black Book* where the soul flies away.)[912] I interpreted the soul flying away as the anima disappearing into the unconscious. Something happened with the soul then: she was sort of absorbed into the unconscious.[913] Then it came about that I was no longer permitted to belong to myself. From then on my life and I myself belonged to the collective. The soul prophesied to me once that I would be quartered, and these pieces would be weighed and sold—such a gruesome thing![914] So I am sort of dispersed into the whole of humanity. Then as it were I consecrated myself to the soul. For that was the only possibility of bearing my existence at all.

The things that came from outside, then and later, all stand under the sign of inner experience. I very soon came to the insight that when there was no solution to things from inside then outer things also mean nothing.[915] Outer circumstances cannot replace the inner. That is why my life is actually poor in outer events. I cannot tell you much about that. It would seem empty or insubstantial to me. I am to be understood only from inner events. And fullness and riches were always present there. Behind that, everything else recedes.

---

[910] See *ETG*, p. 385, and below, pp. 320–21.

[911] Heinrich Zimmer (1890–1943), German Indologist, with whom Jung collaborated. He held a chair at University of Heidelberg from 1924 and 1938. After being dismissed by the Nazis, he moved to England, and then to the United States. The first work of his that Jung read was his *Kunstform und Yoga im indischen Kultbild* (Berlin: Frankfurter Verlags-Anstalt AG, 1926); translated as Heinrich Zimmer, *Artistic Form and Yoga in the Sacred Images of India*, ed. and trans. Gerald Chapple and James B. Lawson with J. Michael McKnight (Princeton, NJ: Princeton University Press, 1984). On Jung's relation to Zimmer, see Giovanni Sorge, ed., *Jung and the Indologists: Jung's Correspondences with Wilhelm Hauer, Heinrich Zimmer, and Mircea Eliade*, Philemon Series (Princeton, NJ: Princeton University Press forthcoming).

[912] *BB* 5, April 19, 1914 (pp. 212–12). See *ETG*, p. 195, *MDR*, p. 191.

[913] See *ETG*, p. 196, *MDR*, p. 192.

[914] Cf. *BB* 5, September 14, 1915 (p. 236). In *LN* this speech is attributed to Philemon.

[915] See *ETG*, p. 12, *MDR*, p. 5.

[916]The soul, the anima, creates the relationship to the unconscious and likewise the relationship to the collective of the dead; for the unconscious is also the land of the dead. So when the soul disappears in the unconscious or in the land of the dead, then a secret activity of the anima arises in the kingdom of the dead, and she animates this kingdom. Like a medium, she gives the dead the possibility of manifesting themselves. That is why very soon after the disappearance of the soul, the dead appeared to me, and the *Septem Sermones* emerged.[917] These conversations with the dead, they form a type of prelude to what I had to communicate to the world. Their content is like a prelude to the ideas in my books.

Back then and from then on, the dead became ever clearer to me as the voices of the unanswered, of the unresolved and the unredeemed. And since no such questions and demands came to me from outside that I had to solve, therefore they came from the side of the dead. [258/259]

But the *Septem Sermones* are only *one* case where the dead direct crucial questions towards the living. That greatly astonished me, even then, and today to a greater extent. One should think after all that the dead would have knowledge, they would know more than we do. But evidently they only know exactly as much as they knew at the moment of death, but nothing beyond that; hence the strong desire of the land of the dead or of the dead themselves to keep intruding into life in order to participate in the life of the living. That is why it seems to me very meaningful that in China everything important that happens in a family must be shared with the spirits of the ancestors. I do not believe that development ceases after death, but it seems to me to continue only in the sense that the consciousness of the living has continued. However, there are many people who are far behind what has already been achieved in consciousness in individual cases; people are not always ready to accept it. Then when they die they are behind their own possibilities; and hence their claim now, demanding their portion that they did not acquire in life. So, for example, whoever has not seen his shadow will realize it and will develop to the extent that he can see it. The absolute consciousness that has already been achieved in the world is the upper limit of what the dead can also achieve. This is why life is of such supreme importance. I saw very early on how supremely full of significance it is. This is why it is so important that one knows things, including these connections to the beyond. I am telling you about it but I can't prove it. Our life means

---

[916] See *ETG*, p. 195, *MDR*, p. 190.
[917] See above, pp. 131–33.

becoming conscious. They also never understand why I say God is unconscious and needs man in order to become conscious. This becoming conscious can only be here, because here God touches his other side. He converges with this nowhere else, but here he is incarnated, here he merges with this dark brother. It is exactly the same with the dead. I often have the feeling and I have experienced it: the dead stand directly behind us and are waiting to see what sort of answer we will give them and how we will respond to life.

If you study the spiritualist literature and [259/260] all the nonsense, you can find a general feature running through it that the "spirits," or whatever manifests there, are actually seeking increased psychic insight. It appears as if the dead first of all would like to demand what they should have achieved in life; next they're keen to learn what is happening here. That would also explain, for example, why, for a ghost, the same things keep being repeated; because the one thing that the dead person should have achieved is where he has got stuck and hasn't got any further.

I don't know whether the things I'm telling you have any value for you and I'm sorry if I am repeating certain things. I also did that in my books; I keep coming back to certain things and am always regarding them from a new "angle."[918] My thinking is sort of circular: I am always revolving around these questions anew. This is a method that suits me. It is in a way a new kind of peripatetics.[919]
[276]

DECEMBER 13, 1957

The idea of the microcosm—that we humans as organic beings are primarily an opposing counterpart of nature, or conversely nature is a counterpart to the human microcosm—played a great role in the Middle Ages. We have hair, these are the grass or plants, the mountains, that's the head, as it were. Blood, that's the rivers, the turbulent water is the juices in the

---

[918] "angle": in English in the original.

[919] Pages 261–75 of the protocols of the Interviews are copies of pp. 249–60, so are not reproduced here. On December 7, Aniela Jaffé wrote to Kurt Wolff that there needed to be a chapter dealing with Jung's inner development between the chapter regarding Freud and Jung's contemporaries and that on the years of "disorientation and darkness."

On December 12 Jung wrote to Cary Baynes, "the autobiographical notes, Mrs Jaffé is taking down, give me a welcome chance to reconsider the manifold contemplations of the *res gestae* of my existence. It's the manifold summing-up of sense and nonsense." (JP).

body. The bowels correspond to the bowels of the earth, where gold is hidden in the caves, or metal. You see, such vague analogies were rolled out in the Middle Ages. Basically, they are the expression of a psychic experience. As a matter of fact, we do have a sun in us, that is consciousness, and also a type of nocturnal consciousness, the moon and the stars. Paracelsus also recognizes a relationship between plants and illnesses. On the one hand these are determined by the stars, the planets, and so on, on the other hand by the organs which in turn correspond once again to certain heavenly bodies. Every inner organ is under a star sign, the feet under Pisces. . . . These are elucidations on the visible level; ultimately however they are projections of psychic facts. Such that, for example, there is in us a psychic factor calling itself sun, or moon, or even fish, or horned goat and so on. The moon corresponds to the "mind." In the *Upanishads* it says: The moon is born from *manas*, the mind.[920] The external world is the likeness of the Anthropos. Hence comes the idea of the *homo maximus*, the idea that the world has the form of a "great man." This was linked to the idea that after death the souls of scholars enter into the brain of this great man, while others, according to their nature, enter the stomach, and everyone goes where they belong. So, there are liver people and kidney people and head people and so on. That is actually also the prototype for the Kabbalist idea of Adam Kadmon who contains everything.[921] He is the "unus mundus" *par excellence*.[922]

Now, you see, all of that actually expresses the fact that there is a naïve feeling for an analogy between psychic phenomena, namely [276/278] consciousness *par excellence*, and the nature of the world. "Were the eye not like a sun."[923]—According to this schema the expectation exists in us, often expressed by the alchemists, that the great world, the world of

---

[920] Cf. *Rig Veda*, "Purusa-Sukta," where the Gods create the world through dismembering Purusa: "The moon was born from his mind; from his eye the sun was born. Indra and Agni came from his mouth, and from his vital breath the Wind was born." *The Rig Veda*, trans. Wendy Doniger (London: Penguin Books, 1981), verse 13 (p. 31). Purusa thus corresponds to the Anthropos in Jung's next comment.

[921] In the Kabbalah, Adam Kadmon was the primordial man. Jung had recently referred to him repeatedly in *Mysterium Coniunctionis* (1955–56), CE 24; CW 14.

[922] The "unus mundus" (one world) featured prominently in the work of the Paracelsian philosopher, translator, and alchemist Gerhard Dorn (1530–1584). Jung took this up in *Mysterium Coniunctionis* to refer to the indivisible unity underlying psyche and world. CE 24; CW 14, §§ 759–60.

[923] "If the eye were not like the sun, it could never gaze at the light of the sun." An epigram of Goethe's from the introduction to his *Zur Farbenlehre* (1810): Johann Wolfgang Goethe, *Theory of Colours*, trans. Charles Lock Eastlake (revised) (Cambridge, MA: MIT. Press, 1970 [1840]), p. liii.

heavenly bodies, cosmic space, is an equivalent of our soul, or conversely, that conscious contents are correspondences to the cosmos and one does not know what came first. This leads to the idea of the *unus mundus*, which is this world and an unfathomable spiritual one. Here also lies the root of the idea of the incarnation of God. That God manifested himself in this world, psychologically: that an analogy exists between the unconscious and the world. And this fact is probably the reason that we understand anything at all of the world: because in us, that is, in our souls, resides a counterpart to the world. So the mathematician is able to introduce equations that correspond to the behavior of things that he does not know at all. At first he thinks that maybe it's a gimmick, but afterwards it becomes clear that he has expressed a process of nature through the mathematical formula. It is in the essence of mathematics that it corresponds to the actual event in the finest detail. So the idea of a microcosm is absolutely not some crazy notion, for the psyche is actually able to mirror the being of the world in a fitting way. A further consequence is that human consciousness is a light that illumines the world, and it is even the second prerequisite for the world to be actual. For if it is not known, neither does it exist nor have any meaning; it is irrelevant. That is why one can rightly say: Man is the crown of creation because he *knows* what exists. He knows that is the world. If only cows and dogs and sheep are present, then there is no world, but only the question of whether or not I have enough to eat. Then that would be the only reality. So if this is how it is—if I'm arguing this case which of course proves nothing but is a question only of whether it is conceivable—then the psyche of man, or our capacity for perception, is a counterpart to the world. Not man, but only the spiritual man, is a counterpart to the world. [277/278]

It's an incredibly impressive thing that man, who, in one respect, is an anthropoid, on the other hand has perceptions that extend to immense vastness. For example, among such perceptions are those about the galaxies. Or perceptions that reach into the infinitely small, that the human spirit can perceive the structure of the very small and the most minuscule. To this belongs our inherent tremendous ability to combine things in advance, so for example highly complex situations that contain so many factors that one could not grasp them even with a computer. It is impossible that the questions that we can solve as human beings could be solved by such machines. In order to calculate a game of chess it would require a machine so large that it would take up an entire urban quarter, and only a very mediocre game would come out of it. Our psychic abilities are so great that they can properly utilize and arrange an incredible number of factors. The more factors that come into question, the more intuitive the solution must be. But even the ordinary mind must survey far more than what a computer would be able to solve. We have an unconscious that is more or less fitted to incredible multiplicities of factors. So when the unconscious with its subliminal perceptions meets conscious comprehension, then the ability to comprehend is directly unimaginable. The unconscious can give us information that exceeds all probability: clairvoyance, precognition, dreams that come true, and so on. We have in the unconscious a reservoir of subliminal perceptions that we—under favorable circumstances—also have at hand to us for our use. Or that press into consciousness through dreams, for example. Factors come into consideration that we cannot recognize. These are things that we have never once conceived: without hope of any sort of answer, maybe one lets a question run through one's head, and the unconscious responds perhaps in a dream. If one wished to build a computer for such perception it would have to be the size of half the world. I would say that the most overt analogy between cosmos and psyche is [278/289] this: just as we have a sun that illumines the world of the earth, in the same way we have an I-consciousness that illumines the surface of the psyche. But as our sun orbits within a massive system of suns, in the same way our consciousness is only one of billions of living consciousnesses.

The whole of humanity corresponds to a stream of stars, like, for example, the galactic Milky Way system, and this whole stream of stars orbits around the center of the Milky Way. But it is only one galactic system, there are infinitely many of them, separated by enormous space from each other. In the same way, the human self is separated from other selves. But all are under the galactic law, which, psychologically interpreted, looks as if there is a much higher self. This corresponds—so I would say—to our concept of God. There are galactic groups, galaxies that somehow are linked. That then would be, as it were, many Gods, and this grouping linked with infinitely vast systems; they would be nothing but Gods who disperse themselves universally, and in this speculation, we are expressing the actual being of our psychic system. Now we discover that the entire universe is apparently expanding; that is a theory, not a certainty. The analogy to this would be that our consciousness is capable of an almost infinite expansion, developing with ever-increasing speed. Just take the monstrous development that has taken place in the last hundred years that's always getting faster. We are now experiencing a worldwide development of consciousness. It's being extended fantastically through our knowledge of the immeasurably small and the immeasurably great. Through this a mystery of the psyche is also being revealed. For us, the world has become unprecedentedly large. It's interesting in this context that the original estimates of galactic distances have proved too small. They've had to increase all galactic distances. And this means that our consciousness has not achieved the level needed to integrate the corresponding ideas. We have underestimated it. Our psychic apparatus, that's the light through which all that becomes visible.

Now it is said that the universe is expanding more rapidly [279/280] than the speed of light.[924] Correspondingly, consciousness is not able to contain infinity, and we are and remain contained within it. For us the world is infinite, and we are always contained within it. At the same time galactic systems are only the smallest point in this world: the further we get in understanding the psyche and reality, the more we will become conscious of the fact that we are contained in the psyche, and not the other way around. Just as we—religiously speaking—are contained in the Godhead, the light of consciousness is simply unable to conceive of the whole because that is infinitely greater than the human being.

There is also the theory that interstellar material is continuously forming itself anew. This corresponds to a psychic ability as yet unknown. The psyche has a relationship to matter, and the new creation of matter is linked to a type of radiant energy that remains in a closed system, and so cannot escape into another system. But what becomes of the radiated energy? Energy = mass.[925] Light is also energy and mass. The universe would have to be filled with light, and one cannot assume that those parts of space that have not yet, through expansion, reached the self-expanding cosmos, are filled with light. One must rather much more assume that they are dark. In this way an unimaginable amount of energy is constantly being transformed into matter; but how that works we, of course, don't know. The analogy to it is this: the psyche can be conceived as an energetic phenomenon,[926] also as a kind of radiation, and it is self-explanatory

---

[924] In the 1920s, the astronomer Edwin Hubble (1889–1953) established that the universe was expanding, and calculated the rate of expansion, known as 'Hubble's constant'. This was widely understood to indicate that the universe was expanding faster than the speed of light.

[925] Cf. Einstein's theory of special relativity ($E = mc^2$: energy equals mass times the speed of light squared.)

[926] On Jung's understanding of the psyche as an energic system, see his "On the Energetics of the Soul" (1928), CE 11; CW 8.

that this cannot go on to infinity. The radiated psychic energy would have to transform itself again into a departure point for the psychic. What that is we do not know. But that is probably linked with the materiality of the psyche. Somewhere the psyche has a material component, otherwise it would not be able to move matter. There must be a common property present. I have the idea that the indication of "very heavy matter" is what the alchemists understood as psyche, [280/281] and that this contains a hint about the materiality of the soul.[927]

Just as there are very big atoms, there are also very large psychic atoms in the psychic world. These are then its point of departure and are somehow related to matter. How that is to be understood is naturally superhuman. One cannot imagine it.[928]

---

[927] Jung may be referring here to dark matter, first posited by the astronomer Fritz Zwicky (1898–1974). Jaffé noted here, "Cf. Myst Conj. II." See Jung's reference to Gerhard Dorn's *Theatrum Chemicum*: *Mysterium Coniunctionis* (1955–56), CE 24; CW 14, § 41 n. 34 and § 715, where he describes giving the quicksilver an "immense weight and indivisible wholeness" in the production of the stone. (On Dorn, see n. 922 above.)

[928] Pages 282–87 of the protocols of the Interviews are copies of pp. 276–81, so are not reproduced here.

On December 15, 1957 Aniela Jaffé wrote to Kurt Wolff that she had heard from Jolande Jacobi that he had approached her regarding Richard Wilhelm's article on Jung. Jaffé took this occasion to insist at length that she alone had to be responsible for the work (BL). On December 25 Georg Gerstner published an interview with Jung in *Die Weltwoche* in which Jung spoke on the symbolism of the Christmas tree (McGuire and Hull, *C. G. Jung Speaking*, pp. 353–58).

On December 18, a friend from Jung's student days, Gustav Steiner, wrote to Jung asking for some reminiscences for the *Basler Jahrbuch* regarding how he came to psychiatry, archetypes and associations studies (JP). On December 30 Jung replied declining his request:

You are quite right. When we are old, we are drawn back, both from within and from without, to memories of youth. Once before, some thirty years ago, my pupils asked me for an account of how I arrived at my conception of the unconscious. I fulfilled this request by giving a seminar. During the last years the suggestion has come to me from various quarters that I should do something akin to an autobiography. I have been unable to conceive of my doing anything of the sort. I know too many autobiographies, with their self-deceptions and downright lies, and I know too much about the impossibility of self-portrayal, to want to venture on any such attempt.

Recently I was asked for autobiographical information, and in the course of answering some questions I discovered hidden in my memories certain objective problems which seem to call for closer examination. I have therefore weighed the matter and come to the conclusion that I shall fend off my other obligations long enough to take up at least the very first beginnings of my life and consider them in an objective fashion. This task has proved so difficult and singular that in order to go ahead with it, I have had to promise myself that the results would not be published in my lifetime. Such a promise seemed to me essential in order to assure for myself the necessary detachment and calm. It became clear that all the memories which have remained vivid to me had to do with emotional experiences that stir up turmoil and passion in the mind—scarcely the best condition for an objective account! Your letter 'naturally' came at the very moment when I had virtually resolved to take the plunge.

Fate will have it—and this has always been the case with me—that all the "outer" aspects of my life should be accidental. Only what is interior has proved to have substance and determining value. As a result, all memory of outer events has faded, and perhaps these "outer" experiences were never so very essential anyhow, or were so only in that they coincided with phases of my inner development. An enormous part of these "outer" manifestations of my life has vanished from my memory—for the very reason, I now realize, that I was never really "in" them, although it seemed to me then that I was participating with all my powers. Yet these are the very things that make up a sensible biography: persons one has met, travels, adventures, entanglements, blows of destiny, and so on. But with few exceptions they have become phantasms which I barely recollect, for they no longer lend wings to my imagination.

On the other hand, my memories of the "inner" experiences have grown all the more vivid and colorful. This poses a problem of description which I scarcely feel able to cope with, at least for the present.

Steiner subsequently published his recollections of Jung as "Erinnerungen an Carl Gustav Jung: Zur Enstehung der Autobiographie," *Basler Stadtbuch* (as the *Basler Jahrbuch* had by then become), 1965, pp. 117–63.

On December 31 Jung went to Bollingen and started writing his memoir, "From the Earliest Experiences of my Life."

On January 1 Jaffé wrote to Wolff,

There are two further protocols for the autobiography which I will send to you soon. It has not yet been possible to get an answer to your questions—at the moment he is so fascinated by thoughts, or better: fantasies and hypotheses about the transcendent, about the "beyond," that only conversations about these topics have any life about them. Once I asked him about Zimmer—on my own initiative—but the answer was terse! I think it best not to swim against the tide. I am sure the time will come when those questions which he has already seen and which he is absolutely keen to answer will have their moment again.

I have thought much about the particular discrepancy between the autobiographical and the intellectual content, and also about the fragmentary nature of the material about the recent years or decades, until it occurred to me that one could perhaps call the book "Memories, Dreams, and Reflections." Then one would be much freer and could string together a chain of precious and less precious pearls. Jung would concur with this. What do you think about it?

For me the autobiography really belongs to what was most essential about the past year. It was a modification of what a benevolent fate has granted to me for many years: Friday afternoons spent (after struggling my way through the heaven, earth, and hell of a personal analysis with Jung) in the gift (or even the habit!) of personal conversations with him. Although he always overflowed with what he had to say and to describe, and memories have always played a significant role, it was not as concentrated on his life as it is now; and I know that this concentration on what is past, this retrospective and prospective view are extremely important for him today, being on the threshold of the beyond. But perhaps that still remains to be seen.

I have the impression that Jung is once again in the grip of the creative daimon. Mostly it starts with a phase of sleeplessness, unsettledness, restlessness, increased

JANUARY 10, 1958[929]

On January 9, 1927 my friend Herman Sigg died.[930] Six months earlier, so in June 1926, I dreamed: I am with Hermann Sigg on a car journey around Lake Geneva.[931] We are traveling from Lausanne towards Vevey.[932] But in the dream I know that Vevey is in fact Luxor; so we are not on the banks of Lake Geneva but on the banks of the Nile. When we arrived at the Place de la Ville in Vevey, Hermann Sigg says, "I must have something repaired on the car. It'll take about an hour. You can go for a walk in the meantime. We'll meet at the town's eastern exit, in the direction of Montreux." I agree and go for a walk in the town and after an hour I wait for Hermann Sigg at the agreed place. But he does not come. So I go further along the road to see if he was perhaps waiting further ahead. Suddenly a car stops behind me. It's Hermann Sigg. He is furious: "Honestly, you can very well wait for me and you don't need to run away from me!"—That was the end of the dream. When I gave it some thought, it occurred to me that Luxor is on the left bank of the Nile, unlike Vevey which is on the right bank of Lake Geneva—if one follows the direction

---

irritability (even grumpiness!). That's how it was the last Friday afternoon allocated for this purpose; we had more of a conversation about it; I also spoke about myself and only began to take shorthand notes when we began to converse on a subject we were both keen on: the stars. He drew a comparison between the macrocosm and the psychic microcosm and I only hope I can capture the difficult ideas from my sketchy notes. That protocol will follow later. [BL]

On January 8, Cary Baynes asked Jung if she could lend Kurt Wolff her transcription of the *Red Book*, and asked if Jung was intending to speak about Bollingen, Freud and his patients, and that "K. W. would like you very much to speak of the 'academic years' as he puts it, the lectures at the University, the E.T.H., etc. *I* would like a saturnine account of how long it took academia to know who you are." (JP). Jung agreed to her lending her transcription of the *Red Book* to Kurt Wolff.

[929] Jaffé noted in *Reflections*, "During my work on the book *Death Dreams and Ghosts*, we often spoke about the subject of precognitive experiences and dreams shortly before or after the death of loved ones in which they appear as dream figures." (p.156).

[930] Hermann Sigg (1875–1927) was a businessman, a close friend and neighbor of Jung's, and the founder, in 1904, of Haus Sigg & Co., which specialized in olive oil and had plantations and factories in Tunisia, Spain, and France. The company was responsible for most of the olive oil imports in Switzerland. Sigg's obituary in the *Neue Zürcher Zeitung* described him as a "very kind, very upright, farsighted businessman" (January 14, 1927). In 1927 Jung painted an image of the map from his Liverpool dream in the calligraphic volume of *LN* to which he gave the following inscription: "D. IX januarii anno 1927 obiit Hermannus Sigg aet.s.52 amicus meus." (January 9, 1927 my friend Hermann Sigg died aged fifty-two.)

[931] Jung noted this dream in his entry for January 9, 1927 in *BB* 7 (pp. 238–39).

[932] Vevey is on the shore of Lake Geneva, not far from Lausanne (driving in this direction would be the route one would take to go to Zurich).

of the Rhône. But it's on the right bank of the Nile, opposite Luxor,[933] that the city of the dead is to be found!

[934]On the day after Hermann Sigg's burial I had an extraordinarily strange experience. I was lying awake and thinking about him. I was very preoccupied with him because his death had been so sudden; he died of a paralytic attack. I couldn't sleep and suddenly had the feeling that he was there standing at the foot of my bed and demanding that I go with him. I had a visual inner image of him. It was my inner picture, and I didn't have the feeling of its being an "apparition." I said to myself: Yes, now, that's a fantasy. But then I began to wonder: Have I evidence that it is a fantasy? If it were not a fantasy and he was really there, if I were then to say he was a fantasy, then it would be a cheap shot,—I recalled the fantasy of a girl that I had had many years before and had to take as real.[935] So I said to myself: Now, I have no evidence! [288/289] Evidence either way! I could just as well say: You are really there.—The very moment I thought that, he went to the door and I went after him in my thoughts. Then I went inside—still in my thoughts–and he led me into his study where a tall bookcase stood behind his desk. I had no idea what sort of books he had there. He pointed at the first of three red-bound books on the second uppermost shelf. With this, the vision stopped.—But these red books were so high up that it was not possible to see from below what they were. In the vision, my friend climbed up on a footstool in order to show them to me.

On the next morning the experience seemed so puzzling and strange to me that I went to his widow and asked her if I might go into in the library of her deceased husband. So I went into the library and behind his desk on the second uppermost shelf I saw in actual fact three red-bound books. As I could not recognize from below what their titles were, I fetched myself a footstool, stood upon it and then I saw that they were translations of Émile Zola's novels. The title of the second volume was *Das Vermächtnis der Toten* [the legacy of the dead].[936] I then read the whole thing, but it is nothing of relevance, just a really stupid novel.

---

[933] Luxor was part of a complex of six temples founded in 1400 BCE. It contains the ruins of Thebes, capital of Egypt in the Middle and New Kingdoms. Jung had a series of postcards from the temple complex of nearby Karnak, indicating that he had visited it, presumably in 1925.

[934] See *ETG*, p. 315, *MDR*, p. 312. Jung noted this dream in his entry for January 13, 1927 in *BB* 7 (p. 240).

[935] See Jung's fantasy of December 28, 1913 in *BB* 2 (pp. 202–9).

[936] A German translation of an early Zola novel, *Le voeu d'une morte* (1867), translated into English by Count C. S. de Soissons as *A Dead Woman's Wish* (London: Greening and Co., 1902).

After his death, when Hermann Sigg was already buried, so at least fourteen days or three weeks after his death, I had another strange dream.[937] In the dream we were now in Luxor for real and[938] were sitting in a restaurant with small white marble tables and plush armchairs. We were sitting on a sofa in a corner. I knew that I was with Sigg in Luxor— and (as you will see) that is very significant because of the earlier dream of him—and I was waiting for him. Then he came to me in a hurry, and full of emotion, saying, "You do know that I am alive. You don't need to pretend that I am dead. I'm as much alive as you!" This scene repeated the dream on the road from Vevey to Lausanne. He came at me in a threatening way. And suddenly a powerful corpse stench was pressing in on me. I knew: "Now something dangerous is happening." Then I pulled my bush knife out of my bag, a sort of dagger, and brandished it in the air between him and me and with it I kept him away from my body. That was the final dream I had of him.[939]

[293]

---

[937] Jung noted this in his entry of January 13, 1927 in *BB* 7 (p. 241).

[938] The remainder of this entry is on a separate fragment of paper.

[939] Pages 290–92 of the protocols of the Interviews are copies of pp. 288–89, so are not reproduced here.

On January 10, 1958 Aniela Jaffé wrote to Kurt Wolff,

Today I was in Bollingen and something so wonderful and significant happened that I had to write to you immediately: Jung is writing his autobiography afresh once again in his own right. Only at the end of November did I intuit that such a thing might be possible and perhaps this is why I was so intensely involved in everything connected to this.

He said that while he was narrating his life to me it all became so clear to him, above all the significance of his life which apparently until then he had not been able to see to its full extent. I have read what he has written so far: it is wonderful. Simple and profound, like a fairy-tale. Much that he has already told me, some that is completely new, some completely reworked, some parts amplified further. Some parts are missing still.

I wanted to make available to him the Protocols (which he has never seen), but he said he would rather formulate it anew. [BL]

On January 11 Jaffé wrote again to Wolff, replying to his letter of January 7. She had spoken with Jung that morning about his work, and Bennet's project. She had been worried about how this would affect her work: "But Prof. Jung takes the view that Bennet's and my work would not overlap, not only because we are two quite different people and characters, but because in the end my point of view will be a different one from that of Bennet." She had since spoken with Bennet. She was very thankful for Wolff's suggestions and questions, but noted that she couldn't ask Jung about matters such as his views on different nationalities. "However, his relationship to animals will play a role—for example, a pair of snakes that had taken up residence on the banks of his tower for whom regularly a bowl of milk was put out—as well as a dog out of whose eyes he saw his deceased father, or a bird who sat on his space when he was digging up potatoes in whom he greeted the spirit of a

JANUARY 31, 1958

[940]In the winter of 1923/24 I was in Bollingen. The tower was then newly built. No snow was on the ground as far as I can recall, so it was heading towards spring. I was alone in the tower at that time, perhaps for a week, perhaps rather longer. It was, as you can imagine, indescribably silent. I had never experienced it so intensively as that time. Then—I can still recall: I was sitting by the fire in the hearth and I had a large water kettle

---

deceased love one. This is sort of his 'style.' The proximity of the dead, I'd almost like to say: the proximity of the beyond, together with an unusually strong bond with nature. My guiding principle would be: Jung and the natural world, within and without. Nature within is dreams and everything that belongs to that. External nature is the earth [. . .]. Questions about Freud and Charcot will of course probably be dealt with by Bennet [. . .]. As far as the further development is concerned, Jung would prefer it if I keep to the 'inner material,' so dreams and fantasies." She noted that conversations with Bennet had tired Jung: "I did the post with Jung every day, and I often had the desire or the idea to pose one question or another to him. I did not do it as he so easily tired." (BL).

On January 19 Jaffé informed Wolff that Cary Baynes had written a letter to Jung in which "she repeated your questions (significance of practice, academic teaching activities etc.) and so I think these will now finally be discussed." She then reproduced Jung's reply to Steiner's letter (see above, n. 928) (BL).

On January 24 Jung wrote to Cary Baynes, who had responded to what she had been sent of the material, "Thank you very much for your kind and beautiful letter. As I am continuously in doubt about my subjective material, it has given me a bit more confidence in my actual work: it consists in the most peculiar and to me unexpected fact that I try to work out the history of my early days, seen as I have seen it in my youth without knowing what it meant and unable then to express it in words. Now I have the memories and the words but I am continuously disturbed by my own subjectivity. It is curious how one has an absolutely certain feeling of value on the one side and on the other an equally certain doubt about its value." He added that he had no objection of her lending Kurt Wolff her transcription of *The Red Book* (JP).

On January 26 Wolff wrote to Jung that it was clear to him that the book was becoming much more important than he had envisaged. He proposed the title "Memories, Dreams, Reflections," noting, "I believe that nothing that you have written in books, spoken in lectures, will speak so directly to the heart, to the innermost center of the reader or listener than the revelations that you are entrusting to A. J.; for here you are not speaking to scholars and students but to the human heart in general." The fact that Jung was now writing his memoirs was a wonderful expansion of the project.

On January 29 Jaffé wrote to Wolff that Jung "has suggested several times to me—but this from a feeling of taking something away from me—that I should publish the protocols and he, his records. (I, in English, he, in German!) But this was not meant entirely seriously, as I saw straight away, and I also protested against it." On January 31 Jaffé thanked Wolff for his letter to Jung, which had resulted in a good conversation: "The conversation was not altogether straightforward. It was chiefly to do with J.'s doubts as to the value of what he had written and the fear that it would not be worthy of publication." She had suggested that Wolff be asked for an objective opinion, which Jung thought was a good idea (BL). On January 31 Jung returned from Bollingen.

[940] See *ETG*, p. 232, *MDR*, p. 228.

on the fire to make hot water for washing up, when the water began to sing. It sounded like many voices, like wind instruments, and they were playing exactly as in an orchestral piece. Quite modern music that I can't stand, but terribly interesting: one orchestra was inside the tower, and the other was out on the lake. They intertwined like waves. I sat there and listened quite fascinated for far more than an hour, listening to this concert, this quiet melody of nature that was quite indescribable, like a many-voiced orchestra, completely polyphonic music.

That vividly reminded me of another experience: when I was a student, already in the clinical semester. I once came home very tired and sat down on the sofa and was almost falling asleep; and then very quietly and distantly I heard a beautiful alto voice singing an aria in the style of Handel, and then I fell more deeply asleep but without *actually* sleeping, and then I heard this voice quite close, much closer than before. As if it had come into the next room. A beautiful voice. I listened for a long time, and I also perceived something like a distant accompaniment. "Curious," I thought, "there is no one there. And anyway: no one can sing like that, no one has such a wondrous voice. That's a great artist." Then I got closer to waking up and the voice was further away again. But it still sounded ravishingly beautiful. I could not understand at all what it was.[941]

I recalled that voice as I sat there in Bollingen. Only this time the music, this quiet music, had all the disharmonies of nature. [293/294] For me nature was never harmonious, but rather terribly oppositional and it had a chaotic character. That is what this music was like: a stream of sounds somehow embodying the nature of the water and the earth and the wind; so wondrously that one can barely describe it.

[942]And there was another strange experience in Bollingen. That was also on such a silent evening. I was still lighting the stove. It must also have been early in the spring, perhaps even still in winter. Around two o'clock in the morning, I dreamed that I had been awoken by footsteps going around the tower. But there was only a lightly trodden footpath along the lake. Then I heard distant music coming closer and closer and then it was as if people were speaking and laughing outside. I thought: Who on earth is walking around out there? What is that then? I was convinced I would

---

[941] Cf. above, p. 142.

[942] See *ETG*, p. 233, *MDR*, p. 229, where this experience is dated to early spring, 1924. See the entry for February 8/9, 1924 in *BB* 7 (p. 234), where the horde is first identified as "peoples of the future, the unborn dead," whom Jung invites into the tower, "Philemon's temple." See Bennet, *Meetings with Jung*, January 10, 1957 (pp. 79–80).

see some people. By now I was awake, and now in reality, I went up to the window; I opened the shutters and—there was absolutely no one there, nothing to hear, no wind, nothing.

That is so strange: I'd thought the footsteps and the laughing and talking were real, but not a trace of it! So I only dreamed it. I went back to bed and thought about how one can deceive oneself, and how I had been woken by these noises. With these thoughts in my mind I went back to sleep, and—immediately the same dream began again; again I heard the steps, the talking and laughter, and an accordion playing. And I thought: What the hell! I thought it had been a dream but now it is true after all. It's real! Again, I jumped up, opened the window and shutters, but there was the same deathly silence as before. I thought: It's simply a ghost! I was so convinced that I was awake and that it was real! [294/295]

Then, of course, I wondered: What does it mean when a dream insists on its reality to that degree? Normally that only happens with ghosts. The dream wants me to consider what I have heard or seen as a reality. In the dream I had the impression that I was really awake. But this only means that I came out of a deeper layer of the unconscious, closer to the consciousness of day, similar to my experience, as a student, of the alto voice. This experience of the voice later repeated itself once again. That night in the tower everything was so absolutely real that I was quite confused. I could not make any sense of it at all. What did these peasant boys mean as they passed by in a long procession? It was as if they had come to look around the tower.

Back then I was not yet familiar with the chronicle of Cysat.[943] He was a native of Lucerne in the seventeenth century and he describes in his chronicle,—on an alp on Mount Pilatus that was particularly notorious anyway,[944] because Wotan was supposed to be up to his tricks around there[945]—so this Cysat was disturbed in the night by a procession of people streaming past both sides of the hut, with music and singing. The next day he asked the neighbors about it. But they said that they had heard nothing, yet they knew very well what that had been: it must have been the "sälig Lüt" [blessed folk]. What I experienced was a genuine shamanic experience. I experienced it with every one of my senses.

---

[943] Renward Cysat (1545–1614), *Collectanea chronica und denkwürdige Sachen pro chronica Lucernensi et Helvetiae* (Lucerne: Diebold Schilling Verlag, 1961–77).

[944] Pilatus: a mountain overlooking Lucerne.

[945] Wotan: a major deity in Germanic and Norse mythology. He is portrayed as a complex, multifaceted God associated with wisdom, poetry, war, magic, prophecy, and the dead. For Jung's encounter with Wotan, see below, p. 267.

And I had as clear an idea of the people as if I had really seen them. All the while it was dark and I lay in bed and was absolutely certain that I was mistaken the first time, and yet it was real. What does the unconscious intend by this? I couldn't make any sense of it. Why are they all young peasant boys? Why all men? I imagine that I had been so sensitized in my solitude that I had perceived the procession of the "sälig Lüt" as it went past. Later I never experienced anything of the kind again, nor did I dream anything like that. [295/296] That experience left me quite speechless. Nor could I recall ever having heard of anything similar.

At that time Hans was once with me in Bollingen for about ten days.[946] We were alone there—perhaps it was fourteen days—and it was also this early springtime, and it was quite cold. We were in the kitchen cooking. Suddenly I heard someone calling my name outside. Hans did not hear anything. I go to the door, no one there. I went right around the tower but there wasn't a soul there. Not ten minutes passed, then again someone called my name. "But this time!" Hans interrupted me: "Now I heard it too." We both went to the door, but there was nothing.—This experience also took place at that time.

One can say that these were phenomena caused by solitude, that the "sälig Lüt" compensated for the external emptiness and presented a crowd of people. But that does not satisfy me. And, why does the unconscious insist on this reality? That is what the hermits hear, such things, which of course might also be compensatory. But we do not know what realities these stories point to. It was not at all frightening. Cysat says the same, by the way: that the "sälig Lüt" were absolutely joyful, and whoever has seen them belongs to them. In any case, it is a phenomenon of the collective unconscious. And there is a general disposition for such things. One can hardly explain it. One only knows one has perceived it, whether as a projection from the collective unconscious or in the physical realm, it's exactly the same. It is only a different way of explaining it. My explanation at the time, that it was a psychic compensation, never satisfied me. I felt obliged also to take into consideration its sense of reality. To say it was a hallucination is not enough. Especially when one reads a parallel report from the seventeenth century. Synchronistic phenomena prove after all that incidents that we claim to know or believe to be collectively unconscious must have a correspondence in matter, because it behaves in a correlated way. It behaves according to psychic experience. [296/297]

---

[946] Hans Kuhn: see n. 333 above.

Such processions of young men took place in actuality as they marched—mostly in the spring—from central Switzerland to Locarno to the Casa di Ferro.[947] From there they were transported to Milan as soldiers for the Sforzas.[948] So it could have been one of these processions which regularly take place in the spring, taking leave of their home town with singing and joviality. There is also the Bizozero song. (That's a village near Milan where a battle took place in which many young Swiss men were killed.) "I think it will be a hot summer . . ."—this, or something like it, is what the young people sing as they make their way south. "In the Rose Garden in Milan there was a lot of room."[949] A crowd of Swiss mercenaries, that was the character of the procession that I experienced. Back then I also wondered whether it might be a funeral procession, but the cheerful character spoke against this. With singing and joviality, they passed by each time, but the majority of them were slaughtered in battle. Perhaps some of them went on to become officers, but the majority of them died.—It cannot be ruled out that this experience was something similar to Ravenna, that I was somehow taken back in time.[950] Whenever I was in Bollingen, and still today, I'm in my "no. 2 personality," and I saw and see life on a large scale, as it comes about and fades away and is already long since past. That would be the timeless aspect of life.

[951]I built the tower when my mother had already died. I always thought it was like a correspondence to the mother. Because the "ancient man": that's the no. 2 personality, that has always lived and still lives and that is, in alchemical language, "the primeval son of the mother."[952] That is expressed with infinite wisdom. This "primordial man" later became Philemon in my fantasies. And this is why I carved into the door of the tower "Philemonis sacrum, Fausti poenitentia."[953] Later that spot was bricked up, and then I carved it on the entrance to the chapel. [297/298]

---

[947] The Cà di Ferro was a base near Locarno for mercenaries, dating from 1560.

[948] Sforza: the ruling family of Milan in the Renaissance period.

[949] These are lines from an old Bernese folksong, "Der Rosengarten zu Mailand" (a mercenaries' song by Karl Geiser), viewable at https://ingeb.org/Lieder/baldfang.html (accessed April 25, 2025).

[950] See above, pp. 134–37.

[951] See *ETG*, p. 229, *MDR*, p. 225.

[952] On October 24, 1953 Jung wrote to Wolfgang Pauli, "In this *matriarchal* sphere, the spirit is the son of the mother (alchem. The 'primeval son of the mother.')" C. A. Meier, ed., *Atom and Archetype: The Pauli–Jung Letters 1932–1958*, trans. David Roscoe (Princeton, NJ: Princeton University Press, 2001), p. 126. Cf. *Psychology and Alchemy* (1944), CE 17; CW 12, § 26.

[953] The motto translates as "Philemon's sanctuary, Faust's penance."

[954]Once in January or early February in 1923, even before I had built the tower, I was in Castagnola. There I received the telegram that my mother had died.[955] The same night I took the train from Lugano to travel home. I was very distressed by the news, for her death came very suddenly. But it was perhaps not wholly unexpected. For shortly before I had dreamed a terrible dream related to Wotan.[956] I dream—it might also have been in the night before—that I am in a dense dark wood, a primeval forest, with massive trees and enormous rocks. It was a heroic, primeval landscape. Then, all of sudden, I heard a shrill whistling. It seemed to echo throughout the entire universe and my knees became weak with fear. Then a huge wolfhound came crashing through the bushes, a terrifying animal, and I knew: That is the Wild Huntsman, and he has sent his dog to fetch someone. I awoke in a state of mortal terror. Quite soon afterwards I received the news of my mother's death.—As I was traveling home that night I had the feeling of great sadness but at root I could not be sad because for the whole journey I heard dance music and laughter and joyful noise and I had the feeling: Now a wedding is being celebrated!

[957]In November 1922 I had a dream of my father that made a strong impression on me. Since 1896 I had no longer dreamed about him, this being from his death until 1922. But then he came in a dream, quite suddenly, as if he were returning from a long journey. (That was always the case: whenever I dreamed of my father it was as if he was returning from a long journey). Now he came again from a long journey and looked very rejuvenated; and not at all fatherly and authoritative. I was extremely pleased to learn how he had fared, I went into the library with him and was looking forward to introducing him to my wife and children and to telling him what I had done workwise and what I had become since he had been gone. But I saw immediately that it was not possible, [298/299] because he seemed preoccupied by something and apparently wanted something from me. I felt that quite clearly and I made myself available to him. And then he said to me that as I was a psychologist, he wanted to consult me on the question of marital psychology. I prepared myself to

---

[954] See *ETG*, p. 316.

[955] Jung's mother died on January 9. See *BB 7*, January 9, 1923 (p. 232).

[956] See *BB 7*, January 2/3, 1923, pp. 224–26. From the account there it is clear that this wasn't a dream, but an active imagination. Jung's encounter with Wotan reverberates in his 1936 essay, "Wotan," in which he attributed the upheaval taking place in Germany under National Socialism at that time as the reactivation of the archetype of Wotan. *CE* 14; *CW* 10.

[957] See *ETG*, p. 317, *MDR*, p. 315; and above, pp. 81–82. The dream occurred on the night of January 8, 1923, and Jung wrote it down on January 12 (*BB 7*, p. 232).

give him a long talk on the complications of marriage and then I woke up.—I could not properly understand it for I did not think that this might refer to the death of my mother. Shortly afterwards my mother had a small mucous membrane tumor in her mouth, something quite harmless in itself. But I thought: Now the body is getting out of control. I recalled the dream of my father, and soon afterwards in February, my mother died.

The experience of the Wild Huntsman was an elemental dream, fantastic; massive rocks lay all around, vast, primeval trees and the giant wolf broke through; at the sight of him blood froze in the veins when one saw what terrible jaws he had. He shot past me, and I knew: Now the Wild Huntsman has commanded him to fetch someone. I found that an extraordinarily gruesome picture, that a person was to be carried away. And I wondered: Why, for God's sake, is it being depicted like this? Why is it the Fenris wolf,[958] and not an angel, coming to fetch them? Death was portrayed in this dream as a terrible catastrophe of nature, caused by furious Gods. A violent act of nature.—And then, soon after, came the experience in the train; it was just the opposite. There was cheerful dance music, jolly laughter and it was impossible for me to be sad. Repeatedly sadness tried to overwhelm me and in the next moment I was caught up in these cheerful melodies again. There was a feeling of warmth, joy with not a trace of fear and mourning. As if death had been portrayed once from the perspective of nature and once *sub specie aeternitatis*[959]—The experience in the dream where I also heard this cheerful music took place later.[960] In that case there was no question of someone having died, it was a friendly and peaceful thing, utterly harmless: young people who are full of life. Quite simple. Then I had not yet thought of the Milan processions.[961]—In Cysat's case there's also the strange story, later taken up by Athanasius Kircher,[962] that a young farmer was suddenly seized by a whirlwind and the next moment found himself in Milan. He had to find his way home from there. It was assumed that it was Wotan who transported him that way. Probably the ambulatory syndrome is the basis of this story, that I once wrote a case history about. In this, people are as if gripped by travel fever, forget the past and simply set off on their travels. I know of one man, a banker, who took off in state of mind like

---

[958] Fenris wolf: a monstrous wolf from Norse mythology.
[959] *sub specie aeternitatis* (Lat.): "from the standpoint of eternity."
[960] Cf. *ETG*, p. 231, *MDR*, p. 228.
[961] See above, p 266.
[962] Athanasius Kircher (1602–1680), Jesuit scholar and polymath. Jung cited his work on a number of occasions in his alchemical studies.

this and suddenly found himself in Bombay. In French pathology such cases are well known.[963]

In my life I had always to follow the inner personality, No. 2. This is why I also had to give up my academic career. I was faced back then with the choice: either I make my career as an academic—that was readily available to me—or I follow my higher reason: I continue these remarkable things, the fantasies, that I had begun then but which I could not come out in public about. Either my career, or I build upon what appears to me to be more important *sub specie aeternitatis*. What does it mean, whether or not I have been a professor. Just as little as whether I have the title of doctor or not. I was annoyed about it, of course; I had incredible rage and it upset me in many regards. But these emotions are only temporary, in essence they mean nothing. On the other hand, the other is what is important. And when one concentrates on what No. 2 wants and says, then the whole pain is finished with. I did not experience that only when I gave up my academic career as a young man, but in my life as a whole. I was in fact very short-tempered; but always when the issue reached its climax it somehow overturned and then came the silence of space; I was removed from everything as if it had taken place in the past. And I thought: Yes, that's quite unimportant.

I told you about the experience on Lake Lucerne as a young boy when I was scolded for disobedience, which I perceived as quite appropriate,[964] and yet [300/301] I had such a rage that he could scold *me* when I was such an important personality who should not be subject to such a ragging. Back then I was still very naïve, I was still identified with the "second" personality, the greater personality. Later I noticed that I am not that at all. That was "No. 2," but this personality kept increasing over the course of the years. In all decisive moments of my life this reaction came, the voice of the second personality. I drew the inference: that must be a very powerful archetype. I described it then as the "Old Wise Man," who could observe everything *sub specie aeternitatis* as if it were already long since in the past. The things that were important to him, dreams, thinking about the whole, that was the real thing for him. It was completely indifferent to me whether I had an academic career. I had to make a

---

[963] See Philippe Tissié, *Les aliénés voyageurs: Essai médico-psychologique* (Paris: Doin, 1887).

[964] See above, p. 55.

decision back then: do I want to continue on the academic track or not. And you know what I decided.

When I got to know Freud, and when I joined Freud, I knew that I was risking my career. But then No. 2 said: If you act as if you did not know Freud, then that is a deception, and one cannot base life upon a lie.[965] And with that the matter was settled. The second such case came when I was a very successful associate lecturer. When I was called on by the inner figures to "teach us the deep things." And then I had to choose to risk sending my academic career to the devil. And it was like coming out of a moment in which I was transported by the "Wise Old Man": "you know all that is nothing, that is all only empty pomposity. What you are doing in this intellectual business has no value. The only value is that you have access to the depths and say goodnight to the academic career!"

[966]It was like that too when I decided for psychiatry. My friends could not understand that. "Something so stupid, without prospects!" During my studies I continued to read the philosophers: Kant, Nietzsche, Nicolai Hartmann,[967] Schopenhauer, and it was impossible for me to bring together medicine [301/302] and philosophy. And then I read the introduction to Krafft-Ebing in preparation for my exams, I was overcome by a crazy excitement and inner certainty, and everything else was rubbish.[968]

I was often amazed by myself: No. 1 wishes something, and No. 2 says something quite different, but that's what stands. As No. 1, I always had the feeling of uncertainty: something can happen, yet his world is only relative. What matters is the world of No. 2. This was also true with my writings.

---

[965] Cf. *1925*, pp. 15–16. Jaffé incorporated passages from this into the chapter on Freud in *MDR*.

[966] See *ETG*, p. 118, *MDR*, p. 111.

[967] Nicolai Hartmann (1882–1950) was a twentieth century German philosopher; here Jung evidently meant Eduard von Hartmann (1842–1906), whose works he studied (see above, n. 270). On Jung's philosophical readings, see Alessio di Fiori, "*Principium individuationis*: C. G. Jung et la philosophie allemande; Élaboration de l'œuvre de Carl Gustav Jung (1875–1961) et étude de ses sources philosophiques," PhD thesis, University of Strasbourg, 2021.

[968] See above, n. 437. Richard von Krafft-Ebing (1840–1902) was a prominent German psychiatrist, best known today for his *Psychopathia Sexualis* of 1886, a foundational text of sexology. After several previous appointments, he became professor of psychiatry at the University of Vienna. In *VA*, Jung recalled that it was on reading Krafft-Ebing's statement in his preface to his *Textbook of Psychiatry* regarding the "subjective character" of psychiatric textbooks that he took the decision to specialize in psychiatry, as it united the two currents of his interests. *ETG*, p. 115, *MDR*, p. 109.

What I have written was always, so to speak, an assignment from No. 2. And it was always things in which the slightest attention to the world was not permitted. That began with alchemy. Think of the book on Job. And today it's still exactly the same: if I write about Flying Saucers,[969] I risk placing myself in an impossible light with intellectuals of every stripe; and ultimately the same applies to the autobiography and to what I am attempting to relate honestly within it. [302/303]

I write in my notes mainly of my inner experiences.[970] Along with all the little things, the smaller memories fade away. They say too little. Now I am writing of how I came into philosophy from theology, which so fundamentally disgusted me. But my life and my passion are in it. The representation is very difficult as it is only a concern of the inner man (I call him "No. 2") who has led a very isolated life in "No. 1" because he was able to speak with no one. It was a secret and an uncanny life which also led to considerable depressions for me.

[971]Starting to write up my memories was a vital necessity. If I neglect writing about them for one single day, immediately extremely unpleasant physical symptoms begin. Toxic feelings, loss of appetite and such things. As soon as I write, all of that disappears and I get a quite clear head. Such things as I am writing there, there is something immeasurable in it. A book of mine is always a destiny. I can neither prescribe nor intend anything myself. It has already taken a quite different path than I had imagined before I started. It takes such a different path.[972]Now I am at a point where I do not know exactly how I got to Schopenhauer. It occurred to me that first I first read the history of philosophy. He was the first of the newer philosophers whom I read. At school I heard a lot about Plato and so on. But Platonic philosophy never really enthused me. But Schopenhauer, he directly struck a chord because of pessimism. That connected to my depressions at that time. Schopenhauer was the first person I encountered who spoke *my* language. [303/304][973]

---

[969] "Flying Saucers": in English in the original. Jung refers to *A Modern Myth: Of Things Seen in the Skies* (1958), CE 26; CW 10.

[970] Jung is referring here to his memoir, "From the Earliest Experiences of my Life," which he was concurrently writing.

[971] See *ETG*, p. 2, *MDR*, p. vi

[972] See *ETG*, p. 74, *MDR*, p. 69.

[973] On February 1 Jung wrote to Kurt Wolff,

Mrs. Jaffé has told me that she wrote to you that I am now writing my early childhood memories myself. This is indeed the case, for when I was narrating my

February 13, 1958

In life, or on the path of individuation, one must also bargain with mistakes, for without them life would not be complete. There is no guarantee, at any moment, that we will not end up in error or in mortal danger. People always think there is a safe path. But the safe path is the path of the dead: then nothing more happens. Those who take the safe path are in fact spiritually dead. The fear of life is justified, but only up to a certain point when one sees that if one does nothing then one will break down; yet if I do it then I'll have half a chance. We can encounter danger in the most civilized of worlds: the more we have physical mastery of life, the more it happens psychically. And besides, there's always a chance that we will have an automobile accident or a railway crash. People say, "Now we're quite free of fear," but that's really crazy!

[974]Something like this happened to me when I broke my foot in 1944. Of course, I immediately said to myself: It's my attitude that's broken, that was quite clear. I slid down a slope: so my attitude was probably too high up. I had somehow been standing high over and above it, above what belonged to me. Then I had enough time to reflect on everything. But I did

---

recollections to her the desire formed in me to engage with the task more seriously. One often does not value sufficiently what one carries within oneself. In this, I am conscious that, in a certain sense, I am on a collision course with Mrs. Jaffé's work but I believe this difficulty can be resolved by establishing a relationship of collaboration. I am throwing my contribution into the ring, as it were. As the whole issue is still in a state of flux there are as yet no acute publication problems. These will arise only when the structure of the book is being considered. I do not know myself how far my preoccupation with my early memories will take me. For the time being, it seems to me that I will only take the narrative as far as the starting point of my scientific activities. But for me every book is a destiny and for this reason I cannot be sure where the boundary will be found.

You can be assured that I have no tendency unnecessarily to shout loudly about my current work. I have always observed this principle whenever I was preparing a book. As long as the matter is still in formation, I forbid myself any speculation about the future of what I have written.

Jung suggested that they discuss the matter (BL). On the same day, Cary Baynes wrote to Wolff, "I must say I am dubious about his taking the pen from the hands of the gentle Aniela. It does indeed show that he is up to the hilt in the project, and so will bring it through to a finish. But, just suppose his ambition gets into it, and ambition is one of his besetting sins. All the magic will then go out of it—it would have a purpose. That would be a real catastrophe." (BL).

Jaffé for her part noted that "even though I told Jung I would be delighted if he were to write about the whole of his life, he insisted on continuing our conversations about his life and work." *Reflections*, p. 75.

[974] See *ETG*, p. 293, *MDR*, p. 289.

not know exactly what I should make of it. And yet I simply had the feeling that I must somehow be responsible for what had happened. Perhaps I still had too many principles back then, such as, for example, saying nothing that I cannot prove and not believing anything without sufficient evidence or rationale. I also thought it was an important function of consciousness to be able to say a substantiated yes or no. I had all these things that one ought to be able to say out of decency. Then I thought: But it might also be the case that things happen to you that you cannot judge at all and that might just as well be true as false. And these could be taken in such-and-such a way or quite the opposite, and where there are no longer any criteria. Then I reminded myself of my experience concerning Basel cathedral.[975] [304/305] Back then, my judgment had also said, "No, not that," although I knew only that it was something quite terrible, but I did not know what it was. So perhaps it might also be that I would have to say yes to something quite terrible. That my attitude was still too high. That my judgment is no longer required because a higher necessity of fate is present, or the will of God which cannot be discussed away. And then I'm simply up the creek, completely perplexed, and if I do not surrender then I am simply in error even if I am justified before the whole world. I had the feeling that if I have no more foundation, then I am a useless instrument. I imagined that it would be of the greatest significance to world affairs to preserve the freedom to say yes or no. But now it's a question of my saying yes to a fundamentally purely chaotic condition, to an event unknown to me, that I do not understand at all and that I do not value. So in fact it's a question of a sin against myself, or at least that is how it looked to me. And yet it was not clearly conscious to me what it was that was being forced upon me. But I thought that's another case like the one back then, where a surrender was expected of me *à tout prix*,[976] which means a dissolution of myself. Now it's got me—what else can I do? Back then I could not cope with the arguments. Then came the heart infarct, the unconsciousness, the delirium. Then I fell all the way into death: I had to pull myself together again painstakingly afterwards. That is why the problem remained untouched for a long time until I could pick it up again. After the illness came an extremely fruitful time for me. Then I worked and wrote and tried not to state my view about the thoughts, but rather to entrust myself to the stream, to what was happening. I said to myself: I just don't understand it, but this is simply how it must be. Not

---

975 See above, pp. 55–56.
976 *à tout prix*, in French in the original: "at any cost."

until my wife died did things come to me that brought this problem back up again as the unconscious gave me dreams that I could only understand with supplementary hypotheses. Such as, for example, the dream of the image of my wife that was presented for me.[977] Is that an image of her fabricated only out of my material, [305/306] or is she really here? I must entrust myself completely to my feelings, I must trust that the feeling is right and give up the intellect. So if my feeling says, "That is my wife," then it must be so, I must accept the information I received as real.

When I was in India (1939) I had amoebic dysentery and was in hospital in Calcutta for fourteen days.[978] I was in a British military hospital. In the first night on my return to the hotel I had a dream that I could not understand at all; it made a colossal impression on me. I was very preoccupied at that time with the problem of evil, as to how far it could be assumed that it was also God's will. I had greedily seized upon the invitation to travel to India so that I would have the opportunity finally to be alone with myself and to be able to think about these things. I had a four-week sea voyage, so in total I was at sea for eight weeks, and in India I was often able to be alone with myself. There was also my joy in the completely different environment, and one night this dream arrived.

It began with a sort of idea of an island shaped rather like England [i.e., Great Britain], but it was much smaller. And roughly where Cornwall is was a sort of headland, quite similar to Cornwall protruding into the ocean. There was a medieval castle there and I was with people from the Club,[979] but I can only vaguely recall who was present. For example, Mr. St. was there, and Schl.[980] And some indeterminate ladies. And I was sightseeing there with them.[981] We viewed the castle, a medieval, fortified castle. We were standing in the courtyard of the castle and there was a German professor who immediately made a beeline for me and began discussing something with me critically. I was standing opposite a gate which stood open at the foot of the dungeon in the great tower and you could see right up the tower from below. The door was of

---

[977] See above, p. 187.

[978] Jung was hospitalized in Calcutta on 3 January 1938 at the Presidency General Hospital. Sengupta, *Jung in India*, p. 144.

[979] Jung refers to the Psychological Club: see above, p. 133.

[980] Possibly referring to Hermann Steiger (1889–1978), a teacher who was secretary, then treasurer, of the Psychological Club, and to Eugen Schlegel (1880–1948) who was president of the Club in 1920–21. Schlegel was a lawyer, and married to Erika Schlegel.

[981] "sight-seeing": in English in the original.

iron. Inside, a wide stone staircase led upwards, and above one could see a sort of hall, [306/307] festively bedecked, in candlelight. They said that the Holy Grail was going to be celebrated there. I was very impressed. But there was the professor speaking out critically against it, and I was no longer standing with him on the steps, but next to a side building upon whose wall there was some latticework made of wrought iron, very skillfully done. Upon it hung artistic vines in wrought iron—a magnificent piece: vine branches with leaves and fruits hung along the horizontal rungs, and to my astonishment on every rung there were one or two small houses made of iron, like dwarves' houses—with doors and windows—just like this! I saw that these doors were mobile. And I suddenly saw how something darted forward: that one of the doors opens and out of it darts a small iron man with an iron cap who darts into the next house and shuts the door. I felt immediately: That's impossible, the little man cannot walk, but he was in fact walking. I turned to the professor and said: Now, you see such things simply do happen. He was actually not unlikeable and was very eager[982] to hear about it and to learn something, but he was very uncertain in his judgment.

Suddenly the situation changed: I was with a group of people from the Club, mainly men, and we were marching in a northerly direction. I heard that although the Holy Grail was to be celebrated today, it was not yet here. It was in another house on the same island, in the north, to be precise; quite far away, it was hidden from all the world. Now we are marching in order to fetch the Grail. Suddenly we come to a wide canal or estuary and see that this splits the island into two parts. It is as if we are marching for the whole day, we arrived tired at journey's end. Everything was deserted, desolate. There were no trees there, only grass and rocks, and I thought to myself: Well, how do we get any further? I saw: there's nothing else for it: we must swim over. This thought made me rather anxious. I did not know how we could do that fully clothed, and I was concerned about how the people would get across. We lay down. I thought: [307/308] Dear God, what are we doing here? I had not known that this northern part of the island was separated from the mainland. There was no ship available, no bridge, absolutely no road, and then I said to myself: I must fetch the Grail, therefore I must simply make a decision to swim across on a wing and a prayer. The house where the Grail was apparently hidden I imagined as a small unremarkable house where no one must suspect anything. I wrestled with myself and thought: This Grail simply must

---

982 "eager": in English in the original.

be celebrated this evening. So it must be fetched somehow. In this moment I saw that all the others had fallen asleep so I had to jump into the water alone. It was a very cold affair, the dark of night; but one thing I knew for sure: I must reach the Grail. With that, I woke up.

This dream made one of the most powerful impressions upon me of any dream. These are the disciples in Gethsemane who fall asleep while Christ must go towards his destiny alone.[983] And then I had the answer to the problem of evil and to the question of God's will. It simply must be lived. But only if life counts only as a religious *mysterium*, otherwise no problem can be solved.

[984]My wife was occupied for very many years with the problem of the Grail; I never got involved in it for I did not want to disturb her in her work. But she told me much about it so that I was aware of all the details of the legend. Now the great question is: we have all the symbols of Christianity. What is the the particular meaning of the Grail? It is borne by a woman after all, isn't it? The Grail meal is a variation of the communion remembrance: the Grail is wonderful food and wonderful drink. This motif of communion was steeped in so many chivalric legends in which erotic adventures played a great part. That was the actual theme of the Grail legends: the Grail is an infinitely precious gift for being a good knight. To the Grail circle belonged those who accomplished the greatest deeds out of knightly honor and loyalty to the lady. But otherwise it was certainly not all about gentle deeds. There was murder [308/309] and manslaughter; there were monstrosities to slay and much more besides. A proper hero's life was required in order to be accepted as a knight of the Grail. Dürer's knight—being between death and the devil—, that is the proper picture.[985]

In my dreams the knight played a great role from the very beginning: the crusader, recognized only by me, riding though the town,[986] the row of graves where the knight came alive, the cemetery in Arles where the graves were to be found until the twelfth century, and that was the time when the Grail appeared, and this knight in the grave from the twelfth century, he was my ancestor.

---

[983] Matthew 26:36–46.

[984] See *ETG*, p. 218, *MDR*, p. 215.

[985] Jung refers here to a well-known engraving by Albrecht Dürer, "Knight, Death, and the Devil" (1513). He also possessed Dürer woodcuts: in a letter to his mother in January 1901 he informed her that he was framing two of these (JFA).

[986] See above, pp. 115–16.

That is really how it's been in my life: this visibility of the Grail or of the Grail castle. One comes there, when one is it, and the Grail remains eternally *introuvable*,[987] because one is not it. It is the mystery of individuation, and that is a *mysterium*, and there human understanding ceases. Individuation must be a mystery, for one will never understand it. But if someone wants a mystery then they will find it. But when one wants to communicate it, it is only misunderstood; for it is only for the few. And yet there must have been knowledge of the Holy Grail. The mystery of individuation is a true mystery. It is something different at every level, and yet always the same. It is in each case the deepest mystery for the individual person. So, my life has played out in a series of decisions: for example, should I think that or not? Or other supreme decisions where I simply fell short until a dream then came that brought the decision to me. And it was always another level of mystery.

Another very wonderful figure from the dream is the little iron man.[988] He has to do with Mercurius, and the vines point to the connection with Dionysus.

The solitary search for the Grail is essentially true for every individual. It is the dying before one gives oneself over to the impersonal.—But only a few survive.—The distance from Europe, the completely other environment in which I found myself at that time perhaps contributed to the fact that I was able to find an answer [309/310] to my questions through this dream—supported by an honest affirmation of evil as a force of God. Evil as I found it to be regarded by the Indians: not as a moral magnitude. [310/311]

FEBRUARY 14, 1958[989]

I know that it was often thought that I was arrogant, or that I was prone to gloating. But that was not really the case. For I know I see the humor in certain situations where others see none. And so, you see: pulling someone's leg,[990] that was my forte. It tickled me no end if then they took something literally and fell right into it. I was never really a gloater, but it diverted me to toy with them for not understanding me, they being so dull

---

[987] *introuvable*, in French in the original: "unfindable."

[988] Jaffé noted, "cf. 'Phenomenology of the Spirit in Fairy Tales'" (CE 19; CW 9.1). The reference appears to be to § 406, where Jung refers to a Russian fairy-tale featuring a manikin.

[989] Kurt Wolff was in Zurich this day, and met Jaffé for dinner in the evening.

[990] "pulling someone's leg": in English in the original.

and I so solitary, and having to be on guard, so that I would not disclose what preoccupied and moved me. And then the others thought I was gloating. I remember one experience: early on in driving my car, I was going along Seestrasse in the direction of Dorfbach, and when I got there someone came out of a side street into Seestrasse and through some sort of stupid maneuver the motor stalled and his car came to a standstill. He blocked the street and naturally I could go no further. Then I saw that it was Dr. U.[991] from the epilepsy center and I waved to him and simply laughed because I found the situation comical. I can tell you: he was furious with me. And afterwards he said: I did not know that you were so prone to gloating. At this, I simply wanted to point out to him that he shouldn't take it all in such a tragic way and that it was funny; and yet he still insisted I was gloating.

I know that in my youth I was not understood. I had always hoped that some time someone would ask me about the things that preoccupied me, but no! And I always withdrew into myself and played something that others did not understand. I had become used to being alone, from when I was very small. The first four years of my life I spent in Laufen. Laufen is on the Rhine at the Rhine Falls and the castle is named after it. There was a farmhouse, the church and the castle and the vicarage, and otherwise there was nothing there, and I was always alone there. [311/312]

FEBRUARY 15, 1958

Sophia is a typically masculine phenomenon.[992] In a woman this figure corresponds more to an earth mother, but she can no longer be conceptualized. She is the mystery of being, of matter, the spirit of matter. The anima *in compedibus*.[993] Sophia is the liberated anima, a liberated rule and activity. That is masculine, it appeals to a man.[994] Wisdom commends itself to a woman much less. For her, it is being that counts. Like the maternal suchness. The mother is the mystery of being. It is that suchness; that is something that we cannot imagine at all, we can only imagine being as a process, whereas in fact actual being is being in itself, a repose that remains unimaginable.

---

[991] Dr. Alfred Ulrich (18869–1944), chief physician at the Schweizerische Anstalt für Epilepsie, (see *CE* 3).

[992] On Sophia as the anima, see "The Psychology of the Transference" (1946), *CE* 19; *CW* 16, § 518.

[993] *in compedibus (Lat.)* "in chains."

[994] "it appeals to a man": in English in the original.

I don't know how being after death will be. I don't know what happens to consciousness and of course that is a pressing question.—The problem of consciousness has to do directly with divinity; that is also why so many myths narrate that the soul's spark, the light of consciousness, flies into the sun after death.[995] And that is divinity's concern with man, that consciousness must arise. It is indeed quite possible that this consciousness after death returns to a universal consciousness. But that is a tremendous mystery. Yet it seems to me certain that the process of becoming conscious goes on after death.

I have sometimes wondered whether I am not really an incarnation of an Indian. If that were true, then I am sure I was a Buddhist. Quite definitely. I recall with what indescribable enthusiasm I read Schopenhauer because I learned from him something about India.[996] When I was in India the stupas of Sanchi caused me to be immeasurably emotional.[997] That went way beyond natural bounds. You know the dream that an Indian is meditating me and as long as he is meditating, I am alive. That was also a Buddhist. What affected me most strongly in India is Buddhism; that was a quite tremendous excitement that I had. I was in Benares in the wood where Buddha had given the fire sermon.[998] There is a ruin there, a stupa. They rebuilt it in Sanchi in a wonderful spot, and there I was so overwhelmed that I had to absent myself from others. I

---

[995] Jung refers in *Psychology of Kundalini Yoga* to a Manichean myth of the souls going after death to the moon, and from there to the sun (p. 22).

[996] See *ETG*, p. 281, *MDR*, p. 278. Jaffé added here in *Reflections*, "I felt similarly moved when I read the *Lalita-vistara*" (p. 136). She refers to a Mahayana life of the Buddha, dating from the third century CE, which Jung cited in *Psychological Types* (1921), *CE* 9; *CW* 6, § 297.

[997] Jung visited Sanchi on December 22, 1937. On his impressions, see "The Dreamlike World of India" (1939), *CE* 16; *CW* 11, § 991.

[998] Jung arrived in Benares (Varanasi) on December 27, 1937, and visited Sarnath, an important pilgrimage site with the ruins of a Buddhist temple, which is nearby and where, at Gyasisa Hill, it has been widely thought that the Buddha delivered his first sermon, the *aditta-sutta*, known as the fire sermon. To a newspaper interviewer Jung recounted, "Benares has not impressed me very much [. . .]. I was on the other hand delighted to see the Indian architecture in the Stupas of Sanchi, Kailash temple at Ellora. And again how can one help not being impressed by the beauty of the buildings of the Moghul period of India! All these were exceedingly impressive. The temples of Benares [. . .] are smaller and more crowded. There is absolutely no chance of appreciating their beauty because they are all crowded out by outer buildings. The passages are particularly narrow and the solemnity that pervades in the Stupas of Sanchi or the Kailash temple at Ellora is lacking in Benares. The ornamentation of the buildings at Benares [. . .] is no doubt interesting but it is too concrete and does not appeal to emotion to the extent other buildings do." "Best Place for Study: German Psychologist's Impression of Benares," *Amrita Bazar Patrika*, January 4, 1938.

went away and hid myself, I was so emotional there, I could not contain myself. That was [312/313] a quite incredible agitation. Later it became my life's task to unite East and West. Richard Wilhelm was quite astonished in his day by my knowledge of the Eastern soul.[999] Where do you know all this from? I had not read much about it but I had it all from within myself, from my own experiencing.

I knew that if I had lived in India, I would naturally have been a Buddhist, it goes without saying. That is what gripped me in India most of all. It also explains the theme of my relationship to Europe: being estranged, or being a foreigner. I have never understood that the inner world and what I said about it could be foreign to people. But it was and is. And that too is remarkable: the multiplicity of the archetypes and their fantastic forms that confronted me. That is the situation into which the Buddha was placed. He positioned himself against it, against the unthinking realm of the Mothers, against the fantastic realm of the infinitely expiring images, exactly as I postulate the contemplation of the seen and the lived. Of course, in Buddhism the same happened as in Christianity: Buddha became the imago of self-becoming, whereas he himself thought that through the annihilation of *Nidana* man has *Bodhi* and therefore is himself a Buddha. Through meditation everyone can become a Buddha. That is similar to Christianity where Christ is the pattern that lives as such inside every person. But it led to the *imitatio Christi* just as it also led to an imitation of the Buddha. Everywhere one finds statues of the Buddha. Why? Because he is a pattern and with this, the possibility of degeneration is already a given. That is simply how it is. "Everything comes out perfect from the hands of the creator, everything degenerates between the

---

[999] In his tribute to Jung, "Meine Begegnung with C. G. Jung in China" (*Neue Zürcher Zeitung*, January 21, 1929), in an attempt to explain the parallelism between Jung's thought and that of the Far East, Richard Wilhelm wrote, "Perhaps Dr. Jung was Chinese in one of his former lives and was condemned to be reborn in Central Europe as punishment for his resistance to all dogmatism. In making this transition, however, he may have brought along in his unconscious a rich treasure of the ancient wisdom, which like buried treasure on Walpurgis Night occasionally comes to the surface. However, metempsychosis is a dubious explanation of this phenomenon. Nor does the second possibility seem more likely—namely, that Dr. Jung has telepathic gifts and knows more than can be grasped in the hand or dreamt of in our philosophy. Here too, one would be resorting to a suspect mystical factor which strikes me as a bit superfluous. Hence there remains only one solution: both the Chinese and Dr. Jung have each of their own accord descended into the depths of man's collective psyche and have their encountered states of being which appear so much alike because in truth they exist and are present." Reproduced in the draft translation of *Memories, Dreams, Reflections* (CLM), pp. 525–26.

hands of man."[1000] (*Emile*). One should come to clarity about these things once and for all. They are mysterious and difficult. "The world is deep and deeper than man thinks."[1001] I don't know why I'm using so many quotes today! [313/314][1002]

MARCH 7, 1958

Question about psychotherapeutic practice.

In order to answer the question about psychotherapeutic practice I must go back to my medical activity in the Burghölzli. There I acquired my first definitive impression of practical psychotherapy. And to be more precise, it was the case of the mentally ill patient Babette S. who imparted this to me.[1003] I had absolutely no idea then what was taking place in the mentally ill.[1004]The whole of psychiatric education was designed in such a way that one abstracted from the experience of the sick into statistics. For example, one never thought, "So now he has the fantasy of being pursued by a priest, or another man believes that the Jews want to poison him, and the third fellow thinks that the police are after him." One ignored all

---

[1000] These are the opening lines of Jean-Jacques Rousseau's *Émile: ou de l'éducation* (*Emile: or, On Education*; 1762; in English 1793), which Jung cited here in French.

[1001] The lines echo Nietzsche's "The Drunken Song," ("Das trunkne Lied"), the last chapter (79) in his *Also sprach Zarathustra* (Leipzig: E. W. Fritzsch, 1883–85): "The world is deep: deeper than the day can comprehend." *Thus Spoke Zarathustra*, trans. R. J. Hollingdale (London: Penguin, 2003), p. 330.

[1002] On February 19, 1958 Kurt Wolff met with Jung in Minusio, in Canton Ticino. He presented a plan such that Jung would have the freedom to decide whether his autobiographical material would appear in print or not. If he agreed to publish some of it, it would be combined with what had been communicated orally to Aniela Jaffé, so a single book would result. After the meeting Wolff drew up a memorandum, dated March 4, summarizing what they had agreed, according to which Pantheon had exclusive world rights on spoken communications to Aniela Jaffé, as well as "whatever Dr. Jung is putting down in autobiographical writings himself." In addition, "[i]n order to express their appreciation for everything Dr. Jung has already done and is still doing for the book, the publishers will now pay the amount of Sw. Fr. 10,000 to Dr. Jung on account of his share of all future receipts to be expected from the autobiographical material." Also on March 4, Jung wrote to Wolff, "You have enormously surprised me with the kind gift of twelve bottles of Beaune and I am looking with some apprehension at the task awaiting me on Friday evenings. Anyway I am now in possession of an antidote to help me back on my feet and for this I'd like to thank you very much indeed." (BL). (Beaune is the *appellation* of Burgundy which has the highest number of Premier Cru sites: forty-two.)

[1003] See *ETG*, p. 131, *MDR*, p. 125.

[1004] See *ETG*, p. 121, *MDR*, p. 114. Babette Staub was Jung's paradigm case in *The Psychology of Dementia Praecox* (1907), *CE* 4; *CW* 3, where she was introduced as an unmarried dressmaker, who had been admitted to the Burghölzli in 1887 at the age of thirty-two (*CW* 3, ch. 5).

these contents and simply said: These are just ideas of persecution. One labeled the sick and stamped them with a diagnosis. But one never asked *why* this person has this idea and another one has a different idea. That appeared to be of no interest whatsoever to the doctors back then.—Freud now became significant for me because through him one acquired a path to the further examination of individual cases. He brought the psychological question into psychiatry. In order to better understand the psychological question I took a case like Babette St. She was completely crazy and said the craziest things that one absolutely could not understand. With painstaking effort, I tried to understand these things. I then wrote up the case in *Dementia Praecox*. For example, she described herself as Lorelei;[1005] and finally I figured out that she did this because she always heard the director of the hospital saying, "I don't know what it can mean!"[1006] She constantly brought up such complaints as: she is the Lorelei, she was the "representative of Socrates,"[1007] she was Germania and Helvetia, made exclusively out of sweet butter, or she said: Naples and I must provide the world with noodles.[1008] Or: I am the irreplaceable Double polytechnic! I am the finest garments. I am garments of the snail museum and so on.[1009] I said to myself: What on earth does the good soul want to say with this? And then I said to her: What is this about the Lorelei? And there a heap of further confused rubbish came out. But I kept [314/315] bringing her back to the topic with my questions until she amplified it so that I could see what she meant. So regarding the Lorelei: "The director always says, 'I don't know what that means!'" This is how it went until I was able to understand all of her bizarre expressions and I saw that they were in fact not as meaningless as they appeared. And in this way, I got a very strong impression of the fact that first and foremost the mentally ill are actually not as crazy as they seem, but that it is a question of linguistic confusion. In such people there is a person in the background who is watching, who perhaps is quite "normal," but who is not identical with the I. With this it was clear to me all of a sudden that the ideas of persecution and hallucinations are meaningful, and it is only our fault that we do not understand them and that we do not know that

---

[1005] *Psychology of Dementia Praecox*, §§ 226–27.

[1006] This is the first line of Heinrich Heine's poem, "The Lorelei" (1823): "Ich weiss nicht was soll es bedeuten."

[1007] *The Psychology of Dementia Praecox* (1907), CE 4; CW 3, §§ 216–17.

[1008] *Psychology of Dementia Praecox*, § 201.

[1009] *Psychology of Dementia Praecox*, § 219.

a whole psychology of personality lies behind it. That made an extraordinarily powerful impression on me.

Then I gave the Town Hall lecture on the "Content of Psychoses."[1010] That was a powerful emotional experience for me. I said to myself: So *that* is what's behind it; there is a personality behind it, a life story, hopes and wishes. Fundamentally it's a question of an inner balance. Babette St. said to me that she was the threefold owner of the world, or that she was the silver isles.[1011] I compiled all the material in *Dementia Praecox*. Then I realized for the first time that a general psychology of the personality is present in psychosis. I saw that things that are expressed in rational language by hysterics are the same in cases of schizophrenia but there they are expressed in defective speech. In essence it is the same. I confirmed this supposition in the associations experiment: the picture of hysteria repeats itself in schizophrenia, only in an immeasurably exaggerated way, just as hysteria immeasurably exaggerates the normal picture.[1012]

[1013]When Freud visited me in 1909/10,[1014] I presented the case of Babette St. at the Burghölzli, and then he said to me afterwards, "Do you know, Jung, what you have found out about this patient is extremely interesting for sure, but how on earth were you able to bear spending hours and days with this phenomenally ugly slut?" Then I looked at him completely flabbergasted, for this thought had never once entered my head. She was in a certain sense [315/316] dear and familiar to me because she had such fine if crazy ideas and said such interesting things. She became for me the model for all the many old spinsters[1015] who later became my clientele and who spoke movingly of confused things from their distress. They seemed to me like Babette. With her and with them, out of a cloud of grotesque madness a human presence ultimately emerged.

Therapeutically nothing happened with Babette St.; she was too crazy for that. But I have seen other cases with whom this type of painstaking exploration also has a therapeutic effect. This is why I later never lost my nerve with such mentally ill or neurotic patients. Remarkably, for a long time my main clientele consisted of such characters. I would curse having to treat only English and American spinsters until I saw what I learned

---

[1010] "The Content of the Psychoses" (1908), CE 5; CW 3.

[1011] *The Psychology of Dementia Praecox* (1907), CE 4; CW 3, §§ 232 and 226.

[1012] In the fourth chapter of *The Psychology of Dementia Praecox* (1907, CE 4; CW 3), Jung compared dementia praecox with hysteria.

[1013] See *ETG*, p. 134, *MDR*, p. 128.

[1014] Freud visited Zurich from September 8 to 21, 1908.

[1015] "old spinsters": in English in the original.

from them. As a student I said: Just don't become a gynecologist![1016] And behold: my clientele was then mainly female, but who engaged in the work with exceptional conscientiousness so insightfully and intelligently that through them I have learned an infinite amount. I am exceptionally grateful to these old spinsters. I can say that they have made a considerable contribution to the fact that I could develop therapy along new paths.

At first no one could understand my advocacy for Freud. Two professors from Germany wrote to me to say that it was a pity for my academic career that I had linked up with Freud.[1017] I replied that if what Freud says is the truth then it is the truth and I will be there. Then I will betray my career if that means restricting research and the truth. Then I'm not participating.

So my first patients were a swarm of old ladies, but then also very many students, male and female, and younger colleagues.—Babette was the experience of psychology. The experience of therapy began when I was at Forel's polyclinic where, as in all polyclinics, all sorts of people attended.[1018] [316/317] I also gave lectures at that time. I had about twenty to twenty-five attendees. I demonstrated hypnosis and I took my first therapeutic steps.[1019] In this I applied the knowledge I had acquired with Babette St. In her case, I had seen how very important it is to understand that behind the neurosis of a person there is a story. So even in the second year of my course I began to explore the history of the patients.

[1020]Back then I had a very remarkable case: an older woman came once, apparently religious. She came partly supported by her maid, partly by crutches, she was about sixty-five years old. She was lame in the left leg. I knew that she had been in that condition for seventeen years, she was not able to move her left leg. This is why she used crutches. I had her sit on a chair and asked her about her suffering. She then began to relate how terrible it was—in long-winded detail. I said: Well, now we don't

[1016] See *ETG*, p. 150, *MDR*, p. 145, where the references to gynecology and old spinsters were not reproduced.

[1017] See *1925*, pp. 15–16. One of these professors was Gustav Aschaffenburg (1866–1944), a former student of Kraepelin, whose work on experimental psychopathology Jung drew upon in his associations experiment. See below, p. 380.

[1018] On Forel's demonstrations of hypnosis in the outpatient clinic, see Mirjam Bugmann, *Hypnosepolitik: Der Psychiater August Forel, das Gehirn und die Gesellschaft (1870–1920)* (Cologne: Böhlau Verlag, 2015).

[1019] See above, p. 281. Regarding his demonstrations of hypnosis, see Jung's letter to Rudolf Loÿ of January 28, 1913, "Timely Psychotherapeutic Questions: A Correspondence with Dr. C. G. Jung," *CE* 7; *CW* 4, §§ 578–79. For the case that follows here, see §§ 581–82. See also Bennet, *Meetings with Jung*, January 21, 1955 (pp. 41–42).

[1020] See *ETG*, p. 124, *MDR*, p. 118.

have time; now we'll just use hypnosis.—Hardly had I said this than she closed her eyes and fell into a deep trance without any hypnosis! During the trance I gave her some post-hypnotic suggestions. Then after twenty minutes I wanted to bring her out of the trance again but she did not wake up. I then tried everything possible to wake her. In the course of a quarter hour she came back to herself, jumped up, and was able to walk! I wanted to give her the crutches. She cried, "Away with them!" and would not take them. "Rise up, take up thy bed and walk!"[1021] The students were of course all astonished. Then I said to her: I am not convinced that everything is now okay. You should come back next week. She did indeed come and felt quite sprightly. I repeated the attempt to hypnotize her and the same thing happened again: she fell into a deep trance even before I began. I had the feeling that there was something in particular which was going on with her. But as she was apparently healed she did not return and I did not see her again. The following year she reappeared in the first session. "Aha, what is the matter?" "Well, in the spring suddenly I had some pain in my back. It was not lumbago, but the pain was higher up the back." She had not been able to hold herself upright. She came back, once again leaning on her maid.—I gave the students a short outline of the case. [317/318] "Now we must hypnotize you." I gave her post-hypnotic suggestions and again she came out of the trance only with difficulty and—was healed. But this instant healing was unsettling to me and I did not trust it. She was a reasonably educated person. I said to her: I must speak to you in private. So indeed she came privately to my clinic and what came out? She was married for the second time and had a son from her first marriage who thus had a different surname from hers. She said he was a gifted young man aged twenty-two or twenty-four years. He had a catatonia and was in my department in the Burghölzli, completely incurable.—And what had played out here? For this woman, I was the gifted young man whom she had to help. She had a maternal transference to me! And as a matter of fact: I owe this woman my local fame as a magician! I explained the matter to her in all its complexities and she took it in very nicely. She never pestered me again and never had a relapse. That was my first real therapeutic experience. But, you know, it was a very nice conversation with this old lady! She was intelligent and exceptionally grateful that I took her so seriously and had sympathy for her fate and that of her son. That simply helped her out.

[1021] John 5:9.

She is long since dead, so it is not indiscreet to tell you this. That was my first analysis.

Then came a case of compulsive neurosis, around 1904, in which I saw that Freud had very correct suppositions as far as obsessional neuroses are concerned. In 1904 I presented his views for the first time in the *Münchener Medizinische Wochenschrift*.[1022] There was a congress on obsessional neuroses and Freud was not even named. Then I said in an article that it was inappropriate that one did not mention him in particular when he had achieved such significant things in the understanding of obsessional neuroses. Freud was the most knowledgeable about it and had written the most about it at the time.

Then very quickly I acquired such a large private practice that I could no longer cope with all the work. Then in 1905 I qualified as a private lecturer in psychiatry.[1023] At the beginning of 1909 I left the Psychiatric Polyclinic because it became simply too overwhelming[1024] and I could no

---

[1022] It was in 1906 that Jung published "Freud's Theory of Hysteria: A Reply to Aschaffenburg's Criticism" (*CE* 4; *CW* 4) in the *Münchener medizinische Wochenschrift*. Aschaffenburg had presented his critique at the Southwest German Neurologists and Psychiatrists congress in Baden Baden. Aschaffenburg had argued that psychoanalysis was not fundamentally different from Jung's associations experiments, and that consideration of this demonstrated that Freud interpolated a sexual meaning into harmless processes, and that he and his patients were guilty of autosuggestion. See Mikkel Borch-Jacobsen and Sonu Shamdasani, *The Freud Files: An Inquiry into the History of Psychoanalysis* (Cambridge: Cambridge University Press, 2012), pp. 63–64. The controversy focused on hysteria, rather than obsessional neurosis.

[1023] For his *habilitation* qualification, Jung presented his paper "On the Reaction–Time Ratio in the Associations Experiment" (1905), *CE* 3; *CW* 2. Bleuler wrote a glowing letter in support of Jung's candidacy, concluding that "[e]verywhere the author demonstrates a complete command of the subject, of its literature, independent observation and independent ideas, linked with acute criticism of himself and others." Bleuler to the medical faculty of the University of Zurich, January 5, 1905 (Zurich Staatsarchiv). Jung gave his inaugural lecture on "The Freudian Theory of Hysteria in the Light of our Experience."

In 1908 Jung indicated his intention to step down from his position as *Sekundararzt* (senior physician); Bleuler proposed that Jung be named the director of the psychopathological laboratory of the psychiatric clinic, which effectively already existed, and that this laboratory be formally established as part of the faculty. There was strong opposition to the latter proposal, though it was agreed that Jung could provisionally continue to manage the current set-up. "Auszug aus dem Protokolle des Erziehungsrates des Kantons Zürich vom 12. Februar 1908" (Zurich Staatsarchiv).

Jung resigned from the Burghölzli on March 7, 1909, giving as his reason a desire to dedicate himself more to scientific research. To continue to have access to the clinical material and resources of the Clinic, he requested to become a voluntary doctor. Jung to the Direktion des Gesundheitswesens des Kantons Zürich (Zurich Staatsarchiv).

[1024] "overwhelming": in English in the original.

longer bear it. [318/319] I retained the lectures. Then I also read about the psychology of the primitives.

[1025]From the beginning I had a different view of sexuality from Freud's. For me, it resides where it resides for every biologist. It is a biological phenomenon. Freud differs from me only in that he ascribes much more to sexuality than I do. For him, sexuality is of pivotal significance. For me, its significance is relative. I in no way deny that many things have a sexual explanation, but other things can be much better explained by other disturbances. For example, think of Adler who is quite right: for many people prestige plays a much greater role than sexuality. They even use sexuality in order to acquire power. Or take for example a man with a certain independence who has a dependent job under a boss who gives him no space. He will become neurotic! Freud simply overvalued the importance of sexuality. But that there are repressions and a general resistance to it, that's also true. Yet it is not the be-all and end-all.—The difference between me and Freud cannot be expressed in one word. It is a totally different spirit.

[1026]Freud said he was not responsible for the monotony of his interpretations. And his interpretations seemed to me terribly monotonous. He knows in advance what will come out of an interpretation. One never knows this with me. Because for me even the neurosis is a prospective situation, and it may not be understood only by looking backwards. What once has been can anyway no longer be erased. Think of any sort of significant dream. Its effect does not go away when one has interpreted it. On the contrary, I'd almost like to say, Freud speaks of sublimation, but he does not say how one does that, quite simply because one does not know. Sublimation is transformation. One is transformed if one was an infantile fool, and then something adult comes on top of it, then one is a different person. That is what the medium taught me with whom I did my experiments as a student;[1027] and I am eternally grateful for that even if at the end she tried to deceive me. It was stronger than her.[1028]

The private practice that developed very robustly then was for me the only opportunity [319/320] for me to go on working. For that reason, I did not have any opportunities for the mentally ill in the clinic.[1029]In the

---

[1025] See *ETG*, p. 152, *MDR*, p. 147.
[1026] See *ETG*, p. 157, *MDR*, p. 152.
[1027] See above, pp. 69–75.
[1028] "It was stronger than her": in French in the original, "C'étais plus fort qu'elle." See above, p. 75.
[1029] See *ETG*, p. 123, *MDR*, p. 119.

beginning of my private practice, I still hypnotized, but then less and less.[1030] I gave it up because one is groping in the dark with it. One does not know what to do with it and one does not know how long it is effective. It is an uncertain thing. I always had a resistance to working in the dark and against having to decide what the patient should do. I was concerned to learn from the patients themselves in which direction a development was headed. The idea of development was from the beginning supremely important for me. I often said to myself: These people are ill because they are stuck in a too-great spiritual narrowness because they are fixated. If one allows oneself to develop into a broader personality, then the neurosis ceases. Unfortunately, Freud too was not able to allow broader development to count; that is why he comes across to me as fixated. For Freud the world extends as far as one can rationally explain it. The other "does not exist." For me the world was from the beginning infinitely large and there was very much within it that I did not understand. For this reason, it was no trouble for me to accept the most different and most exotic religious ideas. I was not present there! Perhaps they are true—perhaps not!

When someone indicates to me that his speech is about sexuality, I say: Good, but the world does not consist only of sexuality. I knew that there are repressed, poor, unappreciated people, that there can be tragic concomitant circumstances in a life, and that that all can lead to a neurosis. Yet these things then are not a matter of sexuality, but of accursed circumstances. For example, if someone cannot get free of a father or mother it can be due to him or it can also be the parents' fault. It is even highly likely that it is more due to the parents than one thinks. Probably it is not a matter of the desire to possess the mother as Freud thought (Oedipus complex), that is quite unnatural, but it has much more to do—I like to think—with the mother. Back then I did not yet have the concept of the "puer aeternus," the son who is bound to his mother *par excellence*. But I saw that these people were trapped in a quite specific situation and this entrapment seemed to me the essential thing. It seemed important to me that, for example, the father was a tyrant and the possibility of development was withheld from the daughter, and such things.[1031] To make a sexual theory out of this seemed to me completely

---

[1030] On Jung's use of hypnosis, see Sonu Shamdasani, "'The 'magical method that works in the dark': C. G. Jung and Suggestion," *Journal of Jungian Practice and Theory* 3 (2001): pp. 5–17.

[1031] Cf. Jung, "The Significance of the Father in the Destiny of the Individual" (1909), CE 5; CW 4.

unnecessary. [320/321] In and of itself the psychogenesis of a neurosis, i.e., that a state originates from a psychic precondition, seemed to me an important idea of Freud's, yet his interpretation I found absolutely uninteresting. His whole "zones" theory I found extremely unenlightened and uninteresting, although in fact there were such grubby urchins and countless perversions.[1032] But that is not the whole person by a long shot. In general the entire causal viewpoint seemed to me ultimately to be an escape into theory. Into a theory which enabled the therapist to say that the patient was crazy and "we doctors" are the normal ones! And everything the patient might say against the opinion of the therapist would only be "resistance."—Such things seemed to me much too theoretical and too speculative.

The transference problem was no small thing for me at the beginning of my therapeutic practice. I had many patients with difficult transferences, and I always said to people: For God's sake, you must adapt to the social order so that you get to understand your problem. Sit together with other people who are in the same situation. That led to my founding of the Psychological Club.[1033] With this I had the goal in mind that my patients would learn collective and social responsibility. I made great efforts to make this happen and to bring people into contact with one another. Such were the beginnings of the Club.

[1034]Even very early on American patients came to see me. Here in Zurich, I had several American colleagues with whom I had worked at the Burghölzli on the associations experiment.[1035] That was in the years 1904/05. It was they who arranged an invitation to Clark University in

---

[1032] Jung is referring to Freud's conception of erogenous zones; see Freud, *Three Essays on the Theory of Sexuality* (*SE* 7).

[1033] On the founding of the Club, see Shamdasani, *Cult Fictions*.

[1034] See *ETG*, p. 127, *MDR*, p. 120.

[1035] In 1905 the leading psychiatrist Adolf Meyer hailed Jung and Riklin's paper on the associations experiment: "This remarkable piece of work and its continuation are no doubt the best single contribution to psychopathology during the past year (*Psychological Bulletin*, p. 242)." Meyer recommended psychiatrists to study with Jung. On January 21, 1907 one of them, Frederick Peterson, wrote to Meyer from Zurich: "I have met Von Monakow here and of course see a great deal of Bleuler and Jung. I am delighted with everything in Zürich and am sorry that I spent so long a time at Munich. Jung is in every way charming and I think he has genius." (Adolf Meyer Papers, Johns Hopkins University Archives). Likewise, Meyer introduced Trigant Burrow to Jung, and he traveled to Zurich in 1909. Burrow wrote to Meyer after meeting Freud and Jung that "it was clear that Dr. Jung was the man for me" (September 9, 1909, Adolf Meyer Papers). In 1907, Jung co-authored a paper with Peterson on "Psychopathological Investigations with the Galvanometer and Pneumograph in Normal and Insane Individuals" (*CE* 4; *CW* 2), and with Charles Ricksher, "Further Investigations on the Galvanic Phenomenon and Respiration in Normal and Insane Individuals" (*CE* 4; *CW* 2).

1909 for me to lecture on these experiments. There I received my first honorary doctorate: Dr. of Laws. Freud, who was also invited independently of me, was also awarded Dr. of Laws *honoris causa*.[1036] It was chiefly the associations experiment and the psychogalvanic experiment that established my reputation in America. Very soon I received patients from America. And there was another particularly important case. An American professor sent me a patient in 1906 or 1907. I received a telegram from him, saying that this man would be coming with his wife from Rome on their way to Berlin via Zurich, and he would consult me for help with his alcoholism.[1037] [321/322] As soon as I saw him I realized that the man had a neurosis because he was under pressure from his mother. He cannot break away from her. At first, I undertook the associations experiment with him, which showed me that he was clueless about the matters or the inner associations of his neurosis. He came from a very rich and well-respected family, had a likeable wife, had no worries, the only thing was that he drank too much in a desperate attempt to escape from an oppressive situation. But of course, that offered him no escape. By means of the associations experiment I saw that he had secret matters and that is where I went in. I soon found out that the mother, the owner of a very large business, had chained the son too strictly to herself. The son, being exceptionally gifted, had a high position in his mother's business. In fact he should have quit all that, but he was unable to decide to give up his glittering role. Whenever he was with his mother, he began to drink in order to create a state of his own, a state of freedom, as it were. Or in order to stiffen his back against her. However, in essence he did not want to leave the warm nest. He didn't want to forgo anything of its prosperity and comfort. After a short treatment he stopped drinking, but I said to him: I cannot guarantee that you won't land up right back in the same state if you encounter the same situation again. But he recovered well and returned to America refreshed and in a good state of mind.

[1036] See Richard Skues, "Clark Revisited: Reappraising Freud in America," in John Burnham, ed., *After Freud Left: A Century of Psychoanalysis in America*, pp. 49–84.

[1037] This appears to be Medill McCormick, a proprietor of the *Chicago Tribune*. He suffered from alcoholism, and in the winter of 1908 he had a breakdown and went with his wife Ruth to Europe, where they consulted Jung. In 1910 Jung went to Chicago to treat McCormick, who was in a serious state (Emma Jung to Freud, March 8, 1910, *FJL*, p. 301). McCormick later entered politics as a Republican, serving in the US House of Representatives from 1917 to 1919 and in the Senate from 1919 until his suicide in 1925. See Kristie Miller, *Ruth Hanna McCormick: A Life in Politics, 1880–1944* (Albuquerque, NM: University of New Mexico Press, 1992); Miller, "The Letters of C. G. Jung and Medill and Ruth McCormick," *Spring: Journal of Archetype and Culture* 50 (1990): 1–25.

Hardly had he been with his mother, his drinking began again. Then they sent for me; the mother consulted me. She was a gifted woman, but a power devil of the very first rate.[1038] I saw what the son had to stand up to and that he simply was not strong enough. Even physically he was of a slight build. He was simply no match for her. Then I decided for a *coup de force*:[1039] behind his back I delivered a report about him to his mother that he could no longer fulfill his role due to his alcoholism, and that he should be fired. This was done and of course he was absolutely furious with me. And how did he develop further? Now he was separate from the mother and was able to develop his personality: he had an exceptionally glittering political career. But that was a drastic cure. His wife was wretchedly grateful to me; [322/323] her husband then swore off drinking. For years I had a bad conscience that I had done this behind his back. But I knew exactly that only an act of force would break him free. And with that the matter was resolved. This was my first so-called "miracle cure" that was naturally much talked about and brought me many patients from America.

It was due to my relationship with America that I came to England. When I was there before the First World War, McDougall came to me and offered me the chair of medical philosophy in Oxford which he had held until then.[1040] He wanted to bring me into his role. I could not accept this, however, because Oxford had overwhelmed me: the history of the place, on the one hand, together with the fixed way of doing things, on the other, would have weighed down on me. I would not have been able to undertake experiments there, the hidebound rules would have forbidden it. And the historical contexts would have affected me too much.—I knew then that I still had to do a great deal of experimenting. I still knew far too little about the transference. The Freudian view that the transference is a matter of "being held back" seemed to me a prejudice

---

[1038] "a power devil of the very first rate": in English in the original.

[1039] *coup de force*, in French in the original: "power blow"/"stroke of force."

[1040] On September 16, 1918, McDougall wrote to Jung as President of the Psychiatric Section of the Royal Society of Medicine to invite Jung to lecture. He added that he regretted that he had been prevented by the war of visiting Jung in Zurich in the autumn of 1914. Jung gave a presentation before the society in the following year (JP). McDougall subsequently went to have analysis with Jung, and wrote up some of his dreams and Jung's interpretations of them in his *An Outline of Abnormal Psychology* (London: Methuen, 1923), pp. 181–205. McDougall held the Wilde Readership in mental philosophy at Oxford from 1904. From 1914 to 1919 he served in the Royal Army Medical Corps, and in 1920 took up the William James Chair in Psychology at Harvard. There is no documentation of McDougall inviting Jung to take up his position at Oxford.

and a fear of actuality. So then I engaged with the question: Just what causes people to have a transference? There were some patients who brought me fantastic fantasies and then I gradually recognized what was behind it. It was definitely not infantile images but highly significant contents, mostly religious and cosmic in content. And the actual reason for the transference was to be found in these images.—I described a case in the *Relations Between the I and the Unconscious* in which a God fantasy had developed out of the transference. That was a Polish student who did her PhD here,[1041] a very gifted person with a complete repression of religiosity. And after she had worked with me for some time, the collective contents came and showed what lay behind the transference, and what she saw there and recognized gave her the possibility of not going under. [323/324]

MARCH 7, 1958: POSTSCRIPT TO FEBRUARY 13, 1958

[1042]It is important that one has a mystery; for the *mysterium* is something that one does not know. And yet that is not completely how it is. One has something, and this impression also expresses my participation in the unknown. One is numinously related to it. It is a numen that cannot be realized away. Something unknown from which a numinous effect radiates. One can also say that it radiates out from man. But what causes me to project a numinosum onto it? I can gladly accept that the feeling or the affect of the numinosum is my own issue, and yet it assails me. Whoever has not experienced that is a poor sap.[1043] For the wellbeing of the individual it is important that he lives in a world which is inexplicable to a certain degree. One must have a world in which something could happen that one cannot explain, not only things that are in line with expectation. But the unexpected, the incredible, must be possible; and only when this is how it is can I also expect it from myself. Then I am aware[1044] of it; and I would not be if I were living in a precalculated world.—If something unexpected arose, something numinous, for example a dream, or an event, then something radiates out of it, one does not know what. But it causes people who share in these experiences, or who were present, to sort of fuse together into a group. One is caught up in something, in a

---

[1041] See Jung, *The Relations Between the I and the Unconscious* (1928), CE 12; CW 7, §§ 206–7. (The Polish student remains unidentified.)

[1042] See *ETG*, p. 344, *MDR*, p. 342.

[1043] "a poor sap": n English in the original.

[1044] "aware": in English in the original.

mysterium, that causes something to resonate in the people involved. Through this, a genuine spirit of community arises; for these things create a true group experience. But these are not conscious experiences, nor are they frequent occurrences, but they happen only when an archetype is touched in a group. And that is what holds a group together. So, for example, the primitive group is held together through such numinous feelings. The numinous experience operates within the rites of the tribe, as it were. The Church attempts the same with feast days when supposedly exciting events[1045] are celebrated. Christmas, Easter, above all the experience of Pentecost, that's quite clearly included. The ecclesiastical year with its feasts should actually be the center, it should illustrate how one lives a numinosum, how to be in numinous relationships. [324/325] Yet how far that is from the reality! The numinous is no longer present.

Such numinous events in which the *mysterium* is contained do indeed happen. They come about, and when they are past then it soon seems as if nothing had happened. But I have the feeling that something else carries on although I don't know what. In the unconscious it continues. One could perhaps say such numinous experiences indicate that the process of revelation or incarnation of God continues. An infinitesimal part of God, if one may put it that way, has incarnated, or has become an event, through which the world gains a dimension of depth, or through which another dimension makes itself felt that was not perceptible before.

On the Atmavictu-fantasy:[1046]
I was in England in 1920.[1047] There I remember that I carved two similar figures out of wood, like the manikin I made from the ruler.[1048] Or possibly I carved only the first figure and the other one was made only when I was back home again. I then had them carved in stone, only bigger, and this figure stands in my garden in Küsnacht. I know that this fantasy had preoccupied me very strongly at the time, of this curious earth creature that sort of grew out of the earth. Atmavictu, being a further development of this quasi-sexual object, but which it turns out, in essence, is the breath of life[1049] manifesting in this way, as an impulse to create. The segmentation reminds me of insects or plants: for example, of the equisetum, the horse tail plant, a very archaic plant. This segmentation has insects and

---

[1045] "exciting events : in English in the original.
[1046] See above, p. 46.
[1047] Jung's stay in England was in fact in the summer of 1919. See *BB* 7, p. 199 n. 137.
[1048] See *Art of C. G. Jung*, cat. nos. 67 and 68 (p. 148).
[1049] "breath of life": in English in the original.

plants in common and is also discernible in the human spinal column.[1050]
[325/326]

MARCH 12, 1958

Parents bear a massive responsibility to their children if they themselves
remain unconscious. They then leave behind to the children an enormous
spiritual tension and burden which inflicts a great wound upon them. My
parents bequeathed me a strain like this and I have prevented it from exploding only through my utmost concentration on the essential.

I have never been able to afford myself pleasure.[1051]I was twenty years
old before I ever went to the theater. On the evening of my state examinations, I went to the theater for the first time. And for a long time afterwards
I held myself back as much as possible from all outward engagement and
through the greater part of my life I was boundlessly focused on my
work. My friend Ruedi von Muralt,[1052] assistant medical director at the
clinic, once said to me—later on, "We doctors often used to chat amongst
ourselves at the Burghölzli and we wondered if you might be psychologically abnormal." "How come?" I asked. Then he said, "Well, in the
first six months you were at the clinic you didn't go out once!"

I well knew why.[1053] I felt absolutely inadequate to my task and began
to read through several volumes of the *Allgemeine Zeitschrift für Psychiatrie*, roughly from the middle of the last century onward, to inform myself

---

[1050] On March 7, 1958 Aniela Jaffé wrote to Kurt Wolff after this session,

There was a rich booty: early psychotherapy, patients, old spinsters, sexuality for
him and for Freud. His most recent plan: to write as far as his encounter with Freud.
He described that as a 'demanding task' in its own right; but it would be very signifi-
cant if he turned again to that encounter in old age. But after thinking about it,
I decided to ask him to do it for me critically for my sake—but still 'reconciled.'
Otherwise better not!

He was very impressed with the beginning of my protocol which I showed him for
the first time. I also showed him a couple of attempts at my 'amalgamation' and he
was very much in agreement. I thank you very much for your helpful nod to the
1925 Seminar which I naturally want to keep in mind.

The family storm I feared ("your biography is the family's property") has now
kicked off in earnest. The waves are raging high. But it was not, as I had thought,
predominantly the daughters, but rather his son and his wife! (Keep this for your ears
only!). Jung is remaining resolute but is still somewhat upset—understandably. [BL]

On March 10 Jaffé wrote to Wolff indicating that she would clarify the "Goethe question" with Jung on the following day (BL).

[1051] See *ETG*, p. 117, *MDR*, p. 110.
[1052] See above, pp. 83–85.
[1053] See *ETG*, p. 120, *MDR*, p. 112.

about the development of psychiatry.[1054] No one else did anything like that! That appeared really strange to the others. I lived like a hermit, like a monk, and later on my life was extremely withdrawn. All the time I was at Burghölzli I really didn't go anywhere, but was only concerned about my work. I have always lived as if I had a monastic rule to follow. During this period, I read an infinite amount in order to bring myself up to a certain level. This concentration protected me from the excessive tension and overload that my parents had left to me. I applied myself, otherwise I would simply have exploded; then there would have been only fragments remaining. That is the danger. If one still bears within oneself the fate of one's father and mother, one simply has too much to bear. Then one can only keep oneself "fully" to the goal with extreme concentration. My father gave up on himself [326/327] and my mother kept herself unconscious, and they placed all their hope in their son! Through this, an excessive feeling of duty developed. Thank God I have a strong constitution. That helped me to bear it at all.

I have seen in many people how, when the parents' problem remained unconscious, it cast itself upon the children.[1055] If the parents have too narrow a horizon the children must atone for this. I was always anxiously mindful that my children should remain free of my problems; I did not in any way want this burden for them that I had to resolve myself because my parents had bequeathed it to me. My children should live their own life, that was my wish. And this fulfilled itself. One cannot necessarily expect that children have unusual strengths available to them. [327/328]

MARCH 13, 1958

(Following a cursory perusal of Sykes's essay on Freud and Jung.)[1056]
It is not only sexuality but also any other instinct such as aggression or power that expresses a striving for wholeness, also containing a

---

[1054] The journal *Allgemeine Zeitschrift für Psychiatrie und psychisch-gerichtliche Medicin* was founded in 1844

[1055] Jung discussed this theme on a number of occasions: see "Analytical Psychology and Education" (1924), *CE* 10; *CW* 17, § 154.

[1056] "Sykes's essay" refers to Gerald Sykes, "The Dialogue of Freud and Jung," *Harper's Magazine*, 1958, pp. 66–71. Sykes (1904–1984), an author and literary critic, had written a positive review of Jung's *Psychology and Alchemy* in *The New York Times*, "The Struggle to be Free from the Demon of the Unconscious" (August 2, 1953). He then met Jung in Ascona, in March 1955. Later that year, he submitted a portrait of Jung to *The New York Times*, which was rejected. On hearing this, Jung wrote to him, "You have just encountered the weapon my friends use. You cannot imagine how bitter the fight is when a new idea gets hold of the public. In another century I should have vanished long ago in a dungeon or

mysterium, exactly like any other natural drive. We know just as little of how these drives are constructed as we do of the psyche. The whole is always contained within it. Thus, matter is also only one aspect of actuality and even there, even within that, the whole is contained. But we cannot express it; we are eternally hindered through language. Language, on the one hand, is already an idea and a general conception. But it is also only a word, and that is something limited. Like the alchemists said of the stone: it has *mille nomina*; that means a thousand names are not enough to express the mystery and yet they formulate it and say it is Mercurius or the diamond, or the carbuncle and so on. One can apply a thousand names to it and yet still not express the intrinsic thing.[1057] And that can also be said of sexuality. And equally of power. Power is also a very subtle issue: one crawls on the belly and has power, or uses it for power. This is why it is correct to say: Every tyrant has his valet who is all-powerful.

People do not understand that I grant sexuality absolute validity as an essential expression of wholeness, but not as an exclusive manifestation. That is hard for people to understand because they cannot think as I do. Modern physics also has a way of thinking that not everyone grasps. Also, one does not understand what one has no experience of. It is the same with sexuality. Mostly it is the case that they abstain from it or they come a cropper through it and then properly land up in a twilight zone.

[1058]For Freud sexuality was simply the substitute for the mystical. He once said to me in quite an impassioned way, "Promise me one thing: take up the cause of sexuality!" And indeed, he said it as if he was

---

should have ended my days at the stake or an ecclesiastical grip [i.e., in the grip of the Church]. So if you join arms with me I am thoroughly grateful to you. There are too damned few men in our time courageous enough to swing a sword and I feel you are no mean help." Jung to Sykes August 17, 1955 (JP).

In his *Harper's* article, Sykes argued that the dialogue of Freud and Jung invited comparison with Greek tragedy: they stood for opposing sides of the human mind, and the perspectives of both needed to be combined. On April 6, 1958 Jung wrote Sykes a lengthy critique of his article, indicating that he was attempting to compare incommensurables. While a comparison between Freud and Adler would be possible, as they started from a comparable principle, his premises were quite different. His own "point de départ is 'Personality.' Mental or nervous conditions (in as much as non-organic) disorders were to me— from the very start—maladies of personality—and the pathological twisting of a specific instinct. [. . .]. So my premise differs on principle from the Freudo–Adlerian viewpoint." (JP).

[1057] The alchemist Theobold de Hoghelande (ca. 1560–1608) wrote, "They say also that different names are given to the stone on account of the wonderful variety of figures that appear in the course of the work": cited by Jung in *Psychology and Alchemy* (1944), *CE* 17; *CW* 12, § 349.

[1058] See *ETG*, p. 154, *MDR*, p. 150.

saying, [328/329] "And promise me one thing, my dear son, go to Mass every day!" Or, "Take care that the Eucharist is always celebrated!" For him sexuality was something incredibly important. It was the only form in which he was able to express himself. But scientific materialism is always tantamount to the game of cats and dogs,[1059] although in essence he meant something quite different. That was what made his view so awkward: namely, the biological method of expression. But a man is not interested in understanding sexuality any differently; that is why he mostly does not understand female eroticism either. A man is simply biologically configured. For a woman, sexuality is receptive; it is a suspended issue; for the man it is imperative: it simply *must* be.

There's a good story about this. A well-to-do woman had a laundry-woman, a very nice person and she has a child born outside of marriage. Then the lady asks her, "How did you come to fall like this?" The laundry woman replies: Well, I couldn't do anything about it, it just happened.—Yes, but why didn't you insist he married you first? Well, he said he simply had to have it, at that moment!—That characterizes the whole difference.

For a man, sexuality is intensified in the actual act. And it's good that this is the case too, otherwise nothing would happen. A woman is simply full of expectation, full of longing.[1060] And she thinks that he is actually the one who can release these feelings. And out of these arises the feeling of his uniqueness and that his penis is a miraculous thing from which the entire wonderful experience flows. That is quite naïve: if no penis is present then the woman is not present either, then she is simply uncoupled and then she is suspended somewhere. For a woman, it is not an *imperative*. Yes, it is very pleasant when it happens, and she longs for it. But it does not have to be here and now. This *à point*[1061] attitude is typical of masculine sexuality, and it is also in no way an imperative [329/330] to be bound to *one* woman, but only because she is simply there. That gives masculine sexuality the brutality of actuality. And cynicism arises from this.

But this is only the immediate aspect of sexuality. There is of course alongside this the aspect of the personal relationship; and then sexuality is an experience of wholeness, or it can be. But sexuality is primitive, and it must be that also, otherwise it does not make it through, and it does not happen. And yet it is also a *mysterium coniunctionis*, a great mystery,

---

[1059] "tantamount to the game of cats and dogs": a matter of bitter enmity.

[1060] In the *Septem Sermones* Jung wrote, "The sexuality of man is more earthly, that of woman is more spiritual." *LN*, pp. 528–29.

[1061] *à point*, in French in the original: "on point."

that one can only experience with a person with whom one has a soul connection. Otherwise it is only like a misfortune, or the woman is like a dummy made of papier-mâché that does not entice one to dissect and to eat. That leaves the differentiated man quite cold. Then that is only anatomy, all only fake.—One can never overlook the fact that wholeness also has a sexual aspect. Wholeness expresses itself in many forms, including sexuality.[1062]

[330/331]

MARCH 19/20, 1958

Last night I dreamed I was in a sinister situation.[1063] Apart from me there are another three people there: a woman, and she is quite distinct, then two masculine figures; a somewhat older and a somewhat younger man, both rather hazy. The feeling that I had with both of them is: rather criminal. The female figure is sort of standing between them. She is "drawn to evil,"[1064] but she herself is not evil. This woman is a figure who is totally unknown to me. She is about thirty years old, very slim, in fact she has such long legs. Her figure is very slight. Tall and slight. I cannot see her face clearly, but I see only that she has a saber cut diagonally across her face. The scar begins by her right eye, goes over her nose and carries on down to her left cheek. She is disfigured by it. She is in the grip of an emotion that I cannot understand: she leans towards me, very tenderly or anxiously, something erotic emerges from her, and I know that she is Hungarian and the two men likewise. Apparently, it's to do with something that's happening in Hungary or that has already happened, i.e., it is also here, but the secret is situated in Hungary. It might be related to Bolshevism.[1065]

[1062] On March 17, 1958 Jaffé wrote to Kurt Wolff that Jung explained to her that he didn't want to write about his encounter with Freud, and that the projected endpoint of the memoir he was currently composing was his state exams (BL).

On March 18 Jung wrote to Daniel Brody, the proprietor of Rhein Verlag, proposing the publication of Toni Wolff's collected papers, noting "they are distinguished not only by their intellectual content but by the fact that the author had personally experienced the development of analytical psychology from the fateful year 1912 right up to the recent past and was thus in a position to record her reactions and sympathetic interest from the first." *Letters*, vol. 2, pp. 424–25.

[1063] Jung noted this dream in *Somnia* 1958–1960 (JFA).

[1064] "drawn to evil": in French in the original, "atteinte par le mal."

[1065] In "Present and Future" (1957) Jung had referred to the Hungarian uprising of 1956 (*CE* 25; *CW* 10, § 518n).

There is another association: my father-in-law for a while had a branch of his company in Budapest. (He was an industrial magnate, and had a machine factory in Schaffhausen.) He resided there for a while and my wife was there when she was about two years old, but only very briefly. I myself have no connection with Budapest, except perhaps for Ferenzci who I trained in psychoanalysis, and who then got stuck with Freud.[1066] The dream obviously has nothing to do with Mrs. Jacobi.[1067] It is probably related to my wife.

The last thing I heard in a dream of my wife was that she had accepted my views. Then I immediately wondered: What's up now? What's going to be the next thing? I have an association to Budapest that I cannot talk about. A fateful story, connected to this dream.[1068] [331/332]

In the dream there is a quaternity present: the rather boyish woman and the two somber men in the background, and myself. What my wife had accepted in the last dream was the quasi-incomprehensible, but that was still related to me. So in that dream it was a question of her accepting something to do with me. My shadow. But then of course logically follows the question of her own shadow. The question: what is the correlate in herself? The one in whom it is manifest, they are only the carrier of this problem, and when this is accepted as such, the question comes: how is it for me then? As long as it is not accepted by the other, one does not arrive at the idea that one is also involved oneself. Now she has apparently accepted it in me, and the development is heading in the direction of her also accepting it in herself—whatever it may be.—For me it is certain that souls go on developing in the beyond. The necessity for development exists there just as much as here: that is, the development of reaching those heights that have already been reached by a human consciousness here; or the highest possible consciousness that was achievable by each soul during their life, that it has experienced within its early environment. If this latter were not also the case, then I would have them all clinging to me. One could even say that the further development of my wife is also taking place in me. This is why I am constantly in contact

---

[1066] Sándor Ferenczi (1873–1933) visited Jung in 1907 (see Jung to Freud, June 28, 1907, *FJL*, p. 65). As Ernst Falzeder noted, this appears to have been "the first 'training' analysis according along Freudian principles." Falzeder, *Psychoanalytic Filiations: Mapping the Psychoanalytic Movement* (London: Karnac, 2015), p. 54.

[1067] Jacobi (see n. 376 above) was born in Budapest and lived there till 1919 before going to Vienna, where she remained till 1938, when she moved to Zurich.

[1068] Probably an allusion to the syphilis of Jung's father-in-law, Jean Rauschenbach, which he may have contracted in Budapest. He went blind as a result of this, and was dependent on care from 1894 till his death in 1905.

with her; that is quite clear. Whereas with Toni, the contact is simply over, it is somehow empty.

Now, there is something else in my dream experience: yesterday Miss B. was here.[1069] And she had an exceptionally curious dream: of a bowl edged with pure gold. On the inside of the bowl something like sparks were sparkling, jumping away from an anvil—and it is gold that is sparkling there. But curiously these golden crystals or sparks are returning to the bowl and are attaching themselves to the gold that is already contained within it so that they then disappear within it. Each time a grain jumps away at a distance of about a meter and then goes back inside it again. [332/333] One could say it was finding a renewed point of entry because it has not yet found a place in the bowl where it actually belongs. Then it must get out and then goes back in again afresh.

Now Miss B. is a person who has always had curious fantasies, partly in dreams or in visions. And among them there were quite specific images of splendid gardens, or palazzi, elegant houses or royal buildings and such like. She then told me another dream where she is again going into such a palace. She goes through the entrance hall, arrives in a courtyard attached to a garden where cypress avenues extend, everything is absolutely perfectly beautiful. Nothing ruined or destroyed, and everything looks exceptionally wonderful; there is something about a church connected with it too. A cloister on the ground floor, a fine terrace, just as there can be in actuality. She sees that all sorts of wild animals are walking around in the garden, but they are still far away from her. Between them was a figure of a person walking about untroubled by the wild animals, and that was me, and as soon as she sees that she also has no fear.

I immediately recalled:

Cave, the deepest, protects.
Lions prowl silently—
Friendly, around us,

[1069] Below (p. 302) it is indicated that "Miss B." was Ida Bianchi. She had analysis with Jung and corresponded with him from 1932 onward, and reported on her visions (JP). She contributed a paper to Jung's *Festchrift* volume describing her experiences: "Vom Werdegang des inneren Menschen," in *Die Kulturelle Bedeuntung der Komplexe Psychologie*, ed. Psychological Club (Berlin: Julius Springer, 1935), pp. 493–508. On Jung's eightieth birthday she gave him a manuscript with her visions. He wanted to present her work in a seminar, but nothing came of this: see Cornelia Brunner, ed., *Die innere Welt: Visionen von Giulia* (Zurich: Werner Classen Verlag, 1975), p. 9. (*Die innere Welt* is a pseudonymous account of Bianchi's visions edited and with commentary by Brunner.)

Honored place,
Sacred love's refuge.[1070]

First, I addressed the bowl: evidently a process of integration is taking place: things that do not want to be or cannot be classified, these are projections. That means they are located in the environment, they are experienced there. One could say: They return imbued with memory, and only then do they find their place. (They are integrated into the gold.)

I had to think of my earliest mandala images. There were seeds of black magnetic ore mixed with seeds of gold, they had to be brought into the vessel where they formed the central body, the self.[1071]—And then there was the story of my magician who appeared [333/334] when I was painting these seeds and he then screamed because they flew into his eye.[1072] That means: He received the projection from me and that caused him pain. It was a thing that I did not accept or could not accept: namely, the figure of the magician, the shaman in myself. This is why this figure appeared to me. Only when I recognize that *I* am the shaman is he healed. He is, as it were, a precursor of mine and this is why the seed fell into the correct place: into his eye, meaning consciousness. It must be dissolved out of there. I have spared myself the pain of seeing myself as a shaman; had I done so, then I would have been placed with the animals in one, for example, with the lions who were pacing around me in such a friendly way. The shaman has helpful animals, or—one could also say: He comes at the level of the animal, but I was not yet able to understand this when the figure of the magician appeared to me.

Miss B. does not bring the fantasies to the right place because she cannot accept that she has a backstory. This is how it went: her father was a child born out of wedlock, but he was a strong and leading personality who exerted a strong influence on people. She herself has something particular: her eyes have something psychic about them, she always reminds me rather of Madame Blavtasky.[1073] She has huge psychological experience,

---

[1070] Spoken by the chorus and echo at the death of Faust. Goethe, *Faust II*, Act 5, sc. 7, ll. 11849–54.

[1071] See *LN*, images 80–97.

[1072] This refers to Jung's encounter with Ha, the black magician and father of Philemon. See *BB* 7, October 7, 1917 (pp. 148–57).

[1073] Helena Blavatsky (1831–1891), a founder of the theosophical movement. Jung was critical of theosophy, and had the following books by Blavatsky in his library: *The Secret Doctrine* (1893–97), *Höllen Träume* (1908), and *The Theosophical Glossary* (1930).

quite astonishing. In fact she wanted to be a nun. Her father was Italian. He went to school in a village there and curiously an extremely distinguished lady used to come and observe him without ever talking to him or anyone else, and then she went away again. A man from this village who is older than her father told Miss B. about this. He claimed that this aristocratic lady was her father's mother. This was the origin of the grandiose manner in Miss B.'s father and also of her own feudal fantasies. These are also true of me; I have also seen my spiritual ancestral line and there are also all sorts of aristocratic people in it. For Miss B. I naturally represent a projection of the associated man in her dream; [334/335] the role of Faust also plays a part here.—Miss Bianchi by the way also had another dream, of a play in which she had to play a part. I was the central figure in it and had to play the role of Wotan.

For me it was the memory of these seeds of gold that was most important. The dark seeds they were mixed with consisted of iron ore. And it is known that this comes from heaven. It is meteoric iron. These iron ore fragments attract each other. The gold ones between them are luminous elements, luminous particles in dark matter. Psychologically one might say: the dark particles are empty of libido or consciousness, and the light, the golden ones, these are the original elements of consciousness, but which one cannot at first prove. But they wish to reach the light. There are energies within them that cause themselves to show up suddenly in an image that can then be integrated. When it is integrated it goes to the base of the vessel.

(The following section is unfortunately unclear.)[1074]
And now I saw clearly how a child was born with this treasure (protection?) consisting of opaque luminous gold and dark matter, and now it is being pressed into the earth through its weight where the weakly luminous points find their correspondences. There are then reactions in which light arises, or consciousness. Then certain points become effective or are seen in their effectiveness.

So, for example, I arrive at the tomb of Galla Placidia[1075]—and there it has me! There one of these gold nuggets exploded and returned.—Or when I saw the buckled shoe,[1076] then it flew out and fell back down again. So consciousness gradually came into being out of these reminiscences.

[1074] Note by Jaffé.
[1075] See above, pp. 134–37.
[1076] See above, p. 57.

Only recently did I learn the story from a former patient of mine; she was a very rich woman who was unable to have children. Then she adopted a child from an orphanage. With her husband she owned a large estate with many horses. When the child—it was a girl—grew up her chief interest was horses. From her first days she had been interested in the horses; [335/336] she was two years old when she was adopted. As a small girl she had got along with the horses so well that she knew more about these animals than the horse trainers. She possessed an exclusive interest in horses. Then her adoptive mother thought this should be investigated. So she inquired at the orphanage and learned that the child's father was a horse trainer and the personal servant of a cavalry officer. So these are inherited characteristics. And in this way, via her father Miss B. had dim indications of large buildings or cloisters and impressive houses. They form a constant motif in her dreams. Another constant motif is that the facade was missing from these buildings, or appears as a transparent wall of glass. This means: I am only the facade of my own history. If one sees what is behind, then one sees that this facade does not in fact exist. And then it is also as if the foreground were not representative of what is behind it. With Miss B. I have the idea that in her the foreground has become so transparent that she lives only in the background, as it were. She has had much heartache for many years and always lives on the edge. She always lives in her own background because the environment in which she was born was inadequate to the inner tradition. And that is also true of me: I always saw something in the background. I never yet saw so clearly what individuation is: that all these traces of light from the past life must be integrated. This is why the Buddha had to acknowledge that he had had sixty-five past lives, even as animals and plants.[1077] He lived as an animal and as a plant.—These are necessary insights that one must have although people of today will not be able to countenance it. [336/337]

The attitudes of a man or a woman in a transference to a man are quite different. The woman wants to be it, as it were, and the man wants to act. He wants to act like me, or rather: to act according to my psychology. So then he does this with a crazy enthusiasm that carries him far beyond the limits of his own being. He no longer respects the boundaries which he actually needs. The danger of such a boundary transgression in the transference is very frequently present in the Germans; they no longer

---

[1077] The Buddha told stories of his past lives, known as the Jataka Tales, through the course of his teachings to explain the *dharma*.

have any moderation but function only as my outriders, while I am the general. They act under the authority of the general. The man must learn then that this "general" is essentially a part of himself. I have often seen the acolyte phenomenon in the soul of the Germans; it plays a great role there. This shows the moral attitude that is typical of the German. Just think of Theodor Vischer: "What is moral is always self-evident,"[1078] or the categorical imperative;[1079] all these express his tendency towards absolutism, and in combination with the figure of the "follower" operating within in it, that is very dangerous.—I once experienced something very enlightening in this regard. When I was still working at the Burghölzli there was a German doctor, a psychiatrist from Stuttgart.[1080] He had come to the Burghölzli to learn new psychological perspectives. He soon noticed that I had something to say, and then he immediately fell into the role of follower. You see, what I said was gospel! By the way, he was a very nice fellow, a proper Swabian, from a very good family. Now at that time in the clinic we enjoyed some humorous banter among the assistant doctors, using all the unlikely and comical expressions of the schizophrenics. For example, when we had to be especially kind to an old woman, we would say, "Today I greased up my aunty." Or, "Today I made a nervous attachment to her," meaning I established emotional contact with her. [337/338] Or when we were with the boss begging for annual leave, we used the expression, "I greased up the boss to grant me a vacation"; that is, I sweet-talked him, lathered him up, to get on the right side of him. And when we wanted to be particularly gracious to someone we said, "I'll make a nervous attachment to him." And things like that. We spoke this language quite naturally but always in jest. For example, we said, "By God I have had a thought withdrawal." Or they referred to Schreber saying, "O damn, that is hard to say!"[1081] And such crazy stories. Or, "Someone has merged with me," when something had become

---

[1078] "The moral is always self-explanatory. A proper chap seeks, strives, and does not complain about it but is happy with this misfortune of the rising and never arriving line of life. That is our upper storey." Vischer, *Auch Einer*, p. 21.

[1079] "categorical imperative": a reference to Kant's ethics.

[1080] Wolfgang Stockmeyer, whom Jung met in 1907. In his unpublished obituary of Stockmeyer, Jung described him as a true friend, and the first German to be interested in his work (JP).

[1081] The phrase "Ei verflucht" features in Schreber's *Memoirs*. He describes it as "a remnant of the basic language, in which the words 'O damn, that is hard to say' were used whenever the souls became aware of a happening inconsistent with the Order of the World" (p. 179).

clear to me, by which they meant the manikins who ran around in Schreber's head.[1082]

I once saw this young doctor again later and we always spoke to each other in this jargon. That was good fun.[1083]—Then he died and later a young Swabian came to see me, he was also a psychiatrist. He told me that he had heard a lot about psychology from this German doctor and that he was very interested in it, and that you could tell how important psychology was when you make a nervous attachment with the schizophrenics! Then my ears pricked up! And then came the thought deprivation! My God! What sort of language are you speaking there? That is our assistants' jargon! "Yes," he replied, "that doctor taught me these expressions!"—So he thought they were technical terms!! There you see what blind following can do. "How he harrumphs and how he spits . . ."[1084] And this danger is particularly great in the Germans. However, it is not only about ridiculous imitation, but also that one dares to exceed one's own boundaries far too much too.

I experienced another case, a Mr. von X. I barely knew him personally, he was introduced to me only once. He was a homosexual and immediately had a transference to me. He was a psychiatrist, by the way. [338/339] I knew nothing of his transference. Then he underwent analysis with someone, I don't know who. And he made a great effort and talked him out of his homosexuality. And in his transference to me Mr. von X. thought that this would especially please me. He even married, but naturally that went wrong, and he had to get divorced. One day he came to me and spewed out the whole sorry story to me and reproached me that it was all my fault. "But I don't even know you!" I said to him. Yes, yes, it was all my fault that everything had gone wrong, that he had married and was now divorced. After that he was filled with resentment.—And all the while I had absolutely nothing to do with him! That is what happens to a man: that fellow is right so I'll follow him blindly and free myself of any responsibility. That is exactly what happened in Germany. How marvelous that Hitler came along! Until then one

---

[1082] Schreber referred to departed souls who led "a short existence on my head in the form of 'little men'—tiny figures in human form, perhaps only a few millimeters in height—before finally vanishing" (*Memoirs*, p. 94).

[1083] "good fun": in English in the original. Freud and Jung also employed this type of jargon at times in their correspondence.

[1084] The quotation is from the first play in Friedrich Schiller's *Wallenstein* trilogy, completed in 1799: *Wallensteins Lager* (*Wallenstein's Camp*), l. 207. The First Hunter is criticizing the Sergeant for imitating Wallenstein's mannerisms, such as how he clears his throat and spits, while failing to capture Wallenstein's true genius and spirit.

always had to pay attention to oneself and take responsibility for oneself. But now someone shows up who says, "Responsibility, I'll carry it." And then one goes to the devil as far as Moscow! And are we not the nation of the poets and thinkers?—Something like this also happens to the individual when he pushes himself too far and then can't keep it up. And then the resistances come! That is also what happened promptly with Mr. von X. That's the danger when one sees responsibility in the other. Think of what the Germans say: The British should have invaded! And what would you have said then?! Then all the hate would have fallen upon the British. The man who has such a transference to another must get to the place where he sees the danger and reflects upon his own reality, on what he can truly represent from within himself alone.

I also raised the banner for Freud at that time and stepped into the arena, but only as far as I could do so with my own integrity intact. From the very beginning, and always, I had a *reservatio mentalis* as far as the sexual theory was concerned.[1085] A man [339/340] must know where he stands. That is difficult for a German. He instantly acts as if he's drunk. He gets into a sort of intoxication of consciousness. That is German barbarism, which naturally has its positive sides too, but which can be very negative due to the consequent lack of freedom. So then he damages not only others but also himself. Such people cannot wait to obey. Germany is essentially a monarchist nation. They are waiting for their commander-in-chief to wonderfully liberate them from their own tasks, from having to think for oneself and take responsibility. It was diabolical that Hitler said, "*I* will take over responsibility!" That is what the "outrider" inside the German is waiting for! But one cannot do that. No one can assume total responsibility for someone else. Whoever wants to be whole, or to become it, must themselves bear responsibility and their life and take responsibility for what they do.
[340/341]

MARCH 21, 1958

(Question about academic teaching.)
[1086]In the years 1905–1913 I lectured on psychopathology at the University of Zurich, and of course also on the principles of Freudian

---

[1085] See Jung's reservations regarding the preeminence which Freud attributed to sexuality in his foreword to *The Psychology of Dementia Praecox* (1907), CE 4; CW 3, p. 4.
[1086] See *ETG*, p. 133, *MDR*, p. 117.

psychoanalysis and on the psychology of primitives. These were the chief subjects. Every semester I worked on something new, and I never repeated myself. At first it was lectures about Janet and Flournoy and above all also on hypnosis.[1087] I usually had quite a full auditorium, about sixty attendees. I didn't have any direct pupils working under my direction there. I first directed only the laboratory in the clinic, and I had students there who worked under my direction. In part I published these works myself. These were papers on the associations experiment. There was a series of American students there, Ricksher and Peterson.[1088] I remember only these two because they published in American journals. Ludwig Binswanger did his dissertation with me,[1089] and Riklin, he always worked with me too. We chiefly worked on the associations experiment; that was experimental psychology. At that time, I also did my first therapeutic analyses and a training analysis in the Freudian sense with Ferenczi. He was my student. I taught him Freudian psychology. And even before I split from Freud he returned to Budapest.[1090] Teaching brought me a lot of joy. I always enjoyed doing it.

Beginning in 1925 I regularly lectured in English, namely the seminars on dreams and visions in the Psychological Club.[1091] In 1933 a new teaching commitment began at the Federal Technical University (ETH).[1092] It was Prof. Fierz, the chemist, who got me to teach not only in English, and therefore I became a professor at the ETH. I was exempted from a

---

[1087] See above, pp. 171; 108–10; 284. The titles of Jung's courses were: "Psychiatry Revision with Demonstrations"; "Psychotherapy with Demonstrations"; "Hysteria, Its Social and Medical Contexts"; "Course on Psychotherapy"; "Psychopathology of Hysteria"; "Course on Psychotherapy"; "Course on Psychotherapy with Demonstrations"; "Psychopathology of Hysteria"; "Introduction to Psychoanalysis"; and "Psychology of the Unconscious" (Zurich Staatsarchiv).

[1088] See above, n. 675.

[1089] See Ludwig Binswanger, "On the Psychogalvanic Phenomenon in the Associations Experiments," in C. G. Jung, ed., *Studies in Word-Association: Experiments in the Diagnosis of Psychopathological Conditions Carried Out at the Psychiatric Clinic of the University of Zurich*, trans. M. D. Eder (New York: Moffat Yard, 1919), pp. 446–530. William McGuire showed that one of Binswanger's subjects was Jung himself: "Jung's Complex Reactions (1907): Word Association Experiments Performed by Binswanger," *Spring: An Annual of Archetypal Psychology and Jungian Thought*, 1984: 1–34.

[1090] See above, p. 299. In response to Ferenczi's forthcoming critique of Jung's *Transformation and Symbols of the Libido*, Jung wrote to Freud on January 31, 1913, "Understanding is one of the hardest tasks in the transference." *FJL*, p. 542.

[1091] See *1925*.

[1092] See Falzeder, *History of Modern Psychology*.

professorial dissertation, but I gave a lecture on complex theory.[1093] There, I gave lectures for seven years, as well as seminars. So from 1933 to 1941 I was at the ETH.[1094]—In the winter of 1943 I became a professor ordinarius for medical psychology in Basel. After new year in 1944 I gave two lectures there.[1095] And then I broke my leg, and after that it was all over.

The lectures at the ETH were very important to me because I tried there [341/342][1096] somehow to formulate the more progressive ideas of therapeutic psychology for a broader public and to develop the further parallels. For example, among these were the *Exercita spiritualia* of Ignatius of Loyola, and a Tibetan Tantra. I took these as a foundation, and then of course there was alchemy.[1097] At this time I always had a massive audience, there were about two hundred and fifty to three hundred people present.

[1098]In 1909 I was invited to Clark University to speak on the associations experiment. Freud was also invited.[1099] We traveled together there. I met him in Bremen, Ferenczi was also with us. It was in Bremen that the

---

[1093] Hans Eduard Fierz (1882–1953). Jung obtained his professorship at the ETH Zurich in 1935. See Angela Graf-Nold, "C. G. Jung's Position at the Eidgenössische Technische Hochschule (ETH), the Swiss Federal Institute of Technology, Zürich," *Jung History* 2, no. 2 (2007): 12–15. On May 5, 1935, he presented his inaugural lecture, "A Review of the Complex Theory" (*CE* 13; *CW* 8).

[1094] Jung referred to it here and below as the "Poly."

[1095] In the spring of 1944 Jung taught two courses at the medical faculty of Basel University. On Thursday evenings he lectured on "Methods of Psychotherapy" from 5 to 7 p.m. He would stay overnight and lecture on "Medical Psychology" from 9 to 10 a.m., and then return home. In accordance with Jung's wishes, these lectures were open only to students and alumni (letter of January 17, 1944, University administration to Jung, JFA), marking a departure from the practice of his ETH Zurich lectures. On September 6, 1955 Jung wrote to Werner Kuhn, the rector of the University of Basel, of the "joy I felt when the University of my home town did me the honor of appointing me to a professorship, and on the other hand of those bitter drops that fell into the beaker of joy when severe illness prevented the continuation of my teaching activity in Basel." *Letters*, vol. 2, pp. 270–71.

[1096] Jaffé noted at this point in the manuscript, "March 21 was an extremely introverted day—full of inner images. A 2nd protocol from the morning will follow."

[1097] See the following volumes in the Philemon Series: C. G. Jung, *Psychology of Yoga and Meditation: Lectures Delivered at ETH Zurich, Volume 6: 1938–1940*, ed. Martin Liebscher, trans. Heather McCartney and John Peck (Princeton, NJ: Princeton University Press, 2021); Jung, *Jung on Ignatius of Loyola's "Spiritual Exercises": Lectures Delivered at ETH Zurich, Volume 7: 1939–1940*, ed. Martin Liebscher, trans. Caitlin Stephens (Princeton, NJ: Princeton University Press, 2023); Jung, *The Psychology of Alchemy: Lectures Delivered at ETH Zurich, Volume 8*, ed. and trans. Martin Liebscher and Christopher Wagner (Princeton, NJ: Princeton University Press, forthcoming).

[1098] See *ETG*, p. 160, *MDR*, p. 156.

[1099] See above, p. 290.

story of the bogman occurred.[1100] I was always looking for the bogmen. Bogmen—these are people who are found in the marshes, for example in Holstein or also in Sweden, whether they drowned there or were buried there. So these corpses are lying deep in marsh water and it contains humic acid. This erodes the bones and at the same time preserves the skin. So the skin of such a corpse is perfectly preserved, even the hair. It is as if they had been mummified, but pressed completely flat by the marshland growing over them. These corpses are found while peat cutting, for example, in Holstein, Denmark, and Sweden where these marshes are located. So this was what happened in Bremen: I suddenly thought of these bogmen and I went looking for them in Bremen. But I confused them with the mummified corpses in Bremen cathedral. In the crypt there lead sheets are stored to repair the roof. And the lead has a similar mummifying effect on the corpses. That is the famous story of the lead chambers. There are such mummified corpses in Bremen cathedral, but in my memory, they were subverted by the bogmen. It got terribly on Freud's nerves that I kept looking for these corpses because he believed that I wished his death. And then he got very cross about it. "What is it with you and these corpses?" And then he fainted when he was eating his dinner.

[1101]The second fainting episode was in Munich in 1912 during the first psychoanalytic congress. Someone introduced the subject of Amenophis IV, [342/343] who had such a father complex and out of this complex he destroyed his father's royal cartouche on the steles.[1102] I objected,

---

[1100] In his travel journal, Freud narrated how he and Ferenczi met Jung on August 20, 1909 in Bremen. As Jung knew the town well, he took them sightseeing. This brought them to the lead cellar under the cathedral, where four hundred years previously the mummified corpse of a worker who had fallen had been discovered. Since then, others had arranged to be buried in this basement. The visitors then went to the Rathauskeller, and as there were only great barrels of wine and cold food, they went to the Essinghaus restaurant. They were pleased to hear from Jung that he had given up his abstinence and was drinking again. Freud continues, "We clinked glasses with fine wine. Whether I drank too quickly or because I had not slept the previous night, at the salmon course I began to sweat and felt debilitated and I had to forgo the other courses. I did not risk any further drink. Jung will take care of the drinking for me. Of course, the entire episode is soon over with. Jung remarks: Of course, we let dear papa pay for us and they divided any further expenses between themselves. In the afternoon, Jung took them out in the car." Sigmund Freud, "Reisejournal," Freud Archives, LC. On September 18, 1959 Jung told E. A. Bennet that when he left the Burghölzli in March 1909 he had celebrated by drinking (Bennet Diaries, ETH). Cf. Bennet, *Meetings with Jung*, January 23, 1955 (p. 43).

[1101] See *ETG*, p. 161, *MDR*, p. 156; and Bennet, *Meetings with Jung*, p. 43.

[1102] Presumably this was Karl Abraham, who that year published "Amenhotep IV. (Echnaton): Psychoanalytische Beitrage zum Verstandnis seiner Personlichkeit und des monotheistischen Aton-Kultes," *Imago* 1, no. 4 (1912): 334–60.

"That's not true!" But the others wanted to say that he had created monotheism in protest against his father. That irritated me immeasurably. I attempted to explain: it was not out of resistance to the father but because he was a creative man. At that moment Freud fell from the chair. Everyone stood helplessly around him. I said, "My God, someone do something!" And then I took him in my arms and carried him into the next room and laid him on the sofa. As I was carrying him, he half came round and the look he threw me I will never forget: as if I were his father or his mother. This is how he looked at me in his helplessness. And that seemed terribly strange to me somehow. That is what happened and that is how the thing played out and if other people say something different then they are lying.—That was the second time he linked something with the idea that I apparently wished him dead. He always had the idea that people wished each other dead. That is what he also assumed about my dream of the skeletons that I found in the cellar.

Incidentally the idea of the death drive originated with my pupil Prof. Spielrein who later became professor of psychiatry in St. Petersburg.[1103] After the revolution in 1918 I never heard any more about her. She disappeared. She had already written about the death drive. Her work is published in the *Jahrbuch für Psychoanalyse*. This idea originates with her. I already said back then: Life is oriented not only towards life but also towards death.[1104] Death is a goal. But for me that is not a death drive, but the fact of life and of death are simply objective facts and corresponding processes exist. The word "archetype" had not yet been given to me at that time.

Freud never understood me correctly. When I introduced the concept of "introversion" he thought that was simply narcissism. I said, "No, it is not that!"—"Yes it is, it's narcissism,"[1105] he rejoined. "But I coined this

[1103] See Sabina Spielrein (1885–1937), "Die Destruktion als Ursache des Werdens," *Jahrbuch für psychoanalytische und psychopathologische Forschungen*, 4 (January 1912): 465–503; Spielrein, "Destruction as the Cause of Coming into Being" (1912), *Journal of Analytical Psychology* 39, no. 2 (1994): pp. 185–96. On Jung's relationship to Spielrein, see Zvi Lothane, "Tender Love and Transference: Unpublished Letters of C. G. Jung and Sabina Spielrein," *International Journal of Psychoanalysis* 80, no. 6 (1999): pp. 1189–204. Spielrein was appointed to a chair in child psychology at the First Moscow University.

[1104] In *Transformations and Symbols of the Libido* (1912), Jung wrote, "It is not only as if the libido might be an irresistible striving forward, an endless life and will for construction, such as Schopenhauer has formulated in his world will, death and every end being some malignancy or fatality coming from without, but the libido, corresponding to the sun, also wills the destruction of its creation. In the first half of life its will is for growth. In the second half of life it hints, softly at first, and then audibly, at its will for death." *CE* 6; *CW* B, § 696.

[1105] See Sigmund Freud, "On Narcissism: An Introduction," *SE* 14, pp. 67–102.

term and so I must surely know that it has nothing to do with narcissism" [343/344]—Of course he didn't like that, neither did the others; for no one dared to oppose Freud.—When we met in Munich, I greeted him warmly and asked after his family.[1106] Then he looked at me with astonishment and asked why I was coming with this benevolence. But I intentionally approached him cordially in order to show him that I had no personal resistances but only advocated a different scientific opinion. He, on the other hand, thought that I wished him dead even though I did everything for him and took on more work for him than all of his pupils at the time: I was editor of the *Jahrbuch* and arranged congresses for him, and then he reproached me, alleging personal motives that were not ever present. Something always had to be wrong, but that was mere projection.

At the invitation to Fordham University in 1912, I had to demonstrate a case of hysteria in the psychiatric clinic and speak about the associations experiment.[1107] In the USA there was an extraordinary eagerness[1108] to acquire this technique. Americans had less theoretical understanding, that is more prevalent here in Europe. But theory, that did not interest Americans. This is why they do not understand the meaning, for them it is only about the gadget.[1109] They only want to know how to do it but not what it means, or what it signifies.

In 1937 I was in Yale and then I went to Boston to the Massachusetts General Hospital.[1110] There I gave a presentation on mandalas. Afterwards

---

[1106] The International Psychoanalytic Association Congress in Munich, September 7–8, 1913 was the last time that Freud and Jung met.

[1107] The American neurologist, later psychoanalyst, Smith Ely Jelliffe (1866–1945), whom Jung had first met in 1907, invited him to lecture in the new international extension course in medicine at Fordham University. On these lectures, see Sonu Shamdasani, "Introduction" (2012) in *Jung contra Freud: The 1912 New York Lectures on the Theory of Psychoanalysis*, updated edn, Philemon Series (Princeton, NJ: Princeton University Press, 2012 [1961]). For Jelliffe's correspondence with Jung, see John Burnham, *Jelliffe: American Psychoanalyst and Physician and His Correspondence with Sigmund Freud and C. G. Jung*, ed. William McGuire (Chicago: University of Chicago Press, 1983). Jung received an honorary law doctorate from Fordham University.

[1108] "eagerness": in English in the original.

[1109] "gadget": in English in the original.

[1110] On October 20–22, 1937 Jung delivered the Terry Lectures at Yale University on *Psychology and Religion* (CE 14; CW 11). On October 16 *The New York Times* announced, "Dr. Carl Jung Arrives. Noted Psychologist to Give Terry Lectures at Yale," and Jung was cited as saying that human reactions were based "much more on religious phenomena than on sex" (p. 3). The newspaper covered Jung's lectures: "Jung Views Dreams as a Key to 'Isms" (October 21), "Voice of Dreams Called Superior" (October 22, p. 21), "'Shadow' Carried by All, Says Jung" (October 23, p. 8).

It was in fact previously, in 1936, that Jung was in Massachusetts, to speak at the Harvard University tercentenary celebrations and to receive an honorary degree. On June 15 that

a psychiatrist came to me and said, "If I understand you correctly, that is scientific work?"—"Yes, that is scientific work."—"But, I mean, that is scientific work."[1111] I would have to explain to him that I follow certain principles and if he could understand that then he would recognize that it is scientific work. The Americans understood nothing at all theoretically, they are not interested in knowing what that actually is, they only want to learn the technique. The psychiatrist who asked me wanted to know only whether I had followed a scientific method. And I had to confirm to him that the comparative method was scientific. Accordingly, he was not able to think about what a mandala means, [344/345] that was completely unclear to him, he could not think about it, only the technical, the clinical, that was the only interest, but what that might mean—not a clue!—Yet one cannot generalize this experience of course. This was one experience exclusively with doctors and the medical profession, and one can safely say it was not very intellectual. I know that others in North America have a keen interest in my works; there are infinitely many who want to consider and recognize the meaning, and who have psychological understanding.

The lecture tour to Fordham university was not a special experience for me. I spoke about psychology and neurology there. There I met Jelliffe and White, the director of the Hospital for the Insane, Washington, DC.[1112] And I visited William James whom I had met back in 1909.[1113] I

---

year he had written to Stanley Cobb, a neurologist at the Massachusetts General Hospital in Boston, accepting his invitation to stay with him from September 15 to 19 (JP), indicating that Emma Jung would be accompanying him. Cobb had had dinner with Jung, together with Henry Murray, in Zurich back in 1925; Cobb and Murray were both stammerers, and Murray recalled Jung advising them, "Don't at all costs give up stammering. It is most sexually exciting to women." Benjamin White, *Stanley Cobb: A Builder of the Modern Neurosciences* (Charlottsville, VA: University of Virginia Press, 1984), p. 119.

At his talk at the Massachusetts General Hospital, Cobb committed the faux pas of introducing Jung as "Dr. Freud"; but he was of assistance at the honorary degree ceremony at Harvard, when Jung needed formal attire, including a top hat, which he had not brought with him. Cobb found "his old collapsible opera hat, which was several sizes too small for Jung. However, Jung, who had a sense of humor, carried it along, so that it would seem as if he had just taken it off, and carried the occasion with aplomb." White, *Stanley Cobb*, p. 235.

[1111] This dialogue is in English in the original. In his lectures, Jung had discussed Wolfgang Pauli's dream of the world clock.

[1112] The American neurologist and psychiatrist William Alanson White (1870–1937) invited Jung to St. Elizabeth's Hospital the following year. Jung's observations there were seminal in his formulation of the concept of the archetypes. On White, see Hollman, "White's Restraint."

[1113] See n. 411 above. William James died in August 1910; there is no record of Jung meeting James on his trip to the USA in 1910. In a letter to Virginia Payne he recalled meeting James on two evenings in 1909. *Letters*, vol. 1, July 23, 1949 (p. 539).

met with him again then. And then I once shook Roosevelt's hand. A senator introduced me to him.[1114] But that was no special experience either. I was not a politician, so he was not able to make anything of me, and likewise I of him.—Then I met Peary, the North Pole explorer, he was a very impressive man.[1115]

I met a series of famous people. Did I ever tell you of my encounter with Einstein? He often visited me at the time he was working on his theory of relativity. He was a guest at my home a few times and he told me about his theory and explained its foundations. That must have been around 1910.[1116]—I did not have any great impression of his human personality. He had a soft, sentimental nature. And alongside that he had an autonomous mathematical genius that carried him into the world of ideas; whereas as a man, he was sort of left behind. When you got as far as human concerns, a personality was lacking. He was terribly limp and was a man who simply consisted of a theory. Everything else was sentiment. So a certain sentimental idealism with shallow enlightenment. I could imagine that he played the fiddle with great feeling but very badly. He was probably a feeling type. Thinking was in the unconscious and was autonomous. Music and mathematics belong in one and the same sphere, [345/346] and the two gifts often alternate. One very often finds them together. You saw that in Bernoulli, he was alternately a musician and a mathematician.[1117] Such people can be laser sharp in mathematics and then on the other hand have these limp, lukewarm aspects. Einstein was not a man whose thoughts radiated out of him, at least not then. He was like, "Yes, yes, the soft calves of the youth!" You know, a sort of socialist,

---

[1114] According to Franz Jung, Medill McCormick introduced Jung to Roosevelt in New York in 1912 (cited in McGuire, "Firm Affinities," p. 308). On October 4, 1936, *The New York Times* carried a piece titled "Roosevelt is Great, Is Jung's Analysis," reporting Jung as saying, "Before I came here I had the impression from Europe that he was an opportunist, perhaps even an erratic mind. Now that I have seen him and heard him when he talked at Harvard, however, I am convinced that here is a strong man, a man who is really great. Perhaps that's why many people do not like him." McGuire and Hull, *C. G. Jung Speaking*, p. 88. (Roosevelt had been speaking at the Harvard University tercentenary celebrations, at which Jung had been awarded his honorary degree: see n. 1110 above. His address can be heard at https://www.fdrlibrary.org/utterancesfdr [accessed April 26, 2025].)

[1115] Robert Peary (1856–1920), Arctic explorer. He claimed to have reached the North Pole in 1909. In 1988, the National Geographic Society concluded that Peary's evidence for this was not conclusive.

[1116] See above, p. 159.

[1117] The Swiss mathematician and physicist Daniel Bernoulli (1700–1782) was also responsible for demonstrating that the movements of strings of musical instruments were made up of an infinite number of harmonic vibrations.

or someone who makes the children do math exercises, something so limp, such a limp flaccid hand!

But the theory certainly made a very strong and significant impression on me. I had the feeling that it was something highly significant. But of course, I was not able to imagine the extent of it;[1118] I understood far too little of mathematics for that. As soon as Einstein began to speak of it, he was a different person, then he was the very process himself, the equation itself. Like a musician, who can be quite a weak fellow; but then when he makes music, then you see: he is the music itself and therein lies his greatness. That is what Einstein was: the equations and mathematics themselves. Then one had the sense of something inexorable[1119] to which one basically had no access through feeling. I never doubted that he was an important intellect, but I could not resist doing a couple of tests on the psychological side. One could also imagine that he was a terribly dear, good, acquiescent, even weak father to his family and any tailor could have been married as he was. Freud was completely different. He was a feeling type probably. But he was rather hard, although he had the Viennese gentility. Where Einstein showed a rather limp optimism and was a philanthropist of general goodness, Freud was bitter and resentful, hard and cynical. Freud made a much greater impact as a personality. He was altogether a distinctive personality.

I also consider William James among the most significant personalities I have met in my life.[1120] He was a very impressive man, very fine and distinguished, very likeable. He belonged in the unfortunate period where it was the style [336/337] to be completely objective and to not let oneself be moved by things. But this was the reason he did not properly see the truth. He treated religious phenomena in the same way: the feeling of a presence. That is expressed terribly weakly. That is why this thing also happened to him: an evening reception was taking place in the home of the president of Clark University. That was a university for postgraduates.[1121] This president was a very well-known man in the USA: Stanley Hall.[1122] So, a powerful man with great allure. Freud and I were

---

[1118] "extent of it": in English in the original.

[1119] "inexorable": in English in the original.

[1120] See above, pp. 110–13.

[1121] "post-graduates": in English in the original. Clark University was founded in 1887 as a graduate-only institution; in 1902, undergraduates were admitted.

[1122] G. Stanley Hall (1846–1924), American psychologist, who founded the *American Journal of Psychology* and was the first president of the American Psychological Society as well as the first president of Clark University. Hall was deeply impressed by Jung's *The*

his guests on this occasion. All the professors of the university were invited, and so also was William James, who came over especially from Boston. And at the time there was some smirking at James's interest in his spiritualist séances that he had organized with the clairvoyant medium Mrs. Piper.[1123] Stanley Hall related this and after dinner everyone gathered and Stanley Hall asked him to bring his protocols with him so that it could be discussed. So then William James said to Hall, "A propos, I brought my papers. Perhaps you are interested in those papers,"[1124] then he reached into his pocket and what did he pull out and hand over to Stanley Hall? A bundle of bank notes! Of course, generalized laughter broke out for James had made a terrible fool of himself, but above all the situation was also humorous because Stanley Hall was well known for being very rapacious[1125] and for being very concerned to attract money for the university. It was said, and was well known, that Stanley Hall was very interested in such "papers."[1126] And one had no idea whether this was malice on William James's part or whether he had made a fool of himself! But I did not think him capable of such malice. And he also seemed terribly embarrassed.

When I was with him, I mainly listened. His philosophy and his concepts of these parapsychological experiences, all this interested me very much. Through him I also met Hyslop with whom he made contact after his death.[1127] That is all in his writings. The second time I saw him was shortly before his death. He was complaining of heart pain. He was then seventy or seventy-two.[1128] [347/348]

Einstein was his ideas, or his ideas were Einstein, and that is also true of me.[1129] I made great efforts to assert myself alongside my ideas. There was a daimon in me and he was the decisive factor, and I was always breathlessly behind the "other"; and when I was reckless it was because I was compelled by the daimon. I was never able to hold back with others and their stupid stories. I stormed away from them, but only because I

Psychology of the Unconscious Processes, and offered to arrange to have it translated. G. Stanley Hall to Jung October 29, 1917, JP.

[1123] See above, n. 404.

[1124] James's remark is given in English in the original. Jung narrated this story in a letter to Virginia Payne on July 23, 1949, expressing his admiration for James. *Letters*, vol. 1, p. 531.

[1125] "rapacious": in English in the original.

[1126] "papers": in English in the original.

[1127] See above, p. 112.

[1128] James was sixty-five in 1909, and died in 1910 (see n. 1113 above).

[1129] See above, p. 159.

had the vision in front of me that others did not see. I snubbed countless people: as soon as they had understood something or as soon as I noticed they had not understood the matter was settled for me. Then I was off and running. I had no patience with people, or I was too quick to say: Oh, there's nothing there because I could see immediately that there really is nothing there. And that was the signal for me: don't touch it, or how should I stay with these boring people? The mistakes I made with people based on their being too slow or too uninteresting, or too prejudiced, and as soon as I saw that I was off, and I had no interest in them. What! You're still here?—and I clapped my hat on my head and said "Adieu!"—I always followed the inner law that was imposed on me and permitted me no freedom at all.—That was also absolutely evident with Einstein. He swam away with his mathematical considerations as if on Noah's ark, and it was the same for me.[1130] This is why I was immediately available to certain people who had contact with this inner world, but then it might be that I was suddenly absent because nothing more connected me to them. I had to learn with much effort that people are still there even when they have nothing more to say. Many had with me the feeling of lively humaneness, but only when they became visible in the magic circle of psychology, and in the next moment when the spotlight directed its beam somewhere else, there was nothing left. I could be interested beyond measure in people [348/349] but when I had taken the trick out of it the magic disappeared! So I made many enemies. But what do you want: when one is a creative person one is at its mercy. One is not free and is bound and driven by the daimon. "Painfully / the heart wrests from us a force, / For the heavens wish sacrifice from everyone / but if one misses it / it has never brought anything good."[1131] On the other hand there is something of great loyalty present in me. Despite this it was often as if I were on a battlefield: Can the hand not extend to you. . . . Remain in eternal life, my loyal comrade! Now you are fallen, I must go on! I cannot, I cannot remain![1132]

"For painfully the heart wrests from us a force." I like you, I love you, but I cannot stay! That is something heartbreaking in the moment, but

---

[1130] See *ETG*, pp. 358–59, *MDR*, p. 357.

[1131] Hölderlin, *Patmos*, v. 15, ll. 6–11. Jaffé noted here, "In the poem it says: shamefully wrests from the heart . . . Patmos." She corrected and expanded the reference in *ETG*, p. 359, *MDR*, p. 357.

[1132] The first lines cited quote Ludwig Uhland's song "Der gute Kamerad" (The good comrade) (1809): "Kann dir die Hand nicht geben, / Bleib du im ew'gen Leben / Mein guter Kamerad!" The last line possibly echoes "Es kann ja nicht immer so bleiben," from Auguste von Kotzebue's poem "Ewiger Wechsel" (1802), which was later set to music.

the daimon manages to get one through. Something still remains, and I am myself the sacrifice, I *cannot* stay, my humanity would like to stay, but it won't work. Every creative person is like that. Think of Goethe, for God's sake!

Perhaps I can also say: I need people to a much higher degree than anyone else, and at the same time to a much smaller degree. Inasmuch as one is a daimon, one is always too close and too distant, or in danger of these extremes. Only when the daimon leaves me in peace am I midway, then I am related, and then I have what is called warmth of feeling. But it can always pull me in too far: pro or contra. I can have relationships only with people who sense the daimon and understand its working. They endure, even in times of unrelatedness. Otherwise I must brush them aside. When my children say: The biography belongs in the family, I must simply brush it aside. But I know: they have a normal attitude. The daimon and the creative have prevailed in me unconditionally and ruthlessly. The common had no space in me, but when one says the uncommon thing, it causes anxiety, that is uncanny. One always wants everything to be comprehensible even to the smallest mind.—What I have is *amor fati*.[1133] [349/350] The feeling for destiny. And when I sense that in another, when I sense that in a relationship to myself, then I can accept it, then I can brush aside the dark places, then one brushes aside the hindrances and the relationship exists even when I am unrelated.[1134] [350/351]

[1133] *amor fati* (Lat.): "love of fate."

[1134] On March 25, 1958 Aniela Jaffé wrote to Helen Wolff telling her that the new limit Jung has set for his memoir was his marriage (in 1903): "He said: if he were to write beyond this point, for reasons of honesty he would have to write things that, for reasons of discretion, it were better not to write. Therefore he must remain silent." She went on, "Jung has told me lots about Freud; and I would be very grateful if your husband would integrate these pieces into the mosaic of the Freud chapter as soon as he feels well enough to do so." She hoped then to complete the amalgamation of Jung's childhood memories up to page 39, which she would then send (BL).

On March 30, Jaffé informed Kurt Wolff that she was nearly finished with the amalgamation, which was "not at all a simple jigsaw." She did it in such a manner that one couldn't tell which came from Jung's manuscript and which from her protocol. She added that she didn't have the courage to delete the first sentence (see below). Jung was due to return from Bollingen on the following day (BL).

On April 8 she wrote to Kurt Wolff that Jung had finished his memoir over Easter, and was going to Bollingen at the end of the week. She had finished compiling the chapter "Black and Red Book," and had the raw material for the next chapter, but wanted to wait till Wolff visited (BL) The first sentence of Jung's memoir was, "Since whenever I write, be it consciously or unconsciously, I always have an audience in mind, and whatever I write is always a letter to the world, then you, my dear children, are in the front row of my

APRIL 11, 1958

In 1902 I was in Paris, and I attended Janet's lectures in the École des Hautes Études.[1135] I didn't meet him personally. Charcot was already dead by then.[1136] But I met Binet.[1137] Apart from that I didn't meet anyone else. I was in Paris for about four months from September to December.[1138] Then in the spring I went to London for two months. In Paris and London, I only visited hospitals and spent the majority of my time in the galleries. I was very interested in art at that time. I can't say which art, but from the medieval right up to modern, and then I reveled in antiquity and in the Egyptian and Assyrian collections.

In 1937 the Terry Lectures took place in America.[1139] I was a huge success there. First, three hundred people came, and then on the next evening it was already six hundred, and the third evening it was so full that the

---

auditorium. It is to you that I want to communicate what has formed me, i.e., to tell you the little that I can recall from the darkness of my childhood." (JFA, p. 1)

On May 9, 1960, Richard Hull suggested to Kurt Wolff "to delete the opening sentence in the ozalid and plunge into the narrative, 'When I was six months old . . .' (the proper fairytale beginning!)" (BL).

[1135] On Janet and his course, given in fact at the Collège de France, where he held a chair, see n. 666 above.

[1136] Jean-Martin Charcot (1825–1893), prominent French neurologist.

[1137] Alfred Binet (1857-1911), French psychologist and student of Charcot. From 1894 till his death he was the director of the recently founded laboratory of physiological psychology at the Sorbonne. In 1895 he co-founded with Victor Henri the journal *L'année psychologique*. In the draft translation of *Memories, Dreams, Reflections* (CLM), Jung stated (pp. 316–17), "My original intention had been to work on this matter [the associations experiment] with Binet in Paris. I got in touch with him, and met with warm understanding on his part. But as I considered the project more closely, I was troubled by the fact that I would have to conduct the experiments in French. For such a task I lacked sufficient linguistic feeling, lacked that ability to make fine distinctions which are particularly important in the case of the French language. Discouraged, I therefore let the plan drop, without, however, feeling confident that it was wise to do so."

[1138] Jung left the Burghölzi at the end of August 1902, after which he spent a few weeks on military service. He formally left his post at the clinic on September 30. In October he visited his sister in Château d'Oex to get accustomed to French. From there, he went to Paris at the beginning of November, where he stayed till mid-January, 1903. He then went to London for two weeks (rather than two months as he states below), arriving back in Switzerland for his marriage on February 14. He and Emma then went on their honeymoon, settling in an apartment on Zollikerstrasse in Zürich by the end of April.

[1139] See above, p 311. The annual Terry Lectureship, established at Yale University in 1905 by the gift of Dwight H. Terry of Bridgeport, Connecticut, "invites preeminent scholars in religion, the sciences and philosophy to address issues concerning the ways in which science and philosophy inform religion and religion is applied to human welfare": https://terrylecture.yale.edu/ (accessed April 26, 2025).

police had to suspend entry to the hall.[1140] It held about three thousand people. I explained this to myself as the Americans having an underground connection to me. They have an intuition that must not be underestimated. The academics cannot understand me because they have an intellect that is skewed by statistics, but among the general public in America I was always extremely popular, something the professors could not understand at all because they actually could not understand what I was talking about.

That was where this funny story happened: I went home after the third lecture of this series of Terry Lectures. It was still rather early and afterwards we had a cup of tea and the hostess was the wife of the dean in a college where I was also staying. She was an older lady, very formal. For example, she wore a hat to serve the tea! Something so crazy! So I came into the room and found her crying behind her silverware and the cups. Of course, I wanted to withdraw discreetly but she said, "No, no, do come in, I am just weeping, but it doesn't matter." I asked her what was the matter and she replied, "It was your lecture. It was so beautiful, but I did not understand a word! But it was so beautiful!"[1141] She was not able to express it [351/352] but something had happened to her that I had also felt with all the others: I felt it, I had *reached* the people! But they were all like this person: they couldn't make anything of it. I did not meet anyone with whom I could have had some sort of intelligent conversation. But the public at large were impressed.

The same thing happened to me in the lecture at Harvard University. There I spoke only to a limited audience, only professionals. On the theme "Factors Determining Human Behavior."[1142] I spoke on the unconscious. When it was finished, I went out and two people were going down the steps in front of me and I overheard their conversation. The one said to the other, "Did you understand this lecture?" He replied, "Well I could not follow, but that is a chap who knows what he's talking about!"[1143] There were only about two hundred and fifty people there. But in Yale it was really extraordinary. I had complained that they had booked such a massive auditorium. It is a very unpleasant feeling if it is only a quarter full, and they said to me that usually more people attend the first lecture than the subsequent ones. "It will drop off, and then even fewer will come." I was very irritated. The first time the space was perhaps a tenth full. The

---

[1140] According to *The New York Times*, there were "more than 2,000 persons" at Jung's opening lecture ("Jung Views Dreams as a Key to 'Isms," October 21).

[1141] The quoted remarks in the exchange are in English in the original.

[1142] *CE* 14; *CW* 8. See above, no. 1110.

[1143] This dialogue is in English in the original.

second time there were over six hundred people there, and the third time the police had to limit entry. That amazed me very much.[1144]

I had the feeling of making contact there. That did not often occur in my life, for mostly I had the feeling that I was speaking out through the window.

When I speak of myself then I must mention what lay within me as a fateful compulsion. That also shows itself in my never being able to undertake a commissioned work, but whatever I wrote overwhelmed me from within. [352/353]

In earlier years I was driven by what compelled me from within and only gradually did an inner peace form.[1145] It began when I realized that the mandala is definitive, that there is no ultra, that it is an ultimate expression, and that is the thing in my life through which I arrived at the ultimate for me. I knew that I could not go any deeper. With this I had achieved the deepest or the highest point. This gave me peace and I knew I could not get beyond it. Beyond this I know nothing more. Perhaps someone else knows more, but I do not.

Intuitively I reached this point in 1917 through the pursuit of the inner images. After that I had to develop this in my life and in my science in order to actually arrive there, and from then on everything oriented itself towards this goal. It developed quite alchemically, and the final stage was then the unification of the opposites, the *mysterium coniunctionis*.[1146]

[1147]The encounter with Zimmer did not have the same importance for me as the one with Richard Wilhelm. Zimmer visited me here, and he stayed with us for a few days. We conversed for a long time about mythology, that he had thrown the book about the golden flower against the wall, as I told you.[1148] But after that he wanted to visit me. We spoke a lot about Indian mythology and philosophy. He had already published his book in 1926.—*Kunstform und Yoga im Indischen Kultbild*,[1149] that

---

[1144] See above. On May 28, 1958, Kurt Wolff noted to Jaffé, "Terry Lectures: Cary attended all three. She remembers absolutely distinctly that it happened the other way around: first lecture, say 3000, second lecture 600, third 300 people. She said that there was immense curiosity at the time in Jung's personality and ideas, which explains the attendance of the first lecture. Then the audience became aware that Jung spoke above their heads, and Cary at the time felt that the dwindling audience was an absolutely natural thing." (BL).

[1145] See *ETG*, p. 200, *MDR*, p. 196.

[1146] See *CE* 24; *CW* 14.

[1147] See *ETG*, p. 385. and above, p. 250.

[1148] See above, p. 250.

[1149] See n. 911 above.

was one year before the *Golden Flower*, but I did not know it. Zimmer was an uncommonly brilliant man, a sparkling conversationalist. We went sailing together and ate and drank together.

No. 1 sort of came into me at the start of the *Black Book*.[1150] In it, I positively came to terms with the other side. Finally, this character of *Bardo*-memory fell away from me.[1151] I recognized that it was a question of psychic things. I already knew this much of psychology, [353/354] that there is an unconscious, and that was the other side. At that time the curious and strange things fell away from me, and I recognized that they were psychic actualities and after I had recognized that, it immediately went much further into the depths. All the dreams of corpses point to the other side. Sometimes I also had terrible dreams of corpses that I had to carry, or that were being burnt and were still moving. These corpses are the other side. And also the long row of the dead in the Alyscamps.[1152] But with the *Black Book* the husk fell away that still hung about me from *Bardo*. I penetrated into the life of the actual psyche.

Our *Bardo*-memories are there in an original form until they somehow come into contact with us, then they sort of clothe themselves with modern means of expression and the corpse-like character or the primeval world-like character falls away from them.

In compensation to inner experience, I naturally had a most intensive experience externally so that I constantly oscillated between these two poles. For example, I always had a most intensive relationship with nature, I adored working in the garden, climbing mountains, riding horseback. The beauty of the earth was always enchanting to me. The fullness of external life always very much belonged to this too. This intensive relationship to the beauty of the world could bring me to tears. When Goethe writes of these things, "Where do I capture you infinite nature . . ."[1153] this is exactly how I felt. This is why I also wrote above the door to my house, "Ridenti in loco otioso erigere iusserunt."[1154] I built the house in

---

[1150] The context suggests that Jung was here in fact referring to "personality No. 2."

[1151] On the notion of the Bardo, see Jung's "Psychological Commentary to *The Tibetan Book of the Dead*" (1954), CE 23; CW 11. In his late works Jung equated the Bardo with the pleroma.

[1152] See above, p. 119.

[1153] Goethe, *Faust I*, Act 1, sc. 1, l. 455.

[1154] "They had this house built in a cheerful, tranquil place." A translation of the full inscription that Jung carved would read, "In 1908 Carl Gustav Jung and his wife, Emma Rauschenbach, had this house built in a cheerful, tranquil place." See Andreas Jung, Regula Michel, Irene Gerber, Daniel Ganz, and Arthur Rüegg, *The House of C. G. Jung: The History*

1908. A cousin of mine drew up the plans.[1155] He was professor at the technical university in Stuttgart. But of course, I put my whole weight into it. The house is built in the style of the early baroque, as you often find on the shore of Lake Zurich. In Basel I would have built it in the style of the eighteenth century.—I paid great attention that my cousin did not bring in ideas from art nouveau. [354/355] That was when architectural style was starting to be corrupted.

It was an unforgettable event for me when I bought the land in 1907. That this was *my* piece of earth! That is the piece of earth upon which I will remain. I worked a great deal in the garden, I dug and planted and that was an incomparably exquisite pleasure to me. I had the same feeling later in Bollingen: that is *my* earth upon which I stand like a tree. That is why I also declined the call to Oxford.[1156] I was not able to separate myself from my piece of earth.

Because I love the earth it is often said that I have something of the farmer about me. That is a German prejudice. I have absolutely nothing to do with farming. My ancestors were doctors and lawyers and theologians as far back as the seventeenth century. In Germany they asked me: How many cows does your father have? And I was supposed to yodel! My maternal grandfather was a Faber du Faur and he was a general on the German side in 1870/71.[1157]

In 1933 I was in the Orient—in Constantinople, Athens, Rhodes, in Palestine and Egypt as far as Luxor.[1158] (But I had already been there before). But I can't tell you anything about that. That has already been told

---

and *Restoration of the Residence of Emma and Carl Gustav Jung-Rauschenbach* (Küsnacht: Stiftung C. G. Jung Küsnacht, 2009), p. 17; on the building of the house, pp. 33–34.

[1155] Ernst Fiechter (1875–1948).

[1156] See above, p. 291.

[1157] Jung's maternal grandfather was the pastor Samuel Preiswerk (1799–1871); but the maiden name of his maternal grandmother Augusta (1805–1862) was Faber. She was a Württemberger, but does not appear to have been related to Württemberg's military family descending from the Habsburg *Feldmarschalleutnant* Christian Wolfgang Faber (1710–93), elevated in 1779 to "von Faber du Faur." His descendants who inherited this title included the soldier/war artists Christian Wilhelm (1780–1857), who accompanied Napoleon to Russia in 1812, and the latter's son Otto (1928–1901), who painted scenes from the Franco–Prussian War of 1870–71, in which the Württemberg army participated on the German side.

[1158] In 1933 Jung joined Hans Eduard Fierz, a professor of chemistry at the ETH Zurich on a trip to Palestine and Egypt. They left on March 13. They visited Sicily, Athens, Istanbul, Rhodes, and Cyprus, arriving in Haifa on March 25, and then went on to Jerusalem. On March 27 they left for Port Said, and proceeded to Cairo and Luxor. On March 31 they went on to Corfu and Ragusa. For details, see Andreas Jung, "Carl Jung and Hans Fierz in Palestine and Egypt: Journey from March 13 to April 6," and Thomas Fischer, "1933—The Year of Jung's Journey to Palestine/Israel and Several Beginnings," in Erel Shalit and Murray

countless times. Yes: I saw the Acropolis and this and that. No inner experience is connected to it. Of course, I enjoyed it: Rhodes made a great impression on me, as well as Malta and Sicily.

The journey to India, that was something else, that was in 1938.[1159] I had an unforgettable experience there on the hill of Sanchi.[1160] That's where the famous stupas are. Even my first visit there made an inexplicable impression on me. When I was there the second time I observed Japanese pilgrims visiting the stupas in worship. They sang and that was very beautiful. I was incredibly gripped by this place, I was almost out of my mind. This is when Buddhism captured me for the first time. But I was not able to formulate it at that time. [355/356] This quite exceptional emotional impact upon me showed me that this place represented something central. I later saw what the life of the Buddha means: the realization of the self. And that it is expressed in Buddhism, that the self stands above all Gods and actually represents the mystery of the world and of human existence. But in a quite different sense from Christ, who also represents the self. Buddha is an overcomer of the world, but through insight. Christ is not an overcomer through insight, but as an event. He is the sacrifice. There is much more suffering in Christianity. In Buddhism it is seen and done. And both are correct, but Buddha is in a certain sense, in an Indian sense, a more complete personality than Christ.[1161] He is also much more historical. He is a historical person and therefore is graspable for man. Christ is not a whole person, he is also a God and therefore is not graspable for man. He is also not graspable to himself for he only knew that he must sacrifice himself. That was imposed upon him, was put upon him, a destiny. With Buddha it happens as insight. He lived his life himself and died as an old man. Christ was perhaps only active for a year. And that is all linked to the incomplete incarnation in Christ.[1162] But precisely this

---

Stein, eds, *Turbulent Times, Creative Minds: Erich Neumann and C. G. Jung in Relationship (1933–1960)* (Asheville, NC: Chiron Publications, 2016), pp. 131–38.

[1159] See *ETG*, p. 281, *MDR*, p. 274, and above, p. 186 and pp. 189–90.

[1160] See above, p. 279.

[1161] In the "Commentaries" to *Liber Novus*, Jung wrote, "Christ overcame the world by burdening himself with its suffering. But Buddha overcame both the pleasure and suffering of the world by disposing of both. And thus he entered into nonbeing, a condition from which there is no return. Buddha is an even higher spiritual power, that derives no pleasure from controlling the flesh, since he has altogether moved beyond pleasure and suffering." *LN*, p. 570.

[1162] The following sentence was obscured by overtyping here: "The incarnation of God continues after Christ."

totality, that is what I experienced in India, and this took me over incredibly. Previously I had already read a great deal, I knew the speeches of Buddha and the Buddhist philosophy. But I had never experienced it with this immediacy as well as this magnificent nature. Sanchi is in the state of Bhopal. That made a wonderful impression. I heard the Japanese pilgrims from a long way off. They were all carrying a small gong which they struck after their prayer, *om mani padme hum*. At first I heard only the gong. And then *om mani padme hum! Om mani padme hum!* And in this way, they came with this prayer to the treasure on the lotus, they ascended the hill in this way and bowed down deeply before the Buddha statues. [356/357] A long path led around the stupas. To the north, south, east, and west there were Buddha statues. There they made their bows and sang their hymns, they performed a complete circumambulation of the center with their right hand to the center. That was incredibly meaningful.

[1163]And then the incomparable evening service in the temple of Kandy, the old capital city of Ceylon. There is a small chapel there with golden Buddha statues in the walls before which small lamps burn coconut oil. And young boys and girls strew around whole streams of jasmine blossoms and they were all chanting a prayer, a mantra. I thought they were singing something about the Buddha, but the monk who was my guide explained: No, Buddha is not, he is in nirvana. They are singing about how these flowers decay so quickly, just as our life melts away.—And this is what these young people were singing!

The Buddha is an attitude. Buddha is the enlightened mind,[1164] and if I am Buddhist, I have the chance of achieving the same perfection through fulfillment of the eightfold path. Then my own mind also becomes like Buddha, and then I myself am Buddha.

By far my greatest experience in India was in Sanchi; it was quite incredible, and nothing exceeded that.—And then came—still in India—the dream of the Grail.[1165] And that signified what I must reach: the Grail. The Grail is a symbol of enlightenment, and in the Western sense too, hence also the Christian connotation (the cup in which the blood of Christ was contained and so on.) This dream made an unbelievable impression on me.

And then in India I felt my way into the Hindu mentality. It was through the Goddess Kali Dhurga: the virgin and mother Goddess, and at

---

[1163] See *ETG*, p. 287, *MDR*, p. 283, and above, p. 193.
[1164] "mind": in English in the original.
[1165] In *ETG* there is a full account of this dream (pp. 284–85) (*MDR*, pp. 280–81).

the same time she is the most terrible one that one can ever imagine, with her bloodthirstiness.[1166] Curiously it was the Grail receptacle that filled me with fear and trembling. As Kali was virgin, mother, queen, Goddess and at the same time this terrible being and all in one and the same figure! And [357/358] that was what I simply had not been able to accept. The dream is initiated by an iron demon, all hardness, coldness, and implacability are expressed in it and all terror, I must swim through the sea in order to retrieve the Grail, which—according to my dream—is also evil, in contrast to the usual version. The symbol of the *vas*, the Gnostic vessel, which is also depicted on some cameos, the vase of sin;[1167] that is also the Grail. That is the *vas* of alchemy also containing the blackness. And that is feminine nature in and of itself which I could not say "yes" to; the unfathomable nature of feminine being. Woman has all the rudiments of infinite beauty and equally the most profound unfathomability. And that was simply not acceptable to me, and in India I learned this and saw what I had to subject myself to, otherwise I cannot reach myself. That was the *coniunctio* of opposites. I wanted to keep my head above it and save myself from ethics by resorting to moral precepts. And that was all so incredibly intense. In India I did not experience months, but nearly decades. There I transcended the Christian Western world. Or I could also say: I acquired a new understanding of Christianity and I saw what Christian character was all about, with its "acceptance." What it means if I say to my brother "raca," that then my sacrifice counts for nothing. Or Christ's saying: If you bring your gift to the altar and you have something against your brother, then first go to him and be reconciled with him.[1168] And if one does not do that, then the offering is worth nothing. I then understood these and other things, and I recognized that I must be *one* with myself, one with the human essence imposed upon me, and that I must say "yes" to the fact that woman is like that and that I am like this. And whoever cannot do that has not taken his cross upon himself. [358/359]

[1166] See above, pp. 190–1. Jung had encountered the figure of Kali in a fantasy of December 22, 1913 (*BB* 2, p. 186). In the "Corrected Draft" of *Liber Novus*, Jung noted, "Kali, however, is Salome and Salome is my soul" (cited in *BB* 2).

[1167] "the vase of sin": in English in the original.

[1168] Both references here are to Christ's "Sermon on the Mount." See Matthew 5:22: ("[W]hoever is angry with his brother without a cause shall be in danger of the judgment. And whoever shall say to his brother, 'Raca!' shall be in danger of the council. But whoever says, 'You fool' shall be in danger of hell fire" ("raca" is a term of contempt in Aramaic, the language Jesus spoke); and Matthew 5:22–23.

The cross means the opposites for Christ. These connections explain why I arrived at the problem of the Grail specifically in Calcutta. It was actually the attainment of the feminine in me, and this feminine expressed itself to me in Kali Durga. Kali seen as a whole. In her, the opposites are much less split apart than in Christianity, because the alpha and the omega is the moral sermon.[1169] In India evil cannot be sent into the desert,[1170] doing the right thing includes evil, that is an authentic Indian idea.

The feminine, Kali, or Isis who encompasses good and evil essentially confronts the masculine intellectual principle.[1171] It is impossible for the totality to be only spiritual, it must also be material. God the mother confronts a God the father. Up till now it was God the father, and then sometime comes a pivotal moment, where the maternal steps forward. Not for nothing do we live in the time of the *Assumptio*.[1172]

The journey to India in 1938 signified a caesura in my life, and the next event that caused a caesura was my illness in 1944.

In essence only those events of my life are worthy of telling in which the world of No. 2 broke through into that of No. 1. Everything else—travel, people, family, and environment—others have also experienced, and one can read up on it from them or have them tell you about them. For the most part that eludes me now. But the encounters with the completely other actuality of this collision mark out the particularity of my life. They have burrowed themselves deeply into my memory.[1173] This is why my works can be regarded as stations of my life, particularly of the later years. Each one represents an attempt at bringing the unsayable of the background into the objective world of science. All my works are, as it were, commissioned from within. I was placed under a compulsion which I could not escape, [359/360] and I was able to write only when I was required to in this way.

At the beginning of the Hitler period, I was once invited to Frankfurt to Mrs. v. Sch.[1174] It was said that there was someone from Berlin there,

---

[1169] Cf. Revelation 22:13, "I am Alpha and Omega, the beginning and the end, the first and the last."

[1170] Cf. Matthew 4, recounting Jesus's temptation by the devil in the desert.

[1171] In "Psychological Aspects of the Mother Archetype" (1938), Jung wrote, "In India, 'the loving and terrible mother' is the paradoxical Kali." *CE* 15; *CW* 9.1, § 158.

[1172] A reference to the papal bull *Munificentissimus Deus* (1950), affirming as dogma the Assumption of Mary.

[1173] See *ETG*, p. 225, *MDR*, p. 222.

[1174] Lily von Schnitzler (1889–1981), who was part of Keyserling's circle, and who corresponded with Jung. She was one of the initiators and editors of the *Europaische Revue*, where Jung published. Jung's trip to Frankfurt was part of a lecture tour, which also included stops in Cologne and Essen. He stated that more than a thousand people attended his lecture in Frankfurt (letter to Vera Curtius, November 6, 1933, cited in Fischer, "1933,"

someone with "a large nose," a snooper. There were many people invited and all at once a general silence arose, quite suddenly, and then he stepped forward—but he was not in uniform, and he suddenly spoke to me and basically he said to me he would be very obliged to me if I would give an interpretation of the swastika. Naturally, I was mortified and explained that I would unfortunately have to say that it was an unpropitious sign that portended destruction. He did not like hearing that, I can tell you!

The swastika existed for a long time before it was adopted by National Socialism. I always inquired about its meaning wherever I found it. For example, in South India. It is sometimes found close to an entrance of a house there, or on the ground before the threshold. Its meaning was a sign of welcome or of good omen, but also against evil magic. I once saw a photograph of the Dalai-Lama's throne. To the left is the anticlockwise swastika and to the right the clockwise. The anticlockwise one belongs to the primitive primal religion of Tibet which is feared for its black magic associations. And also disdained. And this is shaped like the Nazi one. It has an evil and destructive aspect. The clockwise swastika signifies the philosophical or spiritual aspect of Buddhism. I have these explanations from a Rimpoche (abbot or bishop).[1175]

APRIL 30, 1958[1176]

My grandfather was a friend of Charlotte Kestner.[1177] She was a niece of Goethe's Lotte. She knew my grandfather well and in her later years she settled in Basel thanks to her friendly relationship with my grandfather.

---

p. 136). Von Schnitzler's husband, Georg was on the board of the chemical conglomerate IG Farben, and was later convicted as a Nazi war criminal.

[1175] On April 18, 1958 Wolfgang Sauerlander wrote an internal memo in which he noted that the style and mode of presentation of the first hundred pages—namely, Jung's own memoir—didn't fit with the rest of the book. He found Jung's memoir so exceptional that he suggested that it be kept intact. It "will be helpful for many people in their difficulties in life and faith and they can awaken belief if they are able to put such difficulties aside. It is an inner success story, combined with *Pilgrim's Progress*." He suggested that the book be split in two: (1) Jung's autobiography, and (2) The protocols of the Interviews enlarged through seminars. The second part could begin with an addendum from the Interviews about Jung's youth. Some things could be directly added, such as the two pivotal dreams Jung recounted to Aniela Jaffé (BL).

On April 20, Kurt Wolff proposed an arrangement to Jaffé: "Part 1, the autobiography, Part 2, the Protocols, arranged in the following chapters: 1) the forebears; 2) Freud; 3) Years of seeking (Red/Black); 4) Contemporaries; 5) Therapist and Teacher; 6) Travels; 7) Late Dreams, Thoughts and Knowledge." (BL).

[1176] This meeting was at Bollingen.

[1177] See above, p. 143.

I have some letters from her brother, the legal counsel Kestner who lived in Rome and in whose arms Karl August von Goethe died.[1178] I even presume that this *Carl* Gustav might even be another Carl August.[1179]

In 1936 I wrote about the Mass.[1180] That engaged me enormously and I wrote the whole thing in the summer, and when I was still working on it—the main part was already written—I found myself in a hugely emotional state. I was unusually moved and of course I was thinking about the fish symbol at that time. Later *Aion* came out of this.[1181] And at that time, at the back in this small waterhole in the outside wall, I found a meter-long snake hanging stock still above a branch with its head in the water. Then I saw that it had a fish in its mouth. I thought: Good God, there are no fish in this hole! The fish was bigger than the mouth of the snake, it was a young perch. How on earth did this fish get here? This is what happened: the snake went into the lake to have a drink, and while doing so it caught this fish. Now the perch had spikes on its fins and it raised them in its mouth thus killing the snake. The perch was already decaying, but not the snake. The spikes of the fish were dug deep into its head so it could not swallow. It had probably tried for many hours in torment.[1182]

And now just think: the fish is the symbol of Christian love and it perishes because it is eaten by the chthonic black snake. But the snake also perishes. And it is like this because the snake and the fish are pure opposites, they are, as it were, the unconscious early forms, the opposites on the animalistic level. [361/362]

The fish refers to the communion meal,[1183] and is also a symbol of Christ. The black snake is a symbol of mercury, it is the philosophical animal of alchemy.[1184] They both perish together because the one is the pure opposite of the other. There is no connection. As a symbol the black snake is something very wicked, evil. It is a dark spirit. The fish as a symbol is something that is only good. Both are unconscious opposites, as if the theriomorphic background of Christianity had not been recognized: the animalistic, instinctual nature of good. Since I was working on the

---

[1178] Goethe's son Carl was born in 1795 and died after two weeks.

[1179] Referring, that is, to Jung's paternal grandfather Carl Gustav.

[1180] Jung presented his work on the Mass in a lecture at the Eranos conference in 1940, "Transformation Symbolism in the Mass" (*CE* 16; *CW* 11).

[1181] *Aion* (1951), *CE* 21; *CW* 9.2.

[1182] Jung related this episode to Wolfgang Pauli in a letter of January 13, 1951: see Meier, *Atom and Archetype*, pp. 68–69.

[1183] Deriving from the "Last Supper."

[1184] See "The Spirit Mercurius" (1943), *CE* 18; *CW* 13.

Eucharist at just that time, this was a truly synchronistic event. I buried the snake properly and placed a gravestone over it. And here (next to the entrance door) I carved it in stone with the fish in its mouth and made an inscription for it.[1185]

Here in Bollingen I can work creatively because the atmosphere here is completely undisturbed and I live together with the spirits of my ancestors. Here I am surrounded by things that are timeless, that contain both past and present. And the living past surrounds me. That is why creative ideas come to me, because they are things that have been there for centuries as unanswered questions, and equally they extend out into the future as questions. Just as they reach into the past, so they also reach into the future, for all that is past also points into the future.

The appearance of the UFO myth, for example, is the past concentrated, but which appears in the most contemporary form and in an unexpected place.[1186]

The family archives were burned in the destruction of Mainz in 1688. Lassaux.[1187]

The concept of the archetype is the Platonic idea, that things had a primal image in heaven. That corresponds somewhat to the archetype. The next entry point was Jacob Burckhardt. He wrote letters to his friend Brenner that *Faust* is a primeval image residing in the soul of the German. Burckhardt was the grandfather of a friend of mine. I knew the family and consequently I read these letters.[1188]

The dream of the storm where I discovered the shadow, where I had to safeguard the light against the storm.[1189] That was a type of anxiety dream. Then, when I was fourteen years old, I had made a poem about a storm, but there I described the storm in the positive sense.[1190] Independently

---

[1185] See C. G. Jung, *Word and Image*, ed. Aniela Jaffé, Bollingen Series 97.2 (Princeton, NJ: Princeton University Press, 1979), p. 142. Jung's Latin inscription can be translated, "The snake suffocates as it has swallowed too large a fish. In this manner both perished, as proof that the mass and the great work are the same and, likewise, are not the same, for their death was an event that occurred concurrently with my observation of it and its analogy. In memory of this fact I placed this inscription in the year 1936 CGJ."

[1186] See above, p. 271.

[1187] Presumably a reference to Virginie de Lassaux (see below, p. 373).

[1188] Jung cited the letter in question in *Transformations and Symbols of the Libido* (1912), CE 6; CW B, § 56n (as published in the *Basler Jahrbuch* in 1901).

[1189] See above, pp. 76–77.

[1190] See n. 315 above.

from the dream, and it was also not at the same time, but some months later when I got intimations of the violence of the storm, terribly cold.

The murder fantasy opened my eyes to how much I was bound to my mother.[1191] When I returned home, I found that nothing had happened and that was quite a remarkable feeling. Then the idea came to me that it was connected to the fact that I must soon go away again. The loss of my mother and sister then came in actuality, and this translated itself into this anxiety. Our time of being together now came to an end. It was terribly difficult to leave my mother behind alone. I was very attached to her and to my sister. I had taken on the role of the father. It seemed to me like a sacrilege that I had to leave my mother behind, but I could do nothing else. That came to me in this image. I was then completely convinced: you'll enter the house and there'll be a bloodbath. This idea came over me quite suddenly.

[1192]I never had the idea of making a chapel, but I wanted to create a place for myself where I could absent myself and that was for me, and where I was lost in reverie, a type of meditation room, like in Indian houses where a family member can withdraw for half or a quarter of an hour in order to do yoga exercises. That is necessary in India because people live so densely together. So they need a room for seclusion. For us Europeans that is perhaps the WC. One is not very clear how many good ideas have been born in the WC! This retreat, that is very contemptuous, but it is indeed a sort of seclusion room, an *adytum*.[1193] No one is allowed inside. [363/364] There in the chapel I am for myself and only very few are permitted inside. There is nothing to behold and I have the keys with me always. No one else enters. I have everything on the walls that leads me into solitude.[1194]

For example, there is a nice corner in the grounds of Schloss Arlesheim.[1195] That's a country house from the eighteenth century, there is a bench in a romantic place, and there it's written: *o beata solitudo, o sola solitudo!*[1196] That sums it up.

I thought about writing that on the external wall. But then I wrote the saying of Saint Ambrose, "In Patientia vestra habetis animas vestras."[1197] It

---

[1191] See above, pp. 75, 78.

[1192] See *ETG*, p. 227, *MDR*, p. 224.

[1193] *adytum*: the inner sanctum of Greek and Roman temples.

[1194] A reference to the murals Jung painted on the walls of his chapel.

[1195] The Schloss Birseck in Arlesheim, near Basel, which was a hermitage.

[1196] In fact "O beata solitudo, o sola beatitudo" (O happy solitude, o sole happiness) is inscribed on the rock at Schloss Birseck above the bench.

[1197] "By patience you possess your souls": cf. Luke 21:19.

is a meditation corner, even for a very unpleasant meditation. Everything is contained within it that takes me out of time, out of the present and the idea that[1198]

The first time I felt this type of peculiar reverie was in the crypt of Oberzell on the Reichenau.[1199] I used to go on pilgrimage there as a young man. That was my "place." The small crypt.

Always in the holidays when I was a student. It was my regular pilgrimage each spring or each summer, when I made that journey. That transposed me—one could also call it a grave—outside of the world, into the non-temporal, into eternity. That is located deep in the vineyards, and that gave me the idea when I built the "chapel." It was also supposed to be a sort of grave.

The African house centers around the fire, and there are compartments designed for the small livestock, the chickens and goats, so that the other section, about three quarters of the house, is inhabited by the family. The entire existence plays out around the center. There are a couple of larger stones, three or four, and then they make a fire and place a pot inside. That made a very strong impression on me as an idea of family wholeness: there is the fire, the cooking place where they eat, where they sleep, and in the evening at 6 p.m. the home shuts down. Then everything is inside, and that's an idea of wholeness where even the animals have a place, and this idea or this image inspired me when I made it.[1200] [364/365] I wanted to make this real, or something like it: a dwelling corresponding to the primal feeling of the human being, and to the feeling of protection, not only physical but also psychically. It's a symbol of wholeness actualized. That is, the food and fireplace in the center. And around them are the family and livestock. Outside is the kraal sheltering the larger animals, which again is enclosed by an impregnable hedge of "wait-a-bit-thorn":[1201] whoever lands in that must wait!

Then I saw that that there is actually nothing.

[1202](The middle house in Bollingen was raised by one storey): that is, the *I* becomes an expression of this threefold wholeness, and with it the actual situation is determined, and then the fourth one followed,

---

[1198] This line breaks off in mid-sentence.

[1199] St. Georg in Oberzell on Reichenau Island on Lake Constance in Germany is a late Carolingian church (tenth century). In its crypt is supposedly a fragment of the skull of Saint George.

[1200] "it": the tower.

[1201] A plant with sharp thorns: the name is given in English in the original.

[1202] Cf. *ETG*, p. 229, *MDR*, p. 225; and see Bennet, *Meetings with Jung* June 20, 1951 (p. 31).

externally. The strange thing was that I did not know that they are actually three structures working out the idea of a threefold unity.

Afterwards I found that it corresponds precisely to the idea of the origins of the Trinity: the Father is the greatest and then comes the Son, and then the Holy Ghost, and that is the smallest![1203] I built the house as a whole.

Every individual motif grew *in situ* out of itself, I did not think about it. I only followed the local requirements. It is something that arose from the form, from the shape. Only afterwards did I see everything that had happened there. I had done it in a sort of dream. It is like an imagination, a type of daydream arising out of itself, and afterwards I saw what had emerged there.

Genesis of the Stone

[1204]When I built the boundary wall at the back I needed to order stones. In my presence the builder dictated the quantity to the stonemason, and he wrote it in a little notebook. When the stones came, with this *soi-disant*[1205] cornerstone it became evident that he had the completely wrong quantity: instead of a ten-cornered stone he had brought an eight-cornered stone, a perfect cube, of much larger dimensions than had been ordered. The builder was furious and said to the boatmen who had brought the stones that they could take it right back with them. When I saw the stone I said, "No, that's my stone. It's exactly the one I must have." I had immediately seen it was a cube and that suited me, I wanted to do something with it, but I didn't yet know what.—The first thing that occurred to me was that verse of Arnaldus de Villanova: "lapis, exilis, lapis."[1206]

[1203] Cf. Jung, "An Attempt at a Psychological Interpretation of the Dogma of the Trinity" (1942), *CE* 16; *CW* 11.

[1204] See *ETG*, p. 230, *MDR*, p. 226.

[1205] *soi-disant*, in French in the original: "so-called."

[1206] "lapis, exilis, lapis": literally, "stone, slender, stone" In *ETG* and *MDR* the citation was given in full in translation. In English it runs,

Here stands the stone, the unprepossessing.
In terms of price it was cheap—
It is scorned by the dumb,
But all the more is it loved by those who know.

Arnaldus de Villanova was a thirteenth- to early fourteenth-century physician, religious reformer, and alchemist, of unknown provenance, but writing mostly in Catalan. The citation was from the *Rosarium* in the *Artis auriferae volumina duo*, p. 210. Jung referred to it in *Psychology and Alchemy* (1944), *CE* 17; *CW* 12, § 246n, noting that this may be of significant in relation to Wolfram von Eschenbach's (1170–1220) naming of the Grail stone as

That's the saying related to the Holy Grail of Wolfram von Eschenbach. That was known to me and what was also known to me was this eye, the mandala, in the form of a pupil, the little doll stands within it, that is the little girl, a type of Kabir, namely the Telesphoros of Asklepios. But he is cloaked in a cowl, and he appeared as a lantern carrier, corresponding to an antique statue and at the same time he is a guide.[1207]

It occurred to me only afterwards when I was thinking about the stone. I kept seeing it over and over again and I always wondered about it and asked myself: What could it mean that one does such a thing at all? It is outside the tower, and an explanation of it, as it were. It is a manifestation of the tower's inhabitant, which in fact people find incomprehensible. And then it came to me: that is "le cri de Merlin":[1208] in other words, his manifestation in the world after he had already vanished into the one world. Then one still heard this manifestation, which however one cannot interpret. There is no telling what sort of state that is. Some assume that he was crazy because, for them, life with the unconscious is inexplicable anyway. [366/367] That is one of my most impressive experiences: how strange in fact that is for people.

How I trained myself to allow the unconscious to come, well, I also followed my blind impulse and carried it out as intelligently as possible. If I had thought: Now I will build a mandala, then I would never have arrived at the idea of representing the house as three plus one.

And then something like the stone; an eye simply stared out at me from it and out of that emerged the mandala.

The texts are also sort of like dreams, pieces out of reality that have merged together. Orphanus is an alchemical reminiscence, stitched together, but it is like a dream. While I have the work in my hands these things stitch themselves together. Only the Arnaldus de Villanova is a quotation.[1209] [367/368]

---

the "Lapsit exillis" in his *Parzival* (see the next paragraph). While most Grail legends refer to the Grail as a cup or dish, Eschenbach describes it as a stone.

[1207] Telesphoros is one of the Kabiri, and the daimon of Aesklepios: see, *Psychology and Alchemy* (1944), CE 17; CW 12, fig. 77. He was also regarded as a God of healing, and had a temple at Pergamon in Asia Minor.

[1208] "le cri de Merlin," in French in the original: "the cry of Merlin." See above, p. 223.

[1209] See above. For the inscriptions on the stone, see *Art of C. G. Jung*, cat. no. 64, (pp. 160–63). Jung can be seen carving and commenting on it in a short unfinished film by Jerome Hill, *C. G. Jung, or Lapis Philosophorum* (available on YouTube: https://bit.ly/LapisPhilosphorum [accessed April 23, 2025]). To Maud Oakes, Jung wrote (January 31, 1956), "All the volumes I had written are 'in nuce' contained in it"; cited in Maud Oakes, *The Stone Speaks: The Memoir of a Personal Transformation* (Wilmette, IL: Chiron Publications, 1987), p. 17.

MAY 7, 1958

When I was in America for the first time it was still a land of pioneers, a land that had not yet filled out its borders. In my lifetime America has completely changed: it has found its borders in every regard. And with that, the question of American culture has only just begun. A pioneer nation must make do with what it has even if it is limited within its borders; it must strive for the completely other side, for the development of culture.

Today people want to transcend their boundaries: because the earth is over-populated, they want to travel to the moon. But the proton radiation of the sun and of other stars out in space, for example the Crab Nebula,—an exploded supernova—is such an incredible thing; if one were to go there—one could live for only five hours. The radiation is one hundred times more than one expected in theory. That is one thousand, six hundred kilometers from the earth. Up to that height the atmosphere still offers protection. It made me anxious to think that it is much less dangerous. But one could not know that in advance. In this way, the greatest longing of man to extend out beyond the self is discouraged. It must no longer continue in the same sense. There is a chance that it will turn inwards.[1210]

[368/369]

[1210] On May 12, 1958 Kurt Wolff wrote to Aniela Jaffé asking whether she thought the issue of Jung and Nazism should be put in the book, forwarding a letter from Cary Baynes on the subject. The issue had resurfaced in a piece in *The New York Times Book Review* the previous day. The April 20 issue featured Joost Merloo's laudatory front-page review of Jung's *Psychology and Religion* ([1938], CE 15; CW 11), and *The Undiscovered Self* ([1957], CE 25; CW 10), "What Makes a Man What He Is? Unlike Freud, Jung seeks the Answer in Our Culture's Myths and Symbols." Merloo had passingly referred to Jung being "infected by the collective mysticism of the Nazi ideology" (pp. 1 and 18). The May 11 edition ran a number of letters picking up on this, criticizing Jung in this regard. One exception was a letter by Irving Fisher, who noted "when he visited New Haven in 1937 [Jung] was a guest in my parents' home. He was outspoken in deploring the rise of the Nazis." (pp. 26–27). Wolff also asked Jaffé to have Jung speak on Charcot (BL).
   On May 16 Jaffé replied that she had given the Nazism issue much thought, particularly after Merloo's article and the ensuing correspondence, but found Cary Baynes's letter discouraging in his regard. She continued, "I personally consider Jung to have integrity in this issue. I began my analysis with him in the most terrible period of the Nazi years and, at the beginning, the Jewish question was dominant. Given my horrendous sensitivity in this area, if I had sensed even a hint of this, I would have run a mile [. . .]. J.'s current attitude to National Socialism is of course also an unusual one [. . .]. If that were to be in the biography it would be completely misunderstood by those who think in years or decades, but not by those who think in centuries. But for Jung, Nazism was never anything other than a devilish affair." However, she did think of asking Jung why he thought the rumor about his

MAY 16, 1958

[1211]I spent fourteen days with the Taos Pueblos in the winter, so at the end of December or the beginning of January 1925. What impression did it make on me? Well, all the things that are in every travel journal. There are mountains there, higher than two thousand meters. The view of the mountains and the whole landscape is incredibly impressive. I drove up the valley of the Rio Grande by car and it was exceptionally cold. In the morning the sun shone, but snow lay on the ground. And so we traveled to the Pueblos. Their village has the skyline of a miniature American city. The houses are five to six storeys high and one goes up ladders to reach them. All are built of adobe mudbricks, that is, lime with straw. All the houses there are made of them. The storeys, they are simply huts built on top of each other, one climbs ladders made of tree trunks with cross steps, so one climbs up crude ladders on the outside. In each hut, so on every storey, lives a family. Mostly it is only one room, sometimes there is an

---

sympathies hadn't gone away. Regarding other issues, she related that "he was unwilling to speak about the Indians. But there was some great stuff about Africa. One could call Africa his spiritual experience." (BL).

On May 18 she wrote a follow-up letter to Wolff. She had taken up the Nazism issue with Jung, following the letters to the editor that she had shown him. She asked if he wanted to address this, but he declined, saying that "he had set the story straight about these things many times. He was not able to stop this witch-hunt and did not want to get into it." She was considering asking him where he stood on Israel, knowing that he had a positive view on this and that this "will generally have a very positive effect for the Jews."

She informed Wolff that she would be sending the previous Friday's protocol, and explained that "my method of questioning has changed somewhat recently. Perhaps it is related to the smaller matters, perhaps to Jung's mood or exhaustion. I explain to him broadly what I would like to know and then I wait. It is not at all easy then to say nothing, or to ask, but I observe precisely how he sinks down into himself and then it comes: a memory, or an emotion. And then the silence returns. Sometimes for a long time. And then towards the end of the afternoon he becomes very enlivened, when the vein has been found and it flows.—At the beginning it was quite different, when there was still so much. Africa satisfied him then and in the morning he said to me he recalled letters to his wife from India and Africa which I could use. I was not to forget! [. . .] I repeatedly ask—by the way, even in office hours, if we are speaking about the biography—about 'external data' and remind him of them. But I fear that this will only yield a meagre harvest. As you will see, I had already made an attempt with Zimmer."

Finally, she noted that she saw certain dangers in the biography which she wanted to discuss with Wolff (BL).

On May 9, 1958 Jung wrote to Cary Baynes, "When one begins to write one's biography, one knows that one is behind the times." (JP).

[1211] See *ETG*, p. 250, *MDR*, p. 247. Jung had written of his experiences in New Mexico in a manuscript entitled "Afrikanische Reise" (JP). On this, see Shamdasani, *Jung and the Making of Modern Psychology*, pp. 317–18, and William McGuire, "Jung in America, 1924–1925," *Spring: An Annual of Archetypal Psychology and Jungian Thought*, 1978: 37–53.

anteroom too. One goes forwards down these ladders whereas we Europeans climb down a ladder backwards. When they saw how I descended the ladder they laughed and said I belonged to the "bear totem" as I did it the same as the bears who also climbed down backwards![1212] In this village I was received by Ochwiay Biano, which means Mountain Lake.[1213] He was a man of above average intelligence, that means above average when compared with the Indians. I had quite a good conversation with him. For example, about their ceremonies. And I also had that extremely interesting conversation with him about the Americans that I have so often related. But that is all completely uninteresting, I have written that countless times. It was an experience for me that I was able to see the world through his eyes: for example, that they do not describe themselves as Americans, but they are "the people who live on the roof of the world." If the Americans did not stop disturbing them in their religious observances (through missionary work) then in ten years the sun would no longer rise. The sun is their father and they (the Indians) help him to rise. The sun is not made by God, it *is* God. And then the other conversation: What is the matter with the Americans? They are crazy, they think with the head and not with the heart. His sorrow made an impression on me, that he was not able to join in with the dances because he had missed the initiation ceremony where he would have been able to identify with the sun. That was naturally an experience: to hear a man speaking about his religious convictions and his fear that the Americans might take these things away from him. They are already Christians and the dead are buried according to proper Christian rites. [369/370] The Mass is said by a Mexican priest who, from time to time, comes up there and also baptizes the children. But each time a dead person is consecrated according to Christian rites, then the corresponding Indian ceremonies are carried out, and only then are things right. They have a dance, the buffalo dance, they danced it into the vestibule of the church. Antonio Mirabal, that was the "civil" name of Ochwiay Biano—all the Indians had a Spanish name along with their Indian names—, that was a real

---

[1212] See *ETG*, p. 251, *MDR*, p. 247.

[1213] Antonio (or Tony) Mirabal (Ochwiay Biano: "Mountain Lake") was a member of the Taos Pueblo Council. As is borne out by his correspondence with Chauncey Goodrich, he was fluent in English, and actively campaigned in defense of the Pueblos, who had been succumbing to moonshine whisky (Goodrich Papers, Bancroft Library, University of California, San Francisco). See Willow Young, "Eros and the Value of Relatedness: The Lineage of an Enduring Friendship Between Carl Jung and Ochwiay Biano," *Psychological Perspectives* 63 (2020): pp. 441–57.

encounter, and this is why it's hard to describe. We sat for hours with each other on the roof of Pueblo, while the others stood for hours on the roofs in order to identify with the sun. We spoke of the sun and of the dead. What the others did, we discussed with words. Then there's a quickening of something primeval in oneself and suddenly one sees things differently. There are countless details on such a journey that one can hardly relate, the way in which people speak to each other, there is so much familiar and so much that is foreign. I ate with people and spent time in their houses. I was able to speak much better with the Pueblos than with the negroes. The negroes I saw, that was still pure wilderness.

I can hardly express what I experienced in Africa. From the very beginning the idea moved me that I would need to be an artist to express it. It was my first encounter with original timeless primitives, that was when I was in the Mombasa plateau. I awoke in the train and pulled back the curtain from the window and we were traveling through a small valley. Above, there was a small terrace in the rock and there stood, stock still, a negro with two spears, completely naked, or with only a belt, and he was like a part of the landscape. The rocks were reddish and a there was a huge euphorbia there, quite dark and high up in the reddish rocks, and a tropical sun was shining—it was below the equator—and with the sight of the negro I was as if transposed into the tertiary age and now: describe that! One cannot describe these emotions at all, one was simply enchanted. This feeling accompanied me in many places in Africa: I thanked heaven that I got to see the living primeval world. I had the feeling that I had been transposed about a hundred thousand years into history, and that produced a curious feeling in me. As a white man I always had to remain conscious of myself. [370/371] On the other side I lived in an unconscious identity with everything, I was transposed into a *participation mystique*, where man and beast and everything belonged together. It was a tremendous unity. There was no dissonance in it, no stylistic flaw. Nowhere had the consciousness of culture sparked into it. Every time I found the trace of the white man, for example when the women carried petrol canisters on their heads instead of earthenware pots, a jolt went through me, as with a wild animal that suddenly encounters the scent of a human: Damn it, now we have entered a reminder of cultural life and have a splinter in the foot! This all sounds so exaggerated, because that primeval time was actual, and it was like a beautiful dream where suddenly a disharmonious wailing of a gramophone rang out in the midst, or something like that. That was not some romantic atmosphere or the like, there was also an incredible brutality in it and a massive futility. There are these

squillions of animals who nod their heads and eat, are born and die, that
goes on for millions of years, and gatherings of little huts stick like wasp
nests on the slopes of the hills. And that is a world at peace with itself, that
is complete, all of massive futility and infinitely beautiful brutality. It was
as if I had fallen altogether outside time. Then of course I had to return
and think about what we are going to eat and where to buy provisions,
and that we were supposed to go here or there. And then suddenly I heard
my friends speaking English and that was all terribly irritating, that these
white swine are in the middle of it all who belong to a completely different
time, and that was also true of myself, I was this crazy disturbance. And if
I was not that, then this whole experience would not be present, and that
is all incredibly emotional. Something in which one would like to remain
forever. I could not imagine that I would never wish to go back there. I
wanted always to return, over and over again, it is too wonderful! But that
originates only where the circumstances are how they always were.

One can be ten years in Africa and never experience something like
that if one entrenches oneself against it in a European way. But something
in me found an open door to this experience and only that made this
experience possible. It is of course a synchronization with the primitive
consciousness [371/372] where actually nothing is, that it is *only* like
this, there are everywhere countless possibilities among them and everywhere one also encounters the scent of the wondrous, one might say!
But of course, one can experience this everywhere. I have also experienced it in the Alps, in lonely places where nature prevails. Then after a
little time nature also begins to prevail in oneself. It is always a sort of
abaissement du niveau mental.[1214] In civilized life, one is always either
collected and expended energy, or expending and spending energy. As if
you had a full purse from which you are constantly paying. But there, in
nature, one is not heaped up, but on the contrary one has become empty
and the other is heaped up. One no longer gives out, but rather it flows
towards one. The potential is reversed. It is not I who deal with nature,
but rather nature deals with me.

So many people in the Tropics turn to drink. It is boring for them, they
are homesick, and that is an expression of the emptiness. One is emptied
there, and nature is overwhelming. This is why it is so important if one is
in such places for a long time to keep the necessary activities in mind: for
example, retaining their European customs. One gets shaved and dresses

---

[1214] *abaissement du niveau mental,* in French in the original: "lowering of the mental
level." Jung adopted this term from Pierre Janet.

formally every evening. I knew two brothers in Africa; they had a farm in the middle of nowhere. They lived alone, but every evening they dressed for dinner and that is how they remained in form. Others, they go black,[1215] which means they become empty and then are absorbed by the environment; that is, they become completely unconscious and do not notice what is happening. But I wanted to see what was happening in me if I am open to this primeval world.[1216] It interested me that I have never dreamed of negroes except once, but that was of my barber in America; in the dream he wanted to curl my hair with some tongs. My unconscious wanted to protect me at all costs by bringing me dreams of home. They all concerned things that were happening at home. By the way, one also saw that a lot in the war, that people dreamed a lot of home. It was also a principle among military psychiatrists: if someone dreams too many scenes of war, they were ready for a holiday because he no longer had any psychic defense against the impressions. I was closest to "going black" when I dreamed that the negro wanted to make my hair kinky (or crinky).[1217]

Two friends accompanied me to Africa. One was a young American.[1218] Before we departed, he had a dream [372/373] that he was in Africa hunting and suddenly a mamba snake convulses itself in front of him; that's a terrifying cobra. He did not tell me the dream because he thought that this dream signified my death. How he got there I cannot understand. When we were in the bush for the second day, in nowhere land, one morning he went hunting. It was terribly hot there, below the equator. And he set off very early and at 10 a.m. he returned to the camp. He looked terrible and was shaking so much that he could not speak. In vain I tried to get out of him what had happened. Then the trackers, or the escorts who make the trail, returned and they told me what had happened, and then gradually he found his capacity to speak returning. So, they had been walking between old termite mounds. The entire land there is *mammelonné*[1219] by these mounds that are between two and three meters high. They are round mounds between which one can stalk the game. So they were walking between these mounds up to a group of trees where guinea-fowl were sitting and suddenly one of the escorts shouted, "Hatari!" That's an alarm call. "Matari nyoka!" That means: Snake! And he ran away. My friend saw nothing but suddenly he sees a large mamba

---

1215 "go black": in English in the original.
1216 See *ETG*, pp. 275–76, *MDR*, p. 272.
1217 See too above, p. 213. "kinky" and "crinky" (*sic*): in English in the original.
1218 George Beckwith. See n. 815 above.
1219 *mammelonné*, in French in original: "dimpled/covered in hummocks."

slipping down from a mound and, at a distance of two meters, he shot it. The negroes said it was seven or eight feet long. A mamba as thick as an arm! That would have been the certain death of my friend if he had not been able to shoot it and injure it. It then crept into a rat hole. In the forest these snakes are dark and in the grassland they are green.

My friend told me of his dream only after this experience. It naturally made a big impression on me for it was an absolute mortal danger. If you are bitten by a mamba then it is absolutely: Good night!

When we came to the Nile we traveled through the contaminated areas. The tsetse fly was there, along with sleeping sickness. This friend was always rather reckless. I said to him that he must put on his mosquito boots every day towards six o'clock. Because the malarial flies mostly bite humans on the ankle. Once we were guests of the governor of Uganda, and a row of petroleum lamps were burning on the table there and just as many under the table so that the ladies were able to wear pretty stockings. For the malarial fly only bites when it is dark.—My friend always tried to forget the danger. I also tried to get his servant boy to give him the mosquito boots on time. One evening when we went for dinner in Redjaf, that is in South Sudan, the highest place a Nile steamer can reach beneath the fast ships; we were there for some time. [373/374] And there were incredible, brilliant moonlit nights, and he went for a walk along the banks of the Nile. He came home at around 7.30 instead of at seven o'clock, and I saw that he was not wearing mosquito boots. I gave him a proper telling off and predicted that he would one day catch a dangerous malaria. And that is what happened. Eleven days later he had serious attacks and nearly died from it. He was taken to hospital in Paris for two to three months in order to recover. Half a year later he returned to America and the next thing I heard, after some months, was that he was driving in the car with his sister. She was at the wheel, and on a bend, she drove down the embankment and he was killed.[1220]

What was curious was this: every time we encountered snakes, he was present. We had two more adventures with mambas, and he was the first there. He was the one who found a snake in his trousers when he wanted to get up in the morning. The snake had slept under his bed! The negroes said he attracted snakes. But that came from this moment, from the first encounter, and he had the first dream about it! He was a charming chap, a gentleman![1221]

[1220] Beckwith died in a car accident in 1931.
[1221] "a gentleman": in English in the original.

Such things are part of Africa. That is life and death, and every day is, in a certain sense, a risk. One sees it so clearly! There is no evasion. One must only be skillful enough to get through, or to have a clue about possibilities.

I cannot say that I never felt fear. When I danced with the negroes there, I certainly felt fear. A kindly spirit gave me the right way of managing them. That was precisely the right language and it amused them no end.

I was in the Mau Mau region. At that time there was of course nothing of that as yet, that was still the old Africa.

Talking of Africa: the experience of Africa is actually the experience of endless primeval time, and that was wonderful.

[1222]For example, there is another point: I got up at dawn every morning and then I ate breakfast immediately and afterwards I put myself in the shade of a tree, on a camp chair. Beneath our camp there was a small valley and on the other side the terrain ascended again. In the valley below there was primeval forest, above it extended grassland with individual silk trees. And when I sat there every morning, I heard the bellbird flying around the whole horizon.[1223] I believed I was going to die of homesickness if I heard that sound again. That was simply wonderful. And then when the sun gradually gained strength—it rises at 6 a.m., and by 7.30 the air is already shimmering a little. And then in the strong sunlight everything became as if made of glass, everything became self-luminous, and then I heard that bird as if a small bell were ringing, a beautiful clear bell sound. I knew that I must carry out this ritual every morning, of sitting there and listening. If we were not on expedition. That was always the most delightful thing. And nearby there were baboons, large apes who lived in the high rocks. They sat there every morning like I did, on the sunny side and I always remembered the great Kynoke-hali, these Egyptian figures, in Abu Simbel, making the gestures of adoration. And they sat above on the rocks, exactly as I did, and probably saw the same as I. That sounds crazy, but back then I felt: Yes, yes, that is how it has always been! I don't know how many thousand years were resonating inside me at the sound of the bellbird. That was not the sound of millennia but of millions of years, of geological time. There I was and outside there were the apes on the rock ridge: we are the same people, dwellers in this region, and we are experiencing essentially the

---

[1222] See *ETG*, pp. 271–72, *MDR*, p. 268.
[1223] Probably referring to the bell-shrike (*Laniarius aethiopicus*), also known as the "boubou," from its distinctive call.

same thing. And these apes of Abu Simbel always tell the same story: time out of mind we venerated this great God who redeems the world by bathing it in a radiant heavenly light out of the great darkness.

One can only stammer when one attempts to portray these things. One cannot do it justice at all.—But these were the essential fruits of Africa.

Before Africa, but at least seven years before, I had a dream that I was climbing a giant tree from the primeval forest and I was pulling myself up with my arms, and I had very short legs.[1224] And when I was sitting upon the tree—do you know, that was a tree, a cotton-wool tree, a giant tree about a hundred meters high—then it suddenly occurred to me, I was fearful that the forester would be able to see me and would shoot me down. Not because I was an ape, but because I had played the "ape" without justification, as if that were a sin! [375/376]

You must imagine that these experiences—the morning atmosphere, the apes on the sunny side of the rocks, the advent of the great night—all this had an undertone of a terrific melancholy and an inexpressible homesickness afterwards. I then understood when one gazes into the eyes of a cow or into the eyes of any type of animal, one senses this grief within. In the eyes of an animal is a grief and one does not know: is it in the eye of the animal or is it a painful sense being portrayed by that being? That is the atmosphere of Africa, of the solitudes of Africa. One can also see it in the eyes of primitives. That is the experience I had in Africa.—I naturally did not know beforehand that it would be that—that was the satisfying experience, the satisfactory answer.[1225] And that was worth more to me than an ethnological harvest where one can show weapons and cooking pots and God only knows what. That is all insignificant. I wanted to know how Africa affects me.

My dreams stood, one and all, on the side of the conscious I, and not on the side of primeval darkness[1226] or of the maternal mystery. I was always disappointed by my dreams. I would have expected that the unconscious would realize this opportunity with joy. But no, not at all!

[1227]This is what I took from it: in the soul resides a longing for light and an inalienable urge to escape the primary darkness. Hence the overwhelming experience of the primitives is the birth of the sun in the morning. God is when it becomes light. One thinks that is an incredibly ab-

---

[1224] No other source relating this dream has been located.

[1225] "the satisfactory answer": in English in the original.

[1226] "primeval darkness": in English in the original.

[1227] ETG, p. 272, MDR, p. 269.

stract thought: not that the sun is God, but the moment the sun appears is God. That is a primeval experience of the moment. The primeval moment is already forgotten when they think the *sun* is God.

That was so immeasurably impressive to me, to encounter this formulation in these people, in this state of primeval darkness to perceive the sunrise as redemptive. They naturally have no explanation for it. "We are glad that the night where the spirits are abroad is now ending." These are rationalizations. In actuality a very different darkness encumbers the land than natural night: it is primeval night, the countless millions of years where it always was as it is today. And then we came to Egypt with the cult of newly created light, of Horus. [376/377]

The myth of Horus is again the story of divine light that was told after it revealed itself out of the primeval darkness of prehistoric times for the first time as redemption through culture. For me, the journey was a drama, one could say of the birth of light, that was connected to me in the most intimate way, with my psychology. That was tremendously illuminating to me. On the other hand, I felt completely incapable of capturing it in words. That said nothing at all to other people! I know that what means something to me means nothing whatsoever to others, so I have never attempted to capture it in words. I would not have been able to bear it if they thought I had invented it: that the Elgonyi had this religion, that God is the blink of an eye.[1228] No one knows that, and now it is already lost anyway. And just think: the young man who accompanied me was the sacrifice and the other one went mad! That is the experience of Africa! The one died from the light, as it were, by the birth of the sun that one experiences in Africa, and the other went mad from it.

Or think: this encounter with the snake, that is a mythological encounter of the first order. Think of the "petit prince,"[1229] who was bitten by the snake when he came to earth. And this American was a "petit prince" like in the book.

The other was already abnormal back then: he uttered nothing more or only very little.[1230] And he began to get affectations. He later died of a

---

[1228] "Elgonyi" refers to the people who lived around Mount Elgon on the Kenya/Uganda border. These comprised the Bagisu, Mbay, Sor, Sapiiny, Koony, Someek, Pook, and Ogiek tribes.

[1229] A reference to the novella by Antoine de Saint-Exupéry, first published in 1943.

[1230] H. G. Baynes (1882–1943; a.k.a. Peter), analytical psychologist and friend of Jung. In Zurich, Baynes worked as an analytical assistant for Jung from 1919 to 1922 and translated several of his works into English. Just before their African trip, his wife Hilda had committed suicide. In Baynes's obituary, John Layard described him as "the leader of the Jung school of analytical psychology in England. His chief interest was not always,

brain tumor. When we were in the camp (I shared a tent with others, and he had a tent to himself) suddenly a shot was heard. The young American immediately jumped out and ran to the other man's tent. When he came back he said (and it sounded as if he were disappointed), "I thought he blew his brains out, but it was the headman cleaning his rifle!"[1231]

We tiptoed around each other and when we were marching, we always left a distance of about two hundred meters between us.[1232] When a European is alone among the Blacks one each becomes very sensitive towards the others anyway.

My impression of Africa: of a gray futility and an indescribable blessedness. [377/378]

I learned something else in Africa that I had confirmed in India: I was never able properly to understand Islam. When we were traveling down the Nile, we had two boats attached to the side of the steamer. A flat-bottomed steamer, a stern-wheeler. In the one boat lay a man who was ill, a Muslim. And from time to time, he cried out in the night, "Allah!" That resounded through the universe! Then I knew: So that's it!

In Delhi in the great mosque, I again heard this cry, "Allah!"[1233] A very far-reaching voice sang it, penetrating everything. That is Islam. I am convinced that this word "Allah" is a call in itself.[1234] Every muezzin begins his prayer with this cry.—And then on the Nile there was this penetrating voice reaching out into space; that was living Islam for me, that is an Eros! This Arabic flute or pipe also became comprehensible to me there, this horrible sounding music, but in the context of the desert I understood it. They go together, that is harmony. It would be too terrifying to hear an organ in the desert, for example. That would simply be terrible. This fantastic ugly wailing, then you hear this screeching music in the desert, and then you know: it is at home here. But if you heard an organ, you could go crazy.—After that I bought myself an Arabic record in order to

---

however, directed towards the intangible gossamer of the soul. He was a man well over six feet high, with breadth not belying his height, and with physical powers that gave him his 'blue' [award for competing at the highest level of sport at Cambridge University] and led him in his university days to row for Cambridge against both Harvard and Oxford." *Nature* 152 (1943), p. 406. His major work was *Mythology of the Soul: A Research into the Unconscious from Schizophrenic Dreams and Drawings* (London: Routledge and Kegan Paul, 1940). See Diana Jansen, *Jung's Apprentice: A Biography of Helton Godwin Baynes* (Einsiedeln: Daimon Verlag, 2003).

[1231] The quoted utterance is in English in the original.

[1232] *EG* corrects the distance to twenty meters (p. 41).

[1233] The Jama Masjid, built in 1656, is in the Old City in Delhi, which Jung visited in December 1937.

[1234] "in itself": "an sich" in the original.

remember. I can still hear it today, but only with the image of the night-time desert before my eyes. Then it's okay. Otherwise, it's not okay.

It's similar with Chinese music: you can listen to it only with the ancient images of the landscape, with the fine images of the Chinese land-scape, with an individually cultivated voice within it. It is a fine land-scape, and within that there's an individual *vox humana*.

But Arabic music cannot be explained at all without the desert, for there it has meaning, by God!

I have also heard Native American choirs, they are terribly discordant, but equally close to the desert.

Indian music is still only culture. They have a morning-midday-and-night melody in the way we have flats or sharps. One can even sing the same melody as a morning or night song![1235]

Among the Africans I have heard choirs, war dances: one even no-tices within them the possibility of bel canto, there are rudiments of beauty within it. Later it is the negro spirituals that bring this beauty fully to expression. [378/379] That is melodious, and I have already heard this among the primitives. These male-voice choirs were not at all bad. But what dominates in negro music is the rhythm. That is connected with the strongly motoric expression of the negro.
[391]

May 20, 1958

On the question of the "split" (pages 1–97)[1236]
[1237]The issue is not that one makes a diagnosis, but rather to see what one does with it. Otherwise, one would have to say that the religions that have always spoken to the "inner man," in contradistinction to the "outer man," have been talking rubbish. If anything, they consider this type of

---

[1235] Jung is referring to the ragas of classical Indian music, patterns of notes which comprise scales and melodies.

[1236] A reference to the interplay of personalities No. 1 and No. 2 described in the manu-script of "From the Earliest Experiences of my Life," to which Jaffé had added passages from the protocols of the Interviews. In *Reflections*, Jaffé noted, "After reading Jung's text, Wolff said he found the narrative form of a number 1 and number 2 somewhat alienating and also felt number 2 was disproportionately represented in our conversation notes. He asked Jung to talk and write more about number 1. To me, Wolff expressed concern that readers might perceive Jung as having a split personality with schizophrenic traits." She noted (p. 76) that Jung's comments here were in response to her report of Kurt Wolff's reaction.

[1237] See *ETG*, p. 51, *MDR*, p. 45.

person (namely, the "inner") as an average figure that is part of everyone. But that does not prove that all people (who have an "inner" and an "outer" person) are schizophrenic. If all people have the same illness, then it is a human characteristic and not an illness. All religions postulate something similar. Otherwise, there would never have been such a widespread phenomenon as "religion."

I am one who cannot be fitted into this dangerous schema and that is the meaning of my life, and I describe this preponderance (that is, from the perspective of the inner man), because it constitutes my life. But that too is what they do not understand.

If I were not to describe that, it would come forth as an apologia. But what I describe is a fact: I am that.

The meaning and the joke of such a biography would be completely lost if one had to squeeze that into a schema. My biography is created in this way. At the most one could say that I am a freak of nature.
[380]

May 23, 1958[1238]

Addition to "Works":
In 1916 work on the "Transcendent Function" and in 1913 a first edition of the *Types*.[1239] The work on the Transcendent Function has remained incomplete, I was half-hearted about it.

On "Red-Black"[1240]
Concept of the "scientific experiment":
It was as if I had undertaken a mescaline experiment where I am inside it without being objective. I could register objectively only what I was experiencing. I had no concepts with which I could comprehend this. It was not a philosophy, but nor was it an intoxication. I had absolutely nothing I could compare it to. It was something into which I surrendered myself

---

[1238] Jung was in Bollingen (*Reflections*, p. 186). This entry commences with Jung's remarks on Jaffé's recent draft chapters.

[1239] "The Transcendent Function" *(CE 8; CW 8)* was first published, in an English translation by A. R. Pope, in 1953 by the Student Association of the Jung Institute. In 1958 Jung published a lightly revised version in the *Festschrift* volume for the seventy-fifth birthday of Daniel Brody, the Rhein Verlag publisher: "A Contribution to the Study of Psychological Types" *(CE 7; CW 6)*.

[1240] Referring to Jung's earlier discussions of *The Red Book* and *The Black Books*. See above, pp. 245, 162–63 and 128–33.

of my own free will, and yet was trapped by as if I had experimented on myself with a toxin.[1241]

What depressed me was the constant disagreeable feeling: instead of now delivering scientific works, I am going after these phenomena. But I wanted to explore whether there was a thread, a meaning within it. I also had to grasp this for my patients. I saw many patients who had similar fantasies; they had them because they were neurotic or psychotic whereas I myself was clear about the fact that (for me) that was not a neurosis, rather I was seeking out this material to capture it objectively as far as possible and to develop my ideas about how to evaluate it. It was all unduly foreign to me. From it I understood that schizophrenic patients are overrun by this material and lose their orientation, and that neurotics seek in vain to repress such fantasies. I would also have been able to repress it if I had wished to do so. But if one wants to know, it must simply unfold. And when it happens to you, then you are simply inside it.

(Question: what was *his* myth?) (Supplement to "Red-Black")[1242]
What my fantasies showed me was a matter of the actualization of the inner man who appears under the symbol of the Anthropos. [380/381]

That simply carried forward the Christian-Judeo-Egyptian idea, and I first saw that when I was editing it. That was when I saw it.

(It was the inner person who broke through into his life as No. 2 during childhood, and that seems to some like a "split.")
That seems to be two from the outside. And when one looks at oneself from outside then one sees two. "That is also you," only our conscious understanding is not enough to see that one is that as well. Either that is the I, or it is the Self (one thinks). In actuality it is both. This split comes only from the inability of consciousness to see both in one. (*Cherubinic Wanderer*: . . . How come both are both? He is as great as I, I am as great as God. . . . Or similar).[1243]

[1241] In 1957, in "Recent Thoughts on Schizophrenia," Jung commented regarding schizophrenia, "Experiences with mescaline and related drugs encourage the hypothesis of a toxic origin." *CE* 25; *CW* 3, § 548.

[1242] "Red-Black" was one of the provisional titles of the chapter "Confrontation with the Unconscious" in *MDR*.

[1243] Jung was recalling the following lines from Angelus Silesius's *Cherubinic Wanderer* (*Der Cherubinische Wandersmann*, 1674; Silesius, born Johann Scheffler, ca. 1624–1677, was a Silesian-German Catholic priest, doctor, mystic, and poet): "I am as great as God, he is as small as I; / He cannot be above me and I not beneath him." (Book1.10). Jung cited these lines in 1921 in *Psychological Types*, *CE* 9; *CW* 6, § 432.

I have attempted to switch off the I and to give free rein to whatever wants to come at me from within. To give the unconscious a chance and to turn off the critique.

Often, I wished that my consciousness was empty, then I felt a word forming itself in the muscles of my mouth. Often it was an inner hearing. Sometimes it was as if these things formed themselves in my speech organs and then I recognized the word. Then an activity stepped forward from within. After I had succeeded in emptying my consciousness. I did yoga exercises, particularly when I felt that an inner excitement would not subside because things were too arresting.[1244]

I was concerned to find out whether these things have a meaning or whether they are actually meaningless. I was strongly influenced by how meaningful these things are even if I could then understand the meaning only a little. My "scientific" question was this: What happens when I switch off consciousness? I notice from dreams that something stood in the background to which I wanted to give a fair chance of emerging. One subjects oneself to the conditions required for it—as in a mescaline experiment—that are required for it to emerge. [381/382]

The most important experiences since 1944 are, on the one hand, that I have written a series of works that give information.—This illness and the knowledge, the intuition of the end of all things, of life, and of death, gave me courage for these works. That is one thing. And the other is that I could only say: Saying yes to the suchness, an unconditional saying yes to what is, without raising any sort of subjective objections against it. Accepting the conditions of being just as I see them, just as I understand it. Accepting my own understanding of what one simply is.

(Objectivity) An I is there that is not driven out of one's skin when it is destroyed, an I that endures. That is actually an I that bears the truth, that is somehow a match for this world. In other words: this is why it is also an achievement, not only a defeat that one must accept; it is a victory. One has in fact experienced a victory in one's defeat. Nothing is disturbed, neither outside nor within. That continuity has stood firm against the stream of life and time. Albeit by not somehow meddlesomely mixing oneself up in it.

For Nietzsche it was the great preoccupation: *amor fati*.[1245] It is hard to determine whether he meant the same thing. With him so much re-

---

[1244] See above, p. 150.

[1245] *amor fati* (Lat.): "love of fate." In *Ecce Homo* (1908), Nietzsche wrote, "My formula for greatness in a human being is amor fati: that one wants nothing to be different,

mained mere words. He never asked the question: So am I really that? This is why one never knows whether he distinguishes himself from the superman. Just think: six thousand feet beyond good and evil.[1246] One does not know: is he Zarathustra? Or who is Zarathustra? He loses the psychological point of view in it. So it came to this: the psychic happened to him without one being certain that he integrally retained his I. Otherwise he would have actually engaged with what happened to him with some form of common sense, as I then did by giving it a psychological or more or less rational justification. To a high degree he got stuck in the Dionysian state of emotion. That is why it is significant that his brain shattered. He increasingly became [382/383] his fate, a human incomprehensibility. Think of *Zarathustra* or *Ecce Homo* or things like that.

Seen from my psychology, he actually did not know what he was talking about, did not know that his essential ideas were the further development of Christian principles. This is why much sounds like an incredible inflation. So that it would not appear that he was saying it himself, he put it in the mouth of Zarathustra, although it is quite transparent as to who is actually meant. He is exposed to the danger of identifying the I with unconscious contents. That is clearly evident. That is due to the primitive character of the unconscious. One sees that in Indian philosophy, where a direct identification is even generated through yoga: I myself am the Atman, the God. The intensification of the I in yoga dissolves the I and one is the universal being. One is the ground of the world itself, and Nietzsche was reached by this. By choosing a Zarathustra he is only wanting to say that he is the great proclaimer of the truth and that shows the inflation.

I have always attempted to say only what I have actually experienced, what I knew, and what I could prove. I might just as well have

---

not forward, not backward, not in all eternity. Not merely bear what is necessary, still less conceal it . . . but love it." Friedrich Nietzsche, *Ecce Homo: How to Become What You Are*, trans. Duncan Large (Oxford: Oxford University Press, 2007), "Why I Am So Clever," § 10 (p. 35). On Jung's reading of Nietzsche, see Bishop, *Dionysian Self*; Martin Liebscher, *Libido und Wille zur Macht: C. G. Jungs Auseinandersetzung mit Nietzsche* (Basel: Schwabe, 2011); and Graham Parkes, "Nietzsche and Jung: Ambivalent Appreciations," in Jacob Golomb, Weaver Santaniello, and Ronald Lehrer, eds, *Nietzsche and Depth Psychology* (Albany, NY: SUNY Press, 1999), pp. 205–27. On the role of Nietzsche in *Liber Novus*, see Domenici, *Jung's Nietzsche*.

[1246] In *Ecce Homo*, Nietzsche wrote that the thought of the eternal recurrence came to him in August 1881 in the woods by Lake Silvaplana, "dashed off on a sheet of paper with the caption '6,000 feet beyond man and time.'" Nietzsche, *Ecce Homo* (trans. Large), "*Thus Spoke Zarathustra: A Book for Everyone and No One*," § 1, at p. 65.

written a book called "Thus Spake Philemon."[1247] Then their reproach that this was Gnosticism would have been correct. But that is simply not true.

(Resonance in the world, small)
Yes, otherwise what I am saying would have no meaning. My contemporary world is created in such a way that something such as this must be addressed to it. So it will react to that with great hostility for (what I say) is the compensation it needs and normally one rejects that. I could not expect to have any sort of resonance. I knew from the very beginning that's how it would be. It had to be like that for otherwise I would not be a compensation. The world has reacted like a patient who has such impossible dreams. "Why must I also have such dreams?" [383/384]

Why must this decent and conventional Germany experience National Socialism? That simply cannot be true! "That's what I did," says my memory. "I cannot possibly have done that," says my pride, so my memory relents.[1248] It's even amazing how successful I am. I could never have expected more. This is why I always seemed so lost to myself (at the start), because I say what no one wants to hear. As Freud said: I only noticed that I had said something exceptional from the general resistance that rose up against it. One might describe me as a heretic or revolutionary, I connect to where our world has simply got stuck or fallen behind where it should have gone further. I go into ridiculous detail, for example, in the doctrine of the Holy Spirit. To the world that's a ridiculous detail, speaking from the world's perspective. When someone has a view about what the Holy Spirit did even after death[1249]—well, who on earth knows that?

I allow the spirit that moves me to come to expression (I look for its traces). Dreams are an incomplete natural language that we must amplify and must understand with intelligence and knowledge so that the content becomes perceptible. The language of our time is a so-called scientific language, and it is essential that one does not make statements that one cannot prove.

[1247] A reference to Martin Buber's critique in "Religion und modernes Denken," *Merkur* 6.2 (February 1952), pp. 101–20, to which Jung responded in "Religion und Psychologie," *Merkur* 6.5 (May 1952), pp. 467–73 ("Answer to Martin Buber," *CE* 23; *CW* 18).

[1248] Friedrich Nietzsche, *Beyond Good and Evil: Prelude to a Philosophy of the Future*, trans. Marion Faber (Oxford: Oxford University Press, 1998), Part 4, "Aphorisms and Epigrams," § 68, at p. 58.

[1249] See "Answer to Job" (1952), *CE* 23; *CW* 11.

[1250]That is why it's so painful for me that I must accept things that I cannot prove. But I am not speaking about this. If I speak about things after death, then I am speaking out of an inner emotion yet I cannot go further than relating the dreams I have about them.

The Taoist idea of reincarnation as a "fly leg," or spokes of a wheel,[1251] is linked with the Eastern characteristic of thinking in a circular fashion. Nothing has a goal, but birth and death are an eternal wheel. One lives and perceives and dies, and begins again from the beginning. It is first with the Buddha that the idea arises that a goal is present. In Taoism there is no goal, [384/385] nor in India. In Indian thought, one is liberated only from the illusion of existence. But then one is not meant to be excluded from reincarnation. It is self-evident that one is reincarnated to another life.

One can no longer separate the doctrine of karma from this. The decisive question is whether karma is personal or not.[1252] The disciples asked the Buddha whether the karma with which one begins life is acquired in a past life or whether it is some sort of karma. He replied that it is an unnecessary question that does not help to liberate oneself from the illusion of being. The disciples asked him this question twice. As soon as one accepts a continuity—of which I am not certain—I have, in other words, no material that would give me certainty in any sort of statement about this question, namely: Is this karma I am living that which I acquired in my past lives, or is it from my ancestors out of whom I am formed? Am I a particular combination of the life of my ancestors and am I incarnating their life again, but as a multiplicity synthesized in me, stepping forward

---

[1250] Jaffé noted here, "Jung does not wish to use the metaphysical speculations expressed in the following."

[1251] Jung may be referring to the eleventh verse of the *Tao Te Ching*:

Thirty spokes
Share one hub.
Adapt the nothing therein to the purpose in hand, and you will have the use of the cart. Knead clay in order to make a vessel. Adapt the nothing therein to the purpose in hand and you will have the use of the vessel. Cut out doors and windows and make a room. Adapt the nothing therein to the purpose in hand, and you will have the use of the room.
Thus what we gain is Something, yet is by virtue of Nothing that this can be put to use.

Tao Te Ching, trans. D. C. Lau (London: Penguin, 1963), p. 15.

[1252] Jung posed precisely this question to the Indologist Emil Abegg, on December 10, 1949, and to the Swiss journalist Lily Abegg, who had spent much time in the Far East, on December 12 (JP).

into the present with a historical question? Or was it *I* who lived back then and did I get so far in that life that I can now attempt an answer? This I don't know. The Buddha left this question open. I would assume that he himself did not know with any certainty.[1253]

According to the assertion of my dreams, [xxx][1254] and at the last moment made its identity clear to me.

I must be reincarnated because, having lived in earlier centuries, I encountered questions there that could not stand up or that were incorrectly answered, and I did not resolve. So when I die, my deeds follow me, meaning that I bring back what I have achieved and then it is decided whether what I have achieved was enough, and it will become clear how long it will take before I need a new life lesson. Or, through my achievements, a question has arisen [385/386] in the world through me to which a response is required. That contains my karma if I perhaps have to return in order to make a better response to this question, for example. To give a more complete answer. Perhaps I do not have to be reincarnated as long as the world does not need me. I could imagine that I would have an entitlement to so-and-so many hundred years of peace until one has need of me again and I would have to give myself fully to the task again. I have the idea that one could now enter into rest until the allotted task that I have posed to the world is recycled. It seemed to me that the dead harassed me terribly so that I would finally give an answer. In hate and fear and expectation and faith and hope that a living person, a conscious man, would give an answer to it, that everything depended on that. For they cannot come out of their timelessness, out of their eternity. Evidently only a person who has come into the world can do this, distant from the Godhead. It seems as if the dead have possibilities of development only in the space that is left to them out of incompleteness. What a person creates or realizes on Earth comes into the beyond as a new thing, with that, space is created for the dead so that they can develop. If they have not yet got that far.

The Godhead has a drive towards being in order to create a higher consciousness, Godhead is the one and the many. All the countless dead make up the Godhead. That is, what is conscious in it. What is conscious of itself, for the Godhead is conscious thanks only to man.

[1253] On the Buddhist doctrine of karma, see Bhiku Bodhi, ed. and trans., *The Numerical Discourses of the Buddha: A Complete Translation of the "Aṅguttara Nikāya"* (Somerville, MA: Wisdom Publications, 2012).

[1254] Illegible—a few words crossed out.

That is an idea that is very important to me, that it matters infinitely to the Godhead to have consciousness in order to convey meaning to unconscious creation. Otherwise, it has no meaning at all. This is why our life is so infinitely important and one makes no mistake by taking one's life very seriously. Otherwise, the Godhead suffers, that means the totality of the dead suffers from the stagnation of consciousness. There must be a state of emergency, for if the Godhead were complete in and of itself it would not need the world's state of emergency.—Yahweh is in terrible distress that his people ultimately could not obey, for then he has played his game in vain. It is always said that he wanted to put his people to the test. No: he wants to convince himself that man has a conscious-ness. This is why he opposes Jacob so that he puts up resistance to him. He wants to convince himself of it. In this, evil has its great meaning: that it reacts against the Godhead. If God wanted to redeem us absolutely, then existence would have no meaning. He is like the potter who makes bad pots and then wants to go and complain about the pots.

This earth will cease at some point. When we consciously return to the forest and bring life down to its simplest forms, then consciousness has triumphed. The ability to endure what happens resides in the distant future. When the evening of humanity dawns, then the highest culture dwells in the greatest simplicity. Then one has recognized the meaning of the possibility of existence and knows that everything is an illusion except living in what is. One cannot bear that at all if one fears mean-inglessness. If I came up with the idea of emigrating to Polynesia, à la Gauguin,[1255] thinking that I would then be complete, or of retreating from the world like a hermit to gain insight into its meaninglessness, no meaning would come from that, but only a reproach to the creator for the craziness he has initiated. I am convinced that nature is a deep prob-lem about which we still have much to learn. It requires great progress in science. That gives us dignity and hope, but the Indian hermit saying, "Now make it all stop, it is all madness," is throwing away the sword and giving up. For evidently one should join in the fight with all the strands of our existence so that the maximum of knowledge and consciousness can emerge about us, about the world, about the eternal and so on. That has meaning; otherwise, the world does not exist at all, [387/388] or it is only the crazy idea of a crazy demiurge. That is the Gnostic view. The true

---

[1255] Paul Gauguin (1848–1903), French post-Impressionist/Symbolist painter, sculptor, and writer, who went to live in French Polynesia in the 1890s, and depicted life there in his paintings. In 1901 he published a journal of his experiences, *Noa Noa*.

God is the God of the good, but he is not concerned about the world. The demiurge is to blame for this world where humanity lives like the animals. I can imagine something of this: a nature that unfolds itself and man who unfolds himself in his consciousness within this nature. He can do that only when he also understands the language of the animals and plants. So that, then, a sort of God's world could arise. Naturally with all sorts of protective measures, for then a higher culture of consciousness must also exist that does not always want to know better than nature. We are a long way from this. But we are only a million years old, and that is nothing yet. It will always grow ever more dangerous, the further consciousness strides.

A final catastrophe is possible, why not? Or it is also possible that humanity will be destroyed, and that another experiment will be initiated somewhere else. Such experiments are probably underway everywhere in the universe, but they all find their climax in a constantly self-renewing consciousness. That corresponds to the secret intention of the creator that the being is transfigured by knowing itself. Otherwise, nothing has happened and creation does not exist if no one knows about it. What I read in Schreber made a deep impression on me, that the Godhead longs for man in order to experience itself in man. He saw something, but went crazy in the process. Whether man can withstand this experiment of God at all? Schreber himself exploded in the process.[1256]

There is tremendous attrition in nature of seeds and possibilities. Look at the pear tree: how many blossoms, how many seeds that perish. And it is exactly the same with man: what incredible fullness of man there is and yet only a few have any consciousness. The tremendous fullness is conceived by the tremendous will of the creator. God must do that so that there is something that can be an object for his consciousness. This idea expresses itself in Indian spirituality, that for immeasurable periods of time [388/389] there was nothing other than the Godhead.[1257] One day God notices that he is completely alone. Then he gives birth to the idea of another being, an opposite, an object. He then splits himself in two and engenders another out of himself. That is how the world came into being. But that is where the philosopher's thinking usually stops, for then the world has come into being in which one then loses oneself. One no longer asks: And what happened to God when he split himself in two?

[1256] On Schreber, see n. 565 above.
[1257] See "Bṛhadāranyaka Upaniṣad," in Olivelle, *Upaniṣads*, 1.4 (pp. 13–14).

One must make everything of life that one can. That is why one regrets what one has not done: that is what one really regrets. "If I could start my life over again, then I would. . . ." Being able to withstand suffering gives life meaning. Meaning that one can withstand God. For he himself is in doubt about whether he can be borne, or whether he can become. That is why he arms his animals with the most unbelievable weapons so that they can defend themselves, and there is such a will to be in everything. But on the other hand it must never be claimed that it is God who is split, who wanted one thing and not the other. The one builds up and the other destroys.

My encounters? I met with Toynbee twice.[1258] I told him something of my ideas, but he gave nothing of himself. And what effect the conversation had, I have never heard. I am glad to see people; but I can do nothing about it if they then get hold of an idea which turns them upside down or that they fail at; I can do nothing about that either. Mostly people come to me with a concern that one cannot or must not even mention.

I met Lowell, the famous astronomer, he was my mentor when I received the doctorate at Clark University.[1259] And my relationship to Pauli? Could I speak about it?[1260] [389/390]

They think I have no friends nor relationships. Not a trace! I have quite an individual relationship to each of my children, children-in-law,

---

[1258] Arnold Toynbee (1889–1975), British historian. Toynbee drew on Jung's work, such as in his *A Study of History*, 6 vols (Oxford: Oxford University Press, 1934–39). On February 29, 1952 Toynbee thanked Jung for receiving him in Zurich the previous week, and for coming to his lecture (JP). On August 26 that year he wrote to Jung that the excitement and stimulus of the first book of his that he read, *Psychological Types*, was still working in him and, referring to his own *Study of History*, added, "I am conscious that these volumes have on them the mark of the ideas that I have derived from you." (JP). He later he referred to a conversation with Jung in his tribute, "The Value of C. G. Jung's Work for Historians," *Journal of Analytical Psychology* 1, no. 2 (1956): 193–94.

[1259] Percival Lowell (1855–1916), renowned for his claims regarding the presence of canals of Mars, observations of Venus, and role in the discovery of Pluto. Lowell spoke at the Clark conference on the planet Venus. On September 14, 1909 Jung wrote to his wife Emma regarding Lowell's photos of the canals, "I have seen the original pictures, as well as the photographs of Jupiter. All perfectly splendid. [Lowell] is firmly convinced that only intelligent beings could have made the canals." Draft translation of *Memories, Dreams, Reflections* (CLM), p. 339.

[1260] Wolfgang Pauli (1900–1958), Austrian physicist, pioneer of quantum mechanics, and winner of the Nobel Prize for Physics in 1945. In 1932 Pauli consulted Jung, who sent him for analysis to Erna Rosenbaum, while following the case himself. He utilized Pauli's material in his 1935 Eranos lecture "Dream Symbols of the Individuation Process," later expanded in *Psychology and Alchemy* (1944), CE 17; CW 12, and in *Psychology and Religion* (1938), CE 15; CW 11.

and grandchildren. The definitive encounters, however, were the encounters with ordinary people who one insults by calling them patients. From them, I learned something. Or my encounter with Mountain Lake or with a simple pandit in India.—What is crucial in these insignificant people is that they are human beings who have given their essence; and that came out without their wanting it; and I encounter the person there. One finds that only where the person is full of what has befallen him, of what has happened to him; but not when he has achieved certain things in the outside world. That is only the foreground. That is what I wanted, that was the definitive thing for me. And there I also found people with whom I could have a relationship. I have very many relationships.[1261]

[1261] On May 16, 1958 Jung had a conversation with Shin'ichi Hisamatsu (1889–1980), a leading Zen philosopher. See "The Jung–Hisamatsu Conversation," in Polly Young-Eisendrath and Shoji Muramuto, eds, *Awakening and Insight: Zen Buddhism and Psychotherapy* (London: Routledge, 2002), pp, 105–8. On May 25 Kurt Wolff wrote to Aniela Jaffé that he had made notes on her chapters on Bollingen and the *Red Book* which he was going to send her. He had gone through these with the Cary Baynes, who had made important suggestions. He asked if the conversation with the Zen Master could go in the book (BL). In an undated reply, Jaffé thanked him for all the suggestions in his recent letters. She wanted to avoid a chapter on religion as "Jung has said such unusual, heretical, and fantastical things that if one were to summarize them in one chapter they would provoke great resistance." She continued, "To hear from Jung about William James will not be difficult. I can ask about 'therapeutic work' although the associations experiment has not been used by him for decades now. Perhaps not since meeting Freud. That can be checked out with him." She was expecting to finish the work in spring 1959. She was looking forward to their lunch in July (BL).

On May 28 Wolff sent a memo to Jaffé entitled "Some General Remarks." He noted that these remarks were the combined view of himself, Cary Baynes, and Wolfgang Sauerlander. As well as commenting on chapters she had sent him, he reiterated his request for more on William James, given that for the "Anglo-Saxon reader, next to Freud, he was the most important figure. If she was unable to get more from Jung on James, he suggested that she "try to put in a simple and colloquial way Jung's main thoughts about James's ideology by rewriting yourself, in a very different style, what you find in the *Works* and asking Jung's blessing for it." He also felt that there was too little of Jung the therapist in the book and insisted that she tried for more. For instance, he noted that the associations experiment wasn't mentioned: "I am thinking of general remarks about his therapeutic experiences with men and women but also a few more case histories. Should the material CGJ may give you be meager, you may perhaps also be able to fill in from other sources." (BL).

On June 3 Jaffé replied that it was clear to her that they held two different conceptions of the final form of the work: "You are commenting more from the world and I am defending the 'non-world' because that is where Jung is after all, and as it seems to me—one does him most justice when the shortcomings are overlooked as much as possible. But the shortcomings are related to the facts of the world." She added, "By the way, as I thought over your comments, I returned to my original plan which I had not adequately elaborated: ordering the sequences à la Eckermann (dates of conversations). Of course, the objective order would underlie it, it goes without saying." She asked Wolff what he thought of this (and judging by her letter to him on June 9, this plan had not gone down well). She also

[23]¹²⁶²

JUNE 13, 1958

The issue of suicide.

In cases of suicide, the majority of suicides are not observed, so one can say nothing. Of those that are under observation, there are some who see no way out and are forced to think of suicide. In these cases one can always say, "Keep looking for what the unconscious offers in terms of suggestions and life possibilities"; for example, even if one knows no reasonable way out for someone. As a rule, thank God, suicidal possibilities are avoided in one's practice because a door opens from the unconscious that one had not thought of. Or the conscious attitude changes. The person acquires a different perspective towards things. And then there is no more talk of suicide. That can change from one moment to the next. That is what usually happens.

Then there are some cases (I disregard psychoses, I am speaking only of psychological suicide). There are people who do not allow anything else to get through to them; but these people do not come into analysis. If they do, then one must make an effort to find a way out for them. If the case is such that they simply accept nothing, then they will slope off out of the analysis, or the doctor must even send them away. It is pointless if someone does not wish it for themselves, they would be treated against their will and one cannot do that. It could be a dramatic situation where

---

recounted that she was working on the chapter "*Works*" and that, "left to me, I would call the Red-Black chapter the 'confrontation with the unconscious,' 'years of searching' also seems quite good to me." (BL).

On June 6 Jaffé wrote to Wolff suggesting that he ask Richard Winston to start translating the *Sermones* and the chapter "from the Black Book," adding, "I have considered 'Izudbar' as a further chapter and could send it over to you." (The version of the manuscript in Wolff's papers already included an excerpt from *The Red Book*, comprising the whole of *Liber Primus*, copied from Jung's draft typescript.) (BL).

On June 3 Wolff wrote to Jung, addressing him as "Distinguished Autobiographer": "In the conversation that I had with you in Minusio in February I became aware that 'our' book might become a real joy for you if I succeed in breaking through to a new class of reader, a readership which may be led to the *Works* via the biography." He went on to discuss preparing prepublication serializations in this regard, adding that more information on two subjects would also be important in this regard: namely, "recollections and experiences of C. G. Jung as psychotherapist" (ideally twenty-five to thirty pages), as well more on William James (eight to ten pages) (BL).

¹²⁶² New pagination. Jaffé noted in *Reflections* that Volume 16 of Jung's *Gesammelten Werke*, *The Practice of Psychotherapy*, had appeared in the spring and attracted a lot of interest (p. 129).

the analyst to some degree identifies with the patient and struggles with him for his life. That could have a good effect. But if the other refuses, the doctor cannot participate either. In these cases a suicide can be the result.

I have had such a case. A twenty-six- or twenty-seven-year-old young girl, with whom it was simply impossible. She had a compulsive neurosis. She once brought a dream that she had written on the torn-off edge of a newspaper: "Listen to me: this ends right now! If you ever bring such a sloppy thing again, then you're going to a different doctor! I will throw you out!" The next time she did indeed come again with such slovenliness. Then I threw her out. [23/24]

But for a while I prudently stood quietly behind the door. Then I heard a gentle knock, and after letting her knock for a little while, I opened the door: "Yes, where have you come from then?"—"I have brought my notebook." That was a case who simply took nothing in. It would have been easier to talk with a stone. Then I knew that the possibility of suicide was present, but I could not identify with her, for I was convinced she would come to nothing. I could not summon any faith for her, and I had to let her go. Half a year later I heard that she had committed suicide.

There was another case that gave me a lot to think about. It was a relatively well-known person. She was rather "at the eleventh hour." She had anxiety and deep depression and was heavily burdened, but a very decent person. In her case, I really wrestled with her for her life and made all sorts of efforts to have her feel something worth living for. But I was concerned to have the unconscious on board. One cannot say, "I will create some life for you now"—that would be completely crazy—"I cannot offer you any possibility of life, but perhaps the unconscious can." Reasonably, she allowed this idea in. But her dreams, by God, always brought only references to suicide. So here was something inescapable. So I even attempted to trick her a little with the interpretation. But her dreams kept insisting all the more on suicide as the only option. I was very fearful about it. Finally, I said to her: from what I know I must honestly tell you that your dreams point to the inescapability of suicide. We want to try to go along with the unconscious in the silent hope that it might then bring another possibility. So I took her through every nook and cranny of the suicide problem: the religious aspect, the ethical aspect. What it meant for her, for her family members—and her dreams insisted all the more upon suicide. I saw her three or four times a week for six weeks, with the result that the dreams further insisted on suicide. We discussed the various ways one might commit suicide. "How would you commit suicide?" "If I were to commit suicide, then I might sit on the railings of a bridge and shoot myself, then if the bullet didn't finish me off, then at least I would drown."—And that was exactly what she ended up doing! She was a very respected person. I really should have communicated it to the family; then they could have locked her up in the Burghölzli. But she was very frightened of that. She also had no symptoms of melancholy. She simply was not able to accept life. She regarded her life as completely meaningless, and the unconscious did not help her either. "I can no longer help you, I can no longer advise you." "No, you gave me the best advice." She was grateful to me for the conversations. She then went to a different doctor so that when she committed suicide the shadow would fall on the other one and not upon me.

That was for me really one of the most difficult cases I ever had because on the one hand she was an ethically valuable person and on the other hand she was possessed by a will to death, and the unconscious did not help her any further either. God did not intervene!

There are cases where no further identification succeeds, nor God, nor nature, where a tendency is present to bring an end to life, where no wellmeaning art and nothing else helps and it also came after me: after the dream of Siegfried, then I knew: I need only make a hand movement and I am dead. That caused me to get up in the night and to seek for an interpretation for such a long time until I found it.[1263]—That can come at one from inside a completely normal life. This is why there are suicides that one can never explain.

Suicide remains murder. It is murder of the self, and the self-murderer is a murderer. This is also true of the family murderer: the self-murderer takes his family with him. But we are all murderers and thanks only to the favorable circumstances in which we live are we not murderers or selfmurderers. Just think of the countless suicides of the Jews before they were transported to the concentration camps. I would rather shoot myself first. That is clear: life would no longer be worth living under such conditions.—But perhaps one cannot say that in advance. [25/26]

Once I had to treat a pre-exilic Jew who lived in Baghdad. It was one of the Jews who have the *Talmud Babli* (in contrast to the *Talmud Jerusalemmi* which is the usual one).[1264] These Jews have the idea (such a madness) that all Western Jews are Ashkenazi Jews, and they regard them as

---

[1263] See above, p. 107.

[1264] The *Talmud Yerusalmi* (or Jersulem/Palestinian Talmud) was competed ca. 350 BCE. The *Talmud Babli* (or Babylonian Talmud) was completed ca. 500 BCE and is actually the more widely referred to and used.

Gentiles. Only they, the Sephardic Jews, are the true Jews. Such a Sephardic Jew came to me; he was an enlightened Westerner and had left the values behind. He no longer understood them, he no longer understood what it meant to live in a godly atmosphere, or to live with God; he no longer knew about it. That came back to him in dreams and then his whole nervous condition disappeared again. That was properly neurotic, he was like a Jew from the fourth century before Christ.

I know how it was for me when I noticed that I myself was no longer a Christian and then gradually I found my own myth. And that works only when we associate with our dead.[1265] Gradually the burden of responsibility has been taken off me: I have done everything I could in this regard. I gave the dead a reply. But who has understood what that means? I gave my dead my answer, and that has nothing to do with anyone else! For they would only want to know what sort of answer it was and would only parrot this because they do not want to give their own dead an answer. That is far too uncomfortable for them! "So cast all your cares upon him, for He will do it!"[1266]

What does "the dead" mean? What does "the ancestors" mean? Are they the physical ancestors, the spiritual ancestors? One does not know. One might just as well say: the legacy Freud left me, I pursued it to the end I was able to pursue it to. That too was a question directed towards me.

Also my patients: these are all the people who have put questions to me. The original questions came from the patients. They had become neurotic because they had made do with fragmentary answers to the questions of life: they were seeking a job, a marriage, a good reputation, believing that one would be happy when one achieved that or something like it. But they are not happy even if they have a heap of money. And then they come and want to hear and learn what novelty might remain for them. Then it becomes clear that their life has no meaning and that they are neurotic because it is quite meaningless.

My therapy has no rules; every patient is a new proposition, and a routine would not help at all. Of course, I must master the "trade." But if it's about the basic questions, then it is no longer enough and one cannot help: if someone is analyzed for long enough then he gets to the fundamental questions, nothing else is possible.

[1265] This theme emerged in *Liber Novus*. In a fantasy of December 26, 1915 the figure of a dead woman informed Jung's I, "Community with the dead is what both you and the dead need." (p. 492).
[1266] 1 Peter 5:7: "casting all your cares upon Him, for He careth for you."

If someone clears out in the face of the transference, then of course he will never get to these problems.—Of course, it is well known that one can give with one hand only, or with one foot, but it is no ideal state, it is a resignation; it is a resignation that is not necessarily present. There are people who can still live in the most unfavorable of circumstances. They settle. But resignation is not the ideal solution. Under certain circumstances one can do nothing else, then resignation is necessary. But when possibilities exist to get further without resignation then it is even a duty to take this path. At least for the doctor. But when the patient can bear it to give up aged forty, then no one can stop him. Whether he is then happy or "normal," that is written on another page. And whether he himself experiences that as meaningful.

I was inside the Christian world view and increasingly I saw that I was falling out of it and then came the question: how can you go on living, what sort of meaning does life have.

Christianity is after all our spiritual landscape, and I did not want to obstruct access to our spiritual world for my children. That is why I had them baptized. I left confirmation up to them. And I did everything to let them explore this Christian path. If they should fall away from it, they should see the possibility of taking up something different. They can only get beyond what is dominant if they go through it, therefore they must first be within it before they outgrow it. Those who fall out of it never come to a positive view (of their spiritual roots). [27/28] With me the first thing of all that I engaged with was Christianity. I seek the lost sheep, not the ones who are in the flock.

[1267](A patient often spoke with the Pope. She went in and out of the Vatican, she was an older lady. And she told the Pope how she had confessed and that the father confessor had been amazed at how she confessed and with what psychological insight she did it.[1268] And then she told him about it, and that the father confessor had been amazed at what she confessed, not the usual things, but real things, not artificial sins. Then the Pope gave me his blessing for my work. The current Pope.)

[1267] The following sentence occurs before this anecdote in the reworked section of the protocols of the Interviews, with the date of this entry: "When believing Christians come to me, both Catholics and Protestants, I try everything to keep them in their religion. I have even taught some Catholics how to make a confession. For I often realized that they were withholding their real sins from their priest confessor. Those, they took to the doctor!" (p. 851).

[1268] Jung narrated this episode in "The Symbolic Life" (1938), CE 15; CW 18, §§ 618–19. The "current Pope" was Pius XII.

Freud was not a psychiatrist, he was a neurologist, he did not know psychoses at all. I often spoke to him about schizophrenia, back then they said: Dementia praecox. Through the conversations with me he learned something about the psychology of the psychoses. He then wrote about Schreber,[1269] but how he approached this case was completely wide of the mark. He completely overlooked the collective material.

Patient: Indian woman from Mumbai, who belonged to the Parsis who have a fire cult. The richest people in Mumbai are Parsis, or many of the rich people. She had studied medicine in England. When I analyzed her the complete psychology of a proper old English spinster[1270] came out, to my great disappointment. She had crazy states of irritability, sometimes became completely beside herself and had absolutely uncontrolled emotions, she was disorientated like someone who was lost. Gradually dreams came in which Sanskrit terms appeared, or scenes from Indian life with Indian details: plants and animals. Something from India. Before that everything in her dreams was only English or from Zurich where she had lived. I asked her, "What do these words mean?" She did not have a clue. Then I found a dictionary. And then religious ideas came to light and that fascinated her tremendously. There she began her inner life. Then she told me that the Parsi receive a string as small children, [28/29] and she cried, "My God, now I completely forgot, my nephew did not get a string!" Immediately she wrote to India to ensure that her nephew got a string. I was myself very interested in this Zoroastrian fire cult.

When I went to India she greeted me extremely warmly and painted a sign on my forehead with sandalwood ash, a type of blessing. She then returned to her Indian life. She is very attached to me and still writes to me from time to time. She lives somewhere in the country as a doctor. [29/30][1271]
[85]

[1269] See above, pp. 149, 202, 354
[1270] "old spinster": in English in the original.
[1271] On June 17, 1958 Jung replied to Kurt Wolff,

Your wish that I should expatiate at greater length on psychotherapy seems to me unfulfillable because I have already written a whole lot on this subject from the scientific standpoint and none of it is suitable for a biography. I would have to expose a mass of empirical material which was very important to me personally, but unfortunately medical discretion forbids me to make use of it. Some of the patients are still alive, and if dead they have relatives who could easily recognize from my account, if it were reliable, whom it concerned. I have to be extremely careful in these matters.

JUNE 23, 1958.[1272]

Long after the death of my mother I had a dream in which I visited her in the place where she presumably now resides. She was living in a house from the last or from the eighteenth century, a small country house, surrounded with roses. The house was in the beyond, and in the dream I was aware of this.

After that came another longer dream. It took place in Mendoza in Argentina, at the foot of the Aconcagua, the highest mountain in the South

As for my meeting with William James, you must remember that I saw him only twice and talked with him for a little over an hour, but there was no correspondence between us. Apart from the personal impression he made on me, I am indebted to him chiefly for his books. We talked mostly about his experiments with Mrs. Piper, which are well enough known, and did not speak of his philosophy at all. I was particularly interested to see what his attitude was to so-called "occult phenomena." I admired his European culture and the openness of his nature. He was a distinguished personality and conversation with him was extremely pleasant. He was quite naturally without affectation and pomposity and answered my questions and interjections as though speaking to an equal. Unfortunately he was already ailing at the time so I could not press him too hard. Aside from Theodore Flournoy he was the only outstanding mind with whom I could conduct an uncomplicated conversation. I therefore honor his memory and have always remembered the example he set me.

Incidentally I have discussed James at some length in my book on types. If I were to write an appreciation of James from my present standpoint it would require an essay in itself, since it is impossible to sketch a figure of such stature in a few words. It would be an unpardonable exercise in superficiality if I presumed to do so.

I regret that my biography, as I envisage it, is in many respects unlike other biographies. It is utterly impossible for me, without expressing value judgments, to remember the millions of personal details and then have such a conceit of them in retrospect as to tell them again in all seriousness. I know there are people who live in their own biography during their lifetime and act as though they were already in a book. For me life was something that had to be lived and not talked about. Also, my interest was always riveted only by a few but important things which I couldn't speak of anyway, or had to carry around with me for a long time until they were ripe for the speaking. In addition I have been so consistently misunderstood that I have lost all desire to recall "significant conversations." God help me, when I read Eckermann's *Conversations* [see n. 650 above] even Goethe seemed to me like a strutting turkey-cock. I am what I am—a thankless autobiographer! [*Letters*, vol. 2, pp. 451–53]

On June 19 Wolff wrote to Aniela Jaffé regarding Jung's reply, that with regard to psychotherapy and William James, "the Master, in my opinion, isn't always aware that the publisher of the autobiographical work is always thinking of something very different from the scholarly work" (BL). On June 25 Jaffé wrote to Wolff that she had finished the chapter "Medical Activities." She informed him that she hardly knew William James's work, and couldn't put together a chapter on him (BL).

[1272] This entry is from *EG*, pp. 85–90.

American Cordillera. It said that my mother was living there and was married to a pharmacist. Then I see a younger woman—they said she was a pharmacist's wife—with bandages around the head and arms. She was wounded.

A couple of days later I read in the newspaper that an earthquake has destroyed the city of Mendoza![1273][86/87] For lack of something better[1274] one could link this dream with a post-mortal actuality of my mother and assume a connection between the earthquake and the wounding of the woman in the dream.

My mother had a powerful love of foreign lands. She projected it onto me and often expressed the fantasy that I would go to the East and marry an Asian woman. "It makes me wonder what sort of woman you will marry, for sure a Japanese or an Indian!" In such images there was an extravagant fantasy that could easily be the impetus of her own compensatory further development.

Mostly we consider the concept of a life after death and apparent "experiences" to be "only psychically determined"—that is, as subjective fantasies. Ultimately, we do not know what sort of actuality the psychic is and we know just as little how far images and phenomena of the deceased possess autonomy and objective reality. We cannot always differentiate it from inner images and fantasies. But I am of the view that, to a certain degree, our fantasies from the unconscious have validity. If with my logical thinking and my reason I cannot conceive of anything verifiable about a life after death, then I feel justified in taking more or less seriously my intuition and [87/88] intimations of the unconscious, as well as dreams. If the unconscious says "Mendoza," at first that sounds like nonsense. But when it shows up in the newspaper . . . !

I cannot say "yes" or "no" to this, but, for my soul's balance, it is important that I consider what my unconscious offers me as a possibility, even if it remains unverifiable.

For all her inner expansiveness, naturalness and multiplicity, my mother lacked greatness. She was the wife of a country parson and yet there lived in her unconscious a more expansive personality that roamed through vast distances and landed in the foreign and strange—and this personality she projected onto me. This is why she believed I would bring home a wife out of the East! That shows that such a woman was within

---

[1273] There was a devastating earthquake in Mendoza on March 20, 1861.

[1274] "For lack of something better": in English in the original.

her. The possibility of a corresponding compensation lay thoroughly in her orbit.

The idea that one chooses one's life before birth is perhaps not too far wrong. In this case one would choose the life that one has imagined in fantasy. One longs for—and until death has fantasies about—what one has not lived. One regrets not having done this or that. Out of this, one creates one's compensations. If it continues according to psychic laws, an impulse would awaken to realize these compensatory fantasies.

I could imagine that I will compensate my current life by becoming a pioneer, but in a different respect from now, perhaps in natural sciences. I well understand how the Buddha finally, after so many incarnations, no longer wished to return to life. I will not claim that I would like to disappear into nirvana. I could imagine a world situation showing up to which I could do nothing but cry, "Encore une fois!"[1275] [88/89]

Now this is not the case. Now I have had enough. The only thing that could attract me would be science—a further insight about the nature of things. Scientific research, I could imagine that! But I do not know whether the motive would be enough. What I find of compelling interest is naturally the situation after death and what one can experience there. Whether one needs time and space in order to have experiences. Here one needs someone who experiences—the I—and an object that is experienced. Whether this separation is also present after death remains uncertain.

It is questionable whether and how much consciousness we will possess after death. That is the big question: whether one simply then is, and is blown by the great wind of the world back into existence. Although the question of reincarnation seems plausible to me, I cannot understand rationally how it would be possible.

What grips me most profoundly is awareness. In my opinion I do not need a new earthly existence for that. It is plausible that in the "beyond," after death, one has infinite access to perceptions. That is absolutely possible if we manifest after death into a universal consciousness, into a being beyond the opposites, where the separation of the one who experiences and what is experienced no longer exists. However, such perceptions would not be comprehensive. For it would be information about facts and contexts: knowledge, as it were, in breadth, but not in depth. It would be an immediate knowledge of things, without the limitation of time and space.

1275 "Encore une fois!" (Fr.): "one more time."

But the awareness of what had bestowed meaning to one's own life would be the converse of this, and insights that one had acquired in one's own life would be attained for the depths. The extension of knowledge in breadth, the acquisition of information, would only be a tool for this purpose.[1276]
[18]

JUNE 27, 1958[1277]

For a creative person, marriage is a terrible gamble. I had an indescribably benevolent fate in that I found a wife who granted me enough space so that I could breathe. Without this, I could not have done my work. I must be able to have thoughts which exceed all boundaries and that would have risked destroying another person. Someone imprisoned in safe ways of thinking would get into one state of panic after another.

In marriage the only question is whether one can live one's own being, whether one can self-realise and can allow the other the freedom for their individuation.

A woman who is further on than the man has him where she wants him and he does not notice it because she gives him so much space that he does not even sense it. [18/19]

AUGUST 1958[1278]

A son of my maternal grandmother,[1279] in his youth people used to think he would become a scoundrel. But later he pulled himself together and became a very good businessman. That was also in the grandmother. This uncle bought himself an island in the River Amazon and "ruled" there like a king.

People want to hear the truth about my attitude towards National Socialism just as little as they want to hear my skepticism in relation to UFOs.

[1276] On June 25 Aniela Jaffé wrote to Kurt Wolff that she had completed the chapter "medical activities." She had sequenced this with fictional dates, so that it read like a spoken diary (BL). See below, Appendix 1.

[1277] The June 27, 1958 and August 1958 sections are from *EG*, pp. 18 and 62.

[1278] Kurt Wolff was in Switzerland from the end of July to September. He met with Jaffé several times. Judging by Jaffé's letter to him of August 8, their relationship and collaboration were breaking down at this time (BL).

[1279] It is not clear who this son was.

One simply cannot engage with the gossip.—For me there was nothing in it at all that I found to be positive or that attracted me. It was to do with the fact that I was vice-president,[1280] so I had to engage and to see that the society could remain viable for as long as possible. If the president had not copped out I would not have had anything to do with it. It is not my style to run away when something becomes difficult.

[1281]One can only understand the Middle Ages if one also understands Latin. I would not have understood anything of psychology if I had not been able to read the ancient Latin texts. It is terribly important to participate in the European past in this way. If historical thinking is missing, then all too easily an over-emphasis of science and technology arises; in some respects that is toxic.

In order to understand alchemy, knowledge of Latin and Greek is imperative. I read hundreds of tracts which have not been translated, even to this day. I preferred to read these things in Latin, even if they had already been translated. They were then easier for me to understand.

Even the German original texts were mostly far more confused than the Latin tracts because the Baroque German was not able to elucidate the thought processes as clearly as the clear Latin language. German is much freer, but also much more haphazard, while Latin has a fixed syntax.

Of course, I also read the Greek tracts in the original. They had been translated into French by Marcellin Berthelot, but the translation is not reliable because the translator did not understand the meaning of alchemy.[1282] [28/28a]

The last language I learned was Swahili. I learned it from a grammar book. But then I had to re-learn it because in East Africa they speak a

---

[1280] In 1930, Jung became the vice-president of the General Medical Society for Psychotherapy. He succeeded Ernst Kretschmer on the latter's resignation in 1934, and the society was renamed the International General Medical Society for Psychotherapy. See Geoffrey Cocks, *Psychotherapy in the Third Reich: The Göring Institute*, 2nd rev. and exp. edn (New Brunswick, NJ: Transaction, 1997); Giovanni Sorge, "Psicologia analitica e Anni Trenta: Il ruolo di C. G. Jung nella Internationale Allgemeine Ärztliche Gesellschaft für Psychotherapie (1933–1939/40)," Dissertation, University of Zurich, 2010; and Sorge, *Bestandbeschrieb der Akten zur Geschichte der Präsidentschaft von C. G. Jung in der Internationalen Ärztlichen Gesellschaft für Psychotherapie, 1933–1940 im Nachlass von C. A. Meier* (Zurich: C. G. Jung-Arbeitsarchiv, ETH-Bibliothek, 2016).

[1281] The following section of this entry is from *EG*, pp. 28–28a.

[1282] The reference is to Marcellin Berthelot, *Collection des anciens alchimistes grecs*, 3 vols (Paris: Steinheil, 1888).

Pidgin-Swahili.[1283] I will give an example of the pictorial quality of this language: once I was changing for dinner and I could not find my necktie. I asked my boy, a native of Mozambique, "Wapi necktie?" (Where is the necktie?)—He replied, "Ndanya mtoto."—My mind boggled at the the literal translation: "Inside the child." I said in a questioning voice, "Mtoto?" (child?) To which he replied, "Ndio. Ndyanya mtoto ya mesa." (Yes, in the child of the table.) But this was the drawer.—Classical Swahili is no longer understood. My palaver with the indigenous boy was all conducted in Pidgin Swahili.

[41] The atmosphere in Africa, the isolations of Africa, were the satisfying experiences that moved me back then, the satisfactory answer. And that was more valuable to me than any ethnological trophies, such as weapons and cooking pots and goodness knows what that one can show off afterwards. All of that meant nothing to me.

The experience of primitive consciousness is naturally not entirely harmless. Both of my friends and I treated each other with extreme caution and when we were on a hike, we always left a distance of around twenty meters between us. When one is alone in this wilderness as a European, one *reacts* to others and they to you with great sensitivity.

Then I recalled a warning dream that I had dreamed a long time before, at least seven years before my Africa trip: how I climbed a massive tree in the primal forest like a monkey, pulling myself up higher with my arms. I had very short legs. And how I sat atop the tree—then I suddenly became afraid, and it occurred to me that the hunter could see me and would shoot me down.—Not because I was a monkey but because I had played the "monkey" illegitimately, as if that were a great sin.

My dreams stood fair and square on the side of the conscious I, and not on the side of the primeval darkness or maternal mystery. I was always disappointed by my dreams. I would always have expected that the unconscious would realize this opportunity with joy. But no, not at all! Not a single dream made reference to the dark continent. [41/42]

[1284]At the palavers of the natives in East Africa one must be very careful. As soon as the Blacks notice what one wants; they report exactly what one would like to hear. If you're not careful, they'll tell you all sorts of nonsense.

[1283] Jaffé noted here, "Pidgin Swahili is a mixture of all possible borrowed words from Arabic, Portuguese, and English."

[1284] The following section of this entry is from *EG*, pp. 42–54.

One must act rather bored, then one perhaps has a chance.[1285] But it is incredibly difficult to steer the conversation towards the essential questions. For there are things that they do not want to elicit under any circumstances. So for example, I was never able to speak about spirits, *seleteni*.[1286] That would have had the same effect as when one makes an inappropriate remark in an English drawing room.[1287] Once I flouted this rule, as yet unbeknownst to me. Then the people were so aghast that I had to terminate the palaver. Such things must not be invoked.

The Black man fears the technological power of the whites. But he also feels spiritually plundered. He is ashamed of his spiritual traditions which seem as pathetic to him as his weapons. What is African *dawa* (medicine) in the face of the magic potions of the white doctors? What are his religious views in the face of the richly endowed missions? He dreams of firearms, shorts and skirts over them, and the women dream of colorful clothes.

No one wants to accept ever hearing of Gods, demons, spirits, teaching of the tribe. Yes—they wanted to claim never to have seen a spirit house! But that went too far for me! For we had discovered countless spirit houses, some quite new ones among them. A very fine one had recently been built completely from stone in the next village. The reason for this was that our female water carrier had become ill. [42/43] The people called on us for help. I sent my friend who had more practical experience than I did.[1288] He diagnosed sepsis following a miscarriage. We were somewhat embarrassed, for we were not equipped for such a case. But, as I learned later from my Black friend, at the same time the people had called for a *mganga* (medicine man) from the western side of the mountain. He looked at the patient in her high fever and then began to circumambulate the house in ever increasing circles and then ultimately declared the trail leading down from the mountain to be a path for the spirits. I learned that both parents of the young patient had died young. The water carrier was their only daughter. Up in the bamboo forest which was considered the forest of the dead they had felt very lonely and sad, and this is why they wanted to fetch their daughter to be with them. In defense a spirit trap had to be built on the trail. On a bed, a clay effigy of the sick woman had to be laid within it. Alongside this they

---

1285 "chance": in English in the original.

1286 *Seleteni*, Swahili: "spirits." Jung refers to this event then alluded to in his preface to Fanny Moser's *Spuck: Irrglaube oder Wahrglaube?* (1950), CE 20; CW 18, § 759.

1287 "drawing room": in English in the original.

1288 H. G. Baynes: see n. 1230 above.

placed water in shards of pots and *posho* (food). The spirit house was, as usual, built in the tangential extension of a sharp bend, so that the spirits had to run directly inside. But meanwhile the actual patient recovers, liberated from the damaging influence of spirits. As a matter of fact she recovered in the space of two days and on the third day she appeared again back in the camp with her water pot. Whether the *mganga* had also used other means I cannot recall.

In this one case it was possible for me to ascertain from a Black friend who had built the spirit house and what purpose it served. It became the subject of various palavers but no one dared to own it, so deep was the awe of the white man—or of the spirits? How deep the fear of the spirits went was revealed on an excursion into a bamboo forest that extended to an altitude of 2,800 meters. When we arrived in the forest, the porters came and desperately begged me for a holiday: they were so tired, they could not go on any further. Could I not turn around and go back? There was nothing to see here, only the forest. Would I not at least allow them to sleep a little here and to wait for me there?—I laughed at them, I even threatened. All in vain, they were completely demoralized. There was nothing else for it but to leave them there. Only one porter, a Masai called Sabié, a brave and strong young man declared, after some hesitation, that he was willing to accompany my friend and me.

The bamboo forest was a green twilight, traversed by buffalo and rhino routes. We crept for a long time along rhino paths, crouching down low, for the thick tree cover began at a height of one and a half meters: that is, above the backs of the rhinoceroses. As usual I was unarmed, in order to convince both man and beast that I posed no harm to them.

I scrupulously avoided destroying any life form. Apart from a tiny puff adder that I found on the path and associated with a child's foot, I did not kill a single animal.—The Masai followed close on my heels and the further we went, the more he pressed closer to me. He seemed upset and was sweating terribly. His eyes were twitching. I asked, "What is wrong with you, Sabié?"—He whispered in my ear, "Selelteni (spirits) ten thousand." It was not rhinos or buffalo that he feared, but the invisible dead. The spirits—they took him to the limit of his courage! [44/45] I never avoided going to all those places described by people as *mbaja*, meaning "inauspicious." Alongside the meaning of "bad," *mbaja* has another magical connotation, rather like "here something is uncanny," "here something is performed." I went to all those places of which it was said that *sheitani*, meaning "devil" in Arabic, lived there.

In many cases I was able to identify a real circumstance which people misinterpreted and then considered uncanny. But one time we arrived at a place where even I felt the numinosum. It was a purely subjective experience. On the slopes of Mount Elgon one can still discern an ancient lava stream that once flowed down from there.[1289] It ends abruptly above the valley and the jungle begins there. On the ground of the expanse of lava where otherwise nothing else grows far and wide, some high trees were growing. They gave the impression of bastions, like safe places from where one could survey the surroundings and easily discover snakes, for example. Close to one of these trees we decided to set up camp. All of a sudden, I had a very unpleasant feeling. It was as if someone was incessantly staring at me from below out of the jungle, it seemed to me to be a massive, huge bird of about two meters. I took the binoculars but could not see the slightest thing. The shape of the bird turned out to be a play of light and shadow in the leaves. But the feeling of the uncanny remained and was so strong that I wanted to get away from there at once. This is what Africa does to you! I said to my boys[1290] the single word "mbaja," and it made sense to them immediately. No one disagreed, and we broke camp without hesitation. I was jubilant to get away from that place, but to this day I do not know what it was that had unsettled me. It was the only place in Africa that affected me extremely adversely. The unprejudiced way my emotional experience was accepted by the negroes made a strong impression on me.

Ghosts and magic are not unknown to Swiss farmers. But I lived here in Bollingen for ten years before I noticed that.—Almost in every village around here live so-called magicians. That is true everywhere, in England too, in Germany, in Italy, etc.—Near Bollingen there is a Capuchin monastery where two exorcists reside.[1291] And there lived Father Hubert, a Franciscan who, with Franciscan love, healed the little elephant from the Knie circus. It is well known that the Knie circus winters several animals in Rapperswil, not far from here.[1292] The regional veterinary doctor from Rapperswil could do nothing more for the elephant. Then someone said, "Why don't you call Father Hubert?"—Then the old Franciscan came, went to the little elephant, stroked his head, looked him in the eyes,

---

[1289] Mount Elgon: see, n. 1228 above.

[1290] "boys": in English in the original.

[1291] The Capuchin monastery in Rapperswil was founded in 1606.

[1292] The Knie family's circus (now "Schweizer National-Circus Knie"), founded in 1803. Long famed for its animals, it is Switzerland's largest circus, and still based in Rapperswil.

stroked his back and said, "He does not want to get better!" Then he stroked his head again and looked in his eyes and said, "No, he still does not want to."—After an hour and a half he said, "Now he wants to!"—And after that the little elephant became well again. The diarrhea stopped. But this terrible climate did not suit him; perhaps the trainer was unkind, and he thought, "I'm not playing ball!"; he let himself go, he gave up on life. The Franciscan was able to convince him that man loved this little animal very much, and that gave him the impulse back to life.

A farmer told me that the same Father Hubert once defeated a barn ghost. One day the farmer came to me and was in a very bad mood. "Is someone ill?" I asked.—"No."—"And how is the cow?"—"I know what is wrong." "You do? So what is it then? Is the cow sick?"—"If you get twenty-five liters of milk from her every day but today you only got ten liters, what do you think? I know what I'll do: I'll go to Father Hubert."—And he said, "Hello, Karli, what is wrong?"—"Well, yesterday I got twenty-five liters of milk and today only ten." [50/51] Then Hubert said (in dialect) "Write her name on a scrap of paper." The finest cow is always called Venes, after Venus. So our farmer writes "Venes" on a piece of paper, and Father Hubert put it in the sleeve of his habit. "Right," he said, "now you can go, everything will be okay." The farmer gives him a five-frank coin, and indeed, everything was okay. And the cow went back to producing her twenty-five liters of milk again.

That is part of the distinguishing features of the Capuchins. They heal with Franciscan love. "Brother wolf!"[1293] This influence of the Catholics creates a revivification of the environment around here and creates a relationship between the Church and farmers, even the Protestant farmers. The land here belongs to the Prince Bishop of St. Gallen.

SEPTEMBER 19, 1958.[1294] WITH K. W. IN BOLLINGEN

The other image that fascinated me as a child in my parental home came from a Basel landscape artist from the beginning of the nineteenth century. It depicted the flat, open foothills with the view in the direction of St. Jacob and on to the Jura.[1295]

[1293] A reference to Saint Francis of Assisi's taming of the wolf of Gubbio.

[1294] The ms. gives October 19 as the date of this entry, but Kurt Wolff was already back in New York by then.

[1295] See ETG, p. 22, MDR, p. 16.

The Fabers (my maternal grandmother was born a Faber) came from Nürtingen.[1296] They were French Protestants who came to Germany after the edict of Nantes.

I am also related to the French on my paternal side, although not as blood relations. My grandfather's first wife was Virginie de Lassaux. Her daughter, Anna Jung, married the publisher Georg Reimer, the publisher of Jean Paul.[1297]

[1296] See above, p. 322.

[1297] Georg Andreas Reimer (1776–1842), German publisher. Jean Paul (1763–1825), born Johann Paul Friedrich Richter, was a German Romantic writer known for his eclectically humorous novels.

Aniela Jaffé. Photographer unknown. Courtesy of Nomi Kluger-Nash.

Appendix 1

I.

[801][1299]The years at the Burghölzli and at the University of Zurich's psychiatric clinic were my years of training.[1300] At the forefront of my interest and research was this burning question: What is actually going on in the mentally ill? At that time, I had as yet no understanding of that whatsoever, and there was no one there who was bothered about this problem. The psychology of the mentally ill did not feature at all.

The so-called clinical standpoint that prevailed back then was never concerned about the human personality of the unwell; it was never about the individual; rather, you had "patient number seventy-five" in front of you with a long list of designated diagnoses and symptoms, and that was the how the patient could never present as a human being. Just think of all these poor devils! The institutions [801/802] are overflowing with

---

[1298] In the winter of 1958 Aniela Jaffé had a plan to group the material into sections as a spoken diary with fictive dates (Jaffé to Kurt Wolff, October 23, 1958, BL). The following is one such section, parts of which were included in *Memories, Dreams, Reflections* in chapter 4, "Psychiatric Activities." Wolff had been pressing her to gather more material regarding Jung's psychotherapeutic practice. The original interviews for this have not come to light. It is reproduced here without the fictive dates.

[1299] Passages from the entry of March 7, 1958 were added into this entry—these have not been reproduced here. See *ETG*, p. 121, *MDR*, p. 114.

[1300] Jung entered the Burghölzli as an assistant doctor on December 11, 1900. On April 1, 1902 he took up the position of the first medical assistant there. On September 30 he left his post. From October 19, 1903 Alexander von Muralt the *Sekundararzt* (clinical director) was on sick leave for six months, and Jung deputized for him. On April 18, 1904, von Muralt's sick leave was prolonged for a further six months. On October 18 von Muralt took another six months sick leave, and finally resigned in March 1905; Jung formally replaced him on April 18. He became a lecturer at the medical school in 1905, resigning this position in 1914 (information from the personnel files, Zurich Staatsarchiv).

them![1301] Of course you cannot expect doctors to be thoroughly familiar[1302] with every case, as an analyst must know his patients, for example. But I saw very soon that this type of classification that was in vogue back then led nowhere. And it is still the same today!

When someone says "schizophrenia," he thinks he has said something specific. But that is basically nothing but empty words.[1303] When he says "hysteria," he thinks he is saying something important. But that can mean everything under the sun! Diagnoses tell us absolutely nothing.

But I don't want to present theoretical explanations to you here; it's better if I relate a couple of examples to show you what I was all about, then and now. Besides, my biography is not the place for scientific medical considerations. I have written enough about psychiatry and psychopathology and my thoughts about these can be looked up in my books. But I can tell you about a couple of examples that seemed interesting and important to me. They also belong to my essential memories.

I well recall a case that impressed me very much at the time, due not only to the uncertainty of the diagnosis.

[1304]It concerns a young woman who had been admitted to the Burghölzli with "melancholia." She was examined as carefully as it was possible to do at the clinic: a case history was taken, tests, physical examinations, etc. Diagnosis: schizophrenia, or "dementia praecox" as they called it back then. Prognosis: bad.

By chance, this woman was in my department. I did not doubt the diagnosis for one minute. I was a young man after all, [802/803] a beginner, and I would not have dared to propose a different diagnosis. Yet the case seemed noteworthy to me, and I thought, "You have never seen a case like this before!"—I had the feeling that it was not a question of schizophrenia, but a normal depression, and I decided to apply my own method. I was undertaking the diagnostic word associations studies at the time, and I carried out the associations experiment with the patient.

In addition, I discussed her dreams with her. In this way I was able to uncover her history which had not emerged in the anamnesis. So I received the information directly from the unconscious and out of it a very dark and tragic story emerged. Before this woman married, she had known a man. She lived in a small town, and he was the son of an industrial

---

[1301] The statistics in the 1900 annual report of the Burghölzli reported five doctors, seventy-three nursing attendants, and a daily average of 377 patients.

[1302] "thoroughly familiar": in French in the original, "à fond."

[1303] "empty words": in Latin in the original, "flatus vocis."

[1304] See *ETG*, pp. 121–22, *MDR*, pp. 115–16.

magnate and all the local girls were interested in him. Basically, she thought she might have a chance as she was very pretty. But apparently he was not interested in her, so she accepted another man.

Five years passed and then an old friend came to visit her. And when they were alone, he said, "Mrs. So-and-So, it was a huge shock for someone when you got married! Namely, for Mr. So-and-So" (the son of the industrial magnate).—That was the moment! In that instant the depression arrived. After some weeks she happened to be bathing her children. First her little girl who was about four years old and then her somewhat older son. She lived in an area where the water treatment was not yet very good; they had pure drinking water from the well and grey water from the river. When the little girl was taking a bath—naturally not in drinking water—she sucked on the sponge. The mother saw this clearly, but she did not stop her! And she even gave her young son a glass of river water to drink.

Of course, she did this unconsciously, or only semi-consciously. For she was already in the fugue state of the incipient depression.

Shortly afterwards, after the incubation period, both children became ill with typhoid fever, and the young girl died. She was her favorite child. Now the depression was full-blown, and the woman was admitted to the institution. [803/804]

From the associations experiment I had already perceived the fact that she was a murderer as well as many details of her history, long before I had spoken to her about it. It was immediately clear to me that this was the reason for her depression.

But then what about the therapy? Up till now she had been given narcotics, and she had been prescribed walks for exercise every day. Physically she was in quite good shape. Now I faced the problem: should I say this to her or not? Should I undertake the great operation or not?—If I had asked other doctors, it is certain they would have said to me, "For God's sake don't say such terrible things to this woman. You will only make her more unwell."—But in the background, I had a "hunch."[1305] I thought, "Perhaps the opposite is also true." In psychology it is the case that every truth can also be reversed. The opposite is also always true. So I thought perhaps in this case, too, the opposite to the rule might have a therapeutic effect. But of course, I knew for certain: if she gets into hot water then so will I! Despite this, I decided to do it and I told her everything. You can imagine it was very difficult and very tragic. It is no small

---

[1305] "hunch": in English in the original.

thing to be called a murderer!—But the effect was this: in fourteen days she went home, and she never returned to an institution again.

There were other reasons that caused me to hold my tongue about this case with other doctors: I feared that they would discuss it in a stupid or tactless fashion. I had to take into consideration that there would then be some sort of legal questions raised and that would have had catastrophic consequences for the patient. She had been punished enough by fate! I wanted her to be able to return to life in order to atone for her guilt. That seemed far more purposeful than a public discussion taking place. And just think what that would have meant for her husband.

This decision represented an unparalleled ethical conflict for me. It was a weighty question of conscience. [804/805] But I spoke to no one about this matter. No one would understand that! They are all so obtuse! So colossally obtuse!

When the patient was discharged, she left there carrying a dark burden. She was obliged to bear it. The loss of the child was terrible for her and she had already begun her atonement with the depression and her admission to the Burghölzli.

[1306]In most cases in psychiatry every single patient who enters our care has a story that is untold and that, as a rule, is known to no one. It is a very personal story and for me, the therapy begins with its exploration. It is the patient's secret that he was not able to bear or that caused him to break down. When I know his story, his *secret* story, then I have the key to the therapy. The doctor must only know how to get to it. The exploration of conscious material is not sufficient in most cases. The associations experiment can hit the spot by chance,[1307] as can a dream interpretation or lengthy and persistent human contact with the patient. In the therapy it is always about the whole person and never only about the symptom. You must ask the questions that concern the whole person; and that is why you must know his background and his actual story.

2.

[807] Since I had learned from my practice at the Burghölzli how important the history is behind every neurosis, I soon began to inquire about the case history in the course on hypnosis, in the cases I presented to the students.

[1306] See *ETG*, p. 123, *MDR*, p. 117.
[1307] "by chance": in English in the original.

One case in particular stays in my mind.[1308] An older lady came, apparently religiously minded. She appeared on crutches led by her maid, about fifty-eight years old. She was lame in her left leg. I knew that she had been in that state for seventeen years.

I sat her on a chair and asked her about her suffering. Then she naturally began to tell her story and to lament how terrible everything was and the whole history of her illness came out, with all the bells and whistles. I interrupted her: "Well, now, we have no time to talk in detail. Now we will hypnotize you!"—I had barely got the words out when she shut her eyes and fell into a deep trance—without any hypnosis!

I was amazed but I left her in peace. But she talked ceaselessly and related the most remarkable dreams portraying a genuine experience of the unconscious. Of course, I only understood that much later. At that time, I assumed she had a type of delirium. But I was filled with anxiety. There were about twenty students there to whom I was supposed to be demonstrating hypnosis! I was nicely in the soup and praying to God for a miracle. I had reached the end of my wisdom.—After half an hour I saw that I simply had to awaken the woman, but it took about ten minutes until I managed it. I did not want to let my students see anything of my anxiety! When she came to herself, she was dizzy and confused. I explained to her, "I am the doctor, and everything is okay." Whereupon she cried, "But I've been healed!"—she threw the crutches away and was able to walk. I blushed and said to the students, "Now you have seen what one can achieve with hypnosis." But I did not have the slightest clue what had happened. [807/808]

That was one of the experiences that caused me to abandon hypnosis; for it might have turned out very badly. I did not understand what had actually happened, but the woman was in fact healed and went away jubilantly. I asked her to keep me informed about herself for I reckoned on a relapse twenty-four hours later at the most. But the pain never returned, and I could only marvel at the grace of heaven.

In the first lecture of the next semester the woman appeared again. This time she was complaining of severe back pain that had only recently started. I immediately wondered whether that was related to the recommencement of my lectures. Whether it was a more or less conscious contrivance in order to see me again and to repeat such a fine and dramatic

---

[1308] See *ETG*, pp. 124–25, *MDR*, pp. 118–19, and above, p. 284. Jung described this case to Rudolf Loÿ on January 28, 1913: "Timely Psychotherapeutic Questions: A Correspondence with Dr. C. G. Jung," *CE* 7; *CW* 4, §§ 579–80.

treatment. So I asked her when the pain had begun and what had caused it. But she could not recall anything that had happened at a certain time.

Rather, she claimed that she had nothing to say about it. She simply had no explanation. I thought: perhaps she read the announcement about my lecture in the newspaper, and I finally managed to elicit from her that the pain had begun precisely at the hour and on the day that she had seen the announcement in the newspaper. That may have confirmed my supposition, but I still did not grasp how the miraculous healing had come about. So I kept her back at the end of the lecture in order to find out more about her life.

It emerged that she had a mentally disabled son who was in the clinic in my department. I knew nothing of this because she used the name of her second husband and the son was from the first marriage. He was her only child, and she naturally had longed for a healthy and intelligent son. Back then I was still a young doctor and so it was I whom she had put in place of her son, as it were. "I want to perform a miracle for him; it is worth doing something for him." And that is what she did. She did her utmost to create a great piece of theater for me. In fact, I owed my local fame as a magician to her, and since the story soon got around, thanks to this, my first private patients. My private therapeutic practice began because a mother put me in the place of her feeble-minded son. [808/810]

Of course, I explained the whole thing to her with all its complexities, and she accepted this very well. After that she never had another relapse.

That was my first actual therapeutic experience, I might say: my first analysis. But, you know, it was a very nice conversation with the old lady! She was intelligent and exceptionally grateful that I had taken her so seriously and had engaged with her fate and that of her son. That simply helped her out of it. She is long since dead, so it is not indiscreet of me to tell you this.

3.

[813] The associations experiment is really a terrific thing. As long as I was at the Burghölzli and in the first years of my practice I worked with it a great deal and wrote about it.[1309] But then the time soon came when I

[1309] The associations experiment had been introduced from experimental psychology into psychiatry by the German forensic psychiatrist Gustav Aschaffenburg (1866–1944).

could no longer confine myself to it. I had to go further and do something else.
[813/814]

Once a well-known criminologist came to see me. He wanted to do the associations experiment with me. I said, "Fine!" and we began. After fifteen reactions it became tedious to him and so I stopped. Normally one can glean nothing at all from fifteen responses, there is far too little in it. But he asked me whether I could tell him something. I replied, "Yes, fine, I can tell you a couple of things that might interest you." And then I said to him, "I learn from the experiment that you are fearful of dying of heart disease. Recently you have been very preoccupied by death, and you also have some financial worries.—You studied in Paris and led a charmed life there and experienced a love affair there." I can tell you: he almost screamed! "For God's sake, that is clairvoyance!" Then he called his wife who was waiting in the next room: "Olga come in, you've got to do this too! Errr, no—I'd rather not!"

When one understands how to apply and interpret the associations experiment one can read an enormous amount from it. Just as in the case of the child murderer: a whole life, a whole history.

4.

I was struck over and over again by how the human soul reacts to an unconsciously committed wrong. At first, that young woman was not conscious that she had killed her child! And yet after doing so, she ended up in such a state that she had to be brought into an institution.

I once saw a similar case which remains unforgettable to me. Since it took place at least twenty or thirty years ago and everyone involved has since died, I am able to tell you about it. [814/815]

From 1891 Aschaffenburg was the medical assistant, then deputy director under Emil Kraepelin (1856–1926), at the Psychiatric University Clinic in Heidelberg. In 1904 he became professor of psychiatry in Cologne. The initial aim of the experiments at the Burghölzli was to provide a tool for the differential diagnosis of mental disorders. This project collapsed. However, the research took a new turn, and attention was redirected to disturbances of response. Jung and his principal co-worker Franz Riklin (who had studied in Heidelberg) argued that the disturbances of response were due to the associations that had been triggered in the subject's mind by the stimulus word. The words evoked what they termed "emotionally stressed complexes." "Experimental Observations on the Associations of Healthy Subjects" (1904), CE 3; CW 2.

[1310]A lady came to my practice without giving her name. She must have possessed a great manor house and from her appearance and her language she might have belonged to the German nobility. But these are only presumptions. She did not tell me her name. She was a doctor and what she had to tell me was a confession: twenty years before she had committed murder out of envy. She had poisoned a woman because she wanted to marry this woman's husband. It was her best friend! But she thought that such a murder would not affect her. If she wished to marry the husband, she would simply remove the friend from her path!

And afterwards? She married the man, but he died very soon afterwards, while still quite young. And then strange things happened.

Her daughter ceased all contact with her mother. She married and then simply disappeared from her horizon—as if she had drifted away. The mother never heard anything from her again.

The woman was a passionate horse rider and very involved in horse breeding. Then one day she discovered that the horses had begun to be afraid of her. Even her best riding horse was afraid of her and she had to give it up.—Then she also had wolfhounds which she was very fond of. And what happened? Her favorite dog became lame—probably due to an emotional conflict, he could still walk on his front legs, but his hind legs no longer functioned.

When that happened, she felt morally undone. She had to confess and so she came to me. She was a murderer, but she had convinced herself that she could simply carry out the murder. You can do this, it's nothing!

In actuality, she had murdered herself. For whoever commits such a great sin destroys his soul. A murderer has already judged himself, and a thief steals himself.

If a person has committed a deed consciously, the punishment reaches him externally. If he did it unconsciously and is unconscious of the moral consequences, the punishment reaches him all the same. For the unconscious knows everything. One must not deceive oneself about this. Even the animals and the plants know this. Whether a crime has been committed consciously or unconsciously is important for the civil circumstances— but not in and of itself.

Through the murder the woman experienced unbearable loneliness. She even became repugnant to animals and in order to free herself of loneliness she made me into her accomplice. She had to have an accomplice who was not a murderer. She wanted to see a person who could

---

[1310] See *ETG*, pp. 128–29, *MDR*, pp. 122–23.

bear it without making a terrible story out of it, as in this way she was able to re-establish some relationship with humanity. That is also the purpose of confession. Though in her case it had not to be a father confessor, but a normal person. With a father confessor she would have assumed that he was hearing her confession as part of his professional role. But she could not expect anything like that from me; I was simply an objective accomplice.

I spoke with her for about three quarters of an hour. But I never learned who she was: she appeared and then disappeared again. I sometimes wondered about how the story might have unfolded further. For at that time, it was not yet finished. Perhaps ultimately, she committed suicide. I cannot imagine how she was able to go on living in her exterior loneliness. But any speculation about it is superfluous; we simply do not know.

5.

[1311] As I already told you, clinical diagnosis is of course good and important; it gives a certain orientation, but it does not help the patient at all. The crucial point is the question of disposition, for that shows the human background and human suffering and it is only there that the doctor's therapy can intervene. To illustrate, a case at the Burghölzli made a great impact on me. [818/819]

It was an old patient on the women's ward, a fifty-seven-year-old woman who had been confined to her bed for forty years.[1312] She had entered the institution nearly fifty years ago but no one could remember her admission; in the meantime everyone who had been present then had died. Only a senior nurse who had been in the institution for thirty-five years still recalled anything of her history. The old woman was unable to speak and could take only liquid foods. She ate with her fingers with a curious shoveling action. Sometimes she took almost two hours to eat one cupful. When she was not eating, she made strange movements with her hands and arms. I always thought, "How awful that is!" but I could not get any further. In the clinical lectures she was always presented as a catatonic form of dementia praecox, but that seemed completely meaningless to me for it did not tell us the slightest thing about the meaning of those curious movements.

[1311] See *ETG*, pp. 130–31, *MDR*, pp. 124–25.
[1312] Jung described this case in "The Content of the Psychoses" (1908), *CE 5*; *CW 3*, § 358.

The impression that this case made on me characterized my whole re-action to psychiatry (of the time). For six months I battled in despair to find my own way but only became even more confused. I felt deeply hu-miliated alongside my boss and colleagues who seemed so self-confident while I groped around cluelessly in the dark. I was incapable of under-standing, and I had such feelings of inferiority that I was not at all able to leave the institute. There I was, in a profession in which I did not have a clue! So I holed up in the building and studied my cases.

Late one evening I was walking through the department, and I saw the old woman and her strange movements, and I wondered again, "What is the purpose of this?" Then I went to the senior nurse and inquired whether the patient had always been like this and whether she knew any more details about the case. "Yes," she replied, "she used to make shoes. I know that from the head nurse on the men's ward." Thereupon I searched in the archives for her old case notes and there it stated that she made movements as if she were making shoes. The shoemaker used to hold the shoes in front of their knees and they pulled the thread through the leather with precisely those actions. (You can still see this today oc-casionally with village shoemakers). [818/819]

When the patient died soon after her older brother arrived.—"Why did your sister become mentally ill?" I asked him. He related that she had loved a shoemaker, but he did not want to marry her for some rea-son, and then she became crazy.—With these movements she had kept his image alive in her!

Through this I acquired a first intimation of the psychogenesis of de-mentia praecox. From then on I devoted all my attention to my cases and noted all the factors that indicated a psychological background to psycho-ses. My book *The Psychology of Dementia Praecox* developed out of this.[1313]

[1314]That reminds me of another patient in the Burghölzli. Through her, the psychological background of the psychoses and above all of the "in-sane delusional ideas" became clear to me, and I understood for the first time the language of schizophrenics that had been declared meaningless up until then. It was Babette S. whose story I published.[1315] In 1908 I gave a lecture about her in the City Hall in Zurich.[1316]

[1313] *The Psychology of Dementia Praecox* (1907), CE 4; CW 3.
[1314] See *ETG*, pp. 131–32, *MDR*, pp. 125–26.
[1315] *The Psychology of Dementia Praecox* (1907), CE 4; CW 3. See above, p. 281.
[1316] "The Content of the Psychoses" (1908), CE 5; CW 3.

She came from the Zurich old town, from the narrow and grubby streets where she came into the world in poverty and grew up in the same conditions. Her sister was a prostitute, her father a drinker. She became ill with the paranoid form of dementia praecox, had delusions of grandeur and of inferiority. She took ill aged thirty-nine and when I met her she had already been in the hospital for twenty years. [820/821] Many hundreds of medical students acquired from her a deep impression of the incredible power of mental decay.

6.

[822] In many sentences a wish fulfillment is being expressed; they were fantasies that were meant to smooth the hard edges of reality. Whoever knows themselves knows that a being lives within that would like to draw a veil over everything questionable in life. In mental illness this being has the upper hand. Reality [822/823] becomes a distant dream. It replaces reality and shackles the patient to itself. Frequently no more knowledge gets through to us of these things that are playing out in the inner world of the mentally ill, because the bridges from there to us have fallen down.

[1317]Engaging with Babette and other similar cases provided me with an enduring impression of the fact that the mentally ill are ultimately not as crazy as they appear. More than once I experienced that in the background of such people a "person" is hidden who can be quite "normal" and who, to a certain degree, is an observer. Occasionally this person can make quite sensible remarks and objections, and it can happen that it comes into the foreground if the patient becomes physically ill. But normally it is not identical with the I.

Once I had to treat an old schizophrenic woman in whom the "normal person" in the background became very clear to me.[1318] I had taken her on only in order to liberate her son from her. He was a young man who could not abandon his mother so for this reason he had a neurosis. I said to him, "Do your exams, and then off you go! I will take on your mother!" I had no illusions about this woman for she had already been in the asylum for two periods. She heard voices that were distributed over her whole

---

[1317] See *ETG*, p. 132, *MDR*, p. 126.

[1318] Jung discussed this case in his presentation to the Second International Congress of Psychiatry in September 1957, which was read for him by his grandson Dieter Baumann. "Schizophrenia," *CE* 25; *CW* 3.

body. It was not a case to cure, but only to safeguard; but every doctor has such cases that he must safeguard.

She heard voices that were spread across her whole body, and one voice, in the middle of her body, was "God's voice." "We must rely on this voice!" I said to her—and I expressed this calmly.

As a rule this voice said very reasonable things, and with its help I got on well with this woman. Once she said, [823/824] "He must listen to you on the Bible!"–So I began to assign to her a chapter from the Bible every time. She had to read it, and I listened to her talk about it the next time. I did that for about eight years, at first three times a week, then twice, then once. After this time the voices on the right-hand side of the body had completely stopped. That was a very unexpected success, I had not intended any therapy with her, I only wanted to help the son and relieve him of the responsibility for his mother. By my regularly listening to her on the Bible she had acquired a certain consciousness. She had to read something, think about it, and re-narrate it. So she remained intellectually alive and did not fall asleep. I would never have thought of the idea myself of assigning something like that to her.

The "voice of God," by the way, occasionally made very humorous comments about certain people. Unfortunately, I could not say, "Yes, I agree!"

7.

Through my work with Babette, it had become clear to me like a bolt from the blue that persecutory ideas and hallucinations contain a nucleus of meaning and we are the ones to blame if we do not understand it. This insight made an extraordinary impression on me. I said to myself, "That is what is hiding behind it! There is a personality behind it, a life story, a hope and a wish!"

[1319]Then for the first time I realized that a general psychology of the personality lies hidden in psychosis and that the ancient conflicts of humanity are also to be found in psychosis, just as in hysteria or neurosis. Basically, we do not discover anything new or unknown to us in the mentally ill, but rather we encounter in them the substratum of our own being and the life problems that we are all grappling with. That became clear to me then and that was a tremendously emotional experience for me. [824/825]

[1319] See *ETG*, p. 134, *MDR*, p. 127.

As obtuse and apathetic as patients like Babette may seem—it is said they are "mentally decayed"—their inner life is rich, as their baroque mish-mash of words proclaims. They are fragments of fairy-tale-like fantasies, or messages of a distinctly otherworldly kingdom, far from the dismal misty land of reality.—Before I spoke with Babette, however, no one had taken the trouble to decipher these mysterious symbols.

It is always astonishing to me that it has taken nearly half a century for psychiatry finally to pay attention to the psychological contents of psychoses, and it's just as astonishing to me—I must say—that my investigations from that time appear to be completely forgotten. I was already doing psychotherapy with schizophrenics fifty years ago.[1320] Today they think they have just discovered this. Back then I was declared insane because of my experiments, because they did not yet understand anything of psychology.

When I was still at the Burghölzli I had to treat a series of schizophrenics in secret because I was afraid it would cost me my job, since schizophrenia, or "dementia praecox," was considered simply incurable. At that time, they were still concerned with the question of whether Freud was correct or not. If schizophrenia could be treated, they simply said it had been a misdiagnosis and not a case of schizophrenia after all.

8.

[1321]In the mentally ill what is seen from outside is only the tragic destruction, but what is seldom seen are the riches of the side of the soul that is turned away from us. My compassion for and understanding of the subjective life of these patients received a notable correction when I once had to treat an eighteen-year-old girl, and through her I learned rather more about it. She came from an educated family and had been seduced by her brother and some school friends when she was fifteen years old. From the age of sixteen she isolated herself. She hid from people and in the end, she only had any sort of emotional relationship with a vicious

---

[1320] On September 24, 1926 Jung wrote to Louis London, "I only treated a limited number of cases, and these were all in what one could call a liquid condition, that is to say, not yet congealed. I avoid the treatment of such cases as much as possible. It is true that they can be treated, and even with the most obvious success, but such a success costs almost your own life. You have to make the most stupendous effort to reintegrate the dissociated psychic entities, and it is by no means a neat and simple technique which you can apply, but a creative effort together with a vast knowledge of the unconscious mind." *Letters*, vol. 1, p. 45.

[1321] See *ETG*, pp. 134–35, *MDR*, p. 128.

guard dog that belonged to other people and which she attempted to re-train to a good nature. She became ever stranger, and at the age of seven-teen she arrived at the asylum where she spent eighteen months. She heard voices, refused food, and no longer spoke. When I saw her for the first time she was in a terrible state.

Over the course of several weeks, I was ultimately able gradually to get her to speak again. And then her fantasy history came out too: every-thing that had intensively preoccupied her during the period of her ill-ness. [826/827]

She told me that she had lived on the moon. The moon was inhabited, but at first she had seen only men. These had immediately taken her with them and brought her to a place under the surface of the moon where there were women and children. In the high mountains there was a vam-pire who plundered women and children and killed them so that the people of the moon were threatened with extinction. That was why the female half of the population resided under the surface of the moon.

My patient now decided to do something for the people of the moon: she made the decision to destroy the vampire. After lengthy preparations that I won't relate in detail here, she awaited the vampire on the platform of a tower. After several nights she finally saw him in the distance, like a large black bird hovering over her. She took a large knife, concealed it in her clothes and awaited his arrival. Suddenly he stood right in front of her. He had several pairs of wings. His face and his whole figure were covered in wings so that she could see nothing but his feathers. She was astonished and shaken and gripped with curiosity to learn what he looked like. She approached him, the knife in her hand. Suddenly he opened his wings and a man of heavenly beauty stood before her, com-pletely naked. He closed her in his wings with an iron grip so that she was no longer able to use the knife. Moreover, she was so spellbound by the sight of the vampire that she would no longer have been able to stab him. He seized her and flew away with her.

At that moment she came to herself and that was the beginning of my treatment.

After that revelation she could speak again without inhibition, and now her objections also flooded out: I had barred the way back to the moon! Now she would no longer be able to escape the earth. This world was not nice, but the moon was nice, and there life was meaningful. [827/828]

After some time, she got very distressed and I had to bring her into the clinic. For a long time she was raving mad.

When she came out two months later it was possible to speak with her again, and gradually she conceded that a normal human earthly destiny was unavoidable. She fought desperately against this inevitability and had to be transferred to the clinic several times. Once I visited her in her cell and said to her, "None of this is any use to you! You can't return to the moon!"—She took this in silently and impassively. That time she was released from the clinic after a short period and resigned herself to her fate.

She took a job as a carer in a sanatorium. An assistant doctor there incautiously tried to get close to her and she countered this with a revolver bullet. Fortunately, he sustained only a slight injury. So she did get hold of a revolver! She had carried a loaded revolver early on. In the final session with me at the end of her treatment, she brought it with her. To my astonishment she declared, "I would have shot you with it if you had failed me!"

When the uproar caused by the shooting had subsided, she returned to her homeland. She married, had several children, and survived two world wars in the East without ever suffering a relapse.

What can be said about her fantasies? Due to the incest she had suffered as a young girl she was humiliated and demeaned in the world, but elevated spiritually. She was raised, as it were, to the level of the hierosgamos.[1322] But in this way a complete alienation from the world occurred: the state of psychosis. She sort of became alienated from the world and lost contact with people. She ended up in [828/829] that strange remoteness, in space, where she encountered the seraphim. She brought this figure into the transference in the treatment with me. It was vital for me to resist the temptation to incest, and I was threatened with death if I failed to carry that out. Through this the "unio mystica," the alchemical marriage, could be accomplished with me as the seraphim, as it were. And after she had experienced that she was able to return to her life and even marry. Since then, I myself have regarded the suffering of the mentally ill with different eyes, for then I also knew about the riches of their inner life.

9.

[1323]I am often asked about my psychotherapeutic or analytic methods. I cannot give a straightforward reply to this. The therapy is different in every case.

For example, I was once treating a man and at the same time I was treating a lady. Both were from America, but at that time they did not yet

---

[1322] See n. 756 above.
[1323] See *ETG*, p. 136, *MDR*, p. 131.

know each other. They met each other only later and found out that they had both been in treatment with me. Thereupon they began to exchange the experiences they had had in treatment. "But you must have been with someone else: what you are telling me is completely incorrect. That has nothing whatsoever to do with what I experienced!"

Here is the explanation: he was a successful American businessman who had remained completely childish as far as relationships were concerned. So with him I had to teach the ABC of psychological relationships.

She was a woman of the world—but she would not have been able to do business! She knew a thousand times more than he did about relationships. So with her I did not need to teach the ABC, but the treatment went in a completely different direction.

When they met, she naturally had completely different things to relate than he did. With him I had not interpreted one single dream, with her a proper analysis had taken place. [829/830]

If a doctor says to me that he conducts one analysis very much like the other, then I doubt the therapeutic effect. Psychotherapies and analyses are as different as the human individuals. While in a certain way all individuals are alike, that is not the important thing. It is the differences that are the crucial thing. It is only individuals in their consciousness who carry life. And the doctor and the therapist must know this.

[1324]I treat every patient as individually as possible, for the solution to the problem is possible only in the individual case, it never arises through methods and rules. In psychotherapy there is no generally applicable principle. A psychological truth is applicable only when one can also invert it. A solution that would be out of the question for me can be just the right thing for someone else.

In the treatment of human individuality, it is a mistake to think that one might "apply a method." Of course, the doctor must be familiar with the method or, better said, the methods, plural. For it is the basic requirement that he understands his trade, and is master of it. But he must guard against settling on one method. The theories are only nomenclature. Today they are perhaps relevant, tomorrow it might be others. In my treatment they do not play a role. With great intentionality I am not systematic. For me, as far as the individual is concerned there is only one understanding, namely an individual one.

[1324] See *ETG*, p. 136, *MDR*, pp. 131–32.

The requirement patients bring with them is infinitely variable. Even the language is different. For every patient a different language is needed. In one analysis you can hear me speaking in an Adlerian way, and in another a Freudian. These are perspectives that are absolutely at my disposal. [830/831]

The decisive point, however, is that I as a human being encounter another human being. Analysis is a dialogue to which two partners belong; and that cannot be captured in any "method." The doctor has something to say, but so too does the patient.

In psychotherapy, since it is not a question of simply applying a "method," psychiatric training alone is not sufficient. I myself had to work for a long time before I had the skills for psychotherapy. Even in 1909 I realized that I could not treat schizophrenia if I did not understand its symbolism. That was when I began to study mythology.[1325]

With educated and intelligent patients, the doctor cannot bring simple concepts to bear, nor purely biological theories. For this reason, he needs comprehensive knowledge. For example, if one is dealing with people who themselves have religious experiences then he must know something about this in depth. The therapist must understand the conceptual background of whatever moves the patient. For this a course of study and education is required that far exceeds medical training.

The soul is incredibly more complicated than the body. With the soul the doctor is dealing with factors out of which the world comes to exist. It is, as it were, the other half of the world: there is no world without our being conscious of it. Therefore, the soul is not only a personal problem, but also a problem of the greatest universal significance.

Today one can see it as never before: the danger that threatens us all does not come from nature but from man, from the soul of the individual and the many. The psychic inconstancy of man is the danger! Everything depends on whether our psyche is functioning properly or not. You know this: if certain people have a tantrum, a nuclear bomb will explode. [831/832]

But the psychotherapist must understand not only the patient; it is just as important that he understand himself. For this reason, the *conditio sine qua non* of the training is one's own analysis. The training analysis.[1326] The therapy of the patient begins as it were with the doctor; and

---

[1325] Cf. *1925*, pp. 25–26.

[1326] Jung argued for the necessity of this in psychoanalysis in "Attempt at An Account of Psychoanalytic Theory" (1912), *CE* 7; *CW* 4, § 450. In 1912 Freud wrote, "I count it as

when he understands how to get along with himself and his own problems, then he can also teach this to the patients. But only then. In the training analysis the doctor must learn to get to know his soul and to take it seriously. If he cannot do that then it is damn well certain that the patient will not learn it either. With that, however, he loses a piece of his own soul, just as the doctor too lost this piece of his own soul which he failed to get to know.

The therapist must at all times give an account to himself of how he is reacting to the confrontation with the patient. I do not react only with the conscious, so I must always ask myself: how is my unconscious experiencing this situation? So I must observe my dreams. I must pay the most precise attention and observe myself as precisely as I do the patient. Otherwise, it is possible that the whole treatment will go awry. I can give you an example of where it did.

While so-called "minor psychotherapy" exists, in real analysis the whole person is called upon, patient and doctor.[1327] There are many cases that one cannot cure without the shedding of blood. When it comes to the important things it is crucial whether the doctor gives himself to it fully or protects himself in a cloud of tobacco smoke. Then hardly anything can come out of it. In the great crises of life, in the supreme moments where it is a question of To Be or Not to Be, the small things do not help; there great things must occur, and there the doctor is challenged in his entire being. [832/833]

[1328]I once had a patient, a very intelligent woman, but for various reasons she appeared a little suspect to me. At first the analysis went very well. But after a while it seemed to me that I was not getting it right with my interpretation of dreams and I also observed a flattening out of the conversation. The analysis appeared completely fruitless. So I decided to say this to my patient, for naturally it had not escaped her that something was not going well. That night I had the following dream.

---

one of the many merits of the Zurich school of analysis that they have laid increasing emphasis on this requirement, and have embodied it in the demand that everyone who wishes to carry out analyses on other people shall first himself undergo an analysis with someone with expert knowledge." "Recommendations to Physicians Practising Psycho-Analysis" (1912), *SE* 12, p. 116.

[1327] In *Mysterium Coniunctionis* (1955–56) Jung wrote, "There is a minor surgery too, and in the same way there is a minor psychotherapy whose operations are harmless." *CE* 24; *CW* 14, § 512.

[1328] See *ETG*, pp. 139–40, *MDR*, pp. 133–34.

I was walking along a country road through a valley in the evening sunshine. To the right was a steep hill. There stood a castle and on the highest tower sat a woman on a sort of balustrade. In order to see her properly I had to bend my head far back. I awoke with cramp in my neck. Even in the dream I had recognized that the woman was my patient.

I understood immediately that if I had to look that far upwards at my patient in the dream, then I had probably been looking down at her in actuality. Dreams are compensations of the conscious attitude.

Of course, I told her of the dream and my interpretation. That effected an immediate change in the situation and very speedy progress in the treatment. By the way, I wrote about this case in my book *On the Psychology of the Unconscious*.[1329]

As a doctor I must always ask myself: what message is the patient bringing me? What does he mean to me? If he means nothing to me then I have no point of attack. The doctor is effective only when he is affected. "Only the wounded one heals." But when the doctor has a persona armor, he is not effective. I [833/834] take my patients very seriously. Perhaps I face exactly the same problem as he does? Often it happens that the patient is precisely the correct plaster on the doctor's weak spot. Very difficult situations can arise from this, even for the doctor. Or precisely for him. For all of these reasons psychotherapists must understand something of the unconscious and their own dreams.

Every therapist should be supervised by a third person so that he gets another perspective. I always advise them, "Get a 'father confessor' or a 'mother confessor'!" Women are actually very gifted in this. They often have an excellent nose and an excellent critique and probably have a lot of insight into the men! They see sides that the man does not see. This is why no woman has ever been convinced that her husband is superman.

After I had split from Freud, I was in the unfortunate position of being without a "father confessor." I was minded to ask a younger colleague to have a look at what was going on behind the scenes with me. Once I had a dream that I could not understand. I had a colleague then who was about

---

[1329] See *On the Psychology of the Unconscious* (1926), CE 10; CW 7, § 189. Jung discussed this case in more detail in "The Realities of Modern Psychotherapy" (1937), CE 15; CW 16, § 546. The case has been identified as that of Maggie Reichstein: see Vicente de Moura, *Two Cases from Jung's Clinical Practice: The Story of Two Sisters and the Evolution of Jungian Analysis* (London: Routledge, 2019).

ten years younger than me to whom I said, "Listen, I had a dream and I can't understand it. Please analyze it for me!" He did not want to get into it for he did not have enough confidence. Then I said to him, "Please react to the dream just as you are; then we'll see!"—And then I related the dream to him.—"That is an extremely significant dream, but I can't understand it," he said.—At that moment I was able to understand the dream! Do you know why? Because I was able to submit to another! I do not imagine that everyone will find the same thing that works as I do. That is why I can entrust myself to another and his judgment.

Because I had submitted my I to the authority of the other, my own inner authority quickened itself and I was able to understand myself. [834/835]

If the doctor himself has a neurosis it is self-evident that he should undergo analysis. But if he is exceptionally normal then at first there is no pressure to do a training analysis, no sword of Damocles: "If you do not do that you will fall ill!"

[1330]But I can assure you that I have had some astonishing experiences with so-called "normality." I once met a "normal person." He was a doctor and came with the best recommendations of an old colleague of mine. He had been this colleague's assistant and had taken on his practice. He had normal success, a normal practice, a normal wife, normal kids, lived in a normal little house in a normal town. He had a normal income and probably also a normal diet. So he came in order to become an analyst. I said to him, "Do you know what that means? That means: You must first get to know yourself. You yourself are the instrument. If you are not right, how can the patient be right? If you are not convinced, how can you convince him? You yourself must be the real material. But if you are not it, then may God help you! Then you will lead patients into error. So you must first submit yourself to your own analysis."—The man was in agreement but immediately said to me, "I have nothing problematic to tell you!" That should have warned me. But you know: normal people have no problems. I said, "Okay, then we can consider your dreams!" He said, "I have no dreams!"—I, "You soon will have some." Someone else would probably have had heaps of dreams by the next day. But he could not recall a single dream. That went on for fourteen days, and it became rather ominous to me.

Then an interesting dream arrived. I will relate it to you because it shows how important it is in practice to be able to interpret the details of

---

[1330] See *ETG*, pp. 140–41, *MDR*, pp. 134–35.

dreams. He dreamed that he was traveling on a train. The train stopped for two hours in a certain town. Since he did not know this town and he wanted to get to know it, [835/836] he headed for the town center. There he found a medieval house, probably the town hall. When he had found the entrance, he went inside. He wandered through long corridors and arrived in fine rooms with paintings and splendid tapestries hanging on the walls. Beautiful old objects stood all around. Suddenly he saw that it had got dark, and the sun had set. He thought: I must get back to the station! In that moment he discovered that he was lost and no longer knew where the exit was. He became afraid and realized at the same time that he had not met a single person in this house. It took a very ominous turn for him, and he quickened his steps in the hope of meeting someone. But he met no one. Then he came to a large door and he thought with relief: Now that is the exit. He opened the door and discovered that he had entered a massive room. It was so big and it was so dark that he could not even see the opposite wall. Then he became deeply afraid and ran through the vast, entirely empty room in the hope of finding the exit on the other side of the hall. Then—right in the center of the room—he saw something white on the floor, and as he approached, he discovered it was a child aged about two. The child was sitting on a chamber pot, smeared all over with feces. In that moment he awoke, screaming in panic.

Now I knew enough: that was a latent psychosis! I can tell you, I sweated as I attempted to lead him out of the dream. I had to present the dream in as harmless a way as possible. I did not go into details at all.

What the dream narrates is roughly as follows: the journey at the start of the dream is the journey to Zurich. But he stays there only a short time and then goes back again. The child in the center is a figure of himself as a two-year-old child. For a small child such bad manners are rather intense, but children can do such things. Feces attract them for they are colorful and smell! When a child grows up in a town, [836/837] possibly in a strict family, then it is easy for something like that to occur.

When I was a child, my mother often told me off for my coarse manners. When relatives came from the city, the children were always terribly clean and well turned out. An aunt of mine and her small daughter were the pinnacle of wonderful manners! When they visited us once my mother said, "Look at this sweet little girl and you are such a thug!" I thought, "You just wait!"—The meadows had just been fertilized with dung. Quite homely[1331] country air! My little cousin was allowed to go

---

[1331] "quite homely" in English in the original.

into the garden with her white shoes on. I observed her for I wanted to see what she did. She sniffed the morning air—suddenly she went into the meadow, picked up something from the ground and put it in her mouth. It was a cowpat! And I cried, "There you have it!"

But that doctor, the dreamer, was not a child, but an adult. And for this reason, the dream image at the center is a malevolent symbol. When he told me the dream it became quite clear to me that he was someone who had compensated for his madness with his normality. I caught him in the nick of time for he was within in an inch of a psychosis breaking out. I had to be glad that I brought him through it, as well as myself. But if I had not understood the dream, a catastrophe would have ensued. Beware of the all-too-normal ones! It is very dangerous.

The dreamer went straight back home. He no longer touched psychotherapy. He only used hypnosis where he could keep himself on the outside. His tendency to normality suggested a personality that would not have developed through a confrontation with the unconscious but would only have blown up.

One of the main difficulties of psychotherapy lies in understanding the psychotic element. Where a latent psychosis lurks in the background, I have always found something ominous. But you don't find the concept of a "latent psychosis" anywhere in the course books. And yet they are—in my view—far more common than the conspicuous ones. That is like tuberculosis whose latent form [837/838]—often the most dangerous from—is probably more frequent. We do not yet know anything certain about the latent form of psychosis. I reckon—cautiously—that there are about ten times more latent cases than conspicuous ones. It is very often precisely these cases that come to psychotherapy, and this is because they do not see that they are psychotic. But these patients always have a quiet fear that something might not be right, or that a psychosis might break out. I have been lucky that in my analyses no patient has gone mad; but I have seen cases of colleagues where it began in the first session and they were not able to immobilize it. Yet one cannot make doctors responsible for this. For such cases, a good psychiatric training is of course necessary.

¹³³²And now we reach the question of lay analysis. I am in favor of this and supportive of the non-medically trained being able to study and practice psychotherapy, but in this point, in the case of latent psychoses, they can easily miss the mark. For this reason, I advise all my lay analysts, "Yes, I am in favor of you undertaking analyses, but under the supervision of a doctor. As soon as you become in the slightest bit uncertain, ask

---

¹³³² See *ETG*, p. 142, *MDR*, p. 136.

him." Even for doctors it is incredibly difficult to recognize and to treat a latent schizophrenia, and all the more so for lay practitioners. But I have repeatedly found that lay practitioners who have been engaged in psychotherapy for years and have also had their own analysis know something and can also do something. In actuality, it is also the case that there are not enough doctors practicing psychotherapy. To do so requires very long and difficult training and a general education that only very few have.

Once I needed an assistant. The health officials wanted Swiss nationals to be appointed. A young doctor was sent to me, but I must say: he was good for nothing. My patients simply would have laughed at him! It was quite unthinkable that I would hire him. He did not have a clue about psychotherapy. [838/839] Back then you could not yet train in psychotherapy. Besides that, he could not speak a word of English or French. But in my practice three languages must be spoken, and I cannot afford to hire someone who not only cannot speak other languages, but chiefly has not the slightest clue about psychotherapy.

The alpha and omega for the psychotherapist is that he knows not only what is happening in the patient, but also in himself. That is why no one can practice real psychotherapy without their own analysis. And without a profound knowledge of dream interpretation. For this, knowledge of the history of ideas is a prerequisite, as well as of the sciences.

10.[1333]

[1334]The relationship between doctor and patient can occasionally lead to parapsychological phenomena, especially if there is a transference from the patient in play or if there is a more or less conscious identification between the doctor and patient. I have often experienced this. Particularly impressive for me was the case of a patient whom I dragged out of a habitual psychogenetic depression. Soon afterwards he returned to America and married, but the woman chose him above all for his money. When I saw her for the first time I knew: something evil is in play there. From the beginning she nagged him to go against me and in the end this led to a disastrous conclusion. It often happens that women who do not really love the man are jealous and destroy his friendships. She wants him to belong

---

[1333] This entry incorporated material from the June 13, 1958 entry on suicide, which has not been reproduced here, and the episode of George Porter's suicide from August 1957 (see above, p. 141). The latter has been reproduced, on account of the additional details and reflections found here.

[1334] See *ETG*, pp. 142–43, *MDR*, pp. 137–38.

completely to her because in fact she does not belong to him. That is the essence of all jealousy. [845/846]

[1335]One year after the wedding the man had another episode of depression. I had agreed with him that he would contact me immediately if something happened. But he had not done so. I heard nothing more from him. At that time, I had to give a lecture in Bern. Around midnight I arrived at the hotel—we went out to eat together after the lecture—and I went straight to bed, but lay awake for a long time. At about 2 a.m.—I must have just fallen asleep—I awoke with high anxiety and thought that someone had come into my room. I immediately turned on the light but there was nothing there. I assumed that someone had knocked at the door by mistake, and I looked out into the corridor, yet all was deadly silent. "Strange," I thought, "someone must have come into the room!" Then I attempted to think back, and it occurred to me that I had woken up with a dull pain, as if something had crashed against my forehead and then collided with the back of my skull.—On the next day I received a telegram that this patient had committed suicide. He had shot himself. Later I learned that the bullet had got lodged in the back of his skull. If one considers the time difference between the city where he lived and Switzerland, I felt the pain at the same time that he took his own life. In this experience there was a synchronistic phenomenon, as is often observed in the context of an archetypal situation—here, death. Through the relativization of time and space in the unconscious it is possible that I am perceiving something here that is playing out in actuality quite somewhere else. The collective unconscious is common to all, it is the foundation of what was called the "sympathy of all things" in the Middle Ages. In the case of this patient, my unconscious had "known" about his state of mind. I had been curiously troubled and nervous all evening. Via the unconscious, I had co-suffered his experience. [846/847]

II.

[1336]I never attempted to convert a patient to something or other and never exerted any pressure. All the same, I paid great attention to people acquiring perceptions of their own. With me, a pagan stays a pagan, and a Christian stays a Christian, a Jew a Jew.—This is why I cannot under-

---

[1335] See *ETG*, p. 143, *MDR*, p. 137. See above, p. 141.
[1336] See *ETG*, p. 144, *MDR*, p. 138.

stand that there are artists who are afraid of being analyzed. They think they might lose their creative powers if they do! If someone is really an artist, then his genius cannot be analyzed away. It is a madness to say that an artist fell away from art after treatment. If something like that happens, then he was incompetent from the start! [847/848]

I 2.

[1337]The majority of my patients were not believers in a faith, but rather those who had fallen away from their faith. I seek the lost sheep and not those who are already in the flock.

For example, the Catholic believer even today has the opportunity of living out a symbolism in the Church. Think of the experience of the Mass, of the *imitatio Christi* and much more. But such experience of the symbolic naturally presupposes a living engagement, and this is very often absent in contemporary man. In neurotic people it is mostly absent. In such cases we are advised to pay attention to whether the unconscious spontaneously generates the symbol. But then there is still the great difficulty as to whether a person who has such dreams is also in a position to accept their meaning and to bear it, as to whether he can draw the moral conclusions. I want to give you an example of this.

A Protestant theologian had been in my orbit for a long time. I observed: this man actually wants to get into analysis. One day he came to me and said he wanted to really experience symbols. I said to him, "That is quite simple: You tell me your dreams."

He was born in the country, in a village. That was close to a mountain with an old, ruined castle. As a child he had often made school trips there.

In the dream that he told me in response to my question he was standing at the exit of the village and was walking along the street in the direction of the mountain. Many memories arose: how he had hiked there as a young man and had daydreamed and how he longed to return to experience it again. Deep in memory he walked along the old street to the castle, but in the dream the landscape seemed changed: between him and the mountain lay a deep, dark ravine. Far below one could hear the roaring of the stream and he saw only a small shaky bridge [852/853] leading

---

[1337] See *ETG*, p. 146, *MDR*, p. 140.

over the stream. On the other side a steep goats' track led up to the castle. And not a comfortable road as before. On the mountain there was no ruined castle, but a fully developed great house, like a castle of the Holy Grail. As he looked down into the ravine and down to the roaring wild stream, he thought to himself, "It's a long way down!"

Then the dream stopped, and when he was finished narrating it he looked at me quizzically. I say to him, "Before the ascent comes the descent." And I remind him of the old mystery saying, "Give away what you have, then you will be received!"[1338]—I never saw him again!

If he had taken the path, then he would have experienced something! A descent *ad inferos*![1339] That was an opportunity to experience a living symbolism. He would have collided with a dark spirit, a numen, and I know what that signifies and what it means to venture down into these depths. He would have landed in the soup!

I do not reproach him for not daring to do it. He is answerable to his own conscience for that. Perhaps he would not have been able to bear it. I know some who have done a U-turn at this crossroads.

[1340]You know the case of another theologian about whom I wrote in "The Archetypes of the Collective Unconscious."[1341] He had a dream that often repeated itself for him. He dreamed he was standing in front of a hillside from where he had a fine view onto a deep valley with dense forests. He knew in the dream that there was a magnificent lake in the middle of the forest. He also knew that until now something had always held him back from going there. But this time he is going. When he gets close to the shore it becomes dark and ominous, and suddenly a quiet gust of wind scurries across the surface of the water.—You will not believe it, but he woke up crying out in fear and panic.—At first one could not understand it. But as a theologian he should have been able to understand it straight away: you know the pool whose water is disturbed by the wind [853/854] where they carried the sick who were healed by bathing in it— the lake of Bethesda. In the dream he had experienced the miracle of the pool of Bethesda: an angel comes down and moves the water which then acquires healing powers. The gentle wind was the Pneuma that blows

---

[1338] A line from the Mithras Liturgy. Jung cited these lines in in a letter to Freud on August 31, 1910, proposing them as a "motto of psychoanalysis." *FJL*, p. 350.

[1339] *ad inferos* (Lat.): "to the depths"; used in law to refer to the substrata of a piece of land considered as included in ownership of the surface property.

[1340] See *ETG*, pp. 146–47, *MDR*, pp. 140–41.

[1341] See "Archetypes of the Collective Unconscious" (1934), *CE* 12; *CW* 9.1, §§ 71–72.

where it will.[1342] And that caused him to be scared stiff. An invisible presence is suggested, a numen, that lives of its own volition and before which a person is overcome with awe.

I know the dreamer should have overcome his terror and should have got behind the panic. But never insist if someone is not ready to take the path and to take on the responsibility. He would then not be up to the suffering and the dangers that a confrontation with the unconscious brings.

Somewhat later he then had another dream in which his wife is bringing her child to this lake to be baptized. There is an altar there, but not the minister, but I am standing behind the altar and am to baptize the child. I scoop water from the lake, but in this moment, he jumps up and cries, "For God's sake, no, the water might be infected!"

When it is a matter of inner experience, of the most personal things, then most people find it ominous, and they run away from it. This theologian did the same. The risk of inner experience, of the spiritual adventure, is foreign to most people. The whole of today's education is oriented around not daring such things. Whatever does not concur with dogma is rejected!

I am naturally aware that theologians are in a more difficult situation than others. On the one hand they are closer to the religious, but on the other hand they are more bound by the Church and dogma.

13.

[1343]It is not always the right thing just to "go along with" the patient and their affects. Sometimes an active intervention on the part of the doctor is required. You know the fine story that once happened to me.

Once a lady came to me. She was from the nobility and used to box the ears of her employees. She suffered from a compulsive neurosis and came for treatment in the clinic. Naturally she immediately dismissed the head doctor. In her eyes he was also only an employee. [854/855] She was paying after all! He then sent her to another doctor and the same thing happened again. Finally, she was sent to me.

She was a very visible personality, six feet tall—she could beat you up, I tell you. So she appeared and we got on very well. Then came the moment where I had to say something unpleasant to her. Furiously, she

---

[1342] John 3:8.
[1343] See *ETG*, pp. 147–48, *MDR*, p. 142.

jumped up and threatened to beat me. I also jumped up and said to her, "Good. You are the lady. You hit first. Ladies first! But then I will also hit back."–I tell you, then she immediately collapsed. "No one has ever said that to me before," she complained. But from this moment on the therapy was a success.

What she needed was a masculine reaction. In this case it would have been quite wrong to just "go with her." Politeness and just accepting her would have been completely impotent here and would have been of no use. And do you know why she had a compulsive neurosis? Because she could not morally create boundaries for herself. Such people are boundaried by nature through compulsions! [855/856]

14.

I once prepared some statistics for Professor Veraguth about the results of my treatments.[1344] I can't recall the precise figures any more, but cautiously put, there were about a third really healed, a third substantially improved, and—rather pessimistically assessed—a third not substantially improved. But the no-improvement cases are difficult to assess because some are only realized and understood years later [856/857] and they might also only begin to be effective then. How often has it happened to me that former patients have written to me, "I only realized ten years after coming to you what actually took place."

I have had a few cases who ran away, very few that I had to send away myself. But among them there were also some who later sent me positive reports. That is why the evaluation of success of a treatment is often highly questionable.

[1344] See *ETG*, p. 148, *MDR*, p. 143. Otto Veraguth (1870–1944), neurologist in Zurich. In 1907 Jung credited him with being the first to do psychological research with the galvanometer and the associations experiment. "Further Investigations on the Galvanic Phenomenon and Respiration in Normal and Insane Individuals" (with Charles Ricksher), *CE* 4; *CW* 2, § 1181. There exists a manuscript of Jung's, entitled "Draft for Veraguth," which contains his calculations: cured: 34.2%, considerable improvement: 31.3%, mild improvement: 21.6%, uncured: 12.6%." (*CE* 16).

Appendix 2[1345]

[1/2]

November 10, 1956[1346]

(From a conversation with theologians who do not understand what a psychologist means by the "numinosum".)
In actuality this is what it is:[1347]once I dreamed of a young person, in the dream they came to me as a patient, a very strange person. I thought I do not understand her at all; I do not understand what she is talking about. Suddenly it occurred to me that she has an unusual father complex. That was the dream.

The next day this was written in my appointment book: four o'clock: consultation. A young girl appeared. I did not think for one minute of my dream. She was terribly elegant. A Jewess. I thought: what a cursed person! Intelligent, daughter of a Jewish banker. A heap of money behind her. She had undergone Freudian analysis. The doctor had a massive transference to her and, on his knees, had begged her to leave as she was disrupting his marriage. This girl was suffering from a crazy anxiety neurosis which had of course only worsened after such experiences. I began to take her anamnesis. There was nothing particular to discover. She was a proper

---

[1345] This excerpt is referred to by Kurt Wolff in his letter to Aniela Jaffé of November 1, 1957 (see n. 794 above).

[1346] This entry was dated October 10, but Jung had other meetings noted on the that date in his "Agenda." However, a meeting on November 10 with the theologians Biber, Frei, Köberle, and Zacharias is noted, suggesting that these notes refer to that meeting. Egon Biber is known to have corresponded with Jung in 1941 (JP). On Gebhard Frei, see n. 340 above; Adolf Köberle (1898–1990) was a German Lutheran theologian who had been professor of systematic theology at Basel in the 1930s. Paulus Zacharias had written an article on religious implications of Jung's psychology: "Die Bedeutung der Psychologie C. G. Jungs für die Christliche Theologie," *Zeitschrift für Religions- und Geistesgeschichte 5*, no. 3 (1953): 257–69.

[1347] See *ETG*, pp. 144–45, *MDR*, pp. 138–39.

Ashkenazi, an assimilated, Western Jewess, enlightened to her bones. Then suddenly I remembered my dream. I thought, oh my God, that is this person!—now I have myself stated: in the case of a father complex, if it does not originate in the father, one should look at the grandfather. So I asked her about her grandfather. And then I noticed how she closed her eyes and immediately I knew: here it is. Then she related that her grandfather had been a sort of rabbi. In a sort of Jewish sect. I asked: do you mean the Hassidim? She said yes. I said: If he was a rabbi, was he perhaps even a Tzadik? She: Yes. They said he was a sort of holy man. But that is all madness.—With that I completed the anamnesis and said to her, "Your grandfather was a Tzadik. Your father betrayed the mystery and forgot about God. And you have your neurosis because you are suffering from the fear of God!" This hit home like a bolt of lightning. [2/3]

The next night I had another dream: there was a reception at my house and, behold!—this little person also came along. She asks me, "Have you an umbrella? It is raining so hard." I found an umbrella, fumbled to open it and wanted to give it to her. But instead, I passed it to her on my knees, as if she were a divine being.—I told her this dream and in eight days the entire neurosis had resolved.

And now the explanation. If I were to write about it they would say: Now we can see what Prof. Jung is up to! But this is really how it is. I saw the presence of the numinosum. I have often seen this presence in Hassidic Jews. And I told her this. My dream showed this to me: she is not only a little seductive minx, but at root she is a holy woman. And this effected the healing. That was the numinosum.

But one cannot say something like this in print because one does not wish to burden science with it. They would say I was a mystic or a fool.

If one wanted to express it correctly, one could say mythology, or one could keep silent. For this is about the "fear of God."

This Jewess had no mythological concepts, so all of her *élan vital*[1348] went into flirting, clothes, sexuality. Because she did not know anything else. If she had had religious ideas, then her spirit could have developed. So I had to teach her mythological concepts. She is one of the many cases in which spiritual engagement is required.

[1348] *élan vital*: French philosopher Henri Bergson's concept of the vital force, elaborated in *L'évolution créatrice* (Paris: Félix Alcan, 1907); in English, *Creative Evolution*, trans. Arthur Mitchell (New York: Henry Holt, 1911). On Jung's reading of Bergson, see Shamdasani, *Jung and the Making of Modern Psychology*, pp. 207–8.

Epilogue

SONU SHAMDASANI

FROM THE AUTUMN of 1958 onward, the making of *Memories, Dreams, Reflections* was beset by disputations, heated discussions, and contractual wrangles. This has been gone into in detail elsewhere, so will only be summarized here.[1349]

As we have seen, leading up to the inception of *Memories*, there were a number of different notions and models of what the book could be: a biography continuing along the lines of Lucy Heyer's project; a work on the curve of development of Jung's ideas based on *The Red Book*, as envisaged by Cary Baynes; recorded and transcribed interviews like Claudel's *Improvised Memories*; a book of table talk like Eckermann's *Conversations with Goethe*; Kurt Wolff's dream of a work which could be presented as being as near as possible Jung's autobiography; and Jaffé's own idea of a work, *Jung and Nature: Inner and Outer*. This was complicated still further by questions as to how best to incorporate Jung's memoir, "From the Earliest Experiences of my Life," as well as the addition of sections from Jung's manuscripts such as "Africa Voyage," and the possible inclusion of sections from *The Red Book*.

These tensions were further compounded by the unresolved question of the authorial roles of Jaffé and Jung, whether the work was a biography or some form of autobiography,[1350] and whether Jaffé was to be

---

[1349] See Sonu Shamdasani, "Memories, Dreams, Omissions," *Spring: A Journal of Archetype and Culture* 57 (1995): 115–37; Shamdasani, *Jung Stripped Bare*, ch. 1; Shamdasani, "Misunderstanding Jung: The Afterlife of Legends," *Journal of Analytical Psychology* 45, no. 3 (2000): 459–72; Alan C. Elms, *Uncovering Lives: The Uneasy Alliance of Biography and Psychology* (New York: Oxford University Press, 1994), ch. 3 ("The Auntification of Jung"); and, from Jaffé's perspective, Elena Fischli, "Historical Commentary," in *Reflections*.

[1350] On this question, Jung wrote to his son-in-law Walther Niehus on April 5, 1960, "I want to thank you for your efforts on behalf of my so-called 'Autobiography' and to reaffirm that I do not regard this book as my undertaking but expressly a book which Frau

working under Kurt Wolff's editorial direction or independently. The issues came to a head when Jaffé submitted her draft chapters to Jung and Wolff.[1351] Added to this now was the contrast between the chapters that Sauerlander and Wolff themselves compiled from the protocols of the Interviews and Jaffé's own drafts.

Jung's own attitude towards the project continued to fluctuate. On October 14, 1958 Jaffé wrote to Helen Wolff informing her that Jung wanted the form of the work to change. At that time, he had only read her draft chapter on the "confrontation with the unconscious." He found it disturbing that Jaffé had put different statements from various interviews on the same theme together in a whole chapter, that in so doing, she had had to introduce much of her own commentary in the first person singular, and that much of what he had said to her had been re-molded. Consequently, he suggested that she add short sections of her own, as Eckermann had done in the case of Goethe, including her reactions and dreams, instead of the connecting sentences.[1352]

Kurt Wolff found this dramatic shift in Jung's position hard to take. Cary Baynes counseled him regarding Jung's volte face:

I have seen that happen again and again. He gets himself straightened out by making [a volte-face] and the other fellow goes off feeling as if he had been kicked in the stomach by a mule. To use his terminology, you had your contract with 'No. 1', but now 'No. 2' is in it and A.J. is wholly incapable of dealing with him. Just as well to expect a rabbit to deal with a boa constrictor. She says it is 'schöpferische Dämon' [creative daimon] at work and is very content.

You will undoubtedly think that if the book is to be turned over to this uncontrolled and uncontrollable 'Dämon' that all your time, energy and the company's money is down the drain. But I don't think that is the way it is going to work out [. . .]. Summing up, I

Jaffé has written. The chapters in it that are written by me I regard as a contribution to Mrs. Jaffé's work. The book should appear under her name and not under mine, since it does not represent an autobiography that I myself have composed." *Letters*, vol. 2, p. 550.

[1351] See, for instance, Aniela Jaffé to Helen Wolff, October 18, 1958 and Jung to Kurt Wolff, August, 1959 (both BL); Richard Hull to Herbert Read, September 2, 1960 (Routledge & Kegan Paul archives, University of Reading).

[1352] On hearing of this suggestion, Cary Baynes wrote to Helen Wolff, "What causes my fear is Jung's telling A.J. that he wanted her to put down what she dreamed about the things he said. That seems to me so out of reality that it is terrifying. The reader has enough on his hands adjusting to Jung's own dreams, and then is asked to heed those of an utterly unknown person!" November 18, 1958 (BL).

think it is wiser to have 'Dämon' working on the book, no matter what come out in the end than to have it inactive and sulking. It's a choice between two evils.[1353]

In August 1959 Jung took up this issue with Kurt Wolff, writing to him from Bollingen:

The present somewhat difficult and delicate situation of the book has arisen because Mrs. A. Jaffé has become overextended due to the nature of the material. I never intended to write a biography of myself, as I knew that it would be no easy thing, but still yet perhaps an impossible undertaking, which I would never dare to approach. If I had ever dreamed that I would have attempted to write an autobiography, it would have to be written according to my view, namely not in a mere two-dimensional way, but three-dimensional, that means with the inclusion of the unconscious and the shadow, which shows that an actual body has entered the beam of phenomenal consciousness.[1354]

He added that as a result of this, he had had to intervene more, so the balance of the work shifted. To rectify this situation, he had now asked Jaffé to insert herself back into the work, and to add her remarks into the text, in footnotes and at the beginning and end of chapters.

However, after Jaffé did this, Kurt Wolff regarded the results as catastrophic, as they broke the continuity of Jung's statements and destroyed the atmosphere. Wolff wanted these additions removed, or else placed solely in footnotes or the introduction.[1355] He complained that he found it hard to contact Jung directly, particularly as Jaffé opened all his letters, and was present when they met. As for Jung's suggestions in his August letter, Wolff felt that the work could have been presented as a dialogue, if it had been conceived in this way at the beginning (and then ideally with someone like Erich Neumann, instead of Aniela Jaffé), but that one couldn't introduce another voice into a monologue.[1356]

[1353] November 18, 1958 (BL).

[1354] BL.

[1355] Kurt Wolff to Cary Baynes, September 18, 1959 (BP). He considered the combination of the 'I' form with the 'he' form to be unworkable: Kurt Wolff to Cary Baynes, September 20, 1959 (BL).

[1356] Kurt Wolff to Cary Baynes, September 20, 1959 (BL).

Alongside these problems regarding the content and form of the work, there was the question of whether the book would be billed as a work by Jung or as one by Jaffé. For Kurt Wolff, the project had from the start been conceived of as Jung's book—Jung as both subject and author—compiled with the assistance of Aniela Jaffé. However, Jung had exclusive contracts with the Bollingen Foundation and Routledge & Kegan Paul for his works in English, and with Rascher Verlag for his works in German. This led to protracted contractual disputes (including with Collins, to whom Pantheon had sold the UK rights). The situation was further complicated by the inclusion in the work of sections directly written by Jung: his memoir, "From the Earliest Experiences of my Life," accounts of his travels, and the chapter "Late Thoughts." Richard Hull highlighted the significance of the issue:

> there is all the difference in the world between a book advertised as "The Autobiography of C. G. Jung" and a book of Jung's memoirs edited by Aniela Jaffé (of whom few have heard). One is an automatic bestseller, the other is not.[1357]

In a meeting between Jung's lawyer, his son-in-law Walter Niehus, and representatives of Rascher Verlag in May 1959, it was noted, "But one still does not even know, whether the book will sail under the flag 'Jung' or 'Jaffé'."[1358] Designating Jaffé as the author was critical in resolving the contractual disputes (though Kurt Wolff still viewed the actual situation as being otherwise). A resolution of the editorial committee of the *Collected Works* was drawn up, allowing the book to be published outside of the exclusive contracts with the Bollingen Foundation and Routledge & Kegan Paul. It contains the following statement:

> C. G. Jung has always maintained that he did not consider this book as his own enterprise but expressly as a book written by Mrs. Jaffé. The chapters written by C. G. Jung were to be considered as his contributions to the work of Mrs. Jaffé. The book was to be published in the name of Mrs. Jaffé and not in the name of C. G. Jung, because it did not represent an autobiography

---

[1357] Richard Hull, "A record of events preceding the publication of Jung's autobiography, as seen by R.F.C. Hull," July 27, 1960, BA.

[1358] "Aktennotiz über Besprechung zwischen Herrn Dr. Karrer, Herrn Niehus, Herrn Rascher sr., Herr Albert Rascher und Fr. Poggensee. 1.5.59," Rascher Verlag archives, Zentralbibliothek, Zurich.

composed by C. G. Jung (letter of C. G. Jung to Walter Niehus dated 5th April 1960).[1359]

On a conference held on the 26th August between Prof. C. G. Jung, Mr. John Barrett, Miss Vaun Gillmor, Sir Herbert Read, Mr. and Mrs. W. Niehus-Jung and Mrs. Aniela Jaffé, C. G. Jung confirmed again that he did strictly consider this book as an undertaking of Mrs. A. Jaffé to which he had only given his contributions [. . .]. The Editorial Committee decides hereby formally that it will not approve any decision of the Executive Subcommittee which would add the book of Mrs. A. Jaffé to the Collected Works.[1360]

The dispute between Collins and Routledge regarding the UK market was resolved through the first edition being co-published.

In January 1959, while at Bollingen reviewing the chapter "Life after Death," Jung informed Jaffé that "[s]omething within me has been touched. A gradient has formed, and I must write."[1361] On January 24 she wrote to Kurt Wolff that this had become a whole new chapter answering the question of what myth he lived in, which could be titled, "The Myth of Modern Man."[1362]

In February the following year, Jung complained to Richard Hull regarding the manuscript, stating that he had been "auntified."[1363] Hull attempted to reverse the bowdlerizations and remove Jaffé's (sometimes lengthy) third person interpolations in the text.[1364] Some members of

---

[1359] See *Letters*, vol. 2, p. 550.

[1360] "Resolution of the Editorial Committee for 'The Collected Works' of Prof. C. G. Jung," (BA), signed by Jung on November 29, 1960 and by John Barrett on December 13, 1960.

[1361] *ETG* p. 2, *MDR*, p. vii. Jaffé informed Kurt Wolff, "He writes and writes and writes." (January 16, 1959, BL)

[1362] Aniela Jaffé to Kurt Wolff, January 24, 1959, BL. She subsequently titled the chapter "Late Thoughts," to differentiate it from the title of Jung's recently published book on flying saucers, *A Modern Myth: Of Things Seen in the Skies* (1958), CE 26; CW 10. (Jaffé to Kurt Wolff, February 7, 1959, BL).

[1363] Hull, "Record of Events." As Hull recounted in 1971, Jung said in German, "They want to 'auntify' me, to play the aunt with me." Interview with Gene Nameche, p. 16, CLM, Jung Biographical Archive. Jung coined a neologism for this: *tantifizieren*.

[1364] See Richard Hull to Kurt Wolff, May 22 and July 7, 1960 (BL). On May 24 Kurt Wolff commissioned Hull to translate the work and compare "the version you receive from Frau Jaffé with Jung's original writing and dictation etc." (BL). Hull revised Richard Winston's translation of the first three chapters (Jung's memoir). Jung was impressed by Winston's translation, and was not keen for Hull to take it on, lest the work came across as stylistically formal as his *Collected Works*. Given the contractual wrangles, Routledge & Kegan Paul did not give Hull the clearance to translate the work, in order to avoid a further

Jung's family became involved in reviewing the manuscript and insisted on further changes.[1365] In July 1960 Helen and Kurt Wolff resigned from Pantheon, having been ousted by the Pantheon board, and set up a new imprint at Harcourt, Brace, called "Helen and Kurt Wolff Books." Kurt Wolff continued to work on *Memories*. In January 1961 he withdrew, as he found he could no longer work with Jaffé.[1366] To Herbert Read he wrote that in fifty years of publishing, he had never devoted so much to a book.[1367] In April Wolfgang Sauerlander also left Pantheon, handing over the responsibility for the text to Gerald Gross. While Jung had reviewed and marked up draft chapters, he never saw the final form of the book.[1368] Indeed, there was considerable editing of the manuscript, including significant deletions, which took place after his death.[1369] In

delay to his translation of the *Collected Works*. Hull continued to be involved in reviewing the translation and attempting to restore the text.

[1365] See Richard Hull and Helen Wolff, interviews with Gene Nameche, CLM, Jung Biographical Archive. One draft manuscript of the first three chapters with a note describing it as "Copy translated by Winston (pp. 1–109) checked through by Hull with final corrections by Jaffé and/or Jung" also bears the following note by Helen Wolff: "Revealing for changes 'toning down' Jung's original—bowdlerized version. Highly interesting for what was done to keep out Jung's frank and true statements about himself! p. 39–" (BL). The cross reference is to the following revision:

> The symbolism in my childhood experiences and the violence of the imagery—the phallus, and God shitting on the cathedral—disturbed upset me enormously terribly. Who makes me think that God destroys his church by shitting on it in this abominable manner?"

[1366] Wolfgang Sauerlander to Kyrill Schabert and George Gross, January 30, 1961 (BL).
[1367] Kurt Wolff to Herbert Read, October 27, 1959 (BA).
[1368] *Memories* was supposed to include a chapter entitled "Encounters" ("Begegnungen"). There is an undated late handwritten letter from Jung to Jaffé, without a reply, in which he asked her what had happened to this. He noted that he had seen and partially spoken about, among others, Theodore Roosevelt, Paul Valéry, Rabbi Beck, Hitler, Mussolini, Goebbels, Miguel Serrano, Scheler, Toynbee, Eddington, Sir James Jeans, the Grossherzog of Hessen, Kaiser Wilhelm and Prince Heinrich, and Leo Frobenius, and that "it is not 'encountered' [begegnet]." (JP). Jung's comments on some of these figures, though not all of them, are to be found in the protocols of the Interviews.

[1369] For instance, the following was noted in a meeting between Jaffé, Max Rascher and Emmy Poggensee (of Rascher Verlag): "Collins have made a few very good suggestions for abridgements, that she has followed. Above all, the 'extraverted' and somewhat superficial accounts of London and Paris should be omitted, Africa somewhat cut, whilst all 'introverted' sections should be extended and somewhat built up in places. The section of the meeting with James and Flornoy [*sic*] should further be cut according to Pantheon as well as those with Oeri and Zimmer, whereas we will retain these." "Minutes of a discussion between Aniela Jaffé, Herr Rascher and Fraulein Poggensee, 22 January 1962" (Rascher Verlag archives, Zentralbibliothek, Zurich). On the discrepancies between the German, UK, and US editions, see Herbert Read to Jack Barrett, August 28, 1962, Routledge & Kegan Paul archives, University of Reading.

August 1962 serializations appeared in *Die Weltwoche*, the first of which was simply titled, "The Autobiography of C. G. Jung." This was followed by serializations in *The Atlantic Monthly* and *The Sunday Times*.[1370]

The book appeared in German in October 1962, followed by the US edition in May 1963, and the UK edition in July. In October that year Kurt Wolff died in a road accident.[1371] In his review of the book, E. A. Bennet trenchantly noted, "It is an unusual book and apparently it has been a great problem to reviewers, many of whom accepted it as an autobiography. Certainly it is not that."[1372] Among reviewers and subsequent commentators, Bennet was almost alone in realizing this. The work swiftly became a bestseller, which it remains to this day.

Despite all the travails of its composition, editing, and publishing, Kurt Wolff's desire that the book should "lead the outsider inside the work" had been greatly fulfilled.[1373] Appearing on the cusp of the 1960s, *Memories* did much to propel Jung's work—volumes of which were progressively appearing in the Bollingen Series—into the cultural limelight, where it was to play a considerable role transforming the spiritual and psychological landscape. In ensuing decades, *Memories, Dreams, Reflections* became essential reading for spiritual and psychological seekers across the globe.

[1370] "Jung on Freud," "Jung on Life after Death," "Jung's View of Christianity," in *The Atlantic Monthly*, November 1962, December 1962, and January 1963; "The Psychiatrist Speaks. Carl Jung: Visions of the Inner Life," "Finding Freud's Complex: Casebook of the 'Doctor of Souls'," and "The Savage in the Cellar: Carl Jung on the Meaning of Dreams," *The Sunday Times Weekly Review*, June 23, June 30, and July 7, 1963.

[1371] *New York Times*, October 23, 1963, p. 41.

[1372] E. A. Bennet, "Jung's Inner Life," *British Medical Journal*, September 23, 1963.

[1373] Kurt Wolff to Cary Baynes, September 18, 1959 (BP).

The Collected Works of C. G. Jung

Editors: Sir Herbert Read, Michael Fordham, and Gerhard Adler; executive editor, William McGuire. Translated by R.F.C. Hull, except where noted.

1. PSYCHIATRIC STUDIES (1957; 2nd ed., 1970)

On the Psychology and Pathology of So-Called Occult Phenomena (1902)
On Hysterical Misreading (1904)
Cryptomnesia (1905)
On Manic Mood Disorder (1903)
A Case of Hysterical Stupor in a Prisoner in Detention (1902)
On Simulated Insanity (1903)
A Medical Opinion on a Case of Simulated Insanity (1904)
A Third and Final Opinion on Two Contradictory Psychiatric Diagnoses (1906)
On the Psychological Diagnosis of Facts (1905)

2. EXPERIMENTAL RESEARCHES (1973)

Translated by Leopold Stein in collaboration with Diana Riviere
PART I: STUDIES IN WORD ASSOCIATION (1904–1907, 1910)
The Associations of Normal Subjects, *by C. G. Jung and Franz Riklin*
An Analysis of the Associations of an Epileptic
The Reaction-time Ratio in the Association Experiment
Experimental Observations on the Faculty of Memory
Psychoanalysis and Association Experiments
The Psychological Diagnosis of Evidence
Association, Dream, and Hysterical Symptom
The Psychopathological Significance of the Association Experiment
Disturbances in Reproduction in the Association Experiment

The Theory of Psychoanalysis (1913)
General Aspects of Psychoanalysis (1913)
Psychoanalysis and Neurosis (1916)
Some Crucial Points in Psychoanalysis: A Correspondence Between
    Dr. Jung and Dr. Loÿ (1914)
Prefaces to "Collected Papers on Analytical Psychology" (1916, 1917)
The Significance of the Father in the Destiny of the Individual
    (1909/1949)
Introduction to Kranefeldt's "Secret Ways of the Mind" (1930)
Freud and Jung: Contrasts (1929)

5. SYMBOLS OF TRANSFORMATION
([1911–1912/1952] 1956; 2nd ed., 1967)
PART 1
Introduction
Two Kinds of Thinking
The Miller Fantasies: Anamnesis
The Hymn of Creation
The Song of the Moth
PART 2
Introduction
The Concept of Libido
The Transformation of Libido
The Origin of the Hero
Symbols of the Mother and Rebirth
The Battle for Deliverance from the Mother
The Dual Mother
The Sacrifice
Epilogue
Appendix: The Miller Fantasies

6. PSYCHOLOGICAL TYPES ([1921] 1971)
A revision by R.F.C. Hull of the translation by H. G. Baynes
Introduction
The Problem of Types in the History of Classical and Medieval
    Thought
Schiller's Idea on the Type Problem
The Apollonian and the Dionysian
The Type Problem in Human Character
The Type Problem in Poetry

The Type Problem in Psychopathology
The Type Problem in Aesthetics
The Type Problem in Modern Philosophy
The Type Problem in Biography
General Description of the Types
Definitions
Epilogue
Four Papers on the Psychological Typology (1913, 1925,
    1931, 1936)

7. TWO ESSAYS ON ANALYTICAL PSYCHOLOGY
(1953; 2nd ed., 1966)
On the Psychology of the Unconscious (1917/1926/1943)
The Relations Between the Ego and the Unconscious (1928)
APPENDICES
1. New Paths in Psychology (1912)
2. The Structure of the Unconscious (1916)
(new versions, with variants, 1966)

8. THE STRUCTURE AND DYNAMICS OF THE PSYCHE
(1960; 2nd ed., 1969)
On Psychic Energy (1928)
The Transcendent Function ([1916] 1957)
A Review of the Complex Theory (1934)
The Significance of Constitution and Heredity and Psychology (1929)
Psychological Factors Determining Human Behavior (1937)
Instinct and the Unconscious (1919)
The Structure of the Psyche (1927/1931)
On the Nature of the Psyche (1947/1954)
General Aspects of Dream Psychology (1916/1948)
On the Nature of Dreams (1945/1948)
The Psychological Foundations of Belief in Spirits (1920/1948)
Spirit and Life (1926)
Basic Postulates of Analytical Psychology (1931)
Analytical Psychology and Weltanschauung (1928/1931)
The Real and the Surreal (1933)
The Stages of Life (1930–1931)
The Soul and Death (1934)
Synchronicity: An Acausal Connecting Principle (1952)
Appendix: On Synchronicity (1951)

Supplementary Volume B. PSYCHOLOGY OF THE
UNCONSCIOUS: A STUDY OF THE TRANSFORMATIONS
AND SYMBOLISMS OF THE LIBIDO ([1912] 1992)
Translated by Beatrice M. Hinkle, introduction by William
McGuire

Notes to C. G. Jung's Seminars
DREAM ANALYSIS ([1928–1930] 1984)
Edited by William McGuire

NIETZSCHE'S "ZARATHUSTRA" ([1934–1939] 1988)
Edited by James L. Jarrett (2 vols.)

ANALYTICAL PSYCHOLOGY ([1925] 1989)
Edited by William McGuire

THE PSYCHOLOGY OF KUNDALINI YOGA ([1932] 1996)
Edited by Sonu Shamdasani

INTERPRETATION OF VISIONS ([1930–34] 1997)
Edited by Claire Douglas

Philemon Series of the Philemon Foundation
General editor, Sonu Shamdasani

CHILDREN'S DREAMS
Edited by Lorenz Jung and Maria Meyer-Grass. Translated by Ernst
Falzeder with the collaboration of Tony Woolfson

*INTRODUCTION TO JUNGIAN PSYCHOLOGY: NOTES OF
THE SEMINAR ON ANALYTICAL PSYCHOLOGY GIVEN
IN 1925*
Edited by William McGuire. Translated by R.F.C. Hull. With a new
introduction and updates by Sonu Shamdasani

*JUNG CONTRA FREUD: THE 1912 NEW YORK LECTURES
ON THE THEORY OF PSYCHOANALYSIS*
Translated by R.F.C. Hull. With a new introduction by Sonu
Shamdasani.

THE QUESTION OF PSYCHOLOGICAL TYPES: THE
CORRESPONDENCE OF C. G. JUNG AND HANS SCHMID-
GUISAN, 1915–1916
Edited by John Beebe and Ernst Falzeder. Translated by Ernst
Falzeder with the collaboration of Tony Woolfson

DREAM INTERPRETATION ANCIENT AND MODERN:
NOTES FROM THE SEMINAR GIVEN IN 1936–1941
Edited by John Peck, Lorenz Jung, and Maria Meyer-Grass.
Translated by Ernst Falzeder with the collaboration of Tony
Woolfson

ANALYTICAL PSYCHOLOGY IN EXILE: THE
CORRESPONDENCE OF C. G. JUNG AND ERICH
NEUMANN
Edited and introduced by Martin Liebscher. Translated by Heather
McCartney

ON PSYCHOLOGICAL AND VISIONARY ART: NOTES FROM
C. G. JUNG'S LECTURE ON GÉRARD DE NERVAL'S
"AURÉLIA"
Edited by Craig E. Stephenson. Translated by R.F.C. Hull, Gottwalt
Pankow, and Richard Sieburth

ON DREAMS AND THE EAST: NOTES OF THE 1933 BERLIN
SEMINAR (by C. G. Jung and Heinrich Zimmer)
Edited by Giovanni Sorge. Translated by Mark Kyburz and John
Peck.

HISTORY OF MODERN PSYCHOLOGY: LECTURES
DELIVERED AT ETH ZURICH, VOLUME 1: 1933–34
Edited by Ernst Falzeder. Translated by Mark Kyburz, John Peck,
and Ernst Falzeder

DREAM SYMBOLS OF THE INDIVIDUATION PROCESS:
NOTES OF THE SEMINARS GIVEN BY JUNG IN BAILEY
ISLAND AND NEW YORK, 1936–37
Edited by Suzanne Gieser